the UCD aesthetic

the UCD aesthetic

celebrating

150
YEARS
of
UCD
WRITERS

edited by Anthony Roche

NEW
ISLAND

the UCD aesthetic
First published 2005
by New Island
2 Brookside
Dundrum Road
Dublin 14
www.newisland.ie

isbn 1 904301 82 7

Typeset by New Island
Cover design by Fidelma Slattery @ New Island
Printed in the UK by CPD, Ebbw Vale, Wales

New Island received financial assistance from The Arts Council
(An Chomhairle Ealaíon), Dublin, Ireland

10 9 8 7 6 5 4 3 2 1

CONTENTS

INTRODUCTION

When President Mary McAleese spoke at the Foundation Day
Dinner in University College Dublin's O'Reilly Hall on Friday, 5
November 2004, she invoked the founding moment of the
Catholic University a hundred and fifty years earlier from which
UCD dates its origin. She did so in two memorable ways: by
broadening the historical moment of UCD's foundation and so
foregrounding the misery of a provincial capital city in the grip
of poverty and the wake of famine; and by employing the
conjoined metaphor of seeds and harvest to provide an image of
what had occurred in the century and a half since. This
efflorescence has been widely acknowledged in the political
context: that many of the key figures of the emergent Irish state,
from Taoisigh on down through other politicians and members
of the judiciary, have been graduates of UCD. But the literary
flowering which UCD has seen from its graduates is equally
impressive and no less deserving of recognition. It might have
been enough to have helped to produce James Joyce, whose
Ulysses was widely acclaimed in 2000 as the novel of the century.
But there is much more than (even) Joyce to UCD's contribution
to the Irish literary scene, and the twenty-eight essays in this
book bear witness to the galaxy of leading poets, playwrights and
prose writers who have passed through its portals (and continue
to do so). The book is a double celebration of writing at UCD,
because each of the authors of the twenty-eight essays also has a
strong connection with the university, either as past or present
members of the faculty of arts (in particular the School of
English) or as former students who have themselves graduated to
teach elsewhere or to become writers. Three of the subjects
discussed in this volume also number among its contributors. All

of the contributors have written to the theme of the UCD aesthetic, looking in turn at what their individual authors chose to develop in the way of a governing stylistic and intellectual aim. The question posed by the title and topic is: can an overall aesthetic be discerned or articulated for the authors who graduated from UCD? I'll leave it to each reader to decide as they read through this rich volume, but would like in my introductory comments to consider several significant strands which contribute to that end.

On the day it opened its doors in 1854, the University admitted the pitifully small number of seventeen students, and by Donal McCartney's reckoning the total number of students for the next twenty-five years was 521, or an average of twenty-five a year. With the arrival of the Jesuits in the 1880s, and the growth into University College, the numbers soon expanded to the stage where hundreds of students sat First Year exam papers then as now, as Gerard Manley Hopkins was to discover to his cost. But the intellectual level of the university had been set high by its founder, John Henry Newman, in his *Idea of a University* and other writings and lectures. Newman promoted the view that the university should allow for the development of the whole individual and so encourage an 'enlargement' of mind and spirit. He did so in prose remarkable for its fluidity and for embodying the movement of mind. Gerard Manley Hopkins may have been a misplaced English exile at UCD who never got to return home, as Newman did, but if Dublin increased his sense of alienation and despair it was also the site in which he wrote some of his greatest poems, poems so original in their intensity and mode of expression that they found neither publication or understanding until the following century. Both writers are imbued with a profound sense of Catholicism, a deep religious faith which does not make life easy for them and which results in writing of the first imaginative intensity. This should be no surprise, given that they both taught at the Catholic University. But many writers who follow display no waning of the intensity of that Catholicism, even though the struggle in which it involves them finds different outlets and guarantees no orthodoxies.

This is clearly the case with Joyce, who was the first of the

2

UCD writers to carry over from his religion to his art many of the concepts informing the first: the key term 'epiphany' is only one example of how his early aesthetic was forged from a secularising of his Catholicism. Stephen Dedalus seriously considers a vocation to the religious life before deciding to become instead a 'priest of the eternal imagination'. A review in the *TLS* of 20 April 2005 remarks that recent studies in Joyce 'suggest a return to something that many early critics took for granted – that Joyce was Irish and that the formative experiences of colonialism and Catholicism lay at the heart of his work.' Placing Joyce in the context of his UCD years does much to advance this under-standing. It shows that he is not an isolated figure but one of many who came to UCD at the turn of the last century and were caught up in the movement towards a political and intellectual independence. This was something Cardinal Newman probably could neither have foreseen nor have wished, but it was an almost inevitable consequence of what he had encouraged.

An extraordinary strand of continuity in this regard is the example and fate of Thomas McDonagh. He was a lecturer in the English Department at UCD, a playwright at the Abbey Theatre who made special contact with Synge, and a poet who created some of his greatest effects in English verse by drawing directly on Irish. He was also one of the leaders of the 1916 Rising, correcting the proofs of his volume *Literature in Ireland* during lulls in the fighting. His execution led to a job vacancy at UCD, which was filled by McDonagh's former pupil and protégé, Austin Clarke. The strain of all this may well have proved too much for Clarke, who subsequently resigned. McDonagh and Clarke share a concern with bringing the rich linguistic, syntactic and metrical resources of Gaelic poetry into the English language and developing a distinctive Irish poetic. The process is carried much further by Clarke and finds a clear line of continuity into its greatest living proponent, Thomas Kinsella, both in his translations from the Irish (*The Táin* and *An Duanaire*) and in his own original poetry. It may have in part derived from McDonagh's contact with Synge at the Abbey Theatre but owed a great deal to the example and presence at UCD of Douglas Hyde as Professor of Irish. Flann O'Brien's MA was in Irish and he drew on both traditions in his ground-breaking novel, *At Swim-Two-Birds*. Not that all is translation. The presence of Máire Mhac an tSaoi as one of the senior living writers in the volume also speaks to the distinctive and powerful authority of Irish-language poetry in the culture.

Mary Colum and Kate O'Brien emerge early in the volume to contest the possibility of an all-male hegemony. The essay on Mary Maguire (as she was then) brings an undeservedly neglected figure to light – part of the concern of a feminist historiography – and shows how she had to make a noise in order to be accorded some literary space in *The Irish Review*, not merely to be left with the role of secretary. She also furthers the Joyce connection which is so central to this volume, not only in the friendship she and her husband Padraic Colum had with J.J., but in the important review she wrote of *Ulysses* for an American readership. Although positive (and welcomed by Joyce), Colum's writings about the novel show an independence of mind in pointing out what she saw as its shortcomings. Kate O'Brien wittily displays what the distaff view of Newman might be in her sharply titled 'My Idea of a University'. For all the fierce independence of her views, not least with regard to her own sexuality, O'Brien managed to negotiate a relationship with her faith by seeing it as part of her connection to European culture, in particular her beloved Spain. Few have written better of the Catholic conscience *in extremis* than O'Brien, and in St. Teresa of Avila she found a mystical role model with which to challenge patriarchal orthodoxy. Another vital female presence is Mary Lavin, the account of whose years at UCD provides quite a contrast and foil to Flann O'Brien's and who is discussed here by another distinguished UCD graduate, her daughter Caroline Walsh.

This book is, among other things, a tribute to the brilliant UCD generation of the 1930s. Flann O'Brien and Kate O'Brien, who brought a contrasting approach to the Irish novel (one surrealistic/parodic, the other realist/subversive), have already been mentioned. But the group also included poets Brian Coffey and Denis Devlin, who managed a joint publication while still undergraduates. Where Austin Clarke turned to native Irish sources, Coffey and Devlin consciously looked to Europe and an avant-garde modernist aesthetic. All combined in turning away from a British poetic, a feature of UCD writers from Hopkins and McDonagh on, and thus can be seen as contributing in distinct but complementary ways to literary decolonisation. Coffey and Devlin (via Beckett) sought to connect themselves with Joyce on the continent and ally themselves with him (rather than Yeats), but eschewed his Irish subject matter in favour of his experimental techniques.

The second half of the book moves into the living stream of still-contemporary writers. There is a formidable quartet of poets in Máire Mhac an tSaoi, Anthony Cronin, Thomas Kinsella and John Montague. Mhac an tSaoi concentrates most of her attention on the domestic and the personal, avoiding the overtly political; the same is true of Mary Lavin in her short stories. But the granting of what Eavan Boland has termed 'permission' for such subjects to be considered as fit matter for literary treatment itself constitutes a radically political gesture. Mhac an tSaoi and Cronin also combine literary careers with an involvement in the world of public affairs. Cronin, in particular, promotes the idea of a Continental man of letters, where the vocation of poet and novelist and an active engagement with the cultural and political affairs of state are seen as a natural corollary rather than a contradiction. Thomas Kinsella and John Montague are two poets whose influence and importance can scarcely be over-estimated, given how much they have contributed to the revival and resurgence in Irish poetry in the 1950s and how much they have made possible for their successors, both in Northern and Southern Ireland.

It is in the contemporary zone that the emergence of leading playwrights from UCD is so striking. There had been predecessors – in particular the plays of graduate Teresa Deevy at the Abbey in the 1930s (and MacDonagh before her). But the appearance of the first two plays of Thomas Kilroy in the late 1960s brought a European sensibility to the Irish stage, the pursuit of a drama of ideas through a range of experimental techniques. Kilroy was a lecturer at UCD for a number of years before going on to become Professor of English at NUI, Galway. And UCD now has as its Faculty of Arts Writer-in-Residence the outstanding younger playwright of his generation, Frank McGuinness. What the examples of Kilroy and McGuinness show is how the creative and the scholarly impulses are by no means separate, but can be fruitfully interwined. This double focus manifests itself in their writing of important English-language versions of plays from other languages and cultures. In his 'translation' (more properly, version) of *The Seagull* Kilroy transposed Chekhov's characters and setting from late nineteenth-century Russia to a West of Ireland Big House estate during the Land Wars. McGuinness has contributed English-language versions of plays by Ibsen (in particular), Chekhov, Brecht and Greek tragedians in ways that have fed his creative endeavour. A major source and resource for the Irish stage (since 1924) has been UCD's Dramsoc, not just for playwrights but for actors, directors, designers and others. Since UCD's move to Belfield in 1970, LG1 has served as the home of Dramsoc and has nurtured (among many others who might be named) the two young playwrights at the close of this volume, Marina Carr and Conor McPherson. When they founded the Abbey Theatre, Yeats and Lady Gregory called for plays that would be written with a 'high ambition': the plays of Carr and McPherson certainly fit that bill. Carr has done more than any other Irish playwright to create original and challenging work by adapting Greek themes to an Irish setting: her home ground of the Irish Midlands where the tortured protagonists of *By the Bog of Cats* and *Ariel* enact their tragic destinies. McPherson has translated the spare aesthetic of LG1 to world stages through his minimal settings and his compelling monologues.

There are more playwrights present in this book than might at first be apparent. Multi-talented writers like Aidan Carl Mathews and Éilís Ní Dhuibne have both contributed noteable plays to the repertoire, even though they are better known for their fiction, and the fact that Roddy Doyle began with plays may be seen in his natural facility for dialogue in his Barrytown trilogy. But the new form that has emerged in the past several decades in relation to a UCD aesthetic is film. And UCD can claim the two filmmakers who have done most to establish a world audience and acclaim for Irish film: Jim Sheridan and Neil Jordan. Sheridan began in LG1 and progressed to directing plays in the important experimental space for the arts that is the Project Arts Centre. His first film, *My Left Foot*, drew on theatre personnel like Brenda Fricker while not being 'theatrical' in any negative sense of the term. Like everything he has done since, the film shows not only what a natural filmmaker Sheridan is but how central to his creativity the act of storytelling is. Neil Jordan has sustained a dual career, as a filmmaker and as a writer of prose fiction. The account of his career in *The UCD Aesthetic* focuses on his short stories and novels, while constantly backlit by his dazzling achievements in the movies.

It seems appropriate that the last word should go to the area of prose fiction and the novel. If no one contemporary author equals James Joyce (and who would wish that on them?), the list of novelists and short story writers is breathtaking in its range and achievement: John McGahern; Éilís Ní Dhuibhne; Colm Tóibín; Aidan Matthews; Roddy Doyle; Joseph O'Connor; and Emma Donoghue. Joseph O'Connor provides a wonderful account of how John McGahern's prose inspired him to try to become a writer by painstakingly transcribing McGahern's short story 'Sierra Leone' word for word. Before there are great writers, as McGahern himself has insisted, there must be great readers. And by an act of writerly desecration O'Connor describes how he makes the story his own. Early in the Bloomsday centenary year of 2004, Roddy Doyle spoke of his ambiguity about Joyce, about how for all of its sterling and innovative qualities, *Ulysses* could have done with some editing. Who better than a fellow UCD graduate and a leading contemporary novelist to criticise James Joyce's shortcomings?

Because they shared the same undergraduate environment, attended the same lectures, and nurtured the ambition to become a writer of note in the same university, the writers in this book can afford to restore to Joyce the complexity and human qualities he had before he was elevated to worldwide sainthood. Nor is this another form of Irish begrudgery, however much it may resemble it. The engagement with Joyce is one of the key strands of the UCD aesthetic. His example is that of an iconoclast, and so what may begin as emulation rapidly mutates into differentiation through rewriting.

John McGahern's prose is as scrupulous as Joyce's; and his breaking of taboos in his early fiction did much to bring down the barriers of censorship which had been stoutly maintained in Ireland through the middle years of the last century. McGahern brings a European sensibility to bear on a fidelity to local Irish experience that is distinctly his own. Éilís Ní Dhuibhne combines the two traditions in Irish writing (the Gaelic and the English) and creatively draws on her professional training as a folkorist in doing so. Colm Tóibín's journalism honed his prose style and provided the groundwork for his forensic fictional probing of the roles of gender and nationality in the construction of identity. Aidan Matthews may be one of the few remaining Catholics in Ireland for whom 'washed in the blood of the lamb' has a real meaning, but his religious fidelity mates with a surreal sense of comedy that Bunuel would have recognised. Roddy Doyle, Joseph O'Connor and Emma Donoghue all pioneered a contemporary Irish novel charting the urban and suburban social realities of Dublin's Northside and Southside, and an Irish present which appeared to have shed all links with or interest in the past. This makes their turn to writing historical fiction all the more interesting, especially when it is so fully informed by the urgencies of the present. The challenging of gender stereotypes which is such a feature of *Ulysses* has been carried considerably further in the work of contemporary writers from UCD, particularly in foregrounding gay experience.

There are younger writers coming to fruition at UCD all the time. And had space permitted, the list of those covered could have been extended well beyond those represented, as I am only too aware. But I am sure of one thing: if there is a UCD aesthetic, the twenty-eight writers represented here have set the bar very high in terms of achieving it.

Anthony Roche
June 2005

I wish to thank Katherine O'Callaghan for her expert editorial assistance in the preparation of this volume.

8

THE EARLY YEARS
(1854–1916)

John Henry Newman (1801–1890)

Michael Paul Gallagher S.J.

'The kind of knowledge by which people live their lives . . . is the knowledge of which Newman wrote' – Bernard Lonergan (1977)

A well-known Italian brand of chocolates puts a quotation in the wrapping around their sweets. On opening one of them, I found 'to live is to change, and to be perfect is to have changed often'. No author was acknowledged. But it is a celebrated sentence from John Henry Newman's study of the development of doctrine, a book that coincided with his conversion to Catholicism in 1845. Indeed it was a life-long anchor of his thought: 'growth is the only evidence of life', he wrote in his *Apologia pro Vita Sua* in 1865. I want to propose here that a key to appreciating Newman's inheritance lies in his relishing of change or movement. Even his famous style is less an aesthetic exercise in language than a subtle rendering of the dynamism of the inquiring mind. To be faithful to this adventure of growth called forth all Newman's energy and honesty. To awaken this capacity in others was at the heart of his philosophy of education. To embody this process in words was the desire underlying the sophisticated performance of his prose. In his own words, spoken in Dublin, 'style is a thinking out into language' (*IU*, 232).

In earlier decades, when secondary schools in Ireland studied compulsory passages of Newman for the Leaving Certificate, the tendency was to speak of him vaguely in terms of ideal prose cadences. James Joyce was more precise in his surprisingly frequent references to Newman. In *A Portrait* Stephen, walking across Dublin to the university, compensates for 'the sloblands of Fairview' by thinking of 'the cloistral silver-veined prose of Newman'. In a late letter Joyce remarked that 'nobody has ever written English prose that can be compared with that of a tiresome footling little Anglican parson who afterwards became a prince of the only true church' (Pribek, 180). The complex mixture of praise and irony is typical of Joyce's long interaction with the inheritance of Newman. The Cardinal's language charmed many unbelieving authors including George Eliot, Thomas Hardy and Aldous Huxley. Believers of course joined in the chorus of praise, as exemplified by Hilaire Belloc's preface to a 1930 edition of the *Apologia*: 'it carries you on like a river, without effort: an amazing achievement'. Practically all the obituaries in August 1890 mentioned his literary style. *The Tablet* spoke of 'the happy turn of its slightest phrase, and the bold yet classic rendering of every mood and feeling'.

However, what I want to underline here is a dimension that these admirers seem to have missed: the connection between the flow and rhythm of his prose and his sense of the dynamism of the mind in motion towards wisdom. If I were to choose just one example of this gift in action, it would be the following passage from a university sermon of 1840, where Newman evokes the ungraspable groping of thought through the image of a mountain climber. In offering a fairly long quotation the object is to invite the reader to imagine these words spoken in the pulpit of St Mary's Church in Oxford, occasions later idealised by Matthew Arnold as 'the most entrancing of voices, breaking the silence with words and thoughts that were a religious music – subtle, sweet, mournful':

> The mind ranges to and fro, and spreads out, and advances forward with a quickness which has become a proverb, and a subtlety and versatility which baffle investigation. It passes on from point to point, gaining one by some indication; another on a probability; then availing itself of an association; then falling back on some received law; next seizing on testimony; then committing itself to some popular impression, or some inward instinct, or some obscure memory; and thus it makes progress

not unlike a clamberer on a steep cliff, who, by quick eye, prompt hand, and firm foot, ascends how he knows not himself; by personal endowments and by practice, rather than by rule, leaving no track behind him, and unable to teach another. It is not too much to say that the stepping by which great geniuses scale the mountains of truth is as unsafe and precarious to men in general, as the ascent of a skilful mountaineer up a literal crag. (*FS*, 257)

Through such an accumulation of phrases Newman is both defending and embodying a 'living spontaneous energy within us', a capacity much more ordinary and extraordinary than the procedures of formal argument. The importance of this zone became a foundational insight of his thought. His singular ability to do justice to these operations is a key to his method as a writer. Hopkins was not alone in suggesting that Newman's paradigm for prose was 'the most highly educated conversation' (Nixon, 61).

Thirty years after that Oxford sermon, Newman placed a significant epigraph from St Ambrose on the title page of his *Grammar of Assent*: '*non in dialectica complacuit Deo salvum facere populum suum*'. [It was not through dialectic that God pleased to save his people.] If dialectic implies what Newman elsewhere calls a static or 'paper logic', its opposite is a fidelity to the flow of both history and life, to 'the more subtle and elastic logic of thought' (*GA*, 359). For him people 'become personal when logic fails' (*GA*, 369) and a major thrust of his writing was to defend this tacit zone of reason beneath or beyond formal forms of argument. This preference for the implicit or intuitive links up with the personalism central in Newman's approach and so often captured in the exploratory cadences of his sentences.

Few authors, seeking to defend the credibility of religious faith, would risk saying that 'in these provinces of inquiry egotism is true modesty' (*GA*, 384). But for Newman words were 'unreal' unless they could evoke and speak to a person's concrete and psychological operations. He often satirised minds that 'have no discriminating convictions and no grasp of consequences': from these shallow waters of complacency 'they talk at random … merely dazzled by phenomena, instead of perceiving things as they are' (*IU*, 10). Newman's whole career in religious or educational fields was dedicated to defending the deeper avenues of human perception, and here the process of his prose was an essential part of his rhetoric. A fascination with the movement of history went hand in hand with his introspective attention to the process of personal discovery. Owen Chadwick captured the core of Newman's temperament: 'never was a mind so unceasingly in motion. But the motion was always growth, and never revolution.' This is true biographically and stylistically.

In a letter of 1836 Newman remarked that he was more of a rhetorician than a philosopher. If so, this talent of his was in evidence in Dublin in 1852. His letters of the time show an awareness that he faced an audience deeply divided over the type of university to be started in Ireland. He wrote back to his community in Birmingham that, although his first discourse had been successful, what was needed was 'a true rhetoric' rather than plunging into a 'maze of metaphysics'. In fact, when he spoke in the assembly room of the Rotunda (a hall he particularly liked) he performed a rhetorical feat, in the best sense, persuading his audience to accompany him to higher ground. But this was not an escape into idealism; rather it expressed a Christian humanism that does justice to both those terms. Take for instance the realism of the following passage dealing with the moral complexity of literature and of 'man' (in the old sense): 'Do not say you are studying him, his history, his mind and his heart, when you are studying something else. Man is a being of genius, passion, intellect, conscience, power ... do not take him for what he is not, for something more divine and sacred' (*IU*, 195). This is Newman the dramatic realist, who relishes the full range of the human adventure and especially its gradual flourishing. It captures his suspicion of reductive theories and abstractions, including theological tendencies in this direction. Perhaps the keyword of the Dublin lectures is 'enlargement', suggesting a constant development of horizon, a process that Newman himself described explicitly in terms of movement: 'We feel our minds to be growing and expanding then, when we not only learn, but refer what we learn to what we know already. It is not a mere addition to our knowledge which illuminates, but the locomotion, the movement onwards' (*IU*, 120–1). Read even today, these lectures still offer an experience of a questing rather than a closed mind, a mind in movement towards worthy horizons.

Newman has too often been quoted at graduation ceremonies in the guise of a high idealist. It would be truer to present him as an empiricist who celebrates self-conscious human growth and who satirises the enemies of human potential. He was an open critic of a utilitarian approach to education, arguing that its real goal should be to facilitate personal integration and a sense of connection. If people merely study or read without thinking, he remarked, they will never find roots. They will be merely 'possessed by their knowledge, not possessed of it'. Such knowledge in his view 'is unworthy of the name, knowledge which they have not thought through, and thought out' (*IU*, 126). For him the slow process of self-appropriation was central. His explorations of education, as with his studies of church history or of the credibility of faith, make their appeal not to external evidence and achievement but to an inner logic of the whole person. To cite the universities discourses once more, 'if we make light of what is deepest within us, nothing is left but to pay homage to what is more upon the surface. To *seem* becomes to *be*' (*IU*, 173).

Thus Newman intuited an anthropological crisis behind the phenomena of his century. The ultimate danger would be to opt for a 'one-sided progress of mind' (*GA*, 396) and hence to be unable to confront the major questions of life. As he said with unusual power in one of his sermons, if 'we dare not trust each other with the secret of our hearts', then our sense of truth becomes 'dim' and our beliefs 'unreal'. As a result of our fear to start from our roots, even 'our religion viewed as a social system is hollow' (*PPS*, V, 127). Newman is rightly presented as a campaigner against 'liberalism' in the sense of a rationalism that would dismiss or water down religious faith. But behind this lifelong battle lay another preoccupation of his as seen in these quotations. He discerned a danger in the emerging self-images of his age. Just as his great hope was to justify religious faith in a context of human self-transcendence, so his great fear was of paralysing forces, intellectual and cultural, that would stunt this enlargement of mind and imagination.

Since several of the authors discussed in this book are writers of fiction, it seems right to give some attention to Newman's two works in this genre. Both of them are novels of conversion. *Loss and Gain* (1848) deals with the conversion of an Oxford student to Catholicism and *Callista* (1855) is a third-century story of conversion to Christianity. The first was written during Newman's year of study and noviceship (as an Oratorian) in Rome just after his own conversion. *Callista* was written over several years and in part during his many journeys back and forth between Birmingham and Dublin. Both books belong to a sub-genre not much in vogue today, that of didactic religious fiction. G.K. Chesterton once remarked about himself that he was not a genuine novelist because he liked to see ideas wrestling naked. Newman tended towards a similar debating style. Although his religious preoccupations may have cramped his potential as a novelist, these two works illustrate, in a different idiom, his fascination with the movement of life, with the adventure of religious discovery. His focus is not doctrine but disposition for faith, as is captured in these words from *Loss and Gain*: 'A man's moral being is concentrated in each moment of his life; it lives in the tips of his fingers, and the spring of his insteps' (*LG*, 260). This is what modern thinkers would call fundamental option, and Newman was typically concerned to explore journeys into new horizons. In fact during his year in Rome he found the Jesuits there to be dry and immobile thinkers: 'There is a deep suspicion of change, with a perfect incapacity to create any thing positive for the wants of the times.' Newman, by contrast, relished the challenge of change and was admired, even among those who could not share his faith, for his capacity to speak to the culture of his day.

In this spirit Charles Reding, the central character of *Loss and Gain*, gradually becomes capable of seeing through the mixture of rationalism and liberalism embodied in Dr Brownside, who comes to preach a university sermon. Here Newman is at his satiric best in exposing a merely optimistic pragmatism masquerading as religion:

> As a divine, he seemed never to have any difficulty on any subject; he was so clear or so shallow, that he saw to the bottom of all his thoughts ... Revelation to him, instead of being the

abyss of God's counsels, with its dim outlines and broad shadows, was a flat sunny plain, laid out with straight macadamised roads. (*LG*, 50)

A digression away from the novels may be useful here. During Newman's year in Rome (1846–7) he prepared a summary of his thinking on faith in the form of twelve theses in Latin. As he said in a letter, he wanted to get 'up the subject catholicly'. This would dispel any clouds of suspicion that hung over this famous convert, previously ignorant of the scholastic tradition of thought. These Latin theses offer a fine summary of his positions, especially as advanced in his Oxford University Sermons. However, what is totally absent is the quality of his thought, the process of his explorations, the 'elastic' flow of his language. In this Latin summary one finds the skeleton of Newman's theology of faith but without the characteristic contours of his prose-as-discovery. Such correct abstractions were alien to Newman's sensibility. His whole temperament had always resisted the merely rational, not only in matters of religion. As a speaker and writer his power lay in inviting his audience to participate in the unfolding of insight. And, as already argued, his style in English echoed not the certainty of conclusions but the 'imperial intellect' in quest for ever more adequate understanding. His real interest lay in the pre-conceptual realm of human attitudes as constituting the 'antecedent probability' for faith. He was an existential and process thinker before those terms came into prominence, and it is precisely that lived sense of performance and process that is missing in his Latin theses. Indeed they fall into the category that he satirised as 'straight macadamised roads'. In preparing these pages he was being unfaithful to his innate distrust of systems.

To return to the novels: although there is a certain playfulness and comedy in *Loss and Gain*, practically all the commentators on Newman's fiction agree that *Callista* is the more successful novel in literary terms. Its narrative is more experimental and it goes well beyond the rather stuffy discourses of Oxford students. Here we are in North Africa in the epoch of St. Cyprian, the age of persecution and of martyrdom, and the author revels in descriptions of a larger historical and geographical canvas than the world of a university. The story focuses on the gradual journey towards Christian faith of a sophisticated Greek statue maker called Callista, who falls in love with a secret but somewhat tepid Christian called Agellius. Indeed it is Agellius who seems closest to Charles of the previous novel, embodying Newman's frequent twinning of intellect and heart: 'He had got a thousand questions which needed answers, a thousand feelings which needed sympathy' (*C*, 93). Callista too, through her relationship with Agellius, comes to envisage a divine fulfilment for 'her intellect and affections' (*C*, 133). What Newman is dramatising in this pagan figure is the gradualness of spiritual perception, how it takes time for the implicit to become explicit, and, once again, that it does so through an informal or intuitive logic of the whole person. Later when Callista is in prison as a suspected Christian (even though not yet baptised), she is confronted with Polemo of Rhodes, a friend of Plotinus, who believes in 'one eternal self-existing something'. To this Callista replies in words that are vintage Newman, expressing his life-long concern with conscience as the ground of natural religion:

> I feel that God within my heart. I feel myself in His presence. He says to me, 'Do this: don't do that' … it is the echo of a person speaking to me … An echo implies a voice; a voice a speaker. That speaker I love and I fear. (*C*, 314–15)

Callista's further step into revealed religion comes after reading Luke's gospel. In terms close to his stress on imagination and real assent some fifteen years later, Newman writes: 'that image sank deep into her; she felt it to be a reality' (*C*, 326). 'By degrees', we are told, she came to walk by a 'new philosophy' and to relish a 'new meaning' for life and death (*C*, 328). Again in this second novel Newman shows himself fascinated by the informal logic of preconceptual imagination.

By way of conclusion, something needs to be said about his particular emphasis on imagination. I recall that one of the passages of Newman studied during my student days in UCD was a satirical piece known as 'The Tamworth Reading Room'. In 1841 Newman was provoked by remarks made by Sir Robert Peel that the fruits of religion could also be acquired through public libraries and science, and he exploded into print in *The Times* with five letters signed *Catholicus*. He poured scorn on any anthropology of a merely 'reasoning animal' as distinct from a 'seeing, feeling, contemplating, acting animal', and he argued that 'the heart is commonly reached not through the reason, but through the imagination' (*GA*, 94, 92). Newman quoted this passage some thirty years later in *The Grammar of Assent*, when he expounded his epistemology of religious truth and focused on a positive role for imagination. His well-known concept of 'real assent' (as distinct from 'notional') was originally called 'imaginative assent', but Newman seems to have feared that people would confuse 'imaginative' with 'imaginary'. His key point, however, in what he called 'the theology of a religious imagination' (*GA*, 117), is that all forms of existential truth involve the human imagination more than our strictly rational faculties. In the tradition of Coleridge, he saw imagination as capable of fusing different levels of awareness and of 'realising' zones beyond the narrowly empirical. Unless something is apprehended by the imagination, it will not touch our affectivity. Without such an experiential convergence, what he called a 'living organon' (*GA*, 316), we cannot arrive at personal certitude in questions of living truth.

It is significant that the final page of the *Grammar* mentions intellect and imagination as working together in the pursuit of religious vision: 'creating a certitude of its truth by arguments too various for direct enumeration, too personal and deep for words, too powerful and concurrent for refutation' (*GA*, 492). Once again the prose and the process are twinned in Newman's typical voice.

Several commentators have explored 'the intersection with Romantic aesthetics' in Newman's work and how his career is also 'an attempt to retailor Romanticism' (Nixon, 61, 81). To the best of my knowledge (and aided by a search of newmanreader.org) Newman never spoke positively of anything 'aesthetic'. On the rare occasions when he used the word it suggested an inordinate cult of external religion, a seeking after fine ceremonies as ends in themselves. So what can be said of his connection with the title of this book? He would happily acknowledge that the aesthetic sense is a rich and enriching zone of the human adventure but only one zone. He would not find himself at ease with a line from the early Yeats: 'Words alone are certain good.' His feel for the flow and power of words was unique but they were servants of a larger adventure.

Perhaps a certain fascination with the verbal is, arguably, a central strand in Irish writing and in the UCD tradition. For the love of word-craft displayed in this tradition Newman may have been a stimulus for some, but he also offers a challenge. He enjoyed the texture of cadences and phrases to the point that Joyce, as was seen, looked up to him as a master, even as *il miglior fabbro*. These pages have sought to situate that literary gift in a larger perspective and one with which Newman would probably agree. He feared various reductive tendencies in the world around him: a crude utilitarianism in education, an arrogant and un-balanced rationality in intellectuals, a cultural kidnap of religion that chose only its more consoling aspects, a closed attitude which he called 'self-contemplation' in life or literature. Instead he wanted to render the movement of human consciousness in its full stretch towards meaning, seeing this as the highest humanist goal, ultimately crowned by the recognition of God. And he embodied this large 'venture' (one of his favourite words) in a mobile prose that echoed a constant converging of mind and heart and imagination.

I have tried to show how his genius as a writer was rooted in an exceptional level of attention to the inner movements of the self. Let Newman have the last word, with another passage from the university sermon of 1840 already quoted, and one that perfectly captures his sensibility: 'We not only feel, and think, and reason, but we know that we feel, and think, and reason; not only know, but can inspect and ascertain our thoughts, feelings, and reasonings: not only ascertain, but describe' (*FS*, 256). 'Describe' is a weak word for what Newman offered throughout his writings: he enacted the flow of our inquiring minds with a unique accuracy and eloquence.

PRIMARY REFERENCES

C = *Callista: A Sketch of the Third Century*, edited by Alan G. Hill
   (Notre Dame: University of Notre Dame Press, 2001).
FS = *Fifteen Sermons Preached before the University of Oxford*,
   edited by Mary Katherine Tillman (Notre Dame: University
   of Notre Dame Press, 1997).
GA = *An Essay in Aid of a Grammar of Assent* (London: Longmans,
   Green, and Co., 1909).
IU = *The Idea of a University*, edited by I.T. Ker (Oxford:
   Clarendon Press, 1976).
LG = *Loss and Gain, or the story of a convert*, edited by Alan G.
   Hill (World's Classics) (Oxford: Oxford University Press,
   1986).
PPS = *Parochial and Plain Sermons*, 8 volumes (London:
   Rivingtons, 1877).

SECONDARY REFERENCES

Jude V. Nixon, '"Steadily Contemplating the Object of Faith":
   Newman, the Apologia, and Romantic Aesthetics', in
   Nineteenth Century Prose 18 (1991): 60–83.
James Pribek, S.J., 'Newman and Joyce', in *Studies: An Irish
   Quarterly Review* 93 (2004): 169–84.

Gerard Manley Hopkins (1844–1889)

Brian Arkins

The circumstances in which the great Victorian poet Gerard Manley Hopkins arrived in Dublin, and those in which he lived there, were difficult. In February 1884, Hopkins was appointed Fellow in Classics of the Royal University and Professor of Greek at University College Dublin. The Jesuit President of UCD, Fr William Delany, wished to appoint academic staff who would equal those in Trinity College, Dublin, and so sought a suitable man from the English Jesuits. The English Provincial, Fr Purbrick, refused to release any of the first six men on Delany's list, but agreed that he could have Hopkins. Despite this agreement between the two Jesuits, Hopkins' appointment was controversial. Several senior Catholic clerics opposed Hopkins, including Cardinal McCabe, the Archbishop of Dublin, and his successor in that post, Dr William Walsh; they put up an alternative candidate, Fr J.E. Reffe, Dean of Studies at Blackrock College. When Hopkins was appointed, McCabe and Walsh resigned from the University Senate. One aspect of the dispute was political: was Irish nationalism to be fostered by Delany's stress on academic excellence, even if this meant bringing in Englishmen, or by Walsh's belief that Irishmen should hold such posts? A further aspect was financial: the Fellowship of the Royal University (which was purely an examining body) was worth £400 a year, and Delany wanted the money for a hard-pressed UCD, since, if a Jesuit was appointed, the money would accrue to the University.

Hopkins' initial view of Dublin in 1884 was negative –

'Dublin itself is a joyless place' – and reflects the squalid circumstances of the city in the late nineteenth century; indeed the houses of UCD on St Stephen's Green were 'a sort of ruin' (197). It was Hopkins' fate to spend much of his life in great houses that had come down in the world socially: Stonyhurst, Manresa, now UCD. Dublin replied to Hopkins' strictures by finding in him an egregious example of an English Catholic aesthete (who had been taught at Oxford by Pater). A number of factors combined to make Hopkins' life at UCD difficult: his separation from his beloved England and from his family; his distaste for rampant Irish nationalism; his inability to complete various projects in the field of Classics; the unsatisfactory type of teaching in UCD; and, above all, a very large amount of examining that he found exhausting. Hopkins' teaching duties at UCD were less than onerous, but it was a very different type of teaching to the tutorial method he experienced at Balliol College, Oxford. He was required to provide elementary lessons to the students, and anecdotal evidence suggests that he was not at ease in this situation and was unable to maintain discipline. Doubtless, his refusal to cover material prescribed for examinations did not endear him to the students.

Nor could Hopkins count on a pleasant life in Dublin, outside of UCD. He was geographically separated from his family, just as he had been spiritually separated from them by his conversion to Catholicism. This conversion also meant that Hopkins did not belong to the mainstream of English society, and now was literally removed from the beloved England in which he had grown up and been educated. Moreover, being English in Ireland in the 1880s ensured that you were regarded with suspicion, a factor that in Hopkins' case was doubtless exacerbated by his eccentricity.

Hopkins' attitude to Irish nationalism was paradoxical. On the one hand, he was a supporter of Home Rule, writing to Baillie in 1887: '[t]hey must have Home Rule with all that it may cost both them and us. You would say so if you lived here' (253). Indeed Hopkins could go even further and envisage an independent Irish state: 'For these steps have done nothing to give [the Irish], but have nevertheless done much to bring them nearer getting, the object of their undying desire and now of their flaming passion. This is what they called Nationhood. The passion for it is of its nature insatiable and Home Rule will not satisfy it ...' (252). On the other hand, Hopkins' innate conservatism and loyalty to England meant that he detested the day-to-day manifestations of Irish nationalism. He writes of 'unspeakable Nationalist papers'. He criticises any breaking of the law by nationalists because 'The cry ... should be Law and Freedom, Freedom and Law' (226). And he is scandalised by the nationalist activities of Catholic clerics:

> Meantime the Catholic Church in Ireland and the Irish Province in it and our College in that are greatly given over to a partly unlawful cause, promoted by partly unlawful means, and against my will my pains, laborious and distasteful, like prisoners made to serve the enemies' gunners, go to help on this cause. (*The Sermons and Devotional Writings of Gerard Manley Hopkins*, 262)

The factors just outlined combined to render Hopkins prone to what he calls 'nervous weakness' or 'nervous prostration'. In modern clinical terms, this seems to involve anxiety with an element of depression, possibly combined with manic phases in what is now termed bipolar disorder. Certainly, Hopkins' descriptions of his mental state are harrowing. In a letter to Baillie in May 1885, he provides the clearest account:

> The melancholy I have all my life been subject to has become of late years not indeed more intense in its fits but rather more distributed, constant, and crippling. One, the lightest but a very inconvenient form of it, is daily anxiety about work to be done, which makes me break off or never finish all that lies outside that work. It is useless to write more on this: when I am at the worst, though my judgement is never affected, my state is much like madness. I see no ground for thinking I shall ever get over it or ever succeed in doing anything that is not forced on me to do of any consequence. (209)

But there were also positive aspects to Hopkins' life in Dublin. His closest friend was a fellow Jesuit (as yet to be ordained) named Robert Curtis, who was Professor of Natural Philosophy at UCD, and of whom Hopkins wrote: 'he is my comfort beyond what I can say and a kind of godsend I never expected to have'

(202–3). He often talked with Curtis late into the night, and the two men went on holiday together twice. And Hopkins used to visit the house of Curtis' father, who was a prominent barrister.

The acquaintance of Hopkins with a number of eminent Catholic families can be illustrated by the fact that he stayed on several occasions with the Misses Cassidy of Monasterevin in Kildare, who owned a large distillery and who were Catholic but Unionist. Hopkins was a frequent visitor to the house in Donnybrook of Dr Francis McCabe, the Director of Dundrum Asylum, who had a son in Stonyhurst and who had heard Hopkins preach there on the Blessed Sacrament. He was also friendly with the poet Katherine Tynan and in the late 1880s visited her house in Clondalkin on Sundays.

Another acquaintance of Hopkins in Dublin was John Butler Yeats, the father of the poet, who asked him to call and then presented him with a copy of his son's work *Mosada: A Dramatic Poem*. Hopkins could not 'think highly of' this poem of Yeats, and, although he praised another poem 'The Two Titans' to the elder Yeats, he deemed this composition of his son to be 'a strained and unworkable allegory' (White, 170–1). Much later in 1937, Yeats (who did not remember meeting Hopkins) got his own back by expressing elaborate doubts about Hopkins in the introduction to *The Oxford Book of Modern Verse*.

A further positive aspect of Hopkins' time in Dublin was the extensive correspondence he conducted with a number of distinguished Englishmen: Robert Bridges, Coventry Patmore, Canon Richard Dixon, and Mowbray Baillie. These men provided Hopkins with much needed support during his five years in Ireland. Although Hopkins failed to finish any of his projects in Classical Studies, he did manage to collect and send in a collection of Hiberno-English words (eighty-nine in all) for Joseph Wright's innovative *English Dialect Dictionary*. A fitting occupation for a man who thought Victorian English 'a bad business'.

These positive features of Hopkins' life in Dublin cannot, however, be said to compensate for his anguish. What Hopkins experienced in Dublin was not the dark night of the soul as expounded by John of the Cross and other mystics. Rather, he suffered from what Ignatius of Loyola calls in the *Spiritual Exercises* 'desolation'. Ignatius defines 'desolation' as:

> darkness and disturbance in the soul, attraction towards what is low and of the earth, anxiety arising from various agitations and temptations. All this tends to a lack of confidence in which the soul is without hope and without love; one finds oneself thoroughly lazy, lukewarm, sad, and as though cut off from one's Creator and Lord.

It is, then, this 'war within' that Hopkins so wonderfully explores in the Dublin 'sonnets of desolation', as he enters into what Yeats calls 'the abyss of himself'.

The picture painted of Hopkins struggling with his interiorised, isolated Self is indeed heart-rending. Hopkins writes:

> I began to enter on that course of loathing and hopelessness which I have so often felt before, which made me fear madness and led me to give up the practice of meditation ... The body cannot rest when it is in pain nor the mind be at peace as long as something bitter distills in it and it aches. (*The Sermons and Devotional Writings of Gerard Manley Hopkins*, 262)

And Hopkins further refers to one of these sonnets as being 'written in blood'. The pain he suffers is without end. In 'No worst, there is none', 'More pangs will, schooled at forepangs, wilder wring'. None of his eminently sensible projects (like those in Classical Studies) comes to fruition. In 'To seem the Stranger', 'Only what word/Wisest my heart breeds dark heaven's baffling ban/Bars or hell's spell thwarts'. It is indeed the case that God seems to have deserted him as though he were damned: the Creator 'lives alas! away', and his decree 'Bitter would have me taste' ('I wake and feel the fall of dark').

In the face of such great desolation, Hopkins feels obliged in the sonnet 'Thou art indeed just' to take issue with God in the manner of Job, of Jeremiah (who provides the epigraph), and of Teresa of Avila. He poses another question that neither he nor we are able to answer, the reason sinners flourish while God's loyal servants do not: 'Oh, the sots and thralls of lust/Do in spare hours more thrive than I that spend,/Sir, life upon thy cause'.

Hopkins is therefore 'Time's eunuch', who must pray for the rain that might bring renewed life.

But it is important to recognise that Hopkins persevered, so that the beginning of the sonnet 'Carrion Comfort' 'I'll not … cry *I can no more. I can* …' anticipates in a very striking way the famous ending of Beckett's novel *The Unnameable*: 'you must go on, I can't go on, I'll go on'. And as Hopkins goes on in sonnet after sonnet, his lament to his friend and fellow poet Robert Bridges that 'I want the one rapture of an inspiration' is ironically rendered untrue ('To R.B.'). For Hopkins, like others, found that a way of dealing with pain is to transmute it into art. He found himself closer than he might like to Nietzsche: 'Only as an aesthetic phenomenon is existence and the world eternally justified.' So when Hopkins begins one of the Dublin sonnets with the assertion 'No worst, there is none' (where the deviant syntax mirrors his desperate state), already the writing of this sentence assuages the feeling that gives rise to it; as Edgar points out in *King Lear* (4.1), 'the worst is not/so long as we can say "This is the worst"'.

Christians believe that Christ's Crucifixion is followed by His Resurrection and that this establishes a pattern for the individual human person. So even in his anguish in Dublin, Hopkins wrote a sonnet about the Resurrection and may be viewed as himself experiencing resurrection after his death. To bring out the significance of the Resurrection, Hopkins, in his magnificent sonnet of 1888 'That Nature is a Heraclitean Fire and of the Comfort of the Resurrection', uses as a foil the doctrine of Heraclitus; as he wrote, 'a great deal of early Greek philosophy was distilled' in the poem. Heraclitus held that the all-pervasive fire of the cosmos is subject to perpetual change according to definite laws, and that unredeemed man (who has a fiery soul) is simultaneously the best of nature and subject to very rapid change into the degrading element of water and ultimately to death. But Christ's Resurrection changes all that because, after death, the body and the soul of the individual human person will rise again. As Donne writes, 'Death, thou shalt die'; as the Easter liturgy of the Orthodox Church puts it, Christ ' by his death has trampled upon death'. The result is that the essential duality in man – who is ordinary, banal, even comic as a person, but who is also a being that will not die – is overcome by Christ's sacrifice whose fire is immortal. Hence the glorious last line of Hopkins' poem: 'This Jack, joke, poor potsherd, patch, matchwood, immortal diamond/Is immortal diamond.'

The sonnet 'To R.B.' is Hopkins' last poem, written on April 22, 1889, seven weeks before his death. A classic example of a poem about not writing a poem, this sonnet sees Hopkins lament his lack of 'inspiration' in a 'winter world', while simultaneously disproving this analysis by producing an excellent poem. The paradox can be extended to Hopkins' whole career. Little could he have thought that the 'trickling increment' of time ('St. Alphonsus Rodriguez') would ensure not only that his poems, including the great Dublin series, would be published by Bridges in 1918, but also that by the 1930s he would be recognised as a major poet. Hopkins died in 1889 in Dublin, in UCD, unknown, unpublished. The mills of God …

Primary references

The Poems of Gerard Manley Hopkins, fourth edition, edited by W.H. Gardner and N.N. MacKenzie (Oxford: Oxford University Press, 1967).
Gerard Manley Hopkins: Selected Letters, edited by Catherine Phillips (Oxford: Clarendon, 1990).
The Sermons and Devotional Writings of Gerard Manley Hopkins, edited by Christopher Devlin, S.J. (London: Oxford University Press, 1959).

Secondary reference

Norman White, *Hopkins in Ireland* (Dublin: University College Dublin Press, 2002).

Thomas MacDonagh (1878–1916)

Declan Kiberd

Universities have always been founded on a dubious assumption: that learning and piety are somehow conducive to one another. You have only to study the more ribald lyrics penned by medieval scholastics to see just how baseless such an equation is. When John Henry Newman founded his college in the Dublin of 1854, he did so with the idea of creating a Catholic intelligentsia which might not only consolidate the social benefits of Emancipation in Ireland but also add weight and mass to the crusade for Romanism in the wider British scheme of things.

Yet, little more than half a century later, University College Dublin would produce graduates with a somewhat different set of agendas. Newman's classic conversion-narrative, *Apologia Pro Vita Sua*, would be rewritten by James Joyce as *A Portrait of the Artist as a Young Man*, lodging an even more pressing claim for the vocation of art over that of religion. Far from integrating a rationalised, Victorian form of Catholicism into British life, a group of writers emerged whose mystical understanding of that religion was invoked to further a claim to full national independence.

All universities must sponsor a comprehensive syllabus delivered with some semblance of objectivity. But those which evolve a distinctive 'aesthetic' often do so by giving shape to the energies of gifted individuals at a concentrated phase of their development. If the Oxford of the later nineteenth century became an outpost of lost causes, Zuleika Dobsons and dreaming spires, the Sorbonne of the 1960s was a place in which

29

intellectuals sought to seize power and remake the world. If Vanderbilt University in Tennessee became home to the Agrarian poets of the defeated post-Civil War American south, Sao Paolo in Brazil could be cited as the meeting point in the mid-twentieth century for the ideas of European Modernism and those of an insurgent Latin America. And of course in the writings of Trinity College, Dublin, graduates from Jonathan Swift to Samuel Beckett may be found a blend of bleak wit and cool comedy that characterises an Anglo-Irish caste always willing to view man as if he were some kind of anthropological witness of himself.

What might a UCD aesthetic be and wherein might it be found? One answer could be to locate it in the attempts of a Catholic intelligentsia to evolve a lay version of that religion, at once mystical and modernist, and often executed in a spirit of high playfulness. This is a strain which links writers as disparate as Hopkins, Joyce, Clarke, Flann O'Brien, Coffey or Devlin. It has definite roots in Newman, who was often accused by his enemies of insincere punning, tricksy rhetoric and sheer play-acting. James Pribek has gone so far as to cite the 'trickster' figure as the major link between Newman and Joyce: and there is every reason to believe that this is correct.

Why has this not been more obvious? Why did it take an American Jesuit such as Pribek to make the connection? A determinedly secular criticism has for decades turned Joyce into a carbon copy of itself; and an Irish intelligentsia, smarting under the censorship of the independent state, rapidly came to disconnect the words 'Catholic' and 'modernist' (ably abetted in that act of disconnection by most of the authorities of the Catholic church). The theorists of intellectual freedom in *The Bell* and other liberal journals were quite unable to admit the technical conservatism of their own favoured art forms (mostly social realist) or to recognise the astonishing formal experimentation of such avowedly Catholic writers as Coffey, Devlin or, indeed, Flann O'Brien. Back in the 1920s the critic I.A. Richards had announced the severance of 'poetry' from 'belief'. The 'radical' intellects of independent Ireland in subsequent decades were so busy seeking a separation of church and state that they were in no mood to sponsor a reconnection of religion and art. Newman had produced his Catholic intelligentsia, all right, but its effects were strangely 'underground'.

Today, with that censorship a distant memory, it is possible to marvel at the number of writers produced by UCD who not only evolved a lay mysticism but also integrated an 'Irish Mode' (based largely on Gaelic syntax and prosody) into the languages of modern English. Here, a line would pass from Clarke and Flann O'Brien through Kinsella and McGahern down to Éilís Ní Dhuibhne.

All of these traditions seem to come to a point of convergence in the writings of Thomas MacDonagh, who was born in Cloughjordan, Co. Tipperary, in 1878 and executed as a British prisoner-of-war in 1916. His parents were teachers, the father a cheerful drunkard, the mother a devout convert from Protestantism. MacDonagh was educated by the Holy Ghost Fathers at Rockwell and returned for some years there as a clerical student. Undergoing a sudden crisis of faith, he produced large quantities of death-obsessed poetry. His early tastes were antique and, like the young Joyce, he made a special study of Elizabethan love songs.

When W.B. Yeats was shown some of his poems in 1903, he told MacDonagh not to publish, 'but to read the great old masters of English, Spenser, Ben Jonson, Sir Thomas Browne, perhaps Chaucer, until you have got feebler modern English out of your head'. How badly this advice was needed can be judged from a poem called 'Róisín':

> Deep in my Irish heart I grieve that I
> Know not to sing my lays in Irish tongue;
> That here no Gaelic heart before my feet
> I place with trusting gladness; – such vain sigh
> In hope of change, its offering has wrung
> From one who yearns to do thee homage meet.

Yeats went one better and told MacDonagh to 'translate a great deal from the Irish – to translate literally, preserving as much of the idioms as possible. It will help you get rid of the conventionality of language from which we all suffer today'.

MacDonagh was on the road to literary modernism. By 1907 his style had taken full measure of the sprung rhythms and compound words of both Whitman and his disciple Hopkins:

> Heart-felt, brain-syllabled, and lip-let-loose –
> Sweet-sung to-day, to-morrow harsh and hissed.

However, the major and happiest influence was the poetry of the man who had given the good advice:

> None would the service ask
> That she from love requires,
> Making it not a task
> But a high sacrament
> Of all love's dear desires
> And all life's grave intent.

('After a Year')

That was, however, as good as MacDonagh's poetry got. More often it remained a proof of the Wildean contention that all bad poetry springs from genuine feeling, being brooding, subjective and often indecipherable.

Part of McDonagh's problem was technical: how to find an objective language for the mystic's states of consciousness. His close collaboration with Joseph Plunkett was based on a shared desire to express the unknown in terms of the known. In an article for *The Irish Review* MacDonagh spoke of the challenge facing 'the mystic who has to express in terms of sound and wit the things of God that are made known to him in no language'. J.M. Synge had confronted the same challenge in the 1890s and had solved it by the expedient recommended by Yeats: word-for-word translation from another language, which if done with integrity would locate the frustrated mystic on a needle-point between official languages. There is reason to believe that Synge shared his ideas with MacDonagh who met him regularly in 1908. MacDonagh recalled that Synge 'read me some of his translations from Petrarch into that wonderful rich language of the Irish peasant'.

Whenever MacDonagh wrote subjectively he wrote badly and without the distinction of a personal style. His poems are often a roomful of old echoes. But when he translated from the Irish, he conveyed the urgency of a man speaking with full force:

> The yellow bittern that never broke out
> In a drinking bout, might as well have drunk;

His bones were thrown on a naked stone
Where he lived alone like a hermit monk.
O yellow bittern! I pity your lot,
Though they say that a sot like myself is curst –
I was sober a while, but I'll drink and be wise
For I fear I should die in the end of thirst.

('The Yellow Bittern')

MacDonagh, in discovering such Gaelic folk authors – the Irish equivalent of the Elizabethan songsters – liberated also the frustrated author and artist within himself. He was, like Synge, an example of an artist whose genius was for translating the effects of Gaelic syntax into English, a language often held to be incapable of conveying such effects. MacDonagh really was a case of the translator as a character in search of an author, one who might free him into pure utterance. He was least of all himself when he wrote 'sincere' lyrics, but once given a mask he told a deeply personal truth.

It was out of triumphs like this that Thomas MacDonagh produced his major critical study, *Literature in Ireland*, arguably the most influential work of literary analysis to come out of UCD. In it he produced brilliant versions in English of Gaelic poetry and song, as rendered by Ferguson, Mangan, Callanan, Walsh and, of course, himself. He identified an Irish mode, rooted in the Gaelic substratum and characterised by the wavering, delayed rhythms pioneered in English by Tom Moore and perfected by W.B. Yeats. MacDonagh's lectures on this topic were delivered to an M.A. class and constituted the raw material for his book. They deeply inspired one student, Austin Clarke, who would refine the ideas further in his own poetic theory and practice. On a visit to his teacher's house at Oakley Road, Clarke discovered at first hand just how seriously MacDonagh took his idea of a bilingual Ireland. While he stood out on the kerb discoursing on Tudor lyrics, his toddler son, Donagh, cried out as a horse-and-cart flew past: 'Look, daddy, at the capall.'

It was, however, for its definition and description of the evolution of Anglo-Irish literature that MacDonagh's book would be remembered. The subtitle was 'Studies Irish and Anglo-Irish' and the essays asserted the essential continuity of the two, seemingly opposed, Irish traditions. MacDonagh contended that by the time of the Penal Laws Gaelic literature had become decadent, but for more than a century afterwards English 'was not yet able to carry on the tradition or to syllable anew for itself here'. (This was a view to be reiterated for a later generation by Thomas Kinsella.) MacDonagh suggested that it was only with the emergence of a writer such as Synge that one had an art 'at once sufficiently Gaelic to express the feeling of the central Irish tradition, and sufficiently master of English style to use it as one uses the air one breathes'.

Rejecting Patrick Pearse's doctrine that a national literature could be created only in the Irish language, MacDonagh went on to declare that modern Irish suffered from the very same defects which affected modern English: journalese, cliché, fatigued imprecision (all those elements which would in due time feed the surreal imagination of Flann O'Brien). The ideal solution to this dilemma had been found in the Hiberno-English dialect of Synge which 'at its best is more vigorous, fresh and simple than either of the two languages between which it stands'. MacDonagh conceded that 'all of us find in Irish rather than in English a satisfactory understanding of certain ways of ours and the best expression of certain of our emotions – so we are expressing ourselves in translating from Irish'. However, he was quick to point out that such translations were just a temporary expedient during the transition to English: 'At present a large amount of translation is natural. Later, when we have expressed again in English all the emotions and experiences expressed already in Irish, this literature will go forward, free from translation.'

Legend has it that MacDonagh was working on the proofs of *Literature in Ireland* during lulls in the firing at Jacobs' Factory through Easter week 1916. A further legend holds that he improvised a game of cricket, using a battered tennis ball, while holed up in the building. Some commentators find it hard to understand how a man who stood so steadfastly for the confluence of two traditions could have become the leader of an insurrection. But MacDonagh saw no contradiction. In his final class at UCD, he simply closed his copy of *Pride and Prejudice* and sighed: 'Ah, lads, there's nobody like Jane!' His rebel comrades also revered English poetry, Pearse sharing his lifelong admiration for Wordsworth, Plunkett his love for Francis Thompson. They were liberal, educated men who simply wanted their country back from a usurping power, much as they had also sought, in their earlier work as a lay intelligentsia, to seize back from the priests of Cullenite Catholicism those godly things which are not narratable in any obvious language.

Like many lay Catholic intellectuals, MacDonagh had his share of disagreements with church authority. He married a Protestant, Muriel Gifford, with the co-operation of a 'modernist' priest who did not insist that she promise to convert, but who enjoined the couple to absolute secrecy. Thereafter, MacDonagh was only a sporadic churchgoer, although it seems that he received the last sacraments before his execution, at which the British officer-in-command observed that 'they all died nobly, but MacDonagh died like a prince'.

After his death, MacDonagh's influence grew rapidly. *Literature in Ireland* was published in Dublin later in 1916, establishing his reputation as a scholar-critic. So worried were the British authorities by the way in which the 'poets' rebellion' was capturing the international imagination that they commissioned special essays from H.G. Wells, John Galsworthy and Arnold Bennett denouncing the cult in American magazines and newspapers. But the tide could not be turned. Even within the British Army itself, a young poet from County Meath, Francis Ledwidge, recreated those internal rhymes and assonance favoured by the *fili* in his haunting lament for the man who had done so much to introduce the Irish mode into English:

> He shall not hear the bittern cry
> In the wild sky, where he is lain,
> Nor voices of the sweeter birds
> Above the wailing of the rain.

> Nor shall he know when loud March blows
> Thro' slanting snows her fanfare shrill,
> Blowing to flame the golden cup
> Of many an upset daffodil.

But when the Dark Cow leaves the moor,
And pastures pure with greedy weeds,
Perhaps he'll hear her low at morn
Lifting her horn in pleasant meads.

('Lament for Thomas MacDonagh')

In December 1917 *The Irish Times* (no friend of the Easter rebels) nevertheless published a poem by AE/George Russell lamenting two fallen Thomases, MacDonagh dead in the Rising and Kettle in the trenches of the Great War, both of them UCD lecturers:

I listened to high talk from you,
Thomas MacDonagh, and it seemed
The words were idle, but they grew
To nobleness by death redeemed.
Life cannot utter words more great
Than life may meet by sacrifice,
High words were equalled by high fate,
You paid the price: You paid the price.

You who have fought on fields afar,
That other Ireland did you wrong
Who said you shadowed Ireland's star,
Nor gave you laurel wreath nor song.
You proved by death as true as they,
In mightier conflicts played your part,
Equal your sacrifice may weigh
Dear Kettle of the generous heart.

('To the Memory of Some I Knew who are Dead and who Loved Ireland')

Newman could hardly have foreseen all this, least of all a UCD involvement in the Easter rebellion. But perhaps in some oblique fashion, his underlying intentions were carried out. After all, he had always proclaimed himself a defender of threatened traditions and on that basis had declared that, if he had been born an Irishman, he would most certainly have been a rebel.

Perhaps it was the spirit of Cardinal Newman which guided the college authorities to appoint Austin Clarke to the lectureship which his charismatic teacher had left vacant. His own versions of Irish poetry would scale even greater heights, providing in turn the inspiration on which a later translator such as Thomas Kinsella could build.

Primary references

The Poetical Works of Thomas MacDonagh, edited by James Stephens (Dublin: Talbot Press, 1916).

Thomas MacDonagh, *Literature in Ireland* (Dublin: Talbot Press, 1916).

Francis Ledwidge, 'Lament for Thomas MacDonagh', in *Field Day Anthology of Irish Writing*, Volume 2, edited by Seamus Deane (Derry: Field Day Publications, 1991): 774.

James Joyce (1882–1941)

Anne Fogarty

Despite his self-assigned role as outsider and unrelenting assailant on the conventional institutions of Irish middle-class society, pedagogy and the business of learning are deep-seated pre-occupations in the writings of James Joyce. Classrooms and scenes of education abound in his work from the descriptions of Clongowes Wood College, Belvedere College and student life at University College Dublin in *A Portrait of the Artist as a Young Man* to Stephen Dedalus's maladroit efforts as history teacher in 'Nestor' in *Ulysses* and the nightlessons sequence of *Finnegans Wake*. Tutelary relationships between pupil and teacher figures are also recurrent features of his texts. Even though partially sinister and fateful, they are depicted as crucial determinants for self-development. Amongst these links between acolyte and mentor may be numbered such assorted pairings as the anonymous child and the errant, but magnetic, Fr Flynn in 'The Sisters', the mitching schoolboys and the 'queer old josser' in 'An Encounter', Stephen Dedalus and a cohort of Jesuit lecturers and professors in *A Portrait of the Artist as a Young Man* and Leopold Bloom and a later incarnation of Dedalus in *Ulysses*. Bloom, whom Joyce himself deemed to be a complete allroundman like his Classical model, Odysseus, typifies the attitudes to learning that pervade his work. He is intellectually inquisitive rather than erudite; his pedantry and his belief in education as a form of self-improvement point more towards the academic *manqué* than the polished graduate.

Indeed, one of the key features of learning and scholarly exchanges in Joyce's texts is that they regularly take place outside of the designated educational structures. His protagonists, moreover, are characterised as much by the unpredictable zeal of the autodidact as the skills imparted by conventional training. The purpose of this essay is at once to explore why Irish institutions of education, including University College Dublin, have such a peculiar centrality in Joyce's two early texts, *Stephen Hero* and *A Portrait of the Artist as a Young Man*, and to examine why extra-curricular learning has as much force as the school and university syllabus. It will be argued that this fascination with schooling and pedagogy must be seen in the context of the vexed and long-standing debates about education in nineteenth-century Ireland. In addition, Joyce's predilection for the renegade scholar-artist who refuses to cede to the ideals and prescriptions of his teachers will be shown to be a result of the fluctuating and divided history of the schools and university that he attends and of the necessarily conflicted nature of educational bodies in a colonial society. 'Malice aforethought' (32) is the phrase used in *Stephen Hero* to describe the honed critical skills deemed necessary by the opinionated protagonist for interpreting poetry in an adequate manner. It may additionally be cited as the basis of the aesthetic that Joyce forges during his formative but turbulent years as a student in inner-city Dublin. Indeed, becoming an artist is the chief means by which Stephen Dedalus resists the paralysing effects of the university environment which he so disdains. Para-doxically, however, the aesthetic he propounds is a curious by-product of the very educational system he deplores.

The nineteenth century was a signal period of educational innovation and expansion in Ireland. Debates about schooling and the so-called university question dominated political agendas as much as the problem of Home Rule and land agitation. For Irish nationalists, education was fastened upon as one of the prinicpal expedients for achieving autonomy and self-deter-mination. By contrast, for successive British governments the provision of universal schooling – although motivated in part by the democratic principles of liberalism – was invariably utilised to ensure political compliance and enforce cultural assimilation. Indeed, all of the institutional and legislative changes of the period had the effect of enhancing state control over education and of increasing the bureaucratisation of this sector. As a consequence, issues of governance, legal entitlement, cultural difference and of religious and political freedom dominated the heated and unabating exchanges about educational planning.

Some of the key reforms allow an overview of the political repercussions of the successive shifts in policy. The establishment of the national school system in 1831 was a landmark development, as it opened schooling to everyone. However, the insistence by the commissions presided over by the Chief Secretary, Lord E. G. Stanley, that these state-aided schools should be mixed and interdenominational proved unpalatable to the Catholic clergy and impracticable in the long run. Stanley's desire to run a system that avoided 'polemical controversy' (Hyland and Milne, 99) belied the imperialist imperatives anchored in these new structures. As John Coolahan has shown, the reading primers that formed the core of the curriculum seized every opportunity to emphasise Ireland's place within the British empire. The Colleges (Ireland) Act of 1845 passed by the Tory government under Sir Robert Peel attempted to resolve Catholic demands for universities of their own by making provision for the foundation of third-level institutions in Cork, Galway and Belfast. Like the national schools these too were designed to be non-denominational, thereby overriding nationalist demands for autonomy and separatism. Further, as a response to debates about the overspecialisation of the university curriculum in Britain, they adopted what was held to be a progressive and more pragmatic programme whereby students read a broad range of subjects in both the Arts and the Sciences. The secular nature of the new Queen's Colleges aroused the distrust of the Catholic clergy; as a consequence, they were formally condemned both by a Papal rescript in 1847 and by the National Synod of bishops in Thurles in 1850.

The setting up of the Catholic University by John Henry Newman in Dublin on 3 November 1854 became a further chapter in the quest to establish a university to meet local needs. Newman's enlightened foundation was imbued by liberal principles. It consciously espoused ideals that were opposed to those of the Queen's Colleges by actively supporting the conjoint study of theology and philosophy. It also countered the utilitarian aims of these rival institutions in its advocacy of the disinterested pursuit of knowledge. However, this new departure was vitiated by a lack of funding and active political support, reaching – as Donal McCartney has argued in his history of UCD – the nadir of its existence in the 1870s.

The university question, nonetheless, continued to be debated as part of the protracted discussions about Home Rule in the latter decades of the nineteenth century. Gladstone's University Bill of 1873 proposed the creation of one overarching national university uniting all of the existing institutions, but allowing for a modicum of Catholic control. It was defeated, thus dashing hopes of a solution being found under the Liberal regime. The succeeding Conservative government under Benjamin Disraeli, as part of its design to 'kill Home Rule by kindness', passed the Royal University Act in 1879 and established a third-level framework modelled on the lines of London University. This new Royal University was to be an examining body only, administering the former Queen's Colleges in Cork and Galway and the Catholic University which was now renamed University College. Further significant legislation under Disraeli's government was the Intermediate Act of 1878 which aimed to secure the existence of secondary schools by making their funding contingent on the examination results of their students. Thus, the innovations implemented by Tory and Liberal governments, while seemingly widening educational opportunity in the country, succeeded not only in sewing Irish educational institutions into a state regime that was overtly imperialist and moulded according to British precedents. It also altered their ethos to the extent that both second-level and third-level teaching now were organised around the often-crude measures afforded by examination systems rather than more lofty ideals. However, at the same time, the new structures and funding arrangements provided indirect and grudging support for denominational education (McGrath, 112–13). The inadequacies and prevarications inherent in these political compromises inflect the vivid representations of schools and university life that we encounter in Joyce's texts.

The university that Joyce entered in Autumn 1898 was a hybrid and unstable entity. It had been taken over by the Jesuit order in 1883. Consequently, some vestiges of Newman's original philosophy might be said to linger. But the institution that the author experienced also answered to the requirements of the Royal University in terms of its curriculum, its emphasis on examinations and its overall aspiration of imparting a vocational training to middle-class students. However, it is vital to note that Joyce's deliberately stylised and emphatically negative account of his college years between 1898 and 1902 is to some degree at variance with reality. Art in this instance is both an illuminating and distorting medium. As will be seen, fiction is utilised in *Stephen Hero* and *A Portrait of the Artist as a Young Man* to highlight the contradictions within the central protagonist, Stephen Dedalus, as well as to expose the conflicting and immobilising ideologies underpinning Irish educational insititutions.

Aubrey Gwynn's history of the staff of the university during Joyce's undergraduate years from 1898 through 1900 reveals them to have been an ill-assorted but gifted group of scholars and teachers. Fr William Delany, the President of University College from 1883 to 1888 and from 1897 to 1909, was an adept administrator and strongly devoted to the cause of Irish education. Although he distrusted political agitation and was chary of the new nationalist movements such as the Gaelic League and Sinn Féin, he nonetheless was a principal agent in creating the lively platforms for student debate that are so central to the formation of Stephen Hero and Stephen Dedalus. After his appointment to a second term as President, Delany revived the L and H (the Literary and Historical Society), which was founded by Newman but had lapsed in the interim, set up the Academy of St Thomas and encouraged the development of *St Stephen's*, a students' magazine. Other teachers included: Fr Joseph Darlington – the Dean of Studies in *A Portrait* – an English convert who held the professorship of English and later of Metaphysics and was interested in scholasticism and Shakespeare; Fr George O'Neill, who published widely on Victorian literature and ardently supported currently modish theories deeming Francis Bacon to have authored Shakespeare's plays; and Fr Tom Finlay, originally a Professor of Metaphysics who later because of his interest in Horace Plunkett's co-operative movement and in economic theory assumed the chair of Political Economy. With his brother Fr Peter Finlay, the latter founded the monthly review the *Lyceum* – which was retitled *New Ireland Review* in 1894. This became a principal forum for the eclectic interests of the group of thinkers based at, or allied to, the university which ranged across philosophy, Irish politics, economics and British, Irish and European literature. In its pages, essays on the Irish railway system sat side by side with translations from the German Romantic poet Annette von Droste-Hülshoff, Douglas Hyde's renderings of the folk songs of Connacht and nationalist broadsides about Irish-Ireland by D.P. Moran.

As C. P. Curran and Richard Ellmann have illustrated, despite his mask of disaffection, Joyce benefited from several of his teachers at UCD, including Fr Charles Ghezzi, Professor of Italian, who nurtured his love of Dante and Gabriele D'Annunzio. Yet what is of moment in *Stephen Hero* and *A Portrait* is how he reshapes his experiences of learning, endows them with symbolic dimensions and subtly remodels them to express a heartfelt cultural critique. Both these texts may be described as conforming – albeit in complex ways – to the pattern of the *Bildungsroman*, or the novel of initiation or education. Franco Moretti, in his suggestive study of this genre, notes that very few novels fully replicate the motifs and structures that characterise the original example of this mode, *Wilhelm Meisters Lehrjahre* by Johann Wolfgang Von Goethe. Additionally, Moretti maintains that Joyce's *A Portrait* should be viewed as a modern variant of this form and subsumed under the category of the counter-*Bildungsroman* that emerges around the period of World War I. Contrary to Moretti's neat distinction, this essay will contend that both *Stephen Hero* and *A Portrait* may be seen at once as reproducing and deconstructing aspects of the *Bildungsroman*. *Bildung*, or self-formation and development, are both foundational and the site of permanent conflict in these narratives. Even though Joyce's protagonist systematically resists the methods used to socialise him, he never relinquishes the grounds of education to his opponents. Rather, in the manner advocated by Paulo Freire, he propounds instead what might be termed a 'pedagogy of the oppressed' whereby he consciously takes over the tools of learning and uses them to forge the prospect of liberation. In this battle, the ambition to become an artist acts as a concerted strategy for countering what Joyce represents as the pernicious effects of a colonial educational system that enjoins slavish conformity and subservience.

Moretti sees the *Bildungsroman* as structured around a conflict between the ideal of self-determination and the demands of socialisation that is ultimately resolved. The endings of such fictions, hence, seek a congruence between social norms and the desire for freedom. Moreover, the initial alienation experienced by the protagonist is allayed by what Moretti terms the comfort of civilisation and an induction into aesthetics which allow him to acquire the art of harmonious living. Although Joyce's fictions borrow all of these essential features of the *Bildungsroman*, they also subvert and recast them. In particular, the smooth integration of the hero into society that acts as the sign of closure in such narratives seems an impossibility in a country in which *Bildung* is contested and definitions of civilisation are a matter of intense debate. Moreover, Joyce's protagonist is increasingly characterised by his acts of resistance and by his solipsism. Indeed, the Irish *Bildungsroman* proves to be the inverse of the European bourgeois novels examined by Moretti, even while it partakes of their besetting concerns. Stephen Dedalus's impervious isolation and his idiosyncratic self-communings betoken his success at achieving a measure of freedom. Extracts from his private diary rather than any act of social intercourse or gesture of reconciliation mark the equivocal ending of *A Portrait*. Rupture instead of cohesion is the alternative, but provisional, stopping-point of this narrative of Irish self-development.

The opening chapter of *A Portrait* revolves around Stephen's childhood and his experiences as a pupil at Clongowes Wood College. Bruce Bradley has argued that this school – akin to University College – was an institution in flux when Joyce joined it as a boarder in 1888. Clongowes had recently amalgamated with Tullabeg, another Jesuit foundation in Co. Offaly, which was governed, however, by very different principles, as it stressed achievement in examinations, discipline and the exercise of sports. Such goals ran counter to the broad programme of learning and the systematic training of the mind advocated by the seminal Jesuit manual on education, *Ratio Atque Institutio Studiorum*, composed by Claudio Aquaviva in 1599. Moreover, the importation of the ethos of Tullabeg also introduced values influenced by the British public-school system which similarly emphasised athleticism, militaristic regimentation and social hierarchy. Stephen's rebellion against this system is thus not merely the reaction of a perplexed schoolboy who has trouble fitting in. By resisting a regime that he finds alien and unjust, he undertakes the first in a series of dissident actions that characterise his dealings with education throughout the novel.

Stephen's discomfiture is most memorably captured in his defiant journey to the office of Fr Conmee, the rector of the school, to protest his wrongful pandying by Fr Dolan for not studying, although he had, in fact, been granted an exemption as his glasses were broken. Stephen's personal mission has decidedly political dimensions. In questioning the validity of authority in the school, he also echoes the watchwords of equality and autonomy that reverberate in nineteenth-century Irish petitions and parliamentary debates about education. His righteous appeal may be given a plausible psychological grounding, but it equally meshes with political demands for national self-realisation which formed the basis of much agitation for educational reform in the period. Although his victory is rendered as a dramatic climax, it is ultimately revealed to be limited. The fluctuations of his burgeoning self-consciousness are captured metonymically in the final sentences of the episode through the sounds of cricket practice on the school playing field. The ideal of athletic prowess which is so susceptible to political coding remains an unavoidable aspect of the charged semiotics of his world. Ideology can be resisted but not fully dismantled.

The surviving fragment of *Stephen Hero*, a portion of the first draft of *A Portrait of the Artist as a Young Man*, is written in a very different style and tenor to the later text. Its use of the conventions of classical realism to depict Stephen's undergraduate career casts his actions in a particular manner. While the Stephen of *A Portrait* is himself caught in a web of ironies which sheds doubt on the authority of his position, the protagonist of *Stephen Hero* is depicted as a truculent and unswerving rebel. His oppositional nature expresses itself through constant attempts to foil the educational system which he sees as degrading and oppressive. He particularly resists those aspects of the day-to-day regime which cut across his philosophical quest for truth and tortuous pursuit of an adequate definition of beauty. His insolence, late-coming, absence from class, idleness and failure to take examinations seriously may all seem like minor undergraduate infractions and to typify commonplace adolescent antipathy. But the insistent emphasis on this errant behaviour underscores his concerted assault on those aspects of educational management which were the subject of so much controversy in the period.

Stephen's interlocutors are given a far greater presence in this text than in *A Portrait*, as he engages in disputes with Fr Butt, his mother, Mr Dedalus, Temple, his brother, Maurice, Lynch, Emma Clery, McCann and Cranly. The calculated egoism that he cultivates, however, undermines the effect of many of his seeming rhetorical triumphs. Thus, his accosting of the President of the University to discuss his censorious objections to his paper on Ibsen develops into bathos as Dr Dillon concedes most of his points to him and even admits to a tentative interest in the notorious Norwegian playwright. Although Stephen's attack on the 'toy life' (191) permitted to his fellow students by their Jesuit teachers is unrelenting, his adversarial stance seems in the end merely nihilistic. His own research and reading provide him with some of the comforts of civilisation, but nothing acts as an adequate counterweight to his own negativity and to the crushing burden of the *Bildung* that he tries to evade.

The character we encounter in Chapter Five of *A Portrait of the Artist as Young Man* takes up a subtly different stance, albeit many of his traits remain the same and his abhorrence of the restrictions of university life is undiminished. His imagined presence in an English lecture – which he has chosen to skip – associatively evokes odours of 'cheerless cellardamp and decay' (192), and his dark musings as he approaches the University buildings on St Stephen's Green lead him to wonder whether the Jesuit house is 'extraterritorial and was he walking among aliens?' (199). As in *Stephen Hero*, Dedalus subverts the curriculum and the proprieties of the college timetable by carrying out all of his philosophical exchanges at unconventional hours and outside the classroom. Education, in effect, spills out into the life of the streets or is absorbed into marginal moments. Pedagogy, instead of being an instrument of oppression, becomes a means by which subalternity might be countermanded. His altercation about aesthetics with the Dean of Studies in the Physics Theatre takes on a different complexion because they are cast as equal sparring partners and because Stephen is driven, despite his self-absorption, to consider his opponent's position and to empathise with his viewpoint 'as a poor Englishman in Ireland' (204). Moreover, the intermingling of abstract philosophical discussion with concrete realities such as the lighting of the fire and the position of language in a colonial culture enhances the import of the exchange and indicates the hybrid and troubled nature of the comforts of civilisation in Irish society. Wittily, too, Stephen's schematic and defensive theory of beauty is turned by the Dean of Studies into a vista of the Irish sublime as he equates it 'with looking down from the cliffs of Moher into the depths' (202).

Indeed, it is through this transgression of spaces and of roles that Joyce succeeds in distilling a radical vision from his critique of the inadequacies of Irish education in *A Portrait of the Artist as a Young Man*. In his morning walk to college, Stephen cross-connects different aspects of the suburban Dublin terrain with his self-manufactured curriculum which ranges freely across European literature. The 'cloistral silver-veined prose' of Newman is inscribed in the sloblands of Fairview and the poetry of Guido Cavalcanti is interwoven with the shops on the North Strand Road (190). In a similar manner, his eclectic conjunction of Aristotelian theory and Thomist philosophy in his conversations with Lynch assumes a fresh force from the streetscapes that define them. Theories of static beauty paradoxically acquire a cogency and vitality by dint of being displaced from the lecture theatre onto a modern urban setting. In addition, through using Aristotle and Aquinas, who were routinely part of the classical teaching programme in philosophy at UCD, Stephen with malice aforethought turns his education on its head and makes his own of it. Ironically, despite his determined apostasy, his referencing at will of theology and philosophy reinstates and ratifies the liberal ideals that underlay Newman's original Catholic foundation and deliberately rejects the more utilitarian outlook of the current Royal University. Above all, in becoming his own teacher, he opens up the possibility of escape.

Although University College Dublin functions in part as a site of colonial abjection, *A Portrait of the Artist as a Young Man* also indicates that it provides the grounds for an aesthetic which at once playfully captures its essence and mercilessly dissects its failings. Richard Rowan in Joyce's play *Exiles* fatefully returns to Dublin to contest the chair in Romance languages at his former university; but his ambition is painfully spurned and dismantled. For Joyce, the aesthetic that he wrested from his period at University College could only lead elsewhere – into the uncharted territories of the fictional works, written over a lifetime of exile in Europe, that recapture the uncomfortable but shaping experiences of his student years and transmute them into the radical subject matter of modernist art.

PRIMARY REFERENCES

James Joyce, *Stephen Hero*, edited by Theodore Spencer, revised edition by John J. Slocum and Herbert Cahoon (London: Paladin, 1991).
—, *A Portrait of the Artist as a Young Man*, edited by Seamus Deane (London: Penguin, 1992).

SECONDARY REFERENCES

Bruce Bradley, '"Something About Tullabeg": A Footnote on the Schooldays of James Joyce', in *Studies: An Irish Quarterly Review* Vol. 93 No. 370 (Summer 2004): 157–68.
John Coolahan, 'Imperialism and the Irish National School System', in *Benefits Bestowed? Education and British Imperialism*, edited by J.A. Mangan (Manchester: Mancester University Press, 1988): 76–93.

C.P. Curran, *James Joyce Remembered* (Oxford: Oxford University Press, 1968).

Richard Ellmann, *James Joyce*, new and revised edition (Oxford: Oxford University Press, 1982).

Paulo Freire, *Pedagogy of the Oppressed*, new revised 20th-anniversary edition, translated by Myra Bergman Ramos (New York: Continuum, 1983).

Aubrey Gwynn, S.J., 'The Jesuit Fathers and University College', in *Struggle With Fortune: A Miscellany for the Centenary of the The Catholic University of Ireland 1854–1954*, edited by Michael Tierney (Dublin: Browne and Nolan, 1954): 19–50.

Irish Educational Documents Volume I: A Selection of Extracts from Documents Relating to the History of Irish Education from the Earliest Times to 1922, edited by Áine Hyland and Kenneth Milne (Rathmines: Church of Ireland College of Education, 1987).

Donal McCartney, *UCD A National Idea: The History of University College Dublin* (Dublin: Gill & Macmillan, 1999).

Fergal McGrath, S.J., 'The University Question', in *A History of Irish Catholicism*, Volume V, 'Chapter 6: The Church since Emancipation' (Dublin: Gill and Macmillan, 1971): 84–142.

Franco Moretti, *The Way of the World: The Bildungsroman in European Culture*, translated by Albert Sbragia (London: Verso, 1987).

MARY COLUM 1887–1957

Taura Napier

In her introduction to *Woman's Part: An Anthology of Short Fiction by and about Irish Women 1890–1960*, Janet Madden-Simpson writes that 'it is often the same writers who achieved astonishing popularity and who were so largely prolific in their lifetimes who are now least regarded or altogether forgotten' (6). This is unquestionably the case with Mary Maguire Colum, a 1907 Modern Languages graduate of UCD and, during her lifetime, a widely acclaimed literary journalist and woman of letters in Ireland and the United States. Yet Colum's present obscurity does not result from the phenomenon Madden-Simpson describes: 'Too few Irish women have entered into the fray to construct critical standards, too few have theorised and articulated the kind of critical ideas which can be so influential in establishing an atmosphere for serious appraisal.' Mary Colum experimented in style, form and content in her published works, from her early literary reviews to full-length critical studies to her autobiography. She wrote one of the world's first books of comparative criticism, refigured the *Künstlerroman* as a fictionalised autobiography and brought to light concise theories of art and the artist that facilitated the reading public's understanding of modernism in literature.

Colum was a product of Irish convent schools, a contemporary of James Joyce as a student of modern languages at UCD, a literary editor of prominent Irish and American publications including *The Nation* and *The New York Times Book Review* and, during her lifetime, a writer of international importance. Her narratives and critical theories, interspersed with ideas regarding the state of society in Ireland, the United States and the world, transcend political and cultural boundaries. Her early experiences included founding UCD's first society in support of the Irish Literary Revival, campaigning for Irishwomen's suffrage, serving on the executive of Cumann na mBan as nationalist retaliation against British rule reached its height and teaching in St Ita's, Padraic Pearse's nationalist school for girls. She was the only woman among the founders and editors of *The Irish Review*, the first periodical of its kind in Ireland. She enjoyed a particularly strong friendship with the Joyce family, having earned the respect of James Joyce for her critical work with an early essay on *Ulysses*.

Known equally for her erudition and lucidity, Mary Colum consciously avoided becoming an Ivory Tower intellectual. She received as much acclaim from housewives and schoolteachers in the US as from W.B. Yeats, Virginia Woolf and other world literary figures. Colum was outside the tradition of academic criticism and literary specialisation, unaligned with any of the critical movements prevalent in her time. The fact that much of Mary Colum's critical writing, her book of comparative criticism *From These Roots: The Ideas That Have Made Modern Literature* (1944) and her memoir *Life and the Dream* (1947) are innovative in approach and content might suggest why their import has remained unnoticed. Colum moved through most of the literary and intellectual circles in the United States and Europe, and was personally acquainted with almost every major writer. Yet because she did not identify herself with any one group, she tended to receive disparagement from all sides. The suffragettes of Cumann na mBan found her too conservative (although she and Maud Gonne were close friends); literary colleagues found her belief that effective criticism was not limited to the academy not conservative enough. Since Colum's ideas were diffused through a wide scope of intellectual pursuits, and because of her lack of alignment with any literary trend, it is often difficult to classify her works. But perhaps this is undesirable in any case: it is the comprehensive nature of Colum's work that gives it its particular value.

Mary Maguire arrived in Dublin from her birthplace of Collooney, County Sligo, in the autumn of 1900. She never looked back. At the age of eighteen, she had already charted her course: a university education in the capital of Ireland, which was itself ancillary to her participation in the Irish Literary Revival and her career in literature. In *Life and the Dream*, she recalls the parting advice of one of her uncles: 'All literature is about the seven deadly sins; you'll never be a writer unless you know about a few of them' (87). In her autobiography, and indeed all of her writings about the period, she describes the Revival as a living entity, a force that shaped Ireland and the world. During her student years, Colum witnessed the growth of the movement; she would become its chief authority and proponent in America.

On the train to Dublin, Mary Maguire met another student who was on his way to study architecture. His dream was realised as soon as he stepped off the train and saw St Patrick's, Christchurch and the long rows of Georgian houses. But for her the dream was just beginning, and would continue throughout her life. She was at the right place at the right time: coming from the west of Ireland into a cultural movement celebrating particularly the heritage of that region allowed her to understand both the foundation of the Revival and its products. She was attuned to complex literary and philosophical theories, understood the life of rural Ireland and had experienced firsthand the resentment of a civilisation under another's rule.

In 1904 the Abbey Theatre was new, Yeats, Lady Gregory and Synge had begun to gain the attention of literary critics outside Ireland and Yeats was fuelling the fledgling movement with ardent determination and energy. Colum had grown up ten miles from Yeats's family seat in Sligo, so his fame was exciting to her as a fellow Sligonian and as a great writer whom she had revered since girlhood. On seeing his plays advertised in Dublin, her interest in the languages and literatures which she was to study at the university waned:

> The thought of seeing a real play by living writers who were Irish and one of whom used to be referred to by my elders as 'old Parson Yeats's grandson' brought a thrill of rapturous expectation as to the wonders of the life that was about to open for me.

The university did not accept the new literary movement at first, so its first-year students were prevented from seeing any plays not on the university course, in other words the new ones. Joyce mentions the restrictions which prevented students from attending Revival plays in *Stephen Hero* (29) but such regulations were even more stringently enforced when applied to female students. However, Mary Maguire and her friends ignored the rule and, through stealth and determination, became the most consistent supporters of the theatre. Twelve of them began a society to celebrate the Irish Literary Revival, called the Twilight Literary Society (after Yeats's *Celtic Twilight*), of which Mary Maguire was president.

The Twilight Society attended every literary, intellectual and cultural function in Dublin, including 'at-homes', and eventually came to be recognised in its major circles. As president of the club, Mary also served as spokesperson, voicing ideas of the society to the greater cultural powers. Even in routine work, she spoke to leading figures. Once, she had to ask for a reduction in Abbey ticket prices for her society and was granted a personal interview with W.B. Yeats, who acceded to her request. The Twilight Society always sat in the front row of the theatre and was present at every performance. Yeats appreciated the young patrons, 'his college girls' as he called them, whose presence visibly augmented the Abbey's audience numbers. 'The pit in the Abbey Theatre,' he said in a lecture in London, 'has an ear for verse; they know at once between one performance and the next if I change a line or a word in a line' (*Life and the Dream*, 117).

Eventually the Twilight Society made it possible for Abbey plays to become part of the university curriculum and for first-year students to be not only allowed but also encouraged to attend them. Yeats continued to be Colum's hero but also became her adviser and colleague. He suggested that she pursue a career in literary criticism, perhaps become a specialist in French symbolist poetry. He also admired her lack of conventionality: 'As I came to know him, Yeats would tell me that I was his ideal of a youthful nihilist. Nihilism was the romantic form of revolt in his early days' (*Life and the Dream*, 117). Her youthful fighting spirit may have reminded the poet of Maud Gonne.

The most detailed and insightful account Mary Colum gives of the Irish Revival is found in *Life and the Dream*. Its portraits of

Yeats, Lady Gregory, Maud Gonne, Synge and the *Playboy* Riots, Countess Markievicz and AE are very probably the most accurate, informative and entertaining of any history of the Renaissance. Because Colum was a student during the Revival, full of wonder at the marvels of the movement but not yet old enough to have grown cynical, her vignettes convey the untainted amazement of seeing a literary revolution occur before her eyes. She gives particular credit to Lady Gregory, in spite of the perception of Yeats's friend and patroness as marginal in the formation and continued existence of the Abbey Theatre: 'It is almost certain that, but for Lady Gregory, the Irish national theatre would have remained a dream. It is very doubtful that Yeats could have produced as much work as he did without her help' (110).

One person for whom Colum reserves uncomplicated admiration, in fact, one she admired possibly more than Yeats, was Maud Gonne. Colum's first encounter with Gonne was at an Abbey play when she walked in with Yeats. The audience shouted 'Up John MacBride!' and began to hiss loudly. Gonne faced her detractors with a smile, although Yeats looked depressed, and Colum knew that she would never look upon a being more striking in appearance and personality. Through her involvement in nationalist and suffragist causes, Mary Colum came to know Maud Gonne well, and to the end of her life she would laud her achievements for Ireland. Her admiration for Gonne had little to do with that for Yeats: one was a political revolutionary; the other led a literary movement. But both represented the epitome of their causes and, consequently, all that was worthy as far as Colum was concerned.

Mary Colum's reasons for her devotion to Gonne provide crucial insights into her own personality and ambitions. Apart from the attraction of a young scholar to a wise and appealing mentor, Colum admires Maud Gonne's multifaceted identity:

> She had three qualities I have seen in all the real charmers I have known: a romantic personality, rich emotions and a warm heart. She had a considerable touch of artistry: she could paint interestingly. Besides these, she had a mind that could brood and think, though it was not the literary mind cultivated in the first quarter of this century. It was a soldierly mind like that of a chief

of staff, and at the same time, mystical and mysterious. She had a sort of Protean personality moving on various planes … She could be a violent fighter; she could be gentle and appealing; she could be fearless; she could be pathetic; she could be coldly realistic and romantically glamorous. (*Life and the Dream*, 131)

To say that Mary Colum patterned herself after Maud Gonne would be an exaggeration. But the dualities that characterise her life and work parallel those in her description of Gonne. Colum was more of a fighter, fearless and determined, than a romantic. Her mind was certainly literary, and she turned from the suffragist to the nationalist cause when she joined Cumann na mBan. But she had a Protean personality of her own, which would prove as appealing as Gonne's to her audiences in Europe and America. Colum's early exposure to the male and female counterparts of the Irish Renaissance shaped her love for the period and provided her with a holistic perspective on its various aspects.

After graduating from UCD, Colum procured a teaching job at St Ita's, Padraic Pearse's school for girls. But while she would later declare that the years on the staff of St Ita's were among the most productive of her life, she also needed an outlet for her desire to write. For four years after graduation, she published book reviews in *The English Review*, a literary forum based in London, as well as some articles for the London *Nation*. It is unclear as to when Colum published her first piece of work; indexes show that she submitted material to the *English Review* as early as 1908, although most of her reviews were published unsigned. These ostensibly inauspicious beginnings allowed her a public voice in the English literary world.

But better opportunities lay ahead. A group of Pearse's young staff members had an idea for a literary monthly that would contain political articles and original artwork as well as poetry, plays, short stories and book reviews. Professor David Houston, of the College of Science, managed the magazine; the editorial board was composed of James Stephens, Padraic Colum, Thomas MacDonagh and Mary Maguire. They named the periodical *The Irish Review*, as an alternative to *The English Review*, and began publication in March 1911. According to Padraic Colum, in an interview with Zack Bowen, Mary had the office of critic-in-chief. But in *Life and the Dream* she remembers her position differently:

> I was the only girl in this group, and being some years younger than the men, I was well bossed and patronised by them. They were determined to write the body of the magazine themselves – the poetry, the stories, the plays, the articles, and the editorial notes. But they decided to let me do some book reviewing in the back pages in small type. (137)

Relegation to the back pages of the *Review* did not discourage Mary Maguire. For the first edition, she wrote an essay review of the *Collected Works of John Synge*, which had just been published. When the *Review* made its appearance, in Dublin, London, Edinburgh and Paris, the attention of English periodicals was chiefly directed at Maguire's article and at George Moore's 'The Flood', whose author had demanded that it be printed on the first pages of the magazine.

'John Synge' marked Mary Colum's entrance into the spotlight of literary Dublin. It is a bold and unconventional piece, comparing the great artist with the maker of melodrama and serial shockers: both find their audience among the multitudes, not in 'narrow-spirited cliques'. She alludes to the *Playboy* riots, still angry that 'a howling multitude of the fine buoyant folk of the pit hissed and outraged [the *Playboy*] … This is one of the things for which their children's children will be ashamed of their forebears.' Mary Maguire reserves special praise for Synge's female characters:

> They are the most live women in modern drama. [Synge] scorned the psychological minuteness of what are called the intellectual dramatists, who break up into little pieces the souls of their personages for examination … None of Ibsen's painfully analysed women are as live and natural as Nora Bourke, or Deirdre, or Pegeen Mike.

From this point on, Mary Maguire was in fact critic-in-chief of *The Irish Review*. She wrote countless book reviews, most of which are unsigned in the back pages of the magazine, but her characteristic of engaging lucidity is recognisable in all of them. Before she left for the United States, Colum wrote six features for the *Review*, including full-length essays and a short story, entitled

'The Artist', which may be read as an early vindication of the woman artist that would characterise Colum's later repertoire.

Mary Colum's articles combine the critical essay, book review, literary history, editorial and position paper. Her *Review* articles are amusing as well as informative. In 'New Irish Poetry', a review of poetry collections by James Stephens and Seumas O'Sullivan published in June 1912, she describes Stephens' effect as a poet:

> When O'Sullivan tells us in verses of exquisitely matched words that he and his beloved walked beneath hazel trees, that her tresses were beautiful as she smoothed them from her face, there should be nothing to tax one's credulity in what he says. Yet I doubt every line of the poem, I doubt the lady and the tresses and the hazel trees. They have the suspicious air of being a make up. But when Stephens insinuates that, like Noah, he walks and talks with God, I entirely believe him.

Mary Colum grew and flourished with the Irish Revival. The movement was nearing its culmination as she prepared to leave Ireland for America, on the eve of the country's most famous political revolution. Colum did not experience firsthand the political turmoil of her native land, but she left her mark on its literary development. She would spread the ideas forged in Ireland throughout the world, gaining fame, like Joyce, by writing from the viewpoint of the self-exile. Colum's articles and short stories in *The Irish Review* provided a practical analysis of the literature of the Revival. Her explanation of Synge's methods and the *Playboy* riots and her unconventional belief that art did not exist to further the nationalist cause, expanded the boundaries of Renaissance thought.

Mary Colum and James Joyce were on friendly terms even before they met. Colum had written an article for American journal *The Freeman*, 'The Confessions of James Joyce' in 1922, which was not only one of the first reviews of *Ulysses* but also the first article published in America that did not condemn the work outright. Joyce sent her a cable that hers was one of three American reviews which he felt represented his book accurately; the others were by Edmund Wilson and Gilbert Seldes, as Colum recalls in *Life and the Dream* (305–6). In the essay, Colum argues that *Ulysses* belongs to the confession class of literature:

It is [...] a most sincere and cunningly-wrought auto-biographical book; it is as if he had said, 'Here I am; here is what country and race have bred me, what religion and life and literature have done for me.' All of Joyce's work gives the impression of being literally derived from experience; and from internal evidence in *Ulysses*, notably the conversation of Stephen Dedalus on Shakespeare in the National Library, one suspects that Joyce believes only in the autobiographical in art.

Colum connects Joyce's ideology with that of Gotthold Ephraim Lessing, often called the founder of modern German literature, in her descriptions of *Ulysses* as 'one of the most racial, Catholic books ever written'. She places the work unarguably within the realms of modernism: 'the author himself takes no pains to make it easy of comprehension' (450). She impugns the American culture that generally condemned *Ulysses* in her comments on Joyce's multifarious style: 'The book presupposes a knowledge of many literatures; a knowledge which for some reason, perhaps the cheapness of leisure, is not uncommon in Dublin and, for whatever reason, is rather uncommon in New York.' Ultimately, she defines *Ulysses* as 'an epic of Dublin. Never was a city so involved in the workings of any writer's mind as Dublin is in Joyce's; he can think only in terms of it' (450).

As in all her articles, Colum's criticism is instructive without being purely academic. In a three-page overview, she achieves a clarity that details *Ulysses* without trivialising it, as other American reviewers did. But when Colum delves into the literary value of the book, she makes very different observations. After 'Oxen of the Sun', '*Ulysses* ceases to be of paramount literary interest'. It becomes a scientific feat, not a literary one. 'To what extent a writer can parody different styles in the historic develop-ment of English is not of literary interest, it is of scientific interest' (451). She affirms Joyce's contribution to modernist literature with the innovations of *Ulysses* but considers it a 'dangerous indication that science will oust literature altogether as a means of artistic expression' (452). Later, in *From These Roots*, Colum would cite *Ulysses* as the first literary work to employ findings made by psychoanalysis, though its use of this type of writing did not necessarily augment its literary value.

By the time she reached her fifties, Mary Colum enjoyed international renown as a literary critic, translator and specialist in French symbolist poetry. Her American editor Charles Scribner decided that a book of her life would be informative to the reading public. But he could not have foreseen what the book, *Life and the Dream*, eventually became. If *From These Roots*, published two years before, was the first work of comparative criticism, *Life and the Dream* would establish a place in literature as an autobiography incorporating the qualities of a novel, as well as Colum's own fictional writings.

Life and the Dream makes use of several forms and techniques, among them literary and social history, fiction, biography and autobiography. It can be divided into three sections based on Colum's geographical movements: in Ireland, America and Europe. Within these lie the details of her life: Ireland is divided into depictions of her childhood in the northwestern countryside and young adulthood in Dublin, America into personal and public identity. Her travels to Europe provide the foundation for discovering new territories of the mind and spirit as she physically enters unfamiliar regions. Throughout are interwoven descriptions of the personalities Colum has encountered, famous and obscure, typical and extraordinary. It is through these that it is possible to discover her own subjectivity.

Colum's story emerges most lucidly in her portraits of W.B. Yeats, Maud Gonne, James Joyce and Elinor Wylie. These personages comprise a composite representation of Colum: Yeats is her childhood hero and adult intellectual idol; Gonne is heroine and mentor as well as feminist inspiration. Joyce and Wylie are contemporaries and intellectual guides; they do not however embody the heroism attributed to Yeats and Gonne. In addition, there are portraits of Lady Gregory, Countess Markievicz, Padraig Pearse, A.E., Sarah Purser, Roger Casement, W.S. Blunt, George Moore, Eleanor Roosevelt, Albert Einstein, Richard Schumann, Marcel Duchamps and countless others. In a three-page review for the *New Yorker*, Edmund Wilson proclaimed it to be superior to both George Moore's and Oliver Gogarty's memoirs of the Irish Literary Revival. He attributed the book's superior account of the Revival to the descriptions of its leaders and praised Colum for 'a portraiture so solid and alive ... and shrewd'.

Mary Colum's self-perception as a writer reveals a single-minded purpose. From her earliest articles in *The Irish Review* to her final lines in *Our Friend James Joyce*, a collection of essays and recollections co-authored with her husband Padraic, Colum adopted as the focal point of her career the difficult task of instilling literary awareness within the reading public. As she 'saw and felt things through a haze of literature' (*Life and the Dream*, 331), Colum sought to instruct readers in this ability. She determined to make all types of literature thoroughly accessible to her audience, which became increasingly diverse as her career progressed. In order to accomplish this goal, she infused her critical articles with attention to such details as the history, psychology and culture of the authors she reviewed. She thus appealed to a large cross-section of the reading public, which contributed considerably to increased literary awareness among the general population in America and Ireland.

Colum believed that artist and audience are frequently separated by misunderstanding. The public cannot comprehend the artist's works, and the artist does not know or care enough to fulfil the public's aesthetic needs. She maintained that a major hindrance to the public's literary-mindedness was the increase of exclusive, tightly knit artistic circles. In each of her *Irish Review* articles, she finds some means to deride these cliques, who produce for and appreciate only themselves and their styles. She admired John Synge particularly because his works were favourably received by a cross-section of the population representing varied lifestyles and professions; though she chastises the *Playboy* audiences for their vociferous disapproval of the play, one detects in the article a strong affection for the 'fine, buoyant folk' of Dublin. Yet 'popular literature', writing whose style and content are dictated by the tastes of the general public and which is sold not to entertain and inform but to make money for its author, was anathema to Colum. In light of such pieces as 'John Synge', it is clear that she never desired to tailor her writing to the social or moral demands of the populace, but instead to reach them through the accessibility and appeal of her writing.

If the purpose of an avatar is, as A.E. ascertained, 'to reveal the spiritual character of a race to itself', the purpose of a literary critic is to reveal the aesthetic temperament of a culture to itself. Mary Colum felt her purpose to be the aesthetic education of all who read her works, so that they might experience their own revelations of character. By 'expressing herself about everything under the sky', she found a way both to employ her diverse intellectual pursuits and to avoid the monotony of a specialised columnist. Her European and American publications are more than just book reviews; they are creative essays worth reading long after the books they critique have been forgotten.

PRIMARY REFERENCES

Mary Colum, *From These Roots: The Ideas That Have Made Modern Literature* (Ithaca, NY: Columbia University Press, 1944).
—, *Life and the Dream* (London: Macmillan, 1947).
Mary and Padraic Colum, *Our Friend James Joyce* (New York: Doubleday, 1958).
Mary and Padraic Colum Archive, Special Collections, Glenn G. Bartle Library, SUNY Binghamton. Unpublished material.

SECONDARY REFERENCES

Zack Bowen, *Padraic Colum: A Biographical Critical Introduction* (Carbondale: Southern Illinois University Press, 1970).
Woman's Part: An Anthology of Short Fiction by and about Irish Women 1890–1960, edited by Janet Madden Simpson (Dublin: Arlen House, 1964).
James Joyce, *Stephen Hero*, edited by Theodore Spencer, revised edition by John J. Slocum and Herbert Cahoon (London: Paladin, 1991).
Edmund Wilson, 'The Memoirs of Mary Colum', review of *Life and the Dream* by Mary Colum, *The New Yorker*, 22 March 1947: 109–13.

IN A NEW STATE
(1916–1959)

Austin Clarke (1896–1974)

Maurice Harmon

When Austin Clarke began his career by writing long narrative poems, *The Vengeance of Fionn* (1917), *The Sword of the West* (1921) and *The Cattledrive in Connaught and other poems* (1925), he was following in the footsteps of W.B. Yeats and other poets of the Irish Literary Revival who believed in drawing from native sources in order to create an indigenous Irish literature written in English. By Clarke's time that enterprise was firmly established, the Revival was a fact of literary history and W.B. Yeats was a major presence. While at University College Dublin between 1913 and 1917, the young poet came under the influence of the Revival and of the Gaelic League. He read the poetry of Yeats, attended the Abbey Theatre and made contact with many writers, including AE, Stephen MacKenna and F.R. Higgins, who encouraged him in his writing. Although he was appointed Assistant Lecturer in English at UCD to replace Thomas MacDonagh, who had been executed for his part in the Easter Rising, Clarke suffered a nervous breakdown and eventually had to leave his position. From 1917 to 1938 he not only contributed steadily, in narrative poems, lyrics, prose romances and verse plays, towards the creation of an Irish strain of literature in English, but also deepened it by writing types of poetry found in the Irish-language tradition and by investigating in *Pilgrimage and other poems* (1929) an area of the past previously unexplored.

The Vengeance of Fionn, which retells the story of Diarmuid and Gráinne, has lines of dreamy reverie, but its decorative style is not suited to narrative. It is a poetry of escape, removed from everyday concerns, although its account of flight and pursuit and passages of hallucination introduces motifs that become more evident in the following work.

When telling the story of Conor, Fergus and Maeve and investigating a mythological world in *The Sword of the West*, Clarke achieves occasional passages of effective narrative, whose descriptive beauty is sometimes marred by verbal excess. The poem expresses real feeling for the West as the place of emotional release, colourful life and magnificent scenery, and the home of Gaelic civilisation. Dectora's disappearance into the Otherworld resembles Gráinne's flight across the countryside, but it also lures Clarke into hallucination and nightmare as he describes figures from the Tuatha De Danann who live in that Otherworld. Cuchullin's mental instability is the focus of 'The Music Healers' section. The theme of unrequited love and the sorrow of love, which are associated with Yeats's early poetry, are also present in both of these romantic narratives and give the impression that Clarke is being over-influenced by his predecessor.

With the publication of *The Cattledrive in Connaught* (1925) he writes a more objective, realistic and less imitative kind of poetry. 'The Pillow Talk of Maeve and Fergus' expresses the individuality of each and is heightened by humour. But it is in the lyrics of this collection, under 'Induction' and 'The Land of Two Mists', that Clarke makes a deliberate and distinctive contribution to the Irish Literary Revival. Where the poetry of the Revival was largely romantic in style, it lacked, in his view, a real understanding of the poetic heritage; most of the poets, including Yeats, did not know Irish and so did not have a direct knowledge of poetic forms and techniques found in Irish-language literature. Clarke knew Irish, studied its poetic forms and in later life would translate several Irish poems. He writes praise poems, satires, curses, itinerary and topographical poems, moral poems, dramatic monologues, confessional poems, all of which he found in the Irish-language tradition. In this demonstration of writing from an informed understanding of native sources, he favoured a classical kind of poetry. Each poem had to be disciplined in structure, organisation and patterns of sound. To create a distinctive music he avoids end rhyme and the iambic foot that shape our response to English poetry.

A number of these poems are organised in single-sentence stanzas with no end-stopped lines. 'The Musician's Wife' has a vague narrative impulse but weaves the threads of the original love story into a tapestry of sound and syntax. 'The Lost Heifer' shows a relevance to contemporary events, since the dark cow, a traditional name for Ireland, is shown to be displaced by the violence of the Civil War. In its pattern of sound and in the suggestive radiance of its imagery it achieves a delicate mood of loss. The portrait of the crazed outcast in 'The Frenzy of Suibhne' is impressively wild, bizarre yet coherent. It is a drama of the mind in which the landscape serves as a metaphor for mental instability. A phantasmagoric and surreal world with strange figures and nightmarish events creates a powerful sense of foreboding, suffering and alienation. The disturbing accounts of fear and hallucination that distorted the narrative in *The Sword of the West* are subordinated here to the poem's aesthetic purposes.

But it is in *Pilgrimage and other poems* (1929) that Clarke moves away from sources associated with W.B. Yeats and invents a new world for imaginative exploration: the Hiberno-Romanesque period that existed from the coming of Christianity in the fifth century to the arrival of the Normans and the Cistercians in the twelfth. The early Irish monasteries were centres of learning, artworks in gold and silver, high crosses and illuminated manuscripts. Combining verbal simplicity with syntactical fluidity, the title poem evokes the splendour of Clonmacnoise and Cashel. Its assonantal patterns and flowing movement create the effect of the speaking voice crossing from one line to the next. An elevated diction adds resonance and conviction to the description.

The less attractive side of medieval Christianity is expressed in 'Celibacy' where the ascetic speaker is a victim of sexual temptation. Images of briar, nettle, thistle and reed convey the torment of one torn between religion and temptation. Here Clarke, in keeping with his wish to create a distinctive Irish kind of poetry, substitutes his own religious imagery for the rose, lily and poignard found in the English tradition. As he begins to face up to what will be a prolonged investigation of his own moral problems he discovers and defines a subject that had not been associated with the Irish Literary Revival.

Crises of conscience are dramatised in the portrait poems, 'The Confession of Queen Gormlai' and 'The Young Woman of Beare', women afflicted by guilt as they alternate between memories of sexual pleasure and fears of moral consequences. In old age and poverty, Gormlai narrates the moral dilemma of her three marriages, which Clarke will tell at greater length in the prose romance *The Singing Men at Cashel* (1936). Unlike the Hag of Beare, who was condemned to everlasting old age, the Young Woman of Beare is doomed to be forever young and therefore unable to escape the temptations of the flesh which are at odds with her wish to remain true to the teachings of the church. She alternates ambivalently between joyful memories of sensual pleasure and the frightening admonitions of the clergy against sins of the flesh. As in all such portrayals Clarke makes the point that her sinful ways began when she was too young to understand the moral consequences of her behaviour. The self as innocent victim is a constant issue in his thinking on these matters.

The poetry of *Pilgrimage* is primarily concerned with the creation of beautiful effects in rhyme and imagery. In 'The Tales of Ireland' Clarke bids farewell to the writing of epic narratives and in that farewell says goodbye also to evasion, displaced representation and self-indulgent language. The next collection, *Night and Morning* (1938), is personal, realistic and agonised. Drawing upon the language and imagery of Catholicism, its moral engagement is fiercely rendered.

The poems in *Night and Morning* have an unmistakable depth of pain. Their portrayal of the suffering persona caught between belief and denial, between inclusion in the communion of the faithful and exclusion, is expressed in a language borrowed from religious sources – the biblical account of the agony of Christ, ecclesiastical arguments in Church Councils, the ritual of Tenebrae, the rebellion of Luther – to dramatise the need of the persona to belong to the church and the need, equally strong, to be intellectually independent. The poems speak in compressed language of the dilemma of the Catholic conscience. The conflicted persona in 'Night and Morning' and 'Tenebrae' has inherited a sinful nature, is responsible for his own salvation but cannot achieve this without God's help. He knows he will receive little sympathy for his predicament within the church or within society. After living for some years in London, Clarke has returned to live at Templeogue, a suburb on the south side of Dublin, and knows what post-revolutionary, Catholic, middle-class Irish society is like.

'The Straying Student' is a portrait of the artist who came back. Having experienced the liberation of sexual expression, intellectual and imaginative freedom on the European continent, he wants to remain true to the freedom represented by the visionary woman who lured him there, but knowing the repressive nature of Irish society, dreads the consequences of his return.

Clarke works out ways in which he can engage imaginatively with that society. By depicting the medieval Christian past he can contrast cultural attainments there with aesthetic impoverishment in the present. By emphasising its extreme asceticism he can mirror the Jansenistic Catholicism in his own experience. By evoking its intellectual independence from Rome he can highlight the absence of intellectual dispute in his own church. By remembering the resolute disputations of scholastics prior to the Council of Trent he can portray the absence of intellectual inquiry in his own day. Had Clarke been able to comply with church teaching, he might have been less anguished. But he was incapable of unquestioning obedience. In the past, men could argue their way to salvation, but a church that stifled dissent left little room for argument. It is to his credit that he embodied these issues with compassion and intellectual conviction in *Night and Morning* and *The Singing Men at Cashel*.

The moral universe depicted in *The Bright Temptation* (1932), *The Singing Men at Cashel* (1936) and *The Sun Dances at Easter* (1952) mirrors the moral climate of Clarke's time and its life-denying constraints. The background for each of these prose romances is the Hiberno-Romanesque era. *The Bright Temptation* is an allegory of what adolescent development would be like, were it not for the distortions of sexual morality. Innocent love, embodied in Aidan and Ethna, is threatened by ugly and monstrous forces, but Oengus, god of love and happiness, triumphs. Ethna is the spirit of life. Her imagination has been shaped by romances. Her sense of landscape and its subliminal region of myth and romance corresponds to 'The Land of Two

Mists' section of *The Cattledrive in Connaught*. Like Diarmaid and Gráinne, Aidan and Ethna are idealised figures whose love for each other grows despite the fears and inhibitions Aidan has absorbed in a monastery. Love's gentle realisation in the context of the natural world and their overcoming of obstacles, both internal and external, is a triumph of natural innocence.

In *The Singing Men at Cashel*, a romantic tragedy about Gormlai, the central issue is the conflict between mind and body she experiences in her first two marriages. Gormlai's marriage to Cormac, king-bishop of Cashel, begins promisingly; she finds his scholarly interests and natural courtesy attractive. But when he takes a vow of chastity and urges her to do the same, she discovers the demeaning view of women in ecclesiastic writings. This is a sympathetic portrait of a refined and intelligent woman, one deeply responsive to poetry and religion, but that attraction is threatened by her discoveries at Cashel. Chastity, she realises, is advocated by male clerics and embodied in a male Redeemer. Her mind rejects this view which undermines her imaginative sense of an Otherworld of myth within the actual.

Her second marriage, to Carroll of Leinster, brings her into a shocked encounter with the physicality of marriage. In desperation she seeks clerical advice and is told with inflexible male authority that she must submit to her husband's sexual needs. Not to do so might drive him into adultery and this would be her fault. As a result she enters into a bewildering state of casuistical analysis. Hers is a divided personality, Clarke's most fully realised portrayal of the tormented conscience. It is unfortunate for the novel's artistic balance that the marriage to Nial Glundub is not fully described. Together they enjoy the imaginative associations of the landscape. With him she can believe again in the essential goodness of mankind but their lives together are not described. Well-structured, coherent, rational and compelling in its exploration, *The Singing Men at Cashel* is flawed by this failure to relate the story of her third marriage.

The Sun Dances at Easter, a joyful work, contains a number of separate, interrelated narratives which have the effect of dissolving the real world. Characters pass from one world of experience to another, from the here and the now to the timeless and unchanging in the Otherworld. Stories mesh and mirror one another in an ingenious and mutually illuminating manner. Various romances come together – that of Orla and Enda, that of Eithne and Ceasan, the world of reality and the world of the unreal. The comic spirit of the novel, so much a contrast with the sombre tone of Gormlai's story, is embodied in the figure of Oengus, God of Love, associated with birds, agility, music and gaiety, who turns up in various stories. The playful ingenuity of the overall construction is a measure of that comic side of Clarke's temperament that is recurrently repressed in the preoccupation with moral issues and prepares us for the mingling of the comic and the serious in his plays.

Although he was keenly interested in the theatre and was co-founder with Robert Farren of the Lyric Theatre Company, only some of Clarke's plays are successful. The better comedies include *The Son of Learning* (1927), *Black Fast* (1942) and three plays in the *commedia dell'arte* manner – *The Kiss* (1942), *The Second Kiss* (1946) and *The Third Kiss* (1976). His more successful serious plays are *The Flame* (1930), *Sister Eucharia* (1939) and the radio play *As the Crow Flies* (1943).

Set in the Hiberno-Romanesque era *The Son of Learning*, a humorous and irreverent account of the curing of the King of Munster by the poet Anier MacConglinne, was part of Clarke's attempt to alter the mood of Irish literature by the addition of humour. The characterisation of Anier leaves room for histrionics and high comedy; the plot is executed in a lively, economic manner. *Black Fast* is lightly comic in its treatment of a dispute between monks as to the correct date of Easter. But Clarke's mastery of comedy is best seen in the three Pierrot-Pierrette plays which are light-hearted and inventive in protean changes of character, improvisation and swift transitions in time and place. Their theme is love, their method openly theatrical. Disappointment and evil exist but are dissolved in the cleansing spirit of comedy.

Two of Clarke's serious plays, *The Flame* and *Sister Eucharia*, deal with rebellion in the enclosed arena of the convent. They are formal in structure and language but of limited range. The clash between a sensitive individual and inflexible authority embodies an issue that turns up also in *The Singing Men at Cashel*. All three works affirm the claims of imagination and feeling. *As the Crow Flies* uses the techniques of the radio play to good effect in the sounds of voices and various noises. Evil is rendered in the destructive Crow, bird of death in Irish mythology, who infiltrates the Eagle's nest and destroys her young. The play's intimation of elemental horror widens its application, but in another significant change of direction Clarke turns his attention to political and social issues.

The appearance of *Ancient Lights* (1955), *Too Great a Vine* (1957) and *The Horse-Eaters* (1960) marked his return to writing lyric poetry. Grounded in the actual, the short poems, often contrasting present-day restriction with former freedom, engage with instances of clericalism and social injustice, such as the Catholic Church's view on the rhythm method of contraception, immodesty of female dress, the place of Limbo for unbaptised children, the Marian Year stamp in 1954, emigration, corporal punishment and the effects of Jansenistic regulations on the natural expression of love. The language is vigorous in its denunciations; some poems are complex, ironic and ambiguous; others move by means of a more open syntax and simplicity of language.

Clarke wrote one long poem of reminiscence in each of these collections, 'Ancient Lights', 'The Loss of Strength' and 'The Hippophagi'. 'Ancient Lights' re-examines the circumstances of his childhood: the religious practices, the fears, the guilt, the dread of the Final Judgment and the trauma of his first confession. The poem absorbs images from the church itself – stained-glass, confessional and crucifix – but goes on to celebrate his release from fear and nightmare when he learned to trust his own judgement and to affirm the right of poetic expression.

'The Loss of Strength', an examination of his own life and of significant moments in Irish history, is permeated by the meta-phor of diminishment. Clarke's strength has been reduced by a heart-attack; rivers have been curtailed by urbanisation and the construction of electrical power stations; man's freedom has been curbed by priests; Irish monasteries have lost independence in the Cluniac reforms. In playful and lively language, with occasional humour, Clarke demonstrates that although he now has to watch his step, his imaginative energy is still vigorous. He can and will write with skilful command of language and syntax. This is one of the abiding messages of his career and of his work.

The less optimistic 'The Hippophagi' also revisits earlier experience and because it refers to autobiographical details may best be read in conjunction with the autobiographical *Twice Round the Black Church* (1962) and *A Penny in the Clouds* (1968).

Clarke's tendency in these collections to write in a compressed manner that sometimes makes comprehension difficult gives way in the high-spirited *Forget-Me-Not* (1962) and the relaxed *Flight to Africa* (1963) to poems that are looser in rhythm, more accessible in language and drive forward in a process of unfolding perception. The former is a playful account of the civilising role of the horse in Edwardian Dublin before the arrival of mechanised vehicles. It expresses delight in the poet's ability to harness language and syntax to his own jaunty purposes and has an unforced assimilation of relevant classical and historical material.

Flight to Africa continues Clarke's role as chronicler of such events as the Second Vatican Council in 1962, the Abbey Theatre Fire in 1951 and the burial of President Douglas Hyde in 1949. He moves easily through poems of considerable length and by means of a succession of concrete and specific images, as in the description of the flight of a crow across south Dublin in 'Cypress Grove'. 'Burial of an Irish President', a poem that focuses on the funeral of Douglas Hyde, founder of the Gaelic League and his teacher at UCD, shows Clarke's control of syntax, delight in rhyme, use of telling allusion and caustic observations on those Catholic V.I.P.s in university and government who, prevented by clerical regulation, could not enter the Protestant St Patrick's Cathedral to honour their President. Modulated by regret, the satire works through mockery rather than invective, despite the example of Jonathan Swift, former Dean of St Patrick's.

The superb 'Martha Blake at Fifty-One' is subversive and forceful. Written in a naturalistic style, it builds a portrait of a pious woman, a daily communicant who suffers constantly from bodily distress. She thinks of saints sentimentally and has no conception of the mystical passion of St Teresa and St John of the Cross. Although she has dreamt of a pious death attended by compassionate nuns, she is taken to Our Lady's Hospice, known as the Hospice for the Dying, where there is no doctor in attendance and where she worries about salvation. Wasted by colitis, knowing no peace, her last breath, as Clarke writes, is disappointed. It is his last word in a portrait of almost immeasurable significance in the context of the church's insistence that such pious lives were exemplary. That the woman described so literally and with such uncompromising accuracy is his sister bears witness to Clarke's integrity.

His supreme achievement is *Mnemosyne Lay in Dust* (1966) in which he dramatises his experiences in a mental institution through the figure of Maurice Devane. Written in a concentrated, vigorous, compact style it is a compelling account of nightmare, hallucination, paranoia, loss of identity, Freudian dreams and terrifying treatment – shock therapy, solitary confinement and forced feeding. Devane's recovery manifests itself in his renewed grasp on reality. The poem is a psychological narrative, a descent to and return from the underworld of mental breakdown, that re-enacts and exorcises the horrors and trauma that have been present in Clarke's work.

During the final seven years of his life, from 1967 to 1974, he continued the pattern of short poems, many of them occasional, and long poems, such as 'A Sermon on Swift', 'The Disestablished Church', 'Orphide', 'The Dilemma of Iphis', 'The Healing of Mis' and *Tiresias* (1971). He writes freely but with varying success about himself, other writers, dreams, sexual fantasies, travel, the war in Vietnam, Vatican Two, social and political issues. The element of pleasant, if superficial, delight is supported by word play, clever rhymes and homonyms, but the content is sometimes shallow.

The longer poems have more substance. 'A Sermon on Swift' commemorates the scatological side of Swift's work and in the process identifies with a poet who could be sexually indiscreet, sometimes despondent, at times angry. This portrait of a complex figure is to a considerable extent a self-defining image for Clarke himself whose vigorous and plain style in this poem resembles Swift's. In saluting Swift's 'The Day of Judgment', which absolves the human race, Clarke recalls the Irish philosopher Eriugena who argues that all men return to God, all receive Eternal Absolution and are therefore not subjected to the Last Judgment. It is the text that gives a moral and philosophical base to Clarke's later work, enabling him to transcend the moral predicaments that had restricted him in the past and to write with jocular abandonment. His erotic poems are a joyous release. 'The Healing of Mis' tells the story of the therapeutic effects on the mad creature of music and sexual union. 'The Dilemma of Iphis' and *Tiresias* also emphasise the normality of sexual pleasure, if too earnestly. The theme of personal liberation, first affirmed in the key poem 'Ancient Lights', is repeated in 'Disestablished Church' in which Clarke, while showing how both Catholic and Protestant religions have failed, affirms that human beings will all be saved.

Clarke holds a unique position in Irish literature because his work is so deeply embedded in native tradition of the early and medieval period, his sensibility so expressive of the Catholic conscience and so directly engaged with Irish life in his later years. The city of Dublin from the relaxed Edwardian era, through the excitement of cultural and nationalist revolution, to the uncongenial modern period of middle-class supremacy is strongly represented in his work. Throughout his career he was a committed craftsman with the result that his technical skills are varied and exemplary. In the areas of moral analysis, psychological investigation and social engagement he has left work of outstanding achievement, marked by compassion and understanding. In these areas he knew what he was talking about and felt obliged to bear witness to what it was like to be alive in the Ireland of his time.

PRIMARY REFERENCE

Austin Clarke, *Collected Poems* (Dublin: Dolmen Press, 1974).

SECONDARY REFERENCES

Maurice Harmon, *Austin Clarke 1896–1974: A Critical Introduction* (Dublin: Wolfhound Press, 1989). Contains a full bibliography of all of Clarke's writings: 267–309.

Kate O'Brien (1897–1974)

Gerardine Meaney

Kate O'Brien is in many ways the emblematic twentieth century Irish woman writer, not least because so much of her work was written and set outside of Ireland. Her writing was inextricably engaged with the politics of her day, starting with her interrogations of Irish identity but moving far beyond it. Just as she drew on a broad European cultural context in her writing, she insisted on understanding Irish politics within the general framework of European history. Her historical fiction ranged from the Spain of Phillip II to late nineteenth-century Ireland.

O'Brien was born in Limerick and educated initially at Laurel Hill convent school. The school epitomised the values of middle class Catholic respectability, but it also gave her a sense of a broader cultural heritage and seems to have helped lay the foundation of her interest in literature. In *The Land of Spices* (1941), a school very obviously based on Laurel Hill provides a haven from family misery and social expectation for its main protagonist, Anna Murphy. Ultimately Anna must leave to fulfil her potential as an artist and a woman, however. 'Anna was for life now, to make what she could of it' (281), we are told at the novel's conclusion. 'She had been set free to be herself. Her wings were grown and she was for the world. In poverty, in struggle, in indecisiveness – but for some those were good beginnings.'

Her own wings grown, O'Brien herself began attending UCD in 1916. She recollected in an article written for the *University Review* in 1963 that she:

came up to a Dublin still smoking from Easter Week. The first European war was on, and all general conditions were sad and miserable. We were a hungry, untidy, dirty lot – we of 1917–19. But did we enjoy ourselves? Did we read, did we think, did we loaf, did we argue? ... we were witty and wild, or so we thought. (5)

O'Brien wrote fondly of her time at UCD on more than one occasion. It was for her a period of intellectual adventure, of political debate and of unprecedented liberty as she rambled around Dublin with her friends: 'we lived as students, we were free'. For her, it was the beginning of a life defined by passionate commitment to art and ideas:

> Already then the world was a very sad and clouded place – as indeed we knew who walked around burned-out Dublin, and read the news from jails and camps and battlefields of all the earth. Already then the future would be grim and earnest enough, and would be with us very soon; and we were poor and would have to get ourselves somehow equipped to earn our livings. But we were indomitably young; we were in free contact, in all weathers with life as it was carried forward by all varieties of our elders and betters; and in nothing were we being spoon-fed. (9)

For the previously sheltered O'Brien it was a vital part of her education and formation that they were 'citizens in a cold, living, extremely interesting, tragic and history-flooded town' (9). That experience fed her lifelong sense of obligation to participate in questioning what Ireland was and what it ought – and ought not – to be. Parallel to this, her courses in modern languages laid the foundation for the lifelong influence of European artists and thinkers on her work. These were eventually to include Marcel Proust and the Spanish philosopher George Santayana.

Her reading interests were too sprawling and too individual to secure her a first-class degree, much to her disappointment at the time. But they gained her rich cultural resources for her fiction and sustained her when Ireland became too insular to accommodate so large an imagination as O'Brien possessed. She loved the 'unceasing political and patriotic argument' (6) of her student years and seems to have attended an astonishing number of plays for a poor student. Her impatience with pomposity and distrust of authority led her to mock 'the Literary and Historical [Society], where all the grandees, later to be our rulers, showed off'. (6) O'Brien's questioning intelligence and her flair for making stories that challenged perceived wisdoms were repeatedly to put her at odds with the society those grandees, so apparently foolish and inconsequential in their youth, were to shape over the next decades. Looking back in 1963, she retained an irreverence for UCD's sacred icons:

> poor Newman, how he dreamt! And little did he imagine that his wonderfully mellifluent evocation of Ireland was to become a depressingly untrue school text! Untrue, because he was an unhappy and ill-used stranger who could not but write good prose, as it happened, but had not head nor tail to [*sic*] what he was in fact writing about. Had he been writing in the abstract about a university his beautiful paragraphs could stand – but by now their awful topicality can only embarrass all of us who were nurtured on them as if they were as important a part of English literature as *Paradise Lost* or *Biographia Literaria*.

O'Brien's literary tastes and ideas on education were in many ways the antithesis of Newman's:

> My idea of university life is this: that we arrive, ignorant but alert, into a society, which will permit us to pursue, along such avenues as we choose, the difficult quarry, truth … Naturally I do not speak of absolute truth, but of the approximations and personal expressions thereof which the individual can strive towards … Arrival is not the point – all is in the travelling – all is in what is learnt, said, claimed, discarded and reclaimed on the way …

In effect her ideas on education were an extension of her ideas on art and her way of life: 'A university should be an open porch where you and I can sit down, and listen, and disagree, and come back, and disagree again … A place of argument, of silence, of perplexity.' She vehemently opposed any dictate in education or art which sought to impose a criteria of usefulness and publicly opposed UCD's move to Belfield in the 1960s on the basis that 'a university should always live through and in dispute with a city' (10). She argued that 'a neat and expensive set of arrangements in the suburbs' (9) would cocoon students from the highly educational experiment of making their own way in the city. 'We must train the young to think – not to learn ... but simply to think ... alone' (5). In many ways a radical individualist, O'Brien understood very well the constraints of upbringing, class, religion and society. Yet her novels return again and again to the point at which those constraints are exceeded.

O'Brien describes mischievously how she and her college friends 'used to track Maud Gonne about, too, when she was out of jail'. The combination of radical politics, cultural ferment and the possibilities of a woman's full participation in both were part of the life they inhaled in war-torn Dublin. *The Land of Spices* gives some indication of this sense of possibility and change and the intellectual and political excitement of Ireland at the beginning of the twentieth century, as its heroine, Anna, considers her future:

> When her father quoted Tim Healy's witticisms at the Irish Bar, she foresaw that shafts of hers would one day hit more deeply and more amazingly. When Father Hogan talked contempt-uously of the Irish Party, and expounded the political doctrines of Arthur Griffith, she pondered the value to herself of a patriot's career; and when she talked with Miss Robertson, she felt her own strong ability to out-Pankhurst Mrs. Pankhurst. (208)

This sense of many and exciting possibilities of effecting change explains the intensity of the disappointment O'Brien and many of her intellectual contemporaries felt with the conservatism and stagnation of the state which emerged after independence.

In her most pessimistic novel, *The Ante Room* (1934), O'Brien locates the origins of this failure of opportunity in the late nine-teenth century. *The Ante-Room* maps the horizons of an intensely confined society. Like many of O'Brien's novels, it is located in a strictly limited geographical and social space. The novel is set over three days; the characters are physically almost static. Spatial confinement is intense and claustrophobic, comparable with that endured by Ana de Mendoza in her later novel *That Lady* (1946), who is imprisoned by a jealous king in a space that is gradually decreased until she is effectively walled up alive. In *The Ante-Room* enclosure is domestic and considerably more comfortable, but the tantalising glimpses of a freedom they cannot achieve torture the Mulqueen household as surely as the gradual erosion of her allotted space tortures Ana. Like her, the Mulqueen family wait for death as the only release possible to them. The Mulqueens also occupy the ante-room to twentieth-century Irish history and their story is O'Brien's analysis of the elements which were to make that history, by 1934, appear a bitter anti-climax. The novel is set during the Land War, though the reader is excluded, with the novel's female characters, from an extended discussion of these issues, which takes place among the men when the 'ladies' have withdrawn. For the *The Ante-Room* evokes, as poet Eavan Boland noted in her preface to the 1980 edition, a forgotten Ireland:

> an Ireland between the mortgaged acres of Maria Edgeworth and the strong farms of Mary Lavin's short stories. It was an Ireland of increasing wealth and uneasy conscience, where the women wore stays and rouged their cheeks, had their clothes made by Dublin dressmakers and tried to forget the haunting of their grandparents.

The novel acutely renders the claustrophobia of this world. Pinioned between Victorian respectability and Catholic scruple, its main character, Agnes, fails to live. Love and desire bring death and destruction in the novel, to the extent that desire seems only to be produced by unbreakable taboos. The relationships that are possible are too limited to be worth pursuing. It is as if this class had failed at the outset, not because of its ambitions for prestige and power, which O'Brien saw fulfilled at the time of the novel's writing, but by the limitations of those ambitions. Agnes's mother, close to an animated corpse through most of the novel, clinging on to life until she has found someone to take care of her dreadful son, provides the novel's most striking metaphor and O'Brien's caustic response to the myth of mother Ireland.

In the decade after she left college Kate O'Brien came to terms with herself as an artist and as a woman. She tried her hand at journalism, working briefly for the *Manchester Guardian*, and rather successfully at playwriting. She seems to have been able to negotiate a relationship with the Catholic faith in which she had been brought up by regarding it as part of her connection to European culture. Her combination of the secular and the mystical in her life of *Teresa of Avila* (1951) is highly revealing: 'I propose to examine Teresa, not by the rules of canonisation, but for what she was – saint or not – a woman of genius.' (10) Admiring Teresa of Avila 'as a formidable writer of prose' (11), O'Brien chronicles both her 'guile' and her bravery in her dealings with a church that regarded her mysticism and her visions as possible heresy, at a time when the Inquisition was still zealously torturing and dispatching heretics. In O'Brien's account, Teresa of Avila becomes a heroine of spiritual audacity:

> to advance into the very face and presence of God, and to insist that it is he who invites the audacity … this is mysticism, this is a territory that millions would choose never to glimpse, let alone examine; and it is understandable if some find even Teresa's unflurried chartings of it alarming. (47)

This is not hagiography in any sense. Teresa's tendency to hurl 'Lutheran' about as a term of abuse annoyed O'Brien intensely – 'I for one do not excuse it in a woman of genius. Any more than I excuse her lapses into the "I am only a woman and therefore …" line of argument' (65). The novelist revenges herself on her icon by pointing out that the figure with which Teresa has most in common was Luther himself, 'passionate, fearless and self-assured' (65). *Teresa of Avila* traces the complexity of O'Brien's relationship with Catholicism. Those elements in it which still attract her are abstract and at odds with its institutional power and its moral blindness, but her assertion of her claim on those elements marks her defiance of that power and those moral strictures.

O'Brien's lesbian identity undoubtedly contributed to her exasperation and despair at Ireland's sexual conservatism in this period. It also contributed to her identification with outsiders in her fiction and that fiction's cool exploration of hidden and forbidden desires. More importantly it helped forge her aesthetic priorities around the persistent exploration of the relationship between sexual, artistic and political freedom. A major factor in O'Brien's alienation from mainstream Irish society was the censorship of her work in Ireland on the slightest pretext as 'obscene'. *The Land of Spices*, set in a convent school and profoundly serious in its exploration of the appropriate relationship of faith and politics, was banned on the basis of a single sentence which referred to two men 'in the embrace of love'.

O'Brien's political and fictional horizons extended beyond Ireland, however. She had lost her second homeland, Spain, when it fell under the dictatorship of Franco. There is some dispute as to whether she was formally excluded from Spain by the Franco regime or simply feared to return after the publication of *Farewell Spain* (1937). Ostensibly a travel book, the latter presciently regards the Spanish Civil War as the harbinger of a greater conflict to come. O'Brien was disdainful down to her anti-fascist bones of Ireland's neutrality during that conflict. She saw Franco and de Valera as similar in their politics, particularly in terms of their imposition of Catholic moral and social doctrine and disregard for personal and artistic freedoms.

Inspired by an experience of claustrophobia and disorientation when she ventured out into the London blackout during the blitz, she wrote her striking historical novel *That Lady*. Set in Spain during the reign of Phillip II, the novel centres on one woman's insistence on her right to personal and sexual freedom and transforms it into a powerful allegory of resistance to fascism and dictatorship. Ana de Mendoza was traditionally seen in Spain as a dangerous woman, a femme fatale and even a traitor. In O'Brien's version, Ana is a dissident, a heroine in the mould of Antigone. Unlike the Greek heroine however, Ana never repudiates life. Instead she is buried alive precisely because she insists on her right to live to the full on her own terms. Ana chooses prison rather than submission: to maintain her independence, she must lose her freedom. *That Lady* is in part O'Brien's response to the Second World War, in part a parable of resistance to dictatorship and the price paid for resistance. Throughout the 1930s and 1940s, her work seems shaped by a sense of foreboding, where totalitarianism at one extreme and bland social conformity at the other threatens to overwhelm life, freedom and art. For O'Brien these three were inextricable.

In *Farewell Spain,* O'Brien lamented that 'this Spanish war ... is only one ulcer on an ulcered world'. Her book uses personal recollection and intimate descriptions of persons and places to seek to penetrate the 'self-protective' nature of 'the individual imagination':

> no one with a vestige of sanity can be unaware of the universal terrors of nationalisms, dictatorships and race-antipathies, to say nothing of the comic policy of sealed lips … our protective dullness is only really penetrated, our nerves only really ache when that which we have personally known, that which has touched ourselves, takes the centre of the stage awhile. (6–7)

In many respects the apparently private histories with which O'Brien's fiction concerns itself seek to negotiate this paradox. They make us personally know and really ache for those whom, in the abstract, we would judge, dismiss or ignore. More than that, in keeping with her view of the function of art, they seek to offer 'a source of strength and courage' precisely because of their 'manifest non-utilitarianism'. O'Brien, of all Irish writers, writes 'in praise of personal pleasure' (11) in the surety that writing and pleasure stand obdurately against oppression and conformity. She celebrates: 'a book, a hand, a first-rate joke; a prayer to God, or the birth of a child; an escape into solitude or a wild night out; a fit of hard work, an attack of romantic love or of marital peace; a visit to the play; a glass of good brandy or good beer. Or a trip abroad – away from it all, as we say' (15).

The texture of O'Brien's writing is sensuous, intimate, sometimes startling. Art in her work offers both a way of living and a glimpse of eternity. Her most eloquent statement of her aesthetic comes in *Mary Lavelle*, a novel in which she adapted her experiences during her year working as a governess in Spain into fiction. Her adulation for bullfighting seems incongruous to contemporary readers. For her, it epitomised the necessarily dangerous nature of art, its strangeness and its ordinariness:

> Death, so strangely approached, so grotesquely given and taken, under the summer sky, for the amusement of nonentities, death made into an elaborate play, for money and cheers, and exacting in the course of the show a variety of cruelties and dangers; death, asking for helpless victims as well as for the hazards of courage; death and pain, made comic, petty and relentless, for an afternoon's thrill … Here was madness, here was blunt brutality, here was money-making swagger – and all made into an eternal

shape, a merciless beauty, by so brief a thing as attitude … here was art in its least decent form, its least explainable or bearable. But art, unconcerned and lawless. (117)

The bullfight for O'Brien was art as a matter of life and death, but also a matter of making a living. Her description of it is probably her strongest statement of her ambition to create an art that, in the words of Santayana, expressed 'the not-given'. It also makes the point that such sublime art is not incompatible with popular forms and genres. O'Brien was a popular novelist, particularly in England. In the Noel Coward-scripted film of *Brief Encounter* (1945), for example, Celia Johnston's character is going to the library to get 'the latest Kate O'Brien' when her first illicit romantic encounter occurs. This would have been *That Lady* and the contrast between Ana de Mendoza's tragic defiance and Johnston's tragic compliance would have been striking to any reader familiar with the novel.

O'Brien's most extended exploration of the relationship between life, art, sex and politics is undertaken in a novel concerned with two artists in a form which explodes the boundary between high and popular art, opera. *As Music and Splendour* (1958) traces the development of two Irish singers, Clare Halvey and Rose Lennane, from disorientated scholarship girls to mature artists. 'Supposing we'd been left where we were,' Clare speculates as they sit drinking wine and discussing their lovers and careers and the prospect of La Scala:

> You'd still be Rose Lennane, your exact, born self, the very girl who was sent to France … And I'd be Clare Halvey, as sure as I *am* Clare Halvey. But that Rose Lennane and Clare Halvey there at home, our identical twins, wouldn't be recognisable to us now; to us, I mean, who are trying to imagine them, here in Rome at this minute. (189)

Rose, less introspective and more comfortable with her role as diva-in-the-making, responds, 'but that's true about anyone who, well, who was once definitely parted from herself, her obvious self, at any kind of crossroads. Isn't it?' (189)

Remade into 'Chiara Alve' and 'La Rosa d'Irlanda' respectively by their training and profession, the two women also remake themselves and, especially in Clare's case, their art. Clare is, for much of the novel, defined both artistically and sexually by her performance in Gluck's *Orfeo ed Euridice* with her lover Luisa:

> The music they both loved had carried them far tonight, together and above themselves. Their descent was slow and reluctant, and their hands did not fall apart when they paused in Clare's doorway. Still Orpheus and Eurydice, their brilliantly made-up eyes swept for each the other's face, as if to insist that this disguise of myth in which they stood was their mutual reality, their own true dress wherein they recognised each other, and were free of that full recognition and could sing it as if their very singing was a kind of Greek, immortal light, not singing at all. (113)

Orfeo ed Euridice is generally regarded as a milestone in the reform of opera and the shift towards greater dramatic realism and lyrical intensity in the eighteenth century, a reform Clare seeks to emulate in the nineteenth. (The novel opens in 1886.) Even at sixteen, 'cross, uncertain and at bay', she wonders: 'Why can we only sing about what isn't true?' (24)

The contrast between the two singers could be described as that between the sublime Clare and the beautiful Rose. O'Brien's own work is consistently concerned with the aesthetics of the sublime. As John McGahern has astutely commented, she was 'a poet working in prose'. This suggests that Clare is an author surrogate. Yet Rose, the 'absolutely honest artist' (155) who manages to live life to the full, is in some ways closer to O'Brien's own artistic practice. Indeed, O'Brien's novels, employing the conventions of popular genres of women's fiction and the realist mode, are closer to Rose's operatic preferences than the poetic and mythic preferences of Clare. When Clare complains that their pampered operatic existences have nothing to do with life, Rose is robust in contradicting her: 'We have to do with life – that's why we sing. Singing is about life. And we can't help having stomachs and senses' (139).

Possibly because it contains O'Brien's only extended treatment of a mature lesbian relationship, *As Music and Splendour* has only returned to print in 2005. Her reputation and popularity as a novelist had already declined by the time of its writing. When I first chanced on a couple of battered and elderly copies of *The*

Ante-Room and *Mary Lavelle* in the UCD library in the early 1980s she was, however, already returning to print, thanks to two feminist publishing houses, Arlen House in Dublin and Virago in London. Her critical stock as part of the canon of Irish twentieth-century fiction has been rising ever since. She is now widely taught and once again widely read. Nonetheless I think she would have appreciated that many of the writers and critics she has influenced, including this one, first read her work as an uncontained and lawless pleasure, unexamined, unsupervised, to help us think, alone.

PRIMARY REFERENCES

Kate O'Brien, *The Ante-Room* (Dublin: Arlen House, 1980 [1934]).
—, *Mary Lavelle* (London: Virago, 1984 [1936]).
—, *Farewell Spain* (London: Virago, 1985 [1937]).
—, *The Land of Spices* (London: Virago, 1988 [1941]).
—. *That Lady* (London: Virago, 1985 [1946]).
—, *Teresa of Avila* (Cork: Mercier Press, 1967 [1951]).
—, *As Music and Splendour* (London: Heinemann, 1958)
—, 'The Art of Writing', *University Review* (1963).
—, 'My Idea of a University', *University Review* (1963).

BRIAN COFFEY (1905–1995)

J.C.C. Mays

Brian Coffey was fond of repeating that poetics is about making. The thought is obvious in an etymological sense since the Greek root means exactly that and applies to shipbuilding as much as to the shaping of plays. Practising poets, like potters and painters, spend their days weighing technical alternatives, solving problems raised by their particular medium or genre, reckoning that, whatever the public prefers, their occupation is to get a job done in the way it deserves. The condition applies to all arts and crafts. However, you get Coffey's point if you come at making from a point of view other than the maker's. If an artist's notion of a good job coincides with that of his public, he will be rich and famous. If he botches too many jobs he will fail to make a living. But if he works only to satisfy consumers, he could fail to earn the respect of his peers and his wider reputation will be short-lived. Readers who position themselves in the maker's shoes understand the logic of a thing made and can properly judge the satisfaction it provides.

Brian Coffey's ideas about poetry as making were formed at a time when Yeats and Joyce towered over the Irish literary land-scape. Eighty years later, what those two writers have in common is as obvious as what divides them but this was not so at the time. Yeats, despite his posing and politicking, was nothing if not a maker, converting his every experience into the material of art. The Cornell edition of manuscript materials is proof, if proof were needed, of the work that binds his poems and plays together. None the less, the idealistic, even rather prim, young

Brian Coffey, living with his parents on Fitzwilliam Square, was indelibly struck by W.B.'s sometimes-unbecoming behaviour when he moved in as a neighbour at No. 42. At the same time, Coffey had been educated in France and inevitably took more seriously the Paris-based Joyce whom he then knew less well. Joyce, at a distance from home, found it easier to preserve the legend of an artist who subordinated his life entirely to his work. In this way, to an extent adventitiously, the idea of poetry as making became involved with available role models and with contemporary ideas about emerging Irish nationhood.

Coffey saw Yeats's Anglo-Irish Revival as an enterprise based upon self-advertisement and self-deception. His father, then President of UCD, followed John Redmond in politics but had declined to accept a knighthood from the British Crown. Brian Coffey was not a political person, but he resisted the imposition of a line of argument that led from Nietzsche to Joe Breen. By contrast, Joyce stood in his mind for an idea that undercut moral and political pretension and manifested, in ways beyond dispute, his integrity as an artist. Yeats's celebration of the Lake Isle of Innisfree was, for Coffey, a fantasy about a place called Rat Island that buried its admirers in the author's self-conceit. Joyce's example, by contrast, opened onto a world of opportunity where humour exploded myth.

Coffey was not isolated in his thinking. He was probably closest to Thomas MacGreevy among his elders, although MacGreevy did not share Coffey's animus against Yeats and the positions he held were arrived at empirically or intuitively. MacGreevy was paradoxically Nationalist and Modernist at the same time, as well as being a devout Catholic. He spent time away from Ireland – indeed, as Joyce's helpmeet in Paris – as an involuntary exile, such as Coffey always felt himself to be. It no doubt helped that Coffey's father was likewise from Kerry, and I remember Brian dressing up in a searing green shirt and scorching yellow tie in order to lunch at the Park with his UCD contemporary, President Chearbhall Ó Dálaigh.

Samuel Beckett, a lifelong friend of Coffey and MacGreevy, was more driven, more productive and of course eventually more famous. His essay on 'Recent Irish Poetry', published under a pseudonym in 1934, remained overlooked and forgotten until 1971, when it came to seem like an agenda for another generation of Irish modernist writers. Beckett separated the alternatives into 'antiquarians and others', writing that either proceeded 'from the *Gossoons Wunderhorn* of that Irish Romantic Arnim-Brentano combination, Sir Samuel Ferguson and Standish O'Grady' or – 'stupendous innovation' – could admit the existence of an author for whom the question of identity is primary.

At the time, the position of most of those grouped under Beckett's second heading was mixed. Denis Devlin simply wanted to leave Ireland although he was happy to represent its embassy abroad, while his aesthetic ambitions were relatively conventional. George Reavey was a Northerner who had been born in Vitebsk, who found it natural to migrate through Cambridge, Paris, London and ultimately to New York, where he confirmed his reputation as a translator of Russian. Other allies, Jack B. Yeats and a number of mainly women artists, were less eager to emigrate. Brian O'Nolan, an inner emigré, wrote parody so intelligent and so delicately poised that it became confused with the modernism it parodied; and he ended sadly, poisoned by his own satire. The agenda rediscovered in the 1960s, in other words, was not as simple as it might have seemed and it is worth drawing a distinction.

In 1930, a few looked to Europe as a lifeline to a wider vision of Irish nationhood and culture that was being lost, and some others were simply glad to be anywhere else. The country appeared to them to be foreclosing its opportunities in the way Tom Garvin's book *Preventing the Future* (Dublin: Gill & Macmillan, 2004) has well described. The 1960s, by contrast, were a time of recovering prosperity and openness, and the recovery of a previous generation inevitably obscured important differences and converted some spokespersons of despair into beacons of hope.

For similar reasons, the situation of the 1960s is equally difficult to recover now when Europe means something else again, that is, less a cultural resource than a business or career opportunity. Irish writers may travel more widely and frequently but they appear perhaps less eager or anxious to measure themselves against Maurice Scève or Paul Claudel (as did the undergraduate Devlin and Coffey), or, a generation after, against François Mauriac or Charles Péguy (as did John Broderick and Conor Cruise O'Brien). If more translations are now published, this is a result of European funding and on different terms. Under today's more bullish agenda, the sixties generation who hoped to recover thirties models to advance with greater *force de frappe* have been overtaken by a generation that promotes national identity in a multicultural marketplace.

Coffey's idea of *poesis*, then, needs to be recovered with care. It does not easily convert into current values; with the best intentions, it gets overlaid with different assumptions or gets dumbed down. A good starting-point is the familiar final section of Joyce's *A Portrait*, where Stephen expounds the way art should separate from its background (*integritas*), possess internal consistency (*consonantia*) and intensify the workings of the two processes to a point where a new artistic truth bursts through (*claritas*). The exposition is reinforced a few pages later when Stephen describes the difference between the truth available to different literary modes, and how drama can best embody truth because it combines self expression (lyric) and story (epic) in the most objective form. The same idea was reinforced for Joyce by the example of Flaubert – what Hugh Kenner called 'the Uncle Charles principle' – and subsequent writers have honoured other exemplars in their turn, from Ford Madox Ford to Ezra Pound. For Coffey, the Joycean idea was anticipated and extended by academic training in Neo-Thomist philosophy.

Whether a reader is meant to know that Stephen's theorising is lifted directly from a student textbook, Rickaby's *General Metaphysics*, remains an open question. But the way Stephen elides Aquinas's *claritas* with Scotus's *quidditas* is no small matter and, from Joyce's practice overall, it might be reckoned that he muddled the distinction too. The lustre or splendour of *claritas* is a theological concept applied to aesthetics. What Joyce secularised as a moment of luminous arrest comparable to a cardiac condition – 'the enchantment of the heart' – is something else again in the *Summa*. I recall Coffey insisting upon the point of difference as crucial, as indeed it is, and it gave Coffey a clear idea of what he wanted to achieve in *poesis*, even if he did not always succeed. His understanding of making is different from Joyce's and also from his counterparts among 1930s writers. It underwrites the distinctive quality of his best writing.

The critical moment in the evolution of Coffey's thinking about poetics occurred in discussions with Beckett over *Murphy*. Their conversations began when the typescript began to circulate in 1936 and ended during March 1938, the month the novel was published. Coffey's position is articulated in his still-unpublished review of *Murphy* and in the collection of poems, *Third Person*, that came together as he was writing the review. He had written a good deal since the volume of *Poems* he published jointly with Devlin in 1930 but it led nowhere. A sense of purpose only emerged as his understanding of Beckett's different aesthetic crystallised and then his new collection of poems came quickly. Beckett was stabbed on the street in January 1938 and spent time in hospital. Coffey became Peggy Guggenheim's lover, as Beckett had been previously, during February. Guggenheim left for London during March, and Brian Coffey simultaneously wrote his review of *Murphy* and completed his stalled collection by the beginning of April. As the brief affair with Guggenheim receded, he revised the collection and fell in love with a young designer he had met through Guggenheim. He became engaged to her during the summer months, when *Third Person* was published, and the couple were married in October. *Third Person* grows directly from different attitudes towards art and out of an understanding of conflicting kinds of love. It is a sequence in dialogue with Beckett's dualism at a profound level, recording their different responses to shared ambitions and experiences.

The six weeks in early 1938 were the turning point and crystallisation. *Third Person* came together as a collection and expressed Coffey's ideas in their distinctive form for the first time. He had discussed with MacGreevy a kind of poetry 'addressed to the intelligence rather than the affectivity' four years before; he had sent MacGreevy early drafts of 'A Drop of Fire' and 'Content'. Yet more poems came and a full statement was achieved as he simultaneously engaged with Beckett's aesthetic ideas, with their recent shared experience of Guggenheim and with Coffey's discovery of the woman he loved. The review of *Murphy* he wrote at the time communicates the pressure of his thinking more directly than the retrospective notes published in 1962, when the review was presumed lost. Its allusive style mimics Beckett's own, but the argument goes to the heart of the matter and is still relevant. Hugh Kenner's early book on Beckett was clever, but it sent exegetes in pursuit of Cartesian centaurs when they would have done better to follow Coffey, picking up the three-legged stool that fell over. Coffey set out the Joycean programme that attracts Murphy but which he is unable to follow, the preoccupation with order and the breakdown of order, the philosophical basis of achievement at variance with intention. When he wrote that 'the philosopher in Beckett is an active being, with whom the poet has to reckon', he was also writing about himself at that time.

Coffey's philosophical training enabled him to understand how the argument about dualism, which the novel sets out with reference to Descartes, Malebranche and Geulincx, is actually driven by an imperfect solution arrived at by German Idealism. He treats Beckett's pre-Socratic allusions as decoration, extending the argument back to the beginnings of philosophy and otherwise for comic effect, and concentrates on the logic of dialectic. History backward from Hegel to Spinoza and forward from Hegel to Marx demonstrates a collapse into a materialist dialectic if the idea of a prothesis cannot be maintained. Or, in terms of trinitarian theology more likely to have been heard in Coffey's UCD, one category cannot pass over into its opposite in anything but a destructive way unless as a mystery guaranteed by revelation. God may be one in essence, but He can be relatively three persons. It is an argument different from the one Beckett heard from the other Irish friend on whom he relied for philosophical commentary, Arland Ussher. Coffey's response has to do with a connected sequence of suppositions: that faith, sustaining belief, is necessary to bring together what has been divided; that the dialectal process is carried forward by virtue of a prior unity to push against; that dialectic is not simply a matter of *natura naturans* and *natura naturata* confronting one another in a dizzying sequence of aporetic reversals but a trinity of forces involving a third person:

By glens of exile
if she turns
love was needed

('Third Person')

And finally, I should mention, since it was my own bridge to understanding Coffey's meaning, that the critique of secular dialectic I describe is not specifically Catholic: it can be found in the later Coleridge as well as in Maritain.

Donal Moriarty has offered exemplary readings of the poems in *Third Person* in his book *The Art of Brian Coffey*. The only point I need to reinforce is Coffey's particular engagement with Beckett's understanding of dialectic. Beckett inserted Henry Macran, the Trinity Hegelian, into *Murphy* as the eccentric and hard-drinking Neary. Coffey inscribed Hegel into *Third Person* in a way more integral to the philosophical argument, with the consequence that Beckett's problem is seen in terms of its historical consequences and is reformulated in a way that affords a solution. Thus, 'A Drop of Fire' alludes very directly to Hegel's image of Becoming as a fire that dies out as it consumes its material, transforming itself, in the process, into Being identical with negation. The materialist dialectic is divisive, gets nowhere, 'Walking like drunkards in two ways'. There are other references that tie the two books together. Moriarty picks up the allusion in 'The Enemy' to *Purgatorio* Canto 19, in which Dante's siren-hag begins to sing; but 'Coeli' in the following line is actually a misprint for 'Caeli', that is, to Caelius, the friend of Catullus who was another lover of Lesbia, an allusion that overlaps the waste experience both Beckett and Coffey had recently come through. And the references are not all one way. Neary is portrayed in Beckett's Chapter One clenching his hands against his breastbone as he attempts to work through the dialectal process – which is surely a comment on the efficacy, or otherwise, of prayer. The solipsism that Mr Endon enjoys and that is forever unobtainable by Murphy is expressed in lines that anticipate the new style of *Third Person* in a curious way:

the last at last seen of him
himself unseen by him
and of himself. (140)

Coffey's review quoted and commented on these three lines as a way of concluding. It is as if his book of poems discovered itself here, in rephrasing an argument Beckett might have borrowed from him. Beckett, by return compliment, supplied Coffey's book with its title.

A connection with Beckett's earlier *Echo's Bones* – which works through the mirroring trope of Narcissus drowning in his own reflection – is reinforced by Coffey's original arrangement and cemented by the late addition of 'One Way': 'Giving what he has not given/he sees what he has not seen'. 'One Way' stands alongside Mary Manning's play *Youth's the Season* as an early acknowledgement of the despairing-heroic 'I can't go on, I'll go on' theme in Beckett's writing that is now frequently senti-mentalised. The poem recognises, with humility, the integrity and desperate need of Beckett's different response to shared concerns. Again, Coffey's thirteenth poem, 'Third Person', acknowledges 'Est Prodest', the programme-poem of Denis Devlin's *Intercessions* that had been published by the publisher of all three collections the previous September. 'Est Prodest' is a poem of 'Frightened antinomies', describing 'Tablelands of ice/Bastions of blocks of light' that in Coffey's 'Third Person' melt into 'rains of fulfilment': 'Such is patience in helpless need'. I have touched on the debt owed by New Writers' Press poets to the thirties generation of modernists. Trevor Joyce takes up the trope of eyes confronting eyes in dizzying infinitude again at a turning point in his career ('Mirror: Of Glazier Velasquez', 'The Opening'), where the theme of antimony is delivered into an antinomian present.

Donal Moriarty also has good things to say about Coffey's way of writing at large. Again, I need only emphasise the connection with Coffey's ideas about *poesis*. *Third Person* is again the place to start because it is the book in which he discovered an appropriate style. All poetry separates words from their everyday syntactical moorings so they connect with each other as well as with their referents, and it does this in different ways which produce different kinds of poetry. Thus, aural and visual connections in a Shakespearean sonnet typically actualise a sense of real-life drama, while Coffey's Neo-Thomist aesthetic takes him in the opposite direction. Interconnections of sound are more widely spaced, overlapped images are less individually realised, syntax is typically paratactic. Sense gathers in a way that allows the clear light (*claritas*) to shine through, like blinding sun filtered through bare branches. Fundamental issues are not hedged about with contingencies. The poems follow discontinuously within a system of their own making as if to frame a paradigm. The collection moves between Hegel's fire and water forming rainbows at which the heart leaps up:

> Who speaks to whom
> of whom
> these three

('Third Person')

Coffey's poetics produce statements that disorient because of their clarity. Like digital sound or images, they connect without cushioning to invoke the Shekinah. Readers who expect something more ordinary have complained that such writing is abstract but they miss the emotional charge. Others, like Blake, have worked in the same way to address the intellectual powers and not the corporeal understanding. But Coffey does so within a central Christian tradition. The fact that he redeems Beckett's *aporia* by substituting a trinitarian argument for a secular dialectic is further modified by a specifically Catholic doctrine of transubstantiation and the special place of Our Lady. There is no reason to quibble about sects; but there is a corollary for those without any belief. Whereas Beckett sought out philosophical analysis to reflect on a personal-aesthetic dilemma, Coffey began at the other end and applied what he had been taught since childhood. Beckett the man is saved by Beckett the writer, who pursued a metaphor as if it was an idea. Coffey's relation to ideas was more secure, by contrast, though his ideas and beliefs were no easier to apply.

A few words on Coffey's theory of translation are apropos, and the focus on making remains. There are parallels with Hölderlin, whose attempts to preserve the vocabulary and syntax of his originals only persuaded contemporaries that he was really mad, and whose practice has since been defended by Benjamin, Adorno and others. But Hölderlin's example was less in Coffey's mind than his own theory of making. Coffey held that word-for-word or phrase-by-phrase equivalence is travesty because it fabricates an automaton. It can display ingenuity, technical facility but nothing more. His commitment is manifestly to explore a different mind in the process of making – manifestly, in that the exercise does not disguise itself as substitute *poesis*. It contrives to communicate the awkwardness of carrying across meaning from one language to another, what is lost as well as what can be preserved. Translation is road-testing the language, exploring the boundaries between ways of encompassing truth, not constructing a surrogate. It connects with the argument evolved in *Third Person* in that it supposes the ordinary supposition that like and unlike can be exchanged is confused: such exchange is only possible when difference is erased or commodified. Coffey's poem 'Xenia' alludes to an economy that existed in Greece prior to monetary exchange and is linked with the idea of grace or *charis*, thus connecting his idea of translation in which differences are preserved back to the trust or divine grace upon which humanity properly depends. His 'Xenia' describes how guilt and fear invade the innocence of children, and how they might be preserved from what life does to what life is. The proper understanding of translation involves ethics and theology, and economics and politics too.

I should also emphasise that, while Coffey's discussion with Beckett over the nature of dialectic reached a conclusion when *Murphy* was published, the discussion remained a point of reference thereafter. Not because he wanted a leg up from a friend who became famous but because the earlier moment defined what he wanted poetry to do. As *Third Person* responds to *Murphy*, so Coffey's last, unfinished poem, 'The Prayers', takes off from a response to *The Unnamable*:

> Where it goes on   Here not anywhere
> when not anywher   Here   Now
>
> For why go probe whose heart

Beckett observed in a diary entry, 'the art (picture) that is a prayer sets up prayer, releases prayer in onlooker, i.e. *Priest*: Lord have mercy upon us. *People*: Christ have mercy upon us.' Coffey's 'The

Prayers' is an attempt to release such a response, to invoke that third person with a backward glance at the first manifestation of grace in his own writing. This notion sustained his elaborate edition of Devlin's *The Heavenly Foreigner*, which records the attempt of his oldest friend in poetry to achieve the same intention. Devlin's mindset was more sceptical, more worldly, more aware of political compromise and its cost; Devlin's writing made many more connections with surrounding literary reputations; but the project, *au fond*, was shared from their setting out.

The last thing to say is that Coffey did not write a great deal – much less than either Devlin or Beckett. A lot of what he wrote is not serious, or simply demonstrates work with words between times when poems came. But *Third Person, Hektor* and *Dice Thrown* are certain masterpieces. They have a sound driven by an extremely fine intelligence. They communicate rare truths in an utterly distinctive way – sometimes with joy, sometimes with sadness, at other times with wonder. All three come from moments of crisis or release in which pressure of belief transformed contraries into opposites, redeemed the time. In addition, the failure to make a life in America that sustains *Missouri Sequence*, the death of Coffey's son, Dominic, that is worked through in *Advent* and a significant body of translation besides has to be taken very seriously.

Coffey's successful writing rests on a truly original application of traditional ideas and beliefs; but the beliefs explain why his career as a writer was exposed to surrounding necessities and was fragile. His own estimation of it was registered by his interest in the fate of Mayakovsky, which began in early days and continued – in collage and artwork as much as in writing – at the end. 'There was the vessel of love smashed on existence, there was someone alone between heaven and earth, as [Mayakovsky's] last poem equivalently says.' The same shipwrecked boat appears in S.W. Hayter's specially engraved frontispiece for the limited edition of *Third Person*. Coffey did not show Guggenheim what he had written before publication and was far more concerned to get the opinion of Reavey's then-wife, Gwenedd Vernon. Guggenheim was in one sense the only begetter of the poems, but in Coffey's understanding not more than in the manner of a fundamental cause. He told Reavey that she would have to be content with a copy of the ordinary edition, but, ever charitable, he gave her a copy of one with the engraving in the end. 'A Peggy, en amité': number 25 out of 25.

PRIMARY REFERENCES

Brian Coffey, *Poems and Versions 1929–1990* (Dublin: The Dedalus Press, 1991).
Samuel Beckett, *Murphy* (London: Picador, 1973).

SECONDARY REFERENCES

James Knowlson, *Damned to Fame: The Life of Samuel Beckett* (London: Bloomsbury, 1996).
Donal Moriarity, *The Art of Brian Coffey* (Dublin: University College Dublin Press, 2000).

Denis Devlin (1908–1959)

Susan Schreibman

Denis Devlin was an exacting poet and translator whose diplomatic career, spanning some of the most horrific events of the twentieth century, deeply informed his creative work. Devlin's untimely death from leukaemia in August 1959 abruptly brought to a close a thirty-year poetic career which began during his years as a student at University College Dublin. During his lifetime he saw two volumes of his poems in print, *Intercessions* (1937) and *Lough Derg and Other Poems* (1946), as well as a collection brought out jointly with Brian Coffey (*Poems*, 1930). After Devlin's death, Coffey, his college friend and literary executor, worked tirelessly to promote Devlin's writings until his own death in 1995, bringing out several editions of his work (most notably an edited and annotated edition of *The Heavenly Foreigner* in 1967), as well as a number of scholarly articles. Coffey's persistence paid off, as it introduced new generations of scholars to Devlin's work, such as J.C.C. Mays, the editor of *Collected Poems of Denis Devlin* (Dublin: The Dedalus Press, 1989); Roger Little, editor of *Translations into English* (Dublin: The Dedalus Press, 1992) and Alex Davis who wrote the first full-length study on Devlin's writing, *A Broken Line: Denis Devlin and Irish Poetic Modernism* (Dublin: UCD Press, 2000).

Despite this critical interest in Devlin's poetry and translations, his work remains, for the most part, unknown outside circles interested in Irish poetic modernism. His poetry is infrequently taught on courses of Anglo-Irish literature, and when it is, it is usually considered in conjunction with the work of Samuel Beckett, Brian Coffey and Thomas MacGreevy, who formed, however loosely, a counter-tradition to the prevalent post-Revival poetic discourse as practised by such poets as Austin Clarke, George Russell and James Stephens.

Devlin's major poetic themes and collaborations as a translator reflected his life as a career diplomat: the horror of the rise of totalitarianism in Europe in the 1930s; the concomitant predicament of sustaining religious belief (in Devlin's case, Catholicism); and meditations on the state of exile – physical, intellectual and emotional. Devlin also wrote love poetry, often informed by a Jansenist sensibility. An exacting craftsman, it is clear from Devlin's manuscripts (deposited at the National Library of Ireland) that his impulse was to write the personal out of his poems, crafting a more universal statement. Devlin believed that particular grief and joy needed to be abandoned so as to harness language to live within the terror of mankind, providing a path of escape with honour.

Foreigners, foreignness, being a foreigner in one's own land, being a foreigner abroad, being foreign to those one loves and is loved by, as well as one's self, is central to Devlin's *oeuvre*. His last published poem, *The Heavenly Foreigner* (first published in *Poetry Ireland* in 1950), is a religious and erotic sequence with each poem taking the name of a place, in most cases a cathedral, that explores the narrator's relationship to an unnamed woman. The foreigner figures prominently in the late poem 'The Tomb of Michael Collins', a tribute to the revolutionary hero whose safe houses were never betrayed to the foreigners, but who was executed by one of his own. That the theme of foreignness was central to Devlin's work is not surprising, as he was a foreigner most of his life. His formative years were spent in Scotland. Born in Greenock to Irish parents on 15 April 1908, Devlin was the eldest of nine children, and in 1920, his family returned to Dublin where his father's licensed premises on Parnell Street became a favourite meeting place of Michael Collins, Eamonn de Valera and their associates. During his years as a diplomat, posted first to Italy (1938) then to the US (1939–47), to London (1947–9), then again to Italy (1950–9), he was at once a foreigner and a representative of his country. He was probably one of the finest translators of the French poet Saint-John Perse, whom Devlin collaborated with in the 1940s. In Perse's preoccupation with exile and statelessness, Devlin found a voice which spoke to his own sense of alienation.

Devlin's first published collection came out in September 1930 when he and Brian Coffey published, at their own expense, a slight volume simply entitled *Poems*. They ordered 250 copies from the printer Alex Thom & Co., but, as Brian Coffey writes in 'Of Denis Devlin: Vestiges, Sentences, Presages' (*University Review*, 1961), anticipating high demand, they ordered a reprint of another 100 pre-publication copies. Unfortunately, that demand was never realised. The volume consists of nine poems, five by Coffey and four by Devlin. By that autumn, both men had finished their BA degrees and wanted, as Coffey writes, to show 'that the pre-treaty tradition of writing from UCD was not dead'. The following month Devlin began reading for an MA in French at UCD, having the previous year been awarded first-class honours in English and French (with a less-distinguished qualification in Irish) in the BA examination, winning an exhibition prize of £20. As a student, Devlin participated fully in the university's intellectual life, as a contributor to the student publication *The National Student*, a founder-member of the UCD Dramatic Society, as well as making the acquaintance of writers such as Donagh MacDonagh, Brian O'Nolan, Niall Sheridan and Mervyn Wall.

Devlin's ultimate choice of career was not an easy one. In 1926 he entered the diocesan seminary All Hallow's College at Cloniffe, but left to attend UCD. During his final undergraduate year he was enrolled as a law student at King's Inns, but did not sit the First Law examination and did not re-enrol. He spent much of 1930–1 travelling in Europe before submitting his MA thesis on *Montaigne intime* (for which he was awarded second-class honours). After receiving his MA, he studied at the Sorbonne, with the intention of taking a docteur-en-Lettres, but instead, in 1933, returned to Dublin without paid employment. Mervyn Wall recalled Devlin during this time, as quoted in *Collected Poems of Denis Devlin*:

> [we spent] many gloomy evenings walking about town, our walk and slow talk interrupted occasionally by Denis pausing beneath

a lamppost to draw a scrap of paper from his pocket and read by the light overhead some new poem which he had written.

In 1935 Devlin became a civil servant in the Department of Foreign Affairs (then, the Department of External Affairs). Devlin may not have joined, however, out of a strong sense of service. On the contrary, he seems to have seen it as a way to be paid to work outside Ireland. In a letter dated September 1932, which is part of the Thomas MacGreevy papers at Trinity College, Dublin, he wrote to MacGreevy: 'I am ... going for a civil service post because my father hasn't a sou for me. And I can't imagine ever becoming reconciled to Dublin' (TCD MS 8112/1). He failed the exam the first time, and in 1934 was fortunate to be appointed to one of four newly created junior positions in the Department of English at UCD. Yet Devlin was not satisfied: he longed for Paris. It was, he wrote to MacGreevy, 'my only correspondence with the cosmos' (TCD MS 8112/5). During his first year of teaching, he re-sat the examination and passed, entering the Department of External Affairs the following year. Although Devlin's reasons for joining the Department may have not been the purest, he became a highly regarded diplomat whose final posting was as Ireland's first Ambassador to Italy.

Throughout, Devlin continued to write. In the co-publication with Brian Coffey, one poem, 'Now', had been previously published in *The National Student*. These youthful poems (the first poem by Devlin in the collection was entitled 'O Paltry Melancholy') differed greatly from his second collection, *Intercessions*, published seven years later by Europa Press (Paris), which was founded and run by fellow Irish poet George Reavey. *Intercessions* came out in an edition of 300, in part at Devlin's own expense and after many months of delay. It was not reviewed widely. Not surprisingly, the most positive reviews came from Samuel Beckett (writing in the Paris journal *transition*), and Thomas MacGreevy (writing in the Dublin-based *Ireland To-Day*). *Intercessions* is a collection of fifteen poems, the majority dating from Devlin's residence in Paris (1931–3). Gone is the melancholia of the earlier collection. In its stead is a confident use of language, heavily influenced by surrealism, in which the reader must journey with the poet through conceits which startle more than delight, through language which jars, through words which jostle against one another into what seems to be at first discordant, but upon further reading melds into a hesitant harmony.

The collection opens with a two-stanza love poem, 'The Alembic', in which the language of love is all but absent. Rather, the reader is invited to partake in a disconcerting rhetoric of a heart beneath a 'monotonous accident' of 'stillblowing wind', 'aromatic' blood, 'poisoned blessing' and 'cloistral lashes shut on folded cheeks'. By the middle of the second stanza, however, the paradoxical language opens out into lines of immense beauty devoid of ambiguity, in which the narrator resigns himself, permits himself, to experience love:

> let the
> Accountant suspend work, wipe his misty glasses
> The wind pads almost noiseless like a cat
> Do not reject its suave caresses, Heart.

Other poems in the collection reflect themes that would persist in Devlin's poetry: war, though viewed from the lens of the diplomat rather than the soldier; places, particularly in France and Ireland; the politics of belief. Devlin's places are not sites of nostalgia, but are of the here and now which, nevertheless, carry on their backs their shadowy pasts, their (as he writes in 'Liffey Bridge') 'foolish reflection'. Devlin's places are not painted in the manner of realism, but surrealism. The reader is offered no charming landscape to rest a weary eye, but is pulled into a vortex of discordant images, as in 'Communication from the Eiffel Tower':

> Tower, that snowy steel town though postulant
> Of full conscience and its confetti of laughter blown about
> In the main street of the sun, then
> Summoned when the trestle-blether texts of poverty are
>   irrelevant
> What can it offer
> More than the pretty tinkling of snowy steel?

In 1939 Devlin was appointed Irish consul at the Consulate General in New York, and the following year was transferred to Washington where he served as first secretary. There, he met such

American writers as poets Robert Penn Warren and Allen Tate and prose writer Katherine Anne Porter. He was also introduced to the French poet Alexis Saint-Léger, who published under the name Saint-John Perse. Perse was a distinguished diplomat, who in 1960 was awarded the Nobel Prize for Literature. During the Second World War he was deprived of his citizenship and possessions by the Vichy regime and from 1941 to 1945 held the post of advisor to the Library of Congress. Although twenty-one years Devlin's senior, the two established an admiration for each other's work. Léger, who would not allow his *Anabase*, written in 1924, to be reprinted until after the war for personal reasons, remained poetically silent until after coming to Washington. Of the poems that ended the silence, 'Exil' (Exile), 'Pluies' (Rains), 'Neiges' (Snows) and 'Poème à l'Etrangère', 'Rains' and 'Snows' were published by the *Sewanee Review* in 1945, with translations by Devlin, and then later reprinted in book form.

In an undated, unpublished fragment from Devlin's papers at the National Library of Ireland, Devlin recounts his afternoons at Léger's Georgetown flat, where the two worked on the translations, painfully aware that the city in which they worked was, at one extreme, deciding the fate of the world, and at the other, a site of carelessness, where their colleagues regularly indulged in the cocktail bars of the Mayflower and Carlton hotels. But in that Georgetown flat, surrounded by their common love of language, these two poets existed outside time, taking their place in a vast and grave 'universal tapestry'. Léger's work which expressed a familiarity with personal exile, as well as with the eternal exile of the human condition, was instantly recognisable to Devlin whose own poetry reflected these themes. Perhaps because of this concomitant sensibility, the work of the poet who wrote 'On too many frequented shores have my footsteps/been washed away before the day' would appeal to Devlin such that he is still regarded as one of the finest translator's of Léger's verse into English. For Devlin, as for Léger, language itself became the one solid substance. As one of his early critics, Stan Smith, has written in '"Precarious Guest": The Poetry of Denis Devlin', Devlin was impelled 'to find in the impalpable community of language a home he could not locate in any specific time or place'. There too 'he glimpsed the emptiness and evanescence of the forms on which the soul relies'. It is as an effort to save language from losing its power – and to read Devlin's poems *is* an effort if only at the level of syntax – that the power of his poetry lies.

In 1946 *Lough Derg and Other Poems* was published by Reynal and Hitchcock and was widely reviewed in Ireland and the United States. This collection of forty-seven poems, with several reprints from *Intercessions*, was Devlin's most substantial. It opens with 'Lough Derg', which many critics regard as one of Devlin's finest. Like Patrick Kavanagh's poem of the same name, it is a meditation on a summer pilgrimage to St Patrick's Purgatory at Lough Derg, County Donegal. Devlin's poem, written shortly after the end of the Second World War, is a meditative poem that begins with an ironic observation of neutral Ireland: 'With mullioned Europe shattered, this Northwest,/Rude-sainted isle would pray it whole again'. The poem, as Alex Davis has noted, is a densely symbolic argument in which the narrator attempts to resolve the discrepancy 'between a human need to believe in divine justice and the palpable cruelty of a world in which prayer seemingly goes unheard'. Despite the prayer of this 'rude-sainted isle', the limbs of Europe still ache.

'Casa Buonaroti', another poem in the collection, is a meditation on the art of Michelangelo, which can also be read as a metaphor for the craft of poetry:

> He struggled all life with pigment, rock, chisel and sun
> To put God in matter, magnify himself;
> Worked against Time, rhetorical skull on the shelf
> To muscle in stone ideas by Time undone ...

Other poems prefigure the shape of his last collection, *The Heavenly Foreigner*, which take as their inspiration specific sites, including 'West Pier' in which it is not clear whether the 'her' of the poem is a woman or Ireland. 'Ank'hor Vat' is a reflection on the sacred Cambodian City hidden in the pluvial forest, where the Buddha, smiling with 'lissom fury', inspires the poet to 'lie down before him/His look will flow like oil over us'. Other poems of place are 'On Mount Muckish', 'Meditation at Avila', 'Anteroom: Geneva', 'Annapolis'. The last two are savagely ironic poems, the latter ending with a nod to W.B. Yeats's 'Among School Children': 'And there a girl-dancer remotely/Flows to the dance.'

Many critics have argued that Devlin's greatest poetic achievement is *The Heavenly Foreigner*, a sequence first published in 1950 in *Poetry Ireland,* and after Devlin's death in an annotated edition edited by Coffey (1967). The sequence was introduced in *Poetry Ireland* by Niall Sheridan, who commented that the poetry makes 'unusual demands upon the reader'. Nevertheless, he said, these are 'the legitimate demand of a poet, and the reader who concedes them will find himself well rewarded'. He went on:

> On one level 'The Heavenly Foreigner' communicates as a love-poem, rich in poignant and tender moods. But sexual love is the incidental and minor theme, as it was in the Catharist songs of the Troubadours. The deeper preoccupation is with the problems of Time and human destiny, the anguished alliance of flesh and spirit. What god had joined Descartes has put asunder and the wound still festers.

In this poem Devlin is concerned with the Self and the Other. One's body can be part of the other, 'the fiery circle cataracting outerworld'. Yet the Other, as Stan Smith has written, is also the 'Heavenly Foreigner', one's own elusive soul, Christ and the Beloved who is anima and completion of one's own true being. As Devlin writes:

> Something there was other
> Always at my elbow ...

> When the foreign power intervened and made all the difference
> Between the bog and the road,
> Making the present, making life ....
> O Heavenly Foreigner! Your price is high.

> ('Irvine')

The poem itself is divided into eleven sections, each titled with the name of a place associated with a different experience of love, and often its accompanying anguish. Although the poems are addressed to 'the face of one I love and one befriended' ('St Malo'), the beloved remains a mystery. Coffey, in his introduction to the Dolmen Press edition (1967), suggests that one woman is the 'abiding presence' in Devlin's love poetry, but goes no further. Coffey also suggests in his introduction that to read *The Heavenly Foreigner* simply as a mystical experience, and not as an experience rooted in reality, would be a mistake. He suggests that the words of St John of the Cross, whom Devlin admired, provide insight to his method: 'Human knowledge is not sufficient to comprehend it nor human experience to describe it, because only he who has passed through it will be able to feel it, but not tell it.' The 'it' is perhaps Devlin's conflicting loves. 'It' might also reflect the imperfection of memory which cannot hope to capture the reality of experience.

Devlin's sudden death in 1959 caught many of his friends and colleagues by surprise. Soon after his death, his wife Caren established a poetry prize in Devlin's memory, to be awarded biannually to an Irish poet or a poet of Irish descent. Its goal was to help a poet concentrate on writing, if only for a short term, by freeing him or her of material worries. The committee establishing the prize was large, and a substantial sum of money was raised by Devlin's American friends. It was administered first by Poetry Ireland, but in more recent years by The Arts Council. In 1963 a *Selected Poems* was edited and introduced by Allen Tate and Robert Penn Warren (published by Holt, Rinehart and Winston in New York). That same year, Brian Coffey edited a *Collected Poems* which was published as a special issue of *University Review*, and reprinted the following year by the Dolmen Press.

Interest in Devlin's work waned in the 1970s and 1980s, despite the best efforts of Coffey and Michael Smith, editor of New Writers Press and *The Lace Curtain*. The new editions of Devlin's poetry and translations in the 1990s, Alex Davis's critical work, as well as an increasing interest generally in Irish poetic modernism, paved the way for a re-evaluation of Devlin's *oeuvre*. Nevertheless, his readership remains small. The difficulty of his poetry, combined with a lack of biographical information and access to personal papers (if any remain) which could help to contextualise the work, keep many potential readers at arm's length. As J.C.C. Mays writes in the conclusion to his *Collected*

Poems, the obstacles to understanding the type of poetry Devlin writes are not those which can easily be footnoted. What is needed is an act of faith, a suspension of belief, a willingness to enter into Devlin's poetic universe in order to internalise the poetry, to feel its rhythms and follow its syntax. Only then can the reader, '[s]eparate and self-absorbed', enter into this remarkable gift.

PRIMARY REFERENCES

Collected Poems of Denis Devlin, edited by J.C.C. Mays (Dublin: The Dedalus Press, 1989).
Denis Devlin, *Translations into English*, edited by Roger Little (Dublin: The Dedalus Press, 1992).

SECONDARY REFERENCES

Alex Davis, *A Broken Line: Denis Devlin and Irish Poetic Modernism* (Dublin: UCD Press, 2000).
Stan Smith, '"Precarious Guest": The Poetry of Denis Devlin', in *Modernism and Ireland: The Poetry of the 1930s*, edited by Patricia Coughlan and Alex Davis (Cork: Cork University Press, 1995), 232–49.

Flann O'Brien (1911–1966)

Anthony Cronin

University College Dublin in 1929, the year Brian O'Nolan entered the college, occupied a large, supposedly Greek classical building in Earlsfort Terrace, off St Stephen's Green, as well as the premises of its predecessors in the Green itself. O'Nolan was to describe the impression the Earlsfort Terrace building made on the newcomer more than once. In his first novel, *At Swim-Two-Birds* (1939), the premises of the College were described as follows:

> ... outwardly a rectangular plain building with a fine porch where the mid-day sun pours down in summer from the Donnybrook direction, heating the steps for the comfort of the students. The hallway inside is composed of large black and white squares arranged in the orthodox chessboard pattern, and the surrounding walls, done in an unpretentious cream wash, bear three rough smudges caused by the heels, buttocks and shoulders of the students. (45)

In *The Centenary History of the Literary and Historical Society, 1855–1955* (1956), he marginally increases the sordidity of the description:

> The hall was quite empty. The plain white walls bore three dark parallel smudgy lines at elevations of about three, five and five-and-a-half feet from the tiled chessboard floor. Later I was to know that this triptych had been achieved by the buttocks, shoulders, and hair-oil of lounging students. (240)

Some of his friends were later to describe his arrival as if it was immediately noteworthy – Niall Montgomery, for example, was to say that he descended on UCD 'like a shower of paratroopers' – but this was not quite the case. To begin with at least he kept, like many another first-year student, a low profile, attending lectures and seeing mostly the friends of his last years at school.

Towards the end of his first year in college, however, Brian began to achieve a certain amount of fame. This was mostly through the figure he cut at meetings of the Literary and Historical Society. Writing a quarter of a century later in the *Centenary History*, he was to describe the venue and the scene:

> The students' many societies, of which the L.&H. was the principal one and the oldest, held their meetings in a large building at 86 Stephen's Green. In my day it was a very dirty place and in bad repair … If I am not mistaken, lighting was by gas, and it was in this 86 in an upstairs semi-circular lecture theatre, that the L.&H. met every Saturday night. It was large as such theatres go but its seating capacity could not exceed two hundred, whereas most meetings attracted not fewer than six hundred people. The congestion, disorder and noise may be imagined. A seething mass gathered and swayed in a very large lobby outside the theatre … This most heterogeneous congregation, reeling about, shouting and singing in the hogarthian pallor of a single gas-jet (when somebody had not thought fit to extinguish the same) came to be known as the mob … A visitor would probably conclude that it was merely a gang of rowdies, dedicated to making a deafening uproar the *obbligato* to some unfortunate member's attempts to make a speech within. It was certainly a disorderly gang but its disorders were not aimless and stupid, but often necessary and salutary … (242)

He had already described the mob and its activities as seen through the eyes of the narrator of *At Swim-Two-Birds* who, unlike O'Nolan himself, takes no part in the proceedings and affects to regard it as an almost meaningless spectacle of disorder:

> Outside the theatre there was a spacious lobby or ante-room and it was here that the rough boys would gather and make their noises. One gas-jet was the means of affording light in the lobby and when a paroxysm of fighting and roaring would be at its

height, the light would be extinguished as if by a supernatural or diabolic agency and the effect of the darkness in such circumstances afforded me many moments of physical and spiritual anxiety, for it seemed to me that the majority of the persons present were possessed by unclean spirits. The lighted rectangle of the doorway to the debate-hall was regarded by many persons not only as a receptacle for the foul and discordant speeches which they addressed to it, but also for many objects of a worthless nature – for example spent cigarette ends, old shoes, the hats of friends, parcels of damp horse dung, wads of soiled sacking and discarded articles of ladies' clothing not infrequently the worse for wear. (66–7)

This mob was the particular terror of the politicians and notabilities who were visiting chairmen at meetings of the L.&H.; but it was not unresponsive to wit and even oratory. By stationing himself near the door of the lecture theatre a dominating and ready speaker could command both assemblies at once, and this Brian O'Nolan now discovered he had the nerve and talent to do.

Positioned by the door, so that he was dimly visible from within, but making sure that he was seen to be more a part of the mob than of the assembly proper, he would engage in contests of readiness and repartee with speakers, visiting chairmen and the auditor of the society, sometimes embarking on a flight of oratory himself by way of interjection and intervention in debate. He was the first who proved able to fuse the two parts of the proceedings, those of the unruly mass outside and the more orderly gatherings within. He began by single quick interjections, to which only his more immediate neighbours in the mob paid attention, and then gradually extended his range. Having experienced the heady delight which a successful interjection in debate can bring, he returned on the following Saturday. Then one Saturday night, towards the middle of his second year, O'Nolan went into the theatre and began to speak from the benches, with such success that he continued to do this hereafter. The new departure was not well received by some of his former adherents, who were inclined to think that it was something of a concession to respectability or to authority. Soon, however, a portion of the mob followed him in, while the majority of those outside the door continued to regard him as someone who was speaking on their behalf and who would not put up with the pretentiousness and phony legalism that frequently reigned within.

The Literary and Historical Society was the only society in UCD with any sort of real tradition. Thirty years after James Joyce delivered his famous Ibsenite address, 'Drama and Life', the society had become much more political. Literature was never debated and history only in the Irish way – as an embittering dimension of politics. In Brian O'Nolan's time, political tensions were particularly acute. Although De Valera had led his party into the Dail, and was already poised to take office, the issues over which the Civil War had been fought and the merits or the demerits of the Anglo-Irish Treaty of 1922 were still inflammable topics.

Whatever his views, O'Nolan did not take part in these wranglings. His stance was already that of the satirical observer who regards the pretensions, hypocrisies and falsehoods of all parties as more worthy of comment than their actual views, and whose shafts are designed to puncture rather than persuade. He was not a mob orator in the demagogic sense; he was a licensed satirist and jester whose aim was to deflate and to amuse. There was, nevertheless, some social content in his contributions. One of the best remembered was his impromptu speech on the motion 'Sweet Are the Uses of Advertisement'. He began by standing in silence while he elaborately searched the pockets of the overcoat he was still wearing. Finally he produced from the breast pocket a crumpled copy of the *Evening Herald*, which he slowly unrolled, opened and searched for the advertisement he wanted. It was for Lux washing powder and its headline read 'I wonder does he see that faded slip?' At this point he proceeded to deal with the ludicrous aspects of the advertisement with frequent references to the text while the house rocked with laughter. Gradually his line of argument turned until in the end it became a savage onslaught on the deceits of advertisement generally and the cruel manner in which it raised people's expectations. This was the speech for which he won the impromptu medal for oratory in that session.

By now O'Nolan was a well-known figure in college and he was making new friends. Like many who had lived fairly sheltered lives and been the victims of bullying, he wanted to be liked by the tough guys or 'hard chaws' as they were known in UCD. But most of his new friends were to some degree his intellectual equals and most of them had literary ambitions. His was an exceptionally talented generation in UCD and it was also the first generation to be educated and to become possible critics of the society they confronted in an independent Ireland. Donagh McDonagh, who had lent or given Brian O'Nolan a precious copy of Joyce's *Ulysses*, began as a poet, whose somewhat Audenesque verses fitted admirably into Faber and Faber's list. A son of the martyred 1916 leader Thomas McDonagh, also a poet, he was a law student who, later in life, found it temptingly easy to claim an inheritance in the new order as a District Justice. Niall Montgomery was a quick-eyed and quick-witted architectural student who was to play an important role in Brian O'Nolan's life, not only as a collaborator in some of his journalistic enterprises but also as a sort of intellectual mentor. His attitude to Joyce was obsessive but ambiguous. According to another friend, Niall Sheridan, Montgomery's conversation was 'sometimes so elliptical and recondite that he seemed to be telling jokes to himself'. A wit and the son of a noted Dublin wit, the Free State film censor Jimmy Montgomery, Niall Montgomery regarded Joyce's works as an intellectual's playground: esoteric, cabbalistic, logomathic. He left out, insofar as it can be left out, the human content and the compassionate purpose of Joyce's works, and he encouraged Brian to do the same. He wrote plays and poetry, both deliberately modernist, neither very widely performed nor published. However in the Dublin of his heyday, a place which preferred promise to performance and where it was in some ways a mistake to publish, he would retain a reputation for brilliance.

Like Montgomery, the poets Denis Devlin and Brian Coffey, who were somewhat older, were both rather deliberate mode ists. Much influenced by French models, Devlin entere Department of External Affairs and wound up a Ambassador to Italy. Coffey, the more considerable p two and the son of the President of the Colleg ambitious socially, being content to teach school fo all this brilliant circle he was the only one who m to have had a wholehearted dedication to his art, but, partly because of the age gap between them, he was less close to Brian O'Nolan than the others. Also the less close, and the only one to have a commitment to fundamental social change, was Charles Donnelly, who within a year or two of leaving the college joined the International Brigade and gave his life for the Spanish Republic. The handful of poems he left behind him testify to an extraordinary talent and make him the missing figure of O'Brien's generation.

Other than Niall Montgomery, the friend who was closest to Brian O'Nolan was Niall Sheridan. He too wrote poetry and shortly after leaving UCD published a small collection jointly with Donagh McDonagh. He shared with the others a consuming interest in Joyce and was even to become acquainted with the master in Paris later on; but his sense of humour was less dependent on literary allusions than Montgomery's and he provided, besides literary converse, that interest in ordinary humanity which one side of Brian O'Nolan's character preferred. Besides being a college intellectual, he was a bit of a 'hard chaw', who was at home in the poker schools or in the bookmakers and he had a streak of humorous realism which appealed to O'Nolan.

Finding the break which Joyce had made and Joyce's dedication to his art beyond them, most of this circle had to find some sort of accommodation with Ireland and its creeds – as well as some sort of a stance in relation to them – while yet retaining and justifying their admiration for Joyce and his ethic of revolt and severance. The result was that literature tended to become an in-joke, a badge of superiority and a freemason's clasp among them rather than something whose impulse would feed back into life. Lacking the sort of final dedication to art that Joyce and the other great masters of the modern movement had given, they yet embraced a sort of 'art for art's sake' doctrine.

True, O'Nolan's position was different from that of some of the others. He did not have a problem in relation to Catholicism inasmuch as he was a believer all his life; and he did not have a problem in relation to nationalism because basically and instinctually as well as by heredity he was a nationalist, at least of sorts. He was not a Francophile or an Anglophile and his elaborate critique of Ireland in later years was based on the rough premise that, with all its shortcomings, it was as good a place as anywhere else; both as Myles na Gopaleen and otherwise he was very quick to resent insults to his country or implications that other countries were inherently superior.

His conformism was therefore of a less ambiguous nature than that of some of his friends; but, even so, he too had to acknowledge that his path was a different one from Joyce's; and he too had to find a stance in relation to Ireland which would enable him to make a career in it – to some extent even of it. The resulting synthesis was largely Montgomery's solution. Joyce and his challenge would be defused by making him a mere logomathic wordsmith, a great but demented genius who finally went mad in his ivory tower. Admittedly he was a great low-life humorist as well, but he was one whose insensate dedication to something called art would finally unhinge him. On the other hand, Joyce and a view of modernism as a predominantly aesthetic philosophy could still provide a sort of absolution and a sort of charm against infection for those who despised the new Ireland while yet conforming to parental and other expectations within it. It was a circular solution, but it had the advantage of neatness.

The sort of academic fare on offer in UCD did not lessen the intellectuals' sense of superiority. There were scarcely any tutorials and most of the teaching consisted of lectures to large numbers of apathetic students. In the English Department these lectures were simply readings aloud of the set texts by lecturers who seemed unable to add any comment of their own. Modern literature played no part in the curriculum; nor had the new criticism yet arrived to impose any sort of a methodology on teachers of English. O'Nolan attended English lectures only in his first year. After that his subjects were Irish and German. The Irish lectures he did not find much of an improvement. The Professor of Irish was Douglas Hyde, the revered founder of the Gaelic League. To Brian's surprise – or so he was later to claim – Hyde spoke Irish 'inaccurately and badly'.

O'Nolan and his friends now constituted, in Sheridan's words, 'a sort of intellectual Mafia, which strongly influenced the cultural and social life of University College, and controlled – through some rather dubious electoral uses – most of the College Clubs and Societies concerned with the Arts' ('Brian, Flann and Myles', 35). They were all regular contributors to the alternative students' magazine *Comhthrom Feinne* which was published by the Students' Representative Council as a rival to the longer established and less adventurous *National Student*. The editorship of this magazine 'usually passed from one member of the group to another' and in it Brian O'Nolan began to deploy, as Montgomery was to put it, 'a myriad of pseudonymous personalities in the interests of pure destruction'. Brian now began to contribute voluminously to *Comhthrom Feinne* under his various pseudonyms. Sheridan's claim that 'he burst on the scene fully equipped' as a writer is not far from the truth, for what is really extraordinary about the UCD writings is how early he found his line. 'Brother Barnabas', the principal pseudonym he deployed, was a proto Myles na Gopaleen. He had the same extraordinary history which had brought him into contact with the great and famous, the same weary prescience, the same amused tolerance of the foibles of human nature and the shortcomings of its Irish audience. Biographies of Brother Barnabas are as oblivious of the laws of time and space as biographies of Sir Myles were to be, and human history, seen through his eyes, is the same sort of surrealist and somewhat pointless romp. He has been a Russian nobleman who escaped across the steppe in a sled pursued by wolves; he has horsewhipped the Kaiser in Vienna in 1912; he has known Bernard Shaw as well as Harry Wharton, Billy Bunter and the boys of the Remove. He has discovered 'and hastily recovered' James Joyce.

But the most remarkable piece in many ways was written towards the end of O'Nolan's student career. It was headed 'Scenes in a Novel (probably posthumous) by Brother Barnabas' and it told how one night when he 'had swallowed nine stouts and felt vaguely blasphemous', Brother Barnabas created a character called Carruthers McDaid. He 'gave him a good but worn-out mother and an industrious father, and coolly neg-ativing fifty years of eugenics made him a worthless scoundrel, a betrayer of women and a secret drinker'. One night, 'fortified with a pony of porter and two threepenny cigars', Brother Barnabas retires to his room and addresses himself to Chapter

Five. At this point, McDaid is to be required to rob a poor-box in a church. He refuses point blank to do it. For this supposedly depraved character has undergone a religious conversion. When the author sent him to 'a revivalist prayer meeting purely for the purpose of scoffing and showing the reader the blackness of his soul', he remained to pray; and two days later he is caught sneaking out to Gardiner Street Church at seven in the morning.

Worse still, the other characters had begun to revolt. Shaun Svoolish, the hero, the composition of whose heroics has cost the author 'many a sleepless day', has fallen in love with a slavey in Griffith Avenue, and Shiela, his steady, an exquisite creature who has been produced for the sole purpose of loving him and becoming his wife, 'is apparently to be given the air'. The author remonstrates with and finally threatens his literary creation: '"Railway accidents are fortunately rare," I said finally, "but when they happen they are horrible. Think it over."' Gradually, all the characters revolt until the novel seethes with conspiracy. McDaid gets hold of a paper knife which was given to another character, Fr Hennessy, simply to give him something to fiddle with on a parochial call. It strikes Brother Barnabas that posterity is 'taking a hand in the destiny of its ancestors'. We leave him sitting at his window 'thinking, remembering, dreaming'. He considers calling the Guards, but 'we authors have our foolish pride'. As the piece ends the clear implication is that he is about to be murdered by the characters he has created. The origin of the revolt of the characters in the novel within the novel *At Swim-Two-Birds* is clearly here.

In the summer of 1932, Brian sat his final BA exam in the subjects German, English and Irish. He passed with second class honours, a reasonable enough degree considering his well-established reputation for not doing any work. In his College Notes for 1932, Brother Barnabas had forecast that O'Nolan would gain a first-class honours degree and a travelling studentship in the end-of-year exams. And the legend of idle brilliance which it pleased him to create was furthered at the New Year by a 'Believe It or Not' item which said 'Mr B Ó Nualláin is reading for his degree'. In fact he worked quite hard for the six months or so preceding the exam, frequenting the college library in the evenings, setting himself a minimum of one and a half hours' intensive reading and even going so far as to write a letter under his own name to the magazine protesting against the closure of the library one evening to allow a dance to be held there.

From the autumn of 1932 onwards, O'Nolan was a graduate student and a senior figure in UCD, famous not only for his L.&H. exploits and his contributions to *Comhthrom Feinne* but also for the short stories in Irish he had begun to contribute to the *Irish Press*, the new daily newspaper of the Fianna Fail party, and to the *Evening Telegraph*. Like most of his stories, these are anecdotes, with a basic idea rather mechanically worked out; but in a milieu where publication in a daily newspaper would have increased the prestige of a professor, they added greatly to the standing he enjoyed. And enjoy it he did. Fame in a closed circle such as that provided by UCD can be sweeter and more intense than the more diffused fame the larger world may provide later on; all the evidence suggests that Brian O'Nolan enjoyed his UCD fame immensely. The curiously sentimental tone of his contributions to such publications as the *Centenary History of the L.&H.*, where he refers to 'the magic those years held', show clearly that he did look back on it with nostalgia. Indeed, UCD had become his world to such an extent that his leaving of it was rather ragged and inconclusive; he was one of those students who are reluctant to leave the scene of their triumphs.

In 1932–3, Brian and his friends were still deeply involved with *Comhthrom Feinne* and it was in January 1933 that he took over the editorship. Not only was he still attending the L.&H., but it was in 1932–3 that he made the decision to stand for the Auditorship of the Society which somewhat clouded his final exit from college. His opponent in the election was Vivion de Valera who had been his classmate in Blackrock College and whose father's party had won the elections of 1932 five years after its entry into Dail Eireann. Vivion de Valera's candidature was, as might have been expected, frankly political and in the prevailing atmosphere the anti-political or apolitical O'Nolan had little chance of election. Even his occasionally serious political contributions to debate had always been couched in ironical terms and were never other than humorous. Thus the true import of a speech in which he guyed and ridiculed the blueshirts was lost and it was easy for his opponents to characterise him as a mere jester. According to R.N. Cooke, writing in the *Centenary History*:

> Unfortunately his fame as a funny man was such that he was 'typed'. The Society expected it from him and he seldom disappointed it, but it meant that his real standing as a first-class serious speaker was never acknowledged ... Vivion de Valera on the other hand was in those days the most serious-minded man in Ireland. It is only right to say that he was probably the most fair-minded also. That proved our and O Nolan's undoing. At the last meeting of the year, speaker after speaker poured out the most nauseating tripe adulatory of the national aspirations which Vivion was alleged, vicariously of course, to personify until it seemed that a vote for O Nolan was a nail in the coffin of the Republic. (250–1)

De Valera won by the fairly hefty margin of 42 votes to 12. When James Joyce contested the same election in 1900, he had lost to a law student, Hugh Kennedy, subsequently a High Court Judge, by 15 votes to 9. (The present writer did rather better than either of them. He lost the same election – also to a law student who would become a judge – by a margin of one vote and the validity of that was disputed.) The defeat, however, was not the end of O'Nolan's connection with the society. The novelist Patrick Purcell remembered a 'magnificent satirical oration made during the 1932–3 session in which O'Nolan equably ridiculed all those who took part in Irish politics under whatever party name' (262); and according to R.N. Cooke 'it was in this year, after he lost the Auditorship, that some of his best speeches were made' (250).

Whether or not he had hopes of an academic career, he had now decided to enrol for an MA, choosing as the subject of his thesis 'Nature in Irish Poetry'. This was arrived at after discussions with the great Douglas Hyde, a man whom Brian now came to know rather better and respect more than he had done as an undergraduate, and also with Agnes O'Farrelly, his thesis adviser. The subject seems, as is often the case, to have been lazily agreed to in accordance with an adviser's suggestion, but it was a surprising choice all the same. Nature plays some part in the 'mad Sweeny' sections of *At Swim-Two-Birds* and his novel *The Third Policeman* and is essential to the pervading wretchedness of *An Béal Bocht*; but the actual observation of it in these books is limited and generalised, as is the language used to describe it. Of course, as the thesis makes clear, the same could be said of Irish poetry, where the descriptions of nature are standardised and Homeric rather than particular and minutely exact as the English tradition demands. The thesis consisted merely of an anthology of Irish poems with a somewhat obvious critical commentary. It was submitted in August 1934 and Brian got a considerable shock when the easy-going Agnes Farrelly promptly rejected it. His story to his friends was that he was simply going to type it out again on pink paper and re-submit it. After the event this is what he claimed to have done, so that the unrevised thesis which he had conned Agnes O'Farrelly into accepting became part of his legend. In fact he did revise it, expanding the essay, though not rendering it any the less pedestrian; and making some alterations in the anthology that went with it. Conned or not, Agnes O'Farrelly accepted the thesis in the following year, 1935, and he was awarded an MA. His reference in the *Centenary History of the L.&H.* to Douglas Hyde and Agnes O'Farrelly having 'hearts of gold' suggests that he felt they had been lenient, perhaps because by then he had begun to earn his living, and that he was grateful.

UCD was not Arcadia for Brian O'Nolan. He did not find there what others found among the dreaming spires of other institutions. His experience of the true, the beautiful and even the good while there was limited, outside literature at least. But it gave him a lot just the same: the converse of near-equals, a test of his powers, much laughter and matter for future laughter, a baptism in the squalor of which he would be the exegete.

PRIMARY REFERENCES

Flann O'Brien, *At Swim-Two-Birds* (London: MacGibbon and
     Kee, 1968).
Brian O'Nolan, in *The Centenary History of the Literary and
     Historical Society, 1855–1955,* edited by James Meenan
     (Tralee: The Kerryman Ltd., 1956).

SECONDARY REFERENCES

Anthony Cronin, *No Laughing Matter: The Life and Times of
     Flann O'Brien* (Dublin: New Island, 2003). The present essay
     is drawn from Chapter Two of this volume, 'The Brilliant
     Beginning', and is reproduced with the permission of the
     publisher.
Niall Sheridan, 'Brian, Flann and Myles', in *Myles: Portraits of
     Brian O'Nolan,* edited by Timothy O'Keefe (London: Martin
     Brian and O'Keefe, 1973): 36–53.
Niall Montgomery, 'An Aristophanic Sorcerer', in *The Irish
     Times,* 2 April 1966.

Mary Lavin (1912–1996)

Caroline Walsh

When I was a student in the English Department at UCD in the early 1970s my mother Mary Lavin came to read at the English Lit Society. Not being a massive crowd-pulling society like the L.&H. which had its meetings in one of the big lecture theatres downstairs in the Arts Block in Belfield, the English Lit's meetings were upstairs in one of the classrooms. Drifting in among the latecomers I was lucky to get standing room inside the door, along the aisle. She chose to read, appropriately for this audience, 'The Yellow Beret', a story about Donny, a Dublin college student who is missing from his home the night a girl is strangled down by the Pigeon House. It was the reverse of the parent being proud of the child. I was proud of her. She was a crowd puller and knowing the self-obsession levels of young students, coupled with their fascination for the macabre, she had picked a story that held her audience spellbound with its protagonist who could have been any UCD student, just like one of us.

I had been on a reading tour of America with her that stretched as far west as St Louis, Missouri; had heard her read in the company of a young John Updike and an old Padraic Colum at the Poetry Center in New York. But hearing her in UCD was different. It had a provenance that reached back decades to the autumn of 1930 when she left her happy, hockey-playing days in Loreto College on St Stephen's Green to travel across Leeson Street and become an Arts student at UCD on Earlsfort Terrace, where it was then located.

If she had been happy at Loreto, she was ecstatic at UCD. An only child of a mediocre marriage she relished the automatic access to a throng of lively, fellow-spirited students. Her home on Adelaide Road by the canal, where she lived with her mother Nora, was only a stone's throw away. She was in her element waltzing up and down Leeson Street every day to college, stopping midway to run endlessly in and out of Fox's Hotel, home of her great friends May and Florrie Fox.

Her father Tom lived mostly in Bective House, Co. Meath, the big house and demesne he managed for his American employers, the Birds of East Walpole, Massachusetts. Though not illiterate – he wrote wonderful block-lettered, phonetically spelled letters analysing his daughter's performance on the hockey pitch – he had no education beyond what he got in the schoolhouse in his native Frenchpark, Co. Roscommon. But he was proud that he came from stock that had in the penal days produced a famous hedge-schoolmaster and proud to have been from the same area and of the same generation as Douglas Hyde who, before becoming the first President of Ireland, was Professor of Modern Irish at UCD. To Tom Lavin, who found material success in the States, education was the pearl without price, the thing he wanted above all for Mary. When he went along to enrol her in UCD he brought a big wad of cash and she was mortified when, on hearing what the Arts degree fee was, he said: 'What kind of a degree is this Arts anyway, Mary, if it's so cheap?' He wanted to know if there were more expensive degrees she could do, medicine maybe. He was prepared – eager even – to thump down big money on the counter so that his only child could have what he never had. Her view of and affection for her father is the mainspring of her story 'Tom' in which she outlines how he, like all poor emigrants, imagined that in the place of his birth time would have stood still:

> the children going barefoot to school, doing their sums on a slate, and mitching every other day, until at last, like him, most of them would run off to England and thence to America with scarcely enough schooling to write their names.
>
> Although my father had a deep and a strong mind, and was the subtlest human being I ever knew, he had had small schooling. He could read and write, but with difficulty. (*In a Cafe*, 60–1)

Mary Lavin was born in 1912, when her Irish parents were still living in America. The only book she could recall in their home in East Walpole was *Pears Encyclopaedia*. Even after they came to live in Ireland in 1921 and she went to Loreto, her father thought nothing of swanning into school and telling the Reverend Mother he was taking her off to Aintree for two or three days or even just out for a stroll because he hated to think of her cooped up on a sunny day. To him, that didn't conflict with his mantra: 'I want you to go to college, Mary, not like me.'

Mary loved UCD but more importantly, perhaps, she was loved there. It is where she met both her husbands: my father Willam Walsh, a law student from Co. Kildare with whom she had three children before he died in 1954; and Michael MacDonald Scott, an Australian Jesuit scholastic sent there as part of his formation for the priesthood. Irish Jesuits had been in Australia since the mid 1860s and though Australia became a separate Jesuit province in 1931, formation continued to be shared between the two countries for a while after that. With its immense Jesuit associations, UCD was a natural habitat for these seminarians. Often in later life Mary Lavin wondered if, when she spotted him on that first day in UCD – and noted he was very handsome – he had been wearing what she called a dog collar, the insignia of the priesthood that would have marked him out right from the start as forbidden fruit. Though a maths student, Michael Scott took an active part in the English Lit Society – to such an extent that he became auditor. Maybe he did so because it was a setting in which it was permissible for a student priest to socialise with a girl student. Because he had fallen for her on that first day too, in a classic *coup de foudre*. Once T.S. Eliot came to read and Lavin remembered not so much what he had to say but how, charged with buying the cakes for the reception afterwards, she toured the then multitude of cake shops in the vicinity, agonising over what to buy before she settled on macaroons from the Swiss Chalet on Merrion Row.

Contemporaries in UCD included many other writers: Donagh MacDonagh, Denis Devlin, Brian Coffey, Brian O'Nolan (Flann O'Brien) and Mervyn Wall; Lorna Reynolds and Roger McHugh, both later prominent professors of English; and Cyril Cusack, even then a talented actor. He remained a close friend of Lavin's to the end, as did future President of Ireland Cearbhall Ó Dálaigh. There was also the poet Charlie Donnelly who had legendary status among them for his social activism and idealism. Singled out by his anger about the poverty of the Dublin tenements and his fears over the rise of fascism in Europe, Donnelly became the defining hero of that generation when he died at the Jarama Front in 1937 fighting for the Spanish Republic. He was the 'first fruit of our harvest, willing sacrifice/Upon the altar of his integrity/Lost to us …' as Donagh MacDonagh put it in his poem 'Charles Donnelly. Dead in Spain 1937. Travelling through Franco's Spain when I was eleven with my mother, Charlie Donnelly and his poetry were like another passenger in the car. We visited endless battle sites and monuments, always with him in her mind.

When Michael Scott went on to study in Innsbruck before returning home to Australia, contact between him and Lavin ceased. He was ordained. She got married. But as her writing career progressed from the first collection *Tales from Bective Bridge* (1942) he followed her literary trajectory through her books and kept up with how her life was unfolding via the biographical notes on their dust jackets. That's how he learned that she had been widowed. Once during their UCD days, wanting to bring Scott to see Bective, Lavin asked her friend William Walsh to spin them there by car. The three of them had a great day out in the country. Scott wrote to say how sad he was to hear of Willam's death and a correspondence began that led to him being laicised in the late 1960s. Shortly afterwards they got married.

Revisiting the Main Hall of UCD Mary and Michael were delighted when the famous head porter Paddy Keogh, who ultimately retired with an MA *honoris causa* after a UCD career spanning fifty-five years, not only remembered them but said he had always felt there was something between them. He must have had great powers of perception because seminarians weren't allowed commingle like other students. So keen was Lavin in their student days to see the object of her affection at every opportunity she timed her passage up and down Leeson St to coincide with the Jesuit seminarians' diurnal bicycle trips in and out to the Juniorate wing of Rathfarnham Castle where they lived.

When she graduated in 1934 it was with a first class honours in English and a second in French. But French was the department she loved best mainly because of its extraordinary professor, Roger Chauviré. Chauviré came to take up the chair of French at UCD in 1919 and retained it until he retired in the late 1940s. While other foreign academics who arrived into the tumultuous and at times violent country Ireland then was might have decided no job was worth this, he embraced it all. Chauviré's sympathies were with the nationalist republican side of Irish politics, as Phyllis Gaffney of the current French department recounts in an essay entitled '"When we were very young": UCD's French Department and the Fight for Irish Freedom'. Many of his books – he was a prolific author – are imbued with Irish history and culture to such an extent that Gaffney says it would not be inaccurate to describe him in the way he once described his daughter: 'Hiberniis hibernior – more Irish than the Irish themselves' (215).

He was seen by the French Consul, who had pushed for him to get the UCD job, as highly suited to countering pro-German prejudices among Irish students. If ever there was an academic who instilled a lifelong love of his native culture into foreign students it was Chauviré. From a sense of genius loci emanating from his home place of Briollay outside Angers, to the work of Racine and Ronsard, Madame de Lafeyette and de Vigny, Chauviré saw, according to Gaffney, his brief as a kind of propaganda agent for French. The effect of this on Mary Lavin, for one, lasted her whole life but also shaped and informed her writing. In the collection of essays A Portrait of the Artist as a Young Girl she says: 'When I was at college I grew to love French literature, particularly Racine, not so much for the content as for the technique. I became tremendously interested in technique, in the music and architecture of words' (91).

All of this was due to Chauviré. It was gratifying to both that he was there to see her career building as a writer. His reaction to this was expressed in an essay in The Bell in October 1945, 'The Art of Mary Lavin: Tales from Bective Bridge'. In her work he found genius though he was keen to point out that he wasn't using the word in the colloquial laudatory sense.

Rather do I mean that you feel in her work that matchlessness, whether it be gift, instinct, uncontrollable spark – who knows? The privilege granted by a non-egalitarian Nature – of the spirit which has something to say which nobody else has to say. There are many distinguished craftsmen of the pen whose work you will read and enjoy; but they will remind you of somebody or something else. Few have that flash of 'never before', that novelty, that uniqueness. Mary Lavin was born with her own vision of the world, and her own way of conveying it.

She had an insight into human nature of an astounding degree that he saw as something of a divination: 'She can read souls as she would an open book.' Having opened her eyes to the treasury of French literature, he obviously found it fascinating to see how it had distilled in her creative imagination. Mary Lavin wrote with an 'infallible perfection of instinct' which he associated with French women writers like Madame de Sévigné, George Sand and Colette, the last two of whom were major influences on her.

There is a strong sense of the teacher being rewarded by the pupil towards the conclusion of his essay. 'It is sweet, and it is a relief, when one has loved a few lovely things, letters, poetry, beauty, dreams and when one begins to feel old, to see young people surging after you, who will love the same things and who will carry the torch on.'

Years later, in a foreword to her collection *In a Café* (1995), Thomas Kilroy remembered how he first encountered Mary Lavin when she came to read at UCD, in Newman House, and how the friendship he later formed with her was 'an education in books', books like Flaubert's *Trois Contes*: 'I can still recall how she talked about the death of poor Félicité in "Un Coeur Simple" and the great parrot in the half-open heavens above her head' (vii). Chauviré's torch had indeed been passed on.

Though it was a pity that Mary Lavin did not feature in Donal McCartney's *UCD: A National Idea – The History of University College Dublin* (1999), it is not altogether surprising as she was at first a timid student, as Zack Bowen points out in his study *Mary Lavin* in the Bucknell University Press Irish Writers series. She was not a public student, politically engaged like many of her contemporaries. She was busy having a good time, often in

127

the company of a gang of girl friends. As her biographer Leah Levenson wrote in *The Four Seasons of Mary Lavin*: 'Thanks to her father's financial situation, Mary was a somewhat privileged student. She dressed well, took occasional trips to the States with her father when he went there on business for the Bird family, and drove a sports car. For a student to have a car – and a sports car at that – in those days was a rarity' (46).

She went on to get first class honours for her MA on Jane Austen and had started a Ph.D. thesis on Virginia Woolf when she began writing a short story on the back of one of its pages. The story, 'Miss Holland', was accepted by Seamus O'Sullivan, editor of *The Dublin Magazine*, where it appeared in the late 1930s. She never finished the Ph.D. Her long career at UCD was over, although her three daughters all went there, as did five of her nine grandchildren. 'That first erratic impulse', that 'sudden sally' at a short story, as she described it once in a preface, turned her into a writer, though she had had no yearning to write up until then. She had made a discovery: 'For me the writing of stories is a way of being.'

Though early in her career she wrote two novels – *The House in Clewe Street* (1945) and *Mary O'Grady* (1950) – she often deprecated them in later life and saw herself as almost totally a short story writer. Her many collections include: *The Becker Wives and Other Stories* (1946); *The Patriot Son and Other Stories* (1956); *The Great Wave and Other Stories* (1961); *In the Middle of the Fields and Other Stories* (1967); *Happiness and Other Stories* (1969); and *A Memory and Other Stories* (1972). She was writing in the great heyday of the Irish short story but stayed away from the political issues that preoccupied many of her contemporary male short story writers. This caused Frank O'Connor to remark: 'Of the principal Irish writers of the period only Mary Lavin has come out of it unmarked ... Like Whitman's wild oak in Louisiana, she has stood a little apart from the rest of us, "uttering joyous leaves of dark green"' (Kelly, 14). Her terrain was family, the domestic world and the vagaries of the human heart, making her in Tom MacIntyre's words, 'the Vermeer of the Irish short story' (Kelly, 176).

She died in 1996.

PRIMARY REFERENCES

Mary Lavin, *In a Café*, a new selection by Elizabeth Walsh
Peavoy, foreword by Thomas Kilroy (Dublin: Town House,
1995).
— in *A Portrait of the Artist as a Young Girl*, edited by John Quinn
(London: Methuen, 1986).

SECONDARY REFERENCES

Zack Bowen, *Mary Lavin* (Lewisburg: Bucknell University Press,
1975).
Roger Chauviré, 'The Art of Mary Lavin: *Tales from Bective
Bridge*', in *The Bell* 11, October 1945: 600–9.
Phyllis Gaffney, '"*When we were very young*": UCD's French
Department and the Fight for Irish Freedom', in
France–Ireland: Anatomy of a Relationship (Studies in
History, Literature and Politics), edited by Eamon Maher and
Grace Neville (Bern: Peter Lang, 2004): 203–23.
A.A. Kelly, *Mary Lavin, Quiet Rebel: A Study of Her Short Stories*
(Dublin: Wolfhound Press, 1996).
Leah Levenson, *The Four Seasons of Mary Lavin* (Dublin: Marino
Books, 1998).

MÁIRE MHAC AN TSAOI (B. 1922)

Máirín Nic Eoin

In an interview with Michael Davitt published in the poetry journal *Innti* 8 (1984), Máire Mhac an tSaoi self-effacingly described herself as follows: 'Banfhile agus mionfhile mise, is maith liom filíocht a scríobh ach ní aithním mé féin mar fhile ach mar dhuine a scríobhann filíocht ó am go ham.' (I am a woman poet and a minor poet, I like to write poetry but I consider myself less a poet as such than someone who writes poetry occasionally.) This self-assessment is borne out when one looks at the extent and content of her five volumes of poetry published sporadically from the mid-1950s onwards. Yet Máire Mhac an tSaoi is undoubtedly one of the most influential Irish-language poets of her generation. This essay will examine her ground-breaking contribution as an Irish woman poet whose aesthetic stance – based on notions of linguistic authenticity and literary continuity – often served to disguise the more challenging and transgressive aspects of her work.

Máire Mhac an tSaoi was born in Dublin in 1922, eldest child of Belfast-born engineer and republican Sean MacEntee and Tipperary-born secondary-school teacher Margaret Browne. Sean MacEntee was a founding member of Fianna Fáil and became an important and influential member of various Fianna Fáil cabinets. Margaret Browne was an independent-minded woman of feminist leaning, whose passion for learning and literature had an abiding affect on her daughter. Máire Mhac an tSaoi was influenced most significantly, however, by her maternal uncle

Monsignor Pádraig de Brún, a multilingual scholar, poet and translator who acted as a father-figure to her and was responsible for her early and regular exposure to Gaeltacht culture during many extended visits to his West Kerry holiday home, 'Tigh na Cille' in Dún Chaoin. Her upbringing was decidedly urban and middle class and her linguistic confidence – often lacking in contemporary Irish-language writers of non-Gaeltacht background – was arguably as much an outcome of a privileged Irish-Ireland background and education as it was a result of her Gaeltacht affiliation. As a young girl she was introduced to the classics of European literature through her uncle's Irish-language translations, and this experience served as grounding for a lifelong interest in languages and literature and a belief in the Irish language as a versatile mediator of European culture. An exceptional student, in UCD she studied Modern Languages and Celtic Studies, and subsequently completed an MA in Classical Modern Irish with a thesis on the seventeenth-century Kerry poet Piaras Feiritéar. She spent the years 1942–5 in the School of Celtic Studies in the Dublin Institute for Advanced Studies, where she edited classical poetry and two Arthurian romances, and the academic years 1945–7 as a visiting scholar at the Institut des Hautes Études, at the Sorbonne in Paris. Though an accomplished Celticist with a particular interest in the classical period, Máire Mhac an tSaoi was to depart the academic life in 1947 for a diplomatic career with the then Department of External Affairs. Apart from a period of four years (1952–6) when she was seconded to the Department of Education to assist in the compilation of Tomás de Bhaldraithe's English-Irish Dictionary, she was to work in External Affairs until 1962 when she resigned on her marriage to Dr Conor Cruise O'Brien, then serving as Irish representative with the United Nations.

Máire Mhac an tSaoi's poetic output follows the trajectory of a richly experienced personal life. Though she lived through troubled times and in troubled places, her poetry eschews the overtly political and focuses instead on the more intimate life of the emotions and of close family relationships. Her most substantial collections are her first book *Margadh na Saoire* (1956) and her most recent volume *Shoa agus dánta eile* (1999).

In between she published the slim volumes *Codladh an Ghaiscígh* (1973) and *An Galar Dubhach* (1980) and the collected works *An Cion go dtí seo* (1987), which also included a section of new poems. *Margadh na Saoire*, the product of twenty years of intermittent versifying, serves to illustrate the thematic and stylistic scope of her work. Organised into sections entitled 'Liricí', 'Eachtraíocht agus Amhráin Tíre' and 'Aistriúcháin', the subject matter of the poems ranges from the restrained finely crafted portrayal of conventional sentiment to the very conscious dramatisation of psychologically intense and morally troubling emotional states. The early lyrics recording or lamenting former times, places and cherished loved ones introduce the reader to Mhac an tSaoi's characteristic use of native idiom and traditional metrics. Poems such as 'Caoineadh', 'Oíche Nollag', 'Smaointe um Thráthnóna', 'Slán' and 'Do Shíle' are illustrative of the emotional charge associated with the poet's Gaeltacht sojourns, just as 'Comhrá ar Shráid' and 'Jack' serve to underline the linguistic gap and social distance between the cultural tourist and the native. These poems – some of which mediate the experiences of other family members – are sentimental without being cloying, as the musical rhythms and traditional rhyme structures serve to modify and depersonalise the overtly emotional content. It is the relationship between narration and commentary, for example, that makes a simple poem like 'An Chéad Bhróg' so powerful a statement about the joys and pains of childhood as observed through adult eyes. It is an early example of Mhac an tSaoi's many poems about children, poems which illustrate that maternal wisdom is not necessarily the prerogative of biological mothers.

Loss – in its various forms – is Máire Mhac an tSaoi's central and over-riding theme. The most memorable poems in *Margadh na Saoire* are those which deal directly with sexual loss and it is in these poems that Mhac an tSaoi comes into her own as a fresh modern voice in Irish-language poetry. Though all her love poetry is heavily influenced by the ironic thrust of the native Irish 'Dánta Grá' – that late medieval body of courtly love poetry, most of which deals with unfulfilled or unrequited love from a male perspective – Máire Mhac an tSaoi's love poems bring a distinctly female per-spective to bear on the subject. A poem of rejection and obsession like 'A fhir dar fhulaingeas …', for example, which is closely modelled on the late-classical models, demonstrates the ability of the inherited form to successfully communicate contemporary psychological states: 'Cruaidh an cás mo bheith let ais,/Measa arís bheith it éagmais;/Margadh bocht ó thaobh ar bith/Mo chaidreamh ortsa, a ógfhir' (50). The use of traditional form in a poem sequence such as 'Ceathrúintí Mháire Ní Ógáin' (where the spurned though persistent lover is dramatised as Máire Ní Ógáin, the female fool of Irish folk tradition), far from disguising the source of frustration, serves to dramatically foreground it. As a poetic expression in 1950s Ireland of the effect of an ill-fated sexual relationship on a young woman, this poem was truly groundbreaking in its open discussion of excruciating longing, passionate abandon and reluctantly acknowledged regret.

Mhac an tSaoi published this poem, and other equally powerful expressions of female desire and frustration, in the section in the collection entitled 'Eachtraíocht agus Amhráin Tíre', where they appear alongside poetic revisions of traditional material such as 'Labhrann Deirdre', 'Gráinne' and 'Suantraí Ghráinne'. Such juxtapositions are significant in that the literary characters on which these modern versions were based were themselves the male-authored subjects of tragic sexual liaisons. Both Gráinne and Deirdre are presented as women who had no choice – when in danger of forced alliance in the interest of patriarchal power structures – but to take the course of action they did. The dilemma presented in 'Ceathrúintí Mháire Ní Ógáin', however, can be read as that of a modern young woman who must deal, on her own, with the unsatisfactory outcome of her transgression. Her problem is less a moral than a psychological one, and yet the poem remains ambivalent (the speaker is a foolish and ultimately unhappy woman) and the dilemma unresolved.

It is hardly surprising that it was as the foremost exponent of the love lyric that Frank O'Brien included Máire Mhac an tSaoi in his own path-breaking study of contemporary Irish-language poetry, *Filíocht Ghaeilge na Linne Seo* (1968). O'Brien's discussion of her work – the first detailed critical response it received – assured her position, alongside Seán Ó Ríordáin and Máirtín Ó Direáin, as one of the major poetic voices of her generation. This critical recognition proved to be of vital importance to Mhac an tSaoi's subsequent reputation as a poet, as she had, as early as 1953, boldly challenged Seán Ó Ríordáin's position as the rising star of Irish-language poetry in a controversial review of his first collection, *Eireaball Spideoige* (1952), published in the Irish-language magazine *Feasta* in March 1953. Here she laid out clearly what were to be the guiding principles of her own poetic *oeuvre*: that the language of the contemporary poet should be closely modelled on the language as spoken in a particular Gaeltacht region; and that the Irish-language poet should avoid the influence of English-language verse and turn instead to native literary and oral models. Ó Ríordáin's early work was lacking on both fronts, according to Mhac an tSaoi, and she was to reiterate this view in a 1955 article in *Studies*, 'Scríbhneoireacht sa Ghaeilge Inniu'. What was remarkable about the critical judgements in these essays was the linguistic authority with which they were made. This note of authority sounds also in Mhac an tSaoi's poetry, where she trusts absolutely in her own aural memory.

Seventeen years were to pass before Máire Mhac an tSaoi produced another collection, the sixteen-poem volume *Codladh an Ghaiscígh* (1973). She had spent most of the 1960s abroad, in Ghana and the United States, but by the time *Codladh an Ghaiscígh* was published the family was settled once again in Ireland and she had become the mother of two adopted children of Irish-Ghanaian extraction. She was already stepmother to her husband's son and two daughters from a previous marriage, and the particular circumstances of her immediate and extended family relationships were to be recurring themes in her poetry. The title poem of this collection, 'Codladh an Ghaiscígh', which draws on a range of traditional motifs, captures brilliantly the emotions of the adoptive mother as she looks down upon her sleeping child, so foreign and yet so familiar to her. Poems such as this, and the short poem of separation 'Ceangal do Cheol Pop', reveal a stoic acceptance of her own inability to bear children in a manner which reveals the depths of understanding and strengths of attachment which can be generated by such losses. A characteristic feature of her poetry is her ability to approach a particular topic from an unexpected subject position. Her lament for the murdered General Kotoka of Ghana, the only poem in this collection to deal directly with political affairs or with her African experience, is a moving personal account of the loss of an exceptional public figure. When it comes to a more immediately personal loss, the death of her beloved uncle Paddy, however, her poetic response is the dramatic 'Muiris ag Caoineadh Phádraig', where she draws the personal histories and emotional ties of the extended family into the narrative.

Máire Mhac an tSaoi's third collection, *An Galar Dubhach* (1980), features a mere fifteen new poems. More sombre in tone than *Codladh an Ghaiscígh*, it includes another poem in memory of Pádraig de Brún, a poem of farewell to her dead mother and a number of works dedicated to her growing children. The poems about childhood are ironic musings on a mother's desire to, but resigned acceptance that she cannot, shape her children's destinies. As a collection about the sorts of accommodation which accompany the ageing process, it is more subdued than her earlier work and yet can surprise us with its audacity, as in the explicit depiction of female masturbation in the poem 'You can't win', which concludes with a witty reminder of the limits imposed on bodily pleasure by physical infirmity. Despite the title, the collection is not melancholic. Rather it is a work in a minor key, full of irony and self-ridicule. The loss of a child's tooth can be experienced in epic terms, for example, but the poet – unlike the truly tragic Parnell – is presented as a stalwart survivor who lives on to tell her less-than-heroic tale.

The image of the ageing woman fighting a battle against time opens the final section 'Dánta Nua' in Mhac an tSaoi's collected poems, *An Cion go dtí seo* (1987). Thus she sets the tone for a series of poems reflecting on the passage of time and the death of loved ones, interspersed with portraits of domestic and family life. The political is sometimes expressed through the personal, as in 'Pádraig roimh an mBál', where the image of her son transposes into the image of other mothers' sons whom fate had placed on opposite sides in the Nicaraguan revolution. It is in poems like this – which acknowledge the contingency of all human alignments – that she challenges most fundamentally any notion of ethical certainty, be it religious or political:

A Íosa, níl iontu beirt ach garlaigh!
Cá n-iompód mo cheann
Go n-éalód ón gcásamh?
Ón míréasún?
Conas is féidir liom mo thoil a chur
Le toil mo Dhé? (116)

While ambivalence about religious belief can be discerned in some of her later poems, particularly in 'Moment of truth' (in *Shoa agus dánta eile*), where it is the women who pose the fundamental existential questions, it is in matters political that Mhac an tSaoi grapples most directly with the unresolved ambiguities and ambivalences of personal allegiances and convictions. A poem of commemoration such as 'Cam Reilige 1916–1966' (published in *Codladh an Ghaiscígh*) compares the dramatic achievements of the generation who fought for Irish independence with the banality of life for their children, while in 'An Fuath (1967)' (also published in *Codladh an Ghaiscígh*) political certitude and blind hatred are interlinked. Her latest collection contains her most sustained meditation on politics and history, the poem to her father 'Fód an Imris: Ard-Oifig an Phoist 1986', which acknowledges that belief systems and ideals can never be transmitted unproblematically from one generation to another: 'Comhaos mé féin is an stát,/Is níor chun do thola do cheachtar' (29). One of the great strengths of Máire Mhac an tSaoi's poetry lies in its unwillingness to smooth over the ambiguities and ambivalences which govern people's actions and emotions. The overall impression generated in *Shoa agus dánta eile*, for example, is one of inconclusiveness. The poetry refrains from any attempt to resolve the emotional conflicts it examines. It can console – especially in its outpourings of maternal or filial devotion – but such consolation is seldom sustained. A palpable sense of physical and psychic unease is present as images and emotions related to the past return to delight or to haunt. The later poems often review and revise earlier positions, as in the poems to her stepdaughters which chart an emotional attachment from the initial acquaintance with two bright young girls seen through the eyes of their father to the mature relationship between an elderly and two middle-aged mothers. Her lament for Kate, 'In Memoriam Kate Cruise O'Brien, 1948–1998' (*Shoa agus dánta eile*), is a particularly moving acknowledgement of the limits of all acquaintance. The only poem of pure disappointment and dismay in this collection is the poem 'I Leaba an Dearúid, an Tarcaisne' in which she bitterly reflects on her changed relationship with the Gaeltacht of her youth. The reason for the poet's anger is the knowledge that the memory of her uncle's presence in Dún Chaoin has faded; a younger generation ensures that she is now a stranger where once she felt spiritually at home. Rather than accepting the change, she points a satirical finger at the community she deems responsible for her loss.

Though Máire Mhac an tSaoi influenced a generation of women poets with self-avowed feminist convictions, her own commentary on women's social position is often oblique and politically ambivalent. The early 'Cad is Bean?' (*Margadh na Saoire*) is an equivocal account of perceived female limitations; she stakes a claim for poetry beside domesticity in 'Cré na Mná Tí' (*Codladh an Ghaiscígh*); she questions the outcome of the efforts of former generations of feminists in 'Mutterrecht' (*An Cion go dtí seo*) and exposes the inevitable compromises, accommodations and dissatisfactions of family life as it was and is lived by many people in 'Pósadh den tSeanadhéanamh' (*An Cion go dtí seo*). Her most overtly feminist statement is to be found in the poem 'Leagan ar Sheanrá' (published in *An Cion go dtí seo* and again in *Shoa agus dánta eile*), a lament for Bríde Ní Chíobháin, Pádraig de Brún's housekeeper in Dún Chaoin, in which the knowledge, wisdom and linguistic skill of this ordinary country woman – presented as going unrecorded during her lifetime – is given public recognition by the woman poet. This use of poetry to make an unequivocal political point is exceptional, but it may be indicative of a greater self-awareness of her own role as a poet who has prepared the way for a younger generation of Irish women poets. Her unique contribution was that she was the first Irish-language woman poet to openly and unabashedly explore some of the more personal and intimate aspects of women's lives through the use of traditional form, idiom and source material. There is no doubt but that she was an enabling presence in the poetic development of Nuala Ní Dhomhnaill and Biddy Jenkinson, whose work she has championed on a number of occasions, but she has also had a strong and

137

abiding influence on the work of Cathal Ó Searcaigh and the *Innti* generation in general. Her poetry has been widely anthologised and examples of her work have been translated into English, French, German, Hebrew and Japanese.

Her contributions as a translator and prose writer are also significant as they illustrate her ability to traverse the boundaries between languages and genres and to open up imaginative spaces between the creative and the scholarly. Her first collection contained translations into Irish from the English of Shakespeare, the French of Charles d'Orléans and the Spanish of Lorca. Since then she has published three volumes of translations of Irish-language poetry into English: a collection of classical poetry *A heart full of thought* (1959); Pádraig de Brún's original collection *Miserere* (1971); and most recently a personal selection of late classical, eighteenth-century and folk poetry *Trasládáil* (1997). The collection *Shoa agus dánta eile* contains translations from Yeats and from the German of Rainer Maria Rilke. These translations, as well as illustrating her linguistic skills and her understanding of native metrics, also provide further insight into the field of literary influence from which her own work emerged. Similarly, her novella *A Bhean Óg Ón ...* (2001), which is an entertaining work of romantic fiction based on a number of love poems by Piaras Feiritéar, reveals the imaginative field opened up for her by her early exposure to classical poetry. While she has drawn on that material in scholarly essays over the years, one senses that the imaginative potential of the poetry was at least as strong as its purely academic attraction. On the other hand, her work as critic and editor has always been informed by a scholarly sense of what is poetically correct. Máire Mhac an tSaoi's affinity with the seventeeth-century Feiritéar, and with the equally romantic fourteenth-century poet Gearóid Iarla, is understandable when one realises that these poets were educated amateurs who straddled the worlds of Gaelic, English and European culture in times of great social and political change. As accomplished but non-professional poets, they both lived in a world where aesthetics were important and where poetry provided the space for the cultivation of a rich inner life.

Máire Mhac an tSaoi's most recent work is the memoir *The*

Same Age as the State (2003), published under her married name Máire Cruise O'Brien. This book provides an eloquent account of a rich and rewarding life where politics was a daily reality, but where aesthetics was never neglected. One could argue that her poetry has also successfully straddled languages and cultures and has created a space for the cultivation and honest exploration of a complex inner life.

PRIMARY REFERENCES

Máire Mhac an tSaoi, *Margadh na Saoire* (Sáirséal agus Dill: Baile Átha Cliath, 1956).
—, *Codladh an Ghaiscígh* (Sáirséal agus Dill: Baile Átha Cliath, 1973).
—, *An Galar Dubhach* (Sáirséal agus Dill: Baile Átha Cliath, 1980).
—, *An Cion go dtí seo* (Sáirséal Ó Marcaigh: Baile Átha Cliath, 1987).
—, *Shoa agus dánta eile* (Sáirséal Ó Marcaigh: Baile Átha Cliath, 1999).

ANTHONY CRONIN (B. 1928)

Colm Tóibín

The copy of Brendan Kennelly's *The Penguin Book of Irish Verse* is dated, in my mother's handwriting, August 1970. I was fifteen then. The poem we were all shown, and which I later contemplated in solitude, was Anthony Cronin's 'For a Father'. It began:

> With the exact length and pace of his father's stride
> The son walks,
> Echoes and intonations of his father's speech
> Are heard when he talks. (2)

Anthony Cronin was born in Enniscorthy where some of his family, like mine, had worked on *The Enniscorthy Echo*. His father, among other things, had taught shorthand in the Vocational School where my mother went when she was fourteen, after the death of her father, to prepare herself for work. She remembered Cronin Senior as kind, mild and likeable, and she loved his son's poem about him because of its last verse:

> And now having chosen, with strangers,
> Half glad of his choice,
> He smiles with his father's hesitant smile
> And speaks with his voice. (2)

That is exactly, she would say, what Mr Cronin's smile was like, it was hesitant. The idea struck her as extraordinary, that she could have known somebody thirty-five years earlier and he could appear now, accurately described, in *The Penguin Book of Irish Verse*.

I was interested in other things about the poem – the expansive, almost loquacious long line, followed by the clipped,

140

factual short line. There was also something new and strange about the poem which was its effort not to come to any conclusion, not to praise or blame, or sentimentalise. The son in the poem was '[i]n some ways better than his begetters,/In others, worse.' Having chosen his life, he is only '[h]alf glad of his choice'. It was a poem without heroes. Also, there was no mention of Enniscorthy in the poem, or indeed Ireland, no Deirdres nor mists, nor names of local townlands. The poet could have been an Englishman, except that everyone in my family seemed to know him; he had been, indeed, special friends with my first cousin; and my mother vouched for the truth of his father's hesitant smile. A few times over the next few years I saw the poet's photograph in *The Irish Times*.

In my last two years at school that idea of escaping not only from the town, but from everything else too, began to interest me. The idea that you could escape also into uncertainty, which was what the poem suggested, was too complex and hidden, but it must have had its secret appeal. I noticed Anthony Cronin's *Irish Times* column in these years, the writing about history and politics as much as art and poetry as though the first two were a proper concern of anyone interested in the second two. I also noticed the arguments with himself, as the many sub-clauses in the prose attest, but also arguments with others, many of whom were not named and I could not identify. His pieces made clear, however, that there were enemies everywhere. It was a useful thing to know.

In the summer of 1973 I was working in Dublin, travelling to the city centre by bus in the morning. For one week of that summer *The Irish Times* serialised Anthony Cronin's book *Dead as Doornails*. I devoured the sections on the journey, hoping the bus would take its time pulling into its final destination at College Green, so I could read the pieces again. They dealt with Cronin's memory of Patrick Kavanagh, Flann O'Brien, Brendan Behan and other artists who died of drink. There was, however, a whole other aspect of the book which interested me, which was Cronin's own meanderings in Dublin and London, France and Spain, at times barely alluded to, often hinted at and never dealt with directly or in detail, thus seeming all the more natural. By keeping himself out of the book, he became for me a more fascinating presence.

In Dublin in those years I saw Anthony Cronin a number of times. He came to speak at University College Dublin twice during my time there. I spoke to him on both occasions and was surprised, to say the least, that his interest in Enniscorthy was, to say the least again, mild. He seemed indifferent to the place where he grew up while remaining interested in almost everything else. That was a new idea for me. He knew some of my family but not others, even though all of them had known him, and his hesitant smile had a hint of wry boredom as the whole matter was discussed. Someone had also told me that he, once a serious drinker, had given up the drink. I wondered if that had anything to do with it, but I thought not. He had abandoned Enniscorthy for the wider world.

I did not know at first that my father had taught him in school, but soon it emerged that he had been at the Christian Brothers in Enniscorthy for a few years where my father had called him Our Travelling Correspondent, because of his tendency not to turn up. Anthony Cronin was always careful with me when the subject of my father's nationalism and Catholicism had been raised. I think he felt deeply oppressed by that school in those years. However, when my father, who had no feeling for poetry, needed a poem read aloud to the class, he always asked Anthony Cronin. Cronin often told me this story as a way of suggesting that maybe things were not all that bad.

In 1978, when I came back from Spain, Anthony Cronin loomed large in the real and imaginary Dublin I inhabited. His reputation was strange. He was a poet who published his first book in 1958 and then no other volume of poetry until his *Collected Poems 1950–1973* in 1973. He was a novelist who published his first novel in 1964 and his second in 1980. He was a critic whose essays had been collected in a book called *A Question of Modernity*. He wrote a column in *The Irish Times* and was regularly on the radio, but did not seem to have a proper job.

His journalism was rational, thoughtful; his radio style could be wry and funny, as were his novel and his memoir; and his poetry too could have a rational edge, using logic and statement of fact, coming to tentative conclusions as though everything in poetry, as in geometry, had to be tested and proved. He used rhyme and regular metre and stanza forms.

It was clear in his poetry that he loved reason – until you went to one of his readings when it became clear that he loved poetry more than reason. He allowed his sense of the magic and mystery of words to rub against his refusal to deal in twilights or easy emotions or the natural world. Sometimes, with his *Collected Poems 1950–1973*, you could turn the page and find a poem that seemed the very opposite of what you thought his poems were. 'A Revenant' deals with the 'amazing grief' which the beginning of autumn can bring:

> For suddenly summer gloaming
> Turns into Autumn night,
> Raindrops spatter the roses
> And the heart cries out.

But such sharp and simple feeling must be interrogated, treated with suspicion:

> How can that identical grief
> Spring on the heart again,
> When the circumstance such as it was
> Made it ludicrous even then?

It would be easy for him then to find some comfort in the concrete world, go back to his old ironies, to shrug off the feeling of pure anguish at an act of nature that is alien to his sensibility. He refuses, however, to deny the original feeling, he merely wishes to tease out what it means:

> What is the meaning of this,
> That the heart is stabbed with grief,
> At the onset of Autumn evenings,
> At memory's twitch on the leaf?

> The meaning is summer going,
> Ridiculous ecstasy, pain,
> And the heart agreeing with something
> Which was, and which ought to be, plain.

I saw him in those last years of the 1980s walking through the city streets. I have a feeling that he preferred the outer edges of St Stephen's Green to the park itself and the outer railings of Trinity College to its interior. He has a wonderful early poem called 'Liking

Corners'. He had moved in those years from Stella Gardens in Ringsend to Curzon Street off the South Circular Road. He wrote about Stella Gardens in 'The End of the Modern World':

> The master bedroom measured twelve by six,
> The other, square but smaller had no window
> Since someone built the kitchen up against it.
> The loo was out of doors. I don't complain. (226)

He had lived in Spain and the United States in the 1960s. Now he was home:

> So here I settled down in seventy-two
> With wife and children, Iseult seventeen
> And Sarah almost eight. I managed two
> And sometimes up to four effusions weekly,
> Facing the bedroom wall, my papers strewn
> Behind me on the bed. There were no stairs
> Or battlements to pace upon in Stella. (226)

He never walked purposefully, nor did he quite meander. His afternoons were filled with dreams of horse races and odds and winners and pedigree and trainers as much as poetry. He seemed as if he never had that much to do; he had a very special skill at marvelling at the good of things, or their strangeness. But he could also be acid and genuinely funny on the subject of vanity and foolishness. He also, in his conversation as much as his column, refused to join in the general opinion on any matter. In 'The End of the Modern World' he alluded to that:

> Then why this vague unease one knows so well?
> When the unanimous resolutions start
> And everybody bleeds for the good cause
> Why is one guilty, with them or against? (251)

The good causes of the time included opposition to Charles Haughey and opposition to the building of offices on the Viking site at Wood Quay. In *Magill* magazine, Cronin mocked the well-heeled protesters who had invaded the site of Wood Quay and were said to be sleeping there. He found them all in a Dublin restaurant having a marvellous self-congratulatory supper. He could hardly keep his contempt for them in check.

It was, at first, hard to work out Anthony Cronin's alliance with Charles Haughey. I understood Cronin to be a Marxist. Even in public, I remember him once saying that he had no enemies on the left. He had been one of the very few who had attended a meeting against the Pope's visit to Ireland, concerned about the possibility of an old pietism merging with a new one. Whereas Haughey's rhetoric was solemn, self-important and bloated, Cronin had fought a long battle against these things. There was also the shame of it. (Cronin's play, produced at the Peacock, was called *The Shame of It*.) Haughey was the least glamorous politician in the Republic; perhaps he was even the most dangerous. Right-thinking people, of whom there were many, indeed I was one myself, had a deep horror of Haughey.

I loved how Anthony Cronin did not care a toss what anyone thought of him as he became Haughey's cultural adviser. I remember a party in Francis Stuart's house in Dundrum for Francis's eightieth birthday and the liberals among the company wondering in whispers how an intellectual could do such a thing, and then wondering out loud, and being told by Cronin himself that he had work to do and he had the right politician and he would see that it was done. I wondered what he was like when he was drinking if he could be so combative and angry and generally disdainful when he was sober.

Out of that association with Haughey came the Irish Museum of Modern Art, Aosdána, the Heritage Council and the refurbishment of public buildings such as Dublin Castle and Government Buildings in Merrion Street. I remember one winter evening meeting Anthony Cronin as he walked along Lincoln Place. I was going home; he was going to Government Buildings. He was always immensely loyal to Haughey, even in subsequent years. He was secretive about his work, insisting that he was not there very much, it was not like having a job. I knew that he was involved in more than cultural policy; he certainly took the view from very early on that dealing with Northern Ireland would involve the two sovereign governments at the very highest level, as much as the two tribes. That winter evening he stopped for a second at that side door of the building, but he was not going to be detained there for long. He was going to slip in. It was strange work for a poet. But it would not be strange in France, he pointed out to me, not in France.

In the years when Haughey was out of power, although he worked briefly for Garret FitzGerald, Cronin wrote two deeply perceptive and wise biographies, one of Flann O'Brien, one of Samuel Beckett. In the 1990s, when I was editing an anthology of new writing, I asked him if he had any new poems. I was astonished by what came by return of post. In the years after Haughey, he had a new life as a poet. The poems collected in *Relationships* and *The Minotaur* have the same fluency and trust in form as the early poems, the same concern with history and ideas as the two long poems 'R.M.S. Titanic' and 'The End of the Modern World'. But they also had a new fresh wit, at times a formal looseness and a concern with a new subject, happiness.

Other poems were public and dealt with the large political issues. Cronin's poem on the fall of communism was called '1989'. Its ending has all the ring of one of Robert Lowell's public poems:

Does that mean we must let things slide,
Trust, like Lord Russell, to Free Trade

While millions die of interest rates
In Paraguay and Bangladesh;
The last brown trout turns belly up,
And acid, sent by corporate fates
Falls like soft dew on all twelve states;

And suffer the great spirit dearth,
The pointless agonies of birth
Whose issue is inanities,
Since no-one now will ever see
The kingdom he proclaimed on earth? (264)

In 1985, Anthony Cronin was living in London, away from the trappings of power. We met one night for supper in those old Soho streets which he had possessed thirty years earlier: Dean Street, Frith Street, Soho Square. There had been a huge exhibition of German Expressionist painting at the Royal Academy, and I was surprised, when we talked about it, how much he knew about painting, as I was also to be surprised later by his lack of interest in classical music. Some of the work from the German show was new to me, especially the paintings of Otto Dix and Lovis Corith. Anthony Cronin seemed to love how these painters had managed urban and industrial images and images of bourgeois anguish.

I remember then going with him and Anne Haverty during that period to see an exhibition at the Tate of paintings from St Ives. All three of us knew Tony O'Malley and were pleased to see paintings by him in the show. I was more at home with this work, as I think Anne was too. The paintings of Peter Lanyon, as though the earth were being painted from the air, and the luscious colour work of Patrick Heron, tactful and beautiful. I had a wonderful time that day looking at what had been an heroic English movement which mirrored American Abstract Expressionism.

In a letter to Anne Stevenson, the American poet Elizabeth Bishop wrote: 'I have a vague theory that one learns most – I have learned most – from having someone suddenly make fun of something one has taken seriously up until then.' As we came to the end of the St Ives show that day, I was seriously moved and inspired and awed by the paintings. Anthony Cronin began to shake his head when Anne remarked how wonderful the work was. It wasn't wonderful, he said, smiling his hesitant smile, beginning to enjoy himself. Some of it was decoration, he said, and insipid decoration to boot. All this colour, he added, gets us nowhere.

But Tony, Anne began. He turned towards her, amused and exasperated at the same time, like a great teacher, delighted at the fact that his pupils have much more to learn. No, Anne, no, he said, and he marched us slowly through the Tate, away from colour field and abstraction towards some paintings of heads by Dubuffet and Francis Bacon and drawings by Georg Grotz. Look at how much more is in these, the anguish, the city, the face, the crowd. This is how we live, Anne. He turned to me, the gaze fiercely amused, a mock-contempt written into it. And that's what the novel should be about too, he said. He was, that day, against nature; he was cheering for culture in all its twisted diversity. He was insisting on modernity against our romanticism. We could not argue with him, even though we tried. He was, of course, right. And he stood alone in the empty gallery in the dwindling light of a winter Sunday afternoon, taking in the work one more time, palpably enjoying the daring of it, going closer, screwing up his eyes to inspect a small corner, taking off his glasses for a second and then turning to us in wonder and certainty as all three of us got ready to walk out of the gallery into the great city which was his refuge now as it had been a number of times in his life.

PRIMARY REFERENCE

Anthony Cronin, *Collected Poems* (Dublin: New Island, 2004).

Thomas Kinsella (b. 1929)

Catriona Clutterbuck

This essay is an attempt at 'easing the particular' of the effect of
Thomas Kinsella's poetry out of the 'litter' of decades of reading
him for multifarious purposes of school and college examinations,
theses, teaching, editing and, throughout, for sustenance towards
'reading the ground' on which one reader has stood at various
stages of her adult life ('Worker in Mirror, at his Bench',125; 'St
Catherine's Clock', 271). Like so many of his Irish readers, I first
met Kinsella as the only living poet in Gus Martin's thirty-years
instituted school Leaving Certificate anthology *Soundings*. Here,
in two early poems, 'Another September' and 'Mirror in February'
(19, 53), dawn figures of garden trees taught the 'brute necessit[y]'
(53) of stripping oneself into consciousness of the interdependence
of loss, understanding and re-growth. As communications of the
urgency and continued possibility of the creative act in conditions
inimical to same, they were significant aids for sustaining youth's
idealism into adult maturity, had we ears to hear. These two poems
were windfalls in an Irish education system bound to the
decoratively purified definitions of success under promotion by a
rapidly modernising post-colonial Irish culture. Across the half-
century of his unbroken writing career, Kinsella's work has
'Exhale[d] rough sweetness against the starry slates' (19) of these
limiting anti-principles as his poems continue to operate as agents
both of disturbance and faith in the Irish body politic.

It is not easy to speak of what one responds to foremost in a
writer who has made the idea of response-ability – with its
commitment to integrated listening – so absolutely central to his
aesthetic. Kinsella's reputation is as a difficult poet. He has long

distanced himself from the public performance of himself as artist: his poems do that instead as a central focus of the interrogation they offer. These texts do not court acclaim. For more than thirty years now, they have emerged in long sequences whose primary publication is in the form of pamphlets from a specialist private press. Though intensely resonant, these poems are difficult of pithy quotation and unamenable to soundbite that doesn't bite one back. Kinsella demands always that his readers discover the work before its meaning. The poems only function by themselves *in* function with their reader *as* a functioning human: open, listening, alert.

Witnessing their engagement of and by their readers is the fascination of teaching Kinsella's poems to 300-strong BA lecture groups in UCD. The initial silently groaning resistance from the serried ranks – undergraduates' typical mass first reaction to poetry – gives way with remarkable speed to pleasure. Because the poems do indeed communicate as Kinsella intends they should, as 'a function of life as it happens' (Abbate Badin interview, 114), it becomes quickly apparent to students that they too are being taken on their own terms as readers who, in his famous words, 'play ... as useful a part in the creative act as a good writer' (O'Driscoll interview, 59). Kinsella tells us that 'poetry needs to include the basis on which the act of communication may be completed' (Abbate Badin interview, 115). This basis includes these students' own ears and eyes, their pasts and the life of this ordinary college day they are living. The poetry empowers them with its invitation: 'The dance is at our feet./*Give me your hand*' ('Exit', 260). Kinsella's poems encourage readings that 'begin at the very beginning' of consciousness in the discovery that that starting point is never quite itself, as comes hurrying forward all the prior life out of which such beginnings are made. Students find in him the grounding in response-ability – in primary reading rather than second-guessing of the text of the world about them – that sanctions and facilitates the impulse towards transferable liberation which first brought them to the study of literature.

All this is enabled, of course, by Kinsella's signature modes of direct address and compressed meaning. The intense sensual immediacy of his rendering of psychic experience and the vital yielding between the objects of his critique and himself in his role as poet, together serve his multiple enfigurements of the central mental process of disengagement from illusions, so necessary to activate the creative drive. Many readers – or many times in a life of reading Kinsella – one will reject the ascetic element this involves, the 'haggard taste in the mouth' of dying to previous habits of reading and knowing required to cultivate such clarity of vision and the new life it supports ('The Monk', 11).

Through the work of austerity and release commanded both of himself and his readers – of himself in his function as reader and of his readers in our function as artists – Kinsella's poetic persona interrogates the assumption of autonomy of the republic of letters while also confirming its necessity. A recurrent figure in his work is the artist-speaker of appealing yet dangerously com-placent 'superior' sensibility and over-arching understanding, most recently embodied in the persona of Goldsmith in *Citizen of the World* (2000). In the final lines of that pamphlet, as so often in Kinsella's work, a female figure who merges the roles of temptress and redresser invites him and us out beyond the limits of such constricted consciousness to 'alter course in reply' to the challenge to 'dispute together/the detail and the whole', as we listen to her most feared and necessary 'stone song' (350). The *Collected Poems* of Kinsella reconfigure strata of aesthetic, emotional, political and social experience. His poetry is a primary aid, a tympanum that transmits together the voices of the given and of the possible, resonating with the challenge of their relationship to our limited powers of listening.

There is general agreement among his critics upon the fundamental element of this revolutionary aesthetic: Kinsella's famously dual technique-cum-ethic of eliciting order *from* experience rather than imposing order upon it. However, no such agreement exists upon the key question of whether or not an ideal of civilisation is recuperable within that aesthetic. Indeed, a sort of spectator sport of judging the ratio of pessimism to optimism in his work is in danger of developing in a Kinsella criticism (to which my own work here is likely to contribute). But we do well to remember the warning in 'Worker in Mirror, at his Bench', that the work of the artist 'has no practical application', rather, that in it 'the passion is in the putting together' (124). To opt for one or other Kinsella, either of dark or of light, is to neglect his qualification of any easy understanding of these categories in its primary call to fullest-possible response in the culture in which it finds itself. This essay explores the nature of that call.

A central contribution of Kinsella is his resistance to the current critical climate's assumption that discrediting the direct relationship between artist and material (including the role of the artist as spokesperson which that relationship implies) is a precondition of rising to the challenges of discontinuity and vital self-interrogatory consciousness. Kinsella instead testifies to that directness of the artist-material link in every aspect of his work. In terms of form, the Kinsella signature is close-up precision of observation of the data upon which the poet trains his eye. Thematic evidence for the link is myriad. For example, there is the recurrent motif of mirroring between present and past using the vehicle of multiple generations within Kinsella's family: in 'Tear', the speaker enters true consciousness by coming so close to his grandmother that that he can taste 'her heart beating in my mouth' (106). Regarding the practicalities of publication, from the early days when he physically set up some of his own early poems on an old Adana machine for the Dolmen Press (O'Driscoll interview, 59), to his later policy of private pub-lication in the Peppercanister pamphlet format, he has always chosen, literally, to be close to his material.

Kinsella foregrounds the physical nature of his texts through the pamphlets' production notes, giving details of typesetting, edition and copy numbers and each pamphlet's place in the accumulating series. In this, he suggests an idea of significant order in art as only existing in relation to the text as produced effect. The 'hands-on' engagement with material this requires finds expression in the interpenetrative mode of composition of the Peppercanister project as a whole. It is conceived as a 'totality that is happening' (O'Driscoll interview, 59) rather than as a sum of material awaiting completion. Each pamphlet draws upon its predecessors, reusing or resonating with sections of earlier poems and commentaries, and causing the earlier work to be itself reread in continually altering contexts. The confidence in his own material shown by Kinsella's policy of standing foursquare inside his whole output, neither disowning (by direct revision) nor canonising (by the refusal to revisit and reuse) any part of it, arises from the sureness of this poet's continued testing of the basis of his claims to that material. Translation, in which two vernaculars provide 'unique leverage' for realising creative potential (*One Fond Embrace: Thomas Kinsella at Home in Dublin*, RTÉ, 1986), is a crucial aspect of this overall scheme of securely flexible linkage between artist and material.

The direct artist-material link in Kinsella operates as the supporting 'third wall' of a triangular contract of principles that I see as foundational to his aesthetic. The first is well-recognised: that the artist must respect the otherness of his material, 'get[ting] close to the whole shambles without changing it' (*One Fond Embrace*). The early poem 'A Lady of Quality' (6–8) dramatises the issue in the poet's awareness that his own control of the woman he addresses as his subject is commensurate with that control over her being exercised by her circumstances of illness and rigid hospital routine, which is the speaker's most obvious focus of critique. However, at this early stage of Kinsella's writing, the poem does not escape its own control sufficiently to make its theme of scepticism of governance felt by its reader other than sceptically. Kinsella will probe ever deeper into the manner in which the refusal to truly engage with the ordeal of given experience draws the creating individual into collusion with life-denying systems leading to the condition of cultural disassociation or 'misbirth' ('Ballydavid Pier', 57). He famously names this condition 'the divided mind' (in the essay of that title).

Yet the paradox of this condition of division is that, once confronted, it can become an enabling inheritance, a basis for authentic creativity. It can spur individual and culture, in their condition of psychic 'precariousness', to 'make the imaginative grasp at identity for [themselves]' ('Divided Mind', 215, 216). That needy 'grasp' at identity results in a 'ghost tissue' of potential form, of potential understanding that, paradoxically, offers more than any pre-securable delivery of meaning ('Ballydavid Pier', 57).

In one's authority and longing, one makes the effort to link to significant experience in the past, present or future, even though one's line of connection to such significance irretrievably be compromised. The dilemma that is both source and result of this principle of effort – which for the writer is the agency of their conscious artistry – is just how the 'alien/Garrison' of such an execution of will, of an authority that is 'in [one's] own blood' as creating individual, *can* 'Keep constant contact with ... the main/Mystery, not to be understood' ('Baggot Street Deserta', 13). How can one's exercise of balance and skill, one's 'ability to say proportionately what one has to say' (Abbate Badin interview, 114), be, not a blockage to, but rather, the necessary condition of, one's witness to the chaos of the real?

It seems to me that recent criticism of Kinsella, in its rightful celebration of his career-long challenge to authoritarian systems of meaning, may have overstretched its focus on his attentiveness to the independent life-force of that raw data of experience. Such criticism may have neglected the second of the three principles I see governing his aesthetic, one which may seem to contradict that close attention to data: that the artist *must* exercise authority over his material. Though the Joycean rather than the Yeatsean aspects of Kinsella's writing may be in critical ascendancy, he pertinently reminds us not to separate the dancer from the dance of meaning: 'The obsession with fact, with specific individual data, wouldn't seem to me to make much sense unless it had some allegorical drive behind it. Experience by itself, however significant, won't do.' (Haffenden interview, 104). The block of that experience 'turn[s] under my hands, an axis/of light flashing down its length' until 'the wood's soft flesh br[eaks] open' ('His Father's Hands', 173). This is how Kinsella testifies to the symbiotic relationship of the 'guardian structure' of the real and the human consciousness engaged in the effort to 'arouse' it ('Worker in Mirror, at his Bench', 124). Kinsella's aesthetic shows that the life force neither of this guardian structure nor of the responding individual can be truly realised without recognising the agency, each of the other *and* of the contract of right balance between them, in ever-adjustment though that balance must be. We remember that the autonomy of raw data is not invalidated but rather reinforced by the allegorising process: in allegory, figurative demands on material return one to the factual rather than leading away from it. Subtexts require constant connection with surface texts and their instigating moments in real time for their implications to register, as the apparent and the other senses of the composition actively negotiate their relationship.

The nexus of the integrity of vision to which Kinsella's readers are drawn is found here: scrutiny of the authoritarian ethics implied in the drive towards transcendent ideal orders. This is only enabled within the command to exercise authority. True artistry involves the imposition of order by a creator-figure, so that it may be elicited from his or her material. The apparent contradiction of principles here is necessary to resolve the actual contradiction that must otherwise arise between them. The conflict between the otherness of material and artistic agency upon it is only reconcilable through the 'third principle': the artist's entry into, or admission of, a direct, personal and up-close relationship of need and co-operation with that material. Detached observance on its own won't do. The writer's personal as well as poetic pulse must tap out his morse code of desire into the void of the Real ('Baggot Street Deserta', 13). The resulting poetry should, in Kinsella's words, 'add dynamically to the understanding' (Haffenden interview, 113). This is a process of re-connection that generates a potent space of intersection between power and powerlessness, 'a mingling of lives, worlds simmering/in the entranced interval … /wriggling with life not of our kind' ('A Technical Supplement' 19, 189).

The dual negative-cum-positive effect of the human agent's necessary application of power in his consumption of the given has been at the heart of Kinsella's themes from the beginning. It is dramatised in 'In the Ringwood' (16), where the unadmitted dark, the abject waste and destruction of that power's blind drive for freedom, dogs the forces of creation into articulation. 'Down-stream' similarly traces the process of reluctant gradual engagement by the psyche with the reality of darkness, in this case the darkness that is World War Two Europe. The collusion of the poet with that global horror through his willed ignorance, and the potential for restoration of innocence through confronting that collusion, are together represented in this poem's central image of 'A soul of white with darkness for a nest' (50). The Blakean co-dependence between good and evil suggested in the early work is more clearly visible in Kinsella's mid-career family-biographical poems. Here, for example, both grandmother figures represent an overwhelming threat to his potential to individuate, but also represent the only route to successful identity formation in their roles as carriers of the essence of humanity. Their capacity to accept and digest any experience is a capacity which will be essential for Kinsella both as man and poet. In 'Hen Woman' (97) the generation of significance from the process of waste is dramatised vividly through a child and old woman's complementary angles of observation of a hen's laying of an egg and its falling and disappearance through the yard grating into the underworld. Significance is yielded in the poem through an extraordinary sequence of interchanges between black holes opening in a white continuum and white holes opening in a black continuum. Such imagery suggests the associated inter-changes of good and evil and of power and powerlessness central to Kinsella's aesthetic.

These spaces of interchange open in every aspect of Kinsella's work. His mode of publication will serve as example. The Peppercanister project testifies to the contingent self-sufficiency of his material where the texts themselves, like every reading of them, are 'Migrants. Of limited distribution.' ('Migrants', 343). I refer here not just to the fact that Kinsella's pamphlets compare with the shifting human consciousness they record, in their accumulative, back-borrowing and circular mode. The interim nature of pamphlet production, in its signalling of the books' function as holding grounds for the long poems and sequences Kinsella writes until their eventual collection in trade editions, in and of itself testifies to a writing 'grown with the thing itself' ('Worker in Mirror, at his Bench', 124). The pamphlet project's origin in the occasional, 'direct-response' broadside and chapbook tradition (most obvious in *Butcher's Dozen*) also contributes to this effect.

The opposite, of course, is also true. Kinsella's mode of publication highlights rather than distracts from the fact of artistic agency and power. The fine-print production of the Peppercanister Press is a revolt against mechanical standards in larger Irish and literary culture. The pamphlets' status as limited editions – collectors' items to-be – deliberately signals writing's security of permanence against the flux out of which it arises, and also is the mark of a controlling consciousness. This is underscored particularly in the Peppercanisters up to the mid 1980s, where a sort of caste system operates in the various editions Kinsella makes available of any one pamphlet. Paper-bound, cloth-bound and calf-bound copies are released and in Peppercanister 7, *Song of the Night and Other Poems* and some others, a signed edition on handmade paper is made available that includes an additional poem in the author's manuscript. These procedures create the sense that the fullest experience of the text is to be had through its most limited and specialised form of publication. Certainly, the trade editions of Thomas Kinsella, including the two versions of his *Collected Poems*, function to reduce the effect of the text as experienced in the original pamphlets. This is due to the practicalities of the elision of illustrations and notes, and the compression and standardisation of spacing in the text. Most readers of Kinsella prefer to read his work in its initial pamphlet form.

His mode of publication is one expression of the 'Open Trap' ('Worker in Mirror, at his Bench', 123) of self-reflexivity at the heart of the creative enterprise. By his mode of pamphlet publication, the poet courts the charge of constructing the value of his own poetic enterprise, with the effect of flushing out criticism's seasonal Darwinian faith in natural selection as the basis of canon-formation. By opting for a form of publication that in this way draws conflictual attention to the idea of value, he is able to unpick the manner in which value is constructed in the response of the consumer to a literary text. By such means, the Peppercanister pamphlets both proclaim and resist their status as works of art, pointing at once towards the release and the containment of the power of the artist. They are indeed an appropriate form for a body of work centrally concerned with just this loss and regaining of authorial power in the act of understanding.

Thomas Kinsella's larger body of poetry and the responses it calls forth vitally dramatise the contract with responsible agency under discussion in this essay. The skills of precision art-making in his *oeuvre* are those of stripping the ego in order to make the self anew, as style enacts a consciousness coming into being. His work explores how one's identity is always being loosened back into the world one is measuring, so that one discovers agency *through* being subject to that world. Kinsella's declaration of his opening of the poem to co-creation by its reader is the natural corollary of his focus on the necessity for that composite rather than competitive relationship between artist and material. The cost of opting for this relationship is visible in the tension between Kinsella's urge towards escaping his own gift of self-conscious scepticism (this is the poet who would, if he could, 'g[ive] his soul up for the gift of thanks' ['An Outdoor Gallery', 15]), and his rejection of any such escape. The achievement in the later work is Kinsella's realisation that this 'gift of thanks' doesn't require such a Faustian sale of his soul, such invalidation of his capacity for austere testing of the ethics of power. This is a capacity upon which his readers have come to rely, and one which is ever more relevant in the relativistic universe of post-Celtic Tiger Ireland where the authenticating of agreeable principles of behaviour in public and private life alike seems increasingly impossible.

In the later work of Kinsella, the capacity to test for right principles of power unites with the gift of thanks. This is the dominant theme of *Littlebody*, the latest of the Peppercanister pamphlets. In the title poem here (354–5), the poet-speaker rejects the temptation offered by the leprechaun-figure Littlebody to claim the 'ghostly gold' of art's superiority to huckstering in the marketplace of significance. To claim this gold, the poet comes to realise, is to instigate a more insidious form of that same huckstering. He comes to recognise that he already has 'all I need' without this ashy form of destructively exclusive self-generating power.

Though Kinsella knows he will inevitably meet again with the temptation of Littlebody, he has achieved a new realisation of self-sufficiency based on connection to rather than distance from needful humanity, including his own. Thus he returns again 'to the main road' (355) of the larger life of commerce as poet with the everyday sources of meaning in a life: the family of the given with which he is connected. In gratitude for this commerce he concelebrates with this family in the luminously understated 'The Body Brought to the Church', where, as the final line of the current *Collected Poems*, together they engage in 'Exchanging numbers. Arranging to keep in touch' (358). In Thomas Kinsella, the creative act is radically reciprocal and transferable, making him stand apart as the most democratic of major Irish poets today.

PRIMARY REFERENCES

Thomas Kinsella, *Collected Poems 1956–2001* (Manchester: Carcanet, 2001).
—, 'The Divided Mind', in *Irish Poets in English*, edited by Sean Lucy (Cork: The Mercier Press, 1973): 208–18.

INTERVIEWS WITH THOMAS KINSELLA

By Donatella Abbate Badin, in *Irish University Review* 31.1 (2001): 113–15.
By Dennis O'Driscoll, in *Poetry Ireland* 25 (1989): 57–65.
By John Haffenden, in *Viewpoints: Poets in Conversation* (London and Boston: Faber and Faber, 1981): 100–13.

John Montague (b. 1929)

Peter Denman

The sesquicentenary of the university coincided with John Montague's seventy-fifth year. In the course of a writing career that germinated during his time as a student at UCD and has lasted over the half-century since, Montague has published a dozen poetry collections, written a book of short stories and a novella, translated two major twentieth-century French poets and edited a major anthology, *The Faber Book of Irish Verse*. His *Collected Poems* appeared in 1995. UCD marked his sixtieth birthday in 1989 with a special issue of the university-based periodical *Irish University Review* given over to essays on his work, and to which he contributed an autobiographical essay, 'The Figure in the Cave', later republished as the eponymous lead piece in a collection of his prose.

He has coined at least one phrase that entered into the lexicon of public and political discourse, when the Taoiseach Jack Lynch, in a speech on the northern situation in the summer of 1970, quoted him on change: 'old moulds are broken'. Conor Cruise O'Brien, then in opposition in the Dáil, was to comment that this was probably the first time a contemporary Irish poet had been so quoted. Over three decades later the Minister for Foreign Affairs Brian Cowen, in the US and addressing the National Committee on American Foreign Policy in the immediate aftermath of the attacks on the Twin Towers and the Pentagon, again used the phrase, this time with an enlarged reach referring to the changes in international relations. The refrain to his 1963 poem 'The Siege of Mullingar', '*Puritan Ireland's dead and gone,/A myth of O'Connor and Ó Faoláin*', has been widely recognised as rewriting Yeats's lines in 'September 1913' to signal a sea-change in Irish society.

The career had its beginnings at UCD in the years immediately after the Second World War. When Montague comments on his experiences in the late 1940s and early 1950s, as he does in 'The Figure in the Cave' and in his introduction to the 1977 revised edition of *Poisoned Lands,* he tends to understate their importance. The first encounter with Dublin and the south that his student years afforded set a course for the formation of his development as a poet. Describing himself retrospectively as 'a marooned northerner', he nevertheless attended meetings of the English Society, made contact with other alienated contemporary figures from the south such as Anthony Cronin and Pearse Hutchinson and began writing poems. That sense of willed isolation was to stay with him throughout his career. Forty years on, after the emergence to prominence of poets a decade younger, such as Seamus Heaney and Michael Longley, he observed of himself in the mid-nineties: 'I don't fit the prescription of what a Northern Irish poet should be. I'm like an uncle the "team" of other Northern poets would rather avoid. I don't play on the team so they don't throw me the ball.' But he then immediately goes on to observe that one of the factors setting him apart is that he has moved more easily than most across the divisions that partition Ireland. To this it might added that, as a slightly older figure, he escaped (for good or ill) being caught up in and carried along by the collective energy that 'Northern Irish poetry' came to signify in readers' minds, especially in Great Britain.

As an undergraduate Montague studied English and History. The initial contact with the university, while it left him feeling an outsider at the beginning, was his introduction to various academic campuses and an environment that provided him with congenial support for much of his life. A successful degree course at UCD led on to formative spells at Yale and other American universities, and this in turn brought him into direct personal contact with vital poets and critics such as W. H. Auden, Robert Lowell, Robert Penn Warren, William Empson, Robert Bly and William Carlos Williams. During the sixties Montague held various short teaching posts at Berkeley, UCD and Vincennes. In 1972 he joined the staff of the English Department at UCC, where he remained for sixteen years and was appointed an Associate Professor. And in 1998 he was appointed the first Ireland Professor of Poetry, a three-year Chair established by the three Irish universities (UCD, Trinity College, Dublin, and Queen's University, Belfast), together with the Arts Councils north and south.

While he was still an undergraduate, some of Montague's very first poems were selected as winners in a Radio Éireann competition organised by Clarke. In interviews and essays Montague has frequently indicated that two exemplary precursors for him were James Joyce and Austin Clarke, both of whom had been through UCD before him; and in an essay on the internationalisation of Irish poetry he was to point up the importance of another alumnus, Denis Devlin. Joyce offered a model for an art that reconciled the native and the international, and the organisation of his short-story collection *Dubliners* was used as a model by Montague when putting together his own stories in *Death of a Chieftain* (1964). Clarke's work contained 'a lot of verse craft from which younger poets could learn'. Devlin aspired to write poetry that would be judged good anywhere in the world. Each of them opened up possibilities for Montague. Furthermore, it was while at UCD that Montague had his first encounter with France and the European mainland, thus setting in train another facet of the internationalist perspective that is such an important component in his poetry. A fictionalised account of one of these student trips provides the material for his 1987 novella *The Lost Notebook*. As he writes there, 'years later such forays abroad would become part of ordinary Irish student life, but in my urgency I was something of a pioneer ... It was a different Europe, of course, not criss-crossed with charter planes, not crammed with package tours and student fares.'

He had already proven to be something of a pioneer by coming south to attend UCD while other school-fellows of his who moved on to university had gone to Belfast. And that journey south was probably more significant and shaping for his work than the eventual travels abroad. The image of travelling up and down the island between north and south recurs as a motif in his poetry. 'Enterprise' in *The Rough Field* is about the train linking Dublin and Belfast, and the concluding poem of that ambitious book is called 'Driving South'. The motif is also prominent in the poems that go to make up his other extended sequence, *The Dead Kingdom* (1984). The reach southward is there extended to Cork, where Montague had made his home for ten years or more, and the returns north are to visit his dying mother. As he writes in 'Border': 'I go North again and again' (154). Cork is also where his father, 'the least happy man I have ever known' as Montague poignantly and memorably says of him in another book, is described in 'At Last' disembarking on his return from a life in America:

A small sad man with a hat
he came through the Customs at Cobh ...

We drove across Ireland that day,
lush river valleys of Cork, russet
of the Central Plain, landscapes
exotic to us Northerners ... (169)

The frequency and ease with which Montague's writing has moved across the border and its attendant partitions were fittingly recognised in his appointment to the Ireland Chair of Poetry. His transitional ability was set in process by that awkward first move from Tyrone to Dublin and UCD. It has meant that, while Ulster and its concerns have always been prominent in his work, Montague has largely avoided being bracketed as a 'Northern Ireland poet'. During the anthology wars of the 1980s, he was pleased by Sebastian Barry's claim, made on behalf of a younger generation of writers, that he was someone who bestrode the 'inherited boundaries' that sectioned the perception of Irish poetry. In his short essay entitled 'The Unpartitioned Intellect' Montague was to advocate a new element in discussions of Anglo-Irish literature, 'an inclusiveness towards which we might all aspire, a passionate welcoming, a fertile balance' (40).

Montague has always written with a lyric confidence about himself and about his life and contacts. This leads him to adopt a mythopeic approach in his poetry, in which personal events tend to be endowed with an emblematic and enhanced significance. It is a legitimate manner of proceeding for a lyric poet, albeit a little at odds with the modern temper and internationalising contemporaneity that characterise his poetry. He has written a late volume of poems (admittedly not the most successful of his books) entitled *Time in Armagh* (1993) which is centred on his secondary schooling with the Vincentians. His time as a university student in Dublin does not figure in his work, either as immediate material or as reminiscence. Nevertheless, the student path that brought him to Dublin and then onwards to a wider arena has had an enduring effect on his work.

For one thing the move to Dublin offered him a first taste of living in an urban setting, a setting to which he returned in the late fifties after postgraduate years abroad. Montague is not often thought of as an urban poet, but a number of his poems have successfully addressed streetscapes and city living. There is an early painterly poem 'Irish Street Scene, with Lovers'. Elsewhere, those years are commemorated vividly in a retrospective poem 'Herbert Street Revisited'. Herbert Street was his home in Dublin, and also close to the publishing address of his first publisher, Liam Miller of the Dolmen Press. In the sixties Montague lived in Paris, and the central section of his lyrically assured 1967 volume *A Chosen Light* is imbued with that city's streetscape and surroundings. 'A Christmas Card' (*The Dead Kingdom*) vividly imagines his father's life in the streets of Brooklyn. In the same collection, an elegiac poem 'Gone' sings 'a song for/things that are gone':

> Tall walls of Dublin
> dishonoured and torn;
> Belfast's Victorian villas,
> rose windows of the Crown;
>
> Like the Great Forests
> of Ireland, hacked down
> to uphold the Jacobean
> houses of London ... (133)

Although *The Rough Field* chooses his rural childhood territory as a sounding board for its investigation of history, a considerable number of his poems are alive to urban modernity. He has lived through and observed the transformation of Irish society in the second part of the twentieth century. When he returned to Ireland in the late fifties, Montague was just in time to witness the radical initiatives taken to open up the Irish economy by Taoiseach Seán Lemass and T.K. Whitaker at the Department of Finance. Montague's first publication, the Dolmen Press chapbook *Forms of Exile*, appeared at the end of 1958. It came out at the same time as the government's ground-breaking White Paper, the first Programme for Economic Expansion. The conjunction was coincidental, but from then on through the 1960s Montague's poetry carries in it signs of recognising the slow but inevitable transformation of society that ensued. The process of change is much more immediately evident in his early poems than in those of his Dolmen colleague and contemporary Thomas Kinsella, notwithstanding the fact that Kinsella at the time worked as a civil servant in Whitaker's department. Kinsella did not really address such issues until 1968, in 'Nightwalker'. The bleak disenchantment of that powerful long poem had already been briefly anticipated by Montague in an early poem, 'Speech for an Ideal Irish Election':

Who today asks for more –
Smoke of battle blown aside –
Than the struggle with casual
Graceless unheroic things,
The greater task of swimming
Against a slackening tide? (200)

And another poem from the early sixties, 'A Drink of Milk', exhibits in its language signs of the impending changes in Irish farming as the country begins to move from being a predominantly agricultural economy to a manufacturing one. The byre is 'girdered', and the stalled cattle are described as 'warm engines' waiting to be connected to a milking machine turned on at the flick of a switch. Meanwhile a cat steals in 'to dip its radar whiskers/with old-fashioned relish/in a chipped saucer'. That contrast between the rather self-conscious modernity of 'radar' and the explicitly 'old-fashioned' approach to the chipped saucer is reprised in the description of the farmhouse interior at the end of the poem, where

A pounding transistor shakes
the Virgin on her shelf … (192)

That transistor image appears again in the often-anthologised 'The Siege of Mullingar':

In the early morning the lovers
Lay on both sides of the canal
Listening on Sony transistors
To the agony of Pope John. (67)

Here the transistor is given a brand-name in what must stand as one of the earliest instances of product placement in Irish poetry. Once again there is a conjunction of the portable radio with a religious figure, although here the mention of the death of Pope John XXIII is at once a reminder of his modernising influence and of a transition. The poem's refrain comments on another transition, particular to the Irish situation:

Puritan Ireland's dead and gone,
A myth of O'Connor and Ó Faoláin

The poem celebrates the energy and freedom of the young as they roam the streets with sexual energy. It has been remarked, rather ruefully perhaps, that the spirit of the sixties did not make its delayed appearance in Ireland until about 1970, but here is evidence that Montague's acute observation had spotted some early indications of its arrival in 1963.

While Montague is known for his lyrical evocations of love and loss, and for his mythopeic approach to history, his poetry has also found room for social commentary. This was to be given full expression when in 1966 he published *Patriotic Suite*, the first of a number of pamphlet publications that would later be collected as sections of *The Rough Field*. The poems in *Patriotic Suite* are significant as an intervention in the official celebrations and national taking-stock occasioned by the fiftieth anniversary of the 1916 Rising. A note on the inside cover (no doubt penned by Montague himself) observes that 'the poets have been strangely quiet during the 1916 Commemoration. Is it because, as Lenin said, the Irish Revolution was premature and bound to turn bourgeois?' The pamphlet shows Montague assuming the role of a public poet, offering a somewhat astringent view of the Ireland of his time. The cover note quoted goes on to link it to an earlier sequence 'The Sheltered Edge', which had been included in his book *Poisoned Lands*. When originally published in 1958, it had been entitled 'Rhetorical Meditations in Time of Peace', glancing back allusively to Yeats's 'Meditations in Time of Civil War'. That some line of affiliation from Yeats the public poet is being claimed is clear, and it is equally evident that Montague is using his poetry to comment on Ireland.

One of the poems, 'The Enterprise' (already mentioned), is named after the train linking Dublin and Belfast and is structured around the journey between the two cities. Crossing the railway bridge over the Boyne at Drogheda is an encounter with the beginnings of industrial urbanism:

> The train crawls across a bridge:
> Through the cantilevered interstices –
> A lace curtain monstrously magnified –
> We overlook the sprawling town.
>
> Row after row of council cottages
> Ride the hill, curving up to the church
> Or down to the docks
> Where a crane tilts into emptiness. (64)

The viewpoint, in so far as it fastens on concrete details, is Larkinesque; the composition of the actual scene is painterly (with the cantilevered interstices in the foreground reminiscent of André Derain); but the poem ultimately makes a comment on the larger Irish 'enterprise', where

> nothing has been planned –
> Assembled, yes, casual
> And coarse as detritus,

with '[o]nly a drift of smoke' to indicate life (65). The poems in *Patriotic Suite* mark a moment of uneasy poise in Irish history, held between an adherence to the traditional values of the past and a recognition of the pressures of modernity. It is a position replicated with more assurance in the fabric of Montague's own poetry, in which he has sought to gain access to the rhythms and techniques of international contemporaries while at the same time taking as his subject matter the durable romantic themes of myth, history and love. The poems interweave allusions to the foundational past, whether the leaders of the 1916 rising or the more distant, even legendary, past represented by the Skelligs and Hy Brasil.

Observational comment is still an element in Montague's poetry. In *Drunken Sailor* (2004), his most recent collection, there is a sonnet-length poem entitled 'Demolition Ireland' in which 'the giant machines trundle over/this craggy land, crushing old contours' (45). Riverbanks and trout pools are bulldozed and dredged clean, driving mystery from the landscape, but in the end 'the rushes rise again, by stealth,/tireless warriors, on the earth's behalf'. The landscape, with its rough fields and dreaming wells, has always been to the foreground in Montague's poems, 'a manuscript/We had lost the skill to read' as he terms it in 'A Lost Tradition' (33). But as part of this there is a keen eco-awareness, as it would now be termed. 'Demolition Ireland' is a reprise of early poems such as 'Old Mythologies' and 'Hill Field', in which the landscape of Ireland contains and transmits the past, at once subject to yet resisting human intervention. 'Hill Field', from *A Chosen Light*, begins with a sight of a tractor-drawn plough '[p]atterning the hill field', as if the needs of agricultural husbandry were to be seen as issuing in an artistic act. But at the end of the poem,

> Still the dark birds shape
> Away as he approaches
> To sink with a hovering
> Fury of open beaks –
> Starling, magpie, crow ride
> A gunmetal sheen of gaping earth. (227)

Written in the mid-sixties, the imagery of this poem with its darkness, predatory birds, fury, gunmetal, and suggestion of a gaping wound on the surface, can now be read as prescient of later troubles on this island.

The consonance between the early and late poems is evident elsewhere. *Drunken Sailor* includes a short poem that previously appeared nearly thirty-five years ago in *Tides* as 'King & Queen' and is given a new placing as part of a short sequence entitled 'Slievemore'. Another poem in the late volume remembers Austin (Clarke), placing him there in company with other poets Montague has known: Robert Graves, John Berryman, Marianne

Moore, and David Jones. The early years of Montague's formation still operate as significant factors in his poetry.

John Montague's poetry reflects the uneasy but productive friction between tradition and modernity in Ireland. He is celebrated as a lyric poet who has written memorable poems exploring love and eroticism; he has encapsulated movements of family and national history in long poem sequences; and he has given a topography of myth to the landscape and its features. But a less readily recognised strand of his work has been the commentary it has provided on social change in Ireland over the last half-century, asserting a place for poetry in the intellectual critique and reassessment of national aims. Enabled by his UCD experience, he commenced writing on the cusp of that opening up and the tensions it engendered. His engagement with international poets in both the US and France, and his importation of some of their techniques into Irish poetry through the medium of his own work, coincided with the opening up of Ireland culturally and economically during the 1960s, gave a long-term basis for the sustainability of his own writing and provided a poetic voice for the Ireland that was ushered in by the government of Seán Lemass and the Programmes for Economic Expansion.

PRIMARY REFERENCES

John Montague, 'The Hag of Beare' from *Tides* (Dublin: The Dolmen Press, 1970).
—, *The Figure in the Cave and Other Essays*, edited by Antoinette Quinn (Dublin: The Lilliput Press, 1989).
—, *Collected Poems* (Loughcrew: Gallery Press, 1995).
—, *Drunken Sailor* (Loughcrew: Gallery Press, 2004).

DECADES OF DIVERSITY
(1959–2004)

THOMAS KILROY (B. 1934)

Christopher Murray

The ideal commentator for this chapter would have been the late Gus Martin. I think of a line in *Twelfth Night* when Duke Orsino calls for a song better than the 'light airs and recollected terms/Of these most brisk and giddy-paced times' but is told emphatically: 'He is not here, so please your lordship, who should sing it' (2.4.5-9). For Gus Martin was an exact contemporary of Tom Kilroy at UCD, in a generation if not a class which included other such luminaries as Tom MacIntyre, Denis Donoghue, Maurice Harmon and John Jordan. A man of many parts, Gus was to return to UCD from his teaching post in Roscrea to join Kilroy as lecturer in English in the 1960s. When I joined the department in 1970 it was just after the move to Belfield and I had, as a Galwegian, missed the exciting times during which UCD had been convulsed with student revolt and disputes over a possible merger with Trinity College.

As outsider, I soon found that Tom Kilroy was already a writer with a reputation. As a graduate student in New Haven I had read Des Rushe's account of the Dublin Theatre Festival of 1968, in which Kilroy's first staged play, *The Death and Resurrection of Mr. Roche*, had made quite an impact; but I had neither seen the play nor read the text. Neither was I aware of Kilroy's venture just then into fiction. At a reception hosted by Denis Donoghue after the first departmental meeting of 1970–1 I met Tom Kilroy for the first time. We chatted amicably enough. I asked him what he was writing and did not hear when he said *The Big Chapel*. Matters were not helped by my ignorance of the dispute in

Callan on which the novel, not then published, was based. Tom, dapper in brown lounge suit, buttoned-down shirt and tie, with trim red moustache and horn-rimmed spectacles, frowned at this ill-prepared newcomer. Instantly, I felt that here was an artist with exacting standards who expected his interlocutors to keep up. Gus Martin smiled somewhere in the background.

In the years that followed I came to appreciate Tom Kilroy's merits as colleague and creative writer alike. His quiet, subdued manner masked great powers of concentration and determination. In temperament he was and remains a fascinating combination of the deadly serious and the richly humorous. There is a depth there, a solidity not to be moved by the everyday pressures of university life. It is hard now to describe the political atmosphere in Dublin in the early 1970s. There was a general ambivalence about Northern Ireland, where 'our people' – the phrase often if unquestioningly used in the media – were suffering internment and daily injustices. Séamus Deane was then a brilliant presence in the English Department, his commitment to Northern affairs tempered by his cosmopolitanism. Denis Donoghue, then in his Yeatsian phase, kept his distance, his urbanity never to be cast in doubt. Donoghue was the first holder there of the chair of Modern English and American Literature through a quixotic arrangement whereby Roger McHugh, having been appointed to English, resigned and the chair in Anglo-Irish was created for him while Donoghue was appointed to Modern. Roger McHugh was by contrast an open nationalist, author of plays on O'Donovan Rossa and Roger Casement, board member of the Belfast Lyric Theatre and unswerving supporter of Mary O'Malley up there. Though Tom Kilroy taught Anglo-Irish literature and was deeply loyal to Roger he seemed to me at this time quite apolitical. I recall Roger's insisting in 1972 that we should debate Montague's *The Rough Field* in the context of the Northern 'troubles', but I don't recall Tom's having anything to say about it or about Kinsella's *Butcher's Dozen*, published around the same time.

What I do recall is Kilroy's description in conversation of a march he joined to the British Embassy just after Bloody Sunday. The embassy was then in a brick Georgian terraced house in Merrion Square, next door to where the Lantern Theatre thrived.

Tom told of the succession of speakers who addressed the large crowd at Merrion Square about the centuries of oppression. Loud cheers greeted every rehearsal of Ireland's woes. The crowd grew ecstatic. Tom noticed one, then two and possibly more men climb on the window sills while the latest speaker gave his peroration about the latest injury, the attack in Derry: 'and now we're going to burn their embassy down'. All cheered once more, Tom along with them until he saw that the men on the window sills had broken windows and started a blaze. Suddenly he realised, 'My God, he means it.' As he told the story it was clear that the playwright's delight in the conflict between rhetoric and action, reality and illusion, was simultaneous with an appalled recognition of the horror of the moment when another country's embassy was being set alight and burned to the ground. I often thought afterwards how exact an account this made of the Irish version of comedy – Synge's *Playboy*, for instance – in which there is a delight in violence as if it were all fantasy and then a sudden recognition of the reality behind it all. Looking back now I see Kilroy's double response as an individual and as an artist: the will to be present and bear witness as dissenter and at the same time the detachment, the need to have nothing to do with such public disorder, however well-grounded the impulse to join in. In a sense, for the artist flight was mandatory. The moral issue was to listen, to see, to record, to exercise the liberal imagination without – as had happened the writers in Paris – physically joining in.

Before he was a playwright Tom Kilroy was an academic. Having taken his BA at UCD in 1955 he went on to do an MA in English, with a thesis on 'Satirical Elements in the Prose of Thomas Nashe'. This brief study of an Elizabethan writer, whose best-known work is probably *The Unfortunate Traveller* (1594), a short picaresque novel with a dark side to it, is a bit of a surprise in the light of Kilroy's subsequent career. Here, however, he seems to dismiss the satirical mode from his own ambitions by declaring that the satirist 'must *necessarily* be cruel and unscrupulous, unmoved by either the dignity or distress of his victims' (7, emphasis added). Time was to show that as a writer himself Kilroy would be critical but never satirical. The values of tolerance, understanding and pity underlay all he was to write.

Two other points arise nevertheless from this dissertation on Nashe and satire. In referring to Nashe's lack of system in his various narratives Kilroy underlined 'the necessity of carefully thinking out one's ideas' (12). Once again, this lack in Nashe was to become a strength in Kilroy.

In play after play what often strikes home is how the intellectual force secures the action and the meaning in tandem with theatrical experimentalism. In *Double Cross* (1986), the symmetry between the careers of William Joyce ('Lord Haw-Haw') and Brendan Bracken (Churchill's Minister for Information during World War Two) works to show up how masks, pretence, role-playing, define the self in conflict with its national or ethnic roots. The ideas in a Kilroy play are always meticulously thought through. Other good examples would be the brilliantly conceived *Talbot's Box* (1977) and the equally inventive *The Secret Fall of Constance Wilde* (1997). Anyone familiar with *The O'Neill* (1969), so carefully working through ideas inspired by Seán O'Faolain's biography, could not be surprised at the dramatic craftsmanship and theatrical imagination Kilroy can deploy in such pieces. The impulse for the theatrical experimentalism, so important a part of Kilroy's achievement, was facilitated during his student and graduate student days when during summers spent working in London, he saw the latest work of John Arden and John Osborne at the Royal Court and of Joan Littlewood at Theatre Royal, Stratford East.

The other point to be gleaned from the thesis on Nashe is the emphasis on style. The term Nashe used was 'eloquence', which Kilroy defined as 'the ability to keep the attention of an audience' (2). It is interesting that he should already, in 1959, be considering 'audience' while discussing rhetoric, letting it be seen that from the outset his interests were mainly performative. A key influence in this area has to be O'Casey, whose Dublin plays in particular exploit that 'eloquence' to an extraordinary degree. Kilroy was to edit a volume of essays on O'Casey in 1975, in the Twentieth-Century Views series published by Prentice-Hall, and in the introduction he had much to say about O'Casey's language:

> One may distinguish between the two languages of drama: on the one hand, that which is so enclosed that its record in print is virtually its final measure; on the other, that which has to be

completed upon the stage. The distinction is admittedly artificial, but it will serve to highlight the fact that writing for the stage differs from all other kinds of writing. It involves, at all times, a kind of submerged writing, ascription rather than description, language as a highly kinetic form of energy involving passage from one creative dimension to another. (10)

That is to say, O'Casey's language was always theatrical, as it were incorporating voices which in turn ventriloquised other voices. Kilroy himself became highly skilled at this art. Significantly, he pinpointed O'Casey's great strength here: 'The foundations of his language ... remain the same throughout: Irish colloquial speech and a more mannered rhetoric. The rhetoric is in the Irish tradition of public oratory and balladry' (13). The use of the word 'rhetoric' makes clear how Kilroy threw a bridge between Nashe and O'Casey to facilitate the use of 'eloquence' on a twentieth-century stage.

What lends his first staged play, *The Death and Resurrection of Mr. Roche*, its distinction is the poetic nature of the piece, its style, its eloquence, allied to the theatricality in the form of a Greek Old Comedy transferred to a seedy setting worthy of Joyce's *Dubliners*. The result is what used to be called, following Jean Cocteau, a poetry *of* rather than *in* the theatre. The climax of *Mr. Roche*, a play in which a scapegoated homosexual appears to die in the flat of a junior civil servant, occurs where the ancient ritual of resurrection, complete with dancing, seems to open up the stage and push aside realism in order to establish a moment of wonder:

MYLES (*after a pause, almost in a whisper*): Did he die, Kelly? Did he really die?

(*As* KELLY *speaks, across the back, approaching the front door, come* MR. ROCHE, *the* MEDICAL STUDENT *and* KEVIN. *They approach like figures in a dance, almost linked, partly to support one another, partly to catch the mood of delirious revelry that grips them. They cross the raised platform in this formation, pulling away towards one another. As they enter the front door they mime silence and surprise for* KELLY.)

KELLY: Oh, he died right enough. It wasn't really our fault. We were visited by him. The time to stop him was long before he arrived. I was against having him in, remember ...

MEDICAL STUDENT [*offstage*]: Open the door and let the
    dead appear.
MR. ROCHE: I am a little ghosty-ghost. Boo-hoo!
(KELLY *leaps up and throws the door open.* MR. ROCHE *is the
first to enter.*)
KELLY: Jesus!
MR. ROCHE: Not quite, my dear chap, but I am flattered by
    your mistake. (60)

In this passage, 'delirious revelry' – virtually a definition of Old
Comedy – meets the sacred on stage, as in a play by T.S. Eliot or
Graham Greene. The scapegoat Mr. Roche seems illuminated by
the power of Dionysus himself, shading over into Jesus Christ. All
of this epiphany transforms the action into a highly charged
moment of mystery and miracle, reminding us of the conviction
of that other poetic dramatist of the 1950s, Christopher Fry, that
comedy is a narrow escape from despair – into faith. At this point
Kilroy also takes his place among the great playwrights of the Irish
tradition, from Yeats and Lady Gregory's *Cathleen Ni Houlihan* to
Brian Friel's *Wonderful Tennessee*.

Having made that point about the beyond-realism of Kilroy's
work one would need to look carefully at *Talbot's Box*. When that
play was first presented at the Peacock Theatre in 1977, in a
splendid production by Patrick Mason, there were nightly in the
audiences certain devout people who held up rosary beads and
holy pictures as the actor John Molloy went through his paces as
the Blessed Matt Talbot. It seemed clear that they thought the
play a straightforward documentation of the would-be saint's life.
But nothing in Kilroy's work is ever straightforward. In the
modernist mode, irony plays over all that he writes. He views
Talbot as a man desperately in need of the space to be himself and
to pursue his one passion once he overcame the racking addiction
to alcohol, namely oneness with God. The mystical side of the
fanatic workman takes on the guise of an artist figure focused
singularly on his obsession. Kilroy is able thereby to find in the
mythic presence of Talbot something of a twentieth-century
hero, the anti-hero or holy fool at odds with the society which
wants to own him, box him in and exploit him for its own
material interests. Accordingly, Talbot is viewed sympathetically,

even though he was a strike-breaker and a craw-thumper of the most naïve kind. Kilroy's compassion makes this history play a deeply spiritual study of a man overwhelmed by God.

In the end, Thomas Kilroy must be regarded as a playwright's playwright. He occupies himself with the world envisioned as tragicomedy, a place best appreciated through the eyes of visionary or artist. In that way Kilroy is a late modernist, one who cherishes the individual imagination and insists on the importance of the great writers before him as aids or contexts for our continuing search for meaning and compassion in the world. In that sense, also, it can be said that after O'Casey he has assimilated Beckett. But where Beckett failed, perhaps refused, to find meaning in the world and felt compelled to shrink representations of human suffering more and more into tiny images, Kilroy feels himself a member of that same alienated Anglo-Irish Protestant tradition ('a Catholic body in a Protestant mind'). He has persisted in the quest for the right equivalents in narrative, the objective correlative for existence in a world run mad and yet a world not to be given up in despair. He avoids minimalism. He avoids monologue theatre. He adheres to a drama where plot and action are still and always (as he once termed it) 'the groundwork for a new theatre', that ever-elusive dream. He has written and had performed three adaptations which confirm his alliance with the great modernist playwrights: Ibsen's *Ghosts* (Peacock, 1989), Chekhov's *The Seagull* (Royal Court and Irish Theatre Company, 1981) and Pirandello's *Six Characters in Search of an Author* (Abbey, 1996). A version of Wedekind's *Spring Awakening* awaits production at present. Similarly, his eight original stage plays (for he has done radio work also) incorporate and re-echo his wide acquaintance with the 'classics' of world drama and his interest in reinterpreting these for our time and place. In a sense, this combination of learning and theatricalism might be termed Elizabethan: one feels that if Nashe had written plays this is what they might have been like.

His concern, at the same time, is as much for the community as for the individual. Perhaps this is why the theatre has held such fascination for him, as a model of what may be done to confront crisis and look for transformation. As Literary Advisor at the Abbey in the later 1970s he lent support to the exciting regeneration of the theatre by Joe Dowling, and bright young directors like Seán McCarthy and Patrick Mason. His long-standing admiration for the ethos of the Royal Court theatre and for the commitment of directors like Max Stafford-Clark kept an ideal alive in Kilroy's mind. Both *Talbot's Box* and his version of *The Seagull* consequently played at the Royal Court. While holding the chair of English at NUI Galway (from 1977 to 1989) Kilroy kept up this interest in working to refresh the theatre by holding workshops there. In 1986 he accepted an invitation to join the board of the Field Day Theatre Company, and characteristically gave the company a play (*Double Cross*) rather than the pamphlet they expected. His second play for Field Day, *The Madam Macadam Travelling Theatre* (1991), while not a success at the time, might be said to encapsulate in its idea of a touring company bringing some kind of art to the people in an 'emergency' period a comic version of the role and healing purpose of theatre in community. Although she can be pompous at times the eponymous Madam speaks for the playwright when she articulates the mission involved: 'If we bear witness to the steady pulse of the world there is no miracle which we may not accomplish upon the stage' (37).

But there is a danger, too, in having a mission. Some critics savaged *The Madam Macadam Travelling Theatre* and probably caused Kilroy's resignation from the board of Field Day. It was to be several years before he wrote for the stage again. But eventually, after Patrick Mason as artistic director invited him to write a version of *Six Characters in Search of an Author*, he was able to recover his sense of purpose. The brilliantly inventive *The Secret Fall of Constance Wilde* was the result. In the remarkable conclusion to this play Constance, a tragic figure close to death, writes to her two sons in defence of their father:

> All his troubles arose from his own father, from the way his father crushed something within the soul of his own son. But your father is a great man. He had this terrible, strange vision. He sacrificed everything to reach out to that vision – that was very brave, wasn't it? You see what he did was to try to release the soul from his body, even when his body was still alive. (68)

180

The Shape of Metal, premiered at the Abbey in 2003, is, in a way, the welding of the characters of Madam Macadam and Constance Wilde and may serve here to provide a conclusion. Like most of Kilroy's plays this latest one has as its protagonist an artist in crisis (the exceptions to this generalisation turn out at the least to be visionaries like O'Neill, Matt Talbot and, in a less obvious way, Mr. Roche, while a play yet to be staged is about William Blake). The key to *The Shape of Metal* may be said to lie in some lines from the actress in *The Madam Macadam Travelling Theatre*: 'Can it be that the very source of our art is also the source of our decline? Can one destroy a talent by grossly overusing it?' (32). The sculptor Nell Jeffrey in *The Shape of Metal* is a female King Lear, four score year and upwards, but one who has destroyed her daughters rather than they her. It is a fearsome portrait of the artist as an old woman, who put her art before all else in life.

Some commentators have noticed the resemblance to Ibsen's final play *When We Dead Awaken* (1899), where the elderly sculptor Arnold Rubek has built his reputation on a massive work entitled 'The Resurrection Day'. In Ibsen's play, which the young James Joyce as student at UCD in St Stephen's Green famously reviewed, the sculptor succeeded in his artistic life only at the expense of Irene, the woman he loved who was also his model and Muse. She reappears in the play like a ghost from the past to challenge him for betraying both her and the art-work they had conceived together. In Kilroy's version – if such a term is appropriate for an original piece running the gamut of modernist art from Giacometti to Barbara Hepworth and Beckett – the artist is herself the woman and the man in the case is nowhere to be seen: in fact news of his death is received in the first scene without much sign of indebtedness. For his part Eddie has died bitterly denouncing her. 'When we dead awaken,' Irene tells Rubek (in William Archer's translation, the one Joyce knew), 'we see that we have never lived.' In Kilroy's configuration, where no men appear on stage, the wounded and mentally unstable woman is the sculptor's daughter, ironically named Grace. Grace is missing, presumed dead, for many years, but her presence haunts her mother Nell, who dominated her and used her head for modelling.

As the play draws to a close Nell imagines Grace's reappearance, '*this time a bronze death head on a plinth, a bronze head which speaks, the mouth moving but the eyes closed over, metallic*' (51). The image is Celtic rather than Ibsenist. What Grace says appeases Nell: 'Mummy shaped Gracie's head into metal', which gave the disturbed girl peace and a sense of deliverance: 'All finished'. This visitation energises Nell to deal with her unfinished sculpture, 'Woman Rising from Water', and she takes a sledge hammer to it, a cathartic act which seems to release her from her guilt and to give her a new realisation of the primacy of life over art. As she puts it: 'Giacometti. Beckett. All the rest of them! They're dead. We're alive. What we know now comes to us from the future' (56–7). She sees the woman of the future having to cope with the final challenge to womanhood when science creates human life in the laboratory: 'Will she have the courage to go with it, the woman of the future?' (57). Nell longs to live to see that 'new woman's art'. On that note the aged sculptor, close to death, decides to go outside her studio for the first time in the play. Her other daughter Judith opens the door at Nell's command and with a symbolic stage direction this extraordinary plays ends: '*They walk together through the open doorway, into the gathering darkness*' (58). This ending, a kind of 'Welcome, o life!' in a new guise, contrasts sharply with Ibsen's pessimism. It marks the high point in this writer's remarkable career.

PRIMARY REFERENCES

Thomas Kilroy, 'Satirical Elements in the Prose of Thomas Nashe'. MA thesis, UCD, September 1959. Unpublished.

—, *The Death and Resurrection of Mr. Roche* (London: Faber and Faber, 1969).

—, 'Introduction', *Sean O'Casey: A Collection of Critical Essays* (Englewood Cliffs, NJ: Prentice-Hall, 1975).

—, *The Madam Macadam Travelling Theatre* (London: Methuen, 1991).

—, *The Secret Fall of Constance Wilde* (Loughcrew, Oldcastle: Gallery Press, 1997).

—, *The Shape of Metal* (Loughcrew, Oldcastle: Gallery Press, 2003).

JOHN MCGAHERN (B. 1935)

Joseph O'Connor

The first short story I wrote was a work of genius. It was austere and lovely, full of elegant sentences and sharp insights. Any reviewer would have called it a tour de force. Because the first short story I wrote was by John McGahern.

It's called 'Sierra Leone' and it appears in the 1979 collection *Getting Through*, a copy of which had been purchased by my father and was lying around the house. In the story, a couple meet in a Dublin bar to analyse their complicated affair. I was sixteen that year. Complicated affairs interested me. My English teacher, John Burns, a wonderful man, said writing could be a beneficial hobby for teenagers. It was the one thing he ever told us that was completely wrong.

Writing was like attempting to juggle with mud. I would sit in my bedroom, gawping at a blank jotter, wishing I had the foggiest inkling as to what might be written. McGahern often wrote about rural Leitrim, but we had no hedgerows or loys in the 1970s Dublin estate I called home. We had no thwarted farmers, no maiden aunts on bicycles, no small-town solicitors, no cattle-dealing IRA veterans. Simply put, there was nothing in Glenageary to write about. You could call it the original failure of the creative imagination without which no writer ever got going.

Whenever I tried to write, there was only frustration. I felt as pent-up as McGahern's lovers. That's how I recollect these youthful efforts at fiction: a haze of self-conscious fumblings and awkward gropings, second-hand sentences, sentenced to fail. One evening, in dismal hopelessness, I found myself copying out 'Sierra Leone' word for word. I ached to write a story. So I wrote one.

I must have felt that the act of writing would make the words somehow mine. But, if so, it was an act of literary adultery. I smouldered to know what that feeling was like: to write out a beautiful text from start to finish. I suppose this was comparable to wannabe pop-stars throwing shapes and pulling pouts in the bathroom mirror. But something richer and more interesting was going on, too. McGahern was teaching me to read, not to write: to see the presences hidden in the crannies of a text, the realities the words are gesturing towards. Perhaps this is what pulses at the core of the desire to read: the yearning for intense relationship with words we love. Not just with what they are saying, but with the words themselves. Perhaps every reader is re-writing the story.

The next evening, I transcribed the McGahern piece again. This time I dared to alter a couple of names. The male lead became 'Sean' (my father's name). I christened his girlfriend 'Deborah' (after the punk singer Debbie Harry). Our next-door neighbour, Jack Mulcahy, had his name nicked for the barman. This felt taboo. It was like editing the Bible. I was raised in a home where books were revered. My parents considered it disreputable even to dog-ear a volume's pages. To interfere with a story would have been regarded as a form of sacrilege. Under the spell of McGahern, I became a teenage blasphemer.

Every few nights I'd guiltily rewrite the latest adaptation, changing the grammar here, a phrasing there. I'd move around events, break up the paragraphs or tell the same story but from a different point of view. I must have written a hundred versions. The heroine's beautiful hair became auburn or black, and finally – exultantly! – 'strawberry blonde'. I learned the importance of punctuation in a story. A question mark could change things. A well-placed full stop had the force of a slap. Before long, I was murdering McGahern's characters, replacing them with my own pitifully scanty puppets. The pub became a discotheque, the couple acquired flares; I engaged them, married them, bought them a house in the suburbs, then a collection of Planxty records and a second-hand lawnmower. The lovers in the story were starting to seem familiar. They would not have appeared out of place in Arnold Grove, Glenageary.

I rechristened them 'Adam and Eve', after a church on the

Dublin quays. I altered their appearances, their way of speaking. I was afraid to admit it, but I knew who they were becoming. They roamed this fictive otherworld, this Eden designed in Leitrim, talking to each other about all sorts of things: how much they loved novels, how books shouldn't be dog-eared. Sometimes they quarrelled. Occasionally they wept. I could almost feel the firelight of that pub on my face as I watched my parents materialise through the prose.

I'd look at 'Sierra Leone'. It became a kind of friend to me. I wanted to know it better, to learn how it ticked. At one point in those years, I feel almost certain, I could have made a fair stab at reciting the entire text by heart. It was breathtakingly simple, as though it had taken no effort to compose. In that, and in other ways, it was like an old Connemara ballad, of the kind I had often heard with my father on our holidays in Galway: so direct, so alluring, so subtly economical. It reminded me of 'The Rocks of Bawn': you wanted to know how it would turn out. It read, in fact, as though nobody had written it – as if it had somehow grown on the page. I recall one of the sentences: 'Her hair shone dark blue in the light' (318). That strange ache in the heart caused by precise words.

Each man kills the thing he loves. And so the vandalism continued, night after night, with me editing and re-writing this once perfect story, until gradually, over the span of my teenage years, every trace of McGahern was squeezed out of the text. Sierra Leone had become Glenageary. The story had been desecrated, but at least the resulting ruin was mine.

Perhaps all writers have the story they will tell forever, the idea they will go on exploring, consciously or not, until they run out of masks or find their own way of seeing the world. McGahern's 'Sierra Leone' helped me find mine. Every fiction I've begun, every story I've struggled and failed with, has been an attempted reaching-back to that heart-stopping moment of first encountering the power of his art. It's a desire as doomed as any in the history of love stories. But you could spend your time chasing worse.

The Miro foundation in Barcelona, a city about which McGahern has written with great grace, is somewhat unfashionably arranged by chronology. You start with the child-artist's naïve little doodles: his cartoon faces and multicoloured animals. Then you walk through the rooms organised year-by-year, through a life of struggle to say anything worth saying. You think of Patrick Kavanagh as you move through the still rooms: a man who dabbled in verse, only to have it become a life. Here are the pictures from the young Miro's figurative phase, the bowls of fat oranges, the wine-bottles on windowsills. Then the warped guitars, the twisted limbs and mouths. You see him wrestle with the central question of Kavanagh's career: how to balance the satirical impulse with fidelity to the sacred. And then the stuff gets stranger, wilder, more revolutionary. The faces are leering, the bodies apparently yearning to flee their frames; the world turns upside down before your eyes. And now paint itself begins to be abandoned: there are crazy collages, sculptures, ceramics, electric with the colours of the Catalonia Miro loved. It is a stunning experience to enter the last room and see the three vast canvases that dominate its walls. They hit you the way the opening notes of Beethoven's Fifth do, or those last short plays of Samuel Beckett, in a way you know you will never quite forget. Each painting is an unadorned field of vivid blue, with a yellow snaking line bisecting the plane. The simplicity moves you with incredible force, the idea that at the end of such a long search there is only the very simple, the plain line across colour, the desire to leave a stain on the silence. To stand before these images always brings McGahern to my mind: the man who knew, again like Kavanagh, that in art there will always be two kinds of simplicity: the simplicity of going away and the simplicity of coming back.

Much more could be said about McGahern and Kavanagh, two rural-born Irish writers who chronicled versions of Dublin more memorably than did many a native. Again and again, the city appears in McGahern's work, sometimes at a distance but often centrally. The exquisite short stories are peopled by migrant characters who see the metropolis as a labyrinth of possibilities. Here is a Dublin of tatty dancehalls and uneasy courtships, of kisses in damp doorways and unfulfilled hungerings. His citizens are stalwarts of the city's rural-born workforce, who take the first available bus home to the countryside on a Friday evening and the last one back to Bedsit-Land on a Sunday night. They are, in short, like most Dubliners were at the time, and as many are now, despite the new prosperity. Their flings and farewells make for writing of extraordinary beauty, with the city as forlorn backdrop to the search for love. Anyone who has ever lived away from home will find bittersweet beauty in these pages.

McGahern's work acknowledges that Dublin (like capitals everywhere) is largely a community of migrants with conflicted loyalties. And I think of his explorations as opening a way for a number of subsequent writers. In that context it is striking that much of the most compelling fiction about the city has been produced by authors who grew up somewhere else. Ulsterman Patrick McCabe's *The Dead School* and London-born Philip Casey's *The Fabulists* offer powerful reflections on a place that changed radically in the 1970s, as political failure and corruption began to wreak havoc. In *The Book of Evidence*, Wexford-born John Banville produced a gripping novel set in the Dublin of that furtive era, a nighttown of whispered secrets and compromised positions. I find it hard to imagine how these novels could have been written without the presence of McGahern on the Irish scene. For me, he looms behind everyone: an Easter Island figure. Every subsequent Irish novelist owes him a debt.

At UCD in the 1980s, encouraged by Declan Kiberd and the late Gus Martin, I read *The Barracks*, *The Dark* and more of the stories. I found them completely strange and always enthralling. At the time, the vogue among my friends was for Latin American 'Magic Realism'. In those years it often seemed that no novel was worthy of the name unless it contained a talking leopard or a fifteen-page sentence. Against this blizzard of vowelly pyrotechnics McGahern's work stood solid, starkly implacable, like a dry-stone wall in the sweep of a windstorm. I loved its quiet faith, its insistence on its own terms. And then came his masterpiece *Amongst Women*, perhaps the most important Irish novel of the late twentieth century.

So much has been written and said about this sparely magnificent book. It does what was done by Joyce, by George Eliot and Miro, by Muddy Waters and Bessie Smith, the Sex Pistols and Miles Davis: it conjures a world that is absolutely specific to itself, down to the most minuscule, seemingly inconsequential detail, but in so doing manages the alchemy of saying something about every life. Not for nothing did this novel become a bestseller in Ireland, as well as being garlanded with literary awards. The family it depicts is somehow every Irish family of a certain era, held together by its secrets, bound by its evasions, by a nexus of loyalties, only one of which is love. Indeed, it is difficult not to read the Morans as embodying the profoundly uneasy nation in which they exist.

The book draws so subtly from that bottomless well of Irish familial images and returns them to us re-imagined, made wholly new. Moran, the disillusioned republican, burnished hard by pain, walks through the book like a living ghost, through drifts of memories of nights on the run, promises broken, responsibilities ducked. The women in the book, especially the older women, are so utterly real, so achingly recognisable that you forget they are products of someone's imagination. They talk about the rain, about children and food, and you know something else is being discussed all the time. And the episode near the end, at Moran's funeral, is the most powerful fictional scene I have read since my adolescence, when its author helped me first know what it is to read. We see the local hacks of the two conservative parties snickering together in the rural cemetery, as the embittered old revolutionary is finally buried. Sometimes great writers know things they don't know. This tableau was composed a decade before the Tiger padded into Ireland, but it is the most forceful comment imaginable on that ambiguous, sharp-toothed beast.

John McGahern's most recent novel, *That They May Face the Rising Sun*, took eleven years to make and surprised many of its creator's admirers by addressing that rarest of Irish literary subjects: happiness. Here on the lakeside, near to Gloria Bog, little is happening beyond the everyday syncopations – yet, as ever, McGahern unearths resonant beauty. Gossip is a currency, as always in Ireland, and his dialogue, so subtle and carefully poised, abounds with the juiciness of popular speech. It is his most audaciously structured book to date, almost completely devoid of plot, suggesting reams about its characters while rarely telling you anything about them. Reading it is like reading every-thing he has written: like moving to a place you've never lived in before, where you don't know the neighbours or how things work. But thanks to McGahern, you want to know them, because somehow coming to know them, even though they might be nothing like you, is to come to know yourself and those you love, and to understand that there is still a kind of hope. The everyday miracle of fiction, perhaps; one of the reasons why we want to read at all, wherever that grace is revealed to be available, in suburban bedrooms, or in bed-sits, alone.

PRIMARY REFERENCES

John McGahern, 'Sierra Leone', in *The Collected Stories* (London and Boston: Faber and Faber, 1992): 316–30.
—, *Amongst Women* (London and Boston: Faber and Faber, 1990).
—, *That They May Face the Rising Sun* (London: Faber and Faber, 2002).

JIM SHERIDAN (B. 1949)

Ruth Barton

Had Jim Sheridan been born in a previous age, we might well imagine him as a *seanchaí*, a spinner of yarns and keeper of the old tales. Like his brother, Peter, Jim Sheridan is a natural storyteller, a raconteur, whose own family narrative is the raw material for multiple other narratives and whose work is rooted in a humanist's fascination with people and individuality.

Peter Sheridan's best-selling memoirs of growing up in Dublin's North Inner City in the late 1950s and 1960s, *44 – A Dublin Memoir* (1999) and *Forty-Seven Roses* (2001), describe a close-knit family, held together by their mother's resilience and enlivened by their father's faith in his winner coming home. Both brothers anchor their childhood memories in two events, the arrival of a new and virtually unwatchable television set, and the death from a brain tumour of their brother Frankie at the age of eleven. The television set, its images obscured by electronic snow, betokens, as it does in so many recollections of the period, a liberation from a repressive, narrow and authoritarian society; it also presides over a domestic space that draws its warmth from the many individuals who wander in and out of it. In the case of the Sheridans, the lodgers the family took in to support their education add extra colour to a vividly described mix of local characters and opinionated family members. Frankie's death was, as Jim Sheridan has so often remembered, the catalyst for the family's coming together in collective grief and Peter Sheridan's first book ends with their father's realisation that he can only work through his loss via performance, and so the St Laurence O'Toole's Musical and Dramatic Society (SLOT) players are born.

In 1969 Jim Sheridan went to UCD, where he studied English and History. Both subjects would inflect his later films, English in his allusions to Yeats and the Anglo-Irish tradition, History more indefinably, in an ambiguous dialogue with the Irish past. By his third year, he was becoming increasingly involved in college theatre productions with UCD's Dramsoc, and made his name with a rock-musical version of *Oedipus Rex* that saw the audience perched around the hall on three-storey scaffolding.

With his brother Peter, Jim Sheridan first seriously explored many of the themes and concerns that would later reappear in his films and which gained both brothers a reputation for experimental, socially engaged work. The opportunity for this collaboration was provided by Dublin's Project Arts Centre, founded in 1969 as a highly politicised theatre, visual arts and cinema space. A vibrant alternative to the Abbey Theatre and successful competitor for a new generation of actors and writers such as Gabriel Byrne, Liam Neeson and Gerard Stembridge, the Project was dedicated to addressing the inequities of Irish society in the 1970s, be it the Troubles in the North, the country's glaring social injustices, unemployment, emigration or gay politics. With its cadre of talented writers, performers and artists, it gave Jim Sheridan the opportunity to mix with like-minded contemporaries and to develop a nexus of connections on which he was later able to draw for his filmmaking. Here he directed his brother's play *No Entry* (1976), about a young man's response to a violent society where the only way out is through emigration. In the following year, the brothers collaborated with Gerard Mannix Flynn on the production that brought them to the attention of international critics, *The Liberty Suit* (1977). The play, in which the principal role of Curley was taken by Mannix Flynn, is the story of a young man sent to prison for committing arson. Flynn had served time in prison for arson and Peter Sheridan wrote his play as a mixture of fact and fiction. It opened at the Dublin Theatre Festival of 1977, an event that had seen its budget harshly cut and was desperate for a success. *The Liberty Suit* was just that, running for two packed weeks at the Olympia Theatre where on its opening night the curtain went down to cheers and stamping feet from a hugely enthusiastic audience. Jim Sheridan's direction was singled out for praise in a number of reviews, with *The Times* noting that 'Sheridan's production of his brother's play is sympathetic and witty and the performances he has drawn from the predominantly male company are extraordinary.' Gabriel Byrne played the part of Grennell, later taking over from Mannix Flynn as Curley when the production transferred to the Royal Court Theatre in London as part of the 1980 'Sense of Ireland' Festival, while Gerard McSorley played Lane, the evangelising IRA prisoner. With its prison setting and emphasis on tense male relationships, we can see in this, as in *No Entry*, the emergence of themes in the brothers' work that were to reappear in Sheridan's own films, notably 1993's *In the Name of the Father*.

Their collaboration continued with *Emigrants* (1978), again written by Peter and directed by Jim, a play about Irish emigration to England in the nineteenth century, this time with Shane Connaughton, who would later co-write the screenplay of *My Left Foot* (1989), in the lead role. Connaughton also took the role of Mick in *Down All the Days*, Peter Sheridan's adaptation of Christy Brown's autobiographical novel, which Jim Sheridan directed in 1982 for the Oscar Theatre in Dublin and which fed into *My Left Foot*. As well as staging *The Liberty Suit* in London, Jim Sheridan also directed James Plunkett's play *The Risen People* at the Institute of Contemporary Arts in 1980, earning some admiration if less praise for an ambitious staging that used every available space but left audience members somewhat in the dark as to exactly what was going on. In the same year, he directed Stephen Rea at the Abbey Theatre in Tom Murphy's *The Blue Macushla*, a black comedy about the links between para-militarism and crime.

Jim Sheridan also wrote a number of plays, again primarily for the Project during this period. One of these, *The Immigrant*, was born out of his own difficulties entering Canada in the early 1980s and anticipates many of the themes of *In America* (2003). In it, a newly arrived immigrant encounters a sequence of perils in the shape of a motley assortment of characters as he tries to enter and settle into Canadian society. As played by the second actor in this two-hander, these are a customs man, a transsexual prostitute, a Ku Klux Klansman, a janitor, an alcoholic bum, a Native American and several others, all of whom cast light on the tragedies and absurdities of Canadian life as seen from the perspective of its poorest members.

By the time *The Immigrant* was staged at the Project in 1982, Jim Sheridan had left Ireland, winding up in New York with his wife Fran and their two older daughters, Naomi and Kirsten (herself now a filmmaker). A third daughter, Tess, was born in America. Arriving in New York with a reputation as a radical playwright and director, Sheridan took over the running of the Irish Rebel Arts Center, which he renamed the Irish Arts Center. He also completed the six-week filmmaking course at New York University that constitutes his only formal film training. Here too, he wrote the screenplay for *Into the West*, which would eventually be directed by Mike Newell in 1992. Back in 1986, however, a career in film still seemed less than probable and Sheridan was struggling to make a living. One day, Gabriel Byrne walked into the Irish Arts Center and Sheridan handed him a copy of his screenplay for *Into the West*. By now a major film star, Byrne showed the script to his then wife, Ellen Barkin, and followed this up by approaching Harvey Weinstein at Miramax, the production company regarded as the saviour of the independent filmmaker. Byrne acted as Associate Producer for *Into the West* as well as taking one of its lead roles as the disillusioned traveller Papa Riley. By the time the funding was eventually in place and the film released, Jim Sheridan had himself broken into filmmaking with his 1989 Academy Award winning *My Left Foot*.

How do we reconcile the radical theatre work of the 1970s and 1980s with the commercially driven successes of the filmmaking years? For some critics, the gap is too great to bridge, with Sheridan's screen productions being commandeered as exemplars of Irish culture's capitulation to mammon, the *Riverdances* of the cinema world. *My Left Foot* was made at a time when it had seemed that a critical, independent filmmaking culture, structured on avant-garde and politically engaged principles, was the way forward for Irish cinema. These low-budget, experimental productions included *Poitín* (Bob Quinn, 1978), *Maeve* (Pat Murphy, 1981), *Our Boys* (Cathal Black, 1981) and *Pigs* (Joe Comerford, 1984). Suddenly, *My Left Foot* reversed the trend, garnering five Academy Award nominations and winning in two categories (Brenda Fricker for Best Supporting Actress and Daniel Day-Lewis for Best Actor). More than that, the film was made to the standards of the high quality, British realist television drama (not surprisingly, since it was funded by Granada Television, thus ensuring that all its profits were returned to Britain). It went on to make $14.7 million at the US box office, which, on a cost of $3 million, made it the tenth most profitable film released in America that year.

Sheridan followed this with *The Field* (1990), *In the Name of the Father* (1993), *The Boxer* (1997) and *In America*. He was the producer of Terry George's *Some Mother's Son* (1996), a film that is often regarded as a companion piece to his own Troubles films. His production company, Hell's Kitchen, formed with Arthur Lappin in 1983, has developed over twenty films, including the much-lauded *Bloody Sunday*, directed by Paul Greengrass (2001). Not all these productions have been as profitable as his first, but overall, in a country still struggling to develop an environment where filmmakers can work consistently and productively, Sheridan's achievement is extraordinary. *The Field* was Academy Award nominated in the Best Actor category; *In the Name of the Father* received seven Academy Award nominations and won the Golden Bear at 1994's Berlin Film Festival; *The Boxer* won the Goya (for Best European Film) in Spain; *In America* was nominated for three Academy Awards and between them the films have received a plethora of awards and nominations over the years.

Of course awards are not the only measure of a film's success, nor is profitability. Yet before moving on to consider some of the themes that emerge from Sheridan's films, we need to understand just how important the recognition he has received for his work has been, not just to him but also to the development of Irish cinema and to the country at large. When *My Left Foot* won its two Academy Awards in 1990, the Irish film industry was little more than a shopping list of aspirations. Despite the critical success of the independent films of the last decade or so, it still remained the case that most Irish stories were being told by outside filmmakers, working out of external industries. *The Quiet Man* (1952) might belong to the past but, in terms of popular filmmaking, little had been made since to counter the suggestion that Ireland was a country of cheerful leprechaun-like individuals always game for a song and a pint and a good communal fistfight. Ireland was now one of the few European countries not to have structures in place to subsidise even a modest level of commercial filmmaking, and Irish television had committed its meagre budget for fiction to successive soap operas.

With *My Left Foot*, Jim Sheridan and the film's producer, Noel Pearson, demonstrated that you could make Irish stories for a global audience, and you could do so on film. Following this, Neil Jordan's cluster of awards and the critical enthusiasm earned for *The Crying Game* (1992) consolidated that moment, forcing the Irish government of the day to recognise the vitality of film as a medium of national expression and leading to the introduction of a tax incentive system that placed Ireland on the filmmaking map and, for the first time, put Irish filmmaking on a semi-secure footing.

The sense of national pride engendered by the achievements of *My Left Foot* is immeasurable. Unemployment and its corollary, emigration, the Troubles in the North, divisive debates over social reform had all contributed to a perennial inferiority complex that insisted that to be Irish was to be geographically, socially and culturally marginalised. In retrospect, Sheridan's film seems like an early harbinger of things to come, a demonstration that international finance could fund Irish ambition and reconnect Ireland to the wider world.

Since then, Sheridan has remained one of the few Irish filmmakers, alongside Neil Jordan, consistently to gain high levels of studio funding for his productions. Undoubtedly he has had to make concessions along the way, and these include casting, plot development and subject matter. The inclusion of the 'Yank' (Tom Berenger) in *The Field* and the many and contentious plot simplifications of *In the Name of the Father* are two obvious incidents of changes made to please financiers. More generally, he has tended to graft indigenous Irish narratives onto universal story structures and, occasionally, shoehorn plots into generic templates. *The Boxer*, for instance, borrows from the conventions of the boxing drama, tracing the trajectory of an exceptional individual whose talents take him beyond the city streets on which he has acquired his skills and pitting him against the corrupt world of business and party politics. The Bull McCabe (Richard Harris) in *The Field* is a character whose provenance could be traced back to the Biblical Abraham, or to King Lear and whose final moments retread Cuchulain's descent into madness in Yeats's *On Baile's Strand*.

To be universal is not, as the last example demonstrates, necessarily to neglect to be Irish. If it renders his stories intelligible to viewers around the world, regardless of their background, it also demonstrably works for audiences at home where Sheridan's films are guaranteed to perform strongly. In part, this comes from the extraordinary performances that are a hallmark of a Sheridan production. Most famously, Sheridan's direction of Daniel Day-Lewis has resulted in three classic collaborations, not just the Academy Award winning role of Christy Brown in *My Left Foot*, but equally those of Gerry Conlon in *In the Name of the Father* and Danny Flynn in *The Boxer*. In all these films, Day-Lewis acts out the structuring conflict of the work, alternating between tragedy and an ironic humour that are in each case compelling. Harking back to Sheridan's days in theatre, the thread that binds all these works, and indeed the other films, is the conflict between masculinity and social structures, with Day-Lewis's character undergoing some kind of incarceration – in *My Left Foot*, it is the entrapment of his own body; in the other two, it is both a literal imprisonment and a socio-political one, that of a young man caught up in a narrow, regressive community. In common with so many Irish narratives, Sheridan's films focus on the rebellion of the son against the father and on a clash of generations that is as much symbolic as literal. The director's remarks about *In the Name of the Father* could equally be applied to his other films: 'The idea behind the film is that the father figure becomes a kind of decimated symbol when you have a crushed culture. Once you destroy the father figure, the figure of authority, then you haven't got a society.'

The 'crushed culture' of Irish society provides the background to all the films. In *My Left Foot*, it is there in the begrudging, narrow-minded neighbours; Mr Brown's (Ray McAnally) own vulnerability – to the comments of his peers, to the vagaries of the employment market – is expressed in outbursts of impotent temper, most frighteningly over his daughter's unplanned pregnancy. *The Field* is constructed around Richard Harris's larger than life performance of the Bull McCabe, a domineering because ultimately ineffectual patriarch, whose single-mindedness destroys first one of his sons, then the other. The competing tensions of patriarchy equally inform the Conlons' story, with Gerry moving from a rejection of his father's (Pete Postlethwaite) belief in state justice, through his embrace of the illegitimate law of the terrorist, embodied by the ruthless IRA prisoner, Joe McAndrew (Don Baker), to his final realisation that he must grasp the system his father submitted to and take charge of it if he is to find justice. *The Boxer* returns to themes of state incarceration, this time offering the young Liam (Ciaran Fitzgerald), whose father is in jail, a range of alternative father figures, just as the community, inevitably weakened by strife, itself must judge which of the male authority figures it must allow itself to be led by. Sheridan's most personal film to date, *In America,* also traces the journey the young father, Johnny Sullivan (Paddy Considine), must make, away from Ireland, into America, and deeper, into his own emotions where he mourns the death of his child and his own inability to prevent that death. In all these films, as in *Into the West*, it is only by making a journey, both literally and emotionally, that the central male protagonist can put behind him the crushed culture of traditional Ireland, and its continuing grip on modern Ireland, and reach some measure of autonomy. Failure to make or complete that journey, as in *The Field*, leads to tragedy.

The corollary to the seeking father/son relationship in Sheridan's films is the presence of the nurturing mother figure. Brenda Fricker's strong (in *My Left Foot*) and long-suffering (in *The Field*) mother harks back to another archetype of Irish culture, the Irish mother, the driving force of Irish family life. If Sheridan's mothers become more youthful after this (Emily Watson's Maggie in *The Boxer* is still a young woman), it is only in *In America* that the Irish mother, this time played by another English actor, Samantha Morton, is free to enjoy sex without guilt, even if her personality is still circumscribed by her motherhood.

This play on archetypes belies a fascination with people and their motivations. Sheridan's characters are animated not just by the performances, strong as they are, but by their director's own engagement with them. It is characters, to a far greater extent than plot, that drive the films, and it is through characters that audiences are expected to relate to plot. Thus, the impact of *In the Name of the Father* is achieved through identification with the individuals, rather than understanding their politics, if, indeed, they have any. Here is the storyteller at work, drawing in his listeners by creating a world of emotion that demands that you submit to it or be left outside of the charmed circle. Sentimentality is never far off, either, in a Jim Sheridan film, though when it seems most like overwhelming the narrative, the moment breaks up in ironic humour, rupturing the bond between viewer and character.

Looking back on a career that is far from over, we can see that Sheridan's early experience in Irish theatre, launched while a UCD student, offered him the space to explore many of the concerns that inform his later film work. The last twenty years have seen him break into the international circuit of film financing and distribution, enabling him to tell his tales to a world audience. His adherence to an aesthetic of realism and his character-led stories place Sheridan within a tradition that lies far outside that of the modernist strain of Irish literary arts and harks back to an older model of entertainment. Yet he also works within that most modern of artforms, cinema, and one with its base in popular culture. His success has been to adapt Irish stories to this model, to work within the compromises this entails and to retain his own, distinct voice.

SECONDARY REFERENCE

Ruth Barton, *Jim Sheridan: Framing the Nation* (Dublin: The Liffey Press, 2002).

Neil Jordan (b. 1950)

Katy Hayes

To line Neil Jordan up in a parade of voices emanating from UCD is to focus attention on the underlying presence of Ireland in his works. Despite his cosmopolitanism and sophistication, the Hollywood presence and the global ambition, the 'home place' is ever present, particularly in the fiction. The boy/man in the short story 'A Love' from *Night in Tunisia* (1976) declares: 'I wondered whether I'd rather be out of step here or in step in London, where the passions are rational' (105). I wonder has that question ever been fully answered. The talent seems to sit uneasily and edgily, not particularly belonging to any genre or scene. Certainly, Jordan is not content merely to be a Hollywood success story, a significant presence in the international celluloid industry. Inevitably he runs back to the more solitary pursuit of fiction. Literary fiction will never reach the market penetration of what one might call 'literary cinema' so the return to the touchstone of literary solitude must fulfill some other, quieter impulse: the need to express oneself without hauling a team of designers and accountants up a steep hill.

In an introduction to the American edition of the short stories, Sean O'Faolain wrote: 'A further cause for special interest in Neil Jordan is that while being thus engrossed in his locale he is in no way, as Joyce also was not, in the least bit parochial or regionalist. In fact, surprisingly and delightfully, the hero of the central story of this group of stories is American Jazz music, the objective correlative of his theme is an alto saxophone and its presiding deity is old Charlie (Bird) Parker.' O'Faolain was alert at this early stage to the international sensitivity and scope of Jordan. He sniffed the parallel with Joyce, another UCD graduate in whose heart there flickered an interest in cinema, as Joyce proved by establishing the Volta cinema in Dublin in 1912. Joyce also conducted a career of international dimensions while maintaining the primacy of the home place in his creative landscape.

Lending support to an organisation aiding the homeless in London, Neil Jordan recalled his own early years in that city living on the edges of society. He described how he always had the sense that for him things might have gone the other way and that, instead of enjoying major international success, he might easily have slipped into the marginal existence of the homeless. Jordan throughout his work displays an affinity with marginalised characters. This condition has been described by Martin Amis as 'tramp-dread': when asked why so many bums litter the pavements of his fictions, Amis replied that he was afraid he would become one, that he suffered from 'tramp-dread'. In 'Last Rites', the opening story of Jordan's first collection, a young builder's labourer takes a shower in Kensal Rise Baths. Having tidily masturbated, he slits his wrists. None of the onlookers, other Irish, Scottish and black labourers who find his body, wonders why he did it because they all have knowledge of the 'pain': 'A middle aged, fat and possibly simple negro phrased the thought: "Every day the Lord send me I think I do that. And every day the Lord send me I drink bottle of wine and forget 'bout doin that"' (19). All of Jordan's narratives contain marginalised peoples: prostitutes, depressives, transsexuals, fugitives and vampires. His talent remains an edgy one; with the occasional foray into the mainstream, he maintains his distinctive originality in what is a highly coercive and market-sensitive industry.

Far from slipping off the edge, Jordan has managed to work the system very effectively. His 1984 film *Company of Wolves*, which could be described as a feminist art-house parable, was cleverly excavated and presented as horror genre. This feminist reworking of the Little Red Riding Hood fairytale presents Rosaleen as sexual aggressor rather than victim and remains an unusual occasion of interplay between any mainstream Irish cultural force and the ideas of late twentieth-century feminism.

The creative partnership with co-writer Angela Carter's lush feminist vision was a touchstone in Jordan's interest in the gothic. Carter died in 1990; Jordan later said he felt her 'ghost' everywhere when he made *Interview with a Vampire* (1994), based on the novels of Anne Rice.

Jordan has placed himself in an angular position *vis-à-vis* gender relations. In *The Crying Game* (1992), the *coup de théâtre* is achieved when Dil first reveals her penis to the unsuspecting Fergus. When you hear this episode receiving a mention by Mayor Quimby in *The Simpsons* you know you've achieved deep market penetration of what are distinctly non-mainstream ideas. *The Crying Game*'s Oedipal crisis in reverse, where the woman is found not to lack a penis but, what's worse, to possess one, is a shocking experience for Fergus and for the unforewarned among the audience. But the scene remains confidently emotionally centred. As Dil later says: 'Even when you were throwing up, I could tell you cared.' Fergus immediately tries to dress Dil as a man, ostensibly to hide her from the IRA psychos who are pursuing him, but also in an effort to shore up the phallocentric norm. Jordan's characters are sexually creative: lesbian (*Mona Lisa*, 1985); incestuous or homosexual (*Shade*, 2004); whilst clearly hetero-sexual Michael Collins spends an awful lot of time in bed with Harry Boland (*Michael Collins*, 1996). It is not particularly useful to think of Jordan's characters in terms of conventional categories of sexual orientation, of the norm. As Col, the enigmatic barman, says in *The Crying Game*: 'Who knows the secrets of the human heart?'

Having briefly considered Jordan as an Irish cultural force, there is much to be said about him as an Irish cultural product. Having studied English and History in UCD, he demonstrates in his work a profound engagement with Irish history and a nar-rative obsession with the Civil War in particular. In the short story 'A Love', a young man home from London revisits his older lover in Dublin while the pageant of Eamon de Valera's funeral unfolds in the background. The romance is revealed in flashback: the motherless boy became lovers with the older woman who kept the coastal boarding house where he and his father stayed. The boy's conflict with his father is played out through her: 'And all the time for me there was my father lying underneath, cold, most likely, and awake and I wanted him to hear the beast I was creating with you ... for your body was like the woman he must have loved to have me' (108). While the boy becomes her lover, his father invites her out; in a particularly galling episode in a hotel the boy is required to pour sherry as his widower father conducts his arid courtship. Later that night, leaving her bed and taking her old civil-war gun, he shoots through the door of the bathroom in an unsuccessful attempt to kill the father.

This Oedipal drama is played out against the background of images of Eamon de Valera, in particular as described by the woman: 'I was taught to idolise him, everyone was. I remember standing at meetings, holding my father's hand, waving a tricolour, shouting Up Dev' (113). The boy/man's knowledge of Dev is mainly gleaned from pictures: 'that rain-soaked politician with his fist raised, clenched. Against something. Something' (108). Crossing the country to Co. Clare after Dev's funeral, their re-union is consummated in Lisdoonvarna, an inland resort spa town where the boy/man everywhere feels the absence of the sea.

Certain of these motifs become familiar when you look at Jordan's *oeuvre* over time. In 'A Love' there is the same motherless household as there is in 'Night in Tunisia'. But now the father and son are in conflict not over music lessons but over the affections of a woman who creates the triangle. Here the lover is a landlady, but in the later novels she is a tutor. She occupies the place of the mother in the household. And the Civil War provides an anvil upon which to grind this Oedipal passion. (His 1991 film *The Miracle* is the most direct version of the Oedipus story, as it mirrors the man falling in love with his actual mother, not knowing who she is, and dreaming the death of his father.)

In the novel *The Past* (1980), the narrator is on a quest to discover his paternity. This brings him to examine the romance of his grandparents, as revealed to him by an old family friend, Lili. Una and Michael O'Shaughnessy live out their extended honeymoon in an English seaside town in 1914, she already pregnant and a little moody, he conducting an affair with a woman he meets on the beach. They marry in innocence of their eventual political differences: 'because that was the first month and it would have still been a honeymoon month and the war hadn't yet broken out or the Parliamentary party been split and their bodies just might have made those shapes on the dampish bed like those maps in which the larger island envelops the smaller one, backwards admittedly, but expressive of an act of union rather than one of buggery or rape' (20). Here, the land mass is invoked to illustrate the relationship between Ireland and Great Britain. The submissive stance of the smaller island is acknowledged, but is not accepted as weakness; it is palpably denied. Una is a republican; Michael, after much deliberation, supports the Free State. Una has her feminine moods and her 'ancient irrationality'. Michael, from a Redmondite family, listens to the debates, and comes to a rational masculine conclusion.

After taking a ministerial post in the Free State Government, Michael O'Shaughnessy meets a fate similar to that of Kevin O'Higgins at the hands of assassins on a pavement in Booterstown. His actress wife, who has risen to become a star in the 'new style of theatre, peasant in emphasis, nationalist in theme' (41), gathers about her 'the last element necessary for nationalist sainthood – the odour of graveyards ... "Mick," she would proclaim to the handful of mourners "was a Republican ..."'(68). The Civil War corpse becomes a site of narrative conflict.

Rene, daughter of these two, and mother of the narrator, is left nearly penniless by the death of Una. She comes to teach Irish in the bohemian household of the Vance family. Of Huguenot origin, the Vances are in social decline, having lost their delft manufacturing business and their Meath estates. James Vance married a Catholic, and their son Luke was reared in that faith though his mother has since died. Rene thus enters this motherless household. The grandfather paints her, and James the father and Luke the agoraphobic son both woo her. The Vances live in Sydenham Villas, a terrace of houses in the seaside resort of Bray which stands perpendicular to the shore, a location which recurs in Jordan's work. Rene too becomes an actress and, now pregnant, joins the MacAllister fit-up touring company (reminiscent of Anew MacMaster), which criss-crosses Ireland on the trains, rolling in and out of small towns and seaside resorts. She is joined on tour by Luke, the vulnerable effeminate boy who finds he feels at 'home' (184) in the theatre. The climax of the novel occurs at the end, with the birth of the narrator. This occurs after a show in a hotel in Lisdoonvarna, where the protagonists are co-incidentally accompanied by Eamon de Valera on an election tour. Now the political circle has turned and the republicans are in government. Unknown to Rene, de Valera's driver Jack had been her father's Free State ministerial driver and a significant presence for her as a child. Rene has her baby, and the reader is uncertain whether it has been fathered by Luke or his father James. 'Could he be called a love-child? asks Lili' (231). The reader remains uncertain whether she is referring to the narrator or to Dev.

In the novel *Sunrise with Sea Monster* (1994) Neil Jordan turns his attention to the story of the Irish in the Spanish Civil War. Donal Gore is incarcerated in a Spanish prison awaiting likely execution, having gone there to fight against fascism. The impulse to join this foreign war was fostered by a conflict with his father Sam, an activist who had taken the Free State side in the Irish Civil War and who became a minister in the first government. As soon as he is old enough, Donal takes the republican side, partly to thwart his father: 'I joined a remnant of the splinters of that conflict, a wayward bunch of Republicans who, having exhausted the litany of betrayal at home, sought new possibilities abroad' (14). Donal denounces his father as a fascist, claiming 'you expounded your Fascist drivel with all the decorum of a gentleman. Where did you learn those words? he [the father] asked, those aren't your words. I'll make them mine, I said' (55). Thus the Free State side is taken by the rational father and the rebellious republican is the irrational son.

But the father and son are also in conflict over a woman. Rose has entered the motherless household as a music teacher. Once again the household is situated in the Bray seaside terrace, 'a line of three-storeyed late Georgian dwellings at right angles to the sea' (21). Once again the father is of Protestant origin. In this narrative (uniquely, I think) we get an account of the death of the mother from illness and the effect it has on the son: 'What I did know was that everything had changed and that my soul would change into a cold hard crystal because it had changed' (9–10).

Rose teaches piano to the musical boy and develops a relationship with him. She enters the household as a girl and grows to be a woman. During this time, Donal matures and the relationship with Rose becomes physical. Sam Gore runs for election in 1932 and loses: 'one morning the gaunt, iconic figure of de Valera himself harangued the Mass-goers from one side of the church railings, my father from the other ... [I] knew even then how unequal a contest it was' (36–7). Sam Gore does, in due course, secure a civil service job with the new republican administration and when he proposes to Rose and is accepted, Donal reacts with violent disapproval.

Incarcerated in Spain, while his cellmates are being systematically executed, Donal is brought before the Nazi Hans who keeps asking him: 'What brought you here?'(57) Donal's journey to Spain is part politics, part romantic chagrin, part suicide, and he has difficulty finding an answer to this complex question. 'My father's world, I tell him [Hans], was an unfinished one. I joined the Republican movement to bring it to some conclusion. His revolt had been stillborn, dissipating its energies in the nonsense of a Civil War. The State resulting from it was one of paralysis, echoed in himself'(63). Hans saves Donal from execution, almost against his will, and so enables him to return to Ireland.

His father has had a stroke and is now paralysed. Unable to speak, he is being nursed by Rose. The Second World War (or the Emergency) is in progress and the Nazi Hans contacts Donal, looking to connect with the IRA in order to promote England's difficulty as Ireland's opportunity. Donal is approached by Irish government authorities, carefully pursuing their policy of neutrality shaped by the 'Chief' Dev (144), and agrees to act as a double agent, to stitch the conspirators up. The IRA hatch a plot to blow up Madam Tussauds. 'Hit them where it hurts most. Their symbols'(128). They are to rendezvous with Hans in the Atlantic seaside resort of Spanish Point, where explosives will be unloaded from a German submarine.

Donal brings his *ménage-a-trois* to Lisdoonvarna under the pretence of looking for a cure for the paralysed father. They cross the country to the spa town, which is like a stranded seaside resort. Once again, Neil Jordan's characters leave the east coast in pursuit of catharsis in the west. Donal betrays the plotters and does Hans the favour of having him locked up in the Curragh for the rest of the war, declaring: 'Your war's obscene –' (162).

The characters are like revenants, like the undead, acting out an obsession with the Oedipal triangle and the Irish Civil War, trying to wrestle those subjects to the ground. These dynamics appear throughout Neil Jordan's work, particularly in the fiction, and like a dog worrying a bone, he seems to be endlessly trying to get it to yield up its value and its secrets. This repetitive methodological tick is mirrored by the presence of Stephen Rea in the films, acting out often very different parts and providing a familiar constant in the unfolding of different stories.

In the film *Michael Collins* (1996), Jordan finally lays the Civil War to rest. The period is lovingly recreated. In the opening sequence, the leaders of 1916 are pulled from the crowd by a brutal Detective Smith (Sean McGinley). One by one, they all emerge from their iconicity, step out of the teatowel representations of the Proclamation of the Republic: the profile of Pearse; the moustache and spectacles of Thomas Clarke; the unruly hair of Thomas MacDonagh. There is careful characterisation of both Michael Collins and Eamon de Valera. Their actions are both carefully motivated, even if the film's favourite is clearly the protagonist. The personal stories seamlessly intertwine with the political. Harry Boland and Michael Collins clash over the affections of Kitty Kiernan. Michael Collins resents Eamon de Valera travelling the globe whilst he is stuck doing the dirty work at home in Dublin. Collins and Dev vie for the loyalty of Harry Boland. With regard to Michael Collins, Neil Jordan said in an interview with Melvyn Bragg on ITV's *South Bank Show* in 1996: 'I had to clarify my attitude towards his capacity for violence.' And so the modern Irish man, happy with Ireland's emergence from under the thumb of the British Empire, must come to terms with his qualms about the niceties of the methods of its achievement. The canonisation of Michael Collins, his veneration in the film, is a repair of the rupture of the Civil War, with an undertow of apology to the (founding) fathers for not having been there. The generation of the forties and fifties was conscious of the price paid for Irish freedom, for the 'stillborn' revolution, not only in the lives lost, but also in the poisoning of the next generation after the Civil War. A particular legacy was the silences and emotional shut-down of the fathers: the brutalised fathers who strut the pages of John McGahern, the 'paralysis' which censored James Joyce and Kate O'Brien. Thus, in *Michael Collins*, the imperfect revolution has been reformatted and presented as perfect art.

And so the Civil War has been put to bed. Jordan's next novel, *Shade* (2004), is also an historical work. It covers the period from 1897 to 1950 (incidentally the half century before the author's birth) but it concentrates on other things. *Shade* portrays a battle, but a faraway one: fighting in the Dardanelles in the First World War: 'There's a war in Europe that pays better than Keiling's farm' (164). The events of the Anglo-Irish War are touched on: the factory belonging to the English father is burnt out, and the house is only saved from being razed by the half-crazy George, who keeps a flame for the heroine, Nina. For this act of love, he receives 'what is colloquially called the mother and father of a hiding. It takes seven of them, with hurley sticks and pickaxe handles, given his size and his strength' (272). But these events are seen as local and personal, rather than impacting on national matters and the emerging state.

This book is very firmly focused on the personal, the stifling nature of family life, love, mental illness. It engages with landscape and myth and folklore. It returns to some of Jordan's touchstones: there is Gregory, the motherless boy; and there is the sea, always the sea. The mud flats oozing between children's toes. The delights of being a child amongst the sand dunes. The Laytown horse races. Above all it portrays the theatre and early cinema, and the necessity of art, the refuge that art provides from life. As Nina says: '[I] walked on stage and put that ache inside me to work' (247). This analysis of the function of art is there in the very early work, in the wealth that the boy in 'Night in Tunisia' finds when he finally plays the saxophone: 'He fashioned his mouth round the reed till the sounds he made became like a power of speech, a speech that his mouth was the vehicle for but that sprang from the knot of his stomach, the crook of his legs' (69).

Primary references

Fiction

Neil Jordan, *Night in Tunisia and Other Stories* (Dublin: Co-op Books, 1976; New York: George Braziller, 1980).
—, *The Past* (London: Abacus/Sphere, 1982).
—, *Sunrise with Sea Monster* (London: John Murray, 2004).
—, *Shade* (London: John Murray; Dublin: Penguin Ireland, 2004).

Films

Company of Wolves (GB, 1984).
The Miracle (GB, 1991).
The Crying Game (GB, 1992).
Michael Collins (USA, 1996).

Secondary references

Emer Rockett and Kevin Rockett, *Neil Jordan: Exploring Boundaries* (Dublin: The Liffey Press, 2003).

FRANK McGUINNESS (B. 1953)

Joseph Long

At one level, Frank McGuinness's play *Carthaginians*, premiered in 1988, can be seen as an exploration of trauma and healing. A small group of people from the city of Derry – three women, three men – is squatting in the cemetery outside the city walls. Each of them in different ways, directly or indirectly, has been shattered by the events of Bloody Sunday, where, on 30 January 1972, thirteen young protestors taking part in a Civil Rights march were shot dead in the street by the forces of the British Army. For the characters in the play, not all the pain was inflicted by the toll of political events. Maela, in particular, has suffered the loss of her daughter who died of cancer on the infamous Sunday but, as she walks home from the hospital, at every street corner the tally of the dead is spiraling upwards and the city itself is becoming a living mausoleum of the slain:

> I'm walking home through my own city … Two dead, I hear that in William Street. I'm walking through Derry and they're saying in Shipquay Street there's five dead. I am walking to my home in my house in the street I was born in and I've forgotten where I live. I am in Ferryquay Street and I hear there's nine dead outside the Rosville flats. (352)

To reach this point of recognition and tell her story, Maela has an inner journey to make.

The central scene of the play is a fantastical and farcical acting-out of the traumatic events scripted and stage-managed by Dido, a play-within-the-play derisively entitled *The Burning Balaclava*, and which takes on the healing function of a psychodrama. Dido distributes the *dramatis personae* on a principle of cross gendering and the reversal of roles. Thus the one-time republican activist Paul is given a blond wig and must play the part of the Protestant girlfriend, Mercy Dogherty. 'How am I a Protestant with a name like Docherty?' he objects. 'You spell Dogherty with a "g",' retorts Dido (332), the relevance of the proposed emendation being far from clear. Most of the characters discover they are to be named as variants on Doherty/O'Doherty. 'Everybody in Derry's called Doherty,' comments Hark, 'it's a known fact' (332). Dido himself is left to play two parts simultaneously, the pram-pushing Doreen – 'one of life's martyrs who never complains' (334) – and the British Soldier, 'in deep torment because he is a working class boy sent here to oppress the working class'. *The Burning Balaclava* is the catalyst which allows the characters in the play to release themselves from the grip of the past, to realise that they are themselves the very Dead whose resurrection they have been waiting for. The play-within-the-play has been compellingly analysed elsewhere in terms of group psychotherapeutic practice and, in particular, the techniques of psychodrama as developed by J.L. Moreno after the First World War. However, without denying the validity of such analysis, it is revealing to examine other strands within the texture and complexity of Frank McGuinness' dramatic writing.

Dido is an openly gay character and when in Scene 5 he enters brandishing the script of his newly written playlet, he is outrageously dressed in drag. As gay playwright, he has assumed the identity of Fionnuala McGonigle. By mischievously playing on his initials, Frank McGuinness has projected a figure of the author into his own text, but this playwright, we learn to our surprise, is French. With a name like Fionnuala? *Sans problème …* it is to be 'pronounced Fionn – u – ala' (331)! Dido-in-Drag reveals his character's mission:

> Oui. I have come to your city and seen your suffering. Your city has just changed its name from Londonderry to Derry, and so I changed my name to Fionnuala in sympathy. What I see moves me so much I have written a small piece as part of your resistance. (331)

The target of this lampooning might well be seen, in general terms, less with reference to the events of January 1972 than to a more recent period, ten years later, when the death of Bobby Sands and the ordeal of the republican hunger-strikers created unprecedented interest and sympathy throughout continental Europe, and brought, specifically, droves of French journalists and intellectuals to Derry. The focused attention of foreign media was generally received with sharp suspicion by the nationalist community of Derry, who had learned by experience to mistrust the appropriation of their situation and their objectives by left-wing ideologues of every hue.

One French playwright and filmmaker had, however, won the trust of the Derry Youth and Community Workshop, and that was Armand Gatti. Through my own mediation, he put in place a community-based film project and, after a lengthy period of preparation, the first week of the shooting schedule in May 1981 coincided, by a painful irony of circumstances, with the death of Bobby Sands and the turmoil that ensued. Gatti's experimental scripting of his film had involved gathering stories and experiences from the unemployed young people (both Catholic and Protestant) attending the Workshop, and also from those of the adult population of Derry who agreed to take part in the project. Having assembled these anecdotes into a formal script, he invited the young people and the adults to play, in the film, the fictionalised version of themselves, as appeared in the script. In most cases, this was agreed. Thus it came about that a real-life episode in the life of the Workshop was transposed into the film, namely an exercise in group dynamics, in which the young people were called upon to act out roles most opposed to their own beliefs and situations. Protestant young people were to re-invent themselves as IRA activists; Catholic youngsters were to project themselves into the role of members of the RUC or the British Army; pacifists were to be militants; hardliners were to be clergymen; and so forth. The Director of the Workshop at the time, who had devised this experiment in self-questioning both in real-life and in the fictional world of the film, was a visionary community leader known widely by the nickname of Paddy Bogside and whose name was Paddy Doherty. The issue which, in the film, challenges the assumptions of the young people is the death of a British soldier who falls victim to a shooting incident and who is revealed to be an unemployed young man from the north of England whose social circumstances have brought him to that end.

Dido's lampooning of stereotypes in *The Burning Balaclava* has therefore some more specific targets than might at first appear. The targets, all in all, are many and varied. They include some sacred icons of nationalist sentiment, from the pathos of Sean O'Casey's evocations of nationalist motherhood in *Juno and the Paycock*, derisively parodied at several points with lines such as: 'Son, son, where were you when my Sacred Heart was riddled with bullets?' (342) or the consecrated media icon of a priest waving a white handkerchief under gunfire, to the cliché of the socialist construction of the working-class British soldier. The wider target is, clearly enough, the inadequacy of any ideology or any form of representation to account com-prehensively for the contradictions of experience, and the way discourse appropriates and distorts the reality it claims to express, an issue which Frank's play has in common with Brian Friel's *The Freedom of the City*.

Frank McGuinness' ironic deconstruction of Gatti's script and indeed of his very presence in Derry is therefore part of a larger scheme, and clearly not a specific score to settle with the French writer. Nonetheless, it has to be admitted that Frank's personal encounter with Armand Gatti had been somewhat fraught. Gatti's own ideological position is complex enough. He has never been a member of any political party: his driving philosophy is a form of utopian anarchism, which he traces back, in part through his own father's experiences, to the Anarcho-Syndicalist movement of the 1920s, and which has as its references, among others, Antonio Gramsci in Italy or, in Russia, Bakunin and Makhno. Frank's engagement with politics is based on personal witness and an acute awareness of the ambiguities on every side. He felt, as he has expressed to me on occasion, that there were enough complexities in the Northern situation without Gatti adding further complexities of his own. On the other hand, his encounter with Gatti's dramatic writing had been a shock and a revelation, and he acknowledges to this day the extent to which Gatti's work first opened up for him the full potential of theatre and the 'utopian space' of the stage.

Frank's encounter with the French playwright dates back to 1977, when Gatti came to UCD for the English-language premiere of his play *The Stork*, which I had translated and staged with the UCD Dramatic Society. In the seventies, as no doubt it does today, UCD Dramsoc offered a space where encounters and commitments could develop, where a production such as *The Stork* could rehearse for three months in spite of little resources and where many of the leading talents in Irish theatre today first began to emerge. Frank and I had already worked together over a couple of years on different theatre productions. The previous year, he had played Henry Bolingbroke in Shakespeare's *Richard II*, with a controlled intensity and presence in his performance that did much to swing the production, as intended, away from an elegiac lament over the dethroned Richard and towards an exploration of politics and power, anticipating the later Henry plays.

In Gatti's *The Stork*, Frank was cast as Engineer Kawaguchi. As often in Gatti's formal drama, the character is based on documented real-life experience. On 6 August 1944, the fictitious Kawaguchi, like his real-life counterpart, was working on a construction site in Hiroshima at the moment the first atomic bomb was dropped. Being a strong swimmer, he escapes by the river from the inferno on either bank. By evening, he makes his way to the shore. He clambers onto a freight train, not knowing where he is or where he's going. Three days later, the train has brought him to Nagasaki, in time to witness the second bomb. In order to dramatise experience of such a scale, both personal and historic, Gatti moves away from the conventions of realism and its contrived plausibility. Thus, Frank McGuinness as performer is not asked to make himself up and move and speak as if he were a survivor who had received two massive doses of radiation within three days. There might seem to be something presumptuous or even obscene about such a mode of representation on the stage. Instead, at the start of the play, the performers present themselves as a group of volunteer workers clearing the ruined streets of Nagasaki. They have decided not to take part in the celebrations to mark the Commemoration of the Dead: instead, they have decided to present a play and each performer has chosen an atomised object from the rubble of the city. Frank McGuinness's character has chosen a burnt-out watch, and that object will conjure up the Engineer Kawaguchi to whom the watch once belonged. The performer may therefore speak *as the watch*, that is, as a carbonised relic, or as the one-time Kawaguchi, or indeed as the volunteer worker in the here-and-now. The play will thus move seamlessly between the 'one-time' before the bomb and the here-and-now. A central issue of the play is: how can those from before the trauma find a language to speak to us in the here-and-now? How can a carbonised watch speak to us and what can it say? And how can we, in the here-and-now, as volunteer workers or as members of their audience, find words to cope with what is an undeniable part of our past and part of what we have now become?

Frank McGuinness's plays of survival, *Carthaginians* and *Observe the Sons of Ulster Marching towards the Somme* (1985), have deep affinities with Gatti's plays of survival, *The Stork* (1971) and *The Second Life of Tatenberg Camp* (1962). Frank saw the latter play at the Lyric Theatre, Belfast, where I directed it in March 1979. These affinities are not on the surface, in the co-incidence of characters or events. They spring from fundamental dramaturgical choices. With both dramatists, the plays centre primarily on a group of characters rather than on individuals. They focus on what constitutes the group, what process brings them together in the first place and what sustains the fragile identity that the group represents. The group has endured an historic and destructive experience, be it, with Frank McGuinness, the Battle of the Somme or Bloody Sunday, or, with Gatti, the annihilation wrought by the atomic bomb or by the experience of a concentration camp. There is a particular tension between personal experience, historic moment and the possibility of healing. The outcome for the group becomes a pointer for ourselves.

The group of volunteers in *The Stork* has come together around a dying child, Oyanagi, a victim of atomic radiation, with the project of making a thousand paper storks to save her life. She dies, and the thousandth stork, which was never made, becomes the central symbol of the play. Here Gatti has transposed the Japanese legend of the crane as giver of health, and the practice of hanging paper cranes, in the origami tradition of paper folding, around the bed of a sick person. His use of the legend echoes the real-life experience of Sasaki Sadako, a Japanese child victim of the effects of radiation, whose vain attempt to construct a thousand paper cranes before she died became the emblem of the Peace Movement in the fifties. In Gatti's play, Tomiko, one-time Hostess of the Tea Ceremony, pieces together a garment for the Day of the Dead: 'Do you know why I took to sewing this kimono today? Because I thought that Oyanagi must have grown. And that she would be happy to see that we think of her as a living person, already of an age to wear a woman's kimono' (119). Her gesture echoes that of Maela, in *Carthaginians*, as she lays out her child's garments on a grave and, in her state of denial, makes ready for her dead daughter's birthday:

> Greta: What age would she have been?
> Maela: You mean what age she is?
> *Silence.*
> I'm saving for her birthday. (*Whispers*) A leather jacket. (300)

The hope of a positive future is invested, in both plays, in the character who challenges the enclosed existence of the group, their self-imposed incarceration and their refusal of a world which is moving on without them. In Frank's play, it is Dido who suggests, in the final scene, the possibility of reconciling past and future, or rather of carrying the past into the future, without denial or capitulation, as he takes leave of the others in a movement of transcendence:

> While I walk the earth, I walk through you, the streets of Derry. If I meet one who knows you and they ask, how's Dido? Surviving. How's Derry? Surviving. Carthage has not been destroyed. Watch yourself. (379)

In Gatti's play, it is the demobilised soldier Enemon who leaves, who sets out to challenge the world, and it is Tomiko, in the final scene, who evokes, like Dido, the possibility of the past speaking to the future, and enters a plea for recognition and acceptance:

> Forgive us if our district is different from yours. Ours faces the sea – Yours faces the sky – Between the two, the ruins of Nagasaki circle the earth. – If one day they come to rest among us, who will be able to recognise them (and who will know how to speak to them)? We are clumsy in what we call life. (162)

Frank McGuinness's writing for the theatre is in the nature of a conscious project, consciously pursued over a quarter of a century. He has extended the accepted boundaries of what can be represented on the Irish stage. He has also explored a full gamut of different modes of representation and has contributed to widening the horizon of expectations which an audience brings to the experience of theatre. His theatre is, in a sense, a theatre of extremes. In *Someone Who'll Watch over Me* (1992), an intimate chamber piece with three characters, he brings us close to a form of realist documentary drama, based as it is on accounts by Brian Keenan of his hostage experience. In *Mary and Lizzie*, premiered by the Royal Shakespeare Company at the London Barbican in 1989, he sketches out an epic canvas, closest perhaps of all his plays to Gatti's 'utopian space', where imagination has only the limits which it invents for itself. In that play, the historic journey of Mary and Elizabeth Burns brings the audience from a time-out-of-time where women chant in Gaelic in the tree-tops to Manchester in the mid-nineteenth century and a dinner party with Karl and Jenny Marx; and from a descent into the underworld to meet a dead father to somewhere closer to present times, to the Stalinist work-camps and the long queues of women in deportation. The scope of the issues which Frank McGuinness opens up in his theatre and the energy of his explorations in dramatic form have placed contemporary Irish theatre in the mainstream of European consciousness and imagination.

PRIMARY REFERENCES

Frank McGuinness, *Observe the Sons of Ulster Marching towards the Somme, Carthaginians*, in *Plays 1* (London: Faber and Faber, 1996).
—, *Mary and Lizzie, Someone Who'll Watch over Me*, in *Plays 2* (London: Faber and Faber, 2002).
Armand Gatti, *The Second Life of Tatenberg Camp, The Stork*, in Joseph Long (ed.), *Armand Gatti: Three Plays* (Sheffield: Sheffield Academic Press, 2000).
Armand Gatti's Derry-based film *Nous étions tous des noms d'arbre* was distributed in the UK with the co-operation of the British Film Council by Other Cinema, under the title *The Writing on the Wall*, and was shown on Channel 4 television in March 1983. Prix Jean Delmas at Cannes Film Festival, 1982.

ÉILÍS NÍ DHUIBHNE (B. 1954)

Derek Hand

Éilís Ní Dhuibhne's UCD background in both English literature and folklore has meant that her writing confronts contemporary Irish life in original and innovative ways. The combination of her literary concerns with her interests in folklore has meant, too, that all of Ní Dhuibhne's writing is marked with a deep concern not only for the stories that she tells but also the nature of the medium through which they are told. Her work – at the level of form as well as content – reflects the uncertainties and the anxieties surrounding the issue of Irish identity, eschewing the stereotypes and closed patterns and expectations of what an Irish writer should be doing and mirroring, opening up many categories for further investigation and consideration. Her work explores the fruitful connections between the past and the present, juxtaposing the folktale form with up-to-date stories. Her writing hopes to be true to the claims of tradition while also being capable of engaging with the challenges of the new. Her difficulty, as is the difficulty for many of her characters, is with discovering a language or a voice or, indeed, a form that might truly map this experience.

One central area in Irish writing and culture where these issues have been worked out is in the city/rural divide. This divide has always been much more than simply a choice of appropriate images and themes. From the Literary Revival onwards, attitudes to country and city have been inextricably bound up with issues of power – with who is speaking and being spoken about. These in turn are connected to concepts of modernity, progress and tradition in an Irish frame.

Many contemporary writers in fiction merely perpetuate either-or stereotypes and do very little to develop any real understanding about urban and rural life as it is lived in the present moment. There are notable exceptions, however, and Éilís Ní Dhuibhne is one of them. Her writing is an intelligent and enlightening engagement with some of the questions surrounding cultural attitudes to both the city and the countryside in Ireland. In relation to the Irish conception of the rural and urban spaces, her work offers the possibility of renegotiating and reimagining, of getting beyond restrictive stereotypes toward a more accurate appraisal of and engagement with contemporary Ireland.

Two pieces, in particular, deal with this issue: her short story 'Blood and Water' (1988) and a reworking of that original treatment in the novel *The Dancers Dancing* (1999). There are obvious and wholly expected differences of form and content between the short story and the novel. However, there is also a purposeful development of numerous themes and issues from the earlier to the later work. Discernible, therefore, is a growing awareness of the complexity of the urban-rural relationship in Irish culture and an awareness, too, of what is at stake in the broadest sense in attitudes to the country and the city in an Irish context.

Both works make connections to the earlier work of James Joyce, especially 'Blood and Water' which, it can be argued, is an updating and rewriting of 'The Dead'. The quandary with the relationship between city and country articulated in Joyce's story remains, as do difficulties surrounding language and style. If Joyce and other writers of his time concerned themselves with discovering 'images and symbols adequate to [their] predicament' (Seamus Heaney) – or, to put it another way, a 'language' or 'words' adequate to their predicament – then this is still a concern for contemporary Irish writers.

This is precisely the situation in Ní Dhuibhne's short story 'Blood and Water'. The unnamed narrator of the story searches for an authentic language that will be true to her being: she is trying to discover a voice. The narrator tells of family visits from Dublin to Donegal in her childhood and her aunt by whom she is embarrassed both as a child and as an adult telling the story.

She returns to Inishowen a number of years later as a student at an Irish summer college. Her position as both an 'outsider' and a 'native' is a problem for her and ultimately leads her into an act of denial when she does not acknowledge her aunt's attempts to greet her on the street of the town. Indeed, she does not acknowledge any connection with her aunt at all.

There is no sense of adequate resolution at the close of the story; rather, there appears to be an awareness – possibly for the reader only – that her difficulties run deeper than merely a problem with her aunt. The predominant sense is of the narrator being utterly disconnected from her surroundings and culture. The echoes here to Joyce's 'The Dead' clearly resonate. Not unlike Gabriel Conroy, the narrator is presented looking eastwards over the Irish Sea with her back set firmly against the west, engaging with foreign languages and cultures. The narrator associates the west of Ireland rural space with tradition, while seeing the urbanised east representing modernity. This relationship is further complicated when it is acknowledged that the division works – as most divisions do – in a hierarchical manner: tradition/ countryside is seen as backward, whereas the city and modernity are thought of as progressive and forward looking.

Confusion, however, is at the heart of the narrator's relation-ship with the countryside. In her childhood holiday visits to Donegal and her aunt's home enchant her and she is excited to participate in the chores and the everyday life of the house. However, we can begin to question the narrator's stance when near the end of the story she tells us:

> My aunt is still alive, but I haven't seen her in many years. I never go to Inishowen now. I don't like it since it became modern and littered with bungalows. (61)

One presumes that the people of Donegal themselves, if anyone bothered to ask them, would be loathe to declare their preference for the hard life of the old days over the comfort possible in the contemporary world.

On one level Ní Dhuibhne is offering the reader a comic portrayal of misreading and misunderstandings on the part of the narrator. However, beneath this veneer of a comic cultural clash,

Ní Dhuibhne is able to investigate the complicated relationship between tradition and modernity. Her engagement with the countryside, when looked at with this in mind, shows that it is one of her being almost a tourist from another land – the Donegal landscape and the lives lived there are as exotic and interesting as if they were some undiscovered country. Thus, that feeling of disconnectedness that pervades the close of the story actually interfuses the entire narrative. This is brought out wonderfully in the image of a 'big splodge of a dirty yellow substance' that the narrator finds in the scullery of her aunt's house. She believes it is a fungus of some kind and is repelled by it. However later, as she says:

> When I was taking a course in ethnology at the university, I realised that the stuff was nothing other than butter, daubed on the wall after every churning, for luck. (56)

She is cut off and alienated from the traditions of her community and culture, and ironically has to go to University to discover knowledge about her own way of life.

The distance between the narrator and traditional culture is emphasised in her use of language. She describes holiday journeys to her aunt's like this:

> The trips were delightful odysseys through various flavours of Ireland: the dusty rich flatlands outside Dublin, the drumlins of Monaghan with their hint of secrets and better things to come, the luxuriant slopes, rushing rivers and expensive villas of Tyrone, and finally, the ultimate reward, the furze and heather, the dog roses, the fuchsia, of Donegal. (53)

This passage would seem to be more appropriate to a travel guide of Ireland than to a middle-aged woman trying to come to terms with her past. Much of her description of her aunt's home seems also to be out of place. The detail she goes into, on one level, is quite brilliant – reconstructing, as it does, the place in words. And yet, it too smacks not so much of the travel guide but of an academic dissertation:

> Residences were thatched cottages ... 'the Irish peasant house' ... or spare grey farmhouses ... My aunt's house was of the

slated, two-storey variety, and it stood, surrounded by a seemingly arbitrary selection of outhouses, in a large yard called 'the street.' (53)

It can be noticed how the narrator is sensitive to her own use of language: the inverted commas of the 'Irish peasant house' and the 'street' take on an ironic quality for her, as well for the reader.

Throughout the narrative there are moments when different forms, and the hint of different discourses, can be discerned. The narrator struggles to discover a voice/language or form appropriate to her, and to the story she is attempting to tell. Seeking refuge in such stylistic imitation serves only to underline her deep-rooted confusion and uncertainty about her position.

Joyce's Gabriel Conroy, too, faced a similar dilemma. He looks toward Europe for cultural sustenance and meaning and is baited by Miss Ivors for his ignorance of his own culture. By using an interplay of images of east and west, life and death, past and present throughout the story Joyce is able to present this problem to the reader. In that last paragraph Gabriel famously declares: 'The time had come for him to set out on his journey westward.' He recognises the limitations of his supposed modernity: that it is not enough to embrace modernity without simultaneously engaging with the past or what is termed traditional. Conceivably what Gabriel learns is that it is *not* actually possible simply to 'escape' the past; but, rather, it must be continually negotiated and dealt with – no other option is feasible. That *is* the modern condition.

Ní Dhuibhne's narrator is not granted such an epiphany at the close of her narrative. She decides nothing at the end. She does acknowledge that her Spanish husband and her posh accent, while outwardly signs of modernity and thus contentment, are possibly only 'camouflage'. Hers is a circumstance worse than Gabriel's position at the close of 'The Dead': he, at least, can imagine a future, can project into the future. She appears to be immobile and stagnant: cut off from her past, but also importantly, cut off from her future.

A decade later Éilís Ní Dhuibhne returns to the circumstances and the world of the short story with her novel *The Dancers Dancing*. The year is 1972 and the action moves between Dublin and the Gaeltacht of Donegal. Orla Crilly is the character holding the narrative together. Her dawning awareness of the changes in herself – mentally and physically – brings a coherence and unity to the story being told. Once again there are echoes of Joyce in Ní Dhuibhne's choice of the *Bildungsroman* genre to tell her story of Orla's maturation.

In a sense, nothing happens in the novel and yet at the same time everything happens: friends are made and discarded; boys loom large and then fade from view. The adult world of the worsening violence in the North of Ireland is the very raw and immediate political backdrop to the story being played out in the foreground. The reality of this crisis is represented by the presence of two girls, Jacqueline and Pauline, from Derry – the scene of Bloody Sunday in January 1972. The issue of the North becomes one more fact to be assimilated and negotiated by Orla and her Dublin friends, as they make their way in the unfamiliar world of the Irish summer school.

Orla's inchoate and developing perception is expressed and amplified brilliantly by Ní Dhuibhne in terms of the form, or forms, operating within the novel. The opening chapter of the novel, 'The Map', is highly self-conscious, raising questions about the nature of stories and storytelling. Like maps, stories are means of seeing and understanding the world; they are, in the words of the narrator: 'Half true like all truisms. Half false' (3). This self-consciousness is continued into the second chapter with the reader being offered a type of 'still-life' portrait of Orla and her friends. It is impressionistic: a mood picture, a piece of a map that must be put together to make a coherent whole. Another piece of the jigsaw puzzle is presented in the following chapter where an opposition is established between Dublin and Tubber – the Donegal Gaeltacht – between the English and Irish languages, between work and play, past and present. The difficulty for Orla is made clear: the map she uses at home will need readjustment in Tubber, for each place operates within its own rules and regulations. These opening chapters highlight a fundamental feature of the novel. If, in the short story, the narrator groped about for a style or a language of her own, then in *The Dancers Dancing* it can be said that she finds herself caught between forms. She strives for a unitary narrative, a complete perspective or map of this fictional world, but can only offer momentary glimpses, disjointed bits and pieces that undermine the creation of an extended, uninterrupted and whole story. In a way, the work exists in a plane between the short story form and the novel form.

Time, too, appears unsettled in the novel. There exists an ironic distance between the very fixed date for the action and the present moment of the narrator. One chapter heading: 'The truce is over (but not to worry it's 1972)' (98), highlights this uneasy relationship. The narrator is playfully signalling that the past or history is never safely done or finished in an Irish context, that there is always the possibility that the past can erupt disturbingly into the present moment. Part of the narrator's difficulty, then, is in trying to come to some form of understanding about the past.

Uncertainty also surrounds the matter of who is telling this story. In 'Blood and Water' it was a straightforward affair with a first-person narrator. In the novel, although it is predominantly a third-person narrative, the narrator is not coldly objective and omniscient. Then, in the final chapter, the reader is presented with Orla, in the present, as the teller of her own story. It can be argued, perhaps, that the struggle toward unique articulation manifested in the short story is more fully elaborated here. There are instances within the novel when different voices and different perspectives are offered and heard. One such intrusion – for it occurs without introduction or subsequent comment – renders the local Donegal accent (42–3). No truly relevant information is communicated to the reader and it seems strange and very much out of place. Another such occasion occurs in the chapter entitled 'A traditional Irish schoolhouse' when the narrative slips from Standard English into a rendering of Irish through English (35–7). While lacking the polish and the poetry of J.M. Synge's use of Hiberno-English, the English in Ní Dhuibhne's work mimicking the forms of Irish grammar makes the English language unfamiliar and exotic to the reader.

So, on a more ambitious level than in 'Blood and Water', we observe Ní Dhuibhne representing a struggle toward expression on the part of the narrator who tries out these various voices and perspectives, playing with the different styles and the accents available to her. Unlike the earlier story, however, Orla's own voice is not lost or subsumed into these others. Rather, the effect generated is one of comparison, of Orla testing these other modes of seeing the world, and through an act of ventriloquism coming to know and appreciate her own individual voice. Certainly Orla requires, it seems, a different voice to some of the other girls at the Irish college. She is not just a 'scholar' visiting from the outside, but also someone with family ties to Tubber through her father:

> She would settle for being anybody but herself, Orla of the double allegiances, Orla of the city and the country, Orla who belongs in both places and belongs in neither. (29)

Her sense of identity is put under pressure as the strict code of difference by which she operates becomes increasingly meaningless.

It is, however, Ní Dhuibhne's brilliant deconstruction of these supposed differences between urban and rural life and the slow uncovering of realities behind apparently uncomplicated preconceptions that open up the narrative and consequently Orla's received conception of herself and her position. In a series of revelations and reversals Orla begins to discover that what she once thought of as certain and unproblematical is very much the opposite. The Banatee of the house Orla is staying in is, she learns, not from Tubber at all but from Scotland. Also, despite her mother's thick Dublin accent, she is from England. Slowly, Orla begins to realise that behind outward signs – such as accents and the place where one lives – can be found concealed facts far more interesting than her own preconceived notions of what ought to be, gleaned from Enid Blyton books (27–8). She learns, too, that her builder father, by whom she is embarrassed, possesses an unexpected romantic side when she discovers his love of poetry.

Her superior and patronising attitude to the rural world is undermined with a short interlude telling the story of Sava, one of the daughters of the house she stays at in Tubber. For Sava, with her life of dances, boys and sex, the rural space is not backward or restrictive. That estimation is one imposed and configured from the perspective of the city. Beneath difference are similarity and numerous points of connection. For Orla this kind of reversal of oppositions and hierarchies possesses a personal resonance. She tells of how her family has had to take lodgers into her home in Dublin. Her lot is similar to that of the Banatee, Sava and their family: each is forced to take in paying 'guests' to make ends meet, in order to survive and supplement income.

This intrusion into her home, as Orla sees it, means a significant loss of privacy for her, as the private space of home is transformed into a very public one. It is not just the physical sphere, though, which these men inhabit:

> Images of men who lived in her house but to whom she would never utter a word, men who did not just invade her bedroom, courtesy of their five pounds a week, but also had the power, unconsciously, to take up residence in her head. (82)

Orla's admission here allows the reader to begin to come to some form of understanding of what is at stake for her in her construction of an 'ideal' identity. It prompts her subsequent recognition of the real choices she must make in coming to know who she might be. It is not simply a discovery of a language or voice that she can be comfortable with but perhaps, more importantly, a place out of which such a voice might emerge. That place is the 'Burn'. There are five visits made – with some of the other girls and on her own – to the Burn throughout the novel. Each visit is accorded a chapter and these punctuate the action of the novel, becoming the site around which Orla's development and maturation are recorded. It is a place outside the constricting maps of either the city or the countryside, at once intimate and mysteriously unknown. In this secret world Orla has access to aspects of herself to this point denied: the wild and forbidden become possible in the Burn. It is a place that Orla can begin to be herself – simply and uncomplicatedly (73).

The holiday comes to an end and the girls return to Dublin and home, back into their previous lives and their previous roles. The last chapter presents Orla, looking back at that time and commenting on what occurred subsequently. The shift from the distance of a third person to the intimacy of the first-person narrator has already been alluded to as a formal expression of the pervasive uncertainty within the novel. It is curious, too, because it fails to resolve sufficiently some of the strands of the narrative. Ní Dhuibhne is wary of wrapping things up neatly, as if she, through her character Orla, is unsure exactly as to what the story she has been telling might actually mean.

As in the short story, it is the figure of the aunt who signals the type of revolution that needs to take place in Orla's head for her to enter into this new realm of possibility. A source of almost unbearable discomfiture for Orla, her aunt for many others is a storehouse of memory and a source of traditional culture. Indeed, in its absence, the Irish language still has a presence in the novel. At one stage, it is seen to have no authoritative purchase on the minds and imaginations of those at the Irish college. When the Headmaster has to impart some tragic news he says:

> Ciúnas! [...] What I have to say is so important that I am going to speak English. (207)

No matter what the official language of the state might be and no matter that in this particular situation the Irish language might be considered appropriate, everyone is aware of the true status of English. However, in the final chapter Orla tells of how the language in the present has more support and outlets for use than ever before, with the advent of the Irish-speaking television station, TG4. The Irish language, therefore, has a future in the present world.

It is only when Orla begins to recognise that she must look at and appreciate people and places in and of themselves, rather than relying on preconceived maps, that she can fully enter into her own future. She has gained the confidence to start thinking of herself in like terms, rather than measuring herself against impossible conceptions of right and wrong, of what is and is not fashionable.

It might be argued that what the reader is presented with in *The Dancers Dancing* is a new kind of narrative, very much alive to the needs of the present moment. Consider how Joyce's *A Portrait of the Artist as a Young Man* ends in comparison. Stephen Dedalus famously declares his intention of rising above the various nets that hold him back in Ireland and of embracing exile. It is, like the close of 'The Dead', a moment of revelation

227

and triumph signalled, perhaps, by the abandonment of the stylistic rigour of 'scrupulous meanness' in order to engage in the transcendent possibilities of a poetic style. Such a definite close is not appropriate in the contemporary moment. What Éilís Ní Dhuibhne does is attempt to create a fiction that engages with the possibility and potentiality of the past and childhood: to open it up to interpretation and investigation, rather than close it down by 'fixing' an end point toward which it inexorably moves. In other words, the kind of knowledge garnered at the close of *The Dancers Dancing* is not hierarchical or oppositional. As with the deconstruction of the differences between the countryside and the city, Ní Dhuibhne desires to move into a new realm.

PRIMARY REFERENCES

Éilís Ní Dhuibhne, *The Dancers Dancing* (Belfast: Blackstaff Press, 1999).
—, 'Blood and Water', in *Midwife to the Fairies: New and Selected Stories* (Cork: Attic Press, 2003).

Colm Tóibín (b. 1955)

John McCourt

In the summer of 1974, Colm Tóibín, second-year student of Arts (English and History) at UCD, was, in common with most of his fellow students, working to earn some money to get him through the following year's studies. His summer job was in the motor taxation office in Wexford and, spurred by the predictable boredom it induced, he passed his free time reading Henry James's *Portrait of a Lady*. As summer reading went, it was to turn out to be very significant for Tóibín, who was hugely impressed by James's novel and found himself returning to it year after year. In the late 1990s, he was asked to do a piece for the RTÉ radio series *A Giant at My Shoulder* and chose Henry James. No great surprise, then, that Tóibín went on, in 2004, to publish his novel *The Master*, a fictionalised life of James.

The Master, Tóibín's most ambitious book to date, elevates the already well-established Irish novelist onto an even more prominent international stage. In turning to James, Tóibín is not in any sense suffering from what Harold Bloom described as the anxiety of influence in his seminal book of the same name. Bloom argued that new poems originate from old poems, that the primary struggle of the young male poet is against the old masters. The new writer must clear imaginative space for himself through a creative misreading of the strong poets of the past. Only strong poets can overcome this anxiety of influence. This theory can be extended across to the novel. In Tóibín's case we might say that while he certainly clears an imaginative space for himself and becomes a 'strong' writer, creating a portrait of James that very much reflects his own preoccupations and his own recurring themes, he never does so at the cost of misreading James or of becoming a fawning or imitative flatterer. He retains, in short, a healthy disrespect for his subject, resisting the urge to copy or emulate him. Tóibín mostly eschews James's intricate, long sentences while at the same time creating an echo of his rhythms and vocabulary. He manages to write against his master, mastering his ample subject within his own elaborate novelistic structure and within the unerringly stable tone of his deeply effective prose.

But then Tóibín has never begged anyone's pardon or laboured under any other writer's shadow. Although he has paid conscious homage to writers from Joyce to Borges (displaying a particular regard for Hemingway's hard-boiled narrative style) and has revealed his wide and deep knowledge of Irish literature in his 1999 *Penguin Book of Irish Fiction*, Tóibín has always struck a singular, independent path. He has refused any neat categorisations that might wish to locate him as an 'Irish' writer or a 'gay' writer, daring instead to plunge in and out of such territories and to take insidious risks, both in terms of his adopted style and of the content of the broad canvas of his narratives. His style is dominated by unadorned, crisp prose (what Terry Eagleton has described as his 'austere, monkish prose in which everything is exactly itself') that relies on the careful accumulation of detail and on accurately chosen observation as a means of portraying character. Always adopting a non-judgemental tone, Tóibín's ongoing thematic concerns see him rework, in engaging and original ways, themes central to literature in general and to Irish literature in particular: exile, displacement and dislocation, loss and isolation, the idea of the family and home which is often challenged by domestic disharmony, loss and death. But his novels also introduce more particular if equally challenging issues present in contemporary Ireland (even if they are sometimes set in exotic locations such as Spain – *The South* – and Argentina – *The Story of the Night*), such as AIDS, politics and corruption, the messy leftovers of nationalism in a supposedly post-national and post-modern Ireland, and the strained gap between different generations, each attempting to adapt to the changing mores of an Irish society.

Style and content blend in Tóibín's belief in letting the facts speak for themselves, in never forcing his readers' hands but in trusting the direct clarity of his style. The following brief quotation from *The Story of the Night*, which announces an irrevocable death sentence, is a worthy if extreme example of this:

> He drew a large L and then put the pen at the top of the vertical line. 'This,' he said, 'is the state of your health now.' Then he slowly drew the declining graph until it hit the edge of the bottom line. 'This,' he said, 'is the way things are going to go. Do you understand?'

The only adjective provided describes the graph. In characteristic Tóibín fashion, many are left unwritten, left for the reader to imagine.

In an interview in *The Independent* of 18 September 1999, Tóibín described Henry James as '[o]ne of the greatest Irish writers … appalled by Ireland but his grandfather came from Cavan. They were displaced Protestants – the most Irish Irish you could have.' But to many of his readers, the choice to write about an expatriate American novelist in England in the 1890s might seem a strange one for a writer so clearly engaged in his previous novels with contemporaneity and with the changing Ireland of which he is so much a part. For a period, before becoming a full-time novelist, Tóibín was – in tandem with his fellow UCD graduate Fintan O'Toole – one of the most vital forces in Irish journalism, as writer and later editor of the current affairs magazine *Magill*. This experience proved a valuable training ground, as he has admitted: 'Magazine journalism gives you all the tricks of fiction. Endings, openings, stopping, starting. You deal with story and you are absolutely reader-shaped.'

Committed journalism also played an important role in forging a mellower Tóibín, a writer ready to sit down and acclimatise himself to the slower rhythms of fiction. Speaking of his activist journalist days, he has described how that time helped 'to get the poison out of me, over the issues that bothered me – the IRA, intellectual nationalism, the Church, conservative soft-spoken government'. Indeed it is true that much of that pain and sometimes venom – especially with regard to education and the

Catholic Church – that is to be found in twentieth-century Irish fiction is treated from a cool but persistent distance by Tóibín. Rarely going for obvious, easy targets in his novels, he prefers instead to explore ambiguities, inconsistencies and paradoxes, to evoke what is missing, what is lost. Not surprisingly he has come to see much Irish writing as antithetic to what he himself seeks to achieve. Writing of the contemporary Irish novel, he has stated: 'The purpose of much Irish fiction, it seems, is to become involved in the Irish argument, and the purpose of much Irish criticism has been to relate the fiction to the argument.' In his novels (with the exception of *The Heather Blazing*) Tóibín is careful to side-step any direct engagement with Irish arguments although this aesthetic stance also has clear political ramifications.

Not that he has not allowed his polemical spirit with regard to Ireland to languish. The opposite is true. From time to time it re-emerges with sparkle in those works he writes between novels, such as *The Irish Famine: A Documentary* or the 2002 biography *Lady Gregory's Toothbrush*. These vintage Tóibín essays, revelling in contradictions and ambiguities, revising and openly challenging received wisdom, queer everyone's pitch, uncovering and problematising the ideologies and agendas that motivate contemporary criticism about Ireland. Thus in his essay on the Famine, he would take direct issue with generations of Irish historians for not writing more about the worst catastrophe in the country's past, for failing to come to terms with it. He specifically describes the failure of historians to deliver the massive study on the subject that de Valera commissioned Robert Dudley Edwards to produce in the fifties. Describing the history faculty two decades later in UCD, he writes:

> In the early 1970s in University College Dublin, I studied with a few of the people involved in the project. It was clear from their bearing, the timbre of their voices and their general interest in source material that their time in British universities had been very important for them, that they were happier reading *Hansard* than going through lists of the names of people who died on coffin ships. It was equally clear that they would never have edited a book about the Famine had they not been

commissioned to do so. If they did not come from a class which was largely spared the Famine and land clearance, then they certainly aspired to it. (*The Irish Famine*, 9)

Although unlikely to win him many friends (at least in the History Department), there is no doubt that Tóibín makes his point in a forceful, lively, irreverent manner and in doing so succeeds in involving a wider readership than might usually be interested in such issues. His 'New Ways to Kill Your Father', on the merits and limits of historical revisionism in Ireland, and his later essay about Augusta, Lady Gregory, both achieve much the same effect as does his earlier *Bad Blood*, an account of a walk he took along the Irish border in the summer of 1986 and the lives he found there, ordinary lives touched by their harsh political context and years of instability and hardship. One may not always agree with Tóibín but it is difficult not to be swayed by the biting, incisive yet often disarmingly matter-of-fact prose and the clarity of the ideas – which are informed on the one hand by his being the son of a nationalist local historian with Fianna Fáil leanings and on the other by his own liberal Catholicism or Catholic liberalism which is very much informed and formed by the moderate, liberal ethos of UCD in the seventies. As an essayist he remains pre-eminent among his contemporaries and has reached a wider audience than any of them.

What links *The Master* with Tóibín's earlier works (both essays and fiction) is the renewed attempt to break through any political, sexual, geographical boundaries that some might use to stunt or curtail the reach of Irish fiction. What binds all his novels together is his lean and measured style. The authorial self-belief allows Tóibín draw back from attempts to persuade his reader or twist his arm. Instead, unembellished description and observation accumulate and achieve their own emotional resonance and power. His description of historian Mary Daly's method in her book on the Famine is a useful key to his own work: 'It allows the reader fill in the emotion' (*The Irish Famine*, 11). In a 2001 interview with Kieron Devlin, Tóibín himself stresses his debt to Hemingway: 'Hemingway's discovery was that in between words there's something which can give you emotion, and you do this in prose as much as in poetry, that in a number of simple statements you can hit the reader's nervous system in a way that the reader doesn't know where that energy is coming from.'

Tóibín's economy or his 'scrupulous meanness' (to give it a Joycean twist) with words, his cool understatement and his ongoing fascination with isolation and loss, exile and cultural displacement, his careful moral portraits of protagonists who choose or simply have to live lives of real or perceived loss or isolation also link his earlier fiction with this courageous new novel. In all his fiction, Tóibín's protagonists are brought through a chronological journey. But they are also involved in inward acts of remembering, frequently painful acts of reclaiming and re-evaluating relationships with their families, sometimes in the shadow of incumbent death, more often in its wake. The novels tend to centre around moments of epiphany in which life catches up with the central characters and they are forced to come to terms with their isolation, their emptiness, their recurring, haunting sense of non-belonging.

This is an apt description of the predicament lived by the protagonist of Tóibín's 1992 novel *The Heather Blazing*. Eamon Redmond, a High Court judge, is struggling to come to terms with the re-emergence of an almost unbearable pain caused by the death of his wife Carmel and his even deeper sense of loss, following the death of his mother when he was a very young boy. In her absence Eamon grew up with his schoolteacher father and 'learned to wait, to be quiet, to sit still' (14), to be self-reliant and solitary. Sometimes his friends came to play in the house 'but they had to play quietly' and 'when they left to go home and have their tea, he felt relieved. He had the house to himself again and could sit opposite his father and work at his lessons' (15). For all Eamon's father's attempts to be close to him there is an unbridgeable gap between them. This is depicted in the scene in which his father tells him of the death of his Uncle Stephen (immediately after that of his grandfather). On hearing the news Eamon 'turned away. He did not want his father watching him across the room. He shut his eyes. His father came over and touched him on the shoulder. He wanted to turn towards his father, but he kept his eyes shut and his fists clenched' (81). Eamon lives his life out in solitude, confessing tearfully to his wife that he does not believe that anyone has ever wanted him. Following the death of his wife, the novel resists any sentimental conclusion, offering only the most tentative of possibilities that Eamon may in some way reform his closed, solitary life with his grandson.

Eamon's solitude, his feeling of hurt and loss, links him to Tóibín's other heroes. Maurice Harmon's description of how Eamon 'is a flawed human being, afraid of emotional commitment, uncertain of being wanted by anyone, afraid of being rejected' might just as easily be used to describe Helen, the protagonist of *The Blackwater Lightship,* but also Tóibín's Henry James. *The Blackwater Lightship* is built around a series of losses lived and suffered by Helen, originally from Wexford but now a school headmistress in suburban Dublin where she lives with husband Hugh and her two boys. Following a brief depiction of their comfortable if somewhat brittle world – an all-too-rare look in fiction into realities of life in middle-class south Dublin – Helen's supposed peace is shattered by the news that her younger brother Declan is dying of AIDS. Declan has hidden his illness from her and her mother and has been cared for only by friends. The novel focuses on Helen's coming to terms with her brother's illness, with the loss that awaits her, but more importantly on her relationship with her own family and a past dominated by a sense of loss and abandonment she had hoped to have put behind her but which must now be confronted.

The novel takes place in her grandmother's one-time guest-house in Cush on the Wexford coast where Helen and her brother stayed while their father was dying of cancer in a Dublin hospital. Now Helen finds herself there again with her mother, her grandmother, Declan and his two friends, Paul and Larry. Having lived apart for years, each harbouring a series of hurts and slights suffered at the hands of the others, Helen, her mother and grandmother are each forced, in this shabby seaside home, to face and tentatively embrace each other and accept the damage each has inflicted on the other. Helen's grief and loss stem from the fact that she was never given space to mourn or express her feelings when her father died. She chiefly blames her mother for this. Family and neighbours busied themselves around her, fussed over her mother, but never considered how she and her brother might be coping. In one of the book's most moving scenes, Helen is seen back in her house the day after her father's death. She is alone and goes into her parents' bedroom. Physically missing her father, she begins to lay out his clothes on his bed, to remake him, almost bring him back to life. She chooses a tie, underclothes, even shoes which she props up with books. The shoes make him seem real, so real that she places herself in the bed beside 'him' in an almost gothic scene of anguish and love:

> She placed herself on her mother's side of the bed, carefully and gingerly so as not to disturb him. She reached out and held the hand that should be there at the end of the right-hand sleeve of the jacket. She reached over and lifted the cap and kissed where his mouth should be. She snuggled up against him. (82)

The event may be a minor one, but in Tóibín's bold, unsentimental and precise prose, it is made to pack a powerful emotional punch. It is as close as Helen will be allowed to get to an open outpouring of grief.

Tóibín's concern with grief and loss continues in *The Master*. Adopting again what Benjamin Markovits in *The Telegraph* (22 March 2004) called 'the third person intimate', Tóibín shows James spending his life running away from personal belonging, from affective attachment. He is a stranger everywhere, an exile with no hope of ever finding a home, a man (self-)condemned to live on the edges of other people's lives. Tóibín's descriptions of James's repression are in many ways a continuation of the stifled, unexpressed emotions of the three women at the centre of *The Blackwater Lightship*. Even more than Eamon Redmond in *The Heather Blazing* and Helen in *The Blackwater Lightship*, James in *The Master* is in a powerful public and authoritative position (the former is a judge, the latter a headmistress). Like Helen he strives to be in total control and greatly resents people (such as his brother) who dare challenge that. He is, by and large, an observer of life rather than a participant. His life is one of avoidance, renunciation, suppression, withdrawal, of consciously willing not to take opportunities. Rather than risk long-term relationships that might make demands James keeps his family, friends, and would-be friends at a safe distance. While he is attracted by certain men and women he always remains on guard against anything approaching commitment: 'He found the waiting for them, the sense of expectation before a visit, the most blissful time of all … [while] he also relished the days after a guest had departed, he enjoyed the peace of the house, as though the visit had been nothing except a battle for solitude which he had finally won' (209).

But his solitude is uneasy and painful as he is haunted by two losses for which he is at least in part responsible. The dominant one is the death by suicide of his friend and would-be companion Constance Fenimore Woolson. This sees him forced to face death directly and to admit his own empty refusal of what she might have offered him. This event echoes James's earlier refusal to take his cousin Minny with him on his first trip to Rome. James's friend, the famous judge Oliver Wendell Holmes Jr., openly blames Henry for abandoning her and for her subsequent death: 'When she did not hear from you, she turned her face to the wall' (119). James is brought face-to-face with his own responsibilities with regard to Constance when he has to go to Venice to dispose of her effects (and to eliminate the revealing letters he had sent her over the years) but does not know what to do with her clothes.

Tóibín's depiction of the scene in which James and Tito, Constance's trusted *gondoliere*, attempt to 'bury' her clothes in the sea is every bit as powerful as his earlier description in *The Blackwater Lightship* of Helen's bringing her father back to life. The clothes keep returning to the surface 'like black balloons, evidence of the strange sea burial they had just enacted, their arms and bellies bloated with water' (270). Even if Tito eventually makes all the clothes sink, the terrifying memory stays with James and mingles with other memories of past grief, which combine to make him aware of his sense of loss, of his lack of a sustaining comfort. In the end all James has left are his books. In his out-of-the-way house in Rye, as he glances at his shelves crammed with his books, Hendrik Anderson, the young American sculptor asks 'But did you not once plan it all? Did you

237

not say this is what I will do with my life?' (310). James does not answer but his eyes fill up with tears he cannot explain. He realises suddenly that he is old, that he has chosen not to partake in so much that life offered him, that he is alone. Like Mr Duffy in Joyce's 'A Painful Case' or Gabriel Conroy in 'The Dead', James stumbles into his personal epiphany too late. There is nothing he can do by the time he realises the depth of his own unhappiness. And he cannot even share it:

> Andersen was perhaps too young to know how memory and regret can mingle, how much sorrow can be held within, and how nothing seems to have any shape or meaning until it is well past and lost and, even then, how much, under the weight of pure determination, can be forgotten and left aside only to return in the night as piercing pain. (287)

One of Colm Tóibín's great achievements in his fiction has been unceasingly to explore that same pain of loss and to do so in a way that is always new, always raw, always revealing.

PRIMARY REFERENCES

Colm Tóibín, *The South* (London: Serpent's Tail, 1990).
—, *The Heather Blazing* (London: Picador, 1992).
—, *The Blackwater Lightship* (London: Picador, 1999).
—, *The Master* (London: Picador, 2004).
Colm Tóibín and Diarmaid Ferriter, *The Irish Famine: A Documentary* (New York: St. Martin's Press, 2002).

SECONDARY REFERENCES

Harold Bloom, *The Anxiety of Influence: A Theory of Poetry* (New York: Oxford University Press, second edition, 1997).
Terry Eagleton, 'Mothering', in *London Review of Books* (24 September 1999).
Maurice Harmon, review of Colm Tóibín, *The Heather Blazing*, in *Irish Literary Supplement* (Spring 1994).

AIDAN CARL MATHEWS (B. 1956)

Harry White

'My very photogenic mother died in a freak accident (picnic, lightning) when I was three' – Vladimir Nabokov, *Lolita*

It is surely a commonplace that the English language is distinguished by its hospitality to strangers. Irish writers attest to this accommodation almost as an invariable condition of their being able to communicate anything to the world at large. In turn, the enrichments that accrue to the language (Yeats and Joyce are pre-eminent exemplars) are out of all reasonable proportion to the global dominion and practice of English, even if we acknowledge that Ireland has a standing army at any given time of ten thousand poets.

Within these regiments, the sheer plurality of voice can sometimes narrow canonically to the prepotent presence of the few, so that Irish writing in the twentieth century invites (at least to my mind) some degree of comparison to the ubiquity and influence of German music in the nineteenth century. It would be odious to force this comparison too far, but Beethoven, Schubert, Schumann, Mendelssohn, Brahms, Wagner and Bruckner comprise an 'imaginary museum of musical works' (the phrase belongs originally to Franz Lizst) which is suggestive of that imaginary museum of Irish literary works dominated by writers such as Yeats, Joyce, Shaw, Synge, Friel, Mahon, Heaney and Banville. Hardly anyone scanning that second list could resist the urge to amend or extend it, so prodigious is Ireland's literary presence in the wider domain of literature written in English. This rollcall of names is immediately vulnerable to change, but the names themselves denote a sphere of international influence in poetry, drama and fiction that few people would contest.

Given this magnitude, the quest for voice in contemporary Irish writing must be a harrowing one. To claim some singularity of style and address which might extend the expressive reach of literature grows more daunting by the day. It is not only the twilight condition of postmodernity that complicates this quest, but that generic permanence ('fiction', 'poetry', 'drama') which signifies the boundaries of literary discourse in its rival relationship to other, more plastic forms and modes of art.

I begin with these preoccupations because they loom so unmistakably in the work of Aidan Carl Mathews. He is surely not unique in this respect, but I shall not hesitate to declare here that it is once more the sovereign paradigm of German music which provides (at least for me) an instructive and – one hopes – interesting perspective on the problems which Mathews so ably encounters in his work. Without pretence to a literal comparison that would surely dismay him, there is nevertheless a valid parallel to be drawn between the anxiety of influence in Mathews's exploration of those three fundamental genres identified here and the strikingly similar predicaments that plagued Robert Schumann in the aftermath of Beethoven's influence. Schumann's demons were unique and terrible, and they are far removed from the anxieties which Mathews admits onto the page, but in both artists one senses an almost excessive reception and understanding of the prior condition of music and literature respectively. In his music for piano, in his chamber music and symphonic works, and in his songs (wherein Schubert joins Beethoven as an especially acute source of anguish), Schumann achieved an originality of voice that countenanced at every turn the immediate anxiety of influence. It is hard not to recognise a similar admixture of originality and reception in Mathews, so that his work becomes a commentary on the condition of Irish poetry, drama and fiction even as it adds substantially to each of them.

I am encouraged in this perspective mainly by Mathews's own

preoccupation not only with the generic sovereignty of Irish writing in the twentieth century, but also with Europe as a valid domain for the Irish writer's account of experience. The ghosts in his writing may be oppressive, but even Joyce, for all his wide engagement with the world, insists on Ireland as the centre of gravity. By contrast, a lapidary moment of brilliance such as 'The Death of Irish' from Mathews's second collection of poetry, *Minding Ruth* (1982), not only signifies a recognition of linguistic abeyance, but also heralds a decisive turn towards those inner capitals in which twentieth-century European history has been determined.

When I first read the title poem from *Minding Ruth* over twenty years ago, my callow reaction was to wince inwardly at this too-close engagement with European history. I resented, irrationally, this skilful if not impertinent Irish address upon complicit German cruelty, even as I admired the breathtaking quality of that poem's closing image. Knowing a partial precedent – as I did even then – in Aidan Higgins's masterpiece *Langrishe, Go Down* (1966), I ought to have reacted differently. Now that the Nazis have become a species of popular entertainment as well as a more ambiguously iconic representation of human culpability, even to the point where we are unnervingly invited to contemplate with some sympathy the Führer himself (as in the film *Max*, or in Bruno Ganz's magnificent portrayal of Hitler), I recognise anew the soft detonations of Mathews' verse as an astonishingly adept illustration of how evil represents itself.

The readiness is all in 'Minding Ruth', so that the little girl whose name it bears, 'a Visigoth in a pinafore' (62), projects an image of innocence ripe for the banal corruption that lies in the heart and awaits its moment of opportunity. Her inadvertence is the very expression of prelapsarian 'grace notes' (63), but it leads inexorably to the damned condition of human existence which is offered at the close. The final image, the last detonation, is unremitting in its disclosure of light overcome by darkness, of laughter subverted by sadism and of good subdued by evil:

Her hands sip at my cuff. She cranes,
Perturbedly, with a book held open

At plates from Warsaw in the last war.
Why is the man with the long beard
Eating his booboos? and I stare
At the old rabbi squatting in turds

Among happy soldiers who die laughing,
The young one clapping: you can see
A wedding band flash on his finger. (63)

Germany is an abiding theme in Mathews's work. It is the touchstone of common assent, the measure of contemporary experience against which schoolboy terrors in the dormitory or staff-room desolations ought to be judged. It is worth remarking, even parenthetically, that Mathews articulates a sense of bewilderment in relation to the War. Many Irish people of his generation share it (I am one of them). It is sounded most notably in 'Train Tracks' from his second collection of stories, *Lipstick on the Host* (1992). The bewilderment stems from trying to reconcile ordinary German life with the horrors of the Nazi state when the latter is only one generation away. Events so terrible that they were hitherto confined to mythology or literature (the descriptions of hell in Dante) turn out to be a matter of historical record, and a frighteningly recent record at that. Even with the horrors of Baghdad instantly before us, there is little to compare with the next-door-neighbour surrealism of terror that the concentration camps energetically, deliberately and systematically engendered throughout the Third Reich. Mathews expresses the shame and puzzlement of a whole generation when the protagonist's father in 'Train Tracks' tells the boy about flame throwers turned on pregnant women and newborn babies kicked like footballs. This is not an indictment of Nazi barbarism alone, but a robust condemnation of the complicities that bred and facilitated such otherwise unspeakable incarnations of cruelty.

It is, nevertheless, the re-integration of these European concerns with Ireland that signifies Mathews's finest achievement as a writer. Here, too, Aidan Higgins offers a precedent, in the sense that all great writers create their own predecessors. But this absorption of recent European history into an unmistakably Irish context entails, I think, a two-way process. Music provides an enlightening parallel.

When Robert Schumann published his famous endorsement of Chopin in 1836 ('Hats off, Gentlemen: a Genius!') he added to this encomium the observation that Chopin in his more mature works had 'shed the excessively Sarmatic aspect of his physiognomy'. Schumann meant inoffensively to suggest that Chopin's work now belonged to the international spectrum of piano music, whereas it had previously been more strongly expressive of Poland. Others have justifiably remarked that Chopin's music nevertheless functions not only as a vital contribution to the international repertory of romantic pianism but also as a narrative of Polish nationalism and political consciousness.

I would propose here that something similar can be said of Mathews, even if it would require a comprehensive survey of his work to press the point home. If we leave to one side the international span of his fictional settings (not only Europe, but also the west coast of the United States are favourite locales), this integration of Ireland and Europe which lies at the centre of his preoccupations as a writer becomes all the clearer in a story such as 'Fathers'.

'Fathers', from Mathews's first collection of short stories, *Adventures in a Bathyscope* (1988), is a formally perfect work of art. Another commonplace which I cannot suppress, and which arises from this declaration, is that it must have been (at best) a mixed blessing to produce two masterpieces within one's first collection (the other is 'The Figure on the Cross'). In any case, the compact genius of 'Fathers' takes the Irish short story beyond Joyce and O'Connor to a new register of sensibility. Those masters undoubtedly inhere in Mathews's fiction: the Jesuitical humiliations in 'Fathers' are a sure acknowledgement of *A Portrait of the Artist as a Young Man* and Frank O'Connor's preoccupation with fathers and sons haunts the whole structure.

The story expresses itself with such unerring intelligence that any attempt to gloss it seems like a detraction. It enjoys the concentrated exactitude of poetry at perfect pitch, so that the strategic juxtapositions of which it is composed are all the more precise and unsettling. The very sentence structure of 'Fathers' has the compressed narrative force of Nabokov ('picnic, lightning'), but it is the reception of German history that holds and horrifies. By 'reception' I don't simply mean the narrator's disturbed awakening to images of Nazi sadism, but also his realisation that a moral point of view informed by this awareness cannot impede the natural appetite for cruelty which supervenes any such consideration. Mathews prefaces 'Fathers' with an arresting epigraph: 'In the lost childhood of Judas, Christ was betrayed.' The narrator's innocence is likewise lost to the ways of the world, despite his father's *ad hoc* history lessons on the subject of Europe. The nightmare from which Stephen Dedalus strove in vain to awake remains unbroken.

All I would add by way of commentary is that 'Fathers' thereby takes possession of European history in ways that make the latter central rather than exotic to the domain of Irish fiction. In that imaginative leap, enabled by a superlative command of narrative technique, the story secures its claim to our permanent attention. In ways that compare to Chopin's Polish mastery of German compositional technique, Mathews's fiction at its best engages Europe and is vitally expressive of Ireland at one and the same time.

For Schumann, the influence of Beethoven, like the presence of the jar in Wallace Stevens's poem, 'took dominion everywhere'. He sought emancipation from the duress of that omnipresence not only in music but also in literature, and wrestled with himself on that account until insanity overtook him and he was left with nothing much more than 'dear Clara [his wife] and my depression'. Had he foreseen his own posterity as a sovereign exemplar of the European musical imagination, he might have written more and suffered less. What George Steiner calls 'the fatal myth of introspection' – the curse of the *Orfeo* legend so central to opera – afflicted Schumann more than any other German composer. His tendency to look back cost him dear.

'Great readers are rarer than great writers,' Borges once remarked. But when the greater writer is also a consummate reader, when he or she also looks back, the difficulties in literature, no less than in music, can be legion. The somnambular economy of direction by which other artists achieve their work is denied in such cases, or comes and goes with maddening unpredictability. The restless and sometimes painful explorations of Aidan

Mathews's less successful work are, perhaps, the high price exacted by his courage as a writer and by his imperishable achievements in fiction and poetry. To acknowledge as much, even in terms of a comparison that some will find audacious, is to salute the work of a master.

Note: I am most grateful to Julian Horton for his comments on Schumann in the preparation of this piece.

PRIMARY REFERENCES

Aidan Carl Mathews, 'Minding Ruth', in *The Inherited Boundaries: Younger Poets of the Republic of Ireland*, edited by Sebastian Barry (Mountrath, Portlaoise: The Dolmen Press, 1986); *Minding Ruth* (Dublin: The Gallery Press, 1982).
—, *Adventures in a Bathyscope* (London: Secker and Warburg, 1988).
—, *Lipstick on the Host* (London: Secker and Warburg, 1992).

RODDY DOYLE (B. 1958)

Brian Donnelly

Roddy Doyle has proven a radical force in Irish writing. Unable to find a publisher for his first novel, *The Commitments* (1987), he produced it privately under his own imprint before William Heinemann Ltd gave it a more conventional release the following year. His fourth book, *Paddy Clarke Ha Ha Ha* (1993), was the first and, to date, the only Irish winner of the Booker prize, an award that afforded Doyle international recognition without silencing a number of influential commentators at home who claimed that his writings were stylistically limited and patronising towards the working classes. All of his works in the novel, for the stage, for television and the cinema have been popular successes. Alan Parker's film adaptation of *The Commitments* (released in 1991) created a world-wide audience for its author who won awards for his part in the adaptation of the text for the screen. The films based on *The Snapper* (1990) and *The Van* (1991) added considerably to his popularity as the author of comic novels dealing with the lives of ordinary folk (mostly unemployed) on a north Dublin housing estate called Barrytown. His trilogy of plays for Irish television, *Family* (1994), and his novel *The Woman Who Walked into Doors* (1996), saw Doyle exploring the personal and social problems confronting women and children in an environment very like the comic world of the early novels.

Doyle has also achieved considerable popularity as a writer of fiction for children. Much of his ability to communicate with young people stems, no doubt, from his thirteen-year career as a teacher of English and Geography at Greendale Community School in Kilbarrack, north Dublin.

Until his recent excursion into historical fiction with *A Star Called Henry* (2000) and *Oh, Play That Thing* (2004), the first two volumes of a projected trilogy, Doyle's fictional world has been that of the housing estates that grew up around Dublin and other Irish cities in the 1950s and the 1960s as Ireland, like much of the developing world, experienced the movement of populations from the countryside to the city. These happenings were marked inevitably by cultural severance and breaks with the past for the families who underwent such relocation. It has been Roddy Doyle's achievement to record imaginatively important aspects of this new urban experience in his fictional north Dublin estate. Consequently, his works have run counter to the traditional preoccupations and conventions of Irish fiction and drama. The historic concerns of nationality, land, language and religion that had engaged Irish writers since the time of Thomas Davis and *The Nation* are absent in Doyle's fictional setting. His world constitutes a striking contrast to the rural world of his older contemporaries such as Edna O'Brien and John McGahern; it is also the antithesis of the Dublin of James Joyce and Sean O'Casey. The world of their works has few points of reference in the Dublin of Roddy Doyle. His is a community experienced, not visually, but in the lively talk of the characters:

> –Where are yis from?
> (He answered the question himself.)
> –Dublin.
> (He asked another one)
> –Wha' part o' Dublin? Barrytown. Wha' class are yis? Workin' class. Are yis proud of it? Yeah, yis are.
> (Then a practical question.)
> –Who buys the most records? The workin' class. Are yis with me?
> (Not really.)
> – Your music should be abou' where you're from, an' the sort o' people yeh come from. Say it once, say it loud. I'm black an' I'm proud.
> They looked at him. (13)

This episode from early in *The Commitments* ignores the political and cultural assumptions on which readers of Irish fiction had been nurtured. Its vigorous, colloquial utterance shows no respect for traditional novelistic decorum. The young people who are organising themselves into a soul band articulate an identity that is constructed more by global culture than by anything transmitted by historic ideals of Irishness. The only reference to the influence of the Catholic church in their lives is the admission that the band's female backing singers came together in the folk mass choir when they were at school. No one utters a word of Irish, the country's 'first offical language', and the political turmoil in the six counties of Ulster that had dominated Irish consciousness for a generation is relegated to a humorous footnote in the formation of the Commitments: '[Ed Winchell, a Baptist Reverend] was watching something on TV about the feuding Brothers in Northern Ireland and The Lord told the Reverend Ed that the Irish Brothers had no soul, that they needed some soul' (27).

The Dublin of *The Commitments* is not the successor to the city of Joyce's works. The metropolis of the older novelist is a place rooted firmly in the political and social realities of the first years of the twentieth century. The location of Doyle's early fictions exists outside of the immediacy of public affairs. In this respect he differs from contemporaries like Dermot Bolger and other writers who were identified as a movement under the heading 'Dirty Dublin Poetic Realism'. In Doyle's early novels, Barrytown is an anonymous suburb where consciousness is shaped largely by imported television programmes, American popular music and English Premier League soccer which was supplanting the G.A.A. in popular affection. One of the local pubs has changed its name from the sentimentally titled 'The Dark Rosaleen' to that of a popular crime series from California, 'The Miami Vice'.

As in such instances Roddy Doyle's achievement has been to keep the focus and terms of reference of his stories within the day-to-day concerns and awareness of his characters, articulated in their own idiom without any mediating authorial voice. These are men, women and young people who are preoccupied with the mundane concerns of school examinations, unwanted pregnancy, male unemployment and the chronic problem of affording a drink in the local. The social and economic consequences of their lives are viewed exclusively within the personal and domestic sphere, never in the perspective of local or national politics.

The community of *The Commitments*, *The Snapper* (1990) and *The Van* (1991) is a self-contained world within an actual historical city. Here chronic unemployment constitutes a personal or a family crisis, never a serious political issue. A pregnancy resulting from the rape of a young woman by the father of one of her friends is the cause of a certain amount of family upset, not the occasion of a legal, spiritual or community crisis. None of these dilemmas in *The Snapper* results in tragic or even deeply unhappy consequences because the story, like its predecessor, operates within the conventions of comedy that presupposes a happy ending. Consequently, these early novels portray aspects of contemporary, working-class, urban life without the obligation to explore the bleaker consequences of its harsh realities. In these novels Doyle's characters bear much the same relationship to contemporary urban history as do the characters in the R.M. stories of Somerville and Ross to rural Ireland of the late nineteenth century.

Within the conventions of the comic form of the so-called Barrytown Trilogy, Doyle succeeds in portraying many of the significant social and cultural mores of late twentieth-century Ireland in which most of the traditional authorities and historic models have begun to cede to the influences of mass culture and life conditioned by the uniformity of large, modern housing developments. Significantly, there is no suggestion that a rural idyll has been lost. On the contrary, the Rabbitte family at the centre of the trilogy represents much that is best in family life, and the Hikers pub constitutes an idealised centre for the wider community's interaction and recreation. The rough and tumble of Jimmy Rabbitte's relationship with his wife and children has a vulgar naturalness and joy, the absence of which constituted the traditional psychic drama of much Irish writing from Synge's *The Playboy of the Western World* to the stories and novels of John McGahern. Indeed, the spontaneity of the relationship between parents and children as portrayed in Doyle's fictions reflects the healthy lack of respect for traditional authorities. In these works concern is for one's own family and friends rather than for the abstract teachings of church and state. In *The Snapper*, for instance, the news of Sharon's pregnancy, a condition that in the Irish novel up until the 1970s would have constituted the central moral and psychological drama, is given a largely comic treatment. There is no serious family dissension among the Rabbittes because, in Barrytown, '[n]obody minded. Guess the daddy was a hobby' (253). Veronica's protests concerning her daughter's pregnancy lack the visceral conviction of the mother in Irish novels of earlier generations. In *The Snapper*, the drama that would traditionally have arisen from an out-of-wedlock pregnancy is replaced by the conflict between a daughter about to create a new life and her father who increasingly feels marginalised both at home and among his mates in the Hiker.

Much of Roddy Doyle's best dramatic and comic writing is in the scenes involving the daughter who is increasingly conscious of her growth into motherhood and her father's mistaken belief that he has now the opportunity to share in the experience of pregnancy and birth that he failed to realise when he and Veronica were making their own family. Indeed, Jimmy Sr's preoccupation with his ambiguous role as the father of a growing family and with his status in the community is one of Doyle's finest achievements as a novelist. Significantly, the opening episode of *The Van* reveals Jimmy Sr vacating the kitchen table to allow his son, Darren, the space to do his school work while he goes outdoors to observe idly the doings of the neighbours. In *The Commitments* Jimmy Sr was little more than a cipher; in *The Van*, the third of the Barrytown novels, we encounter a more complex character who feels his self-worth to be under threat. Like the earlier books, *The Van* is a comedy that skirts close to tragedy as in the scene where Jimmy Sr's employed son slips his father a five pound note, thus reversing the traditional father-son roles. The deteriorating relationship between Jimmy Sr and his friend and business partner, Bimbo, shows Doyle's writing at its most assured. Yet it is in these episodes that the comic mode of the early novels is threatened and it is significant that the story ends with a scene that returns Jimmy Sr to the condition of a child as he asks his wife to hug and comfort him.

The Barrytown trilogy reveals Doyle's singular gifts: an ability to create a lively, contemporary idiom and an awareness of the culture of late twentieth-century life in a nondescript suburb. He treats his characters without condescension and revels in their earthy humour as in the baiting of the young waiter by Sharon and her friends in *The Snapper*:

> The row was over. They nearly got sick laughing. The lounge boy was coming back.
> –Here's your bit o' fluff, Mary, said Sharon.
> –Ah stop.
> –Howyeh, Gorgeous, said Jackie. –Did yeh make your holy communion yet?
> The lounge boy tried to get everything off the tray all at once so he could get the fuck out of that corner. He said nothing.
> –Wha' size do yeh take? Yvonne asked him.
> The lounge boy legged it. He left too much change on the table and a puddle where he'd spilled the Coke. Mary threw a beer-mat on top of it.
> –Jesus, Sharon, said Jackie. – I thought you were goin' to have a miscarriage there you were laughin' so much.
> –I couldn't help it – Wha' size d'yeh take.
> They started again.
> –I mean his shirt, said Yvonne.
> They giggled and wiped their eyes and noses and poured the Coke and tonic on top of the vodka and gin. (196)

As well as displaying Doyle's obvious pleasure in recording the banter of Sharon and her friends, such scenes reveal his ability to record the trivia that goes to make up a culture at a given moment and to convey something of the spirit of the times.

The ephemeral nature of such occasions is splendidly conveyed in the casual remark that concludes the description of the football fever that gripped Ireland during the 1990 World Cup in Italy: 'And then they got beaten by the Italians and that was the end of that' (515). Few contemporary Irish writers serve better the novelistic instinct, apparent since the days of Defoe, to record and preserve the minutiae and spirit of the times. In this regard, if in no other, Roddy Doyle may be regarded as the successor of the author of *Ulysses*.

Doyle is a writer who is unwilling to keep repeating a successful formula. Though there is comedy in *Paddy Clarke Ha Ha Ha* (1993) the comic conventions that governed the trilogy are replaced by a bleak realism in a society rooted firmly in contemporary social history. The Barrytown of young Paddy's childhood is in the process of construction as it eats into the green fields of north Dublin, a phenomenon experienced by Doyle when a boy. Paddy, the narrator, records the encroachment of suburban development into the farmland that had been his playground. These changes are observed disinterestedly by the ten-year-old who is attempting to cope with the emotional consequences of his parents' failing marriage. The narrative follows the perceptive eye of a child who observes the particularity and strangeness of the adult world. The limitations of a small boy's understanding of his world allow Doyle to create episodes of memorable comedy by re-enacting some of the standard experiences of a traditional Roman Catholic nationalist education. We see this, for instance, in Paddy's account of Miss Watkins's lesson on the 1916 Proclamation of Independence and his retelling of the story of the leper priest, Father Damien. These accounts are bravura performances of narration as the child's idiom and memory process inform every detail. Here, too, Doyle uses his fiction to record and memorialise aspects of the Ireland of his own youth, a country whose cultural insularity was being infiltrated by the television set in the corner of the living-room. Paddy's childhood, like his creator's, coincides with and is partly shaped by such events as the U.S.A.'s war in Vietnam, the Arab–Israeli conflict, popular T.V. shows such as *The Man from U.N.C.L.E.* and Gay Byrne's *The Late Late Show* and sporting occasions like Manchester United's defeat of Benficia of Lisbon in the 1968 European Cup final. This was a time when most households owned one of those record players with the multiple dispenser on which, as Paddy observes, 'you could pile six records in it over the turntable. We only had three: *The Black and White Minstrels*, *South Pacific* and *Hank Williams The King of Country*' (89). All of Doyle's books revel in this kind of detail that can be seen to chart Ireland's entry into the global village. His attentiveness to the bric-à-brac of modern life as a significant factor in the shaping of character registers those late twentieth-century forces that were beginning to supersede the historical and religious lessons endured by Paddy Clarke in the classroom.

Doyle's concern in this novel and in his next, *The Woman Who Walked into Doors* (1996), is to articulate the hurt, anger, fear and confusion of one who is powerless and vulnerable. This preoccupation with characters that are weak or marginalised is the most persistent one in his writings. In *Paddy Clarke Ha Ha Ha* his achievement was the creation of a language adequate to the boy's experience of the disintegration of his parents' marriage and the problems at school that follow from it. The narrative voice throughout the novel is a nice balance between the adult's recollection and the immediacy of childhood perception; only occasionally does the oversophisticated simile or an inappropriate phrase intrude upon this compromise. The same is true of Paula's tale in *The Woman Who Walked into Doors* where the voice has an apparent naturalness that is compelling as she recalls her years with the attractive yet violent Charlo. In the television series *Family* Doyle portrayed the sociological context of the syndrome of the battered woman; in the novel he attempted the more complex task of creating the actual construction of the personality of a victim. In this instance, as in all such narratives, the problem was how to remain faithful to the linguistic range of a character of Paula's education and background, a recurring challenge for Doyle in his fiction. His achievement is apparent in scenes like the following where Paula recounts an instance of Charlo's aggression:

> He hit me. He sent me across the kitchen and I hit the sink and fell. I felt nothing, only shock. A spinning in my head. I knew nothing for a while, where I was, who was with me, what I was doing on the floor. I saw nothing; I was empty. Then I saw his legs, making a triangle with the floor. He seemed way up over me. Way up; huge. I had to bend back to see him. Then he came down to me. I saw his knees bending; I saw his hand pulling up one of his trouser legs. I saw his face. His eyes were going over my face, every inch, every mark. He was worried. He was shocked and worried. He loved me again. He held my chin. He skipped over my eyes. He couldn't look straight at me. He felt

guilty, dreadful. He loved me again. What happened? I provoked him. I was to blame. I should have made his dinner. It was my own fault; there was a pair of us in it. What happened? I don't know. He held my chin and looked at every square inch of my face. He loved me again. (175)

No doubt it was writing of this accomplishment that caused reviewers world-wide to praise this male author for his insight into the psychology of women. The achievement, however, had as much to do with Roddy Doyle's developing narrative skills as it had with his understanding of the battered-woman syndrome; indeed, for a novelist, the two things are inseparable. As in all of his work the author has created and sustained a voice subtly expressive of the day-to-day life of his characters. It is not surprising that in an interview given to *The Irish Times* (28 August 2004) Roddy Doyle confessed that he was most proud of *The Woman Who Walked into Doors*, 'because it's challenging, probably the best of them [his novels]. In some ways it's probably the least typical of them as well. I suppose the subject matter is so grim. That's the one I would want preserved if the others had to disappear.'

It is obviously too soon to try to assess Doyle's place in Irish writing. His historic trilogy, based upon the adventures of Henry Smart, the slum child born in Dublin in 1901 who fought with James Connolly and Michael Collins before emigrating to the U.S.A. where he would assist Louis Armstrong, is still in progress. However, in his work up to the mid 1990s, we have a writer whose books and dramas have attempted to articulate aspects of late twentieth-century urban life that had remained largely outside the horizons of most Irish writing and the experience of many people who buy and read books. In his best work he has achieved that ideal intersection between the formal demands of the written word and the distinctly unliterary culture of his creations. He once remarked (appropriately in an interview given to a UCD graduate student) that 'my style of writing may be a complete reaction to Jane Austen'. This was, no doubt, said with tongue in cheek. Nevertheless, it is redolent of the independent creative spirit that has made Roddy Doyle such a significant and entertaining writer.

P R I M A R Y R E F E R E N C E S

Roddy Doyle, *The Commitments*, from *The Barrytown Trilogy* (London: Secker and Warburg, 1992).

—, *The Snapper,* from *The Barrytown Trilogy* (London: Secker and Warburg, 1992).

—, *The Van,* from *The Barrytown Trilogy* (London: Secker and Warburg, 1992).

—, *Paddy Clarke Ha Ha Ha* (London: Secker and Warburg, 1993).

—, *The Woman Who Walked into Doors* (London: Secker and Warburg, 1996).

JOSEPH O'CONNOR (B. 1963)

P.J. Mathews

At the beginning of Joseph O'Connor's early novel *Cowboys and Indians*, Eddie Virago, protagonist and UCD graduate, recalls:

> the chatter of conversation he used to hear on the middle floor of the university canteen, a great full noise which, if you listened to it for long enough, would trip you out better than any drug. (3)

John Henry Newman's idea of a university, it would seem, was alive and well in the UCD of the mid-1980s and had managed to survive the move to Belfield. Not even the 'squat grey buildings full of stark modernist sculpture and its brutal perspex tunnels' (4) could dampen the palpable enthusiasm for intellectual exchange that seeped out of the lecture theatres and into lunchtime and late-night discussions. The built environment may have been somewhat testing but so too was the prevailing mood on campus. As Eddie recollects, 'everybody, absolutely everybody, seemed to have something to prove' (4). His UCD, after all, is a place where classmates aspire to becoming 'Ireland's first anarchist Taoiseach' (136) or to writing 'the Great Irish Novel' (137) and where friendships can be broken in a row over Marxist literary criticism in the Belfield bar. Not all of Eddie's encounters are of the intellectual variety, however. In this novel Theatre L is as much an amphitheatre of romantic possibility – no better place to check out the class talent – as an arena of knowledge.

On the whole, though, *Cowboys and Indians* is more concerned with Eddie Virago's post-UCD adventures. One of the most significant aspects of the novel is the extent to which it captures the mood of pre-Celtic Tiger Ireland *avant la lettre*. Set in the early 1990s it documents the last moments of the particular cultural, political and economic stasis that characterised Irish life in the late decades of the twentieth century. It is hard not to think of James Joyce as an important precursor who famously described a comparable moment of Irish cultural paralysis in *Dubliners* and who, in *A Portrait of the Artist as a Young Man*, also sent his protagonist into exile after his UCD days. Eddie Virago, however, is no Stephen Dedalus. O'Connor's leading character is, in some important ways, a much more representative figure who embodies the frustrations of a generation coming of age in 1980s Ireland. He is not in any way surprised, for example, when he encounters a former college acquaintance – 'some bright spark hot shot who used to be auditor of the UCD History Society' (42) – working at the Ryanair check-in desk. O'Connor portrays this sense of trapped potential in his image of the Irish flag on the ship that takes Eddie to England, wrapped 'hard around the mast where it struggled unsuccessfully to unfurl' (12).

Throughout the novel Eddie Virago betrays an astounding level of moral confusion, which, in many ways, is suitably emblematic of 1980s Ireland – a society which was despairing of itself in a whole range of complex ways. He is animated by the dream of becoming a rock star in London but lacks the talent commensurate with his ambition. To use a Joycean analogy, he is Little Chandler in the world of Ignatius Gallaher – in love with the idea of rock stardom but unable to transcend his own personal circumstances to achieve it. His frequently espoused left-wing pronouncements are, more often than not, strategically deployed for effect rather than securely held beliefs. Proudly sporting his mohican hairstyle well beyond the heyday of punk, he wears the garb of radicalism while living a life of misguided self-interest. Eddie is an incorrigible Walter Mitty who has difficulty reconciling his dreams and fantasies with the brutal realities of everyday life. He is unable to form meaningful and fulfilling relationships and is astonishingly blind to the hurt he causes others as a consequence of his moral cowardice. The break-up of his parents' marriage provides an important mitigating backdrop to all of this and, at the same time, symbolises the wider fragmentation of older certainties of Irish life. In its downbeat ending *Cowboys and Indians* does not offer a way out for Eddie. The novel does, however, diagnose a condition and define a cultural moment with admirable prescience. In its engagement with a range of contemporary issues such as emigration, abortion, the Northern Ireland conflict, unemployment, marital breakdown and the crisis of national identity – albeit from the confused perspective of Eddie Virago – *Cowboys and Indians* bears witness to the challenges and frustrations of bleaker times.

O'Connor's second novel, *Desperadoes*, is more assured and technically adventurous in the presentation of the narrative from the dual perspectives of the central characters. Interestingly, this travel tale extends the scope of Irish fiction beyond the usual confines of the Anglophone world into a challenging Central American terrain. *Desperadoes*, indeed, might properly be considered a bilingual novel with significant portions of dialogue given in Spanish. Ostensibly it tells the story of Johnny Little, a character bearing many striking resemblances to Eddie Virago, who leaves Ireland to pick coffee in revolutionary Nicaragua in the mid-1980s. Among the noteworthy features of this book is the convincingly drawn setting of revolutionary Central America. O'Connor has a keen understanding of the attractions of Nicaragua for a whole range of first-world drop-outs and romantic revolutionaries or 'sandalistas' in search of adventure. The novel is peopled by an array of these characters in the last throes of sixties' 'peace and love'. Many, indeed, are gently satirised for their use of Nicaragua as an exotic backdrop for their own self-fashioning. This critique is succinctly delivered by a journalist who confronts the phenomenon head on:

> It's just like summer camp for you people, isn't it? I mean, down here on your trust funds, down to the bar-stool Bolshevik Disneyland, before you go running back to Greenwich Village to put on coffee mornings for Jesse Jackson. (47)

Desperadoes is also an interesting meditation on intergenerational relationships and is just as much a story of Johnny's parents, Frank and Eleanor. They receive news of Johnny's death and travel to Nicaragua to find their son's body. This forces them to confront the mistakes of the past in their attempt to deal with the trauma of the present moment. In essence, their journey becomes both a love story and a tale of falling out of love. In the unfolding of their stories, O'Connor creates an intriguing, and beautifully detailed, portrait of Dublin life in the middle decades of the twentieth century which is brought into relief, in all kinds of unexpected ways, by the revolutionary chaos of 1980s Nicaragua.

With his most recent novel, *Star of the Sea*, Joseph O'Connor has achieved an astounding breakthrough that puts him in the front rank of contemporary Irish writers. Many of the pre-occupations of the earlier fiction are still in evidence – emigration, an interest in issues of social justice and a fascination with the tensions between espoused beliefs and personal motivations. Setting this story in the historical past of the Irish Famine is a brave, if somewhat risky, strategy for any novelist; it is a familiar and, to this day, a contested context. Yet in the best traditions of the historical novel, O'Connor enlarges and complicates the Irish historical imagination through a potent combination of artistic insight and judicious historical scholarship (acknowledged at the end of the book). As the novel opens, subtle reference is made to the passing of O'Connellite Ireland as the passengers, catching sight of the ship that brought The Liberator's remains home, are moved to spontaneous communal prayer for their dead hero. If O'Connell represented a non-violent democratic tradition within Irish nationalism that strand was eclipsed by more revolutionary tendencies as the nineteenth century progressed. The reader of *Star of the Sea* is left in no doubt about the crucial role of the Famine in this transformation. Significantly, the novel's epilogue is dated 'Easter Saturday, 1916' (405).

The *Star of the Sea* sets sail from Queenstown bound for New York on 8 November 1847. The 403 steerage passengers on board are in various states of destitution and cling on to the hope of a new start in America. Many of the first-class passengers have also been touched by the ravages of the Famine in various ways. Just as in *Desperadoes*, where distressing times force unconventional interactions on an extraordinarily diverse array of characters, so too in this novel the lives of famine victims, aristocrats, revolution-aries, do-gooders, murderers, servants and charlatans come together in unexpected ways on the famine ship. Among its greatest achievements is the plausible reimagining of a period known to most of us in terms of cruel statistics of death and emigration. The characters presented are not fleeing starvation and a broken culture to merely exist elsewhere but have passions and aspirations, wonderfully articulated throughout the novel, to lead fully realised lives. O'Connor skilfully weaves these lives together in a compelling blend of fictional writings – journal entries, newspaper articles, letters, fragments of fiction, ballads and testimonies – which are, supposedly, contemporaneous with the Famine and its immediate aftermath.

Formally, *Star of the Sea* is significantly more elaborate and yet more accomplished than anything Joseph O'Connor has attempted to date. On the surface the novel bears resemblance to the penny dreadfuls and shilling shockers that were so popular during the Victorian period. These were cheap illustrated story-books and novels that were unashamedly sensationalist, often borrowing their storylines from the theatre of melodrama. Many of these publications were designed to appeal to the working classes and, in America, to immigrants. In Ireland they were so popular among a constituency which was gaining competency in the newly acquired English language that Douglas Hyde, in his famous essay on de-Anglicising Ireland, urged those interested in promoting Irish to set their faces 'sternly against penny dreadfuls and shilling shockers' (85). *Star of the Sea* recalls many of the salient features of these publications in the sensationalism of the chapter titles; in the overtly melodramatic tone of the standfirst texts placed below them; and in the engagingly horrific storyline of the 'Monster of Newgate'. There is also an abundance of contemporary illustrations recycled from publications such as *Punch* and *Harper's Weekly*, strategically deployed throughout the novel to confer authenticity on what is presented as a con-temporary account of the Irish Famine.

Yet there is a weightiness to this novel which belies its populist appearance. To some degree, *Star of the Sea* can be read as a sustained meditation on the authority of writing itself. One of the leading characters, the American journalist G. Grantley Dixon, is an aspiring novelist whose various writings are cleverly stitched into this complex narrative. The inclusion of his newspaper report on the Famine in Ireland for the *New York Tribune* is a clever expositional device deployed by O'Connor. The reliability of his account, however, is undermined by the character Merridith, who dismisses Dixon as a 'coffee-house [radical]' (6). Further into the book the reader comes upon a fragment of Dixon's unpublished novel. This extract, combined with Dixon's spectacularly misguided appraisal of the recently published *Wuthering Heights*, might lead the reader to incline more towards his proficiency as a journalist than as a novelist. Significantly though, it is Dixon's reflections on writing that bring the novel to a close as he considers the motivations and constraints that have shaped his own writing career. Ironically, at the end of this complex tale he is left contemplating the radical instability of narrative itself.

The art of the novel, then, is a central concern of *Star of the Sea* with the author paying homage to the great traditions of English fiction. The investment in presenting the narrative as if it were an actual contemporary account of the Famine is reminiscent of the strategies of the earliest novels. O'Connor's debt of influence stretches back to Daniel Defoe whose memorable descriptions of the grotesqueries of disease and death in *A Journal of the Plague Year* may have provided a useful exemplar for the fictional rendering of the horrors of the Irish Famine. In one memorable sequence in O'Connor's book, the face of the corpse of an elderly woman, who dies just as the ship sets sail, is disfigured with a crude blade lest her body drift back ashore to the distress of her former neighbours. The adventures of the wonderfully conceived character Pius Mulvey recall the picaresque escapades of the fiction of Sterne, Fielding and Smollett, albeit with a darker edge. A copy of *Wuthering Heights* plays a pivotal role in the intricate unfolding of the plot while Charles Dickens appears as a minor character in his own right. The demise of Merridith owes something to the nineteenth century novel of decadence and the spirit of Arthur Conan Doyle hovers perceptibly over the 'whodunit' denouement. Even the fleeting insight into the torment of the failed novelist, Dixon, recalls the inadequacies of Virginia Woolf's Mr Ramsay.

Notwithstanding its indebtedness to the English tradition, *Star of the Sea* is without question one of the most noteworthy Irish epics of recent decades. Significantly in this book, Joseph O'Connor turns away from the charms of the contemporary moment and rises to one of the great challenges to the modern Irish literary imagination: the elusiveness of nineteenth century cultural experience. Thomas Kinsella articulates this crux memorably in his influential essay 'The Divided Mind': 'Silence is the real condition of Irish literature in the nineteenth century … there is nothing that approaches the ordinary literary achievement of an age' (208). A society recovering from catastrophic famine and in the process of replacing one language with another, Kinsella implies, does not have much energy to invest in literary endeavour. Nor, indeed, does a dispossessed peasantry leave even the most rudimentary of written archives behind it. It is out of a felt need to somehow restore the dilapidated cultural archive that Brian Friel attempts to imaginatively recreate the complex dynamics of nineteenth century Gaelic experience in his masterpiece, *Translations*. Set in 1833 the play is centrally concerned with the causes and consequences of the decline of the Irish language in the period just before the potato blight descends in devastation. *Star of the Sea* is a fitting prose companion-piece to Friel's drama, moving the imaginatively reconstructed national narrative into the next decade with the harrowing story of Black '47.

Yet O'Connor's novel does a lot more than simply bear witness retrospectively to a traumatic moment of historical experience that passed without due creative articulation. In an imaginative manoeuvre *Star of the Sea* offers itself as a lost epic of the nineteenth century – a missing link in the Irish literary tradition. The genius of O'Connor's method lies in the fact that the narrative, in its intertextual allusions and references, stands up as a plausible, if necessarily fictional, culmination of mid-nineteenth century Irish literature. At the outset the reader is presented with an elaborate infrastructure of narrative framing devices – a preface, a whole series of complex footnotes, an epilogue and a list of sources – all of which allude to 'the first

Irish novel', Maria Edgeworth's *Castle Rackrent. Star of the Sea*, it would appear, is also intentionally derivative of the fiction of William Carleton, most notably in the depiction of famine suffering in *The Black Prophet* and the portrayal of the clandestine workings of agrarian secret societies in *Traits and Stories of the Irish Peasantry*. Perhaps most significantly, in one of the most remarkable passages of the book, O'Connor celebrates that most quintessential of nineteenth century Irish forms, the popular ballad. In the artistic awakening of Pius Mulvey the balladeer, one can see an analogue for the author's own aesthetic:

> The effect you wanted was a kind of easiness. Strong forward motion and easily remembered words. People needed to feel that the words had written themselves, that the balladeer now possessing them was only their medium. He wasn't singing the song. He was being sung. (102)

If this would-be missing link of the Irish literary tradition constructs a pedigree for itself out of the influential texts and genres of the first half of the nineteenth century, it also positions itself brilliantly in subtle and tantalising ways as a fictionally seminal precursor of the literature to come. Surrendering to this fiction, Yeats's poem 'The Fisherman' can be read as a re-imagining of that memorable Connemara man in 'ash-coloured clothes' (xi), Pius Mulvey. The hedonistic downfall of Merridith inspires Wilde's *Picture of Dorian Gray*. Joyce's *Ulysses* appears to have a significant progenitor in the formal experimentation and stylistic virtuosity of this famine narrative. It can seem plausible that the austere portrait of the bachelor years of the Mulvey brothers, who 'slept together in their parents' bed' (89), may have influenced Patrick Kavanagh's poem *The Great Hunger*. The impact of Mary Duane's love affair with the boy from the big house may be traceable in the fiction of Jennifer Johnston which is repeatedly concerned with unconventional relationships on the fringes of the Big House. Even John Banville's postmodern speculations on the limits of narrative can be seen to have their origins in G. Grantly Dixon's admission: 'Everything is in the way material is composed' (397).

When Pius Mulvey discovers his talent for balladry in *Star of the Sea* the narrator observes that '[k]nowing what to write about was the hardest thing about writing' (99). In many respects Joseph O'Connor, like most novelists, circles around the same concerns in all of his work despite the impressive diversity of contexts that have taken hold of his literary imagination. There is a neat symmetry, for example, in the fact that *Cowboys and Indians* begins on a ship with the main character reading *Ireland since the Famine* by F.S.L. Lyons. O'Connor, too, has a fascination with self-styled rebels on the margins who represent, in some way, the dying moments of a movement or era: Eddie Virago is the last of the mohicans, 'Los Desperados de Amor' are the last rebels of rock and roll, while David Merridith is the last inhabitant of the Big House. Nearly all of his central characters have ambitions greater than their talents and live dysfunctional lives, often radically at odds with their professed beliefs. Music is also a common thematic and stylistic thread in his writing – from 1970s punk to classic rock 'n' roll to nineteenth-century ballads. But what seems most significant about O'Connor's work is the profoundly intelligent cultural awareness at the heart of it. This has developed steadily with each novel and has reached a zenith with *Star of the Sea* – a novel of a different order to anything else he has written. For this reason his work to date stands as a significant contribution, not only to the UCD aesthetic, but also to the mapping of the modern Irish consciousness.

PRIMARY REFERENCES

Joseph O'Connor, *Cowboys and Indians* (London: Flamingo, 1992).
—, *Desperadoes* (London: Flamingo, 1994).
—, *Star of the Sea* (London: Vintage, 2003).

SECONDARY REFERENCES

Douglas Hyde, 'The Necessity for De-Anglicising Ireland', in *Poetry and Ireland since 1800*, edited by Mark Storey (London: Routledge, 1988).
Thomas Kinsella, 'The Divided Mind', in ibid.

MARINA CARR (B. 1964)

Cathy Leeney

Marina Carr took a degree in English and Philosophy in UCD and graduated in 1987. One summer during her time in Belfield she was keen to be involved in student theatre. Those were the days when the visitor season offered young student companies a good audience for lunchtime and evening productions at venues such as Players' Theatre in Trinity College or UCD's Newman House on St Stephen's Green. When Marina was not cast as a performer she enthusiastically offered to work on technical jobs, and Exiles Theatre Company, as that provisional summer group was called, presented Shaw's *Village Wooing* and a beautifully conceived anthology of scenes from Oscar Wilde, directed by Jim O'Keeffe. That was when I first met Marina Carr, a young woman from County Offaly of remarkable charm and beauty, and now an important figure in Irish theatre.

That summer was in another life, and before Marina's gradual accession to her current place as the most visionary and daring playwright of her generation. The poet Eavan Boland talks about the 'lived vocation' of the writer or the artist. Marina's work in theatre exemplifies this ideal of dedication and vision. Her plays have attracted the best directors, performers and designers in theatre, both in Ireland and abroad. Her journey thus far has had its nightmares, inevitable in the collaborative and very public art form of theatre, but her respect for the crafts of writing and performance is allied powerfully with a fearless imagination and intoxicating energy. She is unafraid; she is very unafraid.

Marina Carr's use of an idiomatic, heavily accented form of

Irish Midlands English marks most of her plays. The eccentric spelling in the quotations that follow are not misprints, but markers of a very particular and muscular engagement with language. She chooses the landscape of the Midlands, neglected by tourist advertisements and calendar photographers, to create a territory that accommodates a kind of Irish heart of darkness. The geography in her plays works on many levels, paralleling emotional states in the characters, opening Ireland out into a metonym for the world as the vulnerable home sanctuary of the human race.

Despite her youth, Marina's work has been the subject of considerable and ongoing critical attention. Here, I wish to look at her play *Ariel* (2002), and to reflect on how it shows us concerns current in our twenty-first century world, anxieties that arise through our love/hate relationship with planet Earth, and how the human family has its feet in the filth and its head in the stars.

'We live in an old chaos of the sun,' the American poet Wallace Stevens wrote, and *Ariel* creates images of the negotiations of a relatively new species, humanity, with a very ancient universe. The play is an epic tragedy centred in the Fitzgerald family. The action opens on the sixteenth birthday of the eldest daughter, Ariel, and spans the following ten years, during which the father (Fermoy) rises to power in politics, the mother (Frances) separates from him and their younger children (Elaine and Stephen) grow up to become cold and unhappy adults. The family unit is extended to include two observer characters: Fermoy's elder brother Boniface, a monk, and Aunt Sarah, the sister of Fermoy's and Boniface's dead mother. It was she who took the maternal role in the Fitzgerald home after the violent death of the boys' mother.

The ten-years-on scenes of searing recrimination and repressed grief that dominate the second and third acts arise from Fermoy's secret murder of Ariel on her sixteenth birthday, ten years earlier, in Act One. The father destroys the future of his own beautiful flesh and blood not because he hates his eldest child, but because he loves power more, and believes he will gain it through this Abrahamic sacrifice. Ariel's body is never found. In true Greek tragic fashion Fermoy's fate is spiritually pre-ordained from the time when, as a seven-year-old, he witnessed and helped his own father to murder his mother, by tying her up and sinking her to the bottom of Cuura Lake. Fermoy's overweening ambition dooms him in turn.

Act Two opens on the tenth anniversary of Ariel's death, when the family stumble back from the commemorative mass, marking the girl's disappearance. By now, Fermoy is Taoiseach-in-waiting. Observed by his disciple daughter Elaine, we hear his vision of power, to 'cahapult the whole nation ouha sleaze and sentimentalihy and gombeensim … to take this country to the moon' (63), as Elaine later describes it. Fermoy wants the Irish to re-invent themselves without pretense of civilisation, without reference to a gentle Christ figure, accepting pain and championing the underdog. Rather, Fermoy invokes Caesar and Napoleon, for whom 'the world was wan big battlefield' (42). He invokes Piero della Francesca's painting of a vengeful Christ, in *Resurrection* (1463). Elaine adores her father and shares knowledge of his savage deed. When she tells her mother that Ariel will never be coming home, she confirms what Frances has known in her heart without knowing: that Fermoy killed Ariel on the night of her birthday. Frances returns to the house to have it out with him. She listens disbelieving as he blames God for what he did. She is '*weeping like we've never seen*' (57). Fermoy tries to implicate her through her attraction for him as a man who would do anything, who offered her escape from her 'little bungalow life' and gave her 'graveyard excitement and the promise of funerals to come' (59). Frances stabs him repeatedly in a scene so excessively violent that, theatrically, it beggars belief. We may look back to Clytemnestra's murder of Agamemnon in Aeschylus's *Oresteia*, or Medea's murder of her children and of her rival Glauke in Euripides' play, but these deaths take place offstage, and it is widely believed that death in classical Greek tragedy happened out of sight. Athenian audiences may have seen the bodies of the victims displayed on the mobile platform called the *eccyclema*; they did not, most probably, have to confront the hideous act itself. In *Ariel*, we are faced with what we (hopefully) have never seen, or will see, in our lives; we are also faced with what we rarely have to encounter in the theatre. And it is not yet over.

Ariel's decayed corpse, hauled up out of Cuura Lake and placed in an open coffin, is at the centre of Act Three. Frances is on temporary release from prison to attend the belated funeral rite. Elaine, who guards her father's grave 'like an alsatian' (62), is poised in fury since she found that Frances plans to disturb Fermoy's plot, and to bury Ariel with her father. The defeated Stephen has lost even his loyalty to his mother; he rejects her outright and walks out on her, cheered on by Boniface. Every allegiance within the family structure seems to have been blown asunder, except allegiances with the dead.

In an image recalling Hamlet, Elaine takes her long-drowned sister's skull from the coffin and considers her bond with, and her jealousy of, Ariel. Suddenly, the ghost of Fermoy appears, blood-spattered and desolate. Unlike the ghost in *Hamlet*, though, Fermoy does not even recognise his own offspring. The ghost is itself haunted, by his murdered daughter and by his destiny in her destruction. When it leaves the stage it leaves Elaine defeated by its failure to acknowledge her. She turns on her mother in the final moments. We witness the last ghastly assault, the death of the middle generation, the obliteration of the flawed mother figure, the meaningless and inarticulate survival of vengeance for its own sake. As Elaine knifes Frances in the throat she claims the identity of all the dead who have gone before; she claims for the kingdom of the dead. The audience are left with nothing to cling to: no hero or heroine, no sense of right against wrong; only a future formed by bitter recrimination, loss, jealousy and dumb revenge. The extraordinary rhetorical power of the language up to this end game is silenced; Elaine says nothing. There is nothing left to say.

Ariel is excessive, stretched beyond the ordinary, epic in its passions. Its scope reaches beyond life into the world of hauntings, beyond good and evil into the seduction of power and beyond past and future into a terrifying eternity, past im-agination, yet echoing the darkest imaginings of chaos and savagery conceived in the human mind. Yet, on the surface, it is a play about an Irish family. Birthday cakes are baked, the cement business pays the bills and the world of politics and media is reflected and sent up in the television interview scene between Fermoy and Miriam O'Callaghan's clone.

How do these forgings of the domestic and the epic work in the play? Besides the ways in which they echo the tragic families of Euripides and Aeschylus, how do these forgings express the energies circulating outside the theatre, whether national or global? Two aspects of *Ariel* prompt a reading in the play of a wider meaning than the bloody tale of a doomed family, and a wider meaning even than the Fitzgerald family as a parallel for the state of Ireland under the Celtic Tiger, prey to corruption, private ambition and the ruthless self-interest of those in power. The first aspect centres on the presence in the play of the monk Boniface, and how he enables discussion of God, of spirituality and morality and of the divine. The second aspect is the shadow text of the play concerned with the question of what it is to be human.

Fermoy's elder brother Boniface is a figure of wry humour as he describes his chores as the youngest in his religious community, caring and peace-making amongst his failing and dwindling brethren. He is the Last of the Mohicans, but his faith has deserted him. He believes, residually, in gardening and in cornflowers. He can find no moral ground on which to challenge the megalomaniacal rantings of Fermoy. Because of his time away in the novitiate, Boniface has a distance from the traumatic history of his mother's death, yet the moral chaos in Fermoy's soul plays out in Boniface's depression and alcoholism.

Through the talk between the brothers emerges an idea of God as a nexus of ferocity, of blind cosmic energy. This God is perfection, and is perfectly raging with the imperfection of humanity. This God is not merely an Old Testament one, for Fermoy recreates the New Testament with a re-visioning of Christ as a 'big, cranky, vengeful son of God', the way he appears in Piero della Francesca's *Resurrection*. Pasolini's imagining of Christ in *The Gospel According to St. Matthew* (1967) is an unforgettable embodiment of such angry, impatient and unforgiving sternness. However, in *Ariel*, the figuring of God engulfs and sweeps away individual human concern, and floods over into chemistry, the god that is hydrogen, the power of the split atom and the primal big bang. In this cosmic scheme, the span of individual experience is torn open by the life of the cosmos beyond human death and of our utter inconsequence in the face of the seismic workings of the universe and the havoc wreaked on the blue and green vulnerability of the planet that we

269

share. In a moment that makes the hair stand on end in dreaded recognition, Fermoy describes how 'the earth's over … ozone layer in tahhers, oceans gone to sewer … We're goin to lave this place in ashes' (18). The design for the Abbey Theatre production of *Ariel* in 2002 showed us this sense of uncontrolled crisis on the scale of the globe itself. Frank Conway made the floor of the stage a botched map of the world, one corner of which jutted perilously into the auditorium and fell away like a cliff collapsing into the ocean.

When Fermoy describes Napoleon's view of the world as one big battlefield, the conflict goes beyond man-made armies and allegiances to call up images of biological life in man-made jeopardy. Marina Carr is not the only playwright to conjure up visions of the war between the human family on one side and nature and chemistry on the other. In Caryl Churchill's *The Skriker* (1994), the main character is a shape-changer, a demon of multiple identity who mischievously revels in human dislocation and human failure to live in balance with the natural world. S/he (for the figure is all genders and none) vengefully opens the portals to the underworld where madness measures the folly of human greed and *hubris*. The parallel scene in Hades mirrors the world of ashes evoked by Fermoy in Carr's play. Caryl Churchill uses figures and stories from English folk tradition to create representations of the relentless damage done to the earth (embodied by the Skriker) and the cumulated debt amassed by systematic exploitation and despoliation. Elves and goblins, as they embodied ideas of biological and divine order, must be appeased; but for too long they, and the respectful caution they demand, have been ignored. The consequences are beyond calculation. There is no going back. Carr uses religious and environmental imagery as a focus to create an associated sense of inevitable catastrophe. In *Ariel*, religious imagination in the human mind becomes a site where our fears as a species, and as part of a larger creation, take shape.

In both *The Skriker* and *Ariel* individuals are overwhelmed by forces they can only observe, or fall victim to. Carr dramatises this idea in her two on-stage observers, Boniface and Aunt Sarah. They are an audience within the drama, and they comment on the moral situation of the passive onlooker: as Sarah says, 'To watch a thing is ony to half wish ud' (72). Carr develops this theme of our voyeuristic negotiation with reality in the repeated image in *Ariel* of characters pausing in the doorway before they enter a scene, and silently observing the ongoing action. To be only a watcher, then, is not to be free of responsibility, perhaps even to half share it, yet to be powerless to take control.

The role of the individual protagonist as the centre of the drama is usurped in *Ariel* by the overpowering sense of persons in the grip of larger forces, whether they be spiritual, chemical, genetic or historical. The family, in theatre, provides an image of how humans live not only for themselves, but also for the continuance, or otherwise, of the race. The domestic family is a parallel for the human family, for our species. Privileging human concerns over those of other species relies upon a clear definition of the category 'human'. This brings me to the second aspect of *Ariel* that invites us to read the play as concerned with the human condition beyond domesticity or nationality.

Carr, in her use of imagery, consistently begs the question: what is it to be human? The notion, of course, is planted even as early as the title, *Ariel*. Anyone who has seen or read Shakespeare's *The Tempest* remembers Ariel, the spirit who can fly, swim or 'dive into the fire' (Act 1, Sc. II) to serve Prospero and win liberty. Ariel Fitzgerald is a teenager at the cusp of liberty, brimming with youthful promise and beauty, but she is more. Later in the play, her father, haunted by guilt for her murder, has fevered memories of the child as half-angel, with wings budding from her shoulder blades. He had a dream in which God says of the girl, 'she's noh earth flavour' (57), that she does not belong in mortal life, but belongs with God. *Ariel* creates a continuum where, at the apex, lies flashes of the eternal and the divine, while the nadir dips into the bestial and the barbaric, with images of people as half-animal. Fermoy dreams of dining with Alexander the Great, Napoleon and Caesar, where they 'all had tiger's feeh under the whihe linen tablecloth' (14). Civilisation has failed to civilise, failed to separate human beings not only from our savage ancestors in the caves, but also from the amoral beast, the surge of the life force itself. It goes back a long way, the borrowing of animal imagery to describe human nature. 'Homo homini lupus', or 'man is to other men a wolf' is the way Plautus put it; perhaps it is ironic that this human tendency to look everywhere for reflections of ourselves blinds us to anything that is not dreamt of in our philosophies.

In the final moments of the action, as mother and daughter face each other down, Frances spits out a repellent image of bestial progeniture: 'some zebra stallion grafted you onta me' (74). Such words in the mouths of the performers reveal disturbing visions of mutable life forms across the boundaries of species. This extreme category crisis connects with our current anxieties around genetic engineering, cloning and artificial intelligence. Images of the human family are, in our time, a confused patchwork made up from the Garden of Eden, from Darwinian models of species change and interconnection and from the porous boundaries between persons and the technologies they invent. The Fitzgerald family is the human family destroying itself, haunted by the costs of power and ambition, powerless to control its future, reaching for a shred of the eternal and the transcendent.

In common with a number of such earlier plays as *The Mai* (1994), *Portia Coughlan* (1996), and *By the Bog of Cats* (1998), Marina fashions, in *Ariel*, images of water as the element that carries human longing, that calls up life beyond mortality. At the bottom of Cuura Lake lie the bodies of Fermoy's mother and of his daughter, amongst numerous corpses of the unwanted and despised. Ariel rises twice from her watery grave; first she haunts her father with her account of the great pike that will not rest until he has her; then her remains are hauled up and placed at the centre of Act Three. Both these images are of a damaging past, of unavoidable pain and its intent on retribution. Cuura Lake contains the shameful secrets of the Fitzgerald family and, it is implied, of the wider human community amongst whom they live. The lake is a reservoir of crimes past, welling up into the present. In *Ariel*, vengeance belongs to Cuura Lake, to the planet and not to the Lord.

Marina Carr is a writer alert to the currencies of the world around her, and inspired in her imaginings of its shadows, its burdens, its passions and its possibilities. In *Ariel* she writes a fearful and bloody tragedy to rival the excesses of the Greeks and the Jacobeans, while also encapsulating a contemporary mood of anxious concern with our status and our tenure here on the Earth.

PRIMARY REFERENCE

Marina Carr, *Ariel* (Oldcastle: Gallery Books, 2002).

Emma Donoghue (b. 1969)

Eibhear Walshe

'On principle, I'm not going to object to "lesbian writer" if I don't
object to "Irish writer" or "thirty-something woman writer" since
these are all equally descriptive of me and where I come from. And
the labels commit me to nothing, of course. My books aren't and
don't have to be all about Ireland, or thirty-something women or
lesbians' – Emma Donoghue (emmadonoghue.com)

In the short term, labels can be potent symbols in the transformation of oppressive and outmoded tropes about sexual
identity within Irish culture. However, labels like 'lesbian', 'Irish
writer' or 'woman' can also become the most illegible kind of
shorthand. In this essay I want to consider Emma Donoghue's
four novels published in the last ten years, *Stirfry*, *Hood*,
Slammerkin and *Life Mask*. For Donoghue, who was born in
Dublin in 1969 and first published in 1994, the fictive
exploration of a contemporary Irish lesbian identity has been the
most innovative feature of her first two novels. Since then, her
more recent fiction has extended the range and the form of her
imaginative preoccupations with a movement towards the past
and towards historical fiction. Drawing on her experience as a
literary critic and an historian of early modern sexual identities,
she has created powerful historical fictions of eighteenth century
England. In the genre of historical fiction, representations of the
past are usually meditations on the nature of the quotidian and I
would argue that Donoghue is using the eighteenth century as

the imaginative arena for her last two novels to shift her fictive range away from the immediacies of a politicised literary identity.

When Emma Donoghue, already a literary critic and a cultural historian, published her first novel *Stirfry* in 1994, she did so as an openly lesbian Irish writer. Her literary 'coming out' coincided with the emergence of other openly lesbian and gay Irish writers such as Mary Dorcey, Cathal O'Searcaigh, Keith Ridgeway and Tom Lennon, to name a few. Homosexuality was decriminalised in Ireland in 1993 and the importance of that coming out, that self-identification for writers in the years after the decriminalisation, cannot be underestimated. Apart from Mary Dorcey, Emma Donoghue was the first openly Irish lesbian writer and this was a radical departure within twentieth-century Irish writing. The most important figure in Irish lesbian writing in the twentieth century up to this point had been her fellow UCD graduate Kate O'Brien. But O'Brien was never visible in terms of her own sexuality, only in terms of her writings. As well as that, as Donoghue wrote of her predecessor, 'lesbian historians and critics seem never to have heard of her, or know of no context of "Irish lesbian fiction" in which to place her' ('Out of Order: Kate O'Brien's Lesbian Fictions', 37). Thus, when Donoghue produced *Stir-Fry*, a contemporary Irish coming-out narrative and published by Hamish Hamilton, a mainstream English publishing house, she was deliberately troubling the living stream of late twentieth-century Irish writing.

Before this, lesbian identity within Irish writing had been, to say the least, liminal. In her article 'Occupied Country: The Negotiation of Lesbianism in Irish Feminist Narrative', Kathryn Conrad contends that within Irish writing to that point,

> the feminist and queer/positive response to occluding or silencing narratives, however, has too often been similarly contained through an implicit acceptance of 'appropriate' or 'significant' topics sanctioned by the patriarchal state: in the 'public sphere', war and government or in the 'private sphere', heterosexual romance and personal enlightenment. Resistance means finding new ways to approach narrative, rather than repeating the narrowly focused, carefully contained narratives that ultimately reproduce hierarchies of 'importance'. (135)

Donoghue's writings from 1994 onwards have indeed suggested a whole range of new ways in which to approach narrative from the perspective of an Irish lesbian sensibility. Her fictions have drawn upon a range of narrative forms, such as the coming-out novel, the fictive meditation on death and bereavement, the historical novel. All of these forms have functioned as parables for the nature of lesbian sexuality and for discourses around contemporary homophobia and female entrapment. Other hierarchies of 'importance', in particular the hierarchies of Irish cultural identity usually addressed by Donoghue's contemporaries, are of less interest to her. For example, the debate around the burden of the Irish literary past for a contemporary writer is of more relevance to other contemporary Irish novelists. Any need to re-invent or re-appropriate the tropes of the Irish literary canon is of much less importance for Donoghue as an Irish lesbian writer simply because in looking for a past to subvert, she had precious little to re-invent. As she put it herself,

> Foreign savours stimulated my appetite, but I hungered for the local. The wonderful surveys of lesbian literature I tracked down … had next to nothing to say about Ireland; they told me about the novels of Mary Renault, but not of Kate O'Brien. 'Irish lesbian' still had the ring of a contradiction in terms: how was I to conceive of myself as a practising Catholic and a furious lesbian feminist, a sweet colleen and a salty sinner? ('Noises from Woodsheds: Tales of Irish Lesbians, 1886–1989', 159)

Yet, having confronted these apparent contradictions by establishing a lesbian identity in her fictions and in her public self-presentation, the dilemma for any contemporary novelist is to resist the burden of being 'representative'. The moment of public self-definition in the mid-1990s for Irish lesbian and gay writers came at a time of vital political necessity but it was only that, a moment. For many of these writers at the beginning of the twenty-first century, this moment has passed. To a great degree, Donoghue was seen as a spokesperson, or even an exemplar, for an emergent identity asserting itself after a century of criminalisation. The consolidation of legal and political rights meant that some kind of tentative cultural validation was being established for Irish lesbians and gay men. As a result, Irish lesbian and gay writings into the twenty-first century moved away from the directly political and thus, away from the coming out narrative of the mid-1990s. Instead there is what Alan Sinfield has termed the 'Post-Gay' moment where writers reassess the relationship between sexual identity and 'queer' literary discourse beyond the immediate concerns of the political. Being the only best-selling, mainstream Irish lesbian novelist is potentially limiting and constricting and Donoghue's last two fictions have extended the limits of the labels 'Irish' 'Lesbian' 'Woman'. In this essay, I want to chart the development of Emma Donoghue's fictions since her first coming-out novel in 1994 and argue that, in her use of triangular dynamics of desire and power, she interrogates not only lesbian selfhood but also the nature of heterosexuality in her interconnected explorations of the body, of the erotic and of the self.

In Donoghue's first novel, *Stir-Fry* (1994), a witty and likeable college novel set in Dublin, the protagonist, Maria, is a seventeen-year-old first-year student, an innocent country girl new to city life and to the potential complexities of sexual identity. The time frame for the novel is imprecise but this is clearly pre-Celtic Tiger Ireland. The Dublin that Maria comes to live in is slightly impoverished and somewhat conservative and uncomprehending when it comes to questions of sexual preference outside the heterosexual consensus. Maria is attending a university which is unnamed in the text but by its topography is clearly inspired by UCD (even 'The Trap', the old pool hall in the basement of the Arts Block, makes a brief appearance – renamed as 'The Pit'). In her first weeks at university, Maria moves into a flat in the appropriately named Beldam Square, sharing her new home with the slightly older women Ruth and Jael, unaware of the fact that they are, in fact, a couple. The dramatic impulse of the novel, named after the stages of preparation for a stir fry, mixing, heating, waiting, turns on Maria's gradual realisation that not only are Ruth and Jael a couple, but that she is herself lesbian and in love with Ruth.

This first novel introduces Donoghue's distinctive representations of possible lesbian selfhoods in her characterisation of the three young Irish women. Maria, young, unformed, questioning, is seen as gradually moving towards self-realisation yet remains in limbo, a kind of pre-selfhood in terms of her sexual identity. Donoghue focalises her narrative exclusively through Maria's slightly bewildered observations of university life and on the performances of heterosexual identity. She watches for clues as to her own sexual identity by observing the romances of her straight friend Yvonne, and also in her own tentative encounters with other male students. However, there is an unreality for Maria in these observations of heteronormative sexual identity. She is increasingly attracted towards Ruth and, by implication, interested in the versions of lesbian selfhood that the two women offer. Ruth, in her late twenties and a mature student at UCD, is home-loving, economically self-sufficient, domestic, nurturing and, as it transpires, faithful to her lover. On the other hand, Jael is privately wealthy, politically radical, blissfully undomesticated, freewheeling and polygamous.

It is interesting to note that in *Stir Fry*, while there is some connection between Ruth and Jael's lesbianism and their political activism and commitment to radical feminism, there is little or no portrayal of any sustained links between the couple and a wider lesbian community in Dublin. Ruth is not 'out' to her family and she and Jael have stopped drinking in the one lesbian pub in the centre of Dublin because, it is implied, of some love affair of Jael's that has gone wrong. The only other lesbian who features, Silk, is in fact a lover of Jael's and poses an implied threat to the stability of the two women's relationship. On the other hand there is little or no homophobia in the novel, apart from Maria's straight college friend Yvonne, who warns her against the dangers of sharing a flat with lesbians. However, the teenaged Yvonne's strictures against the lavender menace and the perils of associating with dykes are treated with a certain amount of affectionate authorial irony. The novel ends with Maria's realisation that she too is lesbian and in love with Ruth but this is left deliberately unresolved. Maria's coming out is suspended somewhere in the future, without any confrontation scenes between her and her family and friends, without even a love scene between Maria and Ruth. Yet the essential dynamics of desire within a triangular relationship have been established as Donoghue's most characteristic trope as a novelist.

Hood is a fuller and more sustained examination of an Irish lesbian selfhood. It stands, with Kate O'Brien's 1958 novel *As Music and Splendour*, as the most important document of Irish lesbian identity in modern Irish writing. Antoinette Quinn sees the novel as a crucial text within late twentieth-century Irish fiction and argues that 'in refusing to construct a monument to gay pride or to gay victimisation, Donoghue brings the Irish lesbian novel out of the ghetto' ('New Noises from the Woodshed: The Novels of Emma Donoghue', 164). This novel is set in 1992 but, as with *Stir Fry*, the Dublin that it presents is again pre-Celtic Tiger, slightly run-down, distinctly non-prosperous. Within this second novel, Donoghue's polarised versions of lesbian identity, hinted at in *Stir-fry*, are much more clearly delineated. The novel follows the protagonist, Pen O'Grady, a secondary school teacher in her early thirties, in the week after the sudden death of her lover, Cara Wall. Cara is killed in a freak car crash on the way home from Dublin Airport, coming back from a holiday in Greece. Pen is forced by the shock of this abrupt death to confront the shortcomings and contradictions of twelve years of being 'kind of girl friends' with the younger Cara. The two women became lovers when they met as teenagers in secondary school, at the convent school where Pen is now a teacher. Despite the fact that they share a house with Cara's unassuming, discreet father, Mr Wall, few people are told of their relationship and Cara has periodically broken up with Pen because of her affairs with other lovers, male and female. As with the earlier novel, Donoghue presents the lesbian partners as opposite in terms of selfhood – the slightly younger Cara, like Jael, is bisexual, polygamous, politicised and radical, without any regular job or income. Cara is also a politically active feminist whose politicisation connects her with a Dublin lesbian community. Pen, who is the focus for the authorial voice, is a counterpart to Ruth, closeted, faithful, conservative, maternal and domestic. The third figure within this triangular relationship is Kate, Cara's straight sister and Pen's contemporary from school, the original object of Pen's affections.

As the week of mourning continues and the rituals of death

unfold, the narrative observes the gradual challenges to Pen's sense of herself as lesbian and to her self-imposed 'otherness' and isolation from both heterosexual and homosexual communities. Throughout the novel, the ceremonies of mourning and remembrance are viewed through the eyes of the sorrowing Pen yet, in a curious way, this process of mourning is in fact liberating for her. Before Cara's death, Pen had been profoundly closeted about her lesbianism to her mother and to her colleagues. She had also been hostile to the so-called Attic women, a nearby commune of lesbians where Cara has found friends and casual lovers. (This is, perhaps, a covert reference to Attic Press, the Irish feminist press of the 1980s and 1990s.) The process of loss is for Pen a process of re-evaluation, particularly of her closeted, possessive yet compulsive relationship with Cara. *Hood* therefore becomes a much more sustained examination of sexuality and death and of an Irish lesbian selfhood. Death, the brutal intervention of sudden loss, is actually the catalyst for Pen's eventual coming out. Her gradual realisation is that her love for Cara and her faithfulness have kept her closeted and apolitical. At one point, musing on Cara's greater independence and feminism, Pen begins to wonder about the broader idea of an Irish lesbian community:

> I could see all the way across the southside from this knob of rock. The books Cara brought back from England and America were mostly about urban dykes in trench-coats solving capitalist mysteries or rural bare-breasted ones tending wounded deer. But most of the real ones I'd ever come across were quietly rebellious products of the suburbs, wearing waistcoats over ladylike shirts at dinner-parties … Nowadays invisibility was supposed to be the big problem, but the way I say it was, all that mattered was to be visible to yourself. (60)

Invisibility, the kind of invisibility that Pen tried to maintain, was her choice rather than an actual necessity for survival in a Dublin where homophobia never threatens her and where her coming out moments are all met with acceptance and understanding. As Antoinette Quinn notes, *Hood* is a novel about coming out of a ghetto but, in fact, Pen's ghetto is self-constructed, the ghetto of her own closetry and her overwhelming love and need for Cara. As the novel concludes, Pen does seem to have overcome some of her aversion to the Attic lesbian community and is emboldened to come out to a male colleague, then to Cara's sister Kate and finally to Cara's father Mr Wall who wants her to continue living in his house. The novel ends as Pen resolves to tell her mother that she is a lesbian. In the words of Jennifer M. Jeffers in *The Irish Novel at the End of the Twentieth Century*, '*Hood* is giving voice to the idea that rigid boundaries are the things that hurt. The most obvious and seemingly intractable set of boundaries is the heterosexual matrix. Donoghue's text attempts to roll over these boundaries, create new possibilities and [begin to] render the heterosexual norm useless and meaningless' (106–7).

In her next two novels, Emma Donoghue moves away from contemporary Dublin to expand on her examination of sexual selves and the rigidness of the heterosexual matrix. Because of her experience as a cultural historian, particularly with her study *Passions between Women: British Lesbian Culture: 1668–1801*, Donoghue moves easily into the arena of historical fiction. *Slammerkin*, her 2000 novel, takes as its point of inspiration a fragment of real history. Its departure point is the lurid and inaccurate pamphlet on the life and death of the fifteen-year-old servant girl Mary Saunders, who was hanged in 1763 in Monmouth for killing her mistress, Jane Jones. Donoghue imagines the sequence of grim events that led Mary Saunders to such a moment and, in doing so, presents a devastatingly bleak view of working-class women's lives in the eighteenth-century and of the realities of prostitution. Moving beyond labels, Donoghue writes about a heterosexual girl in her late teens in eighteenth-century London, a novel without any reference to Ireland, lesbians or even thirty-something women. The customary triangular relationship around the dynamics of the erotic is the underlying structure for *Slammerkin* but here it is firmly within the context of heterosexuality, with the young servant girl Mary Saunders, her kindly mistress Jane Jones and Jane's husband, Thomas. In this supple, crisply written narrative, profound questions about the heterosexual matrix are dealt with. Donoghue is a very physical writer, always presenting her characters within the context of bodily desires and discomforts and in this novel the body now becomes a place of extreme unease. A young London girl Mary Saunders, pregnant and diseased with the clap at a cruelly early age and abandoned by her family, turns to prostitution for money and for a sense of control and power. When she runs foul of a pimp, Mary runs away to Monmouth where she is taken in by the good-natured dressmaker Jane Jones and given a home and surrogate maternal care. Yet the lesson that Mary Saunders has learnt is that the body is the first point of deception and she returns to prostitution as a means of independence – at one point even seducing Jane's husband. When Jane finds and confiscates Mary's 'immoral' earnings, her running-away money, and puts them into the church poor box, Mary Saunders kills her. Betrayed by heterosexuality too young, Mary kills the only woman who has shown her maternal love. At one point, Mary Saunders, literate but with no respect for books, tells her admirer the scholarly Davey that books are full of lies. However, bodies and not books are the real source of betrayal in this text, not only for Mary herself but also for her good-hearted mistress, Jane, who has lost all but one of her many children at birth or in early childhood. Thus in *Slammerkin*, Donoghue expands on her meditations on the vulnerability of the body and the uncertain nature of sexual identity.

In her latest novel, *Life Mask*, published in 2004 and set in the years 1787 to 1797, Donoghue uses her research on lesbian and gay history to draw a portrait of a homophobic society and of an earlier lesbian selfhood. Her central character is the real life Anne Damer, sister of the Duchess of Richmond, well connected in Georgian aristocratic society and a sculptress of note. The novel examines Anne Damer's relationship with Eliza Farren the Irish actress. The familiar triangular relationship is between the lesbian Anne Damer, the heterosexual Eliza Farren and Lord Derby, the wealthy nobleman who aspires to marry Eliza, the working woman. The developing friendship between Anne Damer and the young actress abruptly ends when the following anonymous poem is circulated and printed, hinting at Damer's sapphism:

Her little stock of private fame
Will fall a wreck to public clamour,

If Farren leagues with one whose name
Comes near – aye, very near – to DAMN HER.

Eliza Farren, whose life as a popular actress places her firmly in the public eye, is a woman of strict and formidable personal integrity and virtue, sought in marriage by the Earl of Derby. Afraid for her reputation, she cuts Anne Damer out of her life. Damer, shocked and terrified, begins to question her own sexuality and the novel ends with the marriage of Lord Derby and Eliza Farren and the coming-out of Anne Damer. Interestingly this is Donoghue's most sustained examination of the effects of a public atmosphere of homophobia on a private life, seen in the conjunction between straight and lesbian desire. Clear historical parallels are drawn here with media hysteria in England at the time of the revolution in France and contemporary North American pressure of public opinion and hysteria against same-sex passion in the wake of 9/11. (At one point, the phrase 'Homeland Security' is used by one of the eighteenth-century English newssheets!) Because of the pressure of political turmoil from abroad, English aristocratic society is the focus for public attack and a fault line within this culture is the notion of same-sex desire between women, a time when so-called 'tommys' or sapphists are ridiculed and attacked. The life mask is the mask of the closet and when Anne Damer confronts her private and public demons, she realises that the slander is true and claims the name of sapphist for herself, finding a life-long partnership with Mary Berry.

In the ten years since her first novel, Emma Donoghue's fictions have been successful in both remaking and then transcending, labels, making her one of the most powerful and distinctive voices in contemporary Irish writing.

PRIMARY REFERENCES

Emma Donoghue, *Passions between Women: British Lesbian Culture 1668–1801* (London: Scarlett Press, 1993).

—, 'Out of Order: Kate O'Brien's Lesbian Fictions', in *Ordinary People Dancing: Essays on Kate O'Brien*, edited by Eibhear Walshe (Cork: Cork University Press, 1993): 36–58.

—, *Stir-Fry* (London: Hamish Hamilton, 1994).

—, *Hood* (London: Hamish Hamilton, 1995).

—, 'Noises from Woodsheds: Tales of Irish Lesbians, 1886–1989' in *Lesbian and Gay Visions of Ireland: Towards the Twenty-first Century*, edited by Ide O'Carroll and Eoin Collins (London: Cassell, 1995).

—, *Slammerkin* (London: Virago, 2000).

—, *Life Mask* (London: Virago, 2004).

SECONDARY REFERENCES

Kathryn Conrad, 'Occupied Country: The Negotiation of Lesbianism in Irish Feminist Narrative', in *Eire-Ireland* 31.1 and 2 (Spring/Summer 1996): 123–36.

Jennifer M. Jeffers, *The Irish Novel at the End of the Twentieth-Century: Gender, Bodies and Power* (New York: Palgrave, 2002).

Antoinette Quinn, 'New Noises from the Woodshed: the Novels of Emma Donoghue', in *Contemporary Irish Fiction: Themes, Tropes, Theories*, edited by Liam Harte and Michael Parker (London: Macmillan, 2000): 145–67.

CONOR MCPHERSON (B. 1971)

Anthony Roche

The still-young Irish playwright Conor McPherson, whose plays have been acclaimed on the stages of London, Dublin, New York and beyond, attended UCD between 1988 and 1993, where he took a BA in English and Philosophy and an MA in Philosophy. In his final BA year, he ended up in one of my weekly Modern English tutorials. It was my first year as a Lecturer in English at UCD, so he had not requested that he be placed there. In the opening session, I asked the students what they did in their extra-curricular time, what college societies they were active in, what possible careers they might be considering for the life after their June exams. The young man with the closecropped red hair and the direct look from behind the steel-framed glasses said: 'I write plays.' I asked what they were about, and in return he outlined a drama about a group of young men who gather to discuss a previous evening involving young women and a good deal of drink which had ended in a rape. As he spoke, I realised – and told him – that I had seen the play, staged some months earlier in Dramsoc. And what I hope and think I communicated was how impressed I was, by the focused intensity, the authenticity and the verbal concision of the writing.

Such was my introduction to Conor McPherson. During this first year at UCD, I had resolved to see as many Dramsoc productions as possible, without quite realising that this meant two shows a week, an hour at lunchtime, a full-length play in the evening: over forty for the academic year. (At the university in the US where I had been teaching, the annual total had been five.)

This attendance meant, among other things, that I saw a great deal of Conor's work. Not only was he writing plays but frequently directing them, scripts both by himself and by the group of which he formed part, subsequently named Fly By Night. One of these was by Coilin O'Connor, who was in the same tutorial group; his work was no less quirky and playful than Conor's but more overtly literary. And McPherson also turned his hand to acting. I recall his appearance in a Harold Pinter play, exuding just the right mixture of comedy and menace; and he managed quite a turn as the academic sociologist Dobbs in Brian Friel's *The Freedom of the City*, suggesting links with the philosophy lecturer Dr Raymond Sullivan in his own later play, *This Lime Tree Bower* (1995).

Both Pinter and Friel were to be important influences in Conor's own development, not least in their deployment of monologue as a profound dramatic resource, and they need to be set beside the (if anything) overstated emphasis on the influence of David Mamet. Certainly, Mamet's star ran high in Dramsoc in those days; his plays were frequently put on there, some of them directed by my colleague Dr John Barrett, who also lectured on Mamet's plays to the undergraduate English students. One of Conor's original plays was as close to an Irish translation of Mamet as it is possible to get. But I felt once he had made that homage, Conor had absorbed Mamet's idiom and rhythm and was free of any overt influence or indebtedness. The style Conor McPherson developed in those years was distinctly his own – dialogue-driven, displaying a great talent for storytelling, inducing frequent outbursts of laughter while remaining utterly serious in what his plays were pursuing, providing a real and recognisable X-ray of the young Irish male and his insecurities, mingling the profane and the sacred.

Both Conor McPherson and Coilin O'Connor attended our tutorial and wrote their essays while maintaining a high profile in Dramsoc, thus giving the lie to the widely held belief that the two activtities are inimical and mutually exclusive. Where Coilin was more low key, Conor kept the rhetorical level of the tutorial high. If I said something was white, he would maintain it was black; or vice-versa. One of the plays he put on that year was entitled

Michelle Pfeiffer and the posters for the production all over college featured a photo of Ms Pfeiffer. 'Conor,' I said during one of our sessions, 'your play entitled *Michele Pfeiffer* has not a single reference to her in the text. Is it not rather a device to use her in the poster and so objectify her as woman?' Conor retorted: 'You have a photo of Sinéad O'Connor on your wall,' pointing at the *Rolling Stone* cover affixed to my filing cabinet. He was one of the very few students I have met who seemed clearly set on a path, looking ahead at something the rest of us could scarcely discern, while remaining true to the pragmatics of the present. He had a rare blend of honesty and outspokenness, always with the humorous edge, which made him stand out even then.

In the year after their graduation, Conor and Coilin joined with Peter MacDonald, Valerie Spelman, Kevin Hely and others to form Fly By Night and stage plays in the International Bar. His first breakthrough play, *Rum and Vodka*, was staged that same year in 1992 in UCD and subsequently in a Fly By Night production in the City Arts Centre by Tara Street train station. What has struck me when I have seen productions of Conor's subsequent plays in both London at the Royal Court or in Dublin at the Gate is how true to the aesthetic of LG1 in Belfield his theatre has remained. One can call it a theatre of poverty (an economic necessity, no doubt) or a theatre of minimalism (if one wants to make an aesthetic virtue of necessity). But it has always relied on an openness of staging and a minimum of props. Increasingly, the mainstream Dublin theatres have had to learn to adapt from their proscenium origins to accommodate writers like Conor McPherson or companies like Galway's Druid and Dublin's Rough Magic who have found their ways to a life in the theatre through the openness and experimentation of college drama societies. When you sit in LG1, you stare into a space of infinite possibility; when someone comes on and stands in the light, you are ready to trust them to take you on a journey. A great deal of Conor's preference for monologues and storytelling comes from working for five years in this space. It underwrites his frequently stated reply when asked, 'Where am I?' 'Where is the play set?': 'These plays [of mine] are set in a theatre. Why mess about? The character is *on stage*, perfectly aware that he is talking to a group of people. I've always tried to reflect that simplicity in productions.'

The recurrent criticism encountered in relation to McPherson's theatre is that the plays are mostly or are entirely made up of monologues. It came around again in an *Irish Times* review I read last month by Mary Leland of a Cork production of *This Lime Tree Bower*. But McPherson's plays are a reminder that Irish drama arguably had its origins at least as much in the communal art of the oral storyteller performed in the home or in the pub as in a fourth-wall drama performed on a proscenium stage. Brian Friel drew on monologue as the exclusive source of his 1979 drama *Faith Healer*, where three characters – the faith healer of the title, his wife Grace and manager Teddy – appear in turn before the audience to tell their versions of the story they have all participated in. McPherson has clearly been influenced by *Faith Healer*, drawing on its four interlocking monologues for *This Lime Tree Bower*. And the visit by the traumatised Irishman to the disturbed psychiatrist in his 2004 play *Shining City* not only brings Tom Murphy's *Gigli Concert* (1983) to mind but stresses how central the monologue is to Murphy's achievement as a playwright. There are formal storytellers in the plays of Beckett and Pinter also, who frequently face their audiences with little more than their story to tell. All of these major twentieth-century playwrights constitute a resource for contemporary Irish dramatists like McPherson, Sebastian Barry and Eugene O'Brien. In 2000 Conor directed O'Brien's debut play *Eden* at the Peacock. In a series of alternating monologues, a man and a woman in their early thirties from the Irish Midlands spoke of the difficulties their marriage was going through. In O'Brien's writing, McPherson's directing and the acting of Don Wycherly and Catherine Walsh, but most of all through the monologue form, the audience gained a more unmediated and intimate access to the two characters' thoughts and feelings. The play toured and transferred to the Abbey a year later. I met Conor while he was rehearsing *Eden* for the mainstage. I asked if he foresaw any problems with this, and he said no, he did not. It was not just his characteristic lack of intimidation at the prospect of the large Abbey stage (a stage which has never given a welcome to any of his own distinctive creations); it was also that he saw no reason to alter his theatrical methods from what he had learned in LG1.

Conor McPherson graduated from UCD in 1991 with a double First in English and Philosophy. The way was open for him to do an MA and in the end he chose to do it in Philosophy. In the main, the Belfield campus rarely makes it into a McPherson play. But an exception occurs in 1995's *This Lime Tree Bower*. One of the three characters is a philosophy lecturer and the play includes a description of the UCD Philosophy Department which can be identified by the fact it is the only department in the John Henry Newman building (or the Arts Block, as it is referred to by one and all) to occupy a fifth floor. As Ray puts it in one of his monologues:

My office was on a corner of the highest part of the college.
  This tickled Tony Regan no end.
  He said that the philosophy department was near heaven
  so that when the questions became too unbearable we could lean
  out the window and ask God. (99)

The Belfield bar, where Ray holes up much of the time, is only too recognisable; and he gives his lectures in Theatre O. Ray himself is hardly an advertisement for the academic profession. Filled with a curious but credible mixture of pomposity and self-loathing, he preys relentlessly on the more attractive of his female undergraduate students. While the Belfield locations may be recognisable, nobody in the Philosophy Department at UCD, so far as I am aware, has been matched up with this archetypal character. I've always wondered whether, if Conor had chosen to do his MA in his other subject, the play's lecherous lecturer would have been a member of the English Department. In *St. Nicholas* (1997), the sole character is a drama critic who again preys on young women, in this instance an actress from an Abbey Theatre production. But the play is quite explicit that the protagonist is not an academic but a theatre reviewer who walks 'out of plays ten minutes before the end' (5) and 'usually had reviews written before the play was finished'. One imagines that any young playwright trying to get a hearing in Dublin would have a few scores to settle with the local critics. McPherson, in the manner of Dante assigning appropriate fates in his *Purgatorio*, has his theatre critic end up in the company of vampires (or blood-sucking parasites, if you prefer). Perhaps it's just as well McPherson did not pursue an MA in English.

In 1993 he was awarded an MA in Philosophy for a major thesis entitled: 'Logical Constraint and Practical Reasoning: On Attempted Refutations of Utilitarianism'. Unlike many contemporary Irish writers who suppress their academic qualifications for the sake of street cred, Conor gave the full title of his thesis in the Royal Court/Gate Theatre programme for *Shining City*, as something of which he is (justifiably) proud, as something which is part of the record and as an avenue along which he might have continued, had he not turned full-time to the world of theatre and (in more recent years) film.

The MA thesis makes for fascinating reading, not least when taken in conjunction with the plays. It is a strong-minded and robust defence of the theory of utilitarianism, arguing that people undertake goals in life not because they are trying to be objectively moral but to satisfy their own wants and desires. These latter can be described as 'hedonistic', particularly when one bears in mind the single-minded pursuit of alcohol and sex to which many of his theatrical creations are dedicated, but the term is expanded to include the entire range of those desires which a person wishes to fulfil. Nevertheless, McPherson is opposed to any hierarchical distinction between 'higher' and 'lower' pleasures, as he makes clear when he criticises John Stuart Mill's classic study *Utilitarianism*. Mill distinguishes between elementary pleasures which are 'fleeting' – eating, drinking, resting and so on – and pleasures of a more distinctively human achievement, which require more effort and which may last for perhaps a lifetime. But, McPherson counters: 'Can Mill say that pleasures involving our "higher" faculties are qualitatively "better" than rolling in the mud?' (48–9).

In seeking to show that no argument for the objective nature of 'the good' can be sustained, McPherson devotes much of his thesis to going one-on-one with Alasdair MacIntyre and John Rawls, in particular the former. The ultimate object of attack is

Aristotle and a 'tradition of enquiry' which locates human activity in a 'telos' or goal that every object moves towards. MacIntyre's conservatism sees the break with this objective goal as occurring in the eighteenth century, with the emergence of scepticism and the triumph of the individual. But McPherson keeps querying just where 'the good' is located, outside of the individual and their desires. Rhetorically he seeks to demonstrate that MacIntyre is forced to rely on utilitarian arguments to prove his case, despite claims to the contrary. His repeated argument against MacIntyre and against Rawls with his concept of a socially agreed concept of justice is that it requires one person to point out 'the good' to another and then have them submit to it, that it is finally located in an invocation of 'authority'. I was reminded throughout of William Blake's dictum: 'I must create my own philosophy or be imprisoned by another man's.'

In *This Lime Tree Bower* Wolfgang Konigsberg, an eminent philosopher with an international reputation, is invited to UCD to give a series of lectures, held in Theatre L and beamed via 'a closed circuit system to the next theatre, where everyone could see him' (114). There are traces of the 'utilitarianism' thesis strewn throughout the play: Dr Ray Sullivan is teaching a 'third year utilitarianism group' (88) and one of his reported dreams features an enigmatic and otherwise unaccountable appearance by the philosopher John Rawls (who is not otherwise identified): 'John Rawls came down from the mountains and his wife was choosy about what she ate' (89). Ray longs for 'the chance of a question and answer session' with the visiting philosopher 'where we could discuss his ideas. I knew I could have this guy on the ropes if I had the opportunity to press him' (99), a boxing metaphor I have already employed to describe the pugilistic way McPherson takes on MacIntyre and Rawls in the thesis. After a great deal of argument, the famous philosopher finally agrees to take Ray's question. When the latter staggers to his feet, very much in the grip of a severe bout of *delirium tremens*, and opens his mouth, 'absolutely beyond my control, a long stream of orange puke shot out of my mouth' (117). Finally, he speaks: 'I would like to ask Professor Konigsberg if, during his long and eminent career, he has ever seen anything like that.' By way of reply, the philosopher doesn't speak but finally, slowly, shakes his head. Ray thanks him politely and departs, revealing: 'I couldn't even remember what I wanted to say' (119). In the play, the scene was entirely conveyed by means of Ray's monologue. In a case of life imitating art, when *This Lime Tree Bower* was filmed as *Saltwater*, the scene was re-enacted under Conor McPherson's direction in a packed Theatre L. It would be tempting if Professor Konigsberg could be identified as either John Rawls or Alasdair MacIntyre. But the description Ray offers of the visitor's philosophy shows its concern to be with the death of language – 'he said that language was an organic thing ... it was born, lived healthily for a while, making other little languages like its offspring, and then it died' (113) – and it in no wise resembles the philosophy of the two opponents of utilitarianism.

It is elsewhere in the play that one must look for the debate that is central to the thesis to be dramatised. For Ray's is only one of three strands that intertwine in the overall narrative. The primary location, as so often in McPherson, is Dublin's northside, especially along the seafront – his young male protagonists are as drawn to this location as those in Neil Jordan's early fiction. The other two characters are brothers, the seventeen-year-old Joe, who is still in school, and his twenty-two-year-old brother, Frank, who works with his dad in the family chipper. Ray enters their lives through his liaison (yet another) with their sister, Carmel. The play's plot hinges around Frank's decision to rob the local bookie and loan shark, 'Simple' Simon McCurdy, who is putting pressure on their hard-working, harassed and widowed father to repay a loan. The title of another McPherson play, *The Good Thief* (1994), seems relevant to the discussion of what Frank proposes and undertakes in the play, and to the discussion of 'the good' in McPherson's MA thesis. In no conventional or Christian reading can the life of a thief be read as anything other than immoral (in the Christian reading, the 'good' thief is the one of the two crucified with Christ who repents and is promised redemption). And there is the Romantic inversion of the Christian ethos which would see the 'bad' thief exuding attractive qualities of rebellion and independence, as in the American gangster films that influence the McPherson-scripted film *I Went Down* (1997).

What is primarily at issue here are consequences and contingency, two key issues in the thesis and in McPherson's dramatic world. Again, a quote from Mill is relevant:

> Who ever said that it was necessary to foresee all the consequences of each individual, 'as they go down into the countless ages of coming time'? Some of the consequences of an action are accidental; others are its natural result, according to the known laws of the universe. The former for the most part cannot be foreseen; but the whole cause of human life is founded on the fact that the latter can. (op. cit. 40)

In the plays, the distinction is not so clear-cut. When Frank has robbed McCurdy's and is about to be caught by a violent henchman, Ray appears in his car and saves him – not because he thinks he is performing a good deed but because he happens to see him. Pure contingency, the arbitrary point at which one narrative strand meets another. When Frank asks McCurdy to open the safe (not even knowing whether he has one), the haul escalates from thirty pounds to nearly thirty thousand. The police come to their house. But it turns out that Joe, the younger brother, has been accused of rape, something we know from his monologue to be untrue. It is his best friend Damien who is guilty and who has in turn shopped him. In the end, Frank emigrates and sends large sums of money back to his father – a 'good' thief, perhaps, because the consequences, though unseen, are just in terms of what he has sought to achieve. Damien is rightfully charged for the rape; but in seeking to shift the blame to Joe, he has betrayed their private personal relationship, the most important in young Joe's life since the death of his mother. And Ray? Well, he gets away with his philandering; but he stands accused by what comes out of his mouth when he opens it to speak.

At the end of *The Good Thief* the title character denies the epithet, not just to himself but to all of the characters in the play. He does so in terms of consequentialism: 'I knew nothing good could come out of what had happened because of everybody's stupidity' (77). In an interview in 2001 with Gerald C. Wood, Conor McPherson describes how his characters reject the maps they are given and asked to accept for the conduct of their future lives: 'go to school, leave school, work, get married, have children, pay a mortgage, go on holiday, your parents die, then you die' (135). Instead, his characters break out and go to the extremes so vividly dramatised in his plays, just as his thesis tries out potential scenarios to illustrate and test philosophical positions. McPherson generalises that they 'always tend to find an innate sense of what's right and wrong ... and usually come back to traditional moral law, which is basically utilitarian: if I don't treat other people well, I may not get treated well myself.' The fear with which they are left is 'the fear of not being loved ... And nobody can answer that for them; everybody learns different ways of dealing with it.' With no ready-made answers, with each of his characters having to work out their own destiny, the number of potential scenarios is infinite. Conor McPherson the playwright, for all of his achievement, still has many stories to tell.

PRIMARY REFERENCES

Conor McPherson, *Logical Constraint and Practical Reading: On Attempted Refutations of Utilitarianism*, MA thesis, Department of Philosophy, UCD, October 1993.
—, *This Lime Tree Bower: Three Plays* [*Rum and Vodka*; *The Good Thief*; *This Lime Tree Bower*] (Dublin: New Island Books; London: Nick Hern Books, in association with the Bush Theatre, 1996).
—, *St. Nicholas and The Weir: Two Plays* (Dublin: New Island Books; London: Nick Hern Books, in association with the Bush Theatre, 1997).

SECONDARY REFERENCE

Gerald C. Wood, *Conor McPherson: Imagining Mischief* (Dublin: The Liffey Press/Contemporary Irish Writers Series, 2003).

NOTES ON CONTRIBUTORS

Brian Arkins is a Professor in Classics at National University of Ireland, Galway. Publications include *An Introduction to the Poetry of Propertius* (2005) and *Hellenising Ireland: Greek and Roman Themes in Modern Irish Literature* (2005). He graduated from UCD with a BA in Classics in 1965, an MA in Classics in 1967 and a PhD in Latin in 1974.

Ruth Barton is O'Kane Senior Research Fellow at the Centre for Film Studies at UCD. She is author of *Jim Sheridan: Framing the Nation* (2002), *Irish National Cinema* (2004) and co-editor of *Keeping it Real: Irish Film and Television* (2004). She is currently writing a book on Irish screen actors to be published by Irish Academic Press.

Catriona Clutterbuck lectures in Anglo-Irish Literature and Drama in the School of English at UCD. Her main research interests are contemporary Irish poetry and Irish women's writing. She was guest-editor of the 2001 *Irish University Review* Special Issue on the work of Thomas Kinsella.

Anthony Cronin is a poet, novelist, critic and biographer of Flann O'Brien (1989) and Samuel Beckett (1996). He was recently elected a Saoi of Aosdána and his *Collected Poems* were published in 2004. He graduated from UCD with a BA in Economics and History in 1950.

Peter Denman is Dean of Arts and a member of the Department of English at National University of Ireland, Maynooth. Among his previous publications are numerous writings on Irish poetry, a book on Samuel Ferguson, and poetry both original and translated. He is a member of the Editorial Board of the *Irish University Review*.

Brian Donnelly is Senior Lecturer in the School of English at UCD. He has written on nineteenth- and twentieth-century Irish literature and on modern American literature.

Anne Fogarty is a Senior Lecturer in the School of English at UCD and Director of the UCD James Joyce Summer School. She is editor of the *Irish University Review* and Vice-President of the International James Joyce Foundation. A collection of essays, *Joyce on the Threshold,* co-edited with Timothy Martin, is forthcoming in 2005.

Michael Paul Gallagher S.J. is Professor of Fundamental Theology at the Gregorian University in Rome. His most recent books are *Diving Deeper: the Human Poetry of Faith* (2001) and *Clashing Symbols: Introduction to Faith and Culture* (revised, 2003). He lectured in the Department of English at UCD from 1972 to 1990.

Derek Hand teaches in the English Department in St. Patrick's College, Drumcondra. He is the author of *John Banville: Exploring Fictions* (2002) and is currently writing *A History of the Irish Novel* for Cambridge University Press. He was both an undergraduate and postgraduate in UCD, receiving his MA in Anglo-Irish Literature and Drama in 1991 and his PhD in 2000.

Maurice Harmon, Professor Emeritus of Anglo-Irish Literature at UCD, has written critical studies of Austin Clarke and Thomas Kinsella and a biography of Sean O'Faolain. He edited a collection of Samuel Beckett Letters and is also a poet. His collection *The Doll with Two Backs and Other Poems* appeared in 2004.

Katy Hayes is a writer. Her novels include *Gossip* (2000) and *Lindbergh's Legacy* (2003). She graduated from UCD with a BA in English and History of Art in 1988.

Declan Kiberd is Professor of Anglo-Irish Literature and Drama in UCD. Among his books are *Synge and the Irish Language* (1979), *Idir Dhá Chultúr* (1993), *Inventing Ireland* (1995) and *Irish Classics* (2000). *The Irish Writer and the World* will be published by Cambridge University Press in late 2005.

Cathy Leeney lectures in Drama at the Drama Studies Centre in UCD. Her research interests include twentieth-century and contemporary Irish theatre, directing for theatre, and gender in performance. She has published on Irish theatre and performance, and is currently completing a book on Irish women playwrights from 1900 to 1939.

Joseph Long is Director of the Drama Studies Centre and a Senior Lecturer in the French Department of UCD. He is an *Officier de l'Ordre des Palmes Académiques* and *Chevalier de l'Ordre de l'Art et des Lettres.* He has been active in the promotion of Irish theatre in France and in the translation of French drama into English.

John McCourt teaches at the University of Trieste, where he is co-founder and co-director of the Trieste Joyce School. He is the author of *The Years of Bloom: James Joyce in Trieste 1904-1920* (2000) and of books and articles on Joyce,

Trollope and contemporary Irish literature. He graduated from UCD with a BA in English in 1988, an MA in Anglo-Irish Literature and Drama in 1989 and a PhD in 1996.

P.J. Mathews is a Lecturer in the School of English at UCD and author of *Revival: The Abbey Theatre, Sinn Féin, the Gaelic League and the Co-operative Movement* (2003). He edited the inaugural volume of *New Voices in Irish Criticism* (2000) and is Director of the Parnell Summer School. He graduated from UCD with a BA and an MA in Anglo-Irish Literature and Drama in 1991. He was awarded his PhD from Trinity College, Dublin, in 1999.

J.C.C. Mays retired as Professor of English and American Literature at UCD in 2004 and now lives in the country. Brian Coffey's review of *Murphy*, referred to in his essay here, will be published in *The Recorder: The Journal of the American Irish Historical Society* (New York), Fall issue 2005.

Gerardine Meaney is Director of Irish Studies at UCD. She is the author of *(Un)like Subjects: Women, Theory, Fiction* (1993), a short study of Pat Murphy's film, *Nora* (2004) and a co-editor of *The Field Day Anthology of Irish Writing: Women's Writing and Traditions,* volumes 4 and 5 (2002). She has published numerous articles on gender and Irish culture, including two on Kate O'Brien.

Christopher Murray is Associate Professor in Drama and Theatre History in the School of English at UCD. His publications include 'Thomas Kilroy's World Elsewhere', in *Irish Writers and Their Creative Process* (1996), ed. Jacqueline Genet and Wynne Hellegouarc'h; *Twentieth-Century Irish Drama: Mirror Up to Nation* (1997) and *Sean O'Casey Writer at Work: A Biography* (2004).

Taura Napier is the author of *Seeking a Country: Literary Autobiographies of Twentieth-Century Irishwomen.* Her recent publications include studies of contemporary Irish poets and their letters, Lady Gregory's 'Emigrant's Notebook' and the history of the Irish book, and the poetry of Ciaran Carson. She received her M.A. in Anglo-Irish Literature and Drama from UCD in 1992 with 'Through Corridors of Light', a thesis on the European writings of Mary Colum.

Máirín Nic Eoin is a lecturer in the Irish Department in St Patrick's College, Drumcondra. Her latest book is *Trén bhFearann Breac: an Dílaithriú Cultúir agus Nualitríocht na Gaeilge* (2005). She studied Irish and Geography at UCD, and went on to do an MA and PhD with the Irish Department in the College.

Joseph O'Connor is a novelist who has also written screenplays and short stories. His books include *True Believers* (1991), *Cowboys and Indians* (1991),

The Secret History of the Irish Male (1994), *Desperadoes* (1994), *The Salesman* (1998), *Inishowen* (2000) and *Star of the Sea* (2002). He graduated from UCD with a BA in English and History in 1984 and an MA in Anglo-Irish Literature and Drama in 1986.

Anthony Roche (the editor) is a Senior Lecturer in Anglo-Irish Literature and Drama in the School of English at UCD. His publications include *Contemporary Irish Drama: From Beckett to McGuinness* (1994) and the forthcoming *Cambridge Companion to Brian Friel*. He is currently the Director of the Synge Summer School.

Susan Schreibman is Assistant Dean and Head of Digital Collections and Research at the University of Maryland, USA. She is the editor of *The Collected Poems of Thomas MacGreevy* (1991) and co-editor of *A Blackwell Companion to Digital Humanities* (2004). She graduated from UCD with an MA in Anglo-Irish Literature and Drama in 1985 and a PhD in 1997.

Colm Tóibín is a writer. His novels include *The Heather Blazing* (1992), *The Blackwater Lightship* (1999) and *The Master* (2004). He graduated from UCD with a BA in English and History in 1975.

Caroline Walsh is Literary Editor with *The Irish Times*. She is the author of *The Homes of Irish Writers* (1982) and the editor of three collections of short stories, most recently *Arrows in Flight: Short Stories from a New Ireland* (2002). She graduated from UCD with a BA in English and History of European Painting in 1973 and an MA in Modern English and American Literature in 1974.

Eibhear Walshe, a graduate of UCD, lectures in modern English at University College Cork where his research interests include Irish drama, Munster Writing and Irish lesbian and gay writing. He has edited *Ordinary People Dancing, Essays on Kate O'Brien* (1993), *Sex, Nation and Dissent* (1997), *Elizabeth Bowen Remembered* (1998), *The Plays of Teresa Deevy* (2003) and, with Brian Cliff, *Representing the Troubles* (2004). His biography of Kate O'Brien is forthcoming.

Harry White is Professor of Music at UCD and President of the Society for Musicology in Ireland. He has published widely on the cultural history of music in Ireland and on the music of the High Baroque. He has recently been appointed Government of Ireland Senior Research Fellow in the Humanities for the purposes of writing a book on the relationship between music and the Irish literary imagination.

The Internationalization Processes of Freight Transport Companies

- Towards a Dynamic Network Model of Internationalization

Susanne Hertz

Akademisk   avhandling

som för avläggande av ekonomie doktorsexamen
vid Handelshögskolan i Stockholm framlägges till
offentlig granskning måndagen den 24 maj 1993
kl.10.15 i sal Torsten å högskolan, Sveavägen 65.

Stockholm 1993

EFI, EKONOMISKA
FORSKNINGSINSTITUTET

The Internationalization Processes of
Freight Transport Companies

THE ECONOMIC RESEARCH INSTITUTE/EFI

Stockholm School of Economics

Address: Sveavägen 65, Box 6501, S-113 83 Stockholm, tel 08-736 90 00

Basic Orientation

The Economic Research Institute, at the Stockholm School of Economics (EFI) is devoted to the scientific study of problems in management science and economics. It provides research facilities for scholars belonging to these disciplines, training advanced students in scientific research. The studies to be carried out by the Institute are chosen on the basis of their expected scientific value and their relevance to the research programs outlined by the different sections of the Institute.

Research Divisions:

A   Management and Organization Theory
B   Accounting and Managerial Finance
C   Managerial Economics
CFR   Center for Risk Research
CHF   Center for Health Economics
D   Marketing, Distribution and Industry Dynamics
ES   Economic Statistics
FI   Finance
F   Public Administration
IEG   International Economics and Geography
I   Information Management
P   Economic Psychology
S   Economics

Research Programs:

Man and Organization
The Foundation for Distribution Research
Policy Sciences

Additional information about research in progress and published reports is described in our project catalogue. The catalogue can be ordered directly from The Economic Research Institute, Box 6501, S-113 83 Stockholm, Sweden.

The Internationalization Processes
of Freight Transport Companies

Towards a Dynamic Network Model
of Internationalization

Susanne Hertz

THE ECONOMIC
RESEARCH INSTITUTE

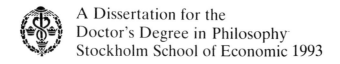

A Dissertation for the
Doctor's Degree in Philosophy
Stockholm School of Economic 1993

ISBN 91-7258-364-9

Keywords:
Transport companies – Europe
Freight transport systems
Relationships
Internationalization
Multinational companies
Dynamics
Domino effects

Gotab 97440, Stockholm 1993

To Rune and Sandra

Preface

This report, carried out at the Economic Research Institute, is submitted as a doctor´s thesis at the Stockholm School of Economics.

The author has been entirely free to conduct her research in her own ways as an expression of her own ideas.

The Institute is grateful for the financial support, which has made this reserach possible.

Stockholm in April 1993

Claes-Robert Julander
Director of the Institute

Lars-Gunnar Mattsson
Head of the Section for
Marketing, Distribution
and Industry Dynamics

Foreword

Writing a thesis is like embarking a sailing ship destined for a journey lasting many years. Planning for achievements during that period could only to a certain extent be made in advance since by necessity much has to be adapted and rearranged according to changing circumstances.

Further,there are many people taking part in the journey, helping out in different ways. Some of the people have followed me during the whole or a large part of the project while others have been of great help in periods of need.

First there are my advisors, without whom this task could not be fulfilled. Among these I will start by thanking Lars-Gunnar Mattsson for his engagement in the project and for having the guts to believe in me when I wanted to rejoin and continue my training at the Stockholm School of Economics after many years in business. During the course of writing my thesis he has spent enormous amounts of time in various advisory capacities, trying to understand my thinking as well as the work of transport companies. It has been a privilege having such an advisor and friend. Further, I would like to thank Håkan Håkansson for his stimulating critque and efforts put into the thesis in spite of varying geographical distances. Finally, Claes-Robert Julander gave me many good advices and ideas for the completion of the thesis. Together they have fulfilled different roles, which all were necessary for making advancements in the process of completing the project. A special thank should also be directed to Lars Östman for putting me on the right track in the very start.

An unlimited curiosity of life and of learning, which are natural characteristics of my collegues in the D-section (Marketing, Distribution and Industry Dynamics) at the Stockholm School of Economics, have encouraged me in the performance of my task over the years. Their indulging in work and in a large variety of interests from mountain climbing, playing the saxophones, writing music and poetry, performing Tai Chi, boxing and workouts en masse really have made life very enjoyable. The enthusiasm and advise of these friends have surely contributed much to my work at the section. I would like to give special thanks to Anders Lundgren for standardising my figures and making them more readable, to Ann-Charlotte for helping with lists and tables and to Patrick Sweet, being indirectly linked to the department, for his comments and corrections in the last stage in the completing of the thesis.

Another very important person putting an enormous effort into this thesis, is George Cook, who has been correcting and changing my English into an understandable form.

Further, Monica von Baumgarten has been of great help in the creation of this book´s cover of the book and Ulla Holmsten has been of special help in listening and reading. Finally, I would like to direct a special thank to Ivan Snehota for his valuable comments and creative critism to my thesis.

However, the writing of this thesis would not have been possible without economic support from the Swedish Transport Research Board (TFB) and from Torsten and Ragnar Söderbergs Stiftelser. I am grateful for the three years of economic contributions that I have got from TFB of Sweden. It was tremendously important in that it made it possible to get the project going, making the interviews and summarize much of the study. The support from Torsten and Ragnar Söderberg´s Foundations became much appreciated and indispensable in that it gave me possibility to complete the thesis into its final form. For that I am very thankful. During my very first stumbling steps in the academic world MTC gave me a certain freedom through their economic "seed money" support.

Furthermore, Rune Castenäs will be remembered for all his engagement and help in organizing my economic and practical situation at the Economic Research Institute (EFI).

Last but not least I would like to affectionately thank all the people from the freight transport industry in the company groups of ASG, Bilspedition and Inter Forward and to them related organizations in Sweden, Belgium, Holland, Switzerland and Germany. Many thanks for your openness, kindness and willingness to assist me in my project. You have given me a lot of support and help.

This thesis is dedicated to my husband and daughter for their love, support and patience over the years.

Stockholm in April, 1993

Susanne Hertz

Contents

3

Part I Background

1. Background and purpose

1.1. Introduction

This study concerns transport companies and their internationalization processes.

To a large extent the choice of subject is attributable to my empirical experiences of this particular industry and of transport companies. Freight transport companies and the way in which they go about their business have fascinated me ever since I joined one over twenty years ago. Up until that time, the world of transport companies was almost unknown to me.

The daily business of handling bulk volumes and large numbers of consignments as well as the administrative activities that stemming from despatching and receiving them to/ from destinations world wide are intriguing.

Further, it is quite common for international transport companies to have a large geographical network of international traffics based on the cooperation of a large number of transport companies. The bulk of volumes and consignments to be handled, the size of these geographical networks in combination with the number of companies involved lead to a very high complexity in the performance of these traffic systems.

The described situation of the transport companies poses a number of questions regarding coordination and integration and how the development of some companies affects the others. How were these international networks of traffics created and developed over a period?

Specific phenomena added to my curiosity. What was it that caused certain transport companies to suddenly restructure their network of traffics causing them to sever their connections with a whole number of cooperating international transport companies at a high cost? And subsequently,why have they taken large shares in other transport companies within such a short period? Why did these changes sever cooperations, seemingly unintentionally, with transport companies not even remotely involved? What could possibly such apparently strange behaviour?

My own interest apart, there are other reasons for studying transport companies and their internationalization. Some of these are specifically related to transport companies and their role while others concern industrial service companies as the suppliers of standardized systems more generally.

Firstly, growing world trade, internationalization of industries and international competition have increased the importance of effective international distribution systems. The importance of effective distribution of products and product related services is further enhanced by the fact that production is more flexible, inventories are held at lower levels and communication is faster. In light of these increased demands on distribution systems, the role of the transport companies would seem to be vital as part of the total distribution system, in creating and developing transport systems. Therefore it would be of specific interest to study to contribute to the understanding of how the transport companies handle the increasing demands for more effective international transports.

Another reason for attention focusing lately on the transport companies and their situation has been the deregulation and harmonization of the existing rules and regulations for transport companies in the EC scheduled for 1993. How will transport companies be affected by this and how will they act to adapt to the new situation? Studying the changes in the internationalization patterns of European transport companies over a long time period would be one way to see how these companies meet new situations of similar types which can be of importance for understanding future behaviour.

Finally, the internationalization of service companies performing standardized services like transport companies, banks, insurance companies seems to have been intensified, making them the subject of growing interest. To the extent that these companies have characteristics in common, a study of transport companies might be of value for understanding also of the internationalization processes of other service industries.

1.2. The focus of the study

Choice of framework

The items of most interest are the internationalization processes and the changes in patterns of internationalization over time and more specifically how such change processes develop for transport companies (see definition p.28).

A prerequisite therefore to the choice of transport companies for the study is that they should have experienced a process of internationalization and preferably a rather extensive process so that the material for studying internationalization patterns will be rich. This implies that the result of the study will show an increasing degree of internationalization over a period. However, since our interest lies in finding different patterns and explaining them rather than discussing more generally why internationalization takes place, the choice is still reasonable.

Moreover, the context of the transport companies would seem to play a very important role in the formation of the patterns of internationalization due to their very high dependence on other companies in their geographical networks. Therefore discussing the patterns of internationalization of transport companies will have to include at least the most important companies featuring in these geographical networks of traffics. These are other transport companies in the roles of suppliers, international representatives, competitors, owners and of partnerships.

However, including a part of the context complicates the study by increasing the number of companies involved and makes it important to limit the context to the most relevant parts. Still to do this seems necessary in order to fully comprehend such phenomena as the huge international changes taking place between groups of international transport companies.

Research into transport companies

A brief overview will be provided of the type of research that exists in this field of goods transports and transport companies and their internationalization.

Research into transports of goods has basically been conducted from a macro perspective and has focused on technical, political or economic issues such as pricing of transports and their importance for society, effects of containerization, monopoly of the railways, of rules and regulations. It has been our observation that the actual development of goods transports and their flows seems to attract rather more interest than the development of the transport organizations creating and changing the systems controlling these flows. In some cases, the prediction of general market changes in different countries, formulated as trends and forecasts, have touched upon the subject of changes in the organizations handling the goods[1]. However, very few examples have been found of any serious studies of the development process of these large multi-faceted transport and forwarding companies. The very few that seem to exist focus on the owners of the means of transportation of the goods like truckers[2], airlines, shipping lines etc., concentrating on structures and strategies rather than processes of internationalization over a period.

From a theoretical viewpoint, the interest in transport companies has been higher because of their role as facilitating agencies seen from the manufacturing companies´point of view. Most logistical studies belong to this category (e.g.Ballou, 1987, Stock & Lambert, 1987).

Lately, three different fields of research which would seem to have shown an increasing interest have enhanced the interest in transport companies. These are services industries in general (Grönroos,1990; Lovelock,1990; Normann,1991; Zeithaml et al,1990) deregulation of transports (Bailey & Friedlaender,1982; Shepherd,1984) and information technology (Browne,1991; Englund,1990). Most of these studies are either too general trying to include all types of service companies or focus on the changes in the industrial structure as a result of the deregulation or information systems development. Not one of these studies has examined the changes for companies in patterns of internationalization over a period.

---

[1] Comén made a study for the Swedish Transport Research Board of the structure and size of the Swedish and world wide airfreight market called " The airfreight in Sweden and world-wide - Forecasts and trends"(1988) a TFB Report 1988: 7.

[2] In Sweden Rask (1984) is a dissertation on trucking companies and their structural poverty. The thesis is focused on the impact of company and industry structure on strategic action for small organizations.

Theoretical framework

What theoretical perspectives would be suitable to describe and analyse internationalization processes and changes in patterns of internationalization over a period?

Firstly, the transport company networks not only depict the geographical spread, they also depict relationships between separate transport companies. The development of relationships between transport companies is necessary for building their international geographical networks of traffics over a period.

Therefore, it would seem natural to use the network approach which is based on development of exchange relationships between companies. The fact that the transport companies create geographical networks for which these relationships are a prerequisite will enhance the contribution of the network approach to the understanding of internationalization processes and the changes in patterns over a period.

This approach also takes the interdependence with the context into account since companies belonging to different geographical networks are basically all related in one way or another.

Further, since the study concerns internationalization of organizations the existing literature on internationalization processes and existing patterns of internationalization will necessarily be of high importance. This field of research will present the issues of importance when discussing the concept of internationalization. A description of the patterns of internationalization found in other studies which might possibly have application to transport companies will make another contribution. The rich field of studies on the subject of internationalization will not only contribute to the understanding of the process, as such, but also reveal the driving forces behind such a process and its development over time. Therefore it seems natural to include the existing theories within this field.

Finally, research on distribution seems to be of interest due to the fact that transporting is a function in distribution systems. The distribution theory is used to handle interdependencies in physical systems of similar types as transport systems and therefore research in this field would seem to contribute to explaining the international development of transport companies. Another matter that is a vital issue in distribution theory is what part of the context should be included in the systems. Even though there are important differences between transport systems and distribution systems this theoretical discussion could add to the understanding of the patterns of internationalization of transport companies.

1.3. Purpose

The purpose of the study is threefold.

First the purpose is to develop a model of internationalization, making use of network, distribution and internationalization theories, that can be applied to transport companies.

Second the purpose is to describe and then to analyse the internationalization patterns of transport companies using that model. My interest here is to show how they internationalize and not why.

The third purpose of the study, which originates from the confluence between existing research and empirical results, is to explain the behaviour patterns of internationalization found for the transport companies. These explanations will be grounded in theories of network, distribution and internationalization. Based on these a dynamic model for internationalization of transport companies will be constructed within the framework of the network approach, complemented by distribution and internationalization theories which present the patterns of behaviour internationally over a period as well as the driving forces for that behaviour.

1.4. Delimitations

In order to reduce the complexity of the study many delimitations are made. This section will focus on two delimitations of the subject which both might have important implications for interpretation of the results of the thesis.

The first is that the study excludes transport companies which have not internationalized or which started to internationalize and chose to stop the process. This way the less successful companies at internationalization will not form part of the study.

Another important limitation of the study is the decision not to include the customers in the study as part of the context in focus.

There is a difference between having the customers as a direct or indirect part of the study. Since the study intends to describe and analyse the behaviour of transport organizations in search of patterns of internationalization changes over a period, an exclusion of customers from the focused context should not be serious, for the reason that the behaviour should be the same whether the customers are directly part of the study or not.

Furthermore a large transport company has normally a large variety and number of customers and especially so in the home country. Then there are the international customers through the geographical network which might be direct customers to the Swedish company depending on how the agreement is made between the industrial company and their customers or suppliers in other countries. Finally there are large multinationals which have partly centralized their procurement of transport services to any location.

The background to the decision not to involve the customers directly in the study is in fact that it is possible to study the behaviour patterns without the direct involvement of customers. I do not deny that the internationalization of the manufacturing industry plays a very important role for the internationalization of the transport companies; it is only that I have chosen to see them rather as a very important group basically setting demands for and through their distribution systems. It is generally the case for most large transport companies and it has always been the case for forwarders that specialized systems for single customers constitute only a minor part of the total activities.

Accordingly, this study concentrates on transport companies, as such, and their interdependence in their many roles towards each other when creating and developing international networks.

1.5. Research method

This section will start by discussing the issues of a contextualist research approach. Then follows a subsection of organizational behaviour. Finally, there is a description of the research procedures in this study. The elucidation of the contextualist approach should be important for understanding the research method chosen while the discussion on organizational behaviour is rather a prerequisite for using the same method.

1.5.1. Contextualist research

There are many different perspectives and theories to the subject of organizational change. One of these perspectives is contextualism and its root metaphor is the historical event (Pettigrew, 1985). Studies describing phenomena seen in their contexts are called contextualist research.

Contextualism is described as focusing on the event in its settings and its descriptions are made "true" through qualitative confirmation, since the context will change and knowledge will also need to change.(Ibid). The important concepts are change in process, change in content and change in context. In practical process terms it implies the importance of the situational and multi-faceted character of meanings in research settings and the holistic study of emergent processes in particular and changing contexts.

Lindholm (1979) comments that contextual paradigm is typical for research on the meaning of concepts. He cites Törnebohm (1977, p 16) saying " If a researcher would like to understand the meaning of X(an action or text fragment, etc.) he needs to put X into one or several contexts". Lindholm (1979) continues by saying that a phenomenon seen from a certain perspective in a certain context has a meaning for a specific person. This means that when studying meanings there are no real objective facts, they are all interpreted by the researcher.

This thesis continues the traditions of contextualist research in describing a phenomenon, the internationalization process, in different historical settings from a perspective chosen by the researcher.

In line with the empirically based purpose of the study to describe and analyse the phenomenon of internationalization, a qualitative method has been used.The aim of this method is not to verify hypotheses but to inductively construct some new hypothesis and perhaps revise or complement some of the existing theories. New concepts will also be developed as a result of efforts to analyse the specific phenomena in their settings.

The methods applied include empirical studies of how transport companies internationalize over a period. It starts with a description which can be seen as a first interpretation searching for the meaning of the internationalization process. This primary interpretation is then a base in this thesis for further interpretation of the process in a theoretically stricter and more formalized way called the analysis.

Even though interpretations are seen as conscious processes (Regnell, 1982) it is not to say that subconscious choices in the process have not been made. In reality a large part of the first interpretation is probably unconsciously chosen based on former experience and theoretical background.

Miller (1982 p 19) argues that in order to be able to explain an event historically, the actual and particular purpose must be linked to the non-accidental, the impersonal and objective. Cause, in general, means a ground or explaining a base, a means of explaining, a condition of, the mode of understanding (ibid p 23). Finally he states that "cause is the reason that places an event in some order.(Ibid p 27) As to teleological explanations involving the purpose of the act he claims that "the essence of a purposive act is not only that it proceeds from a general program but also that it requires the revision of the program in the interests of which it is undertaken." Specific elements in motive or action are both necessary in principle and accidental in their peculiarity"(Miller 1982, p 33).

In this thesis the contextualist approach has been used, which implies that interpretation of complex behaviour of a few organizations is more important than a survey involving a large number of organizations. The explanations of historical events are made from the peculiar, actual purposes of the event to non- accidental more objective and impersonal purposes via theoretical discussions.

1.5.2. Studies on organizational behaviour

Since this study focuses on behaviour of the transport companies in the process of internationalization it seems important to discuss to what extent it is possible to generalize about the behaviour of organizations.

Organizational behaviour is difficult to study since it is difficult to separate the organization, seen as a social collectivity, from the individual (Weick 1979). It is the individuals who act in the organization. Therefore studies on organizational behaviour contain both sociological as well as psychological aspects.

A way to cope with the term organizational behaviour, according to Weick, would be to build theories on particular ways that enduring individual dispositions are expressed in an organizational setting and about effects of this setting rather than to search for unique behaviour. First noting that behaviour can be viewed as responses in search of pretext for expression, he then re-formulates the question into "How are the processes of and contents of attention influenced by the conditions of task-based interdependency found in those settings we conventionally designate as organizations?"

Silverman & Jones(1976) discuss the individual interpretation of the organizational routines which are included in the social structure of the organization. In order to be selected as acceptable for their organization the individuals seem to interpret their discussions with other individuals internally or externally in the light of the rules and routines in the organization. This would indicate that it would be possible to talk about the consistent behaviour of an organization without specifying the individual.

An important point according to Weick (1979) is that organizational activities are social rather than solitary and that if these activities can be specified sufficiently a pattern will be allowed to exist. An organization interacts rather than acts. The pattern of interaction determines the outcome and not the personal qualities of the single individuals.

Weick uses three bases for describing the bulk of organizing activities.These are enactment, selection and retention, basically forming a sequence. These processes help an individual to form social cycles into sensible arrangements.

There may be many cycles within each process and there may even be a reversed direction of the arrows saying "how can I know what I think or feel until I see or hear what I am doing?". The question that Weick poses is "under what condition adaption precludes adaptability" (ibid p 135). Even though the enactment, selection and retention is made in a linear fashion it may be misleading. Since there are many parallel processes going on of various inputs and there is a plurality of cycles, cause maps and enacted environment the complexity will intercept the flows of events.(Ibid p 143) This might be applicable to the interpretation of the organizational behaviour of the transport companies as well.

The contextualist approach recognizes, according to Pettigrew (1985), that the process is contained by structure as well as shaping the structure, whether it leads to preserving or changing it.

1.5.3. Case studies and choice of cases

In light of the fact that we are using a contextualist approach and that the process studied seems to involve large complexities, the case study would be the natural choice. Further, since the purpose is to describe a process over time a longitudinal study should be necessary.

A case study is a research strategy which focuses on understanding the dynamics present within single settings (Eisenhardt, 1989). A case study also involves numerous levels of analysis which makes it possible to understand the different interdependencies creating part of the complexities. Through this it might also be possible to generalize.

Multiple methods for data collection are also a necessity when a process spans as much as 30 - 50 years after which very few people are left who remember the changes.

The decision to make multiple case studies has also been influenced by the interest to describe the process as richly as possible in order to depict in the process repeated sets of actions over a period. The likelihood of finding such sets is higher when studying several cases. The possibility to generalize from the cases will also increase with multiple cases.

What sort of transport companies should be selected then as being most suitable for pursuing our enquiry?
The transport companies chosen for the study are large Groups concentrating mainly on goods transports. They also undertake many different transport company tasks, both domestically and internationally. Their basic international task has been focused on forwarding rather than operating and owning the means of transportation, even if this has changed very much over time. One of the main reasons for choosing transport companies in the freight forwarding business is that they seem to develop large geographical networks and they often utilize several different means of transportation. The role of the forwarder has also lately become increasingly important as combined transports and logistical services have expanded and the size and weight of many products have been decreasing, favouring consolidation. Lately, large multinational

transport companies have combined the roles of operators, owners and forwarders, which have a relevance for the way they internationalize.

I have selected three of the largest international freight transport companies of Sweden. These companies made up more than half of the Swedish market for international freight transports in 1990 partly as a result of their international growth over a period, partly due to large numbers of acquisitions in Sweden as well as abroad. The point in time when they started their internationalization process differs considerably between the three companies which helps to illustrate the impact of the differences in the environment for the three cases.

Since the process of internationalization will involve companies in other countries, the study will have to include some of these as well. These companies are brought into the picture not only as being part of the process of the focal company but also for the specific purpose of showing typical events or very important events in the process of internationalizing.

When trying to depict sets of action in the internationalization process it would also be of interest to look at the sets of action in the internationalization process of the foreign transport companies. Therefore seven of the events are also describing the international development of eight foreign transport companies in another environment. These companies are subsidiaries except for one which is an agent. However, five of the subsidiaries were acquired as international transport and forwarding companies and therefore have a history involving their own international development before the acquisition.

The analysis will then include a deeper and more formalized process of interpretation when the design and definitions are stricter in focusing on important changes in the process of internationalization and put into a model, taking different inter-dependencies into account. In this analysis model, new concepts will have to be developed from the theoretical background which then will focus on certain dimensions of the process seen as important in my interpretation. The analysis contains first a within-case analysis and then a cross-case analysis. It tries to recognize more impersonal and general patterns of actions out of the particular events in the description. The description as well as the analysis focus on organizational behaviour.

1.5.4. Data collection and sources of information

Data is collected through interviews as well as from secondary materials. Even though the case study *per se* is basically a qualitative study it often contains some quantitive descriptions.

The data in this case is based on a combination of interviews and secondary material. Lists of interviews are presented in the enclosure as well as the most important secondary material.The interviews were semi-structured and were of a duration between 2-5 hours. Often there were several contacts with the persons interviewed.

The number of full interviews was thirty two in all, thirteen for ASG, eight for Bilspedition and eleven for Inter Forward. Then there were some ten more persons from the organizations who have played an important role in the collection of information on the companies (Appendix 1).

The interviews were with key informants who had experience and knowledge of the historical background as well as the present. The secondary material consists mostly of annual reports, written historical reviews of the company in question or parts of the company, internal pamphlets and magazines, protocols, etc. The external sources are basically of two kinds. The first kind is articles in newspapers and magazines, press-releases, advertisements, etc. The second kind is from the interviews containing questions about other companies in the business and from other persons involved in other ways like customers, members of the press, etc. Some of the material plays a more important role for the general longitudinal description while other material contributes more to the specific events.

The case descriptions of each company were sent out to a number of key persons in the companies concerned for revision and formal consent.

1.5.5. Validity and reliability

Multiple sources, multiple events and multiple cases have been used in order to increase validity and reliability of the study. As to the construct validity, seen as the ability of the study to describe what it is intended to, the multiple sources, the multiple events looking closer at certain changes and the revision of the key persons would increase this type of validity (Yin,1989). In the case of the external validity, the extent to which the result of the study can be used for theoretical development, multiple cases but also the multiple events would increase this validity. Finally the reliability, the ability to get the same results of the study when repeated, will be enhanced by the multiple sources as well as the description of the process for data collection.

However what is equally important is that the cases are interpreted, formulated and presented by the researcher in a way that it gives the reader a possibility to understand and follow the reasoning in the study. This would lead to an increase in credibility, plausability and trustworthiness of the study (Glaser& Strauss, 1967). The perspective chosen is one of many that can be used on the same material.

1.6. The structure of the book

The book will be divided into four parts. The first is the background (chapter 1 and 2), which will set the frame of the study and introduce the reader to the world of transport companies i.e. information about important concepts, freight transport industry, etc. The second part involves a presentation of the theoretical base (chapter 3 and 4) that will be utilized both for creation of the operational tools to the analysis and as a framework for possible explanations to the process in the last part. This part ends by presenting an analytical model for the study. The third part contains the case studies description and analyses (chapter 5 -9) and the third presents the theoretical results (chapter 10-13). The theoretical implications make up the main part which involves theoretical discussions and construction of a dynamic model of internationalization. Finally there is a small part discussing managerial implications and theoretical results.

Structure of the book

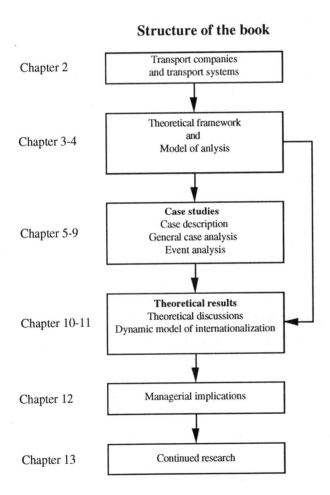

Chapter 2	Transport companies and transport systems
Chapter 3-4	Theoretical framework and Model of anlysis
Chapter 5-9	**Case studies** Case description General case analysis Event analysis
Chapter 10-11	**Theoretical results** Theoretical discussions Dynamic model of internationalization
Chapter 12	Managerial implications
Chapter 13	Continued research

2. Transports, transport systems and transport companies

Before we go into theoretical framework and the empirical studies we will give an overview of change in the context which is not directly part of the study but has a general impact on the development of international freight transports, transport systems and transport companies. A special interest is paid to the international trade and development of the manufacturing industry and the freight industry. Further we will take a closer look at how the distribution and transport systems are connected from a perspective of the manufacturer as well as the transport company. Finally we discuss different types of transport companies and their transport systems, which will help us in clarifying the subject of the study.

2.1. History and development

Historically, transport systems of one kind or another have existed for as long as there has been trading. The developments in freight transport systems have always played a significant role in economic activities in that they have been bridged gaps in time and physical space and as such influenced areal specialization, optimization of production units and extension of the market (White 1983). The existence of effective transport systems have made large scale manufacturing and mass marketing possible for many industries (Chandler 1990).

Changes in transport technology and location and patterns of transport systems have had an impact not only on the possibilities to trade but also the importance of the trade with different areas.

Old gateways to countries and whole areas of industrial activity have declined in importance with the development of new transport systems. The impact of the new technology has varied depending on where the industries are located. The development of rail and long distance road haulage has reduced the importance of some harbours whilst upgrading others, growth of road haulage has caused changes to the railway network, etc. In other cases, the prerequisites for trading in new types of goods like perishables, fashion wear, etc., were met by the development of more advanced and faster ships and airplanes. However, some areas depend more on land transportation due to their geographical location while the development of sea and air transports are vital for others.

Rail and road transports throughout Europe have played a very important role for industrial development in landlocked countries such as Austria, Switzerland and Czechoslovakia, while for countries like U.K and Ireland, the development of faster, larger and more effective ships has made a larger impact on their industries.

In the early part of this century transports by sea, inland waterways and railways were clearly the main forms of carriage. As trains became technically more advanced, a gradual shift in emphasis to rail took place. Very little long-distance road transportation existed. Road transportation has since been taking over the railways' role and has increased its share of the freight transports in Europe. In 1988, road transportation carried over 70% of the volumes (tons) of total transports in Western European countries[1], while sea and rail had decreased to 15% and 7% respectively (see Table 2.1).

On the other hand, sea transports still held the lead, in terms of tonnage, for Western European countries' international transports, with a share of 50% in 1988 while road transports only had 20%. The main reason, of course, is that many countries in the world can only be reached either by sea or by air. The share of road transports for freight is estimated to continue to grow unless there is government intervention on trucking in many European countries.

Mill.-tons	Total	International transports			Total transports (incl.domestic) [2]	
	1970	%	1988	%	1988	%
Rail	230	11	211	7	765	7
Road	177	9	606	20	8491	73
Sea	1165	58	1523	50	1699	15
Others[3]	450	22	678	23	627	5
Total	2022	100	3018	100	11.582	100

Table 2.1. Transports of Western-European countries - modes of transport
Source: Annual Bulletin Transport Statistics for Europe 1991 (Total International transports) and Eurostat-Transport Annual statistics 1970-1989 (Total transports)

Road transportation has changed from having a share of 9% to 20% (tons) between 1970-1988. Behind this shift in volumes from rail to road transportation would lies a combination of factors, such as investments in roads, new technologies for trucks and trucking systems as well as the inflexibility and lack of capacity by the national railways. It would seem that these problems continue to exist even in 1992 despite the EC countries' declared intent to invest in and increase the flexibility of the railways[4] and to reduce the expansion of road traffics on

---

[1]Excluding Italy

[2] Total transports of the same countries as for international transports but Norway, Sweden and Finland are excluded. Transit traffics excluded as in the case of the international figures

[3] Out of which inland waterways was 431 mill tons and air 4,2 mill. tons of *total international transports* in 1988 but of *total transports* all of it is inland waterways

[4] New strategies for European Freight Transport - 91, Conference arranged by TFK-VTI in Hamburg

account of its environmental effects. However, investments planned by the European railways[1] in combined transports rail-road, in new railroad communication systems, etc., estimated at SEK 14 billion, will help freight transports.

The problem is how to finance these. Privatisation and becoming registered on the stock exchange are common solutions put forward.

The shift to road transportation has not resulted in any drastic decreases in volumes for other means of transport due to the growth in the total volumes of international transports (around 50% during the period). Only rail has experienced a slight reduction (-8%) in international tonnage between 1970-1988. Sea actually increased its volumes by over 30% during the period.

Even though we know that airfreight has increased very much during the period, airfreight's total share (in tons) was still too small (under a promille) at this time to be registered separately. For Sweden the increase in exports by air (in tons) between 1976 and 1986 was more than 100% and air freight's share of Swedish export in value was 2,8 % in 1976, increasing to 6% in 1986 (Comén 1988).

There are advantages and disadvantages in a particular situation attaching to each mode of transport and since they partly overlap in suitability they can be both competing and complementary. Though all modes have been subject to technical development the pace has been faster for airfreight and slower for freight on railway.

However, some of the more important technical changes since the second world war have necessitated an application to more than one mode of transport in order to be effective. Examples of such technical changes are containerization, standardization of unit loads, new infrastructure for communication through computers and telefax. Combinations of rail - road, sea - road, rail - sea, road - air have grown in importance as a result of this and have facilitated integration of the different transport systems.

2.2. International trade and internationalization of manufacturing industry

The growth in international trade and internationalization of the manufacturing industry are perhaps the two most important factors for the development of international transports. The functions of the transport in its service to manufacturing industry are threefold: a) the assembly of raw materials b) the transfer of semifinished products between plants c) the distribution of finished products (White 1983). In a wider sense they are all to be regarded as parts of distribution systems for industrial production units.

---

[1] Svensk Export Aktuellt nr 4 1992

A very important indicator of the development of international distributions systems is the growing volumes in international trade since the second world war. During the last decades the increase in world exports has been very high. Between 1970-89 it increased 2,5 times[1]. In Western Europe the growth has been even higher. This not only reflects the increasing trade between different countries of the world but also the on-going internationalization of the manufacturing industries.

An example of internationalization is the increase from 52% to 70 % in the proportion of international sales recorded by large Swedish Groups from 1965 to 1978[2]. Towards the end of the 1980's this share has continued to increase.

The discrepancy between 2,5 times increase in the volume of trade of Western European countries and the much lower (50%) increase in tonnage in international transports during the almost corresponding period illustrates the reductions in weight and size of the units produced during the last decades e.g. computers, refrigerators, etc. The changes in the unit values of world trade during the same period of 3,5 - 4 times[3] partly illustrates the same phenomena.

The growth in volumes, international competition in combination with the increased unit values, higher international interest rates, increased fuel costs, etc., brought the logistical costs into focus for the manufacturing companies in industrialized countries.

The logistical costs include warehousing, inventorying, handling, information systems, transports, etc (Ballou, 1987). In three large empirical studies[4] during 1960-70's the logistical costs in percentage of sales were on average around 21% in the States but differed as between industries. In Sweden they were said to be even higher on average during the 1970's. The logistical costs in percentage of GNP during 1970-80 were estimated at somewhere between 17-18% for Sweden (Tarkowsky & Ihreståhl 1987). A similar figure in the United States was estimated at 15 % during roughly the same period (Ballou, 1987).

In industrialized countries, as a result of the increasing logistical costs, industry is rationalizing by lowering inventory levels, reducing volumes in warehouses, creating greater efficiency in handling, developing new, faster and more effective information systems and better control, etc. When discussing transports the expression "just-in-time"(JIT) is often used, meaning the presentation of an item to a customer at the right time, in the right place and in the right

---

1 World Trade Statistics volumes - Total transports quantum index 1980 =100 from 1965 41- 149 in 1989 and from 62-149 between 1970 - 1989 in volumes (derived from value data and unit value data base period weighted). For Western Europe (EEC and EFTA) the changes were in exports 57/56- 150 between 1970-89 and for imports from 60-149 during the same period.

2 Swedenborg, 1982. (From " De Svenska Storföretagen, 1985, IUI)

3 World Trade Statistics 1970-89

4 Ballou, 1987 p 14-15, Studies made by Bernard, LaLonde & Zinszer 1976, Snyder 1963 and Stewart, 1965

condition, using the right type of carrier and giving right information, etc., price and speed will be less in focus. An introduction of JIT will often result in an increase in the number of and a greater frequency of external transports. Since it is linked with extremely low inventory levels, the work-flow in the total distribution system requires to be carefully and comprehensively planned.

The creation of JIT (just-in-time) during the last decades seems to have been just what industry in Europe wanted. So much so, in fact, that a body of opposition is beginning to awaken in many European countries, since the increased frequency in road transports creates environmental problems. However, the increased international competition to be expected from the single European Market will probably fuse the interest of industry in reducing logistical costs. Some of the large international manufacturers, especially in high-tech (Philips, Rank Xerox, etc.) but also other multinational companies (Unilever, DSM, etc.) have continued to pursue this direction and have largely rid themselves of their transport departments and warehouses.

Accordingly, these industrial companies have come to rely heavily on the services of the transport companies which would seem to have created the need to work more closely with fewer transport companies.

This increase in international trade has been reliant on other very important trade-facilitating prerequisites, such as the changes in trade rules and regulations and decreased or eliminated customs duties, etc. Also in Europe, much of the customs clearance work can now be handled on-line directly with the Customs which has meant a sharp reduction in the time taken to clear a consignment. An important issue for EC has been to harmonize and deregulate the procedures and rules of trade within the Internal Market specifically but also towards other parts of the world.

The growth in trade and internationalization of industry have brought about internationalization of distribution systems and the transport companies have participated through the creation of these international transport systems. Further higher logistical costs and increasing interest for Jit have changed the demands on effective transport systems.

2.3. Freight transport industry
(see glossary of transport terminology appendix 2)

The growth in total transports, in combination with the demands for effective international transport systems, have increased the size and international activities of the transport companies over time. Many transport companies in Europe have become multinational or global as a result.

Shipping and road transport are dominating the volumes of international freight transports according to the trade statistics (see table 2.1.). As international road transports are controlled by freight forwarders one would expect to see forwarding companies along with shipping lines as dominating international freight transport companies. In the normal course, freight forwarders also play an important role for international air and railfreight since they utilize several means of transportation. However, since the UN international statistics on the largest transport companies in Europe does not separate passenger from freight the largest companies are, in fact, railways and airlines. (Among the first twenty transport companies, thirteen are from these two groups). When studying the types of activities one find that airlines[1] and railways perform a large variety of passenger activities while the shipping lines and forwarders have their variety in freight activities.

This is not to say that both railways and airlines might not be large as international freight transport companies but, statistically, their size should be heavily reduced. The railways do have large volumes of freight transports but, on the other hand, are restricted internationally.

Therefore in table 2.2. the largest international freight transport companies are listed excluding railways and airlines. (For the full list see appendix 2)

Large international forwarders being owned by the railways, like ASG owned by the Swedish Railway (SJ), Schenker owned by German Railways (DB), van Gend &Loos owned by Railways of Netherlands(NS), etc are registered separately in the 1988 list with the exception of Schenker which is added to the list. These mentioned companies have all been sold or registered on the stock exchange during the intervening 3-4 years due to economic problems of the national railways.

(1988)	No[2]	(Country)	Type of activities
P&O Co	(5)	GB	Sea/ road etc
Danzas AG	(8)	CH	All types
Schenker[3]		W-G	All types
Bilspedition	(12)	S	All types
Kühne& Nagel[4]	(16)	CH	All types
NFC Plc	(18)	GB	All types
Nedlloyd	(20)	NL	Sea/ road etc
van Gend&Loos	(22)	NL	All types
Panalpina AG	(24)	CH	All types
Lep Group Plc	(25)	GB	All types

[1] The share of freight in the total revenues was for all the large European airlines under 20% in 1986.(Comén, 1988)
[2] Ranking on the total list including railways and airlines ranked by sales
[3] Figures for ranking of Schenker and ASG are from their Annual Reports
[4] International

Hapag LLoyd	(26)	D	Sea/ air etc
Swedcarrier	(35)	S	All types
Kühne& Nagel AG	(44)	D	All types
TDG Plc	(46)	GB	All types
ASG		S	All types
SCAC	(50)	F	All types

Table 2.2 Largest international freight transport companies in Europe (excl airlines and railways) - ranked by sales 1988

Source: U.N (United Nations) International Classification standard by ISIC (International standard industrial classification) Industrial codes 71 - Transport and Storage

In the modified list (table 2.2) consisting of freight transport companies shipping lines and freight forwarders dominate. P&O, a shipping line, is the largest company with 6 bill. dollars in sales. The second, Danzas, and third, Schenker, are two large international freight forwarders. The registered profitability of all companies on the modified list is on average around 4-5% of sales.

When comparing this list to a similar list for 1977 presented by the Commerzbank in Germany (Transportnytt 5, 1979) and focusing on freight transport companies seven, of the 10 largest from 1988 were the same companies on both lists[1]. An important change though was that Bilspedition had moved from being the last to no 4 in size[2]. Both Scansped and ASG were larger than Bilspedition in 1977. Further, between 1977-1988 the 7 largest freight transport companies grew roughly 2,5 times which seems to have been faster than for the average passenger company. The total number of freight transport companies has increased (from 7 to 10) among the first 25 transport companies of the full list.

It is interesting to note that the number of employees in 1988 varied from 4000-56 000 and did not strictly follow the ranking of sales. This phenomenon reflects the degree to which extent the companies are owners of their facilities and means of transportation. Shipping lines like P&O (56 000) and Nedlloyd (22 000) are among the largest while a traditional forwarder like Danzas has much fewer (13 000) employees.

Moreover the variety of services offered by the freight transport companies is large. Their services include warehousing and storing, support services of different kinds, airfreight services, services incidental to transports etc. Reasons for this might be found in higher

---

[1] These were in order Danzas, P&O, Schenker, K&N, Hapag LLoyd, Nedlloyd and Panalpina.
[2] In a list of road-based freight companies in Europe ranked by sales from 1990 (Cooper, Browne & Peters, 1992, pp 198) Bilspedition was ranked as no 3, ASG no 11 and Inter Forward no 16

logistical costs and transport companies taking over some of the logistical activities from industry. The transport companies have added and developed new services in order to meet the demands of their customers. Most of the large freight transport groups have these services.

Many new types of rapidly growing companies have entered the market during the same period, the express and parcel companies, specialist companies, logistical service companies, etc. though only some of the newcomers are European-based. Especially the development of the new express companies or parcel companies such as TNT, UPS, Federal Express, DHL seems to have stressed the importance of integrated transports systems and time-guaranteed transports and pointed to the importance of effective information and communication systems. Some researchers (Browne, 1991) even say that this is the critical issue in the future development for all freight transport companies. Those lacking know-how in this area will not survive. The information systems and communication might be internal or external. Internal systems exist to a large extent for planning systems, operational systems, follow-up systems, etc., while external systems embracing customers, suppliers, agents, etc., demand more adaptions. If direct EDI (Electronic Data Interchange) would not be suitable, for efficiency's sake or due to incompatibility of computer systems between companies, there are other possible ways like using electronic mail box systems and/or a switch board transferring messages electronically, etc. Many of the large transport companies develop their own electronic switch boards for EDI. Cross-border EDI would facilitate their international ambitions but is still in its infancy (Browne,1991 pp 2).

Further the harmonisation and liberalisation of the rules and regulations for transports within Europe, expected to be fulfilled in 1993 or shortly thereafter, will probably underline the importance of information and communication systems and so change the possibilities for more effective transports as well as increase international competition between transport companies.

2.4. The manufacturing industry and the transport companies- two perspectives

In order to describe how changes of manufacturing companies have influences on and are influenced by transport companies, it seems necessary to understand how they are interconnected, starting from the dominating perspective of the manufacturers and then continuing to the perspective of the transport companies.

2.4.1. The manufacturing companies´ view-point.

The dominating picture in business administration and organizational literature is that transport companies are plainly regarded as facilitating agents in the distribution channel for the manufacturing industry.

As facilitating agents, the development of transport companies seem to be totally dependent on the manufacturing companies. The interdependence between the two industries is not taken into consideration when discussing the development of the manufacturing industry.

The distribution channel is seen as an inter-organizational system, consisting of sets of interdependent organizations, that is involved by an exchange of outputs in the process of making products or services available for consumption.(Stern& El Ansary 1977)

The organizations in the distribution channel normally include intermediaries like wholesalers, retailers, etc., which are part of the flows of activities mentioned above and help to fulfil the four basic utilities of form, time, place and possession. In the manufacturing perspective, the transport companies are connected through the transport systems contributing to time and place utilities.

The dyad relations between the companies in the distribution channel to the final consumer can be seen as a separate system, referred to here as the transfer system.

The number of transfer systems varies with the structure of the channel. Normally a distribution channel includes several different transfer systems(figure 2.3.)

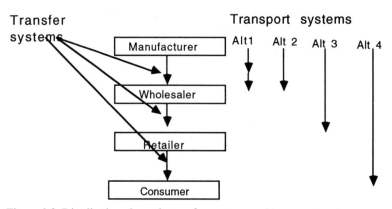

Figure 2.3. Distribution channel, transfer systems and transport systems

A single transfer system is a part of the distribution system having a specified sender and receiver. A transfer system does not have to coincide with the transport system. Sometimes a transfer system includes more than one transport system, at other times it coincides or the transport systems include more than one transfer system (see figure 2.3.). This will vary depending on the the single firms involved being senders and receivers in the transfer systems as well as the extent to which suitable transport systems exist.

No matter how the transfer and the transport systems are inter-connected when used, from the perspective of the manufacturer the systems are seen as a one-way system.

Basically the transport system, as far as the manufacturer is concerned, is a geographically extended system taking the products from one part to another in the distribution channel.

The nodes wherein the transport systems meet the industrial systems may differ depending on the conditions of the connecting systems. An example of this is the extent complementary services have been added, such as warehousing, packing, sorting, etc.. These services have extended the role of transport companies into performing part of the "form utility" as well. In some cases they may even take over part of the role of the wholesaler, with the transport companies storing, sorting, packing, etc., and via their information systems having direct contact with the manufacturer.

Up to this point, the transport systems as well as the transport companies have been presented from the manufacturers' viewpoint, which means being a part of the distribution channel and its transfer systems.

2.4.2. The transport companies´ viewpoint

Turning to the transport companies' viewpoint, the discussion will show a quite different situation.

The linkage between the manufacturing and the transport company is represented by the transport system and the difference in perspective is subsequently based on their different views of the transport system.

First, a transport system from the transport companies' point of view is normally a two-way or maybe a triangular system but not a one-way system and it covers not only one but several transfer systems in both directions.(See figure 2.4.). The number of transfer systems using one transport system might be just a few or run into hundreds, depending on the type of system.

Secondly, the transport systems are normally standardized and thereby utilized for goods from different manufacturing companies. The fact that it is possible to utilize the system for many different customers makes it possible for higher capacity utilization compared to a normal single customer system. The customized system, set up for a specific purpose and/or time limited, is still not so common. However over time, some large manufacturing groups have achieved the volumes to be transported to create a high level of efficiency. Creating special systems for these customers will often be made on a project basis by the transport company as a seller of know-how. On the other hand, it is in the best interests of the customers to increase effectiveness through combining the usage of transport resources in the means of transportation, terminals, etc, with the use of the existing transport systems and net of contacts.

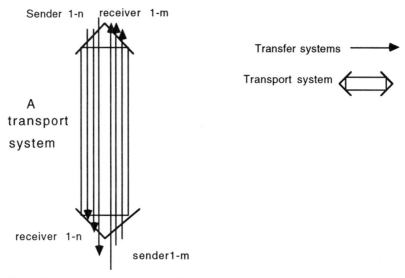

Figure 2.4. A transport system and several transfer systems

From the perspective of the transport company, the transport system is not basically seen as a connection between two parties in the distribution channel. The transport system is rather a specific combination of resources being available at a certain place during a certain period of time that should be organized in an efficient way.

In most cases, the whole system is controlled by one or a few transport companies which, in their turn, have subcontractors who control limited parts of the system. Normally, the transport companies controlling the system are also marketing the transport system. Each transport system can be marketed as a separate service even though this is not always how it happens.

The resources can be made available either because of direct ownership or through leasing, renting or one of many different forms of agreement with subcontractors. Such agreements can be either long-term or short-term and can be close or at arms-length depending on what is standard and the total capacity within that specific branch. It is not uncommon for the most critical resources of the systems to be owned or in some other way guaranteed for a longer period of time by the controlling companies.

A similar situation would seem to apply from the customers' side, in that they are normally interested in making a long term agreement with the transport companies when a specific transport system is vital for their intake or output of goods. In other cases, the industrial companies buy the services of a specific transport system virtually off-the-shelf from the transport company, varying their choice from time to time. The increasingly important role played by the transport companies seems to have resulted in a greater number of agreements made between them and their customers.

The basic flows of activities in a transport system are the physical flow consisting of a technical flow and a flow of goods, the flow of communication/information, the flow of responsibility and the flow of payments. The flow of goods and information is directly related to the transfer system of the customers while the others are mostly related to the design of the specific transport system. The last two flows concern the division between the companies performing the different functions of the transport system. For the transport companies involved in the transport systems, the flows also have longer term and day to day aspects. While the longer term flows might concern the design of the systems in general, the day to day flows might concern the immediate information and quantities of goods moving in the transport system. To the extent that the resources in the flow of goods and information concern the design of the system they are transport system specific (system specific) rather than transfer specific.

Typical functions of transport companies of a long distance transport (A-B) in the flows of goods and information flows are shown in figure 2.5..

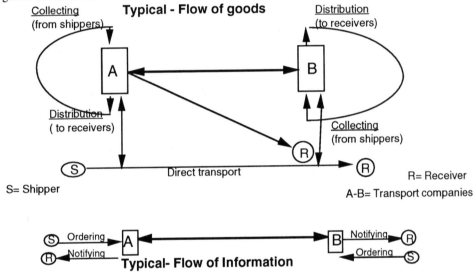

Figure 2.5.Typical flow of goods and of information for a long distance transport

The information flow is typically performed through documents, computers, phone, telefax etc and is to a large extent concerning the other flows. The flow of payment concerns the sharing of incomes and costs and the flow of responsibility concerns sharing the risks. Finally informations of the goods (size, consignments, type of goods etc) are needed not only for the technical system used for planning the continued transport but for the feeding information to next stage of the system.

In summary, the transport companies and the manufacturing companies are basically connected via transport systems which are organized and controlled by the transport companies. In that function, the transport companies are facilitating agents in performing the time and place utilities through undertaking part of thephysical flow in the channel of distribution. From the manufacturing companies' side, the transport systems are a one-direction system between the market and the manufacturing company, for which the demands are set depending on the market situation. The subject of available transport capacity is rarely mentioned when discussing marketing strategies as it is generally assumed to be available. The transport companies, on the other hand, are looking at a two-way or triadic transport system serving a large number of industrial companies. The systems are often standardized and questions as to marketing and efficient use of resources (quantity of resources, alternative combinations and availability in time and place) are very important for their competitiveness.

2.5. Transport companies -definition and classification

The transport company is an organization which organizes and controls a transport system, systems or part of transport system/s without owning the goods transported. A transport system normally consists of several inter-dependent transport companies fulfilling different functions in the system. The companies are often specialized in specific functions.

A classical categorization of transport companies in international transport systems is into a) forwarders/ brokers, that prepare documentation for export and import (like forwarders and brokers), b) owners of the means of transportation/equipment/facilities, and c) operators of the transports/ freight carriers.(see figure 2.6.)

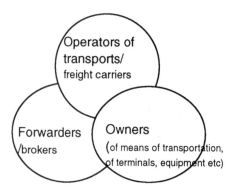

Figure 2.6. Three basic categories of a transport company

Basically these three categories cover the existing types of transport companies but they also include companies that would not be called transport companies according to the definition above. These companies might indirectly be part of the transport system but they do not organize or control any part of that system. Examples of such non-transport companies are ship owners whose interest is purely financial, sub-contractors like companies leasing transport equipment, warehousing specialists, etc. Formerly, it was often taken for granted that the operator was also the owner of the means of transportation, the terminals, etc. This is not necessarily the case any longer. Similarly, in the past the traditional forwarder or broker did not necessarily own facilities, equipment, etc. These traditional stereotypes have been changing. New mixes of these categories have evolved. Reasons for this can be found in changes in laws and regulations, technological development, changes in customer demands, etc. In many instances, the companies have developed partly along all three lines, combining being a forwarder, an operator and an owner of at least certain means of transportation. This has resulted in the development of some very large transport companies.

The services performed by the transport companies can be separated in many different ways. A traditional way has been to divide the services of the transport companies by dimensions of consignment and means of transportation used. The combination of the size of consignment and the basic technologies create specific types of transport systems which are shown in figure 2.7. The figure also shows the typical way that these transport systems were related to certain transport companies.

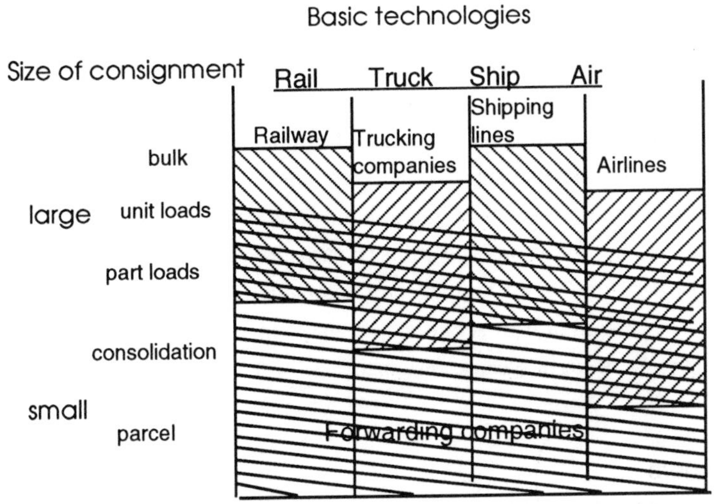

Figure 2.7. The traditional way of specifying transport systems and classifying transport companies

Depending on the means of transportation utilized some transport companies are more suitable for certain types of goods and specialized in transport systems handling these volumes like railway, shipping lines, airlines, etc. Forwarders which often use different means of transportation have traditionally specialized in consolidation. As the unit value has increased and the size decreased, consolidation and packages have become more important to the advantage of the forwarder. The development of unit loads has further increased their field of business. Basically the local transports are performed by truck while the long distance transports can be performed by any mode and type of transportation (sea, air, truck, rail) and any equipment can be utilized (trailers, containers, flats, etc).

In normal circumstances, the smaller the size of the individual consignments the greater the number of customers per transport system.

However, the decrease in size of consignments and the stronger demands on speed, timing and frequency in order to create a more effective distribution of goods, have led to the development of new types of transport services. These are time-based transports, special transports and customized logistical transports. Time-based transports are standardized transports with a time guarantee which are adapted to the new demands of JIT (just-in-time) and more customer integrated. Special transports stem from the development of new technologies utilized for transports of certain types of goods such as hanging garments, bulk, furniture transports, etc. These added services have been at the expense of general transports. The customized logistical transport services are those designed exclusively for a specific customer which include specialized combinations of transport services and logistical services.

The four basic types of transports services (general, special, time-based and customized logistical transports) have caused a development of new transport companies which are less focused on specific means of transportation. Combined transports have been much more common for long distance transports based on standardized equipment like truck-rail, truck-ship or truck-air. Classifying the transport companies in a more modern manner, taking the new service companies into consideration would be possible to do according to their different problem-solving abilities. Figure 2.8 is adapted from Håkansson & Johanson (1982). The general ability reflects the degree to which the transport companies producing standardized services have a low or high standard in their services. The adaption ability on the other hand reflects the ability to adapt to the needs of specific customers.

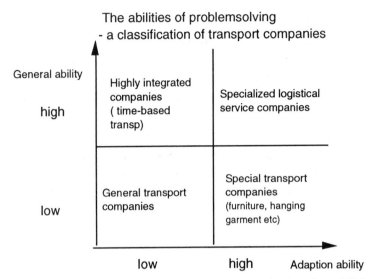

Figure 2.8. Modern classification of transport companies based on abilities of probelmsolving (adapted from Håkansson & Johanson, 1982)

The general transport companies can be exemplified by many of the traditional forwarders, railway, shipping lines, etc and highly integrated companies by the express companies such as TNT, UPS. Special transport companies are of many categories, specialized in taking care of a certain type of goods and customers, which lead to a much higher integration with these customers. The last category is perhaps the least common type, which is specialized in performing complex logistical services for specific customers.

In line with these new services and demands, the transport companies' operational systems have also been changed in order to be more efficient. Different types, like central terminal systems, several terminal systems with direct traffics (network system), hub and spoke systems, central route systems or a mixture of these, have been used (Ljungström, 1986 p. 58). Some have become more frequently used for certain types of goods or sizes of consignments. Central terminal systems are more suitable for many small sized consignments since they concentrate a large number of local traffics(see glossary) to a few large more distant transports. Therefore they are used by IPEC, TNT, Federal Express, etc., specialized in packages, express goods, etc. Network systems, which are the most common in Europe, e.g.used by Kühne& Nagel, Calberson, Bilspedition Domestic, etc, are built on local distribution and collection and then long distance traffics between terminals. The number of traffics will be very high in this case which will lead to low capacity utilization. In the "hub and spoke system" (satellite system) the volumes get much larger, leading to higher capacity utilization.

The development of services has resulted in the development of new types of transport companies as well as a reorganization of the existing traditional ones into these areas.

Therefore the spread of types of transport companies has increased since they have developed into many different areas and/or acquired transport companies representing other areas. Forwarding companies, shipping lines, etc., often cover the whole spectrum of services shown in figure 2.8.

The interest in this thesis is centred on companies going through the process of growing into large international transport companies developing into all basic categories of services. They are all operators and forwarders in combination with being owners of some of the terminals and equipment and part of the means of transportation.

Part II Theoretical framework

3. Three theoretical perspectives

With the characteristics and roles of the transport companies before us, we proceed now to the existing research and theories. On a more general level the intention of the chapter is to gain a better understanding of the behaviour of firms in a growth process such as internationalizing and how this behaviour is assumed to vary in different contextual settings. However, two specific purposes govern the choice of existing research and theories. Firstly based on this review, we want to create a model of analysis that can be applied to the internationalization of transport companies. Secondly, we want to understand what could be possible driving forces to different patterns of internationalizing. While the model of analysis will used for structuring the actual behaviour, the driving forces will facilitate the understanding the observed behaviour and as such will not be discussed until chapter 11.

Since the network as well as the distribution research spring to a larger extent from empirical studies rather than originating from microeconomic models, these research fields will include more of empirical research. The empirical parts will be especially helpful in understanding the problems in connection with the creation of a useful model for the structuring of organizational behaviour.

The focus of the research review, both theoretically and empirically, will be on changes in systems and on firms and their interdependence with other firms. We start, therefore, with the network approach where interdependence between firms is a basic assumption and changes are constantly going on within and between companies. As such, the network approach plays a predominant role in the creation of a model of analysis. Distribution research, being next, contributes specifically to the understanding of distribution systems and changes in firms being a part of these systems, which is important for creating the model of analysis. Furthermore, both network and distribution theories contribute to driving forces for changes which will be applied to the empirical findings. Finally, internationalization theories will have high importance when looking for possible driving forces of explaining how the internationalization process changes as well as for some of the basic concepts of the model of analysis.

3.1. Network approach

Apart from the reason, mentioned earlier, of contributing to the understanding of changes in the behaviour of the transport companies, the network approach simplifies the combining of micro and macro perspectives through seeing the same organization in a limited and then a larger setting. In these settings the organization is assumed to be interacting with other organizations in the network and therefore the context will naturally be included in the study.

Even though the term "network" has been used in many research disciplines like sociology, ecology, communication, etc., the application of the network approach to industrial systems is more recent. Being a young research approach, partly originating from other research fields, it has produced a variety of concepts and definitions. Therefore we shall start by defining what we mean by the concepts used. This will be followed by discussions concerning interdependence and embeddedness and then concerning dynamics in networks. The part on dynamics will be of particular importance in understanding the processes that the transport companies have gone through in the creation of their international networks. The section will end with a short discussion on strategic action in networks and limitations of the network approach.

Definitions and concepts
In general terms, a network is a set of connected exchange relationships between actors. A definition by Cook (1982, p 180), derived from sociology is "exchange relations are defined as connected if exchange in one relation is contingent upon exchange in the other relation". This definition points to the interdependence or interconnectedness between relations. Since the focus here is on industrial networks, the exchange is assumed to include an economic element and it takes place in the relationships of connected organizations (Easton, 1992; Mattsson, 1987).

Easton (1992) comments that the "Industrial network approach differs from other network approaches in terms of its scope. It is concerned to understand the totality of relationships among firms engaged in production, distribution and the use of goods and services in what might best be described as an industrial system." (ibid pp 3)

However, viewing an industrial network of relationships as an industrial system means restricting the relations of the organizations in the network to those concerning industrial systems. In many cases, the discussion will even be limited to a specific production system.

To overcome this limitation, Johanson & Mattsson (1992) have constructed a model that separates the industrial production systems from those of the industrial networks of organizations. It is the separation of the organization/actor, and their respective positions, from the resources and activities which will facilitate the understanding of organizations in the network and their ability to form part of different production systems and still be connected. The actors, at network level, control and coordinate the resources at the production system level via the governance structure. Causal relations are assumed to exist between the two levels (ibid). Since the two levels interact, changes at one level will induce changes at the other.

Further, an industrial network of organizations might be analyzed from three different perspectives, i.e that of the single organization, the relationship and the total network.

When focusing on a single organization/actor the position is important. The concept of position shows how an organization "fits" into an industrial system (Henders, 1992). It is often used in order to describe the role an organization plays vis-a-vis other organizations to which it is related directly or indirectly in the network (Mattsson, 1984). A distinction is made between limited position and extended position (Johanson & Mattsson, 1992), where the limited position purely relates to the network level and the extended position also refers to the role of the single organization/actor in the production system. The position in relation to other firms is relevant for the constraints and opportunities of the single organization/actor in the network and therefore also for their strategies.

In the (industrial) network approach the organizations are assumed to be heterogeneous in their resources and activities. Therefore in the exchange relationships the resources are mostly complementary. Furthermore the type and character of the relationships play a significant role for the organizations. Each relationship is assumed to have different strength and content. (Mattsson, 1985). Strength can be described in different ways depending on purpose. A common way when applying more quantitative analysis is in terms of frequency, intensity and duration (Mitchell, 1969; Lincoln, 1982). Another way, which seems to measure the sum of these, is in terms of the capacity to withstand a disruptive force (Easton & Arujo, 1992). Content is often described in terms of social, legal, knowledge based, technical- and timebased bonds between firms (Hammarkvist et al, 1982).

Through these interdependent relationships the organization obtains access to resources controlled by other organizations in the network. However the coordination of these relationships is often in reality so complex that the parties have to develop close relationships. Empirical studies using the interaction approach have shown that these relationships are typically of a long lasting nature. Due to the efforts put into these relationships in terms of creation, maintenance and development they are not easily broken (Håkansson, 1982).

Even though an industrial network is based to a large extent on complementarity and long term relationships, there are conflicts within the relationships. Both competition and cooperation between actors are both important parts of a network (Mattsson, 1984). Further, stability and change will play a significant role in the development in relations and in the network.

Finally the perspective of the total network consists of organizations and relations. Fombrun (1982) defines the total network as an aggregate of overlapping sets of networks with different transactional content. Further it can be defined in terms of the interdependencies between positions taken by the organizations in the network (Mattsson, 1987) and then described as loosely or tightly structured depending on the degree of inter-dependencies that exist.

There are often clusters of organizations in the total network, however, which show a higher interdependency. These can be called clusters, nets (Mattsson, 1985) or sub-networks (Hägg & Johanson, 1982).

Such nets or sub-networks show similarities to earlier developed, more limited concepts in inter-organizational research of organizational set, action set (Aldrich and Whetten,1981) or trans-organizational systems (Cummings,1984). The organizational set, based on classical role set, is limited to direct relations of a focal company. An action set is based on a number of directly related organizations that have joined together for a specific purpose. The development of the organization set and action set are important in organization theory because they point out the arbitrariness of organizational boundaries.

However, arbitrary boundary setting is in reality applicable not only to an organization but to an even greater extent to networks consisting of inter-organizational relations. On a general theoretical level, the total network might continue almost endlessly into new relations. A vast network would also be under constant change which would make the boundaries fluent. A specific industrial system might have a certain industrial or technical logic though, which could be a base for delimiting the network. There is in reality, however, no single real objective way of delimiting a network (Mattsson 1987). Therefore the boundary setting will be dependent on the subject of research and the perspective of the researcher.

Summarizing, we have described some basic concepts for the network approach and present the three different levels of aggregation of organizations i.e. networks, relationships and clusters/nets and their characteristics. As we shall see, both the concepts and the separation into different levels of analysis will be extremely useful for the construction of our model of analysis. Finally, the problems of boundary setting when making an empirical study will be discussed.

Interdependence - trust and connectedness
Resource dependence theory has received a great deal of attention in inter-organizational theory as a base for explanation of why companies interact and for the increasing interdependence between organizations.This theory claims that in order to understand an organization you must understand the context of that organization.

Pfeffer& Salancik (1978) argue that a key to survival, in a situation of scarcity of resources and interconnectedness of organizations, is the ability to acquire and maintain resources.

Coordination through inter-firm linkages (cooptation, trade association, cartels, joint ventures, social norms, etc.) help to stabilize the organization´s exchanges with its environment and to reduce uncertainty of the context. However these linkages not only create certain advantages of reduced uncertainty but also further increase the level of interdependence to the environment.

Coordination is equally important for firms in networks since it is based on interaction and interdependence between organizations. Cummings (1984) indicates that there is an inherent change towards higher interdependence in networks through the process of coordination, in that coordination is made for increased effectiveness. As the level of effort increases it affects the level of coordination. The argument is that the level of effort (degree of intensity) and coordination of efforts are among the most important factors influencing effectiveness of a limited net, such as an action set, but also that the level of effort is positively connected to coordination of efforts. More specifically, Cummings states that the degree of intensity in interaction (the level of effort) is positively related to coordination of efforts such as formal agreements, centralized decision making and structural agreements like standardization and formalization. The strength of a relationship is positively related to the degree of coordination.

However, interconnectedness in networks or between networks seems to both have a positive and a negative side. It creates interdependence between organizations which might create a higher achievement but at the cost of a higher level of uncertainty and a more unstable environment for the organizations.

Interconnectedness between organizations might lead to uncertainty but does not necessarily lead to disorder involving conflicts, as many economists claim (Granovetter, 1985). Further the degree to which stability and trust, as well as generalized standards for behaviour, are developed in a network will be more important for the level of uncertainty and any pressure for change than disorder due to opportunism and conflict (Ibid).

In the relationships of an industrial network both stability and trust play an important role in coping with the uncertainly of interconnectedness. Trust is the base for the social exchange in the relationships. Trust in a relationship is seen as "one party´s belief that its need will be fulfilled in the future by actions undertaken by the other party" (Anderson & Weitz, 1986). Johanson & Mattsson (1992) have formulated that "Through the exchange relationships the actors learn about each other and develop trust." Furthermore, this is the base for long term relationships.

There are benefits in building up long term social relationships in that it gives cheaper, better, richer and more accurate information about other organizations forming part of the network than merely relying on institutional arrangements or on the fact that firms would not willingly risk damage to their reputation (Granovetter, 1985).

However, the degree to which trust and stability are present in a relationship is often dependent not only on the single relationship but also on its connectedness to other relations in the network. The expression of positive and negative connectedness in relations reflects complementarity and competition between relations. Relations are positively connected, to the extent that exchange in one relation increases the likelihood of exchange in another relation, and negatively connected when the likelihood is a decrease of exchange in another relation (Emerson, 1972; Cook, 1982). Positively connected systems are exemplified by distribution systems or vertically integrated markets (Stern & El Ansary, 1972) and negatively connected networks by competitive economic market structures (Emerson & Cook, 1978).

The distinction between a negative and positive connection is seen as important for unifying theories on competitive processes with exchange processes based on complementarities. For example in the framework of Cook (1982), negatively connected exchange relations represent competition over valued resources within an exchange network.

By adherence to this, in an industrial network there would be a number of desirable alternatives for coordination with a high value of exchange and another number of possible alternatives due to the resource situation for each organization. These would also be in constant change due to actions of other organizations, in order to change the balance of power in the network, which in turn shows how the embeddedness of organizations in the network context changes interconnectedness over time (Cook,1982).

In summary, we have discussed interconnectedness and interdependence between organizations, which is reflected in the embeddedness in networks of organizations. Seeing organizations as embedded in the networks of organizations seems to be vital for the understanding of how transport companies will develop their international networks. A necessity when coping with uncertainty of interconnectedness is coordination between organizations which in turn seems to increase the interdependence further. Important driving forces for coordinating within and between relationships are trust and stability and the degree to which companies are positively or negatively connected in the network. These concepts will play a vital role in the theoretical discussions later on.

Dynamics in network

Due to the inter-dependencies in a network, changes of positions, relations and nets will have effects on the total network. Changes in positions of single firms will be discussed in the section dealing with strategies in networks.

On a relational level, much of the changing takes place in ongoing relations between organizations (Håkansson 1987). In this case it would be a question of maintaining, developing and strengthening a relation over time. Other relational changes taking place are the establishment of new relations and leaving relationships. The relation, as such, may even go through its own life-cycle over time. Dwyer,Schurr &Oh (1987) and Liljegren (1988) have presented two similar models on a relationship life cycle. The model of Dwyer et al shows five phases. The first two phases concern the formation of the relation (awareness and exploration), the next two phases the development of an established relation (expansion and commitment) and finally dissolution of the relation. In the formation process the awareness phase is just a recognition that a party is a feasible exchange partner and the exploration phase refers to the search and trial process. The relation can still be very fragile in this stage.

The first establishment phase, expansion, refers to a continual increase in benefits and increasing interdependence for the partners. Th next phase, commitment, is based on a pledge for continuity of and parties are engaged in maintaining the relationship.

The fifth phase, dissolution, is one of withdrawal or disengagement involving emotional and physical stress. It seems mostly to be initiated unilaterally.

Liljegren (1988) constructed a four phased model based on an empirical study of the evolution of a relationship over a period of 10-15 years which to a large extent supported the model of Dwyer,Schurr &Oh. He called the phases "building up", "development" and "maintenance" and the phase of "uncertainty". Liljegren found that the stage of uncertainty did not necessarily develop into dissolution but could equally well be developed into a stage of uncertainty leading to a renewal from the building up stage again.

Underlying this life-cycle, however, might not only be changes in the focal relationship but also effects of changes in other relations in the network. Gadde & Mattsson (1987) argued that not only the direct but also the indirect relations would have to be taken into account in order to understand changes going on within the relationship. In Liljegren (1988) such effects were shown.

On a general level, applied basically to populations and communities, Fombrun (1986) argues there are two basic types of evolutionary changes in networks, convergence and contradiction/divergence.

Convergence and divergence is also used by Lundgren (1991) in his thesis on "Technological Innovation and Industrial Evolution". He found three network stages as the technology developed over time. These were genesis- identification, coalescence-legitimation and dissemination- adaption. Genesis was characterized by ascendancy of interrelated clusters of innovations in which the actors were separated but gradually developing relations and creating a network. In coalescence the development converged towards a core technology leading to a tightly-knit network. Dissemination is the establishment of user-producer interaction leading to breaking the existing tightly-knit network structure which would be more of diverging from existing technology and converging into pre-existing technologies.

The phases of coalescence and dissemination are seen as the two dominating ways of network evolution by Håkansson & Lundgren (1992). They also discuss different patterns of changes which might lead to network evolution. These are the three dichotomies of generalization-specialization, structuring-heterogenization and hierarchization- extrication.

Mattsson (1987b) discusses network changes in terms of expansion or contraction of the network size, taking the degree of homogeneity, hierarchization, structuredness, and exclusiveness into consideration.

According to Astley &Fombrun (1983) there are three different forms of economic inter-dependencies taking place over time, leading to structural evolution of industries, which can be seen as patterns of change in networks. These are horizontal, vertical and diagonal interdependence. The first two take place within a single functional chain, a set of loosely coupled firms performing a specific social function and being symbiotically related, while diagonal interdependence takes place between functional chains.The horizontal interdependence is exemplified by relationships between competitors within cartels, trade associations, etc., while vertical interdependence is exemplified by complementary relations from suppliers and buyers in value added chains. The diagonal interdependence is seen as an indirect interrelationship between different industrial sectors or functional chains. This interdependence can take both the form of diagonal competition as well as a diagonal symbiosis. "Diagonal interdependence reflects convergence of two functional chains, which come to act either as substitutes or as complements for each other." (Ibid).

Diagonal relationships are seen as the most important for organizations when coping with a turbulent situation leading to more interconnectedness in the environment (Emery & Trist, 1965). Astley & Fombrun (1983) state that the same bilateral structures ranging from agreement and contracts to joint ventures and mergers are also used by organizations of functional chains to cope with interdependence as they converge. These diagonal linkages between functional systems or chains will fuse into a business cluster which together help to serve a major social function. Diagonal interdependence spreads through multiple intermediaries and elaborate networks of relationships are needed to coordinate activity. Business clusters are seen as basic sub-systems of such networks joined together by linking pin organizations (Aldrich & Whetten,1981) whose function is to integrate network activities by providing channels for communication and general services for facilitating interaction.

Astley &Fombrun (1983) are using the works of Chandler (1962, 1977) to exemplify how companies grow first by horizontal penetration, then by vertical integration and then finally by diagonal diversification. In a historical analysis made by Scherer (1980), a similar development was found for small family businesses and for waves of mergers. This development is combined with changes in the internal firm structures, from unifunctional to integrated multi-unit and then diversified multi-divisional conglomerates, as well as with inter-organizational structures like cartels, joint ventures, clusters/ nets etc.

The dynamics of organizations in nets or network seem to have certain similarities with those of populations and communities in ecology in that there are many unities consisting of homogeneous/heterogenous resources performing similar/different functions consisting of interdependent organizations of cooperating and conflicting interests as expressed by Astley (1985), Fombrun (1986), Astley & Fombrun (1983).

Astley (1985) in his article comparing population and community ecology points out that population ecology limits the investigation to evolutionary change while community ecology focuses on the rise and fall of populations. Population ecology emphasizes the stability and the homogenizing of organizations where community ecology simultaneously tries to explain homogeneity and heterogeneity between organizations.

On population levels, Astley refers to "phyletic gradualism", the natural selection that progressively transforms the population through a gradual one-by-one selection and "the bandwaggon effect", exemplified by what DiMaggio & Powell (1983) have called the mimetic processes, which encourages organizations to copy each other. In this way homogeneity increases and variety in the population decreases.

Technologies of different populations are then linked into larger complexes. These inter-dependencies between technologies fuse those organizations into functionally integrated systems or organizational communities.

"Organizational communities are functionally integrated systems of interacting populations : they are emergent entities that, over time, gain a certain degree of autonomy from their environments." (Astley, 1985, pp 234).

Such autonomy occurs as the populations, being part of the community, begin to function by exchanging resources with each other, rather than directly with their environment. In this way, they shut themselves off from their environment. By locking their members into a given set of relationships, communities approximate closed systems as the environmental space is filled. As the community reaches closure stage it is assumed that no new population can be added without disturbing the functional integration of the system . The complexity developed when the system has reached the closure stage leads to stability but also provides an inherent possibility of collapse. Such a community experiences disturbances over a certain threshold level, some may disintegrate because of the domino effect while others go into periodic waves of instability and then extended states of equilibrium. Severe disturbances upset the equilibrium and destroys the community and recovery of such a state of equilibrium occurs through succession i.e.change in both competition and symbiosis. As a community is destroyed new environmental space is created.(Astley,1985)

These changes in population level as well as community level take place in networks as well. The patterns of changes presented by Astley seem to sequentially combine the patterns of networks such as exclusiveness, heterogeneity, homogeneity, structuredness.

In the reasoning in this section, changes have been described on a more general level without really taking into account the driving forces behind them. There are some ideas of more general driving forces for change on network level, like changes in technology or quantitative or qualitative imbalances (Mattsson 1987a). Quantitative imbalances are between capacities of different types while qualitative imbalances are referred to as missing complementary activities in technological change processes.

In summary, this section about dynamics showing different ways of change of relationships and networks is of vital importance for development of the model of analysis. As far as networks are concerned, not only were changes mentioned such as expansion, contraction, changes in inter-dependencies, converging, diverging, etc., but also patterns of developments over time that have taken place through these changes, such as a movement towards a closure stage, combinations of inter-dependencies, etc. These ways are all of importance for understanding of changes and patterns of changes going on in networks. Finally, quantitative and qualitative imbalancies were mentioned as possible driving forces for changes on relational and network levels.

Strategies in networks

Strategies in the network can be formulated for a single organization and sometimes for a dyad or a cluster/net but never for a total network. Instead it is assumed that there is no master plan for the total network since the organizations are too interdependent, the activities too numerous and resources too diverse (Hägg & Johanson, 1982).

In research on industrial networks, the strategies of single organizations would be connected to strategic actions taken from a specific position which is defined in terms of network properties (see p.24). Strategic actions are seen as efforts made by actors to influence their position in network/s the intention being to increase effectiveness and to create a base for future development (Johanson & Mattsson, 1992). The effectiveness of an organization is defined as the ability of an organization to attract and gain control over the necessary resources. It is seen as an external standard applied to the output or to the activities of an organization while efficiency is an internal standard of organizational performance. These two are interdependent standards (Pfeffer & Salancik, 1978).

Strategic action according to Johanson & Mattsson (1992) is based on the firm´s position, its resources and the actor´s "network theory". The "network theory" means the subjective intention and interpretation of the network by the actor. When influencing other actors through breaking, establishing, preserving or changing the character of existing relationships, etc., one important way might be to change other actors' perceptions of the connections between relationships i.e influencing their "network theories". This reasoning applies not only to single firm strategies but also to relational strategies.

Granovetter (1973) analysed the importance of weak ties for the diffusion of influence and information, etc. for an individual actor in an effort to link the micro and macro levels in a network. He came to the conclusion that the weak ties being bridges to other parts of the network are seen as indispensable for individual opportunity and integration into communities. Strong ties, on the other hand, defined as a function of time, intimacy (mutual confidence), intensity and reciprocal services, lead to fragmentation into small groups (Granovetter, 1973). The possibilities for information and change would increase depending on to what extent the number of weak ties form bridges to other parts of the network. In an industrial network indirect relations are often assumed to be weak ties as a result of their distance and thereby lower impact. Strategies based on this reasoning have been used by many researchers of networks (Knoke & Kuklinski, 1983; Mattsson 1987b).

Drawing from the Morecambe Gasfield studies (Easton & Smith 1984), Laage-Hellman & Smith (1992) have used bridging as one of five ways for transformation of small groups. These are bypaths, combination, bridge, displacement and separation (elaboration and blocking). Bypaths are described as changing a relation from indirect to direct and in so doing, by-passing an existing direct relation, while combination is described in terms of joint venturing or creating alliances for keeping others out. Bridging is using a non-member of the group to influence one of the members. This is in a slightly different usage to that of Granovetter (1973) where bridging was a way to reach other nets or networks and to create change but did not say much about the purpose of the change. The two last types of transformations are displacement and separation where displacement includes interruption or severing of a dyadic relationship by a third party. Separation is when a direct relation is changed to an indirect or when the member of a group establishes an indirect relation to a non-group member rather than a direct relation to a group member. The changes here as well as in the Granovetter (Ibid) example are to a large extent taking place through exchange with non-members of the small group or net.

Cummings (1984), discussing performance strategies for smaller action sets, concentrates on internal strategies for the whole group in order to reach common desirable outcomes. He makes the assumption that these performance strategies are primarily affected by performance norms and, if these are not agreed upon, presents four different ways to develop shared norms. These are direction setting, diagnosis, frame-breaking collective definitions and changing networks. The first three involve changing the base of the existing values either legitimating or clarifying existing norms through learning or internal discussions and perhaps creating new common values. The last strategy involves changes in the relationships among the participants in the net. Cumming (1984) comments upon the fact that the degree to which organizations are loosely or tightly connected affects the possibilities for change in the norms. Tighter coupled networks are assumed to be more difficult to change than loosely coupled ones. Boje (1982) proposed that modifying power structures (through campaigns, pressure tactics, coercion, etc) might change strategic coupling within the network.

Cook (1982) also discusses the changes in power structures in the smaller network, in terms of the possibilities for powerful players to maintain their power advantages and the processes by which the less powerful players can gain power. According to her, there are two types of power-balancing mechanisms that apply to a network, network extension and network consolidation. Network extension is an increase in the number of exchange alternatives through the creation of new relations or the addition of new members while network consolidation is a decrease in the number of exchange alternatives either by a reduction in members or by collective action. One of the conclusions was that coalitions of the less powerful players in a network occurred frequently under conditions of power imbalance.These strategies do not limit changes to the existing net but include adding new relations to the group or a decrease in the number of members in the group.

In summary, strategies formulated for the single actor, the relationship or the small group were discussed. The single actor strategies basically concern the changing of its position in the network. The strategies of nets/clusters, actions sets, etc., are changes, both within the group and between groups, through changes in relationships. The possibilities to change are a result of many things, however, and among these are the structure of the network and the existing position of the single actor, dyad or small group in the total network.Strategies can be seen as important driving forces for changes in network postitions of actors or nets of actors and will as such be discussed in the theoretical discussions.

Limitations of the existing research into the network approach
As industrial network theory is a rather new field of research, there are opportunities rather than limitations in the theory since so much is left to do. As in most other fields of organizational research much of the existing study has been confined to the manufacturing industries.

Network theory is based on a different philosophy than the traditional market theories. It assumes that companies are less autonomous, that they are embedded in their context and that organizations, both in cooperation and conflict, are solving many different problems together. Yet we know very little of how networks are formed and how they continue to change over time. Also changes, not just between two parties but over a larger net or in a whole network, are in need of closer study. " There is an urgent need to obtain descriptions of various industrial networks over time in order to categorize them and try to understand the way they operate in terms of reaction patterns, propensity to change and so on" (Axelsson, 1992 p 247). Not only is this needed from a more general point of view but also from a focal company´s point of view.

Since the interdependence would appear to be important for organizations (Pfeffer & Salancik, 1978; Johanson & Mattsson, 1984) it seems that it would be possible to apply the network thinking to many other areas and contribute to new ways of understanding structures and changes. There have been attempts to apply this kind of thinking theoretically to the internationalization of companies (Johanson & Mattsson, 1984) but to date, there have been only a few scattered empirical studies (Forsgren, 1985, 1990). This thesis, by applying the network approach to transport companies and the way they change in their interdependencies over time, aims at contributing to a further understanding of a process like internationalization .

3.2 Distribution

Purpose of this section
The purpose of including the field of distribution is to understand the behaviour of the transport companies, within the framework of the distribution systems of which transport systems are part.
There are certain differences between transport systems and distribution systems that might be of importance when comparing the role of transport companies to that of intermediaries in a distribution system. The reversibility in the transport system leads to a greater interdependence between the organizations in the system. Since they do not take ownership of the goods, transport companies probably give higher priority to the creation of effective transport system rather than the goods *per se*. These differencies will have to be kept in mind when scanning existing distribution research for our purposes in this thesis.
The difference in the theoretical perspectives between transport companies and manufacturing companies (discussed in chapter 2) shows that neither of them includes the other directly in their system. The transport systems controlled by transport companies do not include the

"trading organizations" (Breyer, 1950) in the distribution channel, i.e. the owners of the goods transported. This is also in line with the tradition in the literature on distribution. Transport companies are not generally seen as being directly involved in the distribution channels. Seeing transport companies only as facilitating agencies (Revzan, 1961; Stern & El Ansary, 1988) or as non-trading companies (Breyer, 1950), has left them outside the studies of the formation, dissolution and structure of distribution channels. However, the development of logistics has brought about a certain change in attitude towards transport companies (Ballou, 1987; Stock & Lambert, 1987). As transport companies are, to an increasing extent, assuming activities in the distribution channel formerly performed by the "trading organizations", it would seem more logical and natural to include them in the channel.

Concepts of distribution and channel integration

Distribution is mostly defined as the flow of activities fulfilling the gap between production and consumption (Stern & El Ansary, 1982; Reve, 1986; Revzan, 1961).

The basis in all distribution systems/channels is the exchange of transactions between the organizations in the channel (Alderson, 1954; Cox, 1965; Dixon & Wilkinson, 1986; McInnes, 1964).

Further, the degree to which different intermediaries are involved in channel exchange, what type of intermediaries and the number of intermediaries will define the structure of the channel. The structure is normally a result of coordination of flows of activities and the specialization of the organizations.

Alderson (Ibid p 23) argued that "to act effectively a channel must act as if it were an integrated whole i.e. a program or policy advocated by one unit must be accepted by other units to achieve coordination." Coordination between organizations in a distribution channel made with the intention of "seeing things as a whole", is called *integration* and in the terms of Alderson, is of importance for the effectiveness of a distribution channel.

However, in the channel literature in contrast to that of network (Breyer, 1950; Bucklin, 1960; Reve, 1988; Anderson & Weitz, 1986) integration is mostly used in the form of internalised coordination based on ownership rather than coordination between separate organizations.

Discussions on the channel structure have focused on the degree of vertical integration in the meaning of formal legally based integration like fully integrated, hybrid or mixed and market channel (Anderson & Weitz, 1986; Anderson & Gatignon, 1986; Klein, Frazier & Roth, 1990). Often the discussions have even been restricted to a choice between internal or external transactions, the "make or buy" question.

In the transaction cost approach Williamson (1985) argues that, under uncertainty and high transactional frequency and asset specificity, ownership integration hierarchly is more effective in controlling opportunism than both integration based on contractual arrangements and the arm´s length market relations. Even though the studies of channel choice have found support for this approach they have also pointed out certain problems when applying the transaction cost approach, its dichotomy of market and hierarchy and its reasons for integration.

Chisholm(1989) found, in a case study of the San Francisco Bay Area Rapid Transit System, that under a variety of circumstances the informal mechanism for coordinating activities of independent agencies can be more effective than hierarchically organized ones. Some of the reasons for this were that authority based formal structures can create interdependencies that would not exist otherwise, leading to internal disputes. They may suppress rather than encourage sharing of information due to internal rivalry.

Inter-organizational coordination is, in contrast to hierarchies, based on voluntary linkages or relations to other organizations. Its primary benefits are to provide information about the activities of others, to be a channel of communication, to obtain commitment of support from important elements of the environment and legitimize the focal organization (Pfeffer & Salancik 1978, p 144-145).

Even though integration in distribution literature often assumes ownership there are authors, such as Törnqvist (1946), who recognize ways other than via ownership to reach integration and of making the distribution system into a whole. Mattsson continued this tradition and developed the concept further in his " Integration and Efficiency in Marketing Systems" (1969) by creating three major dimensions of the concept as regards integration, i.e. the execution integration, the decision integration and the institutional integration. The three aspects are present to different degrees in a marketing system. Institutional integration takes into consideration not only full ownership but also other different ways to integrate like part-ownership, contractual cooperation, etc., as lower levels of institutional integration. As for execution integration, it is expressed as a continuous scale and concerns the ways activities are performed. Decision integration is also a continuous scale and takes the degree of centralization in decisions in the marketing system into account. These three different aspects of integration were found to be interrelated.

In our study, the institution integration is not of primary interest, but rather the intention of the coordination in the channel and how it is implemented.

Changes that are taking place for many organizations such as decentralization, just-in-time deliveries and franchising agreements seem to support this wider definition of integration.

Summarizing, the same reasoning as applied to a distribution channel in terms of its structure and the importance of integration seems as easily applied to transport companies and transport systems. Integration, in a wider sense seeing ownership as only one aspect of integration, will as a concept be of vital importance for understanding changes of transport companies and transport systems and as such be used in the model of analysis.

Economies of scale and scope

One of the reasons for the importance of coordination and integration is that it is a prerequisite for economies of scale and scope of a single organization or of a channel.

In Dixon & Wilkinson (1986), the distribution channel is divided into two main interrelated flows, the more physical matter-energy flow carried out by the technical sub-system in an organization and the flow of information carried out by the administrative sub-system. Both are of vital importance for the economic performance of the channel.

Economies of scale and of scope concern the effectiveness and the efficiency (productivity) of the channel, since the degree to which economies of scale and scope are gained by the company influences the cost functions of the technical and administrative sub-systems.

Economies of scale , a widely defined and commonly used economic concept, are based on the principles of bulk transactions[1], of multiples[2] and of massed reserves [3]. These different principles have effects on the costs of an organization in the channel as the total volume grows. The first two principles relate to the indivisibility of certain inputs and and an unproportionality (Dixon & Wilkinson, 1986) between processes performed by the firm. The third is a special case of the principle of postponement (Bucklin, 1960) which in turn says that marketing costs are economized by deferring as long as possible the commitment of a unit of material to a specific use. Economies of scale are seen as effects of the growth of one single product in volumes and in the long run.

Lately the concept of economies of scale has been complemented with the concept of *economies of scope* , which is defined as " when a single firm can produce a given level of output of each product line more cheaply than a combination of separate firms each producing a single product at a given output level."(Bailey & Friedlaender, 1982 p.1026) The concept concerns shared or joint utilization of inputs. Chandler in his large study on "Scale and Scope - The Dynamics of Industrial Capitalism" uses the term in the sense of joint production and joint distribution. Economies of scale and scope quite often support the existence of each other (Bailey & Friedlaender, 1982)

When discussing effects of scale and of scope on the technical or on the administrative sub-systems for a company as a result of intra or interorganizational coordination, they may be present in different ways. The technical system and the administrative systems usually have

---

[1] Principle of bulk transactions in when transaction costs do not rise in direct proportion to the size of the transaction (Florence 1933)

[2] Principles of Multiples when the optimum output is considerably different between two mechanical units.(Florence 1933)

[3] Principles of massed reserves is aggregate stock can be smaller centralized than dispersed (Cox& Goodman, 1956; Florence, 1933)

different unit cost optimum volumes and for different products which makes it necessary to take both into account in order to find the optimum cost functions for the single firm in a marketing channel. A common argument is that the optimum of administrative unit costs probably is reached at lower volumes than for the technical system. In the end, the increasing administrative costs for communication and coordination will outweigh the decreasing technical costs for the firm (Dixon & Wilkinson, 1986). This will happen in spite of the fact that the firm will try to change the structure over time in order to take advantage of all possible economies of scale and scope. "The Visible Hand" shows how firms change structure over time in order to cope with the problems of communication and coordination (Chandler, 1977). A typical such change as increased diversity meant that firms altered from a functional to a multi-divisional organization.

Economies of scale and of scope might be present at different degrees but the exploitation of these economies in the channel rests upon the assumption of coordination taking place between the firms.

In summary, economies of scale and scope can be seen as important driving forces for changes in coordination and as such play a vital role for the understanding of the behaviour of firms in systems.

Conflicts and cooperation in the distribution channel

The bases for conflicts in a distribution channel, according to Stern&El Ansary (1988 p 282), are the degree of interdependence, scarcity of resources and trade-offs between members and these might lead to potential or actual conflicts. Stern&Reve (1980) characterized a conflict by mutual interference or blocking behaviour.

Further, channels cannot exist without a minimum level of cooperation among the parties. Thus cooperative and conflicting processes will exist simultaneously in any channel. However, the degree to which conflicts exist in a channel will affect the possibilities to achieve effective coordination.

Mallen (1964) argued that there exists a dynamic field of conflicting and cooperative objectives between organizations in a channel and if the conflicting objectives outweigh the cooperating ones the effectiveness of the channel will be reduced.

Palamountain (1955) recognizes three different forms of distributive conflicts; horizontal competition, inter-type competition and vertical conflict. The horizontal competition is defined as competition between middlemen of the same type in the channel while inter-type competition is competition between middlemen of different types in the same channel sector. Vertical conflict is a conflict between channel members at different levels.

The concept of inter-type competition and distributive innovation will in turn give rise to three other forms of conflict i.e. traditional inter-type competition, innovative inter-type competition and intra-firm innovative conflict (Mallen,1964). The competition can be divided into actual and potential competition as well (Reve,1986).

A conflict might have different intensity, depending on the stake in the relationship, the age of the relationship, etc. The intensity as well as the inclination to develop into an actual conflict will, in turn, be dependent on the cognitive and effective states of the members as well as their perception of the power relations (Stern&El Ansary ,1988).

Heide & Miner (1990) studied the effect of the expectations of future cooperation, based on Axelrod´s tit-for-tat theory, taking into account trust and communication as well as open-endedness of the relationship, performance ambiguity, and frequency of delivery. As a result, not only do trust and communication but also a high frequency of deliveries, lack of ambiguity and expectation for future meetings increase the likelihood of cooperation rather than turning to opportunism. The fact that development of trust and communication are interlocked increases the likelihood of continued cooperation and solved conflicts instead of leading to dysfunctional conflict (Anderson & Weitz,1986).

The amount of conflicts in a channel depends to a large extent on goal incompatibility, domain consensus and differing perceptions of reality, which only seem possible to solve through communication and a certain amount of mutual trust.

All methods to solve conflicts within a channel seem to involve increased communication in different forms.

However if a conflict is leading to a dissolution in one distribution system this normally would lead to a dissolution of other connected systems which shows the dynamics in the character of conflicts (Breyer 1950).

In summary, the coexistence of cooperation and conflicts in a channel, the bases for conflicts and the different types of conflicts will play a role for changes taking place between organizations in interdependent systems. Further, the extent to which the potential conflicts will change to actual ones, is dependent on frequency and intensity of communication, stake in the relationship, etc. This will contribute to understanding the bases and timing of actions taken by the organizations being part of distribution systems.

Dynamics - Evolution of channels or groups of channels
Changes in a channel or a group of channels can be seen from many different perspectives, from an institutional perspective (Betancourt & Gautschi, 1986); from a relational perspective

(Dwyer, Schurr & Oh, 1987; Reve, 1986; Anderson & Weitz, 1986); from a single channel system or group of channels perspective (Breyer, 1950) or even a society perspective (Cox, 1962).

Since exchange is seen by many authors to be the core phenomenon in marketing (Alderson, 1965; Bagozzi, 1975; Frazier, Spekman & O'Neal, 1988, Mattsson, 1992) changes in exchange within a channel and between groups of channels will play an important role in understanding the dynamics of the behaviour in marketing channels.

Changes of a channel or groups of channels have been a subject of interest for several authors (Breyer, 1950; Coughlan, 1988; Wilkinson, 1990).

First, Wilkinson (1990) discusses changes and stability within a distribution channel based on equilibrium models, recognizing differences between structural system changes due to internal cyclical variations such as the accordeon theory (Hollander,1966) and structural changes as a result of interaction with environment. He argues that structural change arises from instabilities emerging from the underlying system of activities ,and that a sequence of structuring constitutes structural evolution.

Differentiating between process structure (patterns of activities) and organization structure (procedures and rules embodied in the organization) he constructs a process model based on recent developments in system theory and urban dynamics.[1] The model grows in complexity taking more and more account of inter-relations with environment and intra-system changes. Three different types of processes would be involved: variation/ mutation, selection/retention and copying/reproduction of more stable structures. There are also assumptions that a shift of structures arises spontaneously through self-organization and that there are critical points of limits to the stability of an existing structure.

An equilibrium can be more or less stable and the structure process and organization structure do not need to be in equilibrium at the same time. The structure process is related to the flows of activities divided into matter energy and information. These two flows are both related to the organization structure in their own way.

The dynamic properties of the stable equilibrium's point on a curve can show how a continuous change in certain parameters can lead to a discontinuous change in the equilibrium size of the intermediary (Wilkinson,1990 p 21).

Coughlan (1988) studied the international semiconductors industry from a model concerning manufacturers being on a market consisting of either independent middlemen (pure private case), middlemen integration with manufacturer (pure integrated case) or a mixture between the two alternatives. Some of the results of the study were that the presence of a pure private

---

[1] A system definition by Jantsch(1980) is used which says that a system is a set of coherent, evolving, interactive processes which temporarily manifest in globally stable structures that have nothing to do with the equilibrium and solidity of technological structures".

channel at the time of market entry makes it more likely that the entrant also will use such a channel and likewise for integrated channels. Caughlan also found certain support for the fact that the same actions which turn a pure private channel into a mixed one, in general, also result in competitors following suit until the channel becomes a pure integrated channel". She argues that once the structure seems to be broken, the only stable equilibrium is the pure integrated channel.

Finally, Breyer (1950 p 25) comments that a single firm very seldom utilizes only one isolated channel but rather a group of channels and from this standpoint he discusses the formation and dissolution of a single channel and a group of channels. He differentiates between a highly flexible " easy to switch"channel, a channel with lower flexibility based on exclusive agreements and finally an ownership integrated channel with a very low flexibility.
In the highly flexible channel situation, a channel can be added or dropped without much difficulty.
In the second situation, the flexibility is lower due to trading relations persisting over time. Therefore formation and dissolution are slower since substantial commitments are involved. If the trading agreements do not involve the whole channel there might still be some flexibility left.
Finally the channel of integrated ownership has the lowest flexibility due to the investments involved.
The reason Breyer has concentrated the discussion to the formation and dissolution of single channels is the difficulty there is in telling when a group is formed or dissolved. A single channel is formed when the gap between the producer and the consumer has been fully complemented. There is no such definite and fixed point for formation of groups of channels.
Breyer states that the best way to study how a group of channels is set up is to focus on the sphere of interest of a trading concern or a common group. The identification of such a focus serves to map the channel group.

Furthermore, other studies also using external channel variables suggest that there are meaningful interactions between internal and external channel variables (Dwyer & Welsch, 1985, Etgar, 1977; Achrol & Stern, 1988).
Etgar (1977) combined external channel conditions with degree of control and found an increase in control with declining and unstable demand and strong channel competition.
Dwyer & Welsch (1985) found that environmental heterogeneity was associated with more decentralization, less formalization and more retailer control.
A work by Achrol, Reve & Stern (1983) adopted the view that external uncertainty affects conflict, coordination, integration and power balances. Then Achrol & Stern (1988) continued to study uncertainty in the output environment and its effects on a channel.

Summarizing, Wilkinson differentiates between structural system changes generated by internal cyclical variations and structural change generated by environmental changes. He creates a model taking both intra and inter- organizational changes into account where changes in process structure (patterns of activites) lead to changes in the organization structure over time. A shift in the organization structure comes spontaneously at some critical point as instabilities arise in the pattern of activities. This kind of reasoning is of special interest for the creation of a model of analysis taking not only relationship changes within a channel but also the context into consideration.

Then there have been discussions of how the use the different types of channels, such as private channels and integrated ones, influence one another. Finally the possibilities of dropping or adding channels to a group seem to be different depending on the flexibility in the channel organization. This also has a certain importance for the channel behaviour and as such on the transport companies in their transport systems.

Limitations

As mentioned above, the studies within the distribution field are mostly focused on internal matters within a single channel involving only the organizations belonging to it. Studies of inter-dependencies with external organizations are limited.

Mullen (1990) argues that there is a need for more research on the role of international channels in facilitating economic growth and development as well as taking the distribution channel context into consideration. He points at the increasing importance of international channels in the future.

Future research perspectives that could be fruitful in international marketing would be those combining socio-political and economic variables like the political economy and the relational contracting together with network studies (Mullen 1990).

3.3. Theories of internationalization

The purpose of this section is to contribute to the understanding of the behaviour of the firm in the process of internationalization, to generate certain important concepts for the model of analysis and to contribute to explanations of the empirical results.

As in the case of distribution, the perspective taken in the literature has mainly been that of the manufacturing companies. Subsequently, the great majority of theories are developed for products and not for services. However, there are, as we shall see, some attempts made by the researchers if not to include at least to comment upon the possibilities of including industrial services in the leading existing theories.

Research on internationalization of business relates to a variety of different theories derived from many other fields of research like microeconomics, industrial organization, strategic management, network approach, transaction cost theory, etc. What they have in common is that they all apply theories from their own field of research to the phenomenon of internationalization either for industries or companies.

Toyne (1989) defines three streams of research: a) studies of international operations of the individual firm b) comparative studies between countries, and c) explanations of the multinational enterprise as an institution. The first and the last of these are of most interest for this study. However, we shall divide the last part of the explanations of multinational enterprises (MNEs) into two, stressing the phenomenon of global network organization.

As in the case of network and distribution approaches, the focus will be on changes and patterns of changes and contextual interaction but applied first to the individual firm and then to more general driving forces for the process. However, we start with a short discussion of the concept of internationalization.

The concept of internationalization

A widely accepted definition of internationalization characterizes it as a process of increased commitment of resources to foreign activities, i.e.activities performed outside the home country. The increasing degree of commitment over time implies that internationalization is a growth process.

However different driving forces are stressed in the process. The Uppsala School (i.e. Hörnell, Vahlne & Wiedersheim-Paul, 1972; Forsgren & Kinch, 1970; Johanson & Vahlne, 1977) stressed the importance of knowledge as a driving force while others stress the importance of market imperfections (i.e. Pavitt, 1971; Vernon, 1966) and intangible assets (i.e. Buckley & Casson, 1976; Magee, 1977; Caves, 1982). Most definitions of internationalization of organizations seem to include two dimensions, the number of countries to which the company is committed and the degree of commitment by a company in these countries. However Johanson&Mattsson (1988) developed the concept of internationalization from three dimensions also bringing integration into the analysis. These dimensions are extension, the amount of commitments to a country, i.e.penetration and coordination of activities between countries, i.e.integration.

An underlying assumption regarding international commitments is that the company initially starts to grow in its home country from which it internationalizes. Some authors (Porter, 1989; Vernon, 1977) specifically stress the significance of the home country as an important determinant of performance in the process of internationalization. In other later or more general studies (Casson, 1990; Johanson&Mattsson, 1984; Lindqvist, 1990; Nordström, 1990), the subject of the growth in the home country is not so highly stressed or is not considered so important since the studies either concentrate on relative changes in internationalization or on other factors speeding up the process.

International operations of the individual firm

How would an individual firm behave and what could be the explanatory factors to that behaviour? What would be the reason for starting and continuing to internationalize? How does this change over time?

As Aharoni states concerning the motives behind the start of the process " in any specific case it is very difficult if not impossible to pin down one reason for the decision to look abroad or to find out precisely who was the initiator of the project" (1966 p. 55).

The motives might come from within the organization (e.g.individual interest of high ranking managers, etc.) or exogenous (e.g.competition, customers) to it. The decision to look abroad is undertaken as a result of a chain of events including organizational environmental forces, personal trait and sheer accident.

In contrast to this study of the very start of the process, the study presented by Chandler(1990) describes the development process for many individual firms for a period extending over a hundred years. In this study, the basic motives for industrial growth including international growth were found to be economies of scale and economies of scope (joint production or distribution) or reduction in the transactions costs from investments made in production, distribution and management.

Another model was presented by Johanson &Vahlne (1977). They argue that the bases for internationalization are found in the combination of market knowledge and commitment decisions, current activities and market commitment. These factors form a cycle of "learning by doing" in international growth through a knowledge-based model. "Internationalization is seen as a result of gradual acquisition, integration and use of knowledge concerning foreign markets. Market knowledge and markets commitments are assumed to affect both commitment decisions and current activities, which then in turn will affect the first two" (Johanson, Mattsson, Sandén & Vahlne, 1977).

This theory resulted from many studies made by a group of researchers at Uppsala University (Hörnell & Vahlne & Wiedersheim-Paul, 1972; Forsgren & Kinch, 1970, Johanson & Wiedersheim-Paul, 1975; Johanson & Vahlne, 1977). The model which is based on empirical studies from some of the largest Swedish international companies not only describes why companies internationalize through the model of gradually increased knowledge but also how and where. How companies internationalized was explained through the sequential establishment chain starting with no regular export, exporting through an independent agent, developing sales subsidiary and finally investing in production abroad. Further, more sales subsidiaries were often established by acquiring the agent or taking over the people from the agent (Forsgren & Kinch,1970).

Where the investments were situated was explained by the concept of psychic distance between host and home country (Hörnell & Vahlne & Wiedersheim-Paul, 1972; Johanson, Wiedersheim-Paul, 1974). Psychic distance was based on general differences in industrial development, education, language, culture and commercial connections between countries (Johanson, Mattsson, Vahlne & Sandén, 1977) and it was assumed that internationalization started in markets where the psychic distance was small.

This theory of gradual learning leading to the sequential establishment chain and the importance of psychic distance for the choice of country has been confirmed in many other studies (e.g.Bilkey & Tesar, 1977; Bilkey, 1978; Johanson & Nonaka, 1983).

Criticism has also been levelled at this model. Basically the critisism relates to the fact that the sequential establishment chain does not take market opportunity, competition or other contextual variables into account (Hedlund & Kverneland, 1984; Sölvell, 1987; Nordström, 1991).

Also, the idea that the psychic distance between countries should decide the sequence of countries being subject of internationalization has also been criticized for the same reasons (Sölvell, 1987; Nordström, 1991). Nordström (1991) claims that the psychic distances decrease in the world of today and should therefore be less valid as an explanation for sequences observed.

Johanson and Mattsson (1988) make a point of taking the context into account in the theory of internationalization of a firm, including both the specific firm characteristics and the degree of internationalization of the market, which they argue have importance for global competition and cooperation in industrial systems.

Johanson & Mattsson show that the internationalizing firm´s situation is different if it starts the process of internationalization early or late in comparison to other companies on the market. They discuss four different situations for a focal company with reference to its own degree of internationalization and that of the market context: the *early starter*, the *lonely international*, the *late starter* and*the international among others*. However this model is a comparison between static situations and is therefore basically not dynamic.

When analyzing these four situations it is really only in the case of the early starter that the sequential establishment chain plays an important role, according to the authors.

The three dimensions of internationalization used by Johanson & Mattsson i.e.extension, penetration and integration are said to vary in importance over the process of internationalization. While extension and penetration have a higher importance in the beginning the importance of international integration seems to increase over time. Further, extension and penetration will only lead to marginal changes in a firm´s degree of internationalization when it is already highly international.

Forsgren (1985) has compared the propensity to invest on foreign markets via acquisitions or greenfield investments, since these were not differentiated in the establishment chain. In his study Forsgren concluded that location, industrial structure and the firm´s degree of internationalization are of crucial importance for the company´s choice of investment.

Further, he argued that many companies starting with greenfield investments continued acquiring firms on the market and that it was possible to keep existing suppliers and customers to a larger extent when making a greenfield investment. This would also imply that existing customers play a more important role for a greenfield investment than for a acquisition.

In summary, the motives for starting to internationalize are difficult to pin-point (Aharoni 1966). It is probably a chain of exogenous and endogenous events. Chandler (1990) as well as Johanson&Vahlne (1977) have, based on their empirical studies, pointed at important driving forces. Chandler (ibid) argued that economies of scope, of scale and reduction in transaction costs were the most important driving forces for both domestic and international growth. Johanson &Vahlne (1977) described a process of gradual "learning by doing" as a behaviour for reducing uncertainty and sequential establishments explaining increased degree internationalization over time. The concept of "psychic distance" was used as an important explanation for sequence of countries chosen for establishment.

Finally, Johanson &Mattsson commented that changes of the market had to be taken into account and not only a product of the firm when discussing the the patterns of internationalization of firms. Forsgren (1985) arrived at the conclusion that location and industrial structure as well as their existing degree of internationalization were of importance for the choice between greenfield investments and acquisitions. All of these studies are extremely important when it comes to understanding how transport companies might internationalize and what the possible driving forces can be to different patterns.

Explaining the existence of international business

In the traditional international trade theories, by authors such as Heckscher,Ohlin, MacDougall and Leontief, explanations of trade and production before the second world war focused on country specific factor endowment, such as differences in raw material, capital and labour supply. Export and import were supposed to take place within an arm´s lenght market relations and not within companies.

As companies internationalized and MNE s were created in the post-war era, the question in focus for the researchers shifted from traditional trade theory to why foreign direct investments (FDI) were made and why MNEs existed (Buckley & Casson, 1976; Casson, 1987; Calvet,

1981; Caves, 1971; Dunning, 1977; Hirsch, 1975; Hymer, 1960, Kindleberger, 1969; Vernon & Wells, 1976).

The existence of MNE has then been explained as a result of structural and of transactional market imperfections, starting with the former and turning to the latter.

Hymer (1960) was one of the first to state that to make FDI foreign companies must have a counteracting advantage over local firms assuming the existence of market imperfections. Kindleberger (1969) saw imperfections of goods markets, of factor markets, scale economies and government imposed disruptions as dominating explanations. Caves (1971) claimed product differentiation in the home market as being the critical element giving rise to FDI and Vernon (1966) suggested the importance of product life cycle where firms react to the threat of losing markets through expanding abroad.

Even though these structural market imperfections did explain much of the basic reasoning behind the existence of the MNE they did not actually explain the very reason for its formation, i.e.the internalisation.

Instead, this fell to be explained through development of transactional market imperfections during the 1970's (Buckley & Casson, 1976; Magee, 1977; Caves, 1971). The theory assumes that there is a flow of intermediate products within a firm in the form of knowledge and skills, expertise, etc and that markets for these are difficult to keep control over (Buckley & Casson, 1976). The result is internalisation in order to control and protect these intangible assets and when this is made across boundaries it creates MNEs (Calvet, 1981).

Magee (1977) argue in line with this reasoning that the main questions are the appropriability of and returns on information. He claims that information is a durable good which brings decreasing returns over the technological life-cycle of an industry. The appropriability problem is based on the fact that the availability of the information to a second party reduces the privileged nature of the returns on the information created by the first party. The probability of leakage and the costs of preventing leakage increase with the number of and the geographical dispersion of operations.

Dunning (1977, 1988), building on the studies made by Caves (1971), Hymer (1960), Knickerbocker (1973), Vernon (1966) and others formulated the "eclectic theory" in which he argued that both the company´s ownership-, internalisation- and location advantages were necessary components in order to explain foreign direct investment.

This way he combined both tangible and intangible assets as well as structural and transactional market imperfections.

The locational specific advantages were seen as external to the companies and available for all companies in one country. Ownership advantages were internal, on the other hand, and included both tangible and intangible assets. Many of the ownership advantages stem from the size of the company, monopoly power, cheaper inputs as well as the multinationality per se, i.e. the advantage of having a global network. As for internalisation advantages, he states that the ownership advantage not only arises from specific company assets but also from the ability and willingness to internalise those assets. Here he relates his idea to the writings of Coase (1937), Alchian & Demsetz (1972), Williamsson (1971) and Magee (1977) when discussing the importance of internalisation and transaction costs.

Dunning argues that the reasons for internalising might not only be a question of capitalizing on an advantage but also of avoiding disadvantages such as hindering the competitors or the suppliers to the competitors from gaining advantages.

According to Dunning, the eclectic theory will also be relevant for service industries like banks and insurance companies. It has been tested on internationalization of banks (Kang Rae Cho, 1985) and found to give a good explanation.

Buckley & Casson (1976) have criticized the eclectic theory arguing that imperfections in international intermediate product markets are both necessary and sufficient conditions to explain the existence of the MNE. The differentiation between ownership advantages and internalising of these would not be necessary. According to this reasoning, the location advantages also seem to have less importance in explaining the existence of the MNE.

The criticism has caused Dunning (1988) to restate some assumptions for international production as well as to discuss certain extensions, specifically into a more dynamic point of view. In this restatement he points out the importance of the distinction between structural and transactional market imperfection. They are both important and interrelated in a dynamic situation.

However, Dunning agrees with the argument that the theory does not allow for firms to have specific behavioural differences.

Further, Dunning (ibid), in differentiating between multinational and uninational companies, means that the greater the efficiency of the MNE as a coordinator of activities the more international production is likely to take place.

In summary, perhaps much due to the fact that earlier trade theories were so concentrated on trade between autonomous units and did not take the MNE into account, post war models have focused on reasons for the existence of the MNE leaving relationships to autonomous units out. Therefore in these post war models ownership and reasons for internalisation will be very important factors. The existence of the MNE is basically explained via structural or transactional market imperfections. While the first developments of a model concerned structural market imperfections (Caves, 1971; Kindleberger, 1969; Vernon, 1966) and internalising of goods markets, later contributions have concerned transactional market imperfections and internalisation of intangible assets such as know-how, skills, information (Buckley & Casson,

1976; Magee, 1977). The underlying driving force for internalising would be to make use and protect the existing advantages. Dunning (1977) combined both location advantage from trade theories as well as having structural and transactional market imperfections with the willingness to internalise.

The global network organization

The importance of a MNE´s global network has been a subject of increasing interest over time as more companies seem to have reached the situation of being established as MNEs with several subsidiaries in several countries.

Basically the interest has been focused on the advantages of having a global network for MNEs.(Dunning, 1977; Chandler, 1990; Johanson & Vahlne, 1990; Kogut, 1983; Magee, 1977; Vernon, 1979; Vernon & Wells, 1976, etc.)

The advantages of a global network for an MNE according to Kogut (1983) stem from the fact that the MNEs can transfer resources across borders by optimizing a global network. Kogut (1983) saw three general categories of factors as important attributes for an MNE.These categories are the ability to arbitrage international restrictions, to capture the externalities of information or learning and to derive economies of scope in production and marketing.

Vernon & Wells (1976) specifically utilized exploitation of global scanning capabilities as an important strategy of an MNE along with other strategies like exploiting technologies, having a strong trade name and exploiting economies of scale. Global scanning capabilities were seen as capabilities to find cheaper sources of supply or to find low cost production sites. This strategy has been stressed by them as a strategy possible to use even though the products have lost their technological lead and competitive advantage.

Johanson and Vahlne (1990) discuss what they call "the advantage cycle" for an international firm. The concepts are based on the Uppsala School of increasing international knowledge and commitment in the sense that the strengths and weaknesses change in relation to a particular environment i.e." the advantage package". Over time as the size and composition of the advantage package changes it will lower the transaction costs for the multinational firm, which might lead to an advantage cycle.

Chandler (1990) showed that companies made up of many independent unities, whether as a result of internal growth or by acquisitions, cannot fully exploit the advantages of scale and of scope unless the unities are fully integrated. He shows that when companies ignore the gains of economies of scale and scope due to lack of coordination they lose their competitive advantage.

The advantages of the global network do not come without effort though, the company has to be organized in order to be able to exploit these advantages. Bartlett (1986), Goshal &Nohria (1987) and Martinez and Jarillo (1987) are some of the authors that argue for utilizing the contingency theory when discussing the design of the global network. They claim that when designing such a network the complexity of the environment and the amount of local resources and independency versus inter-dependency have to be taken into account.

Martinez and Jarillo (1987) discuss the problem of " how to make the most of the far flung and diverse activities of an MNE". They came to the conclusion that the crucial mechanism was coordination and integration.

Martinez & Jarillo (1987) studied vast amounts of literature on internationalization from the aspect of coordination, finding that this term was hardly of any interest before the 1980's. To the extent that coordination was present in literature the more subtle mechanisms of coordination like lateral relations, informal communication and organizational culture seem to have been lacking before the 1980's.

Bartlett (1986) discusses what he calls the "transnational organization". He starts by stating that the stage model for different structures of international companies, where companies advance from an international division to world wide product division or area division in order to end up in a global matrix as suggested by Stopford & Wells (1972), is to simplistic. It does not reflect the complex tasks and problems of such a company.

Bartlett (ibid) argues in support of the importance of the administrative heritage as well as industry characteristics, the strategic position when an organizational choice is made. In many cases it would not be possible to make the changes without considering also administrative heritage. Further, he comments that the forces on the MNE are complex and diverse and, bearing in mind their organizational effects, that they can be divided into two categories, namely, global coordination and integration as a result of scale economies, spread of technological development costs, etc., on the one hand, and national differentiation and responsiveness on the other. The intensity and balance of these forces varies from one industry to another.

Companies have to cope with national differentiation and responsiveness and simultaneously coordinate and control their activities in order to gain efficiency and effective global competition and this leads to inter-dependencies between the units rather than dependency from one side. Such companies are referred to by Bartlett (1986) as the "trans-nationals".

Further research undertaken in Uppsala by Forsgren (1991), Forsgren &Holm (1991), discuss changes in the locus of decision within large multi-centered MNEs. They see the changes as a result of internationalization of the subsidiaries in the MNE which they call a secondary degree of internationalization. The result is that subsidiaries will act more autonomously and that the parent country decreases in importance. Contributing to this development have been foreign acquisitions over time.

In summary, the MNE, being a global network organization and due to market imperfections on markets for tangible and intangible assets, seems to have advantages such as economies of scope, skills, learning costs, scanning capabilities, etc. However, in order to be able to exploit these advantages the company has to coordinate its activities. This will in turn have effects on the organizational structure in order to exert a stronger control of their total activities but has to be weighed against the need for national differentiation and responsiveness. Furthermore, a complexity in this situation is that where subsidiaries internationalize the locus of decision seems to move more to the advantage of the subsidiaries.

The advantages of coordinating a global network seem to be several and gaining these advantages might be seen as important driving forces for the behaviour of MNEs and concerning the design of the network. Th analyzing coordination within global network organizations should be of importance for the transport companies and the network that they create.

Limitations of the existing theories

There are many limitations to the existing theories on internationalization and researchers in the field have also alluded to this fact.

Some of those most frequently discussed (Dunning, 1988; Casson, 1990; Johanson & Mattsson, 1988; Mattsson, 1992) are the problems of taking dynamics into account, to include the context in the reasoning, the lack of explanation for the internationalization of the service industry, looking at parts rather than taking a holistic view and contrasting markets to hierarchies rather than seeing a variety of alternatives of intermediate solutions.

Dynamics for the single firm can be attributed to many theories but they are not explicitly there. Taking the Uppsala School approach from the 1970's, one of the reasons for its attention was perhaps the fact that it pointed out changes over time for an individual firm.

Even though there are many critics, very little would seem to have be done showing the dynamics of the firm after the sequential establishment chain. Some researchers (e.g.Johanson & Mattsson,1988; Nordström, 1991; Lindkvist, 1991) have pointed out that when starting to internationalize late in an internationalized world the sequential establishment is less valid and the investments come faster and leap-frog certain stages.

Seeing the firm as a part of a changing environment seems to attract even less study. The conceptual analysis by Johanson & Mattsson (1984) takes changes in the context into account over a period but not what happens to the individual firm, as part of this changing context. Other researchers have discussed the context, focusing on competitors (Knickerbocker, 1973; Porter, 1980) or on more general demands from context (Porter, 1988).

Casson has pointed out that existing theories do not in a satisfactory way explain how technological advantages develop. He also argues for new insight through adoption of a system view of production and emphasizes the complementarities as well as the substitution possibilities. This would mean a step towards taking part of the context into the analysis. The discussions of the context should also bring in the problem of a more holistic view, not studying just single functions like R&D but the whole production systems (Casson, 1990)

Dunning (1988) expressed the opinion that one important possible extension of the eclectic paradigm would be to include other forms of international business transactions e.g. arms-length trade, joint ventures and non-contractual agreements. He means that an integrated approach between production and trade should be promising here. As a result of these views, studying alternatives to market and hierarchies ought to be enhanced.

Internationalization of service companies that has taken place over time seems to have been the subject of very few studies as a separate industry in itself. When dealing with the subject the service companies have rather be seen as complementarities to the manufacturing industry. Much of the recent development taking place in the service industry should lead to an interest in analyses of international business operations in this sector.

The limitations such as a strong focus on ownership and relative lack of dynamics, contextual analysis, holistic studies, etc., which are part of the characteristics of the network approach, would speak for a fruitful combination of the network approach and internationalization research.

Final comments

Judging from the limitations of three different theoretical approaches, the conclusion seem to be that the network approach in particular would add further dimensions to the field of distribution and internationalization. On the other hand, the network approach would gain by taking cognisance of the problems and complexities of the types discussed in these other two more established fields of research, i.e. distribution and internationalization.

In the model of analysis to be used in this study I will therefore integrate concepts from distribution research and internationalization research into a network analytical framework.

4. Model of analysis

In the construction of a model of analysis of internationalization processes, the concepts allowing for change should be in focus. In a contextual analysis, these changes would concern not only focal companies but also other organizations taking part in the process. However the context is limited to those transport companies which are connected to the focal companies as representatives, suppliers, owners or competitors. These also play the dominating role when studying the behavioural patterns of transport companies in the process of internationalization.

In this chapter, in order to distinguish patterns we intend to choose concepts that separately or taken together are suitable not only for describing internationalizing but also facilitate differentiation between changes in the process of internationalization. Then we try to find ways to categorize and operationalize these concepts in order use them in the analysis of the cases.

We start by presenting a model for change deriving from the network approach and by applying it to transport companies. In the process some basic concepts are crystallized as important for understanding change. Research from the distribution field contributes specifically to the understanding of critical problems and dynamics of systems of high interdependence.
Secondly, the dimensions of internationalization to be used in the model are chosen and adapted to the characteristics of transport companies, thereby giving an understanding of the internationalization dimensions in a slightly different way than that traditionally applied to manufacturing companies.

The three dimensions of internationalization are then operationalized and categorized utilizing the concepts of systems, nets and networks when describing changes for transport companies. In the processes of operationalization and categorization, which are made for the different dimensions of internationalization, the different theoretical approaches are combined. The change processes categorized for each of the three dimensions and the discussion of interaction between them which follows will then be the core of the model of analysis. Finally the model will be complemented by discussions and categorizing of effects mainly based on research from network theory.

4.1. Basic concepts

General concepts
Applying the network model for analysis of industrial systems by Johanson & Mattsson (1992), which distinguishes between the production systems and the network of exchange relationships between industrial actors, would allow context and changes to be brought into the

analysis. Companies are assumed to form exchange relationships at the network level through which they control[1] and coordinate the production systems. Change in the network relationships influence the production systems. Changes in the resource interdependencies at production system level might then induce changes at the network level. Therefore the two levels interact. This model could easily be adapted to transport companies and transport systems (as shown in figure 4.1). Thus transport companies form and control transport systems (production systems level) through exchange relationships between different transport organizations (network level). Transport companies seen as parts of the network separated from the resources in the transport systems will make it possible to discuss change on one level and its effects on the other.

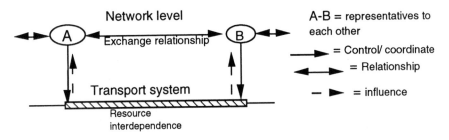

Figure 4.1. A model of transport system/s and transport companies (A, B)
(Adapted from Johanson & Mattsson, 1992 p 209)

Changes in transport systems would derive from changes in the relationships between transport companies or from changes in the resources employed (personnel, facilities, know how, equipment, capital etc) in the transport system.

However, these changes might go in different directions leading to effects for other transport companies being part of the same transport system. Interdependence in a distribution system shows a positive connectedness between the organizations (Cook 1982). This should also be appropriate to transport systems being part of the distribution system. Positive connectedness means that changes in one relation have positive effects on the organizations in other relations. A negative connectedness is the reverse situation, a positive change for one relation leading to a negative effect for the other.

The transport system is assumed to be based on a dyadic relationship consisting of the representative and a focal company. However in a reversible transport system the focal company and its representative are representing each other for a specified geographical area and

---

[1]Control means the degree to which a company can decide when, how, where, how much and how long the resources shall be used. (Pfeffer& Salancik 1978)

all functions including operations have to be performed by both parties. Changes for other transport companies being suppliers to the same system will be positively connected while those of other systems might be either positively or negatively connected. The effects on transport companies being suppliers, competitors and owners are analysed separately.

Groups of companies related to each other could be seen as clusters or nets having a higher interdependence between the organizations than to other part of the network. When such a net of transport companies is formed at the network level it is assumed that the transport systems of the organizations in the group will also be interconnected.

The position of a transport company in such a net is defined not only by its relationships to others at network level but also in the production systems, i.e. the extended definition of position according to Johanson & Mattsson (1992).

In this study the concept "net" will be used from the perspective of a focal company including its direct relationships and its indirect relations via subsidiaries or important agents. However, the positions of these companies to the focal company might vary from being on the border of the net to being very close to the focal company. Being a representative will therefore automatically lead to being part of the focal net. However, there are other ways, such as being owner or supplier, for a transport company to be part of focal net . The study will focus on the representatives because of their importance for internationalization.

The relationship is the base both for net and system level. The net level will be seen as a macro level in contrast to that of system level, which is micro level. The system level is seen as a dyad of organizations controlling and coordinating the single system. The relationships all belong to the network level which includes all companies in the transportation industry. However, creating a macro and a micro level of relationships would facilitate the possibilities to analyse changes from a contextual perspective through interaction between single system changes (micro) and net changes (macro).

Figure 4.2. illustrates a net of organizations governing the transport systems in a very simplified way. A focal company of today might be part of large numbers of transport systems which in turn can be divided into sub-groups. The dyad coordinating the single transport system is one of several relationships that together constitutes the net.

The advantage of adding the concept of a net is that it will give the possibility to take several parallel and sequential processes into account with many organizations involved and thereby take a larger part of the context into the analysis. Since the changes for transport companies in relationships at system and net level seem important in order to understand how patterns of internationalization of transport companies will change over time, the study will include both levels.

Who should be defined as an autonomous organization and therefore a separate representative of an international transport system and who should be defined as just being a part of the parent company? This is an intrinsic problem, which has consequences for internationalization analysis.

While the network approach has focused on inter-organizational relations characterized by non-ownership, many internationalization models have concentrated on ownership relations. In distribution research on the other hand the system, as such, is in focus rather than ownership.

We can assume that the increasing interdependence in the context leads to the need of increased coordination causing different types of cooperations (Pfeffer & Salancik, 1978). Further, we have from network studies learnt that relationships are frequently long term and have many dimensions apart from the legal tie, which is only one. Moreover the distinctions between different types of cooperation have in reality become less clear as new types develop such as franchising, management contract, leasing etc. This has led us to believe that ownership as such has become less of an issue when discussing cooperation.

In addition to this, the representatives of a transport company, whether a subsidiary or agent, are separate organizations for operations and marketing regarding a specific area and as such, have to handle their own relationship, which makes them relatively autonomous. Further, based on the development of freight transport companies in general there are strong reasons to believe that subsidiaries to transport companies like in the case of manufacturing companies seem to become increasingly autonomous through developing internationally on their own (Forsgren 1990). This emphasizes the importance of seeing the subsidiaries as separate companies when studying internationalization. Therefore, in this study, the representatives can be either agents, subsidiaries or joint ventures.

The main difference is to be found at net level since the subsidiary will always be part of the focal net. So will also the agents of the subsidiary even though they are conceived of as indirect relations to the focal company (see figure 4.2). In an extreme case the net could form a group where all the organizations are fully owned by the focal organization.

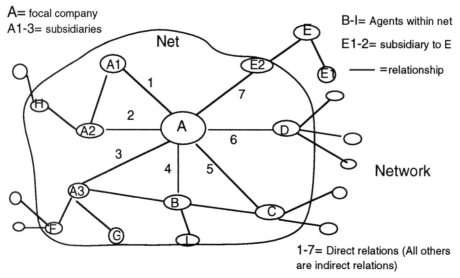

Figure 4.2. Illustration of a net of transport companies

Finally, whatever position a representative has in the net, both directly and indirectly controlled resources for a transport system only concern the engaged resources for the operations in common with the focal company. Thus, the resources of an agent only concern the resources set aside or available for utilization for their activities in common with the focal company at system level and with relations in focal net at net level. Even though an agent might have very large resources the resources available for utilization in the transport system in common with the focal company might be very limited. As the extent to which a transport company is internationalized is interpreted in terms of the resources committed to foreign activities, it seems necessary to have a distinction between the agent´s resources available and not available for use in cooperation with the focal firm. On net level this also shows a difference between a subsidiary and an agent since basically all resources of a subsidiary can be made available for use of the focal company in due time.

Internationalization and the three dimensions

Since the process of internationalization has been developed from the perspective of a manufacturing company there is a necessity to reformulate the definition of internationalization in order to make it fit the purpose of the study and to adapt the concept to the characteristica of the transport companies.

Seeing the internationalization of a focal company as a change process towards an increasing commitment of controlled resources to foreign activities, there seem to be several differences in terms of how the concept can be modified due to the characteristica of transport companies.

First, the assumption that companies first grow in a home market and then internationalize, which is important for several models of internationalization, is not always true for transport companies. Many transport companies have never been fully domestic but started as international companies, e.g.forwarders, airlines and shipping lines. In such cases the process of internationalization over time takes place through relative increases of resources committed to foreign activities.

Furthermore, the different forms of commitments, e.g.direct exports, exports through agents, and establishment of sales subsidiaries do not have the same meaning for the transport company. As the transport companies being mutual representatives to each other normally have to have all functions including operations available in the foreign country, a sales subsidiary cannot take over the full role of an agent. It must be combined with an agent or with several agents on a specific market. Therefore the only commitment abroad that can take over the role of the agent is an operating subsidiary with all functions included. One important result of this is that both mutual representatives must find another partner if the cooperation comes to an end and that the new transport systems will mostly be a competing with each other.

Therefore the alternative of the sales subsidiary used in several models of internationalization as an important entry mode lacks interest. The available alternatives are basically reduced to representation by an agent or an operating subsidiary or a combination of an agent and a sales subsidiary.

Moreover, since the transport systems are mostly reversible systems the commitment is not as much a question of export or import but rather of a balanced or an unbalanced flow of goods, which implies there is an interdependence between exports and imports for transport companies. Both distribution and internationalization models seem to be based on the idea of one way systems to foreign countries. The network approach here seems to be much easier to apply to the situation of the transport companies.

Finally, the interdependence between the representatives of a transport system, the existence of foreign activities performed in home country and the possibility to use transferable resources mean that the change in the commitment to foreign resources will have to include resources committed for that purpose in the home country as well.

From these characteristics it seems that mutuality and interdependencies are vital for the understanding of the process of internationalization of transport companies and the increased commitment of resources and activities will take place mainly in their transport systems. How and where these increasing foreign commitments are performed, however, might differ due to the location of the system. The conclusion is that:

Transport companies internationalize through controlling and coordinating transport systems between home country and foreign country, between foreign countries or within foreign countries. This will also include resources and relations in home country specifically engaged for a foreign transport system.

Considering the importance of interdependence and mutuality a model of internationalization for transport companies should take these aspects into account. Therefore the concepts used by Johanson and Mattsson (1988) in the three dimensions of *extension, penetration* and international *integration* would seem to be valid, since the integration dimension is included. This makes it possible to include the home country resources as well as transferable resources when deciding the positions and resources committed for the transport company in the foreign country. It is also possible to take into account not only the resources controlled directly via having a subsidiary but also resources controlled indirectly via agents.

Giving the concept of internationalization three different dimensions will lead to a more complex concept and will create problems of measuring the total growth. If one variable increases and the others decrease an important international change for future growth might still have taken place but it could in reality look like a stagnation or even a slight decrease. This will lead us to include stagnation or negative changes of the dimensions into the concept of internationalization under the assumption that there will be an overall growth in the internationalization.

Based on the discussions above, the internationalization process is defined as being a change process for growth of increased commitment of controlled resources to foreign activities which might involve short periods of stagnation and decrease.

Before leaving the concept of internationalization for transport companies, it would seem necessary to point out that there is a case of indirect international commitment which is not included in this definition. This case seems relevant when the internationalization process starts. It can be exemplified by a domestic transport company being involved in international business indirectly as a supplier to another international company with the same country base. Going back to the definition of internationalization as meaning committing controlled resources to foreign activities, the definition does not really say much about this type of problem. Has such a company started internationalizing or not? The only indirect international commitment discussed in the traditional literature is the situation where a manufacturing company utilizes a trading house, which hardly covers the situation of being a normal supplier without having any control of the connection to the international activities. In this case, instead of including all domestic suppliers to an international company in the internationalization process, the concept is restricted to companies whose resources are directly coordinated to resources and activities of a foreign organization.

An example of a change for the supplier above would be if Volvo Sweden decided that the Swedish supplier should send the goods directly to Volvo in another country in the future. Even though all social contacts, procurements and payments were made to Volvo Sweden a direct coordination would have to be made to foreign activities.

Therefore the definition of the concept of internationalization must be complemented to include not only the increasing commitment of controlled resources to foreign activities but also the assumption that there is a direct coordination with the foreign resources and activities. *The process starts as the controlled resources become directly coordinated with the foreign resources and activities.*

In this definition coordination gets an important role for internationalization in general but this seems even more important for the transport company coordinating and controlling transport systems with high interdependence.

Of these three dimensions to be used, the concept of integration, being a process of coordination with a specific purpose, is of basic importance since the existence of a transport system assumes a certain degree of integration. Therefore, integration plays a very important role in the creation of a transport system. Furthermore, changes in relationships between transport companies reflect changes in interdependencies, which implies that integration is vital when studying dynamics from a network perspective.

Based on distribution research (e.g.Alderson, 1954), it can be said that an important reason for increasing integration would be the intention to reach higher efficiency or, seen in a wider perspective, higher effectiveness. Integration seems even more important for effectiveness for a transport system being subject to even higher interdependence than distribution systems due to its reversibility.

4.2. Forming a model of analysis

Integration- operationalization and categorizing

In order to operationalize the concept of integration we will go closer into what the concept stands for.

Even though the concept of integration is seen as an important concept in all three theoretical approaches, the way the concept is used differs and more detailed specifications and operationalization of the concept are rare. One of the exceptions is Mattsson (1969) and his approach to the conceptual scheme will be a base for the development of the concept in this study. Another reason for choosing Mattsson´s approach is that integration is used in a wider sense and does not limit the concept only to ownership integration. This would allow for integration not only with subsidiaries but also with agents, suppliers, etc.

Integration is defined as a *process* over time of combining separate parts into a whole (Webster). It is a coordination process with the common goal of combining the parts. Utilizing the concept of integration defined in this way in respect of relationships, transport systems and nets would mean that increasing integration is the relative change from looser to higher integration.

Coordination of the production system takes place through a governance structure, in this study a network structure. Integration processes will therefore be assumed to be initiated at network level (Johanson & Mattsson, 1992). For transport companies, integration will concern transport system activities. Even though the integration process is initiated in the dyadic relationship at network level there will be subsequent changes over time in the transport system that in turn influence the network level also outside the intitial dyad. Changes in the positions in the net will thus be influenced by changes within and between transport systems.

The different aspects of integration elaborated by Mattsson (1969), i.e.institutional, execution and decision integration, were applied to marketing systems. The institutional aspect of integration was described by ownership characteristics and contractual arrangements. The decision integration concerned the degree of centralization of decisions. As for execution integration it concerned the way activities were performed and the characteristica of the flows in the channel. A high degree of adaption between the organizations through activity transference, exclusiveness, internalisation and homogeneity, increased the level of integration between the organizations. Furthermore the three different aspects were found to interact.

In order to make these aspects dynamic and to be able to put them into a more contextual setting, certain modifications of Mattsson´s framework are necessary. The institutional aspect will be called the *legal aspect* and includes legal ties in terms of ownership, joint ventures, formal agreements of various kinds. As for *execution integration* the cooperation between the organizations might change in terms of closeness depending on the will to adapt to each other and to increase the interdependence between the resources. This type of integration concerns the four flows i.e.the physicial , the information , the payment and the responsibility flows. It will include changes in asset specificity in the specific relationship and new techniques necessitating new adaptions and more communication or new routines leading to higher adaption to each other.

Decision integration is here treated as the *control aspect* and is seen as who controls what and the degree to which companies in a relationship have control over each other´s resources. It includes changes in the total resources controlled by the companies, by the relationship and by the net for their activities in common. Finally, an aspect underlying the three mentioned above is the *social aspect* of integration which is assumed to play an important dynamic role and to include the degree of trust between organizations.

The legal, social and control integration are characteristics at network level and execution integration in the transport system at system level.

Not only are the first three aspects of integration interacting but the social aspect of integration could also be assumed to interact with the other aspects which might increase the effects leading to increasing integration once the process starts. The interacting aspects of integration exist not only at system level but also at net level due to the interconnectedness of the company positions as well as their controlled transport systems.

Categorizing

The concepts of relationships, nets and transport systems are the base for differentiation of integration changes of single systems and nets. Changes in integration of relations at network level such as creation of new relations or changes within existing ones influence network positions. Such changes are assumed to interact with changes in two ways both in the transport system and in the nets of transport companies. Therefore the analysis will be divided into integration on these two levels.

Even though the changes of the relationships might be of similar types they cannot be the same since changes at system level is looking at an in-depth change of single dyadic relationship and are its interaction with single transport system/s, while changes at net level concern several relations and their interaction with changes of the total net. First, the assumption is that if the two controlling organizations of an existing transport system increase their integration, the transport system will become more integrated. Another assumption is that transport companies create new transport systems by combining transport systems from different geographical areas. This will be defined as integration between single systems. This assumption is based on the fact that transport systems have always existed and through combining parts of or smaller local existing transport systems new systems are created.

A growth process such as internationalization would indicate that only increases are taking place. However, the definition of internationalization includes periods of stagnation or even negative changes.

The change in integration is studied from the focal company´s point of view. The change in the level of integration within/between systems is either combined with developing an existing or with creating a new relation.

The different integration categories are shown in two matrices of system integration (fig.4.3.) and that of net integration (fig.4.4.). These categories are different types of change processes showing the direction of a relative change to a former situation. Therefore comparisons between integration changes in relationships and nets can only be made as to their differencies in direction and to the type of change process involved.

Integration at system level

The *single system* matrix is divided into four types of changes in integration taking place either within or between systems using newly established relation or an existing one. A relation is here defined as a direct relation to the focal company.

	Existing relationship	New / leave of relationship
Within system	Change in closeness of cooperation	Switch of representive i.e.Leave of relationship/ new relationship
Between systems	Change in field of cooperation	New /cessation of (system) cooperation

Figure 4.3. Integration at system level

The changes in each square of figure 4.3.have been interpreted as follows and are discussed below. As has been mentioned earlier, the integration within the transport system is handled by a dyad, i.e.a focal company and its representative.

Change in closeness of cooperation follows from increased integration within an existing relationship of the focal company and a representative within a transport system. This increased integration in terms of any of the four aspects, can be legal, social, execution or control. An increased integration within an existing relation would lead to stabilizing the relation between the two controlling parties. Changes in closeness of cooperation are based on the assumption that the changes of the systems are smaller alterations and not larger structural changes leading to changes in the type of systems. An increase in closeness is assumed to automatically happen when the focal company acquires the agent. The result of internalising a focal company gets more directly controlled resources which is seen as closer cooperation in the legal aspect.

Change in the closeness of cooperation might also involve the adding new complementary activities within the same transport system e.g.warehousing, packing.

Switch of representative (leave of relationship/new relationship) is built on the assumption that the transport system, as such, is basically unchanged in functions and design and that the new agent will perform almost the same activities as the old. It might also mean leaving an agent when the focal company makes a greenfield investment.

Change in field of cooperation is the case when there exists a cooperation between two organizations which will be enlarged include more or other types of transport systems or be restricted to a more limited field. It is based on the assumption that the new field of activity is separate from the existing ones. In practice, *enlargement* of the field of cooperation might be exemplified by adding another transport system (traffic) together with the same representative.

New / cessation of (system) cooperation means that a new transport system is created that is different from the existing one, involving a new representative at the other end. In contrast to that of switching representative, the change will include larger changes of the transport systems like restructuring, changing to a new type of system, etc. The negative parallel to the new cooperation would be when the cooperation and the specific type of transport system cease to exist either through leaving the area or changing into a new type of system.

Integration at net level
As the number and interdependence of different systems controlled by organizations increase at systems level it seems reasonable to believe that this will result in integration within or between *nets of companies* rather than just dyads.

When does a cluster or net of organizations exist? How many organizations have to be involved? Where should the borders for the net be set?
The net is defined as limited to include representatives which are directly related to the focal company or indirectly related through some of its existing important direct relations.

The transport companies are not all part of a net. In order for a net to be said to exist there should be an awareness in the net of the interdependence. Operationally, reorganization of international activities, choice of representatives, changes in representatives, etc. can be a sign that the focal company might be aware of the interdependency between the organizations in the net. Changes at system and net level interact. However, several relationship changes taken together are assumed to be needed in order lead to a change at net level. A single system change influencing only a dyad will have a too marginal effect to be accounted for at net level.

What are the possible changes taking place at net level? The basic changes seem to concern either changing the size of the net and/or the cooperation between and within the relationships of the net. This can be seen and described in different ways. Håkansson & Lundgren (1992) mentioned coalescence and dissemination as the two dominating change processes. Mattsson (1987) discusses changes in terms of expansion and contraction of the size of the network. Cook (1983) talks about power balancing using extension and consolidation of net as examples of changing power of a net. Astley (1985) discusses closure of a net which means that the number of direct relations within the net increases. Finally quantitive network analysts discuss this in terms of distances, number of paths, etc. in the network which then is the base for identification of cliques and clusters.

Utilizing the concepts of relations and net, the changes in the degree of integration of a net will be classified into four different types of change processes, based on whether they occur within or between nets and with existing or new relations (see figure 4.4.). The changes are seen from the focal company´s net perspective. The change is assumed to involve two or more relations to be registered as a change of the net.

	Existing relations	New/leave of relations
Within a net	Change in closeness of cooperation	Closing up/ Opening up
Between nets	Drifting (closer/ away)	Joining/ leaving net(s)

Figure 4.4. Integration of net level

These categories have been interpreted as follows and are discussed below.

The category *closeness of cooperation* is important from the network perspective when two or more existing relations within a net are changing in the same direction within a limited period. An example of this is attempts to homogenize the transport systems within a net, for instance adopting the same type of communication systems.

Drifting closer or drifting away is a form of development of existing relationships between organizations which belong to different nets which over time are moving closer to or further away from each other. Drifting implies a gradual change over a period of time. It is based on a change in priorities of certain relations that will lead to integration between two nets of transport systems. Drifting means that through an increase or decrease in integration in a relation between specific organization/s, a number of organizations of another net will move closer to or away from the focal net. The change in integration is assumed to be made through changes in the existing relations of the net or with the consent of firms involved in existing relations. An example of this might be that the focal company and some of its subsidiaries in existing relations cooperate closer to an agent and a sister company/ subsidiary of another net leading to infrequent cooperation with other sister companies or subsidiaries of the agent in other areas. Some of these changes might be a result of gradual switching for specific agents belonging to another net as well. Such a change could be a result of continued closer cooperation and enlargement of a specific relation at system level. Another example of drifting closer is when a company acquires another company having many other international traffics. Through this acquisition the nets of the agents of the acquired firm are drifting closer to the focal company. Drifting does not change the net size but it affects the possibility for changing the net size in the future.

Closing up/opening up reflect changes in terms of number of relations in the net and the density of the net. Closing up is defined as an increase in the number of relations between the existing organizations in the net and might lead either to unchanged or a reduced net size. The final stage can be compared to what Astley (1985) discusses as "closure of a net". This case could be interpreted as moving towards a closure of a net leading to high interdependence between organizations and high complementarity in the net. It will then be increasingly difficult to let new organizations into the net.

Opening up, i.e. dissolving and/or widening a net is assumed to lead to a lower density in the net and the net will be more loosely structured. The density can decrease if the number of relations between the existing organizations within the net decreases or when a marginal change is made by adding an organization from the outside. The changes through widening are seen as marginal for the existing net. Making marginal changes of this type, adding organizations one by one through establishing new (system) cooperations at systems level over time, would lead to a gradual expansion of the net.

Joining or leaving net/s means that a large and major part of the net is changed. Through leaving or joining a net a number of relations begin or end within a very limited period of time. Quite often these are radical changes for the focal company. An example of this is the acquisition of a large international company with many subsidiaries and agents that would lead to many new relations with the existing net. Another example could be splitting a highly integrated net when a large group of companies are leaving the net almost at the same time.

Changes in resources in the domestic market for foreign activities will be taken into consideration indirectly at net and system level as prerequisites for changes in integration when the number of international transport systems increases or decreases. Cooperation taking place in many different functions like marketing, operation, finance, etc., with many agents presumes certain amounts of the same types of resources in the home country.

The changes taking place in the process of internationalization discussed in these matrices on integration show different ways to internationalize but they do not consider the actual time that it will take to go through the changes or when they start. Theoretically the discussion of *speed* and *timing* have played an important role, in general, for analysis of the internationalization process. However the concepts have not been specifically applied to the process of integration as in this case. Speed applied to the concept of integration will concern the time it will take for the companies involved to reach the degree of change intended. It can be exemplified by the speed with which the opening of a net lets new organizations come in or the choice of alternative ways to integrate such as taking a faster route through joining an existing net. The definition of timing is simply when something happened.

Operationalization of integration . Legal integration is rank-ordered as follows - no formal legal agreement, formal agreement, minority ownership, joint ventures, majority ownership and full ownership. Social integration is defined in terms of the existence of personal contacts. When a new relation is created it is assumed to involve social integration. The degree of social integration changes with frequency and number of personal contacts. Signs of increasing social contacts are personnel exchange between organizations, common marketing campaigns, adding new services needing common activities, etc. Control integration concerns the division of the control of the transport systems or net and to what extent the resources are shared between the organizations. It will be measured in terms of the extent to which the organizations add or take away responsibilities or new controlled resources to the system or net and to what extent they share and give the other party access to these. It concerns not only the division to the representative but includes also changes in the total resources controlled for the dyad and for the focal company in relation to other companies at net level. Examples are to share strategic planning activities, to share important information about customers and suppliers to a larger extent, set up new routines for better communication and access to each others technical and marketing resources. Finally, execution integration will be measured via actions taken to increase the efficiency of the physical flow of the transport system leading to a better utilization of the resources of the focal company and the representative.

Extension - definition and operationalization

Extension is an important concept for internationalization since it concerns the number of countries with or within which a company has business activities. The concept is more structural than processual, making us think in terms of a certain structure of a number of countries. A possible way to make the concept more dynamic would be to discuss the possibility of waves of widening and contracting of the extension dimension.

Increases in extension is defined by Johanson & Mattsson (1988) as establishment of positions in relation to counterparts in national nets that are new to the firm. It means that a new country is involved as well as a new relation is established.

Extension is changed stepwise and once the focal company has a direct relation to one country it is extended to that country. The concept accumulates the number of countries to which a company is related. Extension has a limit when all different countries of the world are covered for the focal company.

Further, extension is a key concept for the internationalization theories since to extend to another country is a base for continued internationalization. Extension is also discussed in many different ways in terms of the number of countries that the company is extended to but also the speed, the timing and sequence of extension.

The extension of the focal company would be dependent on the net size. The extension at system level is always direct for the focal company while at net level the focal company can be extended through the focal net via a representative

Waves of changes in extension such as widening and contracting of nets would include an increase and reduction of the number of transport systems. The fact that a subsidiary internationalizes would lead to certain problems when we discuss the extension of the focal company. Suppose the focal company situated in Sweden has a subsidiary in Germany which has internationalized to several other countries in Europe. To what extent will this increase the extension of the focal company?

As has been discussed by Forsgren (1990) and Forsgren & Holm (1990), when companies grew larger internationally over time, the same type of process that took place for the focal company seemed to apply to its subsidiaries. The subsidiaries will often change into centers of their own and internationalize. This is called secondary degree of internationalization and the whole net of the focal company is discussed in terms of such a multi-center firm. In line with this, we will call the creation of the first new relation between a specific pair of countries a secondary degree of extension. This way the focal net will show increased extension for the focal company indirectly and directly for the focal net. (See figure 4.5)

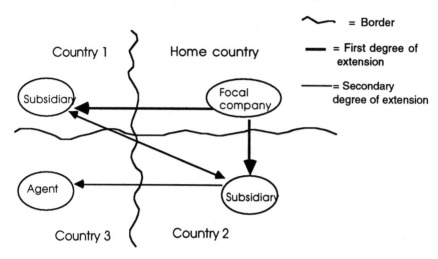

Figure 4.5. Extension dimension

First degree of extension to a specific country cannot take place more than once for the focal company, while the secondary degree of extension can take place several times.

Operationally extension for the focal company will be measured in first degree as the number of countries to which it is directly related. Secondary degree of extension concerns number of foreign countries to which the focal company is indirectly related via internationalization of subsidiaries or agents. The order in which the focal company is extended to different countries will show the sequence of the extension. The speed is defined as the length of time in which the sequence is performed. Finally the timing is defined as when a company starts to establish a relation between two specific countries .

Penetration - definition and operationalization

Penetration is the third dimension of internationalization. It is an important complementary dimension to the other two since it concerns the resources and relations of the focal company that are engaged for a specific country.

Johanson & Mattsson (1988) define penetration as developing the positions and increasing the resource commitments in country nets (markets) abroad where firms already have positions.

This definition concerns basically the extended position concept (Johanson & Mattsson, 1992), i.e. the relationships and the resource commitments.

An increased resource commitment might involve either more resources of the same type or a differentiation of the resources. When many different types of resources are available this is assumed to lead to a higher flexibility towards customers' demands and give rise to more contacts. Types of services are used as a proxy for measuring differentiation of resources. This is based on the assumption that new types of services lead to higher differentiation.

The other part of the concept concerns the relations in the foreign country. Discussing the position of a focal company, the number of relations engaged in a foreign country will be of importance. Assuming that representatives each adds new relationships, the number of subsidiaries and/or agents in the country can be used as one proxy when measuring the position and the types of services as another proxy.

Changes can take place either through new relations and/or through changes in resources. The term position in a network is seen as a result of investments in relationships. This would indicate that the two conceptual parts, relations and resources, interact.

Penetration at net level will also change with the degree of indirectly controlled and directly controlled resources, since all the resources of the subsidiary are automatically included. The amount and differentiation of the resources of the subsidiary are dependent on their total activities. If the subsidiary internationalizes this will increase the resources of the subsidiary whether it concerns the existing types of services or new types of services. Internationalization of an agent also give the focal company more resources related to net level as well, if the focal company uses the agent´s international traffics.

In this study, we shall have to include the focal company resources and relations engaged for a transport system or for a net wherever they are situated geographically since relations and resources might be geographically dispersed. This is especially so between the home country and a foreign country. Therefore resources and relations engaged in home country for a specific foreign country should be included in the measure of penetration.

An intrinsic problem defining the engaged resources of an agent is that only small shares of the total resources of an agent might be engaged. These small shares might on the other hand be spread out on many different types of resources. When changing to a subsidiary the differentiation of resources will therefore sometimes decrease. This phenomena could be explained in terms of asset specificity where the directly controlled resources have a higher asset specificity and cannot perhaps be used as easily for other purposes.

Based on the assumptions above concerning relations and resources, the dimension of penetration is assumed to change depending on existing or new representative relations and existing and new types of services that are involved in the change.

In contrast to integration, a switch from one agent to another does not matter as long as the transport systems do not change in the amounts of resources or differentiation of resources.

The different aspects of penetration for an international transport company are described in figure 4.6.

The assumption in the matrix is that the same type of services for a single foreign and home country use almost the same types of resources, while a different type of service or services to other countries or subsidiaries involve differentiation of the resources. The combination of types of services as indicators of resource differentiation and the number of representative relations engaged for a country will together give the position of the focal company in that country. System as well as net level are represented in the figure 4.6 .

	Existing relations	New/leave of relations
Existing type of services	Size of relations	Spread of relations
Change in type of services	Scope of relations	Diversification of relations

Figure 4.6. International penetration - categories

The first category in figure 4.6. is when change in *size of the relations* leads to changes in the degree of internationalization. For example, a growth in the volumes will probably lead to an increase in quantities of resources for that specific country. At net level it would include a subsidiary expanding within the existing types of services whether they are international or domestic.

For *spread of relations* it is assumed that the number of relations in existing types of services will influence the amount of resources. This category only concerns net level. An example of this is adding more representatives of the same type in a country.

Scope of relations within a specific country concerns both system and net level. This is the case when the types of services performed together with the existing representative/s increase or decrease. This will lead to a differentiation of resources when a new type of service is added. This category has specific importance at net level when the focal company has a subsidiary in the country. As the subsidiary expands internationally it is assumed to increase in the size of relations but also sometimes increases in the scope of the relations due to the adding new types services.

The last category concerns the net situation when both the relation and the type of services are new to the focal company leading changes in *diversification of relations* within a country. An increase is assumed to further differentiation of the resources as well as add to the number of relations in the country.

Furthermore it seems important for reasons mentioned earlier to take the speed and the timing of penetration into consideration.

<u>Interaction between and within the three dimensions of internationalization</u>

The three dimensions of integration, extension and penetration will be combined into a dynamic model to be used for analysis of the internationalization process of the cases. The construction of the final model for analysis is divided into interaction between the international dimensions and effects of the internationalization process. The first part is focused on the dynamics while the second part more explicitly brings the context into the model.

Up to now there has only been a discussion of interaction between different aspects within the three dimensions of internationalization. In this section, we will discuss to what extent there is interaction between the dimensions as such.

A transport system must have at least a minimum of integration in order to exist. Thus in the creation of an international system integration must take place. The integration for a new system will either take place between countries or within a foreign country to be considered international. When the transport system to a new country is created it will result in extension which is a prerequisite for the first penetration in that country. Thus, by definition, there is a certain interaction between the three concepts when creating new international transport systems. The same thing takes place at focal net level but in this case it might be a subsidiary or a very close agent to the focal company that internationalizes resulting in a secondary degree of extension of the focal company.

When extension has taken place to a country, how do the concepts interact then?

The different types of integration at single system and at net level seem to interact with the different aspects of penetration. Basically, adding a new relation will show an increase in both penetration and integration. On the other hand, increased integration does not necessarily lead to any increase in penetration at all in terms of amount of resources. In fact, there are many influences between the dimensions of the process of internationalization that we do not know anything about. To what extent these interact and in what directions the interaction goes we shall hopefully find out through the empirical study.

Johanson & Mattsson (1984) assume that all three dimensions are always present and that some play a more important role for the early starter, late starter, etc., but they do not explicitly discuss to what extent the dimensions interact over time.

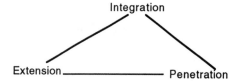

Figure 4.7 Interaction of the dimensions of internationalization

In general, not only will the three different internationalization dimensions interact but so will changes at system and net level as well because the micro and macro level obviously are interdependent.

Since we are interested in the dynamics of the process of internationalization, interaction between the three dimensions would be of vital importance for understanding how patterns of internationalization change over time.

4.3. Effects

In order to show the dynamics of the internationalization process from a contextual perspective, the effects will involve not only focal companies and their representatives but also other transport companies such as suppliers, owners and competitors. These other companies might have direct or indirect relations to the focal company.

The changes and effects on the focal companies will be part of their process of internationalization and will therefore not be presented as effects. This is also true for some of the representatives whose process of internationalization is studied in the empirical specific events.

However, there are direct or indirect effects on other transport organizations such as competitors, suppliers or owners and these will be described to the extent that they are known. The positive and negative connectedness within and between transport systems and nets indicates that there will be effects present.

The effects from the changes of the focal companies or focal nets might lead to changes in positive or negative connectedness for the involved organizations at system level and to changes in the structure of the net .

Positive and negative connectedness are easily understood at systems level based on changes in integration like switching of representative, new cooperation, etc. On the other hand, nets can also be negatively or positively connected but this would seem to be less readily understood. Therefore the concepts of complementarity and overlapping will be used to describe positive and negative connectedness at net level.

Complementarity is a basic concept used in the network approach and means that the resources and activities of two organizations complement each other. For a specific transport system the resources and activities of the companies basically complement each other since each company fulfils different functions.

Nets overlap geographically if they are represented in the same areas and if their activities overlap to another net if they perform the same activities. Overlapping might cause conflicts between organizations and therefore lead to negative connectedness between nets.

There are four different categories describing complementary and overlapping which are of importance between transport companies as shown in figure 4.8.

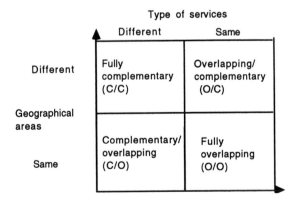

Figure 4.8. Complementary and overlapping areas and services.

If nets are overlapping in one sense and complementary in the other sense this might create possibilities for positive development. On the other hand overlapping in both senses indicates towards full competition.

A discussion of complementarity and overlapping will help us to understand the behaviour of companies in their internationalization processes through seeing changes in the nets of related companies. E.g nets moving from C/C towards C/O or O/C and then toward O/O would have to expect an increasing degree of actual conflicts between the relationships within or between the nets, since competition increases within the net and problems of leakage and spillover of intangible assets will be enhanced. Thereby it will include changes of other organizations in the context.

Indirect and direct relations in combination of the degree of positive/ negative connectedness of systems and overlapping/ complementarity of nets will be of basic importance when describing how the patterns of internationalization interact with that of the context.

Before we turn to the case studies we summarize the model of analysis in figure 4.9.

Internationalization processes of transport companies

In Nets of Representatives
Relationships
Transport systems

Measured in terms of

Three Dimensions of Internationalization

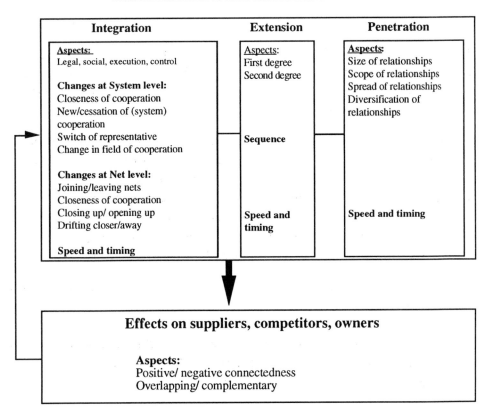

Integration	Extension	Penetration
Aspects: Legal, social, execution, control	**Aspects:** First degree Second degree	**Aspects:** Size of relationships Scope of relationships Spread of relationships Diversification of relationships
Changes at System level: Closeness of cooperation New/cessation of (system) cooperation Switch of representative Change in field of cooperation		
Changes at Net level: Joining/leaving nets Closeness of cooperation Closing up/ opening up Drifting closer/away	**Sequence**	
Speed and timing	**Speed and timing**	**Speed and timing**

Effects on suppliers, competitors, owners

Aspects:
Positive/ negative connectedness
Overlapping/ complementary

Figure 4.9. Major concepts in the model of analysis

Part III   Case studies - description and analysis

The case studies are presented one by one in time order and will be discussed in the terms of the concepts and the model developed above. The cases will be divided into decades except for the first period. In the case of ASG, the first period and the second period are prolonged to 15 years since the material during these early periods is less rich than during the last 20 years. The first period of Bilspedition was for the same reason also 15 years. Inter Forward on the other hand has only existed from the beginning of 1988.

In the ASG case their overseas development is included and divided into the same periods as European development. However in the general cases analysis overseas and European development are joined. This gives a richer description of ASG than in the other cases.

There are three main parts involving the case studies a)the description of each case b)the general case analysis c) the event analysis. The first two parts are discussed for each case separately in chapter 5, 6 and 7. The general case analyses of the three cases are then summarized and compared between the three cases in chapter 8.

The descriptive part of the cases include both the general development of the companies and the specific events while the general case analysis is concentrating on the general development of the focal companies using the specific events as a support for details and for interpretation of the development. In the third part, the event analysis, we focus on dynamics and the context analysing specifically the events and use the general development of the firms as support in order to seek for sequences of changes and effects over time. The dynamic analysis will then be the base for the construction of a dynamic network model of internationalization.

Finally the total empirical results based on the general case analyses as well as the event analysis are summarized at the end of chapter 9.

For those of the readers that are less interested in the details and want a quick skimming of the case, read the general development and the summaries at the end of each period and each event.

5.   ASG
5.1.   Case description
5.1.1. Group- international development
5.1.2. Europe - development (general development and specific events)
5.1.3. Overseas international development (general development and specific events)

5.1.1 ASG - Group international development

General development and ownership-structure

ASG was established in 1935 as the inland transport arm of a Swedish shipping line, Svea Rederi AB.

The international side of ASG's activities started during the war with transports for the Aid organizations in Sweden which were sending necessities to refugees in the war-devastated countries in Europe.

	1967	1970	1975	1980	1985	1990
Parent turnover[1](Msek)	412	610	1012	2187	3200	5489
Group turnover (Msek)			1296	2761	4279	7312
Result (Msek)-Parent [2]	- 0,5	16,5	15,8	36,2	6	135
Result (Msek)-Group				19	2	218
No of employees-Parent	1784	2447	2705	3357	3117	3512
" " - Group				4695	4289	5171
" " abroad				422	597	1066

Table 5.1. Some facts about ASG

The international activities grew at a very rapid rate, particularly in connection with the re-building of European industry directly after the war.

Over time, the international side of the Group has increased its share of total Group turnover, which amounted to SEK 7,312 million in 1989, to around 46%[3]. Within that figure, foreign subsidiaries had a turnover of around SEK 1,308 million in the same year, in other words some 17-18%.

The ownership structure has changed five times during ASG's 50 year history but the major shareholders have always been transport companies, with Svea Shipping Line and SJ always the predominant owners, the latter for the last 30 years (see figure 5.1.2.).

The fact that other transport companies have been the owners of ASG has had both negative and positive effects on the development of the company. The fact that the services offered by ASG were complementary to those of the owners contributed to some extent towards expansion but resulted in restrictions being imposed in other respects. One specific restriction was that ASG should not own the means of transportation. Exceptions to this rule had to be

---

[1]Excluding VAT and Customs duty

[2]After depreciation and finacial income and expenses but before extraordinary income and expenses and appropriations and income tax

[3]Concerns the degree to which the turnover comes from international activities both in Sweden and abroad

made occasionally where trucking companies vital for the geographical traffic network faced crises of one kind or another.

At the same time there have also been conflicts of interest as between the owners when it came to investment priorities. Periodically these conflicts have been quite intense, especially as between ASG-T and the Swedish Railway.

1935-41	Svea Shipping Line 100%
1941-59	Svea Shipping Line 50% and Swedish Railway(SJ) 50%
1959-65	Swedish Railway(SJ) 100%
1965-67	Swedish Railway (SJ) 95% and Association of the trucking companies engaged in ASG (ASG-T) 5%
1967-80	Swedish Railway (SJ) 67,5% Rego (Broström, Transatlantic, Lloyd, JohnsonLine) 25% ASG-T 7,5%
1980-90	Swedish Railway 75%(from 1986 via Swedecarrier[1]) ASG-T 25%
1990-	Introduction to Swedish stock exchange Swedecarrier 59% of the votes, 41% of the shares Other owners (Trelleborg, Skandia, private persons, etc) 41% of votes, 59 % of the shares

Figure 5.1.2. Owners of ASG to date

Even though ASG commenced operations as a domestic transport organization, linked first to Svea and then to SJ, the situation changed over time. The development of the door-to-door concept and consolidation traffics, but particularly the former, played an extremely important role in this context. To offer a door-to-door service meant taking full responsibility for the total transport of the customer's goods instead of merely playing a complementary role to that of the owners. This development also increased competition between ASG and its owners. A disturbing factor was that SJ marketed its own domestic consolidation traffics in direct competition with ASG. Very often SJ and ASG even operated out of the same terminals, hardly a satisfactory arrangement. This situation grew steadily worse until 1987 when SJ decided to leave its costly consolidation traffic to the forwarders. ASG benefitted by taking over a large part of these operations. For ASG, the addition of SJ's consolidation traffics meant increased utilization of existing facilities which had positive effects on profitability. This caused a slight increase in the share of the domestic activities and a decrease of the international share of ASG.

---

[1] Swedecarrier was a newly established holding company fully owned by the Swedish Railways. This change brought new members to the Board of ASG which came from the Swedish industry instead of from SJ.

The role of the ASG trucking companies, which were normally rather small, was mostly that of partners and subcontractors. Certain conflicts in the division of work did occur between ASG and the trucking companies which, lacking marketing resources of their own, regarded ASG as their marketing organization with themselves as the dominant partner when it came to domestic traffics. SJ and the shipping lines had their own marketing resources. As the international business grew, the role of ASG increased in importance while the importance of the role of the domestic trucking companies decreased. This created certain conflicts with ASG-T, part-owners in ASG, since they were dominated by domestic trucking companies and their interest in international development was limited.

5.1.2. Europe- development

5.1.2.1.Period 1940-54
Development of services
By 1939, ASG had already developed domestic traffics that spanned the country. Using a combination of agents and 140 trucking companies they had established what they called door-to-door traffics throughout the whole country. As a result, they had developed into being one of the dominant transport companies in Sweden.

ASG's first international transports, for aid organizations both during and directly after the war, were to the Nordic countries, Austria, Hungary and Switzerland. The contacts created during these first transports were very valuable when establishing more regular traffics later on. As the roads in Europe had largely been destroyed and as trucking transports were subject to many restrictions, the railway provided the only alternative over long-distances and the first regular international transports by ASG followed the form of railway consolidation.

Regular traffics were established to several destinations in Europe within a few years of the war-end. In the beginning of the 1950's ASG serviced a large number of the European countries with railway traffics.

The ASG takeover directly after the war of the domestic railway consolidation of another company, TransportKompaniet (TK), facitlitated the creation of an operational and knowledge base for the rapid expansion in railway consolidation in Continental Europe. ASG, as the leading forwarder at the time, had concluded an agreement with the Swedish customs in 1942 to carry bonded goods -transit goods not yet declared- to the customs inland warehouse, which was another important factor in its development.

The growth in trade made for expansion, although export transports were to remain greater than imports for some years after the war. Industry in the war-devastated countries was in course of reconstruction. Imports increased when industrial production re-established itself in Europe.

ASG became very successful in its railway consolidation, combining its railway know-how with its proven door-to-door concept. In some areas, such as Eastern Germany where ASG had about 80% of all consolidated goods, ASG totally dominated the market.

In order to develop international door-to-door transports, a fixed price had to be set for the whole international transport. Competitors came out in strong opposition to this, as they regarded all-inclusive pricing of this nature to be a way of dumping prices on the market. As a direct result and for many years, ASG was shut out from becoming an associate of the Forwarders´ Association in Sweden.

Basically what ASG had done was to assume a greater level of responsibility towards the customer than was normal for the traditional type of forwarder. This responsibility, which was mainly for consolidated goods, helped to create efficient door-to-door traffics.

Another important development towards the end of this period was the extension of the use of pallets, previously mostly confined to local transports, to long-distance transports so as to gain greater efficiency in the railway consolidation traffics.

However, as it transpired, the European railways had the greatest difficulty in coping with the enormous increase in railway transports in the period directly after the war. Their capacity was too low at the beginning of the 1950's, resulting in many disruptions, long transit times, heavy pilferage, loss of goods, etc. This situation, in combination with the rebuilding of roads and the new truck technology, shifted the competitive advantage in favour of road transportation. It was in 1953 that the economic result per ton for ASG's railway consolidation traffics actually decreased for the first time.

Representation in foreign countries

As ASG developed railway consolidation traffics in Europe between a number of European areas and Sweden during the 1940's and beginning of the 1950's, choosing agents was one of the more important tasks of management.

Representation in the form of agents was the natural choice at the time for ASG after the war and many of the agents were already established railway agents and as such well known to SJ.

As a result of the development in railway consolidation, ASG had agents in a large number of countries in Europe in the beginning of the 1950's. In 1953, however, the ASG Board decided that ASG should concentrate on land transportation and on what were considered the twelve most important countries which were East and West Germany, Switzerland, Czechoslovakia, Hungary, Italy, Bulgaria, Yugoslavia, Austria, Poland, Norway and Denmark.

There were more agents than countries, however, since in some countries, such as West-Germany, agents were restricted to smaller local areas. There were other countries, such as Finland, where ASG also had agents. These were of lower priority because their traffics partly involved sea transportation. France was another country where ASG had an agent but consolidation traffics, via boat to Antwerp, had failed.

The agreements between agents and ASG during the 1950's and the 1960's were highly informal. The cooperation could therefore be terminated by any of the partners at short notice. Most of the agreements between ASG and the different agents, whether written or unwritten, were based on the agent being granted exclusive coverage of a certain area. Basically, all agreement were bilateral.

The new agent Natural will illustrate in more detail some of the important changes during this period (p.105)

Organization and investments

An effect of the growth in international activities was a new way of working, since international traffic involved new functions and new personnel both in operations, marketing, communication, etc. The requirements placed on international personnel were also different due to the need for knowledge of languages, foreign cultures and more complicated routines and rules. The international operations remained highly dependent on the domestic operations for facilities, sales, administration, etc.

The growth, the higher qualifications needed and the travel even made the international side of the company more attractive, causing internal competition for personnel.

The risks were higher in the international than in the domestic traffics since the fixed costs were higher. In the domestic traffics, the basic agreement was that ASG got a commission on the revenue of transports sold while in international traffics ASG got paid according to mileage and time. In the domestic traffics the trucking companies took the main risks while it was the other way around internationally.

During this period of growth in the international transport systems, the Swedish organization changed both in size and structure. The international activities, which were limited in size compared to the domestic, were organized at head office level into a department for international transports and a special department for international railway tariffs. The operations were performed by only a handful of the local offices in Sweden. In all, the separate investments made for the international traffics during this period were mainly, with a few exceptions, in know-how and people and less in offices and terminals.

Summary of period 1940-54

ASG developed door-door railway traffics with local agents to 12-14 foreign countries. The agreements with the agents were exclusive and mostly informal. The international development, which was very successful, led to the creation of some new departments at head office. The international know-how and number of employees increased.

5.1.2.2.Period 1955-69

Development of services

From the mid 1950's and during the 1960´s ASG trucking services grew as a complementary service as well as in substitution for rail consolidation. However, the combination of ASG's strong position and high profitability in railway consolidation and the ownership and opposition of SJ had caused a delay in the acceptance and expansion of international road transports for ASG. Another factor that probably contributed to the delay was that the agents were mainly railway agents, in many cases owned by the railway companies. Few of these agents had any interest or know-how in road transportation.

ASG applied to Biltrafiknämnden (the Board of International Trucking) for international trucking permits several times in order to organize road transports to European destinations but the bulk of these applications were rejected, SJ being part of the Board. In 1958, ASG had only 6 trucks in regular traffics on the continent of Europe. It was not until the beginning of 1961 that ASG received a larger number of permits (137) from the Board of International Trucking and a year later they received another 324 permits as well as the possibility to expand a hundred existing destinations. Also, as the permits were mainly restricted to transports to/ from specific areas in a given foreign country.

At this time the railway consolidation had declined considerably in importance, which ASG had begun to feel. In 1963, railway transports decreased by 400 tons while trucking transports increased by 27.000 tons.

An important step towards more effective transports was taken in 1962 when ASG obtained permission from the Customs to take bonded goods to an approved and controlled warehouse in ASG's own inland terminal.

Not only trucking transports but also airfreight and later on sea-freight were developed during this period. This caused ASG to place emphasis on the fact that they could offer international transports choosing between the different means of transportation. Moreover, during this period ASG assumed full responsibility towards the customer for all goods transported by ASG in its own name. When Nordic Forwarding Association (NSF) finally accepted these practices in 1974, ASG had been working in this way for several years. This responsibility on the part of ASG for the total transport system as a freight carrier and forwarder facilitated the possibility to choose the most suitable means of transportation.

The technological development increased the competition between air and sea transports. As the airlines grew and the aeroplanes were further developed, it became possible to organize airfreight on a larger scale and it became an alternative to other means of transportation for certain categories of goods. At the end of the period when containerization in combination with faster ships was developing, this competition became obvious. Containerization made it possible for ASG to establish its own international traffics for sea-transports.

Representation in foreign countries

The demands on the agent were very different for trucking transports than for rail consolidation. In order to have a profitable road transport the truck also needed goods for the return trip. This implied that the agent had to market the service to customers in order to establish a regular traffic. It was a new way of thinking for many agents. Many of the existing rail agents were not able or not willing to take on this new type of service. This resulted in the number of agents being extended further. This was especially the case for short and medium distances where the truck offered a competitive alternative. Due to this development the conflicts increased between ASG's agents. For some agents like Natural i Switzerland, Saima in Italy, etc., this change did not create any big problems since they had had their own earlier development into trucking services or due to the fact that the rail continued to exist as a competitive alternative because of the long distance.

In the beginning of the 1960's, when ASG had got most of the trucking permits they had applied for, many of the rail agents lost market shares to trucking services. Some rail services over shorter distances had to close down after a period of competition. Even though some of the railway agents left and some of the existing agents took on the new services during this period, quite a few new trucking and airfreight agents seem to have been appointed. Therefore the total number of agents increased.

During this period ASG established its first international offices. The very first was a sales office in Berlin established in 1955. An airfreight subsidiary was established in Copenhagen in 1959 and one in Hamburg in 1960 for trucking services. In Denmark, as well as in West-Germany, the subsidiaries were situated in transit places for their type of traffics and they had a certain coordination function to begin with. In both cases, there were other agents in the country. In Denmark there was another agent for land-transportation and in West-Germany there were a large number of local agents but in other local areas. The sales office in Berlin was closed down after a couple of years and the agent took over the main part of the activities. New sales offices were opened in Düsseldorf and London in the mid 1960´s but even these new sales offices were closed down after a couple of years.

The functions of these sales offices were basically to support existing operating agents in the country in their marketing activities, to get "routing orders" for freight being paid by the receiver, give feed-back of the market development to the Head Office, give information as to the quality in the transport services offered by the agents together with ASG and finally to be supportive to the Swedish customers abroad. Most offices only had 2-5 persons employed.

In the discussions with the agents, ASG always demanded the right to handle the procurement of the long-haul trucking services. If the agent did not agree, either because it had the same policy or did not want to accept this type of domination, the cooperation did not come through. It was only in very specific cases that ASG accepted some other type of agreement for trucking services. Therefore the normal agreements specified that ASG should decide what subcontractors to use for the trucking traffics.

Adherence to this one reason for starting the early representative offices was that ASG was responsible for setting the price for the main part of the transport system. This caused difficulties for the agents to make special agreements with the large customers.

The specific event involving Switzerland and West-Germany can well illustrate some of the changes taking place during this period.

Organization and investments

In the re-organization in 1967, the international transports were combined in a functional organization with domestic activities. The new functional organization was divided into operational, traffic, marketing, administration, accounting and planning and development departments. The new traffic department were divided into special sections for road, rail, air and seafreight. The new departments were all working in close contact with the local Swedish offices and agents as well as with the international agents and offices according to their specific function.

The main investments made for the international transports were investments in terminals in Sweden. Even though the terminals were to a high degree made for the purpose of the domestic traffic, large handling and office space was also created for international traffics. Very few landtransport terminals were built primarily for international purposes.

Over time, the international activities started to create resources of their own, like the building of terminals specifically for international traffic, specialized marketing resources, administration, etc. Services like airfreight and seafreight were developed later than the European land transportation and the dependence to begin with was as much on the domestic services as on the existing international activities. The local resources for airfreight as well as seafreight were, however, to a large extent separated from both the domestic and the international transports for trucking and railway since they needed special offices at the airport or at the harbour, close to the airport or for sea-freight close to the harbour, etc.

In 1967, a smaller part of the head office sales force was specialized on larger European transport projects and also performed direct selling to large European customers.

In the same year, ASG also acquired 50% of Road Ferry and 100% of Transfrigoroute, both small Swedish firms, which had trucking operations and owned certain trucking equipment used partly in international operations. The year after they acquired 25% of the Finnish agent.

Summary of the period 1955-69

Trucking traffics took over both in expansion and dominance. ASG started to develop airfreight and seafreight services. The number of agents and countries increased further. Three sales offices were established and two operating offices, one in Denmark and one in West-Germany. The responsibility towards the customers increased, which made it easier for ASG to choose the suitable mean for landtransports. Investments were made in more efficient terminals and transport equipment. Further, ASG acquired a minority share of the Finnish agent. The international activities gained in importantance. Separate departments were developed for air and seafreight, special salesmen were employed for direct selling in Europe and the contacts with the foreign agents increased.

5.1.2.3.Period 1970-79

Development of services

The services of ASG became increasingly diversified during the 1970's. In addition to the basic services of consolidation, full loads and some charter transports, ASG developed new specialized services like bulk transports, hanging garment transports, furniture transports, project transports, trailer transports, etc. Most of these services resulted from technological changes and some in combination with a further adaption to the problems of the customers which made it possible to create more effective transport systems for certain type of goods.

In the course of time, ASG has created other types of services in conjunction with its customers which included logistical functions previously undertaken by the customers themselves. Among these services were warehousing, packing, consultancy on customer logistics, custom-painting of refrigerators, cutting carpets, etc. Some of these are individual services for one or two special customers while others have developed into being an important integral part of the company´s total business, like warehousing, which comprised around 300,000 square meters at the end of 1970´s. For example, an importer wanting to have a quick delivery could be very interested in this service in the host country and nearly all international agents and subsidiaries had or developed a warehousing capability since this became an important complementary service for the total transport system.

In 1974, there was a change which led to further possibilities to increase efficiency in the international traffics. The new customs regulations in Sweden allowed customers or their agents, the forwarder, to make their own customs declaration after a registration. ASG, like many other forwarding agents, expanded their services to customers by making customs declaration as well.

Representation in foreign countries

At the end of the 1960's and during the 1970's ASG decided to re-assess the whole network of agents in Europe. Basically, ASG was rather dissatisfied with the marketing activities of many of the existing agents, the profitability of the traffics, etc . The reasons for this, as they saw them, were their agents' expansion into other countries, a lack of marketing resources, too small an area of representation, a lack of coordination between their marketing resources and ASG's, lack of EDP development etc. This led to an activation of closer contacts with some agents, a switch to some new agents and finally a restructuring in terms of coverage and representation for local areas. These changes seem also to have resulted in a certain reduction in the number of agents. Several airfreight agents also left their former cooperation with the land transport agents during this period, which will be further discussed when dealing with the subject of overseas transports.

ASG established new sales offices in Hamburg (beginning of 70's), Belgium (mid 70's), Italy and France (end of 70's). These were all closed down within a couple of years after which the agent or a subsidiary took over the sales activities in combination with direct sales to certain customers from ASG head office in Sweden.

In the beginning of the 1970's only the subsidiaries in Copenhagen and Hamburg remained. However, both of these had grown in size and types of services. In 1976, ASG acquired the former agent Atege in Stuttgart and a year later it established a subsidiary in Belgium.The combination of a subsidiary and agents in the same country caused certain conflicts over a period, especially in those cases where both specialized in the same type of services, as in West-Germany. They seem to have caused a certain uncertainty about ASG's future plans. The same would appear to apply in the case of sales offices.

As ASG developed internationally into new areas like airfreight, furniture-, bulk- and project transports during the 1960's and 1970's, the same problem of shifting to a new technology was present as in the case of rail and truck. The result was that many of the existing agents could not, would not or were not even asked to take on the new transport service. This increased the number of agents and subsidiaries further in the different countries in Europe. Furthermore, ASG acquired a new company ERT (European Road Transport Co) in 1979, a company specializing in international trailer transports. ERT already had established agents, different to those of ASG, in certain places in Europe. Since the companies were not merged, this meant that more agents and subsidiaries were added to the existing net.

Norway was an extremely complicated case when it came to the choice of representatives. Due to ASG's increased land transportation freight volumes and the growth of the Norwegian agent NG (Norske Godscentraler), the capacity of the Oslo terminal became insufficient for their needs and the problem was further aggravated by the fact that the agent ran into economic problems at the same time. In the attempts to solve the crises, a joint venture was created between NG and Globe, another Norwegian transport company. This new company became the agent of ASG in 1970. However, the Norwegian Railway (NSB), which was also experiencing operational and economic problems, had been helpful in the construction of the new company with a view to taking over a part of it. This happened after a short period, giving

NG-Globe a new constellation of owners consisting of NG with 1/3, Globe with 1/3 and the Norwegian Railway with 1/3

As the NG-Globe constellation ran into serious economic problems, ASG took over 70% of the agent in 1971. A year later NSB formed a new state owned company (Linjegods A/S) together with a group of trucking companies and demanded to be ASG's agent in Norway in place of the subsidiary NG-Globe. ASG wanted a change, since the company it had taken over was continuing to experience big economic problems, and so in 1973 it reverted to an agent situation in Norway once again. The choice was in part determined by the Swedish and Norwegian Railways which demanded that ASG should take the newly created company Linjegods as an agent in Norway. Therefore the situation changed from an agent to a subsidiary and back to agent again, all within a few years.

In 1976 ASG had the possibility of acquiring 100 % of a Norwegian airfreight forwarder owned by a Norwegian shipping line, but the deal did not materialize due to tax problems. However, in 1979/80, ASG was able to acquire 65 % of Flygods A/S, a company related to the former NG as well as to the agent Linjegods.

Apart from acquisitions and special individual cases, ASG's agreements with agents during this period comprised a mixture of the formal and the informal. In many cases, the cooperation had existed for more than twenty years and yet there was still no formal agreement. However some kind of basic agreement always existed ,whether formal or informal, which set out the economic conditions (tariffs or price-lists) for the different services, agreed policies and routines for marketing, economic transactions between the parties, etc.

Organization and investments

ASG changed the organization from a functional to a divisional structure in 1974-76.

The international divisions were the Nordic, Continental, Overseas (Air/Sea) Divisions, added to which there was the Domestic Division.

The European traffics became part of the three different international divisions depending on geographical area and means of transportation. In this way the agents and subsidiaries were seen as the responsibility of a specific division. Such a separation of the transport systems was facilitated by the fact that land-transportation and airfreight at that time mostly had separate representation in the European countries as well as separate offices in Sweden.

To a very large extent the divisional structure only existed at the head office and did not really affect the situation of the local operating offices in Sweden or abroad very much. The only exception was the air/sea division which also assumed responsibility for the operating offices specialized in air and sea. On the other hand, the air/sea -overseas division was small in comparison to the other divisions of the company at that time. During this reorganization, the company consolidated itself into a Group with a special group staff.

The main investments made in Sweden for the international activities were in terminals, offices, EDP and increased know-how in all new specialized types of transports, through training and recruiting. Specialized terminals for international transports were created in Malmö and at the Skandia harbor in Gothenburg during this period and in many other instances terminals came to incorporate specialized sections for the handling of international goods.

As the international resources were distributed throughout 40 different localities in Sweden it was not only handling but also office space, special communication systems and administrative systems that were demanded. This was especially the case since international traffics needed more space in offices and handling than domestic traffics. In the terminal, the space per ton was higher due to the lower frequencies and the export packing. In offices, more space was needed because the requirements per consignment were 3-10 times greater for export/ import consignments which meant more employees per consignment. Increasingly simplified Customs systems in the different countries and improved communication systems should reduce the additional demands made by international traffics.

Other important investments were the acquisition of Atege in Stuttgart, ERT and the establishment of ASG Belgium. In most cases the investments abroad have been very modest in size compared, say, to the cost of a larger terminal in Sweden. However, there has been a continuous need for working capital for expansion over the years.

It was very advantageous, therefore, that a change in the Customs regulations, allowing ASG - like many other forwarders with a reasonable share of imports - prolonged credit time, enabled the international side of ASG to contribute towards improved liquidity to the extent of SEK 150-200 million over a period of 8 years from 1974 to 1982. This also had positive effects on profits since interest rates were very high in Sweden during these years.

Summary of period 1970-79

ASG diversified into new services such as warehousing, logistical services etc. At the same time they developed special transports for hanging garments, bulk transports, furniture, etc. These new services were performed partly with existing and partly with new agents. This development combined with the downturn in volumes after the oil crisis created problems with non-involved existing agents, which either caused a reactivation of or a departure from their existing relationships with ASG.

Investments were made in more efficient communication systems, terminals and transport equipment in order to perform these new services in the international traffics. Increased training and recruiting also became necessary. Three international companies were acquired. Two were former agents in Norway and in West-Germany and one was a Swedish competitor specialized in trailer traffics. The Norwegian subsidiary failed economically so ASG changed to a new agent after a couple of years. Furthermore ASG made a greenfield investment in Belgium.

Finally, the international activities became as important as the domestic for the total ASG organization.

<u>5.1.2.4.Period 1980-89</u>

Development of services

During the 1980's, the changes in services resulted in ASG splitting up the traditional consolidation and full load transports into certain new categories, with different service standards, according to size and/or time for delivery including or excluding guarantees. Examples were small package transports, guaranteed transport within 24 hours or 48 hours, etc.

Another development resulting from the increasing volume of combi-traffics using trailers, containers or flats was that the choice of carrier became of secondary importance in some cases. This changed the situation both for ASG and its agents. The choice of the means of transportation, especially for temporary traffics, might be solved ad hoc depending on access, price and standard, while the basic and regular volumes transported seem to have been even more strongly tied to a specific supplier.

At the end of 1980's, the transports between Sweden and the individual European countries still dominated ASG's transports, even though there was an increasing share of third country transports between continental Europe and the Nordic countries. The strength of the positions in the Nordic countries contributed to this. The fact that the intra-European traffics in continental Europe had a small share was probably due fact that the ASG subsidiaries in Europe had been directed in their marketing for the Nordic countries and that the agents only had bilateral agreements.

This is also reflected in the business idea for 1988 which was expressed in the 1988 Annual Report as follows "ASG offers high quality transport, forwarding, and warehousing services to the Nordic domestic markets and to foreign markets important to the Nordic business and industry. ASG utilizes efficient transport and information systems to provide competitive advantages for the customers."

Representation in foreign countries

Up to the 1980's, there had been an increase in the total number of agents in Europe when including the expansion of subsidiaries, special transports and airfreight. During the 1980's there was a change towards concentration by having fewer representatives. The few subsidiaries added a few representatives to their existing number but not so as to outweigh the decrease for ASG, Sweden. ASG landtransports as a whole reduced the number of their representatives by 21 between 1976 and 1989 (see appendix 3). The main reduction took place in West-Germany and France while a few agents were added in the Sovjet Union.

A clear example of this concentration is West-Germany, where the number of agents has been gradually reduced(see below):

	Agents	Subsidiaries
1955-75	20-30	1 (est.1960)
1976	18	2 (acq.end 1976)
1979	17	2
1989	3	3 (all included in ASG holding company)

In spite of the move towards having fewer representatives, ASG still has more than one representative in most West-European countries, if air and sea-freight are included. If the agents of the subsidiaries are added, the number increases still further.

However the reduction of the total number of European representatives could have been higher since the concentration of several services to one agent or subsidiary does not seem to have worked out well in every case although much of the concentration has been to existing agents with long relations to ASG. In some cases there were a split again into separate agents or subsidiaries like in Switzerland, Belgium, Finland and Austria.

In 1989, the average period of cooperation with the existing agents was in excess of 20 years even when excluding the Eastern German States. Since subsidiaries numbered only 8-10 and as several were established during the 1980's, their period as representatives is shorter on average than for the agents.

During this decade ASG acquired or established four new airfreight companies in Europe while three companies were added for landtransports. In airfreight, Flygods A/S in Norway was acquired (65%) 1979/80 and ASG U.K.(100%) was established in 1980; later during the period ASG Finland and Nova Traffics in Switzerland were added. A holding company was established in Holland in 1988 for the non-German international companies. Two new land-transport companies were acquired in West-Germany and one in Norway.

Over a period of time the existing subsidiaries developed into transport companies in their own right, with their own area of coverage becoming increasingly more independent of their parent in Sweden. ASG Hamburg and Atege Stuttgart grew internationally from their areas of operation and ASG Denmark developed into one of the largest airfreight forwarders in Denmark. However, they remained much smaller than the Swedish company, with fewer agents than ASG Sweden. In some cases, their representatives are the same as ASG Sweden's but others are different (see list of subsidiaries/ agents in Appendix 3).

During the 1980's, the percentage of shares held in the subsidiaries increased, ASG Belgium, Flygods as well as Nordex becoming fully owned. The only exception was Finland where ASG reduced its share in the company to less than 20% so as to remove the legal impediment against its agent from owning land caused by the previous 25% foreign shareholding in Finland. Later on, ASG established its own wholly owned company.

The expansion by the subsidiaries, however, often resulted in the establishment of new offices or small subsidiaries within their own countries.

In order to adapt to the new type of services with time guarantees and to the increase in combi-traffics, ASG in Germany set up a supporting ASG office in Travemünde to direct, decide and negotiate which companies to choose as carriers for the German traffic. The subsidiary in Stuttgart also had a special trucking company for carrying trailers and flats to/from Travemünde which were used not only for their own traffics but also on behalf of other transport companies being customers. The development of combi-traffic has also changed the usage of the railway. The last decade has seen ASG increase the level of investments made in trailers, containers and flats.

As during the 1970's, changes became especially complicated for ASG in Norway. When the ASG agent Linjegods faced an economic crisis in 1984, ASG did not want to buy the company but Bilspedition did. As a result and within a week, ASG and their Finnish agent had to find a new solution for their goods to/ from Norway of roughly 500.000 tons/year. However, ASG had got to know the Norwegian agent of ASG's Danish agent , TK Nord. This was a rather small forwarding company named Nordex. Through Nordex, ASG obtained access to the facilities and contacts needed to take care of the vast amount of goods that ASG and Finnexpress had daily in their Norwegian transport systems. ASG wanted to buy part of the company, as well as its Finnish agent Finnex, but Finnex refused. Instead ASG bought 60% of the agent Nordex; about a year later, ASG bought the residual 40%. Many Swedish employees were stationed in Norway during the initial period and some personnel from the former agent joined. The total transport systems had to be reorganized and in the beginning period of changes there was a heavy reduction in the volumes of goods. After a year it started catching up again partly through the old contacts with the industry.

As the Norwegian agent was sold to Bilspedition, ASG bought 100% of the former part-owned aircargo subsidiary.

In Finland, Bilspedition did almost the same thing as in Norway, since it acquired the ASG landtransport agent, which was 20% owned by ASG. Within a short period ASG had to find another alternative. However, in this case, a subsidiary ASG Finland already existed even though it was restricted in its services to air and sea. This subsidiary expanded to include also land-transports and with the help of a domestic transport company could take care of the existing volumes. As in the case of Norway, some personnel from the former agents joined the new ASG company.

In Denmark, there was also a change in ownership, since ASG obtained the possibility to acquire a minority (10%) interest in its agent in 1989. As the dominant partner, ASG had held a seat on the Board of that company for almost twenty years.

Furthermore, in 1990 ASg acquired the majority in the Swiss airfreight company and changed in Holland from the very old agent, van Gend & Loos, to a new agent. The old agent had recently been acquired by the Neddlloyd Group.

During this period the cooperation with agents became more formalized. As an example, the first formal agreement between ASG and the agent in Italy (Saima) was written in 1986, with whom ASG has been cooperating since directly after the war.

Organization and investments

In 1983, the Nordic and Continental divisions were combined into a European division and this division was given full responsibility for operations and marketing of international land-transport activities in Sweden and abroad. At that time, domestic transports became entirely separate from the international transports. Eventually, at the end of 1990 and in the beginning of 1991, ASG created one international division out of the European and Overseas divisions, covering all international activities.

Different departments, specialized in international transports, had developed over a period in each location in Sweden having international traffics. In 1989, the European division had more than 30 separate offices in Sweden and the Overseas division had 10 offices at airports, in harbours, etc. These offices were, of course, the base for the international transports on the Swedish side. However, the need for complementing services and for the diversification of services, communication needs, etc., within the transport network involved establishing new activities and functions which implied construction of new departments in the organization like customs declaration department, international projects, etc. These departments were to a greater or a lesser extent dependent on the traditional organization of ASG.

In the main, the offices and terminals abroad were and still are owned by agents.

During this period, the shareholders did not increase their capital investment in the company, in spite of all the investments made during 1970´s and 1980´s. The solidity of the company therefore fell to 8-10% in the early 1980's. It was not until 1985 that the shareholders increased the amount of owners' capital in the company from SEK 46 million to SEK 92 million in comparison with a turnover of almost SEK 5 billion that year.

The dominant area for investments during the 1980's was in communication systems which have grown enormously and are expected to increase further during 1990´s. ASG has tried to reach an investment level in communication systems of around 2 % of turnover but this has not been possible except during some extremely profitable years. ASG has developed several communication systems for different purposes in the European countries for air/sea-freight and their connected offices (Actor, Access etc), for the Nordic offices (Nordcom) and for the Continental Europe (various). However the increasing number of subsidiaries, the new services with time guarantees, logistical services, etc., lead to a need to create effective communication systems for ASG.

Summary of period 1980-89/90

The development of combined traffics continued, which made the choice between different means of transportation less relevant and quality in traffics in terms of speed, timing and frequency increased in importance. There was a concentration to fewer agents and the operating landtransport subsidiaries showed a certain expansion while the sales offices were closed down. One Norwegian company for landtransports and two new West-German companies were acquired As for airfreight, four European new subsidiaries were added over the period. The organization went through several reorganizations leading first to an increase and then a decrease in the importance of international activities. Large investments were made in communication systems.

5.1.2.1 Specific event - Start of cooperation with an agent in Switzerland

Natural was one of ASG's first agents for international traffics. The cooperation between the two companies started in 1946 and is still developing. It has been important for ASG's international development over its duration.

<u>Before the event</u>
Natural S.A. is an old international company, established by E. Natural in Geneva in 1859 . Very shortly thereafter the Head Office moved to Basel due to that city´s strategic position in Switzerland as well as in Europe. Natural were mainly shipping agents and international sea-freight forwarders at that time, utilizing the river Rhein as an important gateway. The importance of the river for transports diminished, however, as new railroads were constructed in Europe during the 19th century (the first railway in the Basel area dates from 1844). As a result of this, Natural diversified into railway transportation. Over time Natural grew and became strong in railway as well as sea-transports.

In 1946 after the war, the manager and owner of Natural wanted the company to develop strong traffics to/from Sweden. Natural had several existing relations in Sweden for shipping, with Svea in Gothenburg, Hillerström & Co in Malmö, United Forwarding and Shipping Agencies in Stockholm (connected to Svea), etc., which had been developed after the first world war. Natural also had a small representative office in Sweden but what they now wanted to confine themselves to was one agent. A dependable and active agent was very important for them since a large number of Swiss firms were selling f.o.b. Swiss border.

In search of an agent, they contacted their existing relations in Sweden and through these contacts they came up with two alternatives of interest. One was ASG, partly owned by Svea. As we know, ASG had been established originally to act as a complementary surface transport company for Svea and, as such, had created an extensive network of domestic traffics in Sweden. It was also by that time 50% owned by the Swedish railways. The other alternative was a shipping agent and international forwarder Wilson & Co, which already had a well-known established agent, Danzas, in Switzerland. Wilson wanted to change agent in Switzerland due to certain conflicts between the companies during the war .

The negotiations between ASG and Natural started in 1945 and lasted half a year. During that period ASG took over the domestic railway consolidation business from Transportkompaniet in Sweden as well as the established traffics to Denmark and Norway.

ASG wanted to develop a fixed price concept with Natural for the total transport including all special charges and it also wanted to become Natural's exclusive agent.

The event

The first layout of an agreement was made in the form of an agreement between United Forwarding and Shipping Agencies (Svea), ASG and Natural.

In April 1946, the final agreement was signed by the two parties ASG and Natural only. They agreed to start a common railway consolidation traffic between Switzerland and Sweden on an exclusive basis, using their existing to/from traffic resources and by mobilizing new resources. Natural's representative in Stockholm (Mr Burri) was sent back to Switzerland and the cooperations with all the other agents were cancelled as a result of the agreement. What ASG-Natural presented to customers was a fixed all-inclusive price for the whole distance, which offered the possibility of quoting door-to-door prices.

After the event

The development of the traffic was very positive, which to a certain extent was due to the high general increase in the trade between Sweden and Switzerland but also as a result of the new way in which the service was marketed and organized. The successful development of the railway consolidation, however, created counter-actions among competitors. The competitors claimed that ASG-Natural had subsidized certain parts of the transports. The formation of joint ventures by their competitors was one form of such counter-action. The new joint ventures were given advantageous freight prices by the subcontractors. This gave ASG and Natural a difficult time and forced them to develop an increasing number of direct rail traffics to different destinations in Sweden.

In 1948-49 long-hauling by truck became permitted in Europe and ASG and Natural wanted to complement their services with trucking services. This was important, especially as trucking services became very competitive since it became possible to collect and distribute partloads directly to/from the customer without extra costs.

The very success of the railway consolidation traffic became a drawback when ASG-Natural wanted to start a trucking traffic. The Swedish Railway(SJ) did not allow its partly owned company ASG to get the rights to start international trucking services until the competition had grown strong. When they eventually got the permission, several of their direct traffics did not exist any longer as a result of loss of volumes. ASG had no wish to stop the railway consolidation services even after they had begun trucking services and in the end the railway services remaining had to be supported by the trucking services. The first Swedish registered lorry in Switzerland after the war was a result of their common traffic. Ever since ASG-Natural initiated their trucking services, the services have dominated the traffic between Sweden and Switzerland.

During the first years of cooperation, ASG and Natural had extensive inter-changes of people selling the common traffics and especially so when new traffics were to be started. The inter-changes subsequently became less frequent and more regulated which was also interpreted as a sign of a higher degree of mutual understanding. In a speech given at the celebration of the 25th year of the cooperation (1971) a director of Natural argued that it was important for the two parties to discuss common policy and planning as well as to continue the coordination between the two companies. The top management from both sides were present during this conference.

Over the years ASG and Natural have developed an assortment of different complementary products to offer customers in both countries and this has increased their cooperation. For a long time and until recently, ASG-Natural have had the largest market-share of the exchange of goods between Sweden and Switzerland. At the end of 1989 they had regular traffics to/from 4 Swedish destinations. They have offered heavy goods transports, project transports, full loads, warehousing, etc. The means of transportation varied but combi-transports had become very important.

During this period of cooperation both ASG and Natural have had an intensive period of international development in other areas as well as in other countries. This international development has in some cases increased the degree of cooperation between the two companies, e.g.in Norway and Finland where ASG has daughter companies with which Natural has a cooperation and in Portugal where ASG works with a sister company to Natural. In Norway and Finland Natural became the agent after ASG had changed to fully owned subsidiaries while Portugal had another history. When ASG needed an agent in Portugal they called Natural, which had been very strong in the traffics on Portugal since the war, and asked them as to their view about possible agents. Natural recommended its own sister company which ASG started to work with and this new Portuguese traffic has been a success for ASG. Natural and ASG do not have the same agents anywhere in Europe apart from Norway, Finland and Portugal[1].

In certain cases this situation has caused an increasing degree of conflict between the partners. Some of the services added by each of the partners during this period did not necessarily develop in step or along identical lines, which led to demands which the other company could not live up to. This often caused someone else in Sweden or Switzerland to be selected as the partner with whom to work, in airfreight for instance. Partly as a result of this and except for a short period, ASG and Natural have been competitors in airfreight. This causes problems, especially as ASG has been part-owner of a small airfreight company since 1990 named ASG. Similar problems are caused by their international development outside their common cooperation forming an international image and the priority that they have put into the different areas.

A smaller conflict developed due to a decrease in the basic geographical area within which ASG and Natural had agreed to work. This was a result of the fact that ASG had chosen another company as their partner for a small but distant part of Switzerland without informing Natural .

The cooperation between the two companies reached a low point and experienced many difficulties because of the many changes in personnel following a reorganization in ASG. From an operations viewpoint, it has changed to the better which facilitates the understanding between the two companies. The establishment of the traffic planning office in Travemünde has increased the operational contacts between Natural and ASG. The office in Travemünde coordinates most transports for continental Europe for ASG but also checks the conditions of the trucks and material utilized.

Another problem as regards to competition that they met with, at the end of the period under study, arose from the merger of Scansped and Bilspedition International, involving all formerly competing international companies like Wilson &Co, Skandiatransport, Fallenius& Leffler, TransportKompaniet and Autotransit. This merger made Scansped very large in resources in Switzerland though Scansped still had many problems to solve towards the end of 1989 with regard to personnel, customers, etc. On the other hand, this merger caused Danzas, the agent of Wilson & Co until 1988, to buy part of a Swedish forwarding company, Rationell Spedition, which in turn has heightened the competition in respect of export/import goods Sweden-Switzerland.

---

[1] In 1991 Natural changed from Lassen in Portugal which was a sister company. As for ASG Lassen remained their agent in Portugal.

Summary of the event

Natural, an old established European forwarder and shipping agent, wished to develop strong traffics to/from Sweden. Through their existing contacts with Svea shipping line they came in contact with ASG. The cooperation with ASG started in 1946 after half a year of negotiations and the sales representative of Natural was withdrawn to Switzerland. The first traffic was by railway and more direct railway traffics were added shortly. Over time the services changed. Railway services decreased, road traffics increased and several other services were added such as warehousing, logistical services, airfreight, etc. ASG also started to cooperate with Natural´s sister in Portugal, Natural used the ASG part-owned company in Finland and as ASG had acquired a company in Norway, Natural started to cooperate with them.

5.1.2.2. Specific event - ASG´s establishment of a holding company, ASG (Deutschland), in West-Germany

ASG Hamburg is the oldest operating foreign subsidiary for land-transportation in ASG.
The subsidiary in Hamburg, and later on the development of ASG (Deutschland), including Atege Stuttgart, has had an important influence on the international development of ASG in Continental Europe. Therefore the start and growth of ASG Hamburg, as well as the acquisition of Atege Stuttgart, are of interest when discussing the internationalization of ASG in Europe. In 1976, ASG Hamburg for practical reasons changed name to ASG (Deutschland) and came to include a few other West-German companies and, as such, was regarded as a holding company in West-Germany, with ASG Hamburg as a base.

 Before the event

After the war, Mr H. Andresen was one of the first persons in Hamburg to start a small company "H.C.Andresen" for international transports. By 1950, the firm had already established contacts in Sweden, Denmark, Holland and Belgium. During this period Mr H.Andresen met people from ASG for the first time. ASG only had a railway traffic to/from Hamburg, together with an agent ,Wendschlag & Pohl. In 1956, ASG was about to establish international trucking traffic to/from Hamburg as well as for other parts of Europe and they needed an agent in Hamburg and a contact point for their total international trucking traffics. The firm of H.C. Andresen provided the answer to their needs and started as to represent ASG in 1957. This agreement only concerned trucking services and did not affect ASG's relationship with Wendschlag & Pohl who were specialized in railway and sea transports.
The operational center for ASG in international trucking services was Norrköping in 1957. In the beginning they had to co-load with a traffic Holland-Sweden (twice a week) since volumes were too small to utilize a full truck. In the two years, the development was rather slow. Then it

changed very quickly, due to more intensive marketing both in Sweden and in Germany. In ASG in Sweden the organization changed in 1958 so that Helsingborg became the center for international trucking transports instead of Norrköping.

A few customers having regular and quite large volumes came to be very important in the attempts to establish a traffic from Hamburg to Sweden. These were Nordmende in Bremen which sold tv-sets to Sweden and a papermill Feldmühle AG. They are both still customers of ASG. The cooperation between Sweden and Hamburg was very close during this period and the company H.C.Andresen became totally concentrated on the transports with ASG. New facilities were needed - instead of the furnished old bus (without wheels) that served as a terminal and an apartment serving as office in a partly burnt-out house!

The event and after the event - in Hamburg

The Scandinavian traffics developed very quickly and as H. Andresen was in need of more capital ASG took over the more important segments of the company in the beginning of 1960 but the company continued to exist a couple of years. Mr H. Andresen became the new manager and stayed on as such for more than 20 years. ASG, Hamburg was registered as a company in the official Hamburg register at that time and in the same year became a member of the Forwarders' Association in Hamburg.

During this period the railway traffic as well as the cooperation between ASG and Wendschlag & Pohl would appear to have ceased.

As Hamburg was a strategic point for the traffics to/from Sweden and large parts of Europe but especially so for West-Germany, ASG Hamburg had to organize certain domestic traffics in order to take care of transit consignments to other parts of Germany. These traffics could be to/from areas in Germany outside the specified area that ASG Hamburg was supposed to cover for ASG Sweden. This caused complaints from the agents with whom ASG had agreements in the areas concerned.

The area that ASG Hamburg should cover in terms of marketing and traffics was Schleswig-Holstein, Hamburg area and a part of Niedersachsen. To the south and east of this area ASG Sweden was represented by other agents. This restricted the possibilities for ASG Hamburg to develop new traffics. Even within this area there were and there still are other agents representing different types of transports where ASG Hamburg lacks the necessary expertise, such as special transports by railway and airfreight. During a period in 1972 ASG Sweden had its own sales representation in the area through E. Westling. When the sales representation office moved to Brussels and became the European Sales Representation, the representation in Hamburg closed down. In most cases, the sales representative was selling together with the agent for the local area.

Through special agreements with different customers ASG, Hamburg extended the borders of its territory as in the case of Gambro, for which ASG Hamburg started a small office and warehouse in Hechingen in order to store their goods and distribute them to different hospitals, etc., in Germany.

The conflicts between the parent company´s agents in West- Germany as well as between ASG Hamburg and its agents have been many over the years. Some agents have suspected ASG of taking their business or getting confidential information about them from head office in Stockholm through the sales representation and the subsidiaries. On the other hand, the agents have on their side developed into other spheres both in Germany and internationally and most cases Sweden constitutes only about 10-20% of their total business. Further, the conflicts are enhanced with the German agents as some customers prefer to use ASG Hamburg and use their domestic traffics to Hamburg and from there onwards the international traffics to Sweden. ASG Hamburg has a higher frequency and direct traffics to more places in Sweden which gives it an advantage. Another complication is the takeover of ERT, a former competitor of ASG's, specializing in trailer traffics to different parts of Europe. ERT were competing and still are to a small extent with ASG Hamburg even though nowadays they also help each other. The manager of ASG Hamburg (J. Andresen) is today also the manager of ERT Germany as well as being a member of the Board of Atege Stuttgart, ASG Belgium and ASG Bielefeld.

ASG in Hamburg was totally concentrated on trucking traffics to/from Sweden during the first ten years. Their cooperation with Sweden was so intensive that the manager in Hamburg even learnt to speak Swedish! They struggled all the time to increase the frequency so as finally to be able to offer daily traffic but they did not get the volume of goods necessary until an agreement was signed with Siemens in Germany in 1965, to transport all their exports for Sweden which before had been transported by sea. ASG Hamburg increased immensely its market-share of the total amount of goods that were trucked between Sweden and Northern parts of Germany. The number of places to which they had direct traffics also increased during this period due to the increase in volumes. In 1966, the turnover of ASG Hamburg was DM 1.2 million and the number of consignments handled was 21,524. This can be compared to the size of ASG (Deutschland) GmbH 1990 with a net turnover of around DM 100 million and 225,000 consignments.

To begin with, the development came as a result of better and more frequent services mainly to/from their own area to Sweden or domestically. They expanded within their area either via larger distribution systems or through the establishment of new offices. One important expansion in 1975 was the office in Travemunde for customs clearance which had previously been handled by Schenker. Shortly after ERT became part of the ASG Group the Travemunde office could handle their customs clearance as well (In 1981, 24,000 trucks were custom-cleared).

ASG Hamburg did not have the possibility of developing any international traffics until the 1970's following which the number of international traffics increased steadily. Today they have established traffics to/from many countries like Italy, Norway, Denmark, Holland, Belgium, Switzerland, etc. ASG Hamburg's agents have changed over time. In Denmark , however, they have, used the same as ASG, TK Nord, for 20 years. In Norway they started with a company Linjegods and then changed to Nortrail in 1985 when ASG changed agent to Nordex. ASG Hamburg then changed to ASG Norway a period after its establishment. In Finland ASG Hamburg has worked with Maaja Meeri for many years but has recently changed over to Teamtrans. In Holland they had an agreement previously with van Gend & Loos, the same agent as ASG used, but when van Gend & Loos was bought by Nedlloyd the agreement ceased. Nedlloyd had their own company in Germany (Uniontransport). At the end of 1980´s ASG Hamburg got an agreement in Holland with Beijer belonging to the Belgian transport company Ziegler instead. In Italy the agent is the same as ASG Sweden's agent. In Belgium, in addition to ERT, they use Gonrand, part of the Gonrand Group. In Switzerland, Berger is their agent and not ASG Sweden's agent, Natural, which already had an agent in the Hamburg area.

The event and after the event - acquiring an agent in Stuttgart

On account of the ill-health of the owner of the agent Atege Stuttgart, ASG acquired the company in 1976. As it so happened, ASG had another agent in West-Germany with the name of Atege but it was not under the same ownership.

For practical reasons, Atege Stuttgart became owned through ASG Hamburg. ASG Hamburg had to change its form to that of a holding company and its name to ASG (Deutschland) GmbH. Important questions concerning Atege Stuttgart were discussed, however, directly with the head office in Stockholm. Traditionally, Atege Stuttgart offered a number of different services to those offered by ASG Hamburg.

Atege's development in international transportation in Europe, which included long and close connections to the well known Swiss families, Gonrand and Girard, dates back to the late 19th century. The Gonrand family owned one of the largest transport companies in Europe before the second world war. Atege Stuttgart was sold to a Mr Vogelsang during the war.

Atege Stuttgart's first connections with Sweden and the Scandinavian countries came after the war in the beginning of the 1950's. At that time Atege Stuttgart concentrated to a large extent on railway traffics and had also started to develop airfreight. Sweden became a very important market for Atege Stuttgart at an early stage and in 1959 Sweden accounted for about 25 % of its total turnover.

While ASG Hamburg concentrated on Scandinavia and trucking traffics in the beginning, Atege Stuttgart started with railway traffics to Switzerland, Italy, etc., as a part of an international transport Group. Atege added trucking traffics later on.

In 1990 Atege Stuttgart, like ASG Hamburg, had many international traffics (see Apppendix 3) and they had its own agents for those traffics which were not the same as those of ASG Hamburg. Furthermore it expanded its area of representation in West-Germany. In 1980, however, it decided to discontinue its traditional domestic services and, in a separate company, started a carrier service for trailers, flats and containers in the international traffics. The new company has developed positively. By the end of 1989 airfreight had become a very important business for them and even though it did not cooperate with other parts of ASG in airfreight, it wished to do so in the future.

In 1987, ASG in Sweden established a company at Bielefeld, through acquiring the assets of the agent , Linie, in Bielefeld. This company is formally organized under ASG (Deutschland) GmbH. When Linie experienced its economic problems, its former agents in Sweden, SKT, changed to another agent, H. Boes, and ASG took over.

Both ASG Bielefeld and Atege Stuttgart have continued their own international traffics and their own agents which only corresponded to a certain extent with those of ASG Hamburg. For Atege Stuttgart ,the agents in Sweden, Italy and Denmark were the same as for ASG in Sweden and Hamburg. In all other places they were working with competitors to the agents of ASG Sweden as, for instance, in Finland, France, Austria and Benelux and also for airfreight the agents are different. ASG Bielefeld on the other hand used ASG in Norway and Sweden as representatives and used the same agents in Italy and Switzerland as Sweden and to an extent in Finland. In other places the agents are not the same as those of ASG in Hamburg and Atege in Stuttgart.

ASG Hamburg, as Atege Stuttgart, have expanded over time into more complex and combined services like hanging garment transports, sea transports, warehousing, including bookkeeping of the products, invoicing, etc., in combination with distributing products to many places within West-Germany as well as abroad. Different destinations can be reached in many different ways, like combi-traffic system using flats, trailers, containers by railway, trucks, ships, barges, etc.

In 1990, Atege Stuttgart, ASG in Hamburg as well as ASG Bielefeld complement each other in many different activities and they have developed a number of international traffics to countries other than Sweden. All this has meant a decreasing share of the Scandinavian business for ASG Hamburg. Sweden traffics have never held such a predominant position for Atege Stuttgart (at maximum 25%) as it has for ASG Hamburg.

The expansion of ASG Hamburg and Atege Stuttgart has resulted in that they have outgrown their terminals over time. The third terminal of ASG Hamburg lasted until 1978 but had to be complemented with other facilities within the area. The terminal in 1990 is built for and owned by ASG with quite large warehousing space. Atege Stutgart also got new facitlites during 1980´s. In addition, over the years ASG has rented warehousing facilities for specific customers. The number of offices in Germany has increased to 9, located in Hamburg, Travemünde, Hechingen, Villingen, Stuttgart, Bielefeld, Ludwigsburg, Hechingen and Rostock.

(In 1991, there was an exchange of shares between ASG (Deutschland) and Atege, the largest agent, giving ASG 30% in Atege and Atege 30% in ASG (Deutschland) GmbH. Atege belongs to a large international transport group called Gondrand. The two other agents in Germany still remain unchanged.)

Summary of the event

ASG wanted to start trucking traffics to/ from Hamburg and to have a support office for other European traffics. HCA became the agent and developed successfully with ASG during late 1950´s. In 1960 ASG Hamburg was established. The managing director and owner of the agent became the manager of the new company. ASG Hamburg expanded over time both in services, in its area of representation in West-Germany and internationally. This caused several conflicts with the existing agents in West-Germany. As ASG acquired Atege Stuttgart, which was an agent to ASG, in 1976 their coverage of West-Germany increased and so did the international traffics to/ from Germany. A holding comany was created in West-Germany with ASG Hamburg as a base. In the late 1980´s another company was acquired in Bielefeld which added to the existing expansion in Germany.

5.1.2.3 Specific event - a greenfield investment in Belgium

Before the event

In the beginning of the 1950s ASG obtained an order from SAS to arrange for the transport of airplane engines from Derby in England to SAS in Sweden.

The transports were supposed to go via Tilbury and Antwerp and on from there to Sweden by truck. To undertake this assignment, ASG needed an agent in Antwerp capable of taking care of the motors on arrival by sea and loading them onto trucks for transport to Sweden. An approach was made to AMA (Agence Maritime Anversoise S.A.), a shipping agent, broker and forwarder who showed interest, although having no experience in trucking services. However, the fact that AMA had an employee (Mr Meier) who had been handling SAS transports from Denmark contributed to the selection of AMA as agent .

Since AMA as a company lacked experience in trucking services they needed a lot of in-put from ASG in organizing their part of the traffic, even to the extent that ASG set the pricing terms. These transports subsequently became the base for the Swedish-Belgian traffic, which developed positively and in due course became very important for AMA.

AMA was also very active in marketing the normal traffic for many years, both in Belgium and in Sweden. The CEO (Chief Executive Officer) and owner of AMA (Ver Holst) had excellent relations with Belgian industry.

For personal reasons, Mr Ver Holst sold the company to the Pluvier Group, although he continued as a CEO of AMA. This gave no reason for ASG to make any changes in the relationship at the time. However, after a few years, certain key persons, like Mr Meier and the sales manager, left AMA and with that AMA´s in interest developing the common traffic with ASG decreased.

Mr Meier joined a competitor (West-Friesland) and wanted ASG to start a cooperation with them. ASG declined, preferring to continue with the then twenty year-old cooperation with AMA.

Although ASG had already had an earlier offer to buy AMA, the Pluvier Group subsequently sold AMA to United Transport Corp, which also owned West-Friesland. West-Friesland also cooperated with TK(Transport Kompaniet) in Sweden.

It was then that the situation in Belgium changed negatively for the Sweden-Belgium traffic and those engaged in the Sweden-Belgium traffic in AMA became very concerned. The new CEO of AMA was also the Chairman of the Board in West-Friesland, the biggest competitor. This was when the stage was set for a change.

The event

In 1976, ASG realized that the situation in Belgium had to change. The traffic that AMA and ASG had together could not possibly continue to develop under the conditions that existed. Personnel in AMA engaged in the Swedish traffic contacted the ASG European Representation Office in Brussels and asked for help. ASG tried to find a solution, looking at the different alternatives such as buying a local company, setting up its own office or finding another agent. To continue with AMA did not seem possible.

In 1977, ASG set up a company of its own and at the same time took over some of the personnel in AMA responsible for the Swedish traffic. In order to get the company operational at very short notice ASG decided to let Gyssens & Co buy a share of the future ASG Belgium. Gyssens & Co, in the main a small airfreight company, had office space available in the right place. The only possibility to start without giving the agent the chance to break the relationship and inform the customers before the new company was ready to operate was to use existing available facilities.

During the period of negotiations with Dr Gyssens, the owner of Gyssens & Co and an active member of FIATA, ASG came in contact with Edmond Depaire SA which was a big transport company in Belgium. Edmond Depaire SA was partly owned by the Belgian Railway and partly by Van Gend und Loos which, in turn, was a Dutch railway-owned company as well as ASG's agent. Both Dr Gyssens and the management of Edmond Depaire insisted of being partners in the future ASG Belgium SA. The result was that ASG got 76 % of the shares. Gyssens & Co and Edmond Depaire got 12 % each. It was important for ASG to have a shareholding as high as 76% in order to have full control over the new company.

Most of the negotiations in Belgium were undertaken by the manager of the ASG European Representative Office (E. Westling). Mr Westling also became a member of the Board and took on some AMA management responsibilities. This did not mean though that his activities at the European representative Office were altered.

The company started its activities over-night, as planned, in order to prevent the agent from taking immediate counter-measures. At the same time a marketing campaign started in Sweden as well as in Belgium to inform customers of the new order and of the new possibilities for transportation between Sweden and Belgium. During the first months ASG Sweden provided the new ASG Belgium with a lot of marketing support by sending down salesmen, making brochures and pamphlets, designing administrative systems and traffic systems, etc. To a very large extent the customers seem to have remained loyal to ASG. Some of them had been with ASG and AMA since the 1950's and were very pleased with the new arrangements. AMA sued ASG for breaking the contract; ASG lost the case being fined some SEK 30,000-40,000.

ASG Belgium was supposed to continue the existing Swedish-Belgium traffic as before which it seem to have done. There were terminal facilities available both in Brussels and in Antwerp from the outset and the trucking companies, being mainly subcontractors to ASG, stayed with the new company.

The company returned a small first year's profit as a result of all these activities.

 After the event

After a period of support from Sweden, problems came very quickly upon the company which seemed unable to manage all the activities according to the terms set by the head office in Sweden. The terminals were too costly for the size of the traffic and the management did not work out quite as expected. In 1979/80, the manager of the European Representative Office also had to take on the role of CEO of the Belgium company but this double role was not satisfactory either for the company or for the Representative Office. The latter closed down in 1982. The company did not develop as expected when it came to volumes or profitability and the terminal and office in Brussels had to be closed on account of the high cost. After a few years, Dr Gyssens ran into problems and could not remain a shareholder in the company.

Edmond Depaire SA also sold its shares in the company to ASG a few years after. The company was totally dependent on ASG in Sweden, both trafficwise and for sales and administration. Another complication was that the Managing Director of the company became very ill and, in spite of several attempts to continue as normal, finally had to leave.

ASG Sweden also required activities to be done in a certain way which led to an increased workload. In many ways it seemed that ASG Belgium was supposed to mirror ASG Sweden. To begin with head office in Stockholm provided the personnel to solve the problems in ASG Belgium but later on many of such personnel came from other ASG subsidiaries. Apart from the management problems, ASG Belgium experienced problems with a computerized system for administration and traffic that they tried to develop. This became an expensive experience for such a small company, which finally led to further changes in staff.

In the first year, ASG Belgium concentrated on the traffic to/from Sweden. They also expanded the number of direct traffics to Sweden in comparison to what AMA had achieved. After that, they started to develop traffic to/from Denmark, Finland and Norway. Even though ASG Sweden was still the dominant partner, the resources were split among several activities.

In establishing other Scandinavian traffics, ASG Belgium tried to work with ASG Sweden's partners in other Nordic countries. This succeeded in Norway and Finland to begin with, but not in Denmark since the Danish partner already had an agent in Belgium to begin with. However, after a couple of years ASG Sweden's Danish agent started cooperating with ASG Belgium. On the other hand, as ASG had to leave its partner Linjegods in Norway, Atege Stuttgart, ASG Hamburg and ASG Belgium also had to look for a new Norwegian partner. The new agent was not the same agent as that of ASG Sweden.

Over time, the Board of the company also changed, resulting partly from the changes in ownership and partly from a change in priorities in ASG Sweden. To start with, the ASG persons responsible for the Continental traffic and the finance director were members of the Board, then also the managers of ASG's subsidiaries in Hamburg and Stuttgart. In 1985, a change in management in ASG Sweden led to another change in the Board of ASG Belgium, the new manager for Continental Europe and another employee from that Division becoming the new members.

Over the years, the company in Belgium has tried to establish different traffics together with other ASG subsidiaries in Europe without much success. By 1990 the company was still very small, with limited resources and the profile of being a Scandinavian specialist. Partly for that reason the ASG subsidiaries in Hamburg and Stuttgart, both having traffic on Belgium, did not cooperate with ASG Belgium.

Further, ASG sea-freight agent in Belgium has been acquired by a competitor, the Nedlloyd Group. This has caused certain complications.

The shareholders capital had to be raised several times during the period, as a result of the low starting capital as well as the losses along the way. By 1990, the Company seemed to have stabilized and was profitable but at a low level.

Belgium as such will increase in importance, with the development of EC and this will probably lead to further changes in the role of ASG Belgium. The Company was owned via ASG (Deutschland) for a while but is now owned via ASG International B.V., the holding company in Holland.

Summary of the event

ASG started a trucking traffic to/from Belgium with Ama as an agent in 1954. Over time ASG and Ama developed more trucking traffics and other complementary services. After a period Ama was sold to the Pluvier group. However, ASG continued the cooperation. In the mid 1970´s, however, the Pluvier group was sold to another large transport group, United Transport, having competing traffics to that of Ama and ASG. Then ASG made a greenfield investment in Belgium in 1977 and took over certain Ama personnel. Gyssens & Co and E. Depaire became part owners in ASG Belgium. A few years later the company became a fully owned ASG company. The company had in 1990 developed international traffics to the Nordic countries but was still rather small and several attempts to develop further had been disappointing.

5.1.3. Overseas development

Overseas in this context is regarded as the world outside Europe, mainly reached by sea and air. Traditionally within ASG responsibility for the overseas markets has been assigned to the air and sea departments within the organization. The development of ASG airfreight and sea-freight development will be described below and now and then the description will also in detail include changes in European activities.

Period 1955-69

Development of services

As the international development, especially in railway consolidation, had been very successful, ASG declared it intention of becoming " a travel agency for goods", which made it open to international development in other areas.

As regards sea-freight, ASG had been connected to sea-freight via the owners from the outset, but this was basically in terms of inland service with some forwarding activities. Sea-freight services were seen as a complementary services to Svea Shipping Line and as such they continued to live a rather quiet and half forgotten life without any support within the organization until the 1960's.

Airfreight also started as a complementary services, with infrequent transports, but the business was young and the development became more intensive.

As industry expanded and its utilization of production capacity was high the interest for faster means of transportation including airfreight increased. Airfreight was mainly used in the beginning for emergency consignments as a result of temporary capacity problems or lack of goods in stock.

ASG really started to get into airfreight when it opened a small office at Bromma international airport in 1954. Before that not much progress seems to have been made, even though ASG had an agreement with SAS, being an agent for the Stockholm area. Even so, in 1955 the small office handled 2980 import consignments and 1139 export consignments. A person from ABA (one of the forerunners to SAS) was employed to start the business. In terms of the traditional IATA (International Air Transport Association)[1] agent agreements with the airlines, ASG received a 5% commission on the freight sum of goods but other important sources of revenue were handling and documentation fees. Cargo was normally only a complementary service to passenger flights as far as the airlines were concerned.

In the beginning of the 1950's, there was really no competition between seafreight and airfreight apart from the fact that in many cases these were the only possibilities of reaching the majority of overseas markets.

In 1959, ASG signed an agreement with a large international American airfreight company Emery. This started not only the first consolidation services in ASG airfreight but also the first regular services with time guarantees. Through Emery, ASG could offer delivery within 48 hours in their consolidation services to/from U.S.A. and Canada.

Another type of airfreight service was developed in 1961 when ASG started a regular full charter of flowers from the French Riviera to Stockholm, Gothenburg and Malmö. ASG had special forwarding agents on the French and Italian Riviera for that specific flower charter traffic.

During the 1960's, the airfreight to/from Sweden continued to grow evenly but at a relatively high pace from 13.000 tons to 40.000 tons (Comén, 1986) and this was partly due to the fact that a new category of goods was transported. These were perishables, in the physical as well as the economic sense. This continued growth created many new traffics for ASG and volume increased. It also created capacity problems for the airlines as regards terminals, handling equipment, etc. Many airports experienced problems with congestion. Furthermore, the fact that airfreight was a complementary service for the airlines enhanced the crisis, since the

---

[1] A voluntary organization for scheduled airlines.

passenger services received priority. This situation, in combination with the growing interest in logistics in the industry, made ASG start its own consolidation traffics.

The rate-structure of the airlines was very complicated and was based on the value of the goods and sometimes of the economic conditions for certain types of goods. In this rate structure, consolidation units were not specifically advantageous for agents in spite of the fact that they facilitated handling for the airlines. The increased control of the goods and the increasing possibilities to create door-to-door transports, however, still made consolidation attractive enough to continue. Adherence to the development of consolidation traffic created a need for more active marketing activities both by ASG and by the agents.

In the mid 1960's, the first regular sea-freight services were established in ASG and these were trailer and container traffics to/from the U.K and the USA.

The large change for ASG sea-freight came in 1968 when Rego, consisting of four large shipping lines (Broström, Svenska Lloyd, Transatlantic and Johnson Line) bought 25% of ASG. This was basically a result of containerization and other new techniques (trailers, flats etc) which made an integration between inland and sea-transports necessary. These new techniques also made it easier for a forwarder or broker with a large breadth of international experience and an inland organization, like ASG, to start their own consolidation traffics which offered new economic terms and a possibility to create door-to-door traffics.

Certain policy problems arose, however, since Rego wanted ASG to give priority to their services while ASG wanted to remain neutral. At the same time, the shipping lines represented by the owners did not want to favour ASG ahead of other sea-freight forwarders who were their customers. Much discussion took place in setting the policies in order not to disturb the market.

The sea-freight services that ASG offered at the end of the period were consolidation and full containers and to a limited degree traditional sea-freight services, with USA, Canada and UK as the most important markets.

Representation in foreign countries
The representation abroad in sea-freight was very loosely structured in the beginning. As the traditional receiving broker or despatching forwarder, ASG only had a corresponding agent, used for specific purposes. In a normal situation, the exporting forwarder took no responsibility for the shipment after it had been accepted by the shipping company. The shipping lines played the predominant role at that time. By the end the 1960's though, as ASG started its own traffics, the establishment of cooperating agents became necessary in USA, Canada and in the UK. The idea was to create door-to-door transports also for transports by sea. In search of suitable agents, ASG sea-freight used existing contacts with the shipping lines, the corresponding agents and agents of ASG airfreight or European traffics.

In the same way, in airfreight the connections to different agents abroad was very loosely structured in the beginning. However, ASG needed agents to take care of the goods in the receiving or despatching country. Since emergency goods were often paid for by the receiver it was important that these agents had economic stability in addition to having sales and the traditional forwarding and distributional function. To begin with during the 1950's and 1960's ASG airfreight used existing agents for the surface transports (rail, road and sea). Gradually there was a change towards a new type of agent specialized in airfreight.

A first crucial change came as a result of the cooperation with Emery Airfreight in 1959. The cooperation with Emery, as an exclusive agent for Scandinavia, became very important for ASG as an airfreight forwarder. It gave ASG an opportunity to be very strong on the US market which was one of the most important markets for the Swedish customers. At the same time, the high quality services that Emery offered with a 48 hour guarantee put high demands on the ASG organization also.

During the same period in 1959/60 Linjeflyg, the dominating domestic airline of Sweden, and ASG started a cooperation. ASG was appointed handling agent at all domestic airports and was supposed to collect and distribute all international consignments for Linjeflyg in Sweden as well as between Copenhagen and Ängelholm. As a result of these agreements, ASG set up an office in Copenhagen in order to solve local handling and transfer problems. In Sweden, ASG started separate airfreight distribution and collecting systems to be able to keep the guaranteed time-table. The Copenhagen office became very important for ASG when negotiating with the airlines and agents.

The combination of the cooperation with Emery and Linjeflyg gave ASG a possibility to create specialized inland transports for airfreight.

The establishment of the joint-venture in the Far East with Schenker in 1961 also came to be very important and created a certain stability for ASG in its representation abroad. As the joint venture with Schenker meant the establishment of more offices in the Far East , ASG built up an even better coverage of the Far East over time. Through the cooperation with Schenker, ASG also obtained access to many other Schenker offices and agents throughout the world. At that time, ASG even had discussions with Schenker regarding establishing a more widespread cooperation for land-transports in Europe as well as Schenker-ASG offices all over the world (outside Europe).

One of the important connections developed during the 1960's through Schenker was the cooperation with Nippon Express in Japan and another example was Lee & Muirhead in India. The existence of the joint venture with a large organization like Schenker made ASG quite strong in the Far East.

Organization and investments

 As a result of the Emery and Linjeflyg cooperation, a separate department for airfreight was created head office in 1960.

The 1960's became an important period for ASG airfreight, since many crucial investments were made in airport offices in Sweden and Denmark, airfreight trucking distribution started, the joint venture with Schenker in Hong Kong was established, etc.

The first investments in sea-freight came in 1966 when a separate department was created for the new U.K./USA unit traffics. Special marketing campaigns were formulated in order to increase the growth of sea-freight and a new office was opened in Gothenburg. As airfreight increased in ASG the differences in demands on speed, size and value of the consignments created difficulties in the ASG organization, which was accustomed to road and rail transports. By the end of the 1960's ASG began to invest in terminals, in better know-how, in operations and in marketing.

The development of larger and faster ships and planes increased the volumes handled and the speed of carriage and this in turn put pressure on handling and transports on land. This worked to the benefit of forwarders with terminals and office space close to harbours and airports.

Summary of the period 1955-69

During this period of growth, airfreight as well as seafreight became established among ASG services. In 1954 ASG set up an airfreight office at Bromma, which became the official starting point for airfreight development. In 1959/60 two important agreements were made, an agent agreement with Emery in U.S. and a handling agent agreement with the Swedish domestic airline, Linjeflyg. Further, ASG also established an airfreight office in Copenhagen in 1960 and a joint venture together with Schenker in HongKong in 1961. This intensified the development for large parts of the Far East. New agent cooperations were established in Japan and India. The existing European landtransport agents were often used for airfreight. As the airlines experienced capacity problems and agents became increasingly important for the creation of effective transports for ASG.

The first regular international seafreight traffics were established in the mid 1960´s to/ from U.K. Shortly afterwards new container traffics were established to U.S. and Canada. The shipping lines of Rego, being the new owners of ASG, facilitated this development. Investments were made in new terminals and new offices for air and seafreight. Specialized domestic transport services for airfreight were set up and separate departments were established at head office.

<u>Period 1970-79</u>

Development of services

The continued growth of the 1960's and then the need for improved fuel economies during the 1970's led to airlines investing in larger and faster airplanes like jumbo jets and eventually these investments created an over-capacity. This over-capacity changed the situation not only for the airlines but also for the IATA agents and forwarders like ASG. The airlines became more open to change in their rate-structure, at least unofficially, and were prepared to offer discounts in order to utilize their over-capacity. As a result of the lower prices, new categories of non-perishable, planned and non emergency type goods were taken over by airfreight. To begin with, new rates did not seem to ameliorate the terms for consolidations, as such, but the advantage of consolidation traffics was the control over larger volumes which normally gave favourable rates. As containerization then developed in airfreight, consolidation became a more accepted service by the airlines and the rate structure took full containers and consolidation into account, increasing the competition between air and sea-freight as a result.

During the 1970's the number of traffics to overseas countries increased both for air and sea-freight. Even though it had become possible to establish unit load traffics in many of those countries, in others it was either not possible or it was not preferable depending on the type of goods. Therefore part of the sea-freight was still traditional forwarding and brokerage and in the same way part of the airfreight continued to be direct airline goods.

When sea and airfreight container traffics became more common, the new demands on communication, handling and inland transportation made it necessary to choose agents having suitable facilities, know-how of the new type of traffics as well as marketing capabilities.

During the 1970's airfreight was evolving into different types of services such as split charter, part and full charter which were combined land-transports and airfreight services. The goods were trucked to/from some larger European airport in Holland, Luxembourg, etc., where the airlines had permission to offer split or part charter.

The predominant markets for airfreight to/from Scandinavia were for a long time Europe and North America though other markets like the Far East and Australia/Pacific have been growing in importance with Europe reducing in importance.

Representation in foreign countries

As airfreight grew in importance and ASG started consolidation traffics many of the existing agents, who regarded airfreight as peripheral and whose principal interest lay elsewhere, were not able to live up to the changing demands.

In the beginning of the 1970's, ASG and many of its agents at the time were members of a group called Constar, made up of strong domestic companies with airfreight departments that worked together world- wide but not on an exclusive basis. For many of the members of

Constar airfreight was regarded more as a complementary service and therefore the necessary commitment to airfreight was not shown. When Constar started to break up, ASG was invited to join a newly formed group called WACO. WACO developed out of parts of the Constar Group but was intended to work under stricter rules, with more commitment to airfreight and with exclusive agents only.

After considering alternatives, such as closer cooperation with Schenker or Emery, ASG joined the WACO Group in 1973 as an associate member. As ASG already had Emery in the States, Schenker-ASG and Nippon Express in the Far East they could not have full membership to begin with. The agreements with these representatives in important areas of the world created problems between ASG and members of the WACO Group. ASG's link to WACO was also a negative factor for the cooperation with Schenker and Nippon Express.

WACO formed a chain of companies, all of whom could claim to be part of the WACO organization. WACO and the effects of WACO for ASG airfreight will be developed separately later on.

The fact that Schenker had established an operation in Sweden, marketing their own services, and that the larger land-transport cooperation did not exist further aggravated the complications between ASG and Schenker in the Far East.

When sea and airfreight became part of one division in 1974/76 which was the time when prices for airfreight were declining as a result of the over-capacity, ASG tried to influence some airfreight agents and subsidiaries to take up seafreight as well, but its efforts really only had effect on some of its own subsidiaries like ASG Denmark. In most cases, the sea and airfreight agents remained separate as in USA, Canada, etc. during this period.

In 1976, there were 19 agents outside of Europe (sea and air) and 15 within Europe (air) in all. Seafreight still had very few agents internationally. Out of the 15 airfreight agents in Europe, 5 agents also acted for ASG in landtransports. A number of sales offices were established in airfreight in Canada (1974), Japan (1976), and USA (1978). Further there were three more sales offices set up in South Africa, Nigeria and Australia together with some of the WACO members.

During this period of change ASG also tried to buy Aircargo Contact A/S, a company in Norway. Since Norwegian government approval was a pre-condition and this was not forthcoming, it did not work out. As a result, the company was sold to some other company and the relationship with ASG was broken off. However, ASG did get the possibility to buy its new agent, Flygods A/S, a sister company to the surface agent, Linjegods A/S, later on in 1979/80.

In some cases ASG representation in an overseas country developed as a result of aid projects. This was the case in Tanzania and Kenya. In 1978, ASG was given the job by the World Bank (IDB) to reconstruct the trucking business in Tanzania. This project came to be the first of several projects for the Overseas Division (at that time called Air/Sea Division). It was placed in a separate company named Transport Development which was used exclusively for projects from 1979 onwards. As a result of this project and some later projects, ASG set up its own offices in markets like Tanzania and Kenya.

Because Emery broke the relationship with ASG in 1978/79, ASG had the possibility to buy a part of the existing regular WACO agent, Intercontinental Forwarders Inc.(IFI), in the USA. Buying into that company eventually resulted in breaking with the whole WACO organization which, in turn, led to breaking off relations with a large number of agents worldwide at the same time. These development will be described later.

Organization and investments

In 1972, ASG invested together with Olson& Wright in a 50/50 joint venture for aircargo handling and distribution, SACT(Swedish Aircargo terminals), in order to improve door-to-door service as well as to expand and economize on the special airfreight collecting and distribution transports to and from the international airports in Sweden. In the long run the idea was that the cooperation should expand into other areas.

The fact that ASG started consolidation traffics and became freight carrier both in sea-freight and airfreight meant that ASG was responsible also for handling the goods when consolidating and stripping the unitloads. Therefore investments had to made not only for operations in Sweden but also by subsidiaries and agents for operations abroad. ASG continued to invest in offices and terminal space in order to meet the growth. The same situation existed for some subsidiaries like ASG Denmark which built a new terminal for office and handling.

Another joint venture Baltic Air was created together with Wilson & Co, to a large extent for marketing flower charters but also for other charter operations. The company was to give service to ASG and Wilson with charter alternatives and to make arrangements for the operations.

In 1974/76 sea freight and airfreight were organized into a separate division. This intensified the investments in those services both in Sweden and abroad. An important difference was that ASG's sea and airfreight overseas division became directly responsible for the operations at the airports and seaports. This made it possible to economize and to be more flexible in the choice of suitable airports for goods leaving or entering Sweden. The new specialized marketing resources were another important factor. Earlier, the sales resources had been combined with domestic and international land-transports, which not only were much larger than sea and airfreight and but also were based on a very different know-how. Being member of WACO, in combination with the development of consolidation traffics, demanded more intensive marketing efforts which the former organizational structure could not handle.

The new division made it possible to gather into one unit the personnel in traditional sea freight forwarding and unit load traffics. The investment in the new organization therefore changed the total situation for sea freight in ASG.

At the end of the period the shipping lines had less interest in common activities with ASG, but sea freight had already strengthened its position within ASG.

Summary of the period 1970-79

The number of services and agents increased both in Europe and overseas. In 1976 there were 19 agents overseas (air and sea) and 15 agents within Europe. New countries were added in Australia/Pacific region, Africa and the Arab States. Development of door-to-door consolidation traffics in airfreight made ASG change to specialized airfreight agents. ASG became a member of WACO, a world wide exclusively airfreight group.

New cheaper service alternatives were developed for intercontinental traffics based on trucking traffics to/from Holland or other European airports. Further air and seafreight started to cooperate closer in ASG as they became part of the same division at head office level. Sales offices were established by ASG in U.S., Canada and Japan and together with WACO in South Africa, Nigeria and Australia. New operating offices were set up in Kenya and Tanzania for aid projects and seafreight services.

ASG created a joint venture with another large airfreight forwarder,Olson&Wright, for handling and distribution of airfreight goods in Sweden. At the end of this period ASG and its U.S agent Emery broke their cooperation. ASG started to cooperate with the new WACO agent, IFI.

Period 1980-89

Development of services

During the 1970's and in the 1980's the actual time spent in the air decreased in relation to the total transport time. Surface transports to/from airports, handling activities increased in importance and a large proportion of the air cargoes for long distance as well as for European destinations were trucked to/from Sweden, a phenomenon that had grown extensively. One important factor contributing to these road transports was the development of the wide fuselage aircraft which with their increased possibilities could lower price on long distances .

When ASG left Waco in 1980 it resulted in many complications and placed ASG under considerable strain. This will be described in detail later. However, it also became a period of fast growth internationally since ASG went on to establish new subsidiaries in three different countries of the world within a year.

The fact that ASG had several international subsidiaries also increased the number of cross-border traffics. In order to achieve profitability the newly opened offices needed to complement services between each other which meant that ASG got cross-border traffics not involving Scandinavia. From these different offices in combination with other existing agents ASG built a new network of international representation . The fact that these offices were established in the name of ASG worried some of the existing agents, however, and caused them to break off their cooperation with ASG and this caused a second wave of changes.

Even though other countries world wide increased in importance for ASG, the total airfreight organization was based on Sweden and Denmark. It was not until the end of the 1980's that the other subsidiaries in the network took over in terms of importance.

During the 1980's there was a development towards more timebased transports which started with the development of Europex, a time-guaranteed service for the European destinations. In 1990 there were a number of service levels from which the customers could choose depending on the quality and price needs. ASG has been cooperating with Federal Express, a large multinational express parcel company from the beginning of 1990. The year before ASG had an agreement with XP, another small parcel multinational, but XP was sold to a competitor so ASG changed to Federal Express.

During the 1980´s the sea-freight services started to diversify into new areas. ASG sea- freight developed a complementary service in the beginning of the 1980's through buying a small agency in Denmark for the Trans-Siberian railway .This small Danish company cooperated with a Swedish transport company recently acquired by ASG in Sweden.The Trans-Siberian Railway was an alternative way for transports to reach countries in the Far East like South Korea, Japan and even Hong Kong. The Trans-Siberian agency soon became integrated in the operations of ASG Denmark and resulted in an intensified cooperation between ASG Denmark and the Overseas division in Sweden. In many cases the Trans-Siberian agency meant a cooperation with agents in the Far East other than the regular agents for air and sea-freight. ASG has since then developed an agency on other markets, both in the Far East and in Europe, for the trans-Siberian railway.

Gradually more sea-freight traffics were developed internationally. The difference can be found in the number of consolidation traffics, the combined transports, express transports, special type of customer transports or special type of goods transports, project transports, etc. To a large extent the existing consolidation and other unit load transports are divided into these different kinds of services. Airfreight within Western Europe in 1989 would seem to have changed to a very large extent into being an express road transport, even though it might still have been called airfreight by the airlines performing some of the transports.

Representation in foreign countries

A development of the representation abroad in both operations and marketing was a basic necessity in order to match the changes in the type and number of traffics.

Through a delay in the separation from WACO until 1980, due to certain technicalities and lack of alternative for WACO, ASG managed to get enough time to form subsidiaries in UK and in Australia as well as to provide for alternative agents for the Scandinavian countries and the

U.S. During this year ASG also acquired part of the agent Flygods in Norway and two small broker companies in Australia.

The establishment of ASG Hong Kong came about a year later, as an indirect result of the separation from WACO.

Schenker had established its own office in Sweden and as the extended cooperation in Europe between the two companies was not effectuated, the climate between the two companies deteriorated. Therefore the joint venture Schenker-ASG decided to split in two in 1981 following which ASG established a fully owned subsidiary, ASG(HK) Ltd. In the late 1970's, ASG had sent a Swedish salesman to protect ASG's interests on the Scandinavian markets in Hong Kong, since the Schenker-ASG company seemed to have increasingly grown into a part of the Schenker organization world-wide. That salesman became responsible for the new ASG company and then part of the staff from the joint venture were taken over together with him. The new company had grown to be the sixth largest airfreight forwarder in Hong Kong in 1989.

In order to find alternative agents in Europe in such a short space of time ASG asked its existing land-transport agents in other areas for help. All of those approached were also able to help. Some of them were still agents of the Overseas division in 1990.

The ASG companies that were established in the early 1980's have led to an increased engagement worldwide for ASG. In 1981, ASG had 26 agents (7 more than 1976) outside Europe and by 1989 that number had increased to 33 despite the fact that in some countries the existing agents had taken on both air and sea-freight. In Europe the airfreight agents had increased to 20 (from 15 in 1976) out of which 9 were the same as the land-transport agents which shows a further concentration between land and airfreight agents in Europe. The sales office in Canada had been closed down and the offices in USA and Japan had turned into companies having operations of their own. The WACO sales offices disappeared with the WACO cooperation.

After virtually having only agents world wide except for one subsidiary and one J/V, the separation from WACO led to having four new subsidiaries. As ASG established more subsidiaries the conflicts increased with partners like Schenker-ASG Hong Kong which had intensive cooperation with a world-wide Schenker network.The newly established companies needed agents, at the same time, in other parts of the world since they could not exist on the profits from the Scandinavian traffics alone. When trying to find these, they soon found out that most of the existing ASG agents, like Schenker, already had partners and did not want to break their relationships.

ASG overseas division also established 12 partly or fully owned companies during 1980's both in Europe and overseas. Examples of these were companies in Norway, Finland, Switzerland,UK, Hong Kong, U.S., Australia, Japan, Taiwan (part owned), Singapore (sales office) etc. The office in Kenya still existed but had been reduced to one person and Tanzania there was a franchising agreement instead.

At the end of the 1980's, not only the Group but also the subsidiaries were acquiring companies in their area of representation. At Group level , ASG European and Overseas Divisions had set up companies in Finland and Singapore and increased to 100% their share in other companies such as ASG U.S., SACT and Nova traffic in Switzerland, etc. As regards the subsidiaries' acquisitions in 1989/90, ASG U.S and ASG Australia both acquired shipping companies, ASG Germany and Norway acquired trucking companies, ASG Hong Kong acquired a company in Taiwan, etc. This illustrates the fact that ASG developed many companies of its own during the 1980's.

Organization and investments

Many acquisitions were made during the 1980's. The first wave of acquisitions came during 1980-82 after the separation from WACO and the next wave came at the end of the 1980's after the company had been registered on the stock exchange.

After the WACO event, where companies were already part owned ASG followed up the investment by increasing its share to 100%. .

As the subsidiaries have continued to grow, further investments in know-how, terminals, offices, handling equipment ,etc., have been necessary. For instance, a large new terminal was built in Hong Kong.The exceptions are the small companies in Africa in which limited investments have been made due to the restrictions on taking any profits out of such companies. In recent years, ASG has purchased a shipping agency and forwarder in the US and has acquired a part of the agent in Taiwan which also represented ASG for shipping services. The investment in the agency for the Trans-Siberian Railway can also be seen as an investment in shipping in the Far East markets.

Perhaps the most important investments to have been made lately are the investments in communication systems, like Access, which are used between the different subsidiaries. Here ASG has had many difficulties in getting the different agents world-wide to invest in the same system. Their willingness to expand is dependent on their relationship to ASG and the joint future they could see for themselves in this cooperation. This led to an even stronger tendency to create fully or partly owned subsidiaries.

Summary of the period 1980-89

ASG airfreight developed time guaranteed and express services during this period. At first they created their own express system within Europe which intensified the cooperation between ASG and the agents in terms of resources and communication. However, at the end of the period ASG made an agreement with XP and a year later they changed to Federal Express. Further ASG became an agent of the Trans-Siberian railway in Denmark. In many cases the

Trans-Siberian service also had its own agents in the Far East. In the late 1980´s ASG subsidiaries in U.S and Australia also became shipping agents through acquisitions.

The total number of representatives for ASG Sweden increased over the period both in Europe and overseas. As ASG left WACO, several new subsidiaries and agent relations were established. In the search for new agents both for the existing and the new subsidiaries cross-country cooperation increased between the subsidiaries. Important investments were made during the period in new communication systems. Acquisitions came in two waves. The first was when ASG left WACO and the second at the end of the period as ASG became registered on the stock exchange.

5.1.3. Specific event - ASG -ISA and the WACO organization

Waco as a specific phenomenon has been of significant importance in the process of ASG's internationalization.

5.1.3.1.ASG and WACO

Before the event

When one of the managers in a company within the Constar Group left for another airfreight company, he had the idea of forming a new Group to be named WACO and ASG was invited to be the member for Scandinavia in early 1970´s and became associate member in 1973. Due to this ASG had to change most of their existing European airfreight agents and acquired some new outside Europe.

The idea of WACO, World Air Cargo Organization, was to create an exclusive net of the predominant airfreight forwarders in each country. All the agents should cooperate on an exclusive basis with each other. This net of agents was to be an alternative to the multi-nationals in transportation like Schenker, Panalpina, etc. The local strength in combination with the world-wide representation would be even better than for some multi-nationals who were strong mainly on traffics to from their home markets. Another advantage would be that it should be possible to invest in new communication and information systems.

WACO created a common logo-type for the total organization which would be a sign of membership and could be used in marketing. Five of the European companies formed an executive committee (EC), which was responsible for control and development. EC decided which countries and companies should be members and also supervised that the members followed the rules. The members of this committee were supposed to meet frequently while all the members of the organization met only once a year. ASG was one of the members of the Group and of its EC.

Being a member of the EC of WACO, ASG had the possibility to influence the choice of new agents in the new markets of interest.

A result of the over capacity of the airlines was that they offered high off-the-record discounts which gave the members of a large organization like WACO certain advantages. At the same time these discounts made consolidation less profitable which in turn made investments in communication and information system less interesting for a period.

After a period of positive development some of the disadvantages started to show. One of the problems was the difficulty to get the members to invest in the common communication system, since the need for such systems varied between a company in a highly developed country and a company in a developing country. Many members were very dependent on demands from specific customers which was also a problem when acting in common as regards investment. As separate companies WACO members gave priorities to short term profits rather than WACO related long term investments. Furthermore were the biggest agents in the Group already had their own agents on the most important markets like U.S., Japan, West-Germany, etc., and were unwilling to break those relations. These agents would indirectly gain access to the communication and information systems that WACO invested in.

Positive spin-off effects for ASG were that ASG together with the English participant set up a representative office in South Africa, in Nigeria and one in Canada. Another project was to set up a support organization at Maastricht airport for split charter traffics.

Certain attempts were made to create a holding company for the organization so that the members could be more closely tied together. This did not work out.

As WACO was looking for a better agent in the U.S., Emery became concerned and decided to leave the cooperation with ASG. This created the need for WACO to find an agent in the States that suited ASG as well. This became a problem since the States, being a very important market, was to a large extent dominated by the multinational transport companies. Finally IFI, Intercontinental Forwarders Inc., an existing U.S.agent for a limited area U.S., they invested in a better coverage of the country and became the exclusive agent. Shortly after that they said they were prepared to let some of the companies buy 50% of their company, but they could not accept having 3-4 owners with different views as to how the company should be handled. They asked ASG to be part-owner, therefore, since ASG had some of the largest traffics and was in the greatest need of finding a satisfying agent.

The event

Thus ASG bought 50 % of the shares in IFI. The basic reason for this was that ASG would owned an agent outside the Nordic market, the area of representation for ASG in WACO. This would make ASG too dominating in the WACO Group it was felt.

A separation from WACO meant a change of agents in 10-20 different places at the same time. Most of those places were to be found in Europe but others were in areas like Australia and South America. Fortunately, ASG had some of the primary countries like U.S., Japan and other places in the Far East not tied to WACO.

Since there were some technicalities in following the rules and members of WACO could not find other agents in Scandinavia as well as in US in such a short time they had to let things continue unchanged for the time being. This gave ASG some time to look for alternatives for the markets of the EC members, who were very eager to leave the cooperation as soon as another agent was found. The other WACO members were prepared to stay on as ASG agents, at least for a while. During this period ASG acquired part of the Norwegian agent

As it was necessary to find a new solution rapidly in most places in Europe, ASG asked its European surface transport agents for help. All were willing to do so. Two very difficult countries were the UK, since the predominant member of WACO was English, and Australia, since the agent did not want to continue with airfreight because of low profitability. In the UK, ASG employed the marketing manager of the WACO member to set up a subsidiary and in Australia they bought two small brokers to form the base for a new company. Both the subsidiary in U.K. and Australia started at the same time in 1980. ASG had just before acquired 65% of the Norwegian agent. With these arrangements, ASG airfreight had the capability of solving the problems that came with the break with WACO. The common sales representation in Canada stayed with ASG while the representation in South Africa stayed with the UK agent.

After the event

After ASG had resolved its immediate problems, the problem then became to get these new agents and newly formed companies to work. The partly owned company in the U.S., being a member of WACO, also lost many of its agents. The newly formed subsidiaries needed agents in other parts of the world. They could, of course, have worked together but this did not solve the problem of the Far East or of many of the European countries. Finding new agents for these companies led to a separation from Schenker in the Far East and the establishment of ASG Hong Kong to support the Scandinavian traffics. Many very large changes stemmed from the severance of the relations with WACO in 1980 and many indirect effects still existed in 1990.

In Scandinavia, ISA, a subsidiary of Wilson & Co, took over the role of ASG in the WACO Group in 1980. The effects on them will be discussed below.

5.1.3.2. ISA and WACO

Before the event

InterScandinavian Airfreight, ISA, was formed as a separate airfreight company in 1974. The basic rationale for it´s formation was the dissolution of the former airfreight company, UAF (United Airfreight), in Stockholm, which had been jointly owned by Wilson & Co and TK (Transportkompaniet). TK was part of the Scansped Group, which had recently formed another competing airfreight company, Scanflight, with some of the parties in the Scansped Group. These conflicts made it impossible to continue the cooperation.

Wilson & Co saw the opportunity to expand in airfreight and by taking over the managing director of UAF, the problem of finding agents to ISA for the necessary markets was facilitated. The agents specialized in airfreight seem to have stayed with ISA to a larger extent than with Scanflight. In areas for which new agents were needed, ISA utilized the contacts or agents of the parent company. Basically all agreements were bilateral and most of the agents were receiving agents, which ISA was as well. As a receiving agent there were very few formal agreements signed. Each company was only interested in exports.

Only in a few cases did ISA have another form of agreement where imports were also important. One such case was in the Far East (Hong Kong) where ISA sold import traffics in their own name.

ISA also entered into two joint ventures, one in Brasil and the other in Singapore neither of which coming up to expectations. It was especially the joint venture in Brasil which created many problems. The cost of establishing traffics worldwide was very high and ISA's resources were not sufficient.

The parent company Wilson had a subsidiary Wilson Inc. in the U.S. which was also an agent for ISA. This company ran into economic problems at the end of the 1970's, which in turn caused the Wilson & Co in Sweden to suffer severe economic damage.

Such was the situation when the WACO Executive Committee contacted ISA concerning being a member in the WACO organization.

The event

ISA was offered the alternative of becoming either a traditional bilateral agent or of joining as a full member of the WACO system. Joining as a full member meant changing agents in about 25 different places, taking over after ASG in most places. Being a full member also offered the opportunity to be a member of the Executive Committee after ASG. In a situation where they would not have made any larger international investments anyhow, ISA decided on full membership in 1980 based on the fact that thereby they would be getting a more extensive and higher standard of agent representation world-wide.

The advantages to WACO were obvious. The volumes would increase, the agents were not only receiving agents but were closer tied to each other, the development of an international communication system would be possible, buying power would be higher, etc. The disadvantages considered were mainly the problem of getting tied up to one total system and the agents in it.

After the event

ISA's expectations from WACO membership were only partly realized. The several advantages, such as getting better partners world-wide, would seem to have been true to a certain degree, but the number of disadvantages was larger also than expected.

As a result of the Waco membership many marketing activities were possible to plan ahead instead of working on an "ad hoc" basis, but it necessitated a reorganization of ISA in marketing and many other areas.

Due to the WACO membership ISA got a change in profile on the Swedish market and established a number of new traffics. Even though the number of customers did not seem to increase, the profitability became better.

As ISA did not at that time have a strategy as to develop a world-wide network of their own, a membership in WACO suited them. Furthermore the WACO cooperation helped ISA in the negotiations for withdrawal from the joint venture in Brasil. It also caused them to reconsider the investment in Singapore.

Being member of WACO gave ISA many international contacts and through these contacts new opportunities developed, like being a partner of UPS (United Parcel Systems) a world-wide integrated chain in Sweden. The WACO member in the UK was already a partner in UPS in the UK.

Being a member of the Executive Committee meant spending time together with the 6 other committee members in managing the total WACO- organization . ISA found it difficult to be in accord with all the members of this Committee. Instead Scandinavia,UK and Holland formed a small group that worked together more intensively. For instance, they formed a new company "Space Air" in Holland for split-charter together, which sold their services also to other members of the Group.

A problem was that many members of the Group did not stick to the rules. This was even the case with some members of the Executive Committee.

The investment in the total communication system ceased, due to the fact that most members were not interested in joining the system due to differences in priorities and lack of knowledge in utilizing computers. It made it too expensive for the few companies utilizing the system.

In the beginning of the 1980's, ISA together with 13-14 members of WACO created WACO-express system. ISA organized a separate department with separate salesmen for the purpose. The system was effective but the numbers of members interested were too few. Even members of the Executive Committee did not join. Either they had a functioning express system already or they did not want the system suggested. In the end only three companies really put their efforts into the system. This resulted in the system developing along partly false premises, since it was based on higher volumes.

Further the large number of members created problems of deciding upon the needed common investments as well as upon changing agents. Waco developed a bureaucracy when it came to decisions. In the case of the communication system this bureaucracy resukted in that the technical development of the suggested system was surpassed.

Shortly after ISA became a member of WACO, the total Wilson Group was sold to the Bilspedition Group. The Bilspedition Group already had a small airfreight company, which was a competitor to ISA.

In 1987, it was decided that ISA and Scanflight, both nowadays subsidiaries of Bilspedition Group, should be merged into one company under the name of Scanflight. The agent situation had to be discussed and a large number of agents had to disappear which caused both new problems and opportunities for the WACO organization in Scandinavia. The new Scanflight developed rapidly and the loyalty to the Waco organization decreased gradually. In the end, therefore, Scanflight changes their status in WACO from an full member taking an active part to an associated WACO member.

Finally it seemed that ISA, due to the cooperation with WACO, became more international and grew in market share in Sweden while ASG concentrated hard on developing their worldwide net of establishments.

Summary of the WACO event

As ASG became a member and exclusively tied to a world wide organization WACO, it had to change many of its existing agents. ASG took an active part in recruiting new agents as members and in the development a new common communication system. As WACO was looking for a more suitable agent in U.S, ASG´s existing agent Emery left. IFI became the new WACO agent. ASG was asked to be a part owner of IFI. This created internal conflicts within the WACO group and ASG was asked to leave.

ASG had to find around 20 new agents in different countries. In solving this problem ASG acquired and set up new companies in Norway, U.K. and Australia. Some of the existing European landtransport agents took on airfreight as well. The newly created companies and existing ASG companies in Sweden, Denmark and U.S had to find new agents in many countries. They turned to each other for cooperation when possible. Schenker -ASG J/V in the Far East was divided into two separate companies and the new ASG HongKong started to cooperate with many of the existing ASG airfreight subsdiaries. Over time many new changes for ASG airfreight resulted from this event.

The new Scandinavian agent, to which the remaining agents in WACO had to switch, was ISA. ISA had to change 20-25 of their existing agents in order to become a member of WACO. They became very active in WACO and the competition with ASG increased. As Wilson & Co, parent company of ISA, was acquired by Bilspedition, ISA was merged with Scanflight. This decreased their loyalty to WACO and they changed into being an associate member.

5.2. General case analysis

The analysis comprises the development of land-transports in Europe as well as that of overseas including air and sea transports in Europe. The specific events are used as examples for better understanding of what has transpired during the periods. The events are analysed in more detail when discussing context and dynamics (chapter 9).

5.2.1 Period 1940-54 - Beginning of internationalization

ASG had existed only seven to eight years when the first international aid transports were undertaken. In spite being only recently established the company was one of the largest domestic transport companies providing trucking services in Sweden. Due to restrictions on trucking transports, some railway traffics were established in the early 1940's.

Integration

During the period from 1945 to 1954 ASG established something like 12- 20 *new cooperations* resulting in even more transport systems. These were basically all railway consolidation traffics.

The first direct international relations were developed through the international contacts of the owners, the shipping line Svea and the Swedish Railway. In some cases former aid transport contacts were used.

In the Swiss event, the contacts were taken in 1946 via relations to the Svea shipping line while in many other cases existing railway agents or former aid transport agents were chosen to represent ASG.

The legal integration was extremely low. In most cases there were informal exclusive bilateral agreements. The social contacts were relatively strong and only in a very few cases did formal written agreements exist. In the Swiss event, ASG and Natural negotiated for more than half a year before agreeing on their future cooperation and transport system in common. The door-to-door concept that ASG demanded necessitated a higher integration of the system to be executed than was normal at that time. The control aspect between ASG and the agent differed depending on the size and international experience of the agent. In the case of Natural, the control from Natural was probably higher during this period, Natural being a more experienced international transport company than ASG. In general, the control seems to change during the period as the balance of trade was changed. In the beginning it was in favour of ASG since exports dominated and most customer contacts were taken in Sweden. However this changed as industries in the war devastated countries developed.

The specialized departments for international transports increased the knowledge and efficiency. This in combination with the high growth led to *closer cooperation* developing between ASG and its representatives. The profitability was high in the railway traffics during this period. In a few cases, the closer cooperation led to an increased number of transport systems in common between ASG and the representative through initiating new direct traffics to other parts of Sweden.

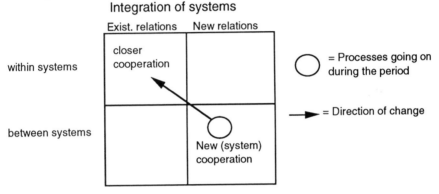

5.3. Internationalization - integration at system level 1940-54

As a result of the establishment of these cooperations, a net of cooperating transport companies was created even though there was very little interdependence between the different companies in the net.

Extension

ASG's activities expanded to 12 different countries through the establishment of the agent cooperations and the transport systems between Sweden and the different countries concerned. The extension was of *first degree* , starting with the Nordic countries in combination with Switzerland, Austria and Hungary. Next in line were West and East Germany, Czechoslovakia, Poland, Yugoslavia, Bulgaria and Italy. There was an attempt to establish a traffic by boat to France via Antwerp which failed.

Penetration

At least 20 different <u>traffics</u> were established together with agents, of which several were in West-Germany and in the Nordic countries. Sometimes the same agents had many traffics with ASG and at other times there was only the one agent for each traffic.

The high growth in volumes caused large increases in the *size of relations* as the resources for the existing type of services increased. The resources for the international traffics increased very much within ASG during the period, both in terms of personnel and terminals. The number of local offices handling international traffics increased in Sweden.The fact that there was more than one agent in West-Germany caused a change towards an increase in the *spread of relations.*

Penetration

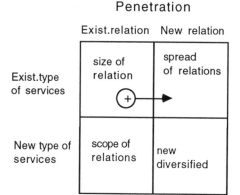
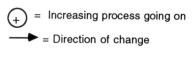

5.4. Internationalization - penetration 1940-54

The home country resources grew as well as the resources in foreign countries through agents. Further the growth resulted in very high market shares in some areas.

Conclusion and effects of representatives
Through a number of new cooperations (12-20) and an even larger number of transport systems created, a gradual international expansion was taking place. This caused first degree of extension to 12 European countries as well as increasing volumes of resources committed for these countries.

Effects on suppliers, owners and competitors
Both Svea and SJ played an active role during this phase. For SJ, the result was a very positive contribution to their railway traffics. As the growth in volumes caused capacity problems for the railways, ASG and its agents took greater control over their consolidation systems.
The trucking companies which had participated in the foundation of ASG were concerned about the increased SJ engagement and the direction in which ASG was developing. Once the war was over, the conflicts arising from these concerns became more open.
At the end of the period, when SJ had a negative influence on ASG's possibilities of getting international trucking permits, the conflicts became severe.

During the period, other Sweden-based <u>competing</u> forwarding companies tried to stop ASG's internationalization process through forming a coalition for international transports, threatening to use their joint power on SJ as well as on ASG.

5.2.2.Period 1955-69 - Expansion of trucking traffics and start of airfreight

During this period the railway expansion slowed down and the trucking transports took over. Enormous increases had taken place since the second world war.

Integration

On the <u>system level</u> the relations to the existing <u>railway</u> agents were changed during this period, especially for shorter distances such as the northern parts of Europe. For many of such agents there was a stagnation in development as the <u>trucking</u> traffics were taking over. In some cases, this resulted in *looser cooperation* or a *ceased* relation to the existing railway agents while in other cases there was an *enlargement* of the existing cooperation. In the Swiss event, the cooperation was enlarged since trucking services became a complementary service to the existing railway services. In the West-German event, on the other hand, the existing cooperation first became looser as a result of the ASG Hamburg establishment then it *ceased* to exist.. A high number of new trucking traffics started during this period and as volumes increased new direct traffics were added.

The aspects of integration were slightly different during this period compared to the earlier. Perhaps the most noticeable change was the increased execution integration as a result the formation of so many new trucking systems, since trucking traffics demand a higher degree of integration in operation including handling, marketing, communication, etc than railway traffics. ASG also increased its terminal and marketing resources and intensified its total marketing efforts both in Sweden and abroad. As a result of the higher level of execution integration the social integration seem to be increase as well, since communication had to increase on many levels.

ASG was more active as regards legal integration, starting a subsidiary including operations in Hamburg but also opening and, within a couple of years, closing four different sales offices. Three of these were situated in West-Germany at different periods. The earliest was established in Berlin in 1955. These sales offices were supposed to lead to intensified social integration with the agents in the country. However they also created certain conflicts since they increased the degree of ASG's control at the expense of the agent. ASG took direct contact with many existing customers of the agents.

Even though these sales offices were to disappear after a while, the customer contacts did not, since ASG shifted the direct selling to the head office in Sweden. Moreover, the trucking transports increased the degree of control exercised by ASG over the agents on account of the fact that ASG insisted on supplying the systems with the trucking resources. This was very obvious in the first *new cooperation* in the Belgian event where ASG supplied not only the trucking resources but also the trucking traffics know-how to the agent.

The changes mentioned above concerned land-transports but during this period ASG started airfreight and seafreight activities as well, on account of which *new cooperations* were established both outside Europe and within Europe. In Europe, many of the agents chosen for airfreight were existing land-transport agents having airfreight as a complementary service. In airfreight, some extremely important agents in the U.S and the Far East caused ASG to make investments and increase their legal integration in those areas. ASG established a subsidiary in Copenhagen exclusively for airfreight in 1959 and started a joint venture in the Far East with Schenker in 1961. These cooperations developed quite quickly into a *closer cooperation*. The American agent had designed a transport system with a very high executional integration, with time guarantees. However, the control of the systems was higher by the agent than by ASG. Other airfreight cooperation, basically concerning direct consignments with airlines, involved only a low degree of integration, since many of the agents were merely receiving agents. As for control, it was divided between ASG and the agent, depending on whether export (ASG) or import (agent) was concerned.

As for seafreight during late 1960's, ASG started new cooperations in the U.K. for the establishment of trailer traffics and new cooperation concerning container traffics to the U.S and Canada. The seafreight transport, whether utilizing trailers or containers, included a reltatively high execution integration compared to traditional seafreight.

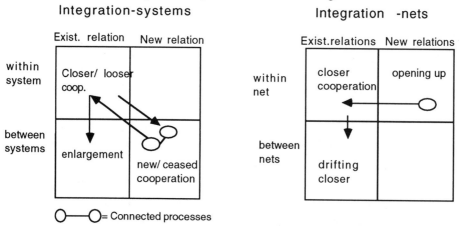

Figure 5.5. Internationalization -integration at system and net level during 1955-69

In the figure, the development for the railway is shown as connected to that of the process of trucking traffics.

On a net level the formerly created net was *opened up*. Some existing railway relations were dissolved and a number of new agents and transports systems for trucking, airfreight and seafreight were added gradually. The intensified cooperation with Schenker and Emery resulted in a *drifting closer* to many of their other offices or agents. Sometimes the cooperation was infrequent and only when there was a specific need and at other times ASG started to do more and actively cooperate with one or two of their agents or subsidiaries over the period.

Extension

During the period *first degree* extension took place to many new countries in Europe such as France, U.K. Spain, Belgium, Holland, etc. The change in extension in Europe was, however, smaller than during the earlier period.

The first extensions to overseas countries to take place during this period were those to U.S, Canada and to a number of countries in the Far East, such as HongKong, Japan, India and Thailand. *Second degree* of extension was a result of the international traffics of the Danish airfreight subsidiary.

Penetration

Resources for railway traffic decreased while resources for trucking traffics, airfreight and seafreight increased heavily. Therefore *size of relations* decreased in the case of existing railway traffics while the others increased. The *scope of relations* increased for agents adding trucking traffics and on airfreight to the existing railway services. It was a case of *new diversifed relations* in other situations where ASG cooperated with new agents for this new type of transport system. Both the latter developments were present at the same time. The development during the period also allowed for a certain *spread of the relations* due to the increasing volumes and the increasing number of new trucking permits.

During this period the total penetration increased, both in terms of quantity and differentiation of resources and relations. Moreover, the expansion in resources committed for international activities in Sweden was equally strong.

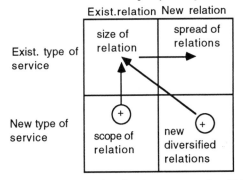

Figure 5.6. Internationalization - penetration 1955-69

Basically the growth came through the new types of services and not through the railway traffics, which decreased in number of agents and profitability. Speed of penetration was also higher during this period than during the former.

Conclusion and effects on representatives
Several parallel processes have taken place during this period leading to changes in different services. Not only have system changes taken place but also changes at net levels. The main part of the changes led to a higher degree of integration at system level through new cooperations and to a lower degree of integration at the net level, since part of the existing relations were dissolved and other relations were added. The extension was still concentrated the first degree and the speed in Europe was lower than in the former period.

The speed of penetration assumed greater importance during this period partly due to the growing volumes combined with the new types of services that were added.

The trucking services agents' connection to the railway services within their own geographical area deteriorated.

Effects on suppliers, owners and competitors
Basically the effect during the period was that of increasing integration with the trucking companies, both legally and executionally and with regard to control. The expansion of trucking traffics which continued over the whole period was made together with trucking companies. Due to this, some of the existing domestic trucking companies related to ASG became internationalized. The risk and the control also seems to have been higher for ASG in the international trucking traffics than in the domestic. As to legal integration, the ASG Truckowners Association (ASG-T) got the possibility to buy 5% of the shares in ASG from SJ in 1965 and in 1967 they acquired another 2.5%.

As for SJ, the integration seems to have gone in different directions during the period. First SJ increased its legal integration with ASG to 100% in 1959. Then in 1965 this decreased to 95% and in 1967 there was a further decrease to 67.5 %. During the period the executional integration between ASG and SJ was reduced in some areas and increased in others. In Sweden many terminals were built together with SJ. On the whole, however, the competition between ASG and SJ seems to have increased. SJ managed to delay development of ASG's trucking traffics for many years by systematically influencing the Swedish Board of International Trucking to refuse ASG's applications for permits. The control of the rail traffics also seems to have increased for ASG since they wanted to choose the type of traffics best suited to the customer.

For the shipping lines, the changes also went in different directions during the period. On the one hand, Svea shipping line sold its shares in ASG and decreased its integration with ASG in most aspects. The trailer traffics to the U.K.were an exception. On the other hand, a group of shipping lines, Rego, acquired 25% of ASG in 1967. The development of ASG seafreight at the end of the 1960's further increased the integration with Rego shipping lines.

Finally, the airlines and ASG also increased their degree of integration during this period both executionally, socially and controlwise. Executionally, ASG and Linjeflyg (a Swedish domestic airline) had made an agreement that ASG should perform the necessary land-transports and some of the administrative work connected with their international consignments. This included transports to/ from Copenhagen. As ASG developed its own international airfreight, the cooperation with SAS increased, since they held the monopoly on Scandianvian international traffics. This meant that the control in airfreight was predominantly in the hands of SAS and to a lesser extent with ASG and its agents.

Period 1970-79 - Specialization and diversification

The growth which had persisted for so many years stagnated after the first years of the decade and did not come back until the end.

Integration

Many *new cooperations* were established during the period both as a result of specialization and of diversification.

The existing relations in land-transportation were under pressure to increase the effectiveness of their transport systems as a result of the stagnation. This resulted in either intensified *closer cooperation* or in a *switch of representative* . In many cases it was combined with an *enlargement* of a former cooperation adding some of the new special transport services.

The aspects of integration demonstrate the wave of changes taking place during the period. The legal integration continued to be low during the 1970's but increased somewhat during the period's last phases. However, there were several events on the way that led to both increases and decreases. In 1971, ASG took over the majority interest in the agent in Norway, but due to economic and political problems that

lasted only two years, after which ASG acquired a new Norwegian agent. A further event was the opening of four new sales offices. First there was an office in Hamburg, which was later moved to Brussels during the mid-1970's, and then there were the two other sales offices opened in Italy and France. All were closed down in the early 1980's.

Finally, ASG acquired two internationally operating companies, the first the agent in Stuttgart, West Germany and the second a competitor in Sweden. In addition, a greenfield investment in Belgium was made during the last part of the period.

Similar changes in the other aspects of integration, representing increases, decreases and a stabilization had taken place before the period was through. For execution integration, there were decreases, *looser cooperation*, which caused ASG and the agents to dissolve some cooperations and to intensify others. However, by the end the period effectiveness of the transport systems had increased. Some of the reasons behind the increased effectiveness were better know-how, new and more efficient terminals and transport equipment, communcation systems development and a specialization and divisionalization within the organization.

Through these changes the social contacts had to increase to solve the problems. Finally Control became more symmetric for ASG and the representatives since the traffics had to be intensified from both sides. The strength in market position came to be more important for the control of the traffics in common.

Air and seafreight developed positively during the period both in Europe and overseas, ASG made a change from its existing airfreight agents to specialized agents who either were or became part of the WACO group. Many *new cooperations* started in airfreight, therefore, and the previous traffics *ceased* to exist. Since several of the existing land-transport agents in Europe were among those affected, there was a *decrease in the field of cooperation* due to this. Futhermore, other *new cooperations* for seafreight as well as for airfreight were being formed in new overseas countries during the period. As regards to airfreight, the number of agents overseas came to exceed the number of agents in Europe.

At net level, several parallel changes were happening. The net was *opening up* both in terms of dissolving a limited number of relations for railway and airfreight transports and adding both some new airfreight and seafreight agents as well as some specialized agents. The internationalization of the subsidiaries was another reason for the net to open up. However parallel to these changes a great deal *closer cooperation* took place between the existing agents due to the increased know-how, the new organization and the new communication systems that were developed.

Two cases of *joining nets* took place in landtransports through the acquisition of ERT and Atege, Stuttgart.

Further, there were changes in priorities, both as a result of new agents being brought into the net as a consequence of acquisitions and because of changed priorities towards some of the larger international representatives. In the former case, the nets of the added agents were *drifting closer* as in the case of many WACO agents. In the latter, ASG was *drifting away* from nets of the large international representatives Schenker and Emery and "drifting closer" to Natural and van Gend &Loos.

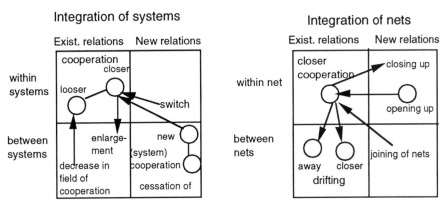

Figure 5.7. ASG internationalization - integration changes 1970-79

Extension

During this period the <u>first degree</u> of extension still took place even though the <u>second degree</u> of extension became much more common, not only through the internationalization of subsidiaries but also due to the acquisition of international transport companies. The first degree of extensions from a Nordic horizon were basically to the outskirts of Europe, like to Turkey, Greece, Sovjet Union, etc., and overseas countries while the second degree of extension was to West-European countries which had already been the subject of first degree extension. In airfreight, ASG gained coverage of a lot of new countries, especially after joining the WACO group. At the end of the decade a large part of the world was covered through airfreight agents. Seafreight expanded to many new countries as well, not only in the industrialized world but also to countries like Tanzania and Kenya. South America and Africa had the lowest coverage in terms of agents or subsidiaries. The speed of secondary degree extension seems to be higher than first degree extension since many countries were added through acquisitions of international companies.

Penetration

Air and seafreight on the whole, and trucking traffics to an extent, increased their penetration during the 1970's. This was basically a result of specialization and diversification leading to increased differentiation of resources shown in the form of increased *scope of relations* in some cases and *new diversified relations.* However, the differentiation of resources into special systems and functions caused decreases, to a certain extent, in the *size of* some existing *relations* performing a more general type of transport system. The addition of so many new functions and the development of special transport resulted in a wave of training of personnel. New offices and terminals were also opened in Sweden especially for international traffics. The number and size of airfreight offices and terminals in Sweden and Denmark grew, partly as a result of the change to consolidation traffics entailing higher risk, greater utilization of resources than traditional airfreight and calling for increased marketing activities. Also during this period, ASG created a joint venture with another large international airfreight forwarder, Olson &Wright, in order to achieve effective handling and distribution of airfreight. At the same time, ASG Hamburg, taking on new functions and new international traffics, increased its penetration, creating the need for more resources for development.

The volumes increased strongly in the beginning of the decade. The oil shock changed the situation and the mid-70's saw the total volumes internationally for ASG decrease (-16% in 1975) as a result of the international recession) following the oil crisis. A slow decrease in *spread of relations* for the general land-transports could be detected, a few of the existing local agents having seemingly disappeared from the scene.

The internationalization of the subsidiaries, essentially made within the framework of services that existed, therefore increased *the size of relations* in the countries in which ASG had subsidiaries as well as in the countries to which those subsidiaries had established traffics.

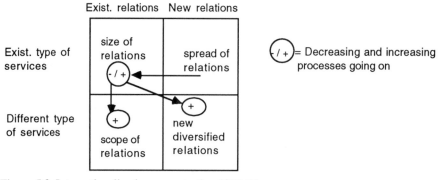

Figure 5.8. Internationalization - penetration 1970-79

Penetration increased subsequently during this period, primarily through adding new functions, special transports and new types of airfreight and seafreight traffics leading to *scope of* and *new diversified relations*. Further, the *size of existing relations* with agents decreased in land-transports and the "spread of relations" decreased slightly. A certain increase in the size of relations occurred for the subsidiaries on net level due to their internationalization.

Conclusion and effects on representatives

During this period there were many parallel as well as sequential changes. To a large extent, the number of parallel changes depended on different changes in airfreight, seafreight, rail and road transports. Through the change in the organization into divisions where the relationships to the representatives as well as to the suppliers became divided between three international divisions i.e.the Overseas, the Continental and the Nordic division the parallel changes became more visible. These part-nets were both complementary and overlapping (O/C and C/O) and fully complementary (C/C). The creation of these part-nets within the focal net also calmed the increasing conflicts between the negatively connected agents in the focal net. The internationalization in combination with the increased specialization and diversification of ASG, as well as that of both agents and subsidiaries, increased the degree of negative connectedness between the representatives.

The period showed an instability leading both to increases and decreases in volumes which also influenced the changes that took place as well as the speed of those changes.

Effects -suppliers, owners and competitors.

During this period ASG decreased its execution integration with SJ internationally since the consolidation traffics continued to decrease. ASG's priorities were changed to the disadvantage of SJ, in spite of the fact that SJ still was the majority shareholder in ASG. SJ was negatively connected to the development in other fields.

Resulting from the diversification of services into bulk, heavy transports, combined transports, etc., there was a need for specialized equipment. To the extent that trucking companies were prepared to invest or adapt, the degree of integration could increase but many of the others had the possibility of facing a decrease in volumes, sometimes resulting in lower degrees of integation. Therefore during this period there seemed to have been a change in priorities. Some of the more effective trucking companies willing to change and invest were cooperating more closely with ASG while the cooperation with others became less .

Similar changes in priorities seemed to take place for airlines and shipping lines.

The shipping lines chosen for ASG seafreight had a positive connectedness to the development of ASG. To the extent that these were Rego organizations, the integration with ASG increased. In those cases where ASG used competing shipping lines to that of Rego, the level of conflicts rose. Other cooperations were initiated, directly with Johnson Line in a cooperation on the Sovjet Union , domestic transports of unit loads, etc. As ASG increased in knowledge and size in seafreight so did its control.

ASG increased its degree of integration with the domestic airlines, SAS and Linjeflyg, in the beginning of the decade due to their agreement of being their agent.

When ASG began developing international airfreight consolidation, the increased integration with airlines in general became varied. Integration with some international airlines increased and decreased with others. On the whole, however, the creation of the WACO group and the overcapacity of the airlines brought about a reduction in the control exercised by the airlines which worked to the advantage of ASG and its representatives.

During this decade the trucking of airfreight goods to/ from Continental airports increased for certain long distance destinations like the Far East. This brought about a reduction in the dependence on the home country or national airlines and an increase in the control over the air transports for the agents.

Period 1980-89 - Overseas expansion and European consolidation

Integration

During this period, the change in integration was dominated by net changes rather than system changes.

The European land-transport net of representatives underwent a period of consolidation and concentration while air and seafreight expanded overseas.

The concentration of the European land-transport induced a *closer cooperation* and a *drifting closer* at the net level during the period . In Europe, the number of land-transport agents in West-Germany decreased from 17 to 3. At the same time the number of subsidiaries increased through the acquisition of two companies. Also a concentration took place in other European countries, such as in France where ASG had several representatives. At system level, there was a *switch of representative* from some agents to other representatives leading to an *enlargment of cooperation* with a few agents and subsidiaries. The concentration was basically to old established agents which can be appreciated by the fact that average period of cooperation extended over more than 20 years in 1989.

New types of services such as time-guaranteed and express systems were developed over this period. These services could be built into the existing general transport systems or they could be constructed as special transports and form complementary transport systems. In either case, they brought about an increased need for integration with the representatives through more effective communication systems, etc. For those representatives prepared to adapt, this resulted in a higher degree of integration through *closer cooperation* or *enlargement.*

Legal integration increased for the focal net during this period more than ever before. For the part net of land-transports, acquisitions were made in Norway and West-Germany followed by the taking of a minority interest in the Danish agent. The change in Norway was necessitated by Bilspedition's acquisition of the then ASG agent. The new Norwegian agent, which was also the agent of the ASG agent in Denmark, started a cooperation with ASG when, after a short period, the company was acquired by ASG, Sweden. In three cases it were legal integration with the agent.

As for the _airfreight_ part-net, many changes took place during the period at the net level and at system levels involving all aspects of integration.

In 1980 the cooperation with the WACO organization broke down and in many countries ASG had to leave 20 agents since the WACO organization was an exclusive, highly integrated world wide organization. The loss of Emery as an agent in U.S. and the acquisition of 50% of the US agent of WACO, caused severe conflicts with the other agents (for more details see the WACO event).

ASG had to *leave* WACO net and *opened up* their net for new agents and a combination of greenfield investments in U.K. and Australia as well as acquisition of the agent in Norway. In Europe several of the existing landtransport agents took on ASG airfreight as well. In some cases this was only a temporary solution. The existing ASG subsidiaries for land-transportation, however, lacked the necessary knowledge to take on airfreight.

A short period afterwards, Schenker ASG in the Far East had to break up since ASG wanted a representative for their new subsidiaries in the Far East. The ASG joint venture with Schenker in HongKong had been *drifting closer* to the Schenker net almost worldwide. The joint venture was disbanded and ASG HongKong established.

The newly ASG opened offices, through homogenizing their activities, increased the integration with Sweden in all respects. The new airfreight subsidiaries also expanded into other airfreight markets important for their countries and increased the integration with their sister companies thereby making an effort to *move towards closing up* for airfreight. Their expansion also led to *new (system) cooperation* s with many agents.

The legal integration increased during this period since formal agreements in writing, as opposed to informal agreements, became standard. Still, many of the formal agreements seem to be focused on exclusivity for a certain system in a certain geographical area and not generally at net level.

Later during this decade, air and seafreight part-nets slowly developed towards a concentration to fewer overseas representatives as in HongKong, U.S., Australia. At the end of the period, ASG even acquired an international seafreight forwarder in US which would help the ASG company in pursuing_seafreight_ traffics. The result was a *switch of representative* and *enlargement* at the system level and *closer cooperation* and *drifting closer* at the net level.

During this period the focal net had been *opened up* , adding many new cooperations overseas. Some of these cooperations, resulting from theTransib railway agency, meant that *new cooperations* were established with several new agents in the Far East. In other cases, the existing representative took on the agency for Trans- Siberian railway.The transport systems of the normal seafreight was negatively connected to that of Trans-Siberian railway.

The organization within Sweden changed became divisionalized into Division Europe and Overseas.

The development of time-guaranteed transports and logistical services in airfreight also created new cooperation with other types of agents like XP and later on Federal Express. These transport companies offered specialized services for which they had a world wide transport net for time-guaranteed transports of small parcels already. ASG first *joined* the XP *net* and then *left* the XP *net* and *joined* the Federal Express *net*. The execution and control integration is higher in those systems than in a general transport system without time-guarantees.

Even though the sales offices in Europe had been closed down, at that time ASG had sales offices overseas in Japan, U.S and Singapore which were changed into operating companies in these areas later during the period.

ASG- Period 1980-89

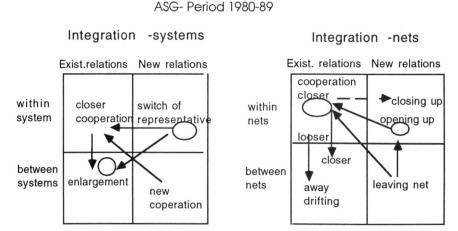

Figure 5.9. Internationalization - integration at system and net levels 1980-89

Finally there was a movement towards the closing up of the focal net at the end of the period since the representatives of the net seemed to be cooperating to a larger extent with each other. This seems to be especially true not only for the newly started airfrieght companies but also for the Scandinavian land-transport companies and within West-Germany.

Extension

During this decade the *first degree* of extension did not increase. Only small peripheral increases and decreases took place . However the *secondary degree* of extension changed very much, primarily as a result of leaving the WACO group which decreased the secondary degree of extension. On the other hand, the number of subsidiaries established both in airfreight, seafreight and land-transports increased the secondary degree of extension.

Penetration

The focal net went through different phases of decreasing and increasing. In Europe there was the concentration to fewer more *closely cooperating* representatives and this decreased the *spread of relations* and increased the *size* and *scope of* the existing *relations.*

However, in the case of the newly established airfreight offices, these were smaller and less differentiated than the former agents and therefore the *scope of relations* often decreased as a result of breaking with WACO. To begin with *size of the relation* also decreased since the WACO agents, being important organizations in their own countries, were controlling an important part of the traffics through their customer relations. Furthermore, for the greenfield investments there were very few, if any, established customer relations in the country concerned. However, the volumes increased over time as the ASG net was marketing the new organization.

On the other hand, since the ASG subsidiaries started up new traffics to third countries very quickly and as investments were made in communication systems, terminals, equipment, etc., the penetration increased the *size of relations,* again at net level, after a short period. At the system level, the penetration could well have continued to be low in comparison with the earlier level.

As regards airfreight, penetration decreased both in size and scope for a period, especially in the countries where ASG started its own offices. This was also the case for some land-transport investments, as in Norway.

Penetration

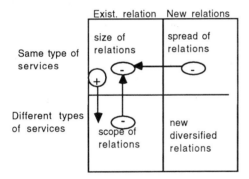

Figure 5.10. Internationalization -penetration 1980-89

In Sweden large investments were made in the international net not only through acquisitions abroad but also in acquiring the necessary resources in the home country. The investments came basically in two waves. The first one came in the beginning of 1980's as ASG broke-off with WACO and the second one when ASG became registered on the Swedish stock exchange and therefore had much more capital available.

Conclusion and effects of representatives

Net level changes predominate rather than system level changes. The clustering into separate nets seems to continue as new specialized fields of services are added and these nets differ in their directions of change.

At the same time as these part-nets are *drifting closer* while many of the former representatives became competitors. The part-net of landtransport Europe, which was C/O (i.e.complementary in services but overlapping geographically) to that of airfreight Europe, was actively used to solve the airfreight problems of finding agents.

The fact that the foreign subsidiaries were expanding domestically and internationally made them negatively connected to many of the international agents either within Europe or on overseas markets. Therefore, the ASG net became more and more overlapping with some of the internationalized agents like Schenker. The same situation of an increasing degree of overlapping seems to have taken place between agents as they grew nationally and internationally and diversified in services. There is also a question of difference in expansion between the types of services. As air and seafreight or other special transports increased in importance in comparison to land-transports, the conflicts between agents and subsidiaries representating ASG in the different services in the same country (C/O) were enhanced and especially so when they were diversified.This in fact occurred in those cases where the agents were acquired by larger international nets competing with ASG. In those cases, there seem to have been a decrease in integration due to real or perceived leakage or spillover of information.

Of importance was also that the increasing number of subsidiaries made a number of the agents lose some of their trust in ASG cooperation. Where subsidaries and agents were internationalized, it was more likely that both deal with many aspects of the same customer's business. Through this the possibilities of competition increase which in turn increases conflicts between the agents and/or the subsidiaries. Homogenizing the nets tend to make the conflicts larger since it shows more clearly which companies are part of the net.

The complexities inherent in all these nets comprised of all these different representatives and agents is exemplified in the figure 5.11.

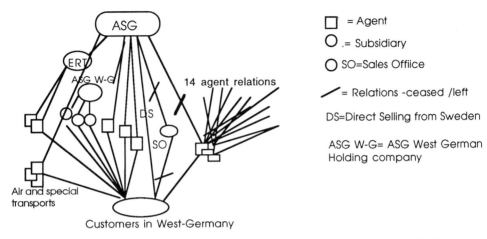

Figure 5.11. Changes in number and types of representatives in West-Germany 1980-89

Breaking relations with many agents when narrowing down to fewer agents means that most of these agents have to find another representative and therefore start cooperating to a large extent in competing with ASG and its agent. This happened both in the WACO event and in the concentration in land-transportation.

Effects- suppliers, owners, and competitors

In 1980 the shipping lines decreased their legal integration with ASG and sold their shares in ASG to SJ and the trucking companies. The Swedish Railways,SJ, increased its share from 67,5 to 75% of the shares in ASG. Both legal and executional integration with SJ increased. In 1984 SJ doubled the total capital invested in ASG and a year later the domestic competition with ASG ceased as SJ discontinued its own consolidation traffics. Part of these consolidation traffics were taken over by ASG.

 ASG expanded the sea-traffics worldwide and some of the shipping lines continued to have a close execution integration to ASG, being positively connected in their consolidation services. The fact that ASG was agent for Trans-Siberian railway gave ASG an alternative to/ from the Far East. The shipping lines were negatively connected to the Trans-Siberian agents.

In spite of an increase in legal integration with the trucking companies from 7.5% to 25%, the continuation of the combi-traffics and the increased costs of Swedish trucking companies led to an increase in the utilization of foreign trucking companies. Many of the Swedish trucking companies, being part-owners of ASG, were negatively connected to the foreign trucking companies, leading to decreased integration for some of them.

Airfreight also presents a divided picture, with increasing integration towards some airlines by performing handling on their behalf, giving priority of cargo to them, etc. and with decreasing integration towards others. In other cases, much of the airfreight within Europe transferred over to carriage by truck in preference to airplanes. Where the airplanes are partly owned by the agent, as in the case of Federal Express, some of the regular airlines are negatively connected to that type of transport system.

Using the same suppliers for many systems in the net also results in some of the suppliers basically being more closely connected to one net than to others. In changing agents or acquiring a company, this will have effects on the suppliers as well.

Interaction between the dimensions of internationalization

Combining the three concepts integration (I), penetration (P) and extension(E) would lead to different combinations over time. During the first two periods(1940-69) the changes took place on system level. The establishment of new cooperations, which created new transport systems led to extension of the first degree to many new countries and then increased the resources and the relations in those countries causing increased penetration (I--> E1---> P-->). Over time, as development continued in the already extended countries increeased integration between companies only added to increased penetration (I-->P).

Further the investments made during these first periods in Sweden as well as in foreign countries in know-how, technical facilities, terminals, etc. for the international traffics, leading to increased efficiency of the transport systems show that increased penetration also led to increased integration (P-->I) .

However, it seems that over time when there was a change in the balance of resources between the focal company and the representatives in other countries there would be a disturbance in the relation which might effect integration between the two partners.

During 1970-79 the balance between several landtransport relations became disturbed which called for a higher interaction between integration and penetration.(I<-->P). As for the overseas development it was similar to what landtransport had during their first period(I-->E1-->P). However, since the few existing subsidiaries were internationalizing there was an interaction between I--E2--P at net level.

In 1980-89 as ASG was extended to most countries the changes were dominated by integration changes on net level having effects on penetration(I-->P). During this period there was a combination of increases and decreases taking place at net level but also on system level. As ASG was leaving the WACO net and making a number of greenfield investments there was an increase in integration in comparison to the earlier situation but at the cost of penetration. However, it seemed that penetration caught up after a while, first at net level and then at system level.

Secondary degree of extension, it played a more important role over time as the net expands and the number of subsidiaries or very closely cooperating agents increases and the first degree of extension become less common as the company net becomes globalized.

6. Bilspedition

6.1. Bilspedition Group- case description

6.1.1. Bilspedition Group- International development

General development and owner structure

When Fallenius & Leffler in Gothenburg took the decision in 1918 to complement their seafreight services in 1918 with domestic trucking services in order to reduce the number of calls at different Swedish harbours[1],they founded a company in the name of AB Göteborgs Skeppselevator. This company, in which Bilspedition has its origins, continued in being until 1936 when the name was changed to Fallenius Godstrafik Göteborg AB. Fallenius Godstrafik Göteborg AB was the first company to offer the Swedish market consolidation services by truck.

The company developed positively during the 1930's but the expansion ceased with the second world-war when new restrictions and regulations were imposed. In 1940, the Swedish Railway acquired a 50% interest in ASG, the other large domestic broker and transport company. Two years later, in 1942, SLF - Svenska lastbilsägare förbundet (Swedish Truck Owners' Association) bought 50% of Fallenius Godstrafik Göteborg AB from Fallenius & Leffler AB. The basic reason was to secure a private alternative for the Swedish trucking companies for the future.

The name of the company was changed in 1944 to AB Godstrafik and Bilspedition (Bilspedition or GBS) which was altered in 1977 to Bilspedition AB.

In 1947 the domestic network of the company had 12 regional offices and agreements with 26 agents in Sweden. Total volumes transported came to 230.000 tons and the turnover was SEK 7.1 million.

Over time Bilspedition established an increasing number of offices in Sweden, to a large extent part-owned by the local agents. As expansion continued, these part-ownerships became a problem when Bilspedition wanted to create a web of domestic traffics between the offices. The problem was finally resolved through a new issue of shares in Bilspedition in 1952 which enabled these local interests to be exchanged for shares in Bilspedition, the parent company. The share issue was directed not only to the agents but at the same time towards other industries, which were offered up to 1/3 of the shares in Bilspedition. As a result, important

---

[1]This situation was similar to that of ASG and Svea Shipping Line which started in 1935.

companies in other Swedish industries like Billerud (Forest), Boliden AB(mining and trading), etc., became part-owners of Bilspedition at that juncture.

The heavy expansion of road transports in Sweden as well as its political effects interested SLF in buying the remaining shares in Bilspedition from Fallenius & Leffler. SLF and indirectly all of its truck-owning members, then became the majority owner of Bilspedition. Only a limited number of these members cooperated regularly with Bilspedition. In 1957 they formed a separate organization called BTF - Bilspeditions transportörförening (Bilspedition´s Truck Owners Association). This association came to play an important role in the development of Bilspedition.

The high growth in road transports continued during the 1950's and in the 1960's. The turnover changed from under SEK 20 million in 1950 to more than SEK 550 million in 1970. This situation created problems for Bilspedition since it needed capital to invest in the necessary facilities to handle the larger volumes as well as to cope with an expanding organization. The industrial shareholders did not want to make further investments in the company and SLF did not have the necessary capital available. The situation became acute in 1964. However, the members of SLF were divided among themselves due to the fact that only a limited number of the transport companies were cooperating with Bilspedition i.e. the BTF truck owners. The other truck owners were very largely prepared to sell their shares in Bilspedition in 1964/65, especially as some were cooperating with competing organizations like ASG. As a result of this situation and the internal problems it created, SLF started to look around for buyers for their Bilspedition shares.

The BTF truck owners reacted negatively to this and canvassed members in order to raise the necessary capital for Bilspedition. They managed to raise SEK 2.6 million which together with the capital of other shareholders (SEK 4 million) gave Bilspedition the necessary capital for expansion at that time. BTF created a separate shareholding company, BTFAB, which bought the new shares in Bilspedition. At this stage SLF decided to stay on as a shareholder in Bilspedition and even decided that 1% of the total turnover for transports made for Bilspedition was to be retained for future investments in the company. Through these measures and investments Bilspedition obtained the capital necessary for survival and expansion in the long-term also. The company was majority owned by the truck owners in BTF and SLF until the beginning of 1983 when it became registered on the Swedish Stock Exchange. BTFAB(ACC) still dominated after that through their voting shares of 44%. However their domination decreased over time and was 35% in 1990.

Figure 6.1. Ownership of Bilspedition

1918 - 1942 Fallenius &Leffler
1942 - 1952 Fallenius&Leffler 50% and SLF 50%
1952 - 1953 Fallenius&Leffler 1/3, SLF 1/3 and Industry 1/3
1953 - 1965 SLF 2/3 Industry 1/3
1965 - 1983 SLF and BTFAB majority owners, transport companies (e.g. Salen Shipp.
            Line, Wilson & Co, Skandiatransport, etc)
1983 - 1985 BTFAB largest owner 44% of voting shares 31% of
            capital
1985 - 1989 ACC(BTFAB) largest single owner 39% of voting shares
            20% of share capital, Wallenius Shipping line, Skandia
            Assur. Comp., Trygg-Hansa Assur. Comp., etc.
1990 -   ACC(BTFAB) largest single owner 35% of voting shares

Sources: Annual Reports, ACC - ett kvartssekel and Special Prospectuses when issuing new shares

Bilspedition remained predominantly domestic until the mid-1980's when a large acquisition increased the share of international activities to more than 50% of the total turnover. However, the first international transports started to the Nordic countries during the mid-1950's and a few years later to Continental Europe.

The growth in the newly started international traffics was very high during the 1960's. The number of trucks used increased by around 20 % yearly and turnover by even more.

After the rapid growth of the 1960's, the 1970's became a period of stagnation and instability leading to structural changes for the company. Rationalization was necessary both for the trucking companies as well as for Bilspedition. Large investments were made in terminals, warehouses and special terminal equipment for more efficient handling. Trucking companies were in need of concentration to larger units and BTF even created a special company BTUAB (Bilspedition Transportörer Utvecklings AB) in 1975 to take care of the reconstruction of trucking companies.

The international expansion slowed down during the 1970's even though the international share of Bilspedition's total turnover rose from 20% in 1970/71 to 24% in 1980.

In 1977 the company changed its name from AB Godstrafik and Bilspedition(GBS) to Bilspedition AB and the share capital was further increased by a new share issue.

The structural changes and the investments made during the 1970's also resulted in a low level of profitability for the Bilspedition Group until the early 1980's. Due to regular new issues of shares, the solidity was kept in the range of 20% over time in spite of the low profitability. The company suffered from a scarcity of capital during this whole period.

The situation changed in the 1980's when Bilspedition obtained access to new and larger amounts of capital through its introduction on the stock exchange. This allowed for a total reconstruction of the company and an immense growth by acquisitions. In 1982/83 Bilspedition acquired the transport and forwarding activities of Wilson &Co, an old family owned company. Wilson & Co was one of the larger international companies in Sweden with a turnover of SEK 1.6 billion but with low profitability. The owner of Wilson & Co had shares in Bilspedition before the acquisition and through the acquisition increased the size of his participation to around 8%.

Through the acquisition of Wilson &Co the international activities of Bilspedition grew in one year from 35 to 50% of the total turnover.

In 1985/86 Bilspedition bought another large Swedish group of international forwarders Scansped(SKT/F&L, NTS and TK), one of the largest competitors in international transports. Scansped was registered on the Swedish Stock Exchange and as a Group was larger than the international side of Bilspedition at the time. Scansped's turnover at the end of 1984 was SEK 3.6 billion on international transports whereas Bilspedition's international transports including Wilson totalled only SEK 2.3 billion. NTS had no desire to belong to the Bilspedition Group once Bilspedition bought Scansped. Since the companies involved in the Scansped Group had worked as separate entities and as the former owners of the different Scansped companies had to a large extent retained control of their companies it was possible for them to leave the Group. NTS therefore left the Scansped Group and joined the investment company Ratos. NTS then became the first company to join the Inter Forward Group, a new international transport and forwarding group created by Ratos. In the end Bilspedition acquired the Scansped Group, less NTS, and formed a new international part to the company.

Cool Carriers, the shipping line that Bilspedition bought in 1987, became part of Bilspedition Group the same year. In 1988, Bilspedition also bought two more large shipping lines Gorthon Lines (specialized in forest products) and Transatlantic.Through buying the different shipping lines the internationalization of the company increased, not only in Europe but through Cool Carriers and Transatlantic also overseas .

In 1988/89, Bilspedition consisted of three different groups of transport companies, namely, the Scansped Group(consisting of Scansped companies, Wilson and ATA), the Scanship Group (consisting of the shipping lines Gorthon[1], Cool Carriers and Transatlantic) and Bilspedition Domestic (the traditional domestic transportation business).

---

[1]Sold in 1991

Table 6.2.Some facts concerning Bilspedition

	1966/67[1]	70/71	74/75	1980	1985	1990
Turnover Group (msek)[2]	310	649	1 485	2 380	5 116	15 432
share international (%)	11-15	20	19	24	52	68
Result - Group (msek)[3]	2	4	5	14	140	733
No of employees - Parent	1092	1321	1343	1822	1431	1608
- " - - Group	1285	1761	1978	3386	4235	10 341
- " - -Abroad	100	116	220	287	847	3387

Through these acquisitions the 1980's became a decade of extreme growth and especially so for the international businesses. The total turnover increased almost 5 times. For international activities the growth rate was 15-20 times. The number of employees abroad increased 11-12 times, decreased in the parent company and increased 3 times for the Group.

The year 1990 became the best year ever in terms of profitability with a profit 10 times as large as in 1980. Furthermore, in 1990 the Bilspedition Group came to an agreement with a large Finnish Group, Spontel, to acquire 100% of Speditor OY, the largest Finnish international transport group with a number of subsidiaries abroad. The international transport and forwarding part of Speditor was to be called Scansped while the domestic transport companies and shipping agents and specialists were to retain their own names. Speditor's turnover for 1990 is not included in that of Bilspedition.

Another important event that took place during 1990 was the acquisition of 50% of Linjeflyg, the leading Swedish domestic airline.[4]

The business concept of the mid- and late 1980's was: "The carriers and forwarding companies in the Group will provide transport and information systems of such high quality and efficiency that they create prerequisites for customers of Bilspedition companies to attain an optimum balance in the tying-up of capital" (Annual Report 1987)

In 1990/91 the economic development has stagnated and the business concept of the 1980's had been changed to " Bilspedition will develop and produce transport and logistics as well as

[1]The period of accounting is set to 1 Sept- 31 Aug until 1975/ 76.
[2]Excluding VAT and Customs Duty
[3]Before taxes and dispositions
[4]These 50% of shares in Linjeflyg was sold during 1992 to SAS.

information services which meet the market demands for quality efficiency and simplicity" (Annual Report 1991). As the company has grown in size and diversification the business concept of 1990 seem to have changed to be less customer oriented and more interested in creating efficient standardized transport systems.

6.1.2. European Development

6.1.2.1. Period 1955-69

Development of services and foreign representation

The international development started mid 1950's together with agents within the Scandinavian countries as a complementary service. In 1960 Bilspedition established its own company, Nordisk Bilspedition, in Denmark and in 1962/63 another subsidiary, Skandinavisk Bilspedition, in Norway . As a contrast in Finland Bilspedition started together with agent in 1966.

At an early stage, Bilspedition also became owner of 10% of Autotransit (ATA), a small international transport company established in 1957. The majority of ATA was owned by several forwarders such as Skandia Transport & Spedition, Nordisk Transport & Spedition and Fallenius &Leffler, etc. and it was used for services complementary to its owners' normal business activities. Further, GBS took over 50% of the company in 1964. In 1965/66 the company became a fully owned subsidiary of GBS. Buying ATA gave GBS a base for an expansion into Continental Europe.

The size of the total Continental traffics were smaller in size than the Nordic traffics to begin with. This probably continued to be the case during the 1960's. As an indicator of this, in 1967 the number of trucks used in the total Continental traffics was 1,577 compared to the 6,527 used in the Nordic traffics; in 1971, the figures were 3,573 and 12,505 respectively. Even though the Continental traffics grew very solidly during the 1970's the Nordic traffics have continued to be very strong for Bilspedition over time.

During the 1960's, GBS had a gradual expansion of traffics to different European countries through ATA and the subsidiaries in Denmark, Norway and, at the very end of the period, in the U.K and through a sales office in Hamburg.

In 1968, ATA, with trucking traffics and its recently started trailer traffics, was represented through 15 agents, 3 subsidiaries and 1 sales office in 14 countries, namely, the Nordic countries, Belgium/ Holland, Luxembourg, Italy, Poland, Switzerland, West-Germany, U.K., Hungary, France and Austria.

The international development both for ATA and the sister companies in Denmark and Norway took place predominantly together with agents. In spite of the growth in Continental traffics, around 80 % of the total international traffics were concentrated to the Nordic countries during this period.The services were only traditional trucking services at first but from the end of the 1960's a few other types of services developed such as trailer traffics, temperated transports and warehousing. As new types of traffics were developed new agents were often added in Europe.

In 1967/68 GBS bought Flyttningsbyrån in Gothenburg, which included several companies and among these Trailer Express, specialized on international trailer transports mainly to the U.K. but also to Holland and West-Germany. Autotransit and Trailer Express were merged into Autotransit Trailer Express AB. TrailerExpress had a subsidiary in the U.K.which increased the importance of the U.K. for GBS. Very soon a new office was opened in Felixstowe and new agents were added. The cooperation with at least one of the former agents in the U.K. ceased as a result of this.

Other companies in which Bilspedition acquired a part-ownership at the end of the 1960's were Scandinavian Ferry Trailers and Scanfreight AB. This intensified the international growth into new countries like the U.S. and Canada.

Organization and investments

In 1950, the company handled under 0.4 million tons while in 1960 it handled 2.1 million tons and had 111 employees of whom only 10 were terminal workers. In 1970/71, the company handled 5.7 million tons and there were almost 1761 employees in total, out of which more than 200 were were employed by the international part. The basic reason for the very high increase in the number of employees was the fact that Bilspedition took over the personnel from the agents in Sweden but was also as a result of the expansion abroad. The need for new terminals was immense during this period and therefore the major portion of all investments was made in terminals. At the end of the period investments were also made in trailers and other transport equipment through acquiring part of Scandinavian Ferry Trailers and the ownership of Trailer Express.

As for the organization, the growth in the number of employees called for changes almost every year. The international side was rather limited to 6 international offices and since ATA did not become fully owned by GBS until 1965/66 it could not become a fully integrated part of the Bilspedition organization before then.

In 1967, one of the larger reorganizations started. Domestically the different profit centers in Sweden changed into fewer but larger districts and at the same time sales and other marketing activities grew in importance. Domestic and international traffics were separated as ATA became responsible for all international traffics to/ from Sweden.

Two years later the work started on another reorganization. A special "department of development" was created at the head office level, which then started to review the total organization. There was a need for managing and controlling the different parts of the organization. The organization became functional with separate departments for traffic, marketing, accounting, development, administration and training. This time the districts were organized into four regions. The marketing activities for both domestic and international traffics were coordinated by a marketing department at head office and at the regional level (except in Gothenburg and Jönköping). New types of personnel joined the company and the interest increased for active utilization of computers not only for accounting routines but also for administration of the operating routines.

Summary of the period 1955-69
Bilspedition started internationalizing in the mid 1950´s through trucking services with agents to Denmark and Norway. In the early 1960´s they established subsidiaries in the same countries and acquired a larger part of a company, Autotransit (ATA), specialized in trucking services to Continental Europe. ATA became fully owned in 1965/66.Then all the international activities of Bilspedition in Sweden were concentrated to ATA. In 1968 they covered 14 European countries through cooperation with agents and sister companies in Norway, in Denmark and in U.K. The U.K.company was a subsidiary to Trailer Express, which was another international company acquired during 1960´s. At the end of the period the subsidiaries started their internationalization and a sales office was set up in Hamburg.

6.1.2.2.Period 1970-79

Development of services and foreign representation
Even though the international development was not as stable and intense during the 1970's as it was during the 1960's, the turnover still increased around three times and the number of employees by 2-3 times during the period.

As customer industries began to concentrate and centralize their activities in the 1960's and 1970's their interest in and demand for distribution increased. Structural changes became necessary in transportation. Bilspedition, wanting to provide the customers with all types of transport services, reinforced its marketing activities and developed new types of services in the late 1960's and 1970's. The result was an increasing number of specialized services like warehousing, consulting and advisory services, hanging garment services, transports for cold or frozen goods, etc.

Bilspedition acquired a part of a large company, Cold Stores, specializing in frozen or cold goods. A new company, Coldsped AB, was constructed for transports of frozen and cold goods partly owned by Bilspedition and Cold Stores. At the end of the 1970's Bilspedition owned most of the Cold Store warehouses as well.

Bilspedition acquired Scandinavian Garment Services (SGS), another specialized company this time in hanging garments, from Wilson &Co in 1971. Setting up small specialized joint ventures for hanging garments in Denmark and Norway, SGS developed international traffics quickly .

A diversification in transports continued as Bilspedition in 1970 created a separate department for airfreight traffic and in 1971 it obtained its IATA licence in the name of ATA/Trailer Express. It also bought 50% of Flygspedition International AB in 1971/72 and acquired the balance in 1974. Furthermore, in 1976 Bilspedition acquired Alpen Parelius, an international seafreight forwarder. All of this meant that Bilspedition had established traffics to all different parts of the world. Before that, its internationalization was basically concentrated to countries which could be reached by truck from Scandinavia. Bilspedition also created customized specialized system transports for single customers, like carrying out internal transports for SKF in Europe. Many of these new businesses were then separated into profit centers.

Apart from the diversification through acquisitions or the creation of separate profit centers there was a continuation of the international expansion through ATA/Trailer Express. The number of employees in the ATA/ Trailer express increased during the period from 126 to around 330. Even then the number of employees of ATA/TrailerExpress will only show the Scandinavian side of the traffics and not the number of employees engaged in the same traffics within the agent companies. The total number of traffics were 140 Nordic and 40 to continental Europe in 1975.

Some new countries were added during the period such as Spain, Ireland, Eastern European Countries and the Middle East. At the end of the 1970's ATA/Trailer Express had around 30-40 agents and 26 international offices in Sweden. In total for Bilspedition at least 50-60.

Much of the transports to the Middle East were connected to the development of Bilspedition International which was specialized in trade fairs and project transports. It even opened a Representation Office in Baghdad.

The subsidiaries in Denmark and Norway showed overall growth from 109 employees to 228 during the period. However the subsidiary in Norway experienced a period of downturn in the early 1970's, as the Scandinavian landtransports were taken over by an agent Transportsentralen.

The high increase in Denmark at the end of the period was partly a result of the acquisition of Eurotrans A/S (Europa Transport & Spedition) and the establishment of Flygspedition International in Denmark.

Table 6.3. Number of employees engaged in the international business of Bilspedition

(No of employees)[1]	1968	1970	1972	1974	1975	1977	1979
ATA / Trailer Exp(S)[2]	117	127[3]	148	192	239	301[4]	330[5]
Skandin Bilsped(N)	42	45	21	24	31	50	58
Nord Bilsped(Dk)	57	64	60	77	103	90	170[6]
U.K.	-	26	55	107	68	-	-[7]
Holland	-	-	-	21	18	18	20
Total International	216	265[8]	284	421	459[9]	486[10]	600[11]

[1] Up to 1975 the number of employees is reported from 31 Aug. and from then on 31 Dec. each year.

[2] The figures are from the first year when ATA came to include not only the Continental traffics but also the Nordic traffics formerly part of the GBS offices in Sweden

[3] Including Trailer Express in Sweden but not U.K and West-Germany.

[4] Year 1977 and 1979 include empl. of Flygspedition in Sweden around 20 empl.

[5] Estimated

[6] Including Eurotrans and the newly established Flygspedition Denmark A/S

[7] In 1980 Autotransit UK was re-established.

[8] At the West-German sales office 3 persons were employed in 1970. In 1971 the office was closed down.

[9] Flygspedition in Stockholm had 4 and Gothenburg 10 employees

[10] Flygspedition International had 20 and Autotransit Italiana (majority owned) had 7 employees

[11] Number of employed for Flygspedition in Sweden and for Autotransit Italiana have increased. The employed of the part owned SGS companies in Denmark and Norway as well as in Switzerland are not included.

During 1970's the development internationally was intensive, the number of agents increased and many new areas in Europe were covered. Through the merger with Trailer Express in 1969 the U.K.became a very important market for ATA at least in early the 1970's.

During the period 1969 - 1974 the subsidiary Trailer Express Ltd in the U.K. expanded quite heavily. The subsidiary established offices in other parts of England and expanded international traffics to Holland, Norway, etc. In mid-1974 Trailer Express Ltd had 107 employees but in 1975 a downturn resulted in Bilspedition selling the U.K. company to Kühne & Nagel, which then became the agent. In 1980 ATA took it back, however, and started ATA, U.K. The cooperation with Kühne & Nagel continued for a while but on different terms.

Later during the period subsidiaries were established in Holland, Italy and part of a company in Switzerland was acquired. In Italy and Switzerland ATA bought 40% of the agents. A greenfield investment was made in Holland for Scandinavian traffics as well as for other European traffics. Thus Bilspedition's international expansion continued.

When Flygspedition International was acquired early in the 1970's and Alpen Parelius in the late 1970's both had agents in Europe as well as outside Europe. Flygspedition had established a small subsidiary in Denmark also. Other specialized companies belonging to the Group like SGS had their own agents in Europe (around 30 in 1980) that fitted their specialization. SGS had part-owned companies in Denmark and Norway also. In this way different agents for Bilspedition existed in many of the European countries.

Organization and investments

As the company specialized and diversified during the 1970's it also became divisionalized. In 1975, the regional organization changed into two divisions and the domestic and international divisions and the four regions were changed into 19 different domestic profit centers. The international division included the international subsidiaries. Then in 1977/78 a Group management and a number of Group staffs were created and the company changed into four divisions. These were the Inland, International, Cold storage (refrigerated and frozen goods) and Finance divisions (including administration).

Further diversification in services led to the creation of a separate division for subsidiaries like Ivers Lee (packing), Ekströms Industri AB (equipment for materials handling), etc., which did not fit into these already established departments. (Appendix 4)

The international growth had large effects on the international operations in Sweden. The international offices in Sweden increased from 6 in the beginning of the 1960's to 26 by the end of the 1970's and in the 1980's there were 30 international offices in Sweden. The various types of businesses also changed from the traditional trucking transport business to several specialities like ATA Bulk, ATA seafreight, special Scandinavian distribution systems, etc. This development increased the need for education and training of personnel not only within the separate businesses but also for management due to the growth of the organization. Large investments were made during the 1970's especially in creating a better know-how in international traffics as well as special transports.

Instead of investing mainly in terminals as during the 1960's, a large part of the investments were made in warehouses and transport equipment such as trailers, containers and flats. This facilitated development of combined traffics like rail/ road, sea/ road, air/ road. Further these investments, in combination with large terminal investments, also increased the risk for Bilspedition and decreased the risk for the suppliers. Additionally, Bilspedition came to take full responsibility for the total transport.

In 1975 all Bilspedition's international activities became part of an international division of around 500 persons including the foreign subsidiaries. The former coordinator of the international activities in Bilspedition became responsible for the total international division. The need to manage not only international operations in Sweden but also abroad increased. (Appendix 4)

As the international organization grew larger and more dispersed geographically the interest for computerized communication systems increased. The development which had been going on for many years but mainly in domestic operations now focused on the international operations.

Summary of the period 1970-79

Growth was almost as much a result of acquisitions as of existing activities. The acquisitions were either in new types of services (warehousing, advisory, airfreight etc.) or in more specialized trucking services (hanging garment, bulk, frozen goods, etc). ATA/ Trailer Express had a high growth. The number of employees nearly tripled. The number of agents in Europe to ATA/Trailer Express more than doubled.

In the first half of the period there was a downturn and the U.K. and Norwegian traffics were fully or partly taken over by agents and the sales office in Hamburg was closed down. At the end of the period acquisitions and greenfield investments were made in Holland, Italy, Denmark, Norway and Switzerland. In Sweden they invested in intensified training, new communication systems, more transport equipment for combitraffics and in an increasing number of international offices. The total international activities of the Group were concentrated to one division.

6.1.2.3. Period 1980-89

Development of services and foreign representation

During the 1980's Bilspedition had changed from being basically a trucking transport company into being a conglomerate of companies within all different types of transports, as well as all possible complementary services. The company was also one of the largest transport and forwarding companies within this area based in Europe and as a group the largest in the Nordic countries. Through the acquisitions during the 1980's Bilspedition had almost all existing types of transport companies within their Group.[1]

The situation had radically changed in 1983 when the Bilspedition Group bought Wilson & Co which had a European network of representatives.This more than doubled the existing number of agents in Europe for land-transportation and even more so if airfreight, seafreight and speciality agents in Europe were to be included.

Many new international services were added to the company's international business like railway transports, more diversified shipping and airfreight services, etc.

ATA's representation in Europe worked in competition with that of Wilson's from early 1983 when Wilson joined the Bilspedition Group. This was especially true for trucking services even though a similar situation existed in air and seafreight.

Wilson had 46 agents and 5 small subsidiaries in Europe (see list enclosed) in 1987 and these were mostly old and established transport and forwarding companies which had cooperated with Wilson over a long time. Most of them were competing with the ATA group of companies and their agents.

However, the ATA group of companies[2] changed during the 1980's and especially so ATA Sweden which had gone through a period of concentration in the number of and types of representatives which had been reduced to 4 agents and 8 subsidiaries (excluding Flygspedition and SGS). ATA Sweden was represented in 12 countries in 1987. The 8 subsidiaries were all given the same name, ATA, a change from earlier when there were several different names. The companies were fully owned subsidiaries with the exception of the Norwegian company, since Linjegods A/S, a large domestic Norwegian transport company with some international traffics, had acquired 40% of Skandinavisk Bilspedition in 1984 and Bilspedition acquired

---

[1] During 1991 they even acquired 50% of an airline.

[2] ATA group of companies is the same as the group of subsidiaries and agents in Europe cooperating with ATA Sweden and belonging to the same organizational Group in Sweden, which in 1987 was Bilspedition International.

20% in Linjegods. Before the deal with Bilspedition, Linjegods was an important agent to ASG.

In Norway, Denmark, Holland, Belgium and West-Germany the number as well as the size of the companies increased. They were actually the outcome of a merger of several companies that had been acquired in those countries as part of the ATA group of companies. In Holland, Belgium and West-Germany there had been several investments in small companies in order to get a better coverage of the different countries. However, the subsidiaries all remained very small until 1986 when Bilspedition acquired West-Friesland which had companies in all three countries. At first the Dutch and Belgian parts were acquired and half a year later the company in West-Germany. West- Friesland was specialized in international trucking services. These acquired companies were all merged after some time with the existing activities of the ATA group of companies in those countries. Sometimes it could take several years before they merged, as in the case of Eurotrans and ATA in Denmark but in other cases it was much quicker. The small acquisitions made by Bilspedition in Holland and Belgium included not only trucking services but also seafreight, warehousing, etc.

When the Scansped companies had joined the Bilspedition Group in 1985/86 the situation got even more complicated since they had representatives (agents as well as some subsidiaries) in most European countries sometimes overlapping because of competition between TK and SKT/F&L.

In 1985/86, Bilspedition also bought the Scansped organization which, when the deal was finally settled, consisted of SKT/F&L and TK as well as a number of specialist organizations which worked as separate companies like Kungsholms Express(removals etc), Aug. S. Andersson (fruits, vegetables etc), Gustav Smith (e.g.chinaware), etc.

At the time of the takeover, not only did SKT/F&L have quite a considerable competition with TK within their own organization but also with the Wilson and ATA international traffics in Europe and overseas. SKT/F&L also had an airfreight company Scanflight which had its own agents in Europe. Most of the specialist companies had some agents of their own within Europe. The large European land-transport organizations were competing intensively with ATA and Wilson. This was also the case for sea and airfreight.

In Europe, SKT/F&L/TK, which was an old well-established transport and forwarding company, was represented at the end of 1987 by 49 agents and 9 subsidiaries covering all countries of importance in Europe (see list Appendix 4). At this stage TK had been merged into SKT/F&L. Through the acquisition of Scansped the number of representatives in each European country increased further through a combination of agents and subsidiaries. In many countries like Denmark, Holland, Norway and the U.K., etc., there were three of more subsidiaries competing with each other (see lists enclosed in Appendix 4).

In West-Germany SKT/F&L had 16 agents which combined with Wilson made 30. This did not include the subsidiaries of ATA or Wilson in West-Germany and agents of specialists like airfreight. However, while many of the agents of other specialists utilizing road transports were the same as the regular agents, others were not. The situation became very complex not only for the competing Swedish parent organizations but also for the agents and the subsidiaries competing with each other.

The three large international groups of companies Wilson, Autotransit and Scansped continued as separate groups and were free to act separately. Therefore there was strong internal competition. Through the acquisition of Scansped the representation not only in Europe but also in other parts of the world was tripled or quadrupled depending on the country. The airfreight companies from Wilson and the Scansped Group, however, were almost directly merged into one of the companies, Scanflight. This did not include the small airfreight company Flygspedition International which existed (until 1991) as a separate company. The largest airfreight company before the merger was ISA, InterScandinavian Airfreight, which belonged to the Wilson Group. ISA was also part of a large international voluntary chain of airfreight forwarders WACO, World Air Cargo Organization.

In 1988, it was decided to merge the companies SKT/F&L, Wilson and ATA. Air and sea and land-transportation were included with the exception of the specialist companies. As for airfreight, Scanflight and ISA merged, with the exclusion of Flygspedition, as had been decided two years earlier. It reduced the number of representations for land-transportation from 126 to 57, increased the volume of their traffics and reduced the variety of services. The total volumes decreased by 10-15 % on the whole during the first year after the merger in spite of high growth on the market. (A more detailed description is found in the Scansped Europe event)

The European land-transport subsidiaries were all renamed Scansped in 1989/90.
For the remaining representatives, whether subsidiaries or agents, the utilization of transport and terminal facilities increased and as well as the frequency in the traffics.

Finally, Bilspedition still had a large number of agents in Europe after the merger if one were to include the agents for separate areas like airfreight, overseas and specialist as well as separately for the shipping lines which were acquired in 1987. This in spite of the fact that the merger of ISA and Scanflight also reduced the number of airfreight agents.

In 1990 Bilspedition acquired the Speditor group of companies, involving international representation in most countries in Europe, partly in competition with the new Scansped group.

Organization and investments

In the 1980's the organization was changed in a number of ways, mainly as a result of the very large acquisitions made. The number of employees was around 9500 in 1988 (from 3300 in 1980) and the net turnover was over SEK 12.5 billion.

The organizational structure first changed when Wilson & Co joined the company in 1983. Wilson continued as a separate unit but placed in the international division and until Scansped was bought. The international companies continued their activities separately.

Another reorganization in 1986/87 turned the divisions into separate companies. The new organization had five companies, out of which one was the newly acquired Scansped Group with the addition of Wilson &Co and reduction of TK..The formerly international division became a separate company, as did Bilspedition International AB, which included ATA, SGS, Flygspedition, TK, etc. Also Finance and Domestic divisions became a separate companies as well as Bilspedition Information Systems. At the same time, it was decided that operative decisions should be decentralized to the new companies. Then around a year later Bilspedition acquired the shipping lines Cool Carriers, Transatlantic and Gorthon Lines, they became a separate group of companies, Scanship and AB Scansped and Bilspedition International AB were combined and merged into Scansped Group.

In 1989, after the merger of Bilspedition International and Scansped, Bilspedition consisted of three transport sub-groups which were Domestic Group, Scansped Group (the largest), and Scanship Group. There were two separate companies for service functions, one called "Biljonen" for financing and Bilspedition Information Systems. The investments during the 1980's were made possible to a very large extent by the fact that the company became introduced on the stock exchanges in Sweden, Norway and Denmark. (Appendix 4)

In 1991 there was a new reorganization where the Domestic Group and Scansped Group became part of the same group, called Transport and Forwarding, while Shipping remained a separate group.

The rate of acquisitions intensified during the 1980's. The investments in different international companies abroad and in Sweden during 1980's involved around 80 companies compared to less than 20 before 1980. Compared to earlier decades not only had the number of companies acquired increased but so had also the size of the companies. (Appendix 4) .

Summary of the period 1980-89

During this period Bilspedition became an international conglomerate through a number of acquisitions and the Group became introduced to the stock exchanges in the Scandinavian countries. In 1982/83 the first large acquisition, Wilson & Co, took place, which increased the international share in Bilspedition from 35 to 50% and more than doubled the amount of agents in Europe and overseas. The next huge acquisition was of another large Swedish competitor, Scansped, in 1985/86. The ATA group of companies and the two new groups, Wilson and Scansped, continued as separate units and international competitors.

Several medium-sized acquisitions were made in West-Germany, Holland, Belgium, U.K., Finland, etc which were accrued to one or other of the three large international groups.

The organization was changed several times, as a result of these acquisitions. First, in order to include the two large competitors into the Group and then after the large merger in 1988.(For a more detailed description of the merger see Scansped Europe event.)

6.1.3. Specific event - merger between Bilspedition International and Scansped 1988

6.1.3.1. Scansped Group in Europe

The merger between Bilspedition International and the Scansped Group resulted in a new and larger Scansped Group. Even though the merger concerned all different types of transports and thereby connected services, the part described here concentrates on the merger of land-transport companies and their operations within Europe. The same event which is described here in total will later be described in more detail through the event of the creation of the new Scansped Sweden, the new Scansped West-Germany and Scansped Belgium.

Before the event

Bilspedition owned two large International Groups in 1986, Bilspedition International and Scansped Group. Competition existed not only between but also within each group of companies. The competition was sometimes even stronger within than between. At the same time the profitability of the different companies was not satisfactory.

The companies in these groups also had some complementary activities in general forwarding, special transports and other activities. The companies of former Scansped were and historically had been more the type of forwarders and acted as such, selecting different means of transportation but not owning the means of transportation. ATA, being part of Bilspedition, majority owned by trucking companies for many years and founded as a complement to forwarders, had to take a certain responsibility for the truck owners' viability. ATA also placed more emphasis on investments in terminals, transport equipment, trucks, etc., which had to pay off. The customers of ATA were often customers of Bilspedition domestically. The demands made by these customers derived to a large extent from experience of Bilspedition's large domestic operations while SkandiaFallenius' average customers could not really compare performance in domestic and international traffics since they lacked these services. The ATA group of companies in Europe were to some extent expected to live up to the same demands as the large Bilspedition in Sweden, by offering warehousing, logistical problem solving, etc. This situation influenced the profiles as well as the profitability of the two different companies. Wilson, finally, was an old and well established company as a forwarder and as agent for different shipping lines. As a result of this it was strong on overseas markets.

On January 1, 1985, Skandiatransport and Fallenius & Leffler merged - in the same year as the company was acquired by Bilspedition. In 1986, the first year as part of the Bilspedition Group, SkandiaFallenius derived some positive experiences from the former merger between Skandiatransport and F&L. It was then decided that TK should be merged into SkandiaFallenius in January 1987. TK, the smallest company, was specialized on certain markets like Denmark, Italy, Austria and the Far East.

The new merged company SKT/F&L/TK made a profit in 1987 while Bilspedition International made a loss.
There was still intense rivalry between the SKT/F&L/TK, Wilson and ATA Groups of companies. Unsuccessful attempts were made to get the companies to cooperate and to divide the companies within the Group as regards company services through taking on some activities and leaving others.

The positive experiences of former mergers set against the continued internal competition and the low profitability of the international activities became incentives to consider a total merger of the international activities.

At the same time, the expected changes in the rules and regulations in the EC, which would in all likelihood increase competition within as well as between countries on the European transport market, made it of interest to have a strong position not only in Scandinavia but also in the European countries. Even though the three international Groups of transport and forwarding companies in Bilspedition were quite large, their activities were concentrated to the Scandinavian markets. Altogether, they had 71 terminals and offices for international traffics in Scandinavia and around 1,250 employees in Sweden, 400 in Norway and 350 in Denmark.

The three Groups together had a number of different subsidiaries abroad mainly in the North European countries. Outside Europe they had only three companies of which Wilson had two in the US and TK had one in Hongkong.

Of the three larger groups of companies, the ATA group had more international subsidiaries including 30 foreign offices which covered 8 foreign countries. Some of them, like West-Friesland in Holland, Belgium and West-Germany, were acquired after the Scansped acquisition. Both Wilson and SkandiaFallenius also acquired international subsidiaries after they joined the Bilspedition Group. For example, Wilson acquired their UK agent, Giltspur, in 1985 and SkandiaFallenius acquired Adams Transport in 1987. Both companies acquired were relatively large international companies with their own international network of agents.

The subsidiaries in the EC countries were mostly situated in the same countries and to a large extent competed with each other within these countries. There were 2 subsidiaries in France, 3 in Holland, 3 in Belgium, 3 in Germany, 3 in Norway, 4-5 in Denmark, 3 in the U.K. and 2 in Switzerland. If the Swedish parent companies merged, the subsidiaries would have had to be merged as well. A merger of the three separate large international groups within Bilspedition Wilson, ATA and SkandiaFallenius/TK would not only have important effects on subsidiaries but also would have meant the loss of many of the agents that the different Groups had. Many of the agents had worked with some of the companies for a long time. This was especially so in the case of Wilson in Europe. SkandiaFallenius/TK had changed agents due to earlier mergers and ATA had their own offices in most countries of importance.

This was the situation when the Board of Bilspedition Group decided to accept the suggestion of the managers within the different groups to merge. It was decided in August, 1988 based on a plan presented by the managers and was supposed to be put into effect in January, 1989.

The event
The event was discussed and planned in advance in Sweden by 75 persons working during July and August, 1988 in seven working groups for different functional areas. More detailed plans were made after the decision to merge was taken. At the same time, in project groups the subsidiaries had started to plan for a change .

The merger was facilitated by the fact that at the time of the merger the Swedish subsidiary of SkandiaFallenius had the same managing director as ATA in Sweden.

A large reorganization had to be carried out both in Sweden and abroad. The number of employees in Sweden was to be reduced from 1250 to 950. The reductions were to be even greater in the other Scandinavian countries Norway and Denmark where the employees would be reduced by 50% or even down to a 1/3. Similar detailed plans had to be made by the managements in the subsidiaries.

Everything was to be changed and many people who had been competitors formerly and who were not in favour of the merger would find themselves having to adapt. Others would have to leave. Apart from the rationalizations, one of the main problems was choosing the design for the European traffics and its representatives. Somewhere in the region of a hundred different agents would have to leave, since there were two or sometimes three agents too many in a great number of countries and in countries like West-Germany more than 20 agents would have to leave. (see the list of the former agents).

The decision, especially for the Swedish parent companies, was to give priority to the subsidiaries and use agents for complementary coverage only.

The fact that the traffics were predominantly south-north traffics to/from Sweden in cooperation with agents or subsidiaries meant that relatively little by way of third-country traffics not involving Sweden had been developed. Where such traffics existed the partners would not necessarily be sister companies. ATA was the only group which had a larger number of subsidiaries in Europe. Giving priority to cooperation between subsidiaries necessitated a higher degree of cooperation between the newly merged sister companies in Europe which would serve to increase traffics not involving Sweden.

The sister companies in Europe would be working under the name of Scansped, with the exception of overseas transport where the name of Wilson was to be retained. The specialist companies like Anton Pettersson, Aug .Andersson, etc. would not only keep their name but also continue their operations as before. The old parent company Scansped AB was to change its name to Scansped Group AB.

All the plans had to be very secret in order to take the agents by surprise. Otherwise they might have left Scansped before the change was fully planned. In the event, however, the timing had to be changed from January, 1989 to October, 1988 due to certain rumours. A mass of information was to be distributed both internally and externally in order to let people know where they would be placed in the new organization in Sweden as well as abroad and to keep customers and suppliers informed.

The Scansped Group was divided into four different business areas, namely, Scansped Sweden, Scansped Europe, Scansped Overseas and Scansped Specialists. At the end of 1988, the Scansped Group consisted of 4.200 employees from the three different groups of companies and had subsidiaries in 12 countries.

<u>After the event</u>

What were the effects of this merger on Bilspedition and Scansped <u>in Europe</u> as a whole?

Internal effects

The creation of the new company was not easy. Almost all routines required changing not only in Sweden but also abroad. The Swedish organization, the merging subsidiaries and many agents experienced big problems in functioning in an efficient manner. Also working with larger sister companies differed from that of working with small and dependent subsidiaries or agents. Further, there were differences between companies in the type of customer and a new common profile had to be created, etc.

ATA and SKT/F&L were strong in different markets which made it somewhat easier to adapt even though their cultures were very different. Wilson on the other hand had its basic strength in dealing with typical European seafreight countries like the U.K.

The managing director of the new Group came from SkandiaFallenius. This was also the case in Holland, Belgium and Norway, where SkandiaFallenius had its own subsidiaries.

In Sweden only, 10-12 new firms were started in competition as a result of the merger. Some of them by managers who left the company. It was mainly ATA and Wilson personnel which left the merging companies, while SkandiaFallenius personnel stayed to a larger extent.

It took a longer time for things to settle than expected. However, the profitability in 1989 changed from negative to positive figures.

In 1989, the Group merged 20 smaller companies into 9 larger transport and forwarding companies in Europe. There remained 1,700 employees out of the former 2,200. Merging different traffics meant higher frequency, lower costs and improved punctuality. Some of the offices in Europe immediately received twice the volumes of goods, which most of them did not have the necessary resources to handle. Nor were they able to satisfy the demands from agents or sister companies as regards quality of services. The fact that the Scansped Group retained the existing subsidiaries and concentrated the services to them meant that an increasing number of subsidiaries were representing each other in different European countries.

Scansped Europe had employees working in 46 different locations in 9 countries in 1989. Many of the companies started building or renting new terminals in order to be able to handle the larger volumes of goods.

Most European subsidiaries cooperated with Scansped within Scandinavia but still competed in several cases in continental Europe.

External effects

In all, Scansped Europe suffered a reduction of between 10-20 % of its total volumes during the first year after the merger (1988) in spite of the fact that the market had a positive development during the same period. Many customers that formerly used Scansped stopped doing so. A large segment of these were probably customers of the former agents.

In most cases the names of the subsidiaries were changed as well as telephone numbers, locations, contact persons, etc. and this had negative effects on customer services. In Holland, Belgium and West-Germany, for example, the name of the company had been changed three or four times within five years.

The restructuring of the companies as a result of the merger also led to a deterioration in services for a short period. In the cases where the subsidiaries lacked the necessary resources to take care of the larger volumes the effects continued for a longer period. Building new terminals, creating new computer systems etc., as was sometimes necessary, took time.

Some positive effects of the merger were the increased frequency in the traffics as well as the size of the Scansped companies. Some larger international customers were able to take advantage of the new Scansped and its international size.

A number of the existing agents to the subsidiaries ended their cooperation because of the merger. Finding new agents had become increasingly difficult. As an example, when Scansped in Holland lost its large international agent, Panalpina, in West-Germany they finally solved the problem of finding a new representative by buying another international company in Stuttgart, Teka Trans. Teka Trans had the necessary resources to take care of the existing traffics between Stuttgart and Holland/Belgium. However this company also had an independent salesman in Belgium stationed at its agent who got transferred and integrated into the newly merged Scansped Belgium.

Scansped was as an unknown name in Europe before the merger since none of the subsidiaries had used the name Scansped before the merger. They had to market the new name heavily during the period of change. The merger therefore led to a large marketing campaign for the Scansped companies in Europe and the contacts with most customers were intensified.

All in all, the merger meant a restructuring of the market so that Bilspedition was seen as one of the larger transport and forwarding companies in Europe, competing with the other MNCs in transport and forwarding.

The growth in volumes for subsidiaries also resulted in positive effects for their suppliers. Only in a very few cases did the merger result in a negative reactions from the suppliers as, for instance, in the case of the trucking company Satraco[1] in Belgium being sold to Inter Forward Group.

Summary of the Scansped Europe event

The merger was made between the two groups Bilspedition International and Scansped. Bilspedition International was dominated by the ATA group of companies and Scansped by the two competing subgroups Wilson & Co and former Scansped companies. These three groups were competing not only in Sweden but also internationally through their subsidiaries and agents in Europe. In several countries there were two or three subsidiaries. The total number of agents was well over 200 if the agents of the internationalized subsidiaries were included.

The event resulted in a merger not only of the companies in Sweden but also of the European subsidiaries. The number of employees was reduced in size from 2200 to 1700, most of which were made within Scandinavia. The sister companies in 12 countries in Europe all got the name Scansped and the cooperation between them increased. All subsidiaries of Scansped Europe were restructuring at the same time. This caused decreases in volumes of between 10-20% depending on the area.

The new merged subsidiaries cooperated with sister companies and agents in many countries. In the case of Germany the strength and knowledge of the subsidiary were not enough as the Dutch company lost its agent in Stuttgart, Germany. Bilspedition had to buy a new company, Tekatrans, to solve the situation in that area. Finally an external result of the merger was that a number of new competing cooperations were established by the former agents and sometimes by former personnel.

6.1.3.2. Scansped Sweden

Scansped Sweden as a company was formed by merging the Swedish parent operations of the three separate groups of companies SkandiaFallenius/TK (SKT/F&L/TK), Wilson & Co (Wilson) and ATA. Traditionally, the Swedish side of the three companies had played a dominant role within their respective groupings, forming the base for their international development prior to the merger.

Before the event

Before the event ATA, Wilson and SKT/F&L/TK were three different competing companies, each in its own right ranking amongst the largest transport and forwarding companies in Sweden. All were old established companies with international operations and with some subsidiaries abroad. Each had developed internationally over time and together were

---

[1]Shortly after Satraco was acquired by IF group it was sold back and the company went bankrupt

represented by more than 100 different agents in Europe (see appendix 4). ATA had been concentrating on creating a European network of subsidiaries during the last years before the merger and had ceased cooperation with many agents. On the other hand, Wilson and the old Scansped companies SKT, F&L and TK all had longer international experience than ATA. They had been competitors for decades but cooperating now and then for specific purposes.

The attempts to get the three different companies to cooperate voluntarily failed. Competition between the companies seemed to be stronger than ever and the profitability was unsatisfactory.

The experience of mergers especially within Scansped had been positive after the mergers in 1984 of Skandiatransport (SKT) and Fallenius & Leffler (F&L) and between SKT/F&L and TK in 1987. This was something, of course, that the three different competing groups were aware of.

The event
The merger of the three different competing operations into one company, Scansped Sweden, resulted in some 300 employees in Sweden leaving the Group within the first year. Quite a number left because they found some other alternative employment and some took early retirement . Only a very small percentage were finally asked to leave.

In Sweden, 71 different terminals and offices were to be reduced to 30 and 22 regions with their own management were to be reduced to 7. This greatly affected personnel as well.
The decision to merge the companies also contained a decision in favour of subsidiaries, where subsidiaries existed, in preference to agents. The concentration of the goods to the existing subsidiaries meant that most of the effects of the merger would be suffered by the agents, as opposed to the subsidiaries abroad.

The excessive number of agents as well as the concentration of the traffics to/from Sweden increased the importance of taking the decision to merge the companies.
The change was to be very visible in Sweden where the three companies were all quite large and well-known.
Since the bulk of services for all three companies engaged Swedish resources in one way or another the effects in Sweden became very apparent.

Reactions from the personnel in Sweden were extensive. The differences in corporate cultures were more visible in Sweden.The cooperation with many of the agents was ended overnight. Others with agreements incorporating a termination clause or a guarantee continued for a while. In some of these cases, like in Finland and Holland, the agents decided to break the relations prematurely.

Large resources had to be engaged in order to handle all the changes simultaneously. The change took about a year, from the beginning of October, 1988 to the end of 1989. During 1989, most of the resources were needed to handle the effects of the merger, which caused problems through other parts of the business, like invoicing, receiving lower priority.

After the event

One of the most important outcomes was that the total international traffic system had to be changed. The number of traffics, the services that could be offered in each place, the contact persons, the agreements, etc. It was especially complicated where the international partner was a subsidiary consisting of the three merged companies, facing the same type of problems that were present in Sweden.

The result of the merger in terms of changes of representatives in the European network for the Swedish parts of the groups can be seen by comparing the three combined lists of agents and offices abroad before and after the merger (see Appendix 4) of November 1989. The number of agents decreased from 99 to 43 and the number of sister companies changed from 24 to 14. Scansped AB cooperated with all the general forwarding subsidiaries of Scansped Group in Europe but in some countries, where coverage of the sister company was insufficient as in Germany, France, UK and Switzerland, in combination with agents.

The fact that Scansped Sweden cooperated with agents where the European subsidiaries did not have sufficient resources led to conflict between Scansped Sweden and its agents and the European sister companies. For example, Hellman in Osnabrück, a very large international company, competed with Scansped in Germany, Scansped Holland, etc., as well as in airfreight and seafreight both in Europe and overseas. Hellman also had a close cooperation world-wide with Nordisk Air Cargo in Sweden and was cooperating with NTS in Denmark. At the same time Scansped had a cooperation with Hellmann using its domestic services for the whole of West-Germany. During 1990 Hellman and Scansped Sweden ceased their cooperation and Hellman switched to ERT, an ASG subsidiary.

The agents of Scansped Sweden were competing with the European sister companies in several different ways either locally in the country of concern, in traffics to/from other countries or in other services like airfreights, seafreight or special transports such as hanging garments, etc.

The competition changed as result of breaking with agents. Some of the companies newly established by Swedish personnel leaving the merging companies were cooperating with former agents. Examples of new companies that started in this manner were ABC transport in Malmö with ATA personnel, Jönköping ATA personnel went to Road Link, Stockholm Wilson personnel started a company for an agent Mahlenstein, in Borås TK personnel left and started on their own. Danzas, the Wilson agent, bought part of an existing company, Rationell Spedition. Further some well known former agents, on losing their Swedish agents, started cooperation and thereby strengthened of existing competitors in Sweden.

Summary of the event

The effects of the acquisitions as well as later the merger were most visible in Sweden. The merger of the Swedish companies drastically changed the number of employees (a reduction of 300), of offices in Sweden (from 77 to 30) and the number of agents (from 126 to 57). Their sister companies abroad were given priority as representatives. Competition increased from former agents and through the establishment of new companies. In 1989 Scansped Sweden had high restructuring cost, which resulted in a loss. In spite of the merger, many conflicts still existed between the internationalized subsidiaries and the agents of Scansped Sweden, so further arrangements had to be made.

Scansped West-Germany

Before the event

West-Germany has always been a very important market for Bilspedition in Europe. Until the end of the 1970's, apart from a sales office for a few years at the end of the 1960's, it's only representation was through a number of agents. In 1980, the first German operational subsidiary, Autotransit GmbH, was established in Hamburg. The operations of the company were limited to the northern parts of West-Germany. In the other parts ATA Sweden was represented by agents.

The company in Hamburg had around 15 employees when it started. Then it grew internationally. Important countries became not only Nordic countries but also other destinations like Italy, Switzerland, France and Holland and Belgium. They also had a small seafreight department as well as warehousing.

In 1986, Autotransit bought Spedition United, formerly West-Friesland, which was owned by United Transport Corporation. Originally West-Friesland, an old Dutch company that started in Alkmeer in 1917, had been family owned. The subsidiary in Germany started in 1951 and was sold to United Transport in 1981. It continued in the name of West-Friesland until 1984 when it changed the name to Spedition United. As Autotransit acquired the company in the beginning of 1986 it did not include the German operations. The company in West-Germany was acquired some months later and was then renamed to Autotransit GmbH and it was decided that Autotransit GmbH in Hamburg and the new international part, Spedition United, should be merged.

At the time of the takeover Spedition United had three offices in West-Germany (Köln, Wuppertal and Frankfurt) and around 120 employees. Very soon after the takeover though, in 1986, the new international part of Autotransit GmbH started three new offices (Stuttgart, Nürnberg and München).

Then in 1986/87 the ATA group of companies, became a part of the larger group of Bilspedition International. Further a new office was opened in Hannover. This new office led to certain complications with one of the most important German agents of their sister company Scansped Sweden, Gebr.Hellmann in Osnabrück. However, Autotransit GmbH agreed to leave the Osnabrück area alone and vice versa for Gebr. Hellmann and the Hannover area .

In West- Germany, most Scansped offices had only trucking traffics, subcontracting the transports out to trucking companies. Before the event, Autotransit in Hamburg and Autotransit in Köln were the only two offices which had trucking traffics as well as certain overseas activities.

The situation of SKT/F&L and Wilson& Co in West-Germany was different. SKT/F&L, as well as Wilson, used agents for all their traffics in West-Germany though Wilson did have a small office in Travemünde for the Scandinavian operations. Further, most of the agents were well-known German transport companies with which cooperation had existed long term sometimes since the second world war or even earlier. The number of agents in Germany was around 15-20 for each of them and the cooperations mainly concerned traffics to/from Sweden.

The agents of SKT/F&L, Wilson and ATA were to a large extent competing on the German market for goods to/from Scandinavia. This situation, in combination with the fact that Autotransit through ATA GmbH and the acquisition of Spedition United had a number of offices and had recently started some new offices, made this competition even harder.

Not only did they compete on the Scandinavian market but Autotransit in West-Germany also had its own traffics to/from other countries in Europe like Benelux, France and Italy in competition with the agents.

The event

The decision to merge SKT/F&L/TK, Wilson and Autotransit activities in West-Germany became rather complicated since almost all the agents of these companies had to be changed. The newly formed Scansped Germany GmbH was supposed to be the main agent for all the three former Swedish parent companies in West-Germany. The German company changed its name from Autotransit to Scansped GmbH in 1988/89. This was the third change of name for the old West-Friesland part of the company since 1984 which made it difficult both for the customers and for the personnel. This time the new name Scansped was also unknown on the

German market. The managing director of the new Scansped GmbH, with head office situated just outside Köln, was former managing director of the former Spedition United part of Autotransit.

Since neither SKT/F&L/TK or Wilson had any offices of their own in West-Germany the offices of the old ATA international were supposed to handle almost all volumes for all three companies to/from the eight areas where they existed. This became difficult since some of these offices were newly established. The former added international part Autotransit GmbH organization had grown from 120 employees to 190 within a period of less than three years. In spite of this, Scansped GmbH did not have the necessary resources to handle all the added volumes within such a short period. When the merger was accomplished the volumes of the company to/from Sweden more than doubled overnight. This was achieved in a period of extremely intense competition from the large number of former agents. As a result of this, the total loss in volumes were larger in West-Germany than in most other areas of Europe.

After the event

Scansped GmbH had no complementary agents in Germany, which Scansped Sweden, Belgium, Holland and many of the other European Scansped offices had. Basically they cooperated with the sister companies in the Scandinavian countries and with agents in Austria, Benelux, U.K.and Italy. In some countries the local offices of Scansped in Germany had different representatives.

In Benelux only the newly established somewhat weaker Scansped offices in the southern part of West-Germany established a cooperation with Scansped in Holland and Belgium. The offices in the Köln/Wuppertal area cooperated with Ziegler in Belgium (a large well-known company) and they even had an advanced project going on for Volvo together with Ziegler. In Italy and Holland Scansped in Köln/ Wuppertal had other agents than other Scansped companies in Europe such as Saima and van der Graf and Karl Hermann.

This made the situation in West- Germany rather complicated because of the combinations of agents as well as Scansped's own offices in eight places.

West-Germany	Before event[1]	After event
No of agents -Swedish Parents	31	10
No of offices of subsidiary	7[2]	8

Table 6.4. Change in agents and number of offices of subsidiary in West-Germany

[1] In 1987 a year before the merger
[2] In spring 1986 the number of offices were only 3+1

The reduction in agents in table 6.3 only shows the changes experienced by Scansped GmbH due to the merger of the Swedish parent companies. Then there are the other sister companies in Europe which also substituted many of their agents with Scansped GmbH in several areas. The old SKT/F&L subsidiaries in particular had very little cooperation with Scansped West-Germany before the merger. These changes, which could have been almost equally large as those in Scansped Sweden added to the pressure on the new Scansped GmbH.

As a result of the merger, Scansped GmbH in West-Germany lost its agents in the U.K., Spain, Italy, Switzerland and France. Scansped GmbH in Köln and Wuppertal were in this case forced to change and find new representatives in these countries. The agents leaving the cooperation declared that they expected Scansped to increase the cooperation within the Group. Therefore they sought new agents which were not developing internationally. It did not seem to work out that way though. Three of these agents started working with subsidiaries to other international transport companies. One was acquired by Schenker.

However Scansped GmbH found new agents in these areas. Even though there were Scansped sister companies in the countries in question, when it came to the point only Scansped Switzerland came to represent Scansped Germany for the concerned traffics since the sister companies in these countries already had agents in Germany and did not want to change there. A similar situation were present for the West-German offices which caused differences in representation abroad between the different offices in West- Germany. The newly opened offices in Southern Germany seem to be more dependent on sister companies as agents while the offices in the Köln/ Wuppertal area already had their own agents in other countries such as Bansard in France and Ziegler in Belgium, etc.

As a rough estimation, at the end of 1987 ATA GmbH in West-Germany had 9-14 agents covering most countries of Western Continental Europe before the merger, out of which 5 were sister companies. After the merger the number of agents would be 17 out of which the number of subsidiaries used 7. Of the agents with which ATA GmbH in West-Germany had regular traffics before the event, 5 agents switched due to the merger. In 4 of these cases the merged Scansped in West-Germany found new agents and in one case they started to cooperate with a sister company.(see Appendix 4)

Another problem has been the fact that the name Scansped in Europe was unknown and that it had to be established in Germany. Many customers have stayed over the years in spite of the changes in ownership in Germany and basically their contacts in the company have stayed the same.

After the merger, Scansped West- Germany was very strong in Scandinavian traffics but had limited capacity in traffics not involving Scandinavia. As Bilspedition acquired Tekatrans in Stuttgart (which was formerly an agent to Scansped Sweden) at the end of 1989, Scansped

Germany became stronger in the southern parts of Germany, especially in the Stuttgart area. The reason for the acquisition was that Scansped Holland BV had lost its partner Panalpina in Stuttgart when Panalpina had started its own business in Holland. This, in turn, was a result of the main Dutch agent of Panalpina, Nedlloyd, had acquired Union Transport in Germany and by doing so Nedlloyd obtained a representation of its own in Germany and left the cooperation with Panalpina. The existing Scansped Stuttgart did not at that time have the necessary resources in order to handle the goods to/from Holland and possible agents would not be prepared to invest in such a traffic since Scansped already had an office of its own in the same area.

Later in 1990 Scansped Group acquired another large domestic as well as international transport company in West-Germany Nellen & Quack. This further strengthened and complicated the situation for the existing offices of Scansped in West- Germany.

Due to all the different changes, Scansped GmbH came to cooperate to a larger extent with some of the other Scansped companies and new traffics to other places started, for instance to Poland where Scansped Group had bought 50% of a newly established Polish transport company Scanspol.

From a concentration on international road transports the acquisition of Nellen & Quack in 1990 added relatively large domestic trucking operations for Scansped in West-Germany.

Summary of the Scansped West-Germany event

In 1980 Bilspedition established a subsidiary, ATA GmbH, in Hamburg. In 1986, Bilspedition acquired a German international transport company, United Spedition, which was incorporated into ATA GmbH. Three new offices were also opened in West-Germany by ATA GmbH.

At the time of the total Scansped and Bilspedition International merger in 1988, ATA group was the only group having subsidiaries in Germany apart from a small Swedish support office of Wilson´s in Travemünde. Wilson and SKT/F&L/TK had 31 agents representing them in West-Germany. After the merger the number of German agents of the Swedish Scansped was reduced to 10, located to areas not covered by Scansped Germany.

The merger Scansped in Germany doubled their goods volumes over night, which resulted in large temporary problems. Five of their own international agents left them. In four of the cases they found new agents in one they started to cooperate with a sister company. The competition in Germany after the event from the 21 agents that had left the cooperation with Wilson and SKT/F&L/TK was extremely strong .

6.1.3.4. The establishment of Scansped Belgium NV

Before the event

The total Bilspedition Group had three separate subsidiaries in Belgium via their subsidiaries SKT/F&L, Autotransit and Wilson. SKT/F&L was represented by Castra NV, daughter company to a fully owned forwarding company van Casteren in Holland and founded in 1960 by Mr P. van Casteren, which had all its basic activities concentrated on Waregem.

The subsidiary of Autotransit was called Autotransit NV and was to a large extent based on the acquisition of United/West-Friesland in Belgium in 1986.

The Belgian company, established in 1934, was part of the same group as West-Friesland acquired in Holland and West-Germany. At the time of the merger the company was situated in Brussels, Zaventem, Antwerp, Zeebrügge and Mechelen.

The third company was Scanroute NV, partly owned by Wilson & Co and partly by Cornel Geerts. It was situated in the Antwerp area. Before the merger, C. Geerts bought Wilson&Co´s shares because he did not want to join the merger. The Scanroute company was more of a trucking company than a forwarder.

The three different companies had over time developed differently. Castra NV was basically a family business which had been sold to Skandiatransport (SKT) in 1980 before the merger with Fallenius and Leffler (F&L). Prior to that, during the 1970's, van Casteren and Castra were partly owned by Holland America Line (from 1971) and later by the Swedish Broström shipping group (1975). Castra NV cooperated very closely with the parent company van Casteren in Tilburg, Holland. They were both located in textile areas. Even though it had many customers in other industries the textile industry had always played a very important role for Castra. It was a stable and profitable company situated in a rather small town where it was possible for the people to give personal service. The company was specialized in international consolidation services. Through the international owners the company got more internationalized. The growth of the company was very high almost from the start. The number of employees had increased from 13 in 1972 to around 60 before the merger in 1988. The name Castra N.V remained the same in spite of the different owners during this period.

Autotransit, formerly West-Friesland, was a larger company with around 90 employees at the time of the merger which started as an inland navigation transporting company. As it was bought by United Transports it developed into international groupage services mainly by truck. The diversity of services (full loads, consolidation, warehousing, storage , bulk transports, customs clearance, brokerage, etc) was larger than that of Castra and the number of locations were spread throughout Belgium. As a result of this the variation in customer industries was larger as well as the average size of the customers.

When Bilspedition was looking for a transport company to buy within Holland and Belgium they found United/West-Friesland through old contacts with ASG which had set up its own company in Belgium in 1976 since the agent AMA had been acquired by United Transport.

Bilspedition bought the United/West-Friesland company in Holland and in Belgium 1986 and early 1987 the company changed its name to Autotransit. In 1987 they bought another company in Belgium, a small customs clearance company in Brussels which also included a small airfreight office in Zaventem, the airport.

The agents of Castra and ATA were very different even though they belonged to the same Group in Sweden. In fact, they were basically competitors and so were their agents. In 1988, before the merger, Castra cooperated in Scandinavia with its parent company SKT/F&L in Sweden and its sister companies in Norway and in Denmark. Only in Finland did they cooperate with an Autotransit company. As for West-Friesland, before it was acquired by Autotransit it cooperated with Adams Transport in Denmark and with TK in Sweden. After the Bilspedition acquisition it had to change to Autotransit in Sweden and Denmark, just a few months before both Adams Transport and TK became part of the same Group. In Norway and in Finland ATA Belgium cooperated with companies other than Autotransit. The policy was, however, that ATA should cooperate with sister companies in Sweden, Norway and Denmark as well as Switzerland.

The two companies were competing in Belgium on the Scandinavian market and some other European markets like France, the U.K., etc. On the other hand they were also complementing each other. For example Castra was strong on traffics within Benelux and Germany while ATA had almost no traffics in these areas. At the same time, ATA was stronger in some traffics to other areas like Italy. Castra had developed express traffics to certain destinations in Europe at attractive prices which ATA did not have.

On the whole ATA, being more diversified in transport services, more divided in location, with an older staff, a low profitability and a tighter budget, had a very different company culture to Castra with its positive development, younger staff and higher concentration both in services, assortment and location. Finally, the board of directors in Castra reported to van Casteren in Holland while the board of directors in ATA reported directly to Sweden.

The event

When it was decided that the companies should merge in Belgium on January 1, 1989, project groups were formed (as in Sweden) in order to form the new company. As the name Scansped was already adopted in Belgium the new company was forced to take the name Castra/Autotransit for the first year but was then able to change to Scansped NV Belgium on January 1, 1990. The new company was a sister company to van Casteren, both being a part of the European division of Scansped. Therefore Castra established dependency on van Casteren in Holland ceased. The new company came to be located in four different places Waregem, Brussels, Antwerp and Mechelen. The office in Zaventem was closed down. The managing director of Castra became the chief executive officer, the managing director of ATA the deputy managing director.

Because the new company was a much larger company with a total of 145 employees some new specialist functions such as controller were needed. The services of Castra and Autotransit were competing in some areas and were complementary in others. In some cases there were too many employees but in other cases, like for accounting and bookkeeping, which van Casteren formerly took care of, this was not so. One specific problem was how to split the traffics between the offices in order to rationalise the traffic system in the best way and at the same time satisfy the customers. Since the companies had had many competing traffics before merging there were several traffics to the same places. Now the traffics became more concentrated. For example, the traffic to/from Denmark was concentrated to Waregem(old Castra) but to/from Sweden was concentrated to Mechelen (old Autotransit). Other problems had to do with the formation and location of a new marketing department, the price structure and the sales personnel of the new company. Castra had been a more marketing oriented company than ATA before the merger.

The differences in culture between the companies made the total change rather difficult for the employees. Since also their sister companies (representatives) in Scandinavia and Switzerland were merged and restructured at the same time the situation became even more complicated. In these countries as well as partly in France (Paris) and Finland they were cooperating with their sister companies. Not only were their sisters reorganized and changed but also the relations to suppliers to these companies were changed. For instance in Sweden the domestic transports for SKT/F&L were performed by Fraktarna and not by Bilspedition domestic which was changed as a result of the merger. In most places where the new company cooperated with agents, the agents of Castra were chosen.

In some cases the Scansped sister companies were not chosen as partners since their existing services were not sufficient. This was the case in the U.K.where Thompson & Jewitt became their agent. In France the Scansped office was complemented with other agents in France as well as in West- Germany. Quite often a combination of agents and subsidiaries was used.

Customers were told that the merger had been made not just to reduce internal competition and to rationalise but perhaps more for the purpose of creating an international network before the changes in EC in 1993.

After the event

It took about 1 1/2 year for things to stabilize. In Belgium after only one year the head office was moved to Mechelen, where neither company had any office even though ATA had some warehouse facilities. As a result, employees in Brussels and some in Antwerp were moved to Mechelen. A new office and a new terminal were built in Mechelen (situated between Brussels and Antwerp). The office in Brussels were closed down. The Waregem office continued to be around the same size as before the merger but the managing director and part of the administration moved to Mechelen. In the beginning of 1990, the employees in Mechelen numbered 75, in Waregem 66 and in Antwerp 5. The sales administration was to a large extent moved to Mechelen even though 2 salesmen were still left in Waregem. In the spring of 1990, the warehousing space had increased and the company owned a fleet of trailers, distribution trucks, conventional equipment, etc., in addition to subcontractors.

Over the last years the cooperation with sister companies in other countries has increased. In all countries where Scansped has its own companies, except for a part of Germany and France and in U.K., the new Scansped in Belgium is represented by such companies.

In other countries like Austria, Greece, Italy[1], Luxembourg and Spain the company was represented by agents. To some limited extent these agents are the same as the parent company´s in Sweden. There is a problem with agents because of the expansion of Scansped overall. This makes it necessary for Scansped to ask the agents for a guarantee clause in order to make sure that the agents will continue the cooperation. One of the more important agents to Scansped NV, Cretschmar Cargo (the agent in West-Germany as well as Spain), expressed their concern when Scansped bought Tekatrans in Stuttgart. Tekatrans, which was a competitor to Cretschmar, had rather large traffics to/from Holland and Belgium. They took the view that Scansped will leave them in the future as agent which will have effects on their interest to expand the common traffic. Another worry was the marketing plan and marketing activities and the problem of transferring information which would be necessary for a development of the traffic. In this case Tekatrans even had one sales representative in Belgium who Scansped NV took over.

---

[1]From 1990 the agent in Italy was owned to 30% by Bilspedition Group

Another type of problem with the agents existed in France with the agent Aveka, which belonged to the Nedlloyd Group. Since the Nedlloyd Group was expanding and merging companies in competition with Scansped all over Europe the guarantee clause was a necessity for both parties. A further problem was that Scansped West-Germany was still cooperating with Ziegler in Belgium, a large international transport company, in competition with Scansped Belgium and their German agents.

New services were also developed to Poland as Scansped had started three joint ventures in Poland,[1] Spedpol,[2] Scanspoland and Transmeble International. Other services had been a result of a cooperation with Patmar Wilson in HongKong.

As a result of the merger the cooperation between Castra and Satraco as a subcontractor in the Austrian traffic ceased since Satraco at that time belonged to a competitor the Inter Forward Group.

In total, the number of representatives, 8 for ATA and 15 for Castra before the merger, changed to 17 for the new merged company. The number of countries in which it cooperates with sister companies has increased from 4 to 8. (see Appendix 4) The new company had a larger number of agents than each of the former companies and the number of countries in which they have subsidiaries has been doubled. The frequency in the traffics has increased as well as the number of services for the new company.

Summary of the Scansped in Belgium event
Each of the three Swedish parent groups had subsidiaries in Belgium. The ATA group had recently acquired United/ West-Friesland, SKT in the former Scansped group had acquired another international transport company in early 1980 and Wilson had a joint venture. The three companies were competing.

However, only the first two companies were merged since the Wilson share in the joint venture was sold. The merger resulted in large changes. Part of the new larger company moved to new facilities and some offices were closed down, the number of competing agents had to be reduced and the cooperation with the subsidiaries increased.

---

[1] Bilspedition owns 35% in Spedpol and 50% in Scanspol and Transmeble International
[2] The ownership is 1991 35% but is agreed to be 50%

6.2. General case analysis

6.2.1. Period 1 1955-69 - Beginning of internationalization
When Bilspedition started internationalizing between 1950-60 the company was specialized in trucking transports.

Integration
The international growth started at the end of 1950's in the Scandinavian countries through *new cooperations* with agents. However, after a few years Bilspedition *switched* from the agents to subsidiaries in Denmark and Norway. In Denmark they started their own activities in 1959/60 and in Norway in 1962/63. In these countries there was a *closer cooperation* between the parent and the representative taking place not only in legal but also in executional integration. Very quickly the change also resulted in *enlargement* of the cooperation in Denmark and Norway through the formation of a number of new direct traffics to/from different places in Sweden as well as in Norway and Denmark. Through these cooperations a small international net was created.

The Continental traffics started through *joining nets* with ATA in 1964-66, when Bilspedition acquired the majority of the company and therefore gained direct access to ATA's existing relations. Through the merger of ATA and the international activities of Bilspedition in Sweden in 1967 a *closer cooperation* was established not only with the Swedish international operations but also with the Scandinavian sister companies.

Based on ATA and the two Scandinavian subsidiaries, Bilspedition continued expansion from Sweden, Norway and Denmark into Europe and later on into other parts of the world *opening up* the net for a a number of *new cooperations* over the period.

As the company grew internationally it obtained permission to have its own customs warehouses in Stockholm, Helsingborg, Norrköping and Örebro, which caused a closer cooperation through increased execution integration with representatives and increased efficiency in the international traffics.

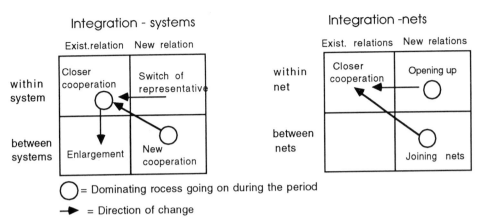

Figure 6.5. Internationalization- integration 1955-69

Through the acquisition of Trailer Express and later the acquisition of the majority of Scandinavian Ferry Trailers, Bilspedition increased integration through better control of the trailer equipment, of the trailer traffics and the representatives taking part in those traffics.

Finally during this period, Bilspedition became a partner and minority owner of the Scanfreight Group. Through this cooperation, GBS established new cooperations in the U.S. and Canada.

Extension

The *extension of first degree* dominated this period, since Bilspedition established traffics to many new countries.

The first countries to which it started traffics were the Nordic countries and then a

a few years later new countries on the Continent were covered through acquisition of the majority ownership in Autotransit. In 1968, the company had representatives in 14 European countries and continued expansion into other Continental countries. Through internationalization of their subsidiaries in Denmark, Norway and U.K., extension of *secondary degree* was also taking place.

The speed of extension was high during the first period. Bilspedition not only managed to cover the most important parts of Europe with trucking traffics but also started some overseas traffics through partnership in Scanfreight.

Penetration

During this period the company increased the international penetration dramatically. First they established direct relations to the Scandinavian countries which, through changes in volumes and creation of new direct traffics to/from different places, soon caused an increase in *size of relations* especially in the Nordic countries.

Starting almost from scratch at the end of the 1950's the company was receiving 17 % of its total turnover from international traffics in 1969/70. New terminals had to be built not only in Sweden but also in Norway and Denmark, which contributed to the increase in the size of the relations as larger amounts of resources for existing relations in the same type of services were engaged in the home country as well as in the foreign country.

In some countries such as West-Germany and the U.K., the increased coverage was made by *spread of relations* in that country through adding more local agents.

The Danish and Norwegian companies in turn developed in continental traffics which increased the amount of resources needed in those countries, as well as resulting in increased *size of relations* at net level.

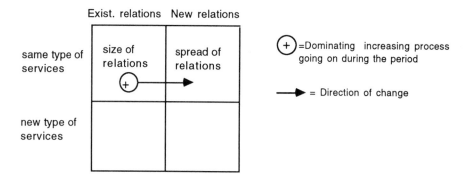

Figure 6.6. Internationalization -penetration 1955-69

The overseas traffics which existed through Scanfreight required only very limited amounts of resources for the three Scandinavian companies.

Conclusion and effects between representatives
The integration during this period took place to begin with at system level, creating a number of transport systems within the Nordic countries. However, they continued quickly to the net level through the acquisition of ATA and even though ATA was a small company it provided a nucleus of transport systems to a number of countries. Through the legal integration with the Swedish international companies ATA,Trailer Express and Scanfreight, Bilspedition gained access to international experience.

Due to the fact that the subsidiaries of Bilspedition also began their internationalization, both first and second degree of extension took place during the period. The internationalization of Bilspedition resulted in international activities accounting for a share of 17% of turnover at the end of the period. During this period the effects between the representatives are still relatively small. However, some negative effects were present in U.K. between the newly acquired subsidiary Trailer Express and existing ATA agents.

Effects on suppliers, owners and competitors

In the beginning, Bilspedition was only performing the domestic transports connected to the in the international traffics of the owner Fallenius &Leffler. It could be said, therefore, that they were positively connected to the development of international transports without having any international relations. Fallenius decreased its integration with GBS through selling 50% in 1942 to the Association of the Swedish Trucking Companies(SLF) and the rest of the company about ten years later. The first change in ownership was made at the same period as Swedish Railway bought the majority of ASG.

At the time that the international business started, 2/3 of Bilspedition was owned by trucking companies via SLF and 1/3 owned by Swedish industry. The increase in international business had positive effects not only for the number of trucking companies which took part in the new traffics but also for the positively connected trucking companies performing domestic transports.The truck owners working exclusively for Bilspedition BTF established a special association in 1957 which increased the possibilities for closer cooperation.

In the beginning of 1960's Bilspedition needed more capital due to high growth and some acquisitions and the largest owners SLF and Säifa, (another Swedish Truck Owners Association), wanted to sell. The BTF trucking companies that were closely tied to Bilspedition wanted to continue and managed to raise the necessary capital and to get SLF and Säifa to stay. The trucking companies increased their engagement in Bilspedition in 1965. Conflicts between the truck owners in SLF and Säifa resulted since many members were working almost exclusively for competitors such as ASG.

During this period, in 1965, the truck owners in the ASG -T association obtained the possibility of acquiring 5% of the shares in ASG from Swedish Railway. Through the acquisition of ATA, Bilspedition started to compete with the other Swedish forwarders. One of these was the former owner F&L.
The acquisition of Trailer Express and Scandinavian Ferry Trailers increased the cooperation with some of the shipping lines.

6.2.2. Period 1970-1979 - Specialization and diversification of services

The period was a period of stagnation and instability but also of growth at the beginning and at the end.

Integration

During the 1970's, many *new cooperations* were established. The main reasons for this were specialization and diversification into new services as well as the gradual development of traditional trucking traffics into new countries. The gradual development which was a case of *opening up* the existing net had resulted in increasing number of traffics and agents

As for specialization and diversification they generally took place through acquisitions and *joining nets*. Through *joining nets* with Flygspedition, SGS, Alpen&Parelius, Cold Stores, etc., Bilspedition added a large number of new agents to the net. At the end of the 1970's Bilspedition had 50-60 agents outside Sweden including overseas, out of which 5 were subsidiaries to Bilspedition. The fact that these joining nets were complementary in services resulted in a creation of part-nets within the total Bilspedition net.

Moreover, the specialization and diversification was sometimes developed together with existing representatives which created a *closer cooperation* and *enlargement*.

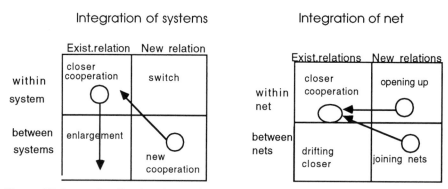

Figure 6.7. Internationalization- integration 1970-79

Generally speaking, in spite of shorter periods of stagnation and decline the *cooperation* became *closer* to most representatives during the period as a result of intensified training and education of personnel, in order to improve the know- how in existing as well as in the new specialized and diversified areas. Other actions leading to closer cooperation were the development of computerized communication systems and unit load transport systems. This also increased the possibilities for Bilspedition as well as the agents to control the transport systems. In one case a separate company BIAB was established in order to increase the control of the trailers, containers and flats that were part of the existing traffics. The diversifying into activities formerly performed by the customers such as warehousing, packing, etc., was another way of increasing control integration during the period.

The level of legal integration also generally increased during the period through acquisitions not only in Sweden but also internationally, even though there were some negative changes. In several of the Swedish acquisitions leading to joining of nets, there was a gradual development over the period as the share initially acquired increased until the company became fully owned, as in the case of Flygspedition, Cold Store, SGS, etc.

On the other hand, the legal integration with representatives abroad went through a period of instability, since it increased by five and decreased by two leading to a combination of new cooperations and closer cooperations and dissolution of cooperation. The additional foreign companies were situated in Denmark (2), Holland, Italy and Switzerland and the reductions were in West-Germany and the U.K.

During this period, the possible effects of the increases and decreases in volumes of the existing trucking traffics on integration were diminished, both by the expansion into new countries, increased specialization and diversification as well as the increased execution and legal integration.

Extension

The *first degree* of extension was increasing both in Europe and overseas mostly to countries in Europe, which were more on the periphery, such as Spain, Ireland, Eastern Europe and to Middle East countries such as Iraq, Iran and Saudi Arabia. Bilspedition even set up a representative office in Iraq especially for trade fair transports. The speed of extension for land-transports seems to have decreased in comparison to earlier periods. However, for overseas transports the speed of extension was faster since many overseas countries were added through the acquisition of Flygspedition and Alpen & Parelius.

By and large, the *secondary degree* of extension increased due to investments in new foreign subsidiaries.

Penetration

The combination of adding coverage to a number of new countries within Europe and the expansion through acquisitions of Swedish based international companies as well as some international companies all resulted in increased penetration in terms of *new diversified relations* and *spread of relations*.

In other cases the *scope of the relations* increased since the representatives added new types of services like temperated transports, warehousing and consultancy to their existing services. The fact that there were many acquisitions increased the resources both in Sweden and in foreign countries.

The *size of relations* both increased and decreased during the period. The decreases were basically taking place in the existing relations while increases were a result of the new acquisitions of international companies.

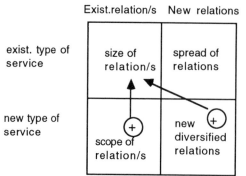

Figure 6.8. Internationalization -penetration 1970-79

Conclusions and effects between representatives

The first period seems to have consisted of both increases and deceases. However, over the whole period, there was an increase in all three dimensions. The share of international activities had increased from around 20% 1970/71 to 24% in 1980.

The new added complementary areas such as airfreight, seafreight, hanging garments, etc., continued to have their own separate net of representatives and transport systems which created part-nets which were C/O (complementary in service and overlapping geographically) within the total Bilspedition net. As a result, the number of representatives in each country increased and so did the latent conflicts between representatives.

In specific cases the conflicts were obvious. In the UK where a large international transport company took over the operations of the subsidiary, other UK agents who were previously complementing the activities of Trailer Express in the UK had to change.

The sales office in Germany which ceased its activities early in the 1970's changed the role of the agents in West Germany leaving a large part of the marketing to them which increased the integration with them.

Finally, since many of the agents of the different part-nets, such as ATA, Coldstores, SGS, Flygspedition and Alpen Parelius, were diversified and internationalized they were competing in other areas.

Effects on suppliers, owners and competitors

During this period the cooperation with <u>shipping lines and airlines</u> became important since Bilspedition became involved in airfreight and seafreight transports through the acquisition of Flygspedition and Alpen & Parelius. Both the shipping lines and the airlines were positively connected to the development of Bilspedition.

The <u>trucking companies</u> had structural problems during these years. Bilspedition took part through the setting up of a specialized company for rationalization and development of trucking companies. Certain larger trucking companies were even acquired by Bilspedition in combination with a company specially established for that purpose by BTFAB. In this way the integration between the trucking companies and Bilspedition increased.

During this period the forwarders, being partly competitors, especially those in Scansped as well as Wilson &Co, increased their shares of ownership in Bilspedition and the share of the truck owners decreased. As Bilspedition continued diversification the competition with the owners increased too.

6.2.3. Period 1980-89 - Acquisitions and mergers

(Since the Scansped Europe event is so important for the total European development it is part of the general case analysis, while the three other Scansped events are analyzed separately in chapter 9.)

During this period Bilspedition became registered on the stock exchange and issued new shares several times. This changed the conditions for development and possibilities to grow via acquisitions.

Integration

During the first 2-3 years of the 1980's Bilspedition developed internationally through changes within the existing international part-nets of the total international Bilspedition net. ATA, Alpen&Parelius, SGS, Flygspedition, as well as the international subsidiaries in Europe, continued their international expansion by changes at system level *switching representatives* and into *closer cooperation..*

There were several small increases in legal integration in the ATA part-net during the early years of the 1980's. In 1980, the cooperation ended between ATA and Kühne & Nagel in the UK and Bilspedition set up its own subsidiary again, now called ATA Ltd. In West-Germany, something similar happened in Hamburg since a new ATA company was set up. The new office in Hamburg was intended to cooperate with some of the other agents in West-Germany. In Italy the part owned company became fully owned in 1982. In Holland, Bilspedition acquired a small international company in 1982/83 which also added seafreight to Bilspedition´s services in Holland. These companies all became part of the ATA international organization. However, these were all basically very small changes in legal integration. Later during the period Bilspedition acquired larger companies such as West-Friesland which were added to the ATA international part-net .

On the whole, during this period there was a strong concentration on subsidiaries and on a few agents. In 1987, the ATA part-net only had as representatives in 12 countries, 4 agents, 8 subsidiaries and one joint venture. Within the ATA -net, the concentration resulted in the existing representatives *cooperating closer* together and the net showed a tendency towards *closing up* trying to get the sister companies to cooperate.

The first really large *joining of nets* that took place during the period was in 1982/83 when Bilspedition acquired the transport and forwarding part of Wilson & Co. This increased the share of the international activities of Bilspedition from 30% to 50%. However the part-nets of Bilspedition and the added Wilson net were not merged but continued as separate part-nets within the total Bilspedition net.

Each of the two large groups, Wilson and Bilspedition with ATA dominant, also continued separately to move into *closer cooperation* within their part-nets through activities such as developing their own communication systems together with subsidiaries, etc.

In 1985/86, another large international group,the Scansped Group, was acquired leading to a *joining of nets*.. As in the Wilson acquisition, the Scansped group of companies continued as separate part-nets being overlapping(O/O) in all parts to that of ATA and the Wilson groups in their activities. Even though there was a joining of nets through legal integration between the Scansped net and the total Bilspedition net, the integration was almost non-existent between the separate part-nets for a couple of years. There were a few exceptions, however, which concerned merging the Wilson and Scansped areas of airfreight and railway agency.

Moreover, the three large international groups of ATA, Wilson and Scansped continued to expand within the separate groups, acquiring companies and increasing the competition between their existing areas. The companies being acquired within the part-nets were either executionally integrated at system level before the acquisition or became quickly so. Examples of this were Adams in Denmark acquired by SkandiaFallenius, Giltspur in the UK (the former agent of Wilson) and the acquisition of West-Friesland in Holland, Belgium and West-Germany for the Bilspedition International group.

However, two of the former Scansped part-nets, SkandiaFallénius and TK, were merged in 1987, which resulted in *closer cooperation* between the nets in all aspects of integration. After the acquisition of Scansped,TK had been formally organized into the Bilspedition International group and not together with SKT/F&L.

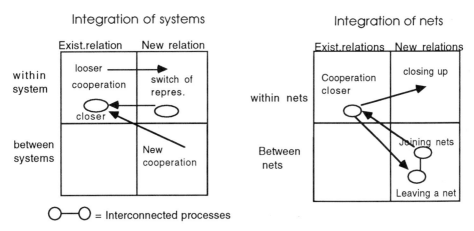

Figure 6.9. Internationalization -integration 1980-89

Finally, as competition between different part-nets decreased the effectiveness of the total international net, Bilspedition decided that the large three part-nets should be merged. Therefore the *joining of the nets* at total level lead to *closer cooperation* within the total Bilspedition net. The large merger resulted in a concentration to the existing subsidiaries and a reduced number of agents on the Continent in the name of Scansped as well as overseas in the name of Wilson.

However, one airfreight company, Flygspedition, being a member of the specialist division, continued a few years as a separate part-net instead of being merged with the airfreight activities of Scanflight.

During this process of concentration, many agents (probably over a hundred including all former part-nets) left or were required to leave. Many new cooperations and switchings were taking place at system level. In some cases Bilspedition had no option other than to buy or start some new companies when possibilities to find new agents were lacking. For example, the Finnish agents left and Bilspedition was forced to start a company of its own in Finland in 1988. In 1990, however, Bilspedition acquired a large international transport group in Finland, Speditor. Another relatively large international transport company acquired was TekaTrans in Stuttgart in West-Germany.

Not only were the Swedish parent companies merged but also the international subsidiaries in the same country. After the merger the international subsidiaries were supposed to give priority to other merged sister companies. This demand was strongest on the Swedish Scansped AB since they were dominating the Scansped Group. However many of the smaller Scansped subsidiaries did not feel an urge to switch or to start a new cooperation with their sister companies in countries other than Scandinavia because their concentration to Scandinavian countries often resulted in weak third country traffics or they might have had an agent of importance. In some cases, however, the lack of agents made them work with a sister company.

Thus, through the merger and the priorities given to subsidiaries, the total net was gradually *closing up* over time.

This was a period of going through waves of different types of integration. Basically, legal integration predominated. As many of the companies were not merged but continued as separate nets they were not integrated executionally at system levels nor were there any changes in control integration. Social integration seems to have increased slightly at management level as a result of the attempts to get the groups to cooperate.

On the other hand, when companies were merged there was then a high increase in social and execution integration within the total net. However, the same change also caused a certain loss in control integration since many of the agents leaving were in control of customer and supplier relations.

The period was totally dominated by net integration and the systems integration changed as a result of this. However, it seems to be important that integration takes place not only at net level but also continues to the execution and system levels for the good of the companies involved and for effectiveness.

Extension
During this period there was very little of first degree of extension since Bilspedition was already extended to most countries in the world. The first degree of extension might have increased marginally for some overseas countries as a result of the acquisition of the Wilson Group. On the other hand, *secondary degree* of extension increased generally during the period since a number of existing subsidiaries have been connected.
However, for some specific part-nets as those of the ATA group first degree extension actually decreased during the period.

Penetration
In beginning of the period, the *size of the relations* increased as a result of internationalization of the subsidiaries and concentration to fewer representatives. The concentration reducing the number of agents in Europe also resulted in a decrease in *spread of relations* .
When Bilspedition acquired Wilson and later the Scansped Group without merging the groups the *spread of relations* more than tripled. Then the merger of the groups eventually occurred it resulted in a strong decrease in *spread of relations* as well as losses of 10-20% of total international volumes. This was combined with a decrease in *scope of relations* since many of the former agents were large companies offering many types of services while the new representatives being subsidiaries were smaller and less diversified. It seem that existing relations with the representatives increased in terms of *size of relations* but this could not

compensate for the loss in *spread of relations* and *scope of relations* during the first period after mergers.

After a year there would seem to be a change towards an increase in penetration both in *size* and in *scope of relations* again adding more volumes and developing new types of services.

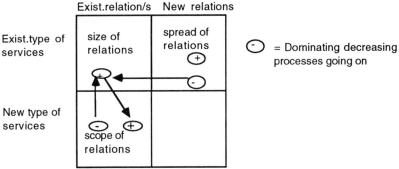

Figure 6.10. Internationalization - penetration 1980-89

Conclusion and effects between representatives

During the period, net changes are totally dominating and systems integration develops as a result of this. The number of O/O part-nets within the total Bilspedition net increased due to acquisitions and then decreased at the end of the period as a result of the mergers. Legal integration was driving other aspects of integration after Bilspedition obtained access to new capital.

Changes of increasing integration through waves of concentration moving towards *closing up* were taking place in the early years of the 1980's. These were then disturbed by acquisitions leading to *joining of nets* as a result of the acquisitions of Wilson and later Scansped Group. Finally after a period of *closer cooperation* after the Scansped acquisition the merger resulted in *leaving nets* and new waves of concentration into *closing up*. Through the acquisition of Speditor in Finland the concentration there was disturbed again.

The number of changes taking place and representatives involved during this period in comparison to earlier periods would seem to be extremely high. The changes also seem to include both increases and decreases to a larger extent.

The effects between representatives of the net were very large during this period. The internal competition seems to have been very strong between the representatives of the part-nets. Many representatives in each country were cooperating with a Bilspedition company and were still competing with each other. In 11 countries there was a combination of both agents and several subsidiaries competing. The fact that Bilspedition in the end seemed to merge its companies in most cases made several agents leave the cooperation with a Bilspedition company directly after the acquisition. In West-Germany, the new Scansped company very soon lost five international agents even though they were not supposed to be affected by the merger.

During 1980's, the reduced number of agents and the increased number of subsidiaries abroad and in Sweden caused large amounts of conflicts within the total Group as well as between agents since the best choice was not always present and the agents leaving the net became competitors. This also caused unexpected changes of representatives for Bilspedition.

Large numbers of existing agents to the competing Groups or part-nets were worried by the internal competition and the number of mergers growing over time.

The effects of the mergers on representatives, both direct and indirect, were numerous at all levels and will be discussed further in the next chapter when analyzing the specific event .

Effects 1980-89 on owners, suppliers and competitors

As Bilspedition grew and acquisitions became more frequent new capital was needed. In 1983 the company was introduced on the Swedish stockmarket which gave the company many new owners such as insurance companies, financial institutions, etc. This diluted the share of the majority owner BTF, the Bilspedition Truckers´Association even though it still dominated in voting shares.

During the period Bilspedition acquired many of the former suppliers such as shipping lines, trucking companies and part of an airline which increased integration of control of the transport systems both in relation to suppliers and towards their agents.

Through the acquisition of Wilson Group, Bilspedition acquired a large competitor which was part owner of Bilspedition at that time. This was partly also the case with the Scansped acquisition which was partly a hostile takeover of another large competitor which had formerly been a part-owner of Bilspedition. The takeover caused one of the freight forwarding companies which was part of the Group NTS (NordiskTransport &Spedition) to break away and continue as a competitor.

The break away of NTS from the Scansped Group became possible through the investment company Ratos. Based on NTS, Ratos then formed a new group of international transport and distribution companies called Inter Forward.

Interaction between the dimensions of internationalization

The interaction between I (Integration), E (Extension) and P (Penetration) has shifted over the periods.

During the 1950's in the first period of 1955-69 internationalization was made through integration at systems level leading to extension of first degree and a certain penetration in the

Nordic countries (I-->E1-->P). Very quickly there were large amounts of Nordic traffics with the same representatives which caused (I-->P).

Later as Bilspedition and ATA were joining nets this resulted in a continued first degree extension and increased penetration (I-->E1-->P).

During the period there was also a further increase in integration (P -->I) due to the large growth of volumes. New more efficient terminals and offices were constructed in order to cope with the traffics and changes in the organization were made. International know-how increased as traffics grew, leading to closer cooperation with many agents. As the Scandinavian subsidiaries started to internationalize secondary degree of extension was involved which also increased penetration in both countries involved. On the whole the period was dominated by the chain of integration leading to extension and penetration(I-->E-->P).

During the second period of the 1970's the interaction was different. Even though the chain of changes(I-->E1-->P) still existed the dominating changes were I-->P. Integration increased in certain systems and decreased in others due to a combination of stagnation in growth, specialization and diversification. Further this caused penetration to decrease in size of and increased scope and diversification. However over the total period penetration increased.

Due to the clustering of the total net into part-nets through specialization and diversification it is more difficult to discern and summarize the total change in integration. The fact that much of the diversification was made through joining of nets, specialization causing closer cooperation as did the new communication systems, it seems that the integration increased in the total net as well.

During this period both secondary and first degree of extension were involved. While first degree only increased, secondary degree both increased and decreased during the period leading to similar changes in penetration (I-->E2-->P).

The last period 1980-89 the changes seem to be faster and larger. On integration the changes were basically taking place at net level and the changes in extension basically concerned secondary degree of extension. First degree of extension was hardly involved for the total net. Joining nets and leaving nets were common which led both to increases and decreases in second degree of extension and penetration (I-->E2-->P). Basically the increase in integration through joining nets would lead to high increase in penetration while leaving a net led to high decrease in penetration. As in the Scansped case, joining the Bilspedition net increased penetration while merging decreased penetration. Merging overlapping nets seems to involve joining part of nets and leaving part of nets. Therefore increases and decreases in integration and penetration takes place at the same time. However, in the end, these parallel processes seem to have led to an increase in integration of the residual net and a decrease in penetration compared to the former situation for the focal company and the focal net. This was what was taking place during the 1980's several times as a result of the mergers going on.

Even though penetration fluctuated during the period, at the end of the period there had been an enormous increase.

7. Inter Forward

7.1. IF Group - Case description

The history of Inter Forward (IF) is necessarily very short as the company was only founded on January 1, 1988. The case consists of the international development of the IF Group during the first three years of its existence. The development of the company as a whole is described first and then the international development over time of two of the largest companies acquired by IF during this period, both before and after acquisition.

7.1.1. General development

IF was essentially established to act as a form of holding company for the transport sector interests of the Ratos investment group in Jan 1988. Two years earlier, Ratos made its first major investment in the transport, forwarding and distribution sector by acquiring NTS, Nordisk Transport &Spedition AB. IF, the outcome of a restructuring and renaming of the NTS parent company, was formally created thereafter with a new group management team. NTS then became the cornerstone of IF's transportation and distribution activities.

As Ratos divested its interest in its traditional areas such as steel manufacturing, distribution of steel and became more of an investment company, it decided to invest in international services instead. Ratos experiences in distribution as well as the expected changes in the rules and regulations on the Common Market led Ratos to focus on transport companies. The restructuring of the transportation industry also increased the likelihood of finding interesting companies willing to sell, according to the management of IF.

When the Scansped Group, of which NTS was a part, was sold to Bilspedition against the will of NTS, the former owners, then part owners of Scansped, and the NTS management looked for a way of getting out of the deal by finding an alternative buy. Personal acquaintance with persons in the Ratos Group led to a contact with Ratos which culminated in Ratos buying NTS from Bilspedition. At that time, NTS was the single largest transport company in the Scansped Group and accounted for a large part of the profit in the Group. After the split-up of the Scansped Group in 1985/86, some parts of NTS had to be restructured and investments made which caused a downturn in the company's profitability in 1986. Further in 1987, acquired two transport and forwarding companies in Denmark, G. Hansen Spedition A/S, which had been its agent since 1966 and Erritzoe A/S. These companies were merged into one company named NTS Denmark at the same time as IF group was established on January 1,1988.

The Group level IF consisted of seven persons, increasing to ten in 1990, with the requisite experience in distribution and management. The IF Group set out with the ambition to create one of the larger transport and forwarding groups in Europe by the time the expected EC harmonization and deregulation became accomplished in 1993.

The first year became very intensive. Business ideas, objectives and strategies for the IF Group were created. NTS was divided into one service company, IF Service, and three operating companies, NTS Sweden, NTS Rail and Nordic Air Cargo (NAC). At the same time four new companies were acquired and negotiations were going on towards even more acquisitions. Three Swedish companies were acquired, Jerre AB (mainly railway and airfreight), J.A.Larsson (transport specialist for plants and bulbs) and Allservice AB (warehousing and distribution) and one West-German company, Schier & Otten (sea and airfreight).

In the beginning of 1989, two larger European companies, Amas in Holland and Züst & Bachmeier (Z&B) in Switzerland and Germany and one smaller U.K. company, Norfreight Ltd, were acquired. These companies were also agents to NTS although on a limited scale. The combined size of the companies acquired in 1988 and 1989 was larger than the whole of the existing NTS group of companies.

Further acquisitions were made in West-Germany, Belgium, Denmark and in Sweden later during 1989. In West-Germany the companies acquired were Fenthol & Sandtmann and a rather small company, DMP. Fenthol & Sandtmann was mainly a domestic trucking company with some international seafreight and DMP was specialized in warehousing and contracted distribution as well as having suitable terminals and office buildings . The company acquired in Belgium, Sartraco, was a transport and forwarding company specialized in trucking traffics to Nordic destinations. However the company was sold back to the former owner in 1990. From early 1990, the Swedish company Air Cargo Express (ACE), one of the larger Swedish airfreight companies, became part of a common airfreight group specifically created for that purpose within the IF Group which included Nordisk Air Cargo (NAC) as well as ACE. The manager of ACE became the managing director of the airfreight group. The two companies continued as separate subsidiaries within the airfreight group.

Another company acquired during this period was ITM, a Danish company specialized in furniture transports and cooperating with Amas in Holland. Amas also acquired a company in Belgium named Sasse & Co, which was an old established general forwarder in air, sea and roadtransports.

A further four international transport and forwarding companies were acquired in France during 1990. These were Beyer, SMTS, Rambaud, and Alltransports. Basically they were all general forwarders together representing all types of transports. Two more companies were acquired in the U.K., namely, London Carriers International (LCI) and Bondelivery. Both of these were engaged in third party logistics, working very closely with specific customers.

At the Group level, IF formed a new company, International Cash Management & Administration AB (ICMA AB), offering cash management and other financial services the Swedish export industry.

Table 7.1. IF acquisitions

Time	Name	Turnover [1]	Employees
MSEK			
1 Jan 1988	NTS Group	2300	1180
1988	J.A.Larsson		7
1988	Sped.AB Jerre	400	100
1988/89	Schier,Otten & Co		50
1988/89	Allservice AB/WMS	36	70
1989	Züst&Bachmeier	750	400
1989	Amas	360	500
1989	Sasse&Co	50	100
1989/90	Norfreight	60	60
1989/90	Satraco	54	100
1990	ACE	315	120
1990	Fenthol&Sandtmann	185	220
1990	ITM	90	70
1990	DMP	10	14
1990	LCI	400	900
1990	Beyer	220	405
1990	Rambaud	80	65
1990	SMTS	105	118
1990	Alltransports	45	37
1990	Forsblad &Son	72	70
1990	Bondelivery	170	500

The companies bought were all small to medium sized, with between 10 to 500 employees. An exception was LCI who could be compared with NTS which had around 1,000 employees at the time of takeover.

After a period of three years, the number of companies within the IF Group had increased to around 20 larger operating companies. (see above) These companies, in turn, were often divided into smaller groups of companies. Some of them were already divided into smaller companies at the time of takeover as was the case with Amas, which consisted of 21 different companies. All in all, there were around 70 different companies.

As a result of this, the work load at the Group level on the seven persons involved had changed radically. One way of handling the workload of having so many companies in the Group was to create holding companies. IF therefore established a holding company in Germany in the beginning of 1989 and other IF holding companies in Belgium, France and U.K. in 1990. A

---

[1] Estimated

holding company already existed in Holland through Amas and a Danish holding company had been established through previous acquisitions in Denmark.

As a result of all these acquisitions, the turnover of IF doubled over the first two years 1988, 1989 and almost tripled during the third year. Profits doubled during the first two years but changed to a loss in 1990 as a result of increasing costs of the acquisitions.

Table 7.2. Some facts of the IF Group

IF Group	1987	1988	1989	1990
Turnover (msek) [2]	1.997	2.232	3990	5.659
Profit [3]	23	33	52	-6
Employees (Sweden)	914	954	1144	1325
Employees (Abroad)	273	323	1365	2714

Expansion through acquisitions has been restricted therefore after 1990. During 1990, however, the intention still remained to acquire new companies in order to achieve the objective of being one of the larger transporting and forwarding companies in Europe.

Policies, services and business concepts

Once established, the first task of IF was not only to create a business concept, objectives and strategies for the IF Group but also to create the necessary systems for their implementation.

The business concept and the strategies were the outcome of discussions which included over a hundred persons involved in the business, basically the NTS organization.

The business concept of the Group was to become a large multinational forwarder offering services to industry in the fields of international delivery and distribution. A common feature of the companies acquired was that they had their base in Europe. Up to 1989, the companies acquired were all situated in northern parts of Europe and with services complementary to those of NTS. During 1990, however, a number of French companies were added.

The services within IF covered a wide spectrum of activities within transporting, forwarding and distribution. The first company in the Group, NTS, an old established international forwarder, was founded in 1919 and was establishing their first three international subsidiaries in 1920´s. Over time NTS had developed general transport and forwarding activities encompassing rail, truck, air and sea transports in combination with some specialized activities.

---

[2] Turnover excl.Vat and customs duty
[3] Profit after net financial income and expenses

In Norway, West-Germany, France and Denmark, it had its own subsidiaries which became sister companies in due course, being part of the holding companies in these countries instead.

On the whole, the IF Group focused on Europe as its market which, on the face of it, meant that airfreight and seafreight would play a less important role in acquisitions. However, airfreight and seafreight activities have, in fact, increased through the acquisitions. Some of the companies like Schier, Otten & Co, acquired by NTS Germany, and more recently ACE were specialists in sea and airfreight. In late 1990, IF has a number of companies working with sea and airfreight. In the beginning of 1989, the goals were still not settled for these areas. For airfreight, its only policy was that it should use agencies instead of investing in airfreight companies.

Through acquisitions IF within a short space of time became able to offer almost all types of transportation, forwarding and distribution services within large parts of Europe. Most of the companies acquired had intercontinental traffics and some of them even had subsidiaries on other Continents. Therefore, through these acquisitions IF achieved a coverage of large segments of other Continents as well.

Since many of the companies were new to the Group they knew very little about the other companies within the Group. This meant that almost no one in the Group had a complete knowledge of all the services and the different types of know-how that were available within the total Group.

To begin with, the intention was to own neither the means of transportation nor the buildings used for same but to procure such services when needed. Over time, however, large numbers of trucks and substantial transport equipment and terminal facilities have come into ownership through some of the companies acquired in Europe.

Companies acquired did not have to be integrated with the other subsidiaries of the IF Group if they did not want to. They had the freedom to keep their agents and their own culture. It was stated that all cooperation should be voluntary and on a strictly business basis. It was not supposed to be dictated by the Group management. To an extent, the same policy applied in respect of the communications and informations systems. The different companies were given advice and support to develop a suitable system. These policies seem to have changed to some extent over time as the financial situation deteriorated. Consolidation would seem to have come more into focus which partly included internal restructuring within the different countries as well as between countries.

Organization and investments

The organization of IF is functional at the Group level. It is made up of a President of the Group and persons responsible for operations development, financing, human resource management and Info/PR, control, accounting and administration. People from the Group management are also members of the boards of directors of the companies.

During the first year NTS was reorganized into four separate companies, NTS Rail, NTS Transport Sverige AB for general forwarding, Nordisk Air Cargo and Inter Forward Service AB. The other NTS companies, NTS SA France, NTS A/S Denmark, NTS A/S Norway, NTS GmbH West-Germany, became organized directly under the Group management. The reorganization would seem to have made the IF Group more of a holding company for the total Group.

NTS subsidiaries continued with their own international activities and the cooperation with NTS Sweden constituted only a minority of the total business activities.

All acquired companies had to start by going through a process of strategic planning and budgeting together with people from the IF Group. The intentions were to give the acquired companies a high degree of latitude within the frame of agreed strategies, budgets, demands on ROI and reporting of different kinds.

Most companies acquired during these years although unchanged to begin with went later through a process of restructuring and reorganizing. A new overall organizational structure was decided upon at the end of 1990. In practice, the total activities within IF were to be divided into six different fields of services. These were General Forwarding (including special transports), Airfreight, Rail, Third Party logistics, Projects and Consulting.

Basically, in all the changes in organization made for Europe hardly any cognisance seems to have been taken of the intercontinental traffics, even though many of the companies had extensive oversea activities.

Although large investments were made in order to acquire suitable transport companies, other important investments were also made during this period, such as investments in communication and information systems as well as planning and budgeting systems for the companies in the IF Group. In Germany, France, U.K. and Benelux where IF had holding companies in 1990, the separate companies in that specific country were formally part of that company.

7.1.2. Europe

<u>General development</u>

Within a period shorter than three years IF had managed to acquire international transport and forwarding companies based not only in Sweden but also in West-Germany, France Holland, Belgium, the UK and Denmark. These acquisitions have gradually increased IF's coverage of Europe. NTS was the first company in the Group and also the largest. Next largest in turnover was Z&B which was less than one third the size of the NTS group of companies. The IF Group covered traffics to/from Sweden through NTS to all important parts of Europe either via agents or subsidiaries. They also had third country services through NTS subsidiaries in Norway, France, Denmark and West-Germany. The acquisitions of Jerre and J.A. Larsson early in 1988 were small and rather specialized. Both cooperated with NTS and gave a certain increase in the number of services being offered, partly parallel and partly complementary to NTS. NTS Rail and Jerre AB together owned Railcarriers Oy in Finland and Woodtrans in France. Since Jerre and J.A. Larsson had only a limited international representation in Europe, they were mainly complementary to IF's existing activities in their services. Jerre had on the other hand an airfreight department which had a certain international coverage even though there had been some drastic changes due to the loss of a very important international agent. Jerre's airfreight was merged into NAC after the takeover.

Another early acquisition was a rather small company Allservice/WMS, specialized in warehousing and distribution in the Stockholm area, which did not add to the international coverage of the Group.

Until the end of the first year IF was basically a company very much concentrated on Scandinavia and traffics to/from that area. A European customer could not use IF to transport goods east-westbound other than in parts of France and in a limited part of Germany. The acquisitions of Amas and Z&B with their bases in Germany and Holland respectively provided IF with a change in their coverage not only in Europe but also overseas. These companies or rather groups of companies also added new types of services to the Group. Some of their services were in competition with parts of IF at that time, like NTS Germany, but mostly they were complementary so that they increased the degree of internationalization.

The next company was Norfreight which did not add much to the coverage since it was specialized in traffics to/from the Scandinavian countries.

On the other hand buying Fenthol & Sandtman GmbH, Sasse&Co, Beyer, SMTS, LCI and Bondelivery in 1990 introduced something new since these companies were to a large extent companies with both domestic and international services. DMP, ITM and ACE, out of which

ACE was by far the largest, were each specialists in their own areas. As far as the change in coverage in Europe was concerned, DMP and ITM were concentrated on Europe while ACE, being an airfreight company, added more to the Group on overseas markets.

By the end of the second year the IF Group had changed from being basically a Swedish international company to being a European company. Sweden was from the beginning the country of predominant importance in the Group with a large slice of the activities. In 1987 around 80% of the total number of employees were working in Sweden. By late 1990 the share had switched to 1/3 in Sweden and 2/3 abroad.

Services and representation

As companies were acquired, the number of services as well as the coverage offered by the Group increased, as did the volumes. Many of these services might already have been obtainable from parts of the Group through existing companies, but not with the necessary coverage.

Even if NTS had subsidiaries in France, West-Germany, Norway, Denmark and Finland, Europe was predominantly serviced via cooperations with agents. Some of those agents, like Z&B, Amas and Schier&Otten were then acquired by IF and brought into the Group. In their respective roles as agents, the resources of these companies had been available for the Group before the acquisitions but had been utilised only to a very limited degree. Scandinavia was only of marginal interest to European companies like Z&B and Amas. Scandinavia was more important for other companies like Satraco and Norfreight . Therefore Z&B and Amas meant very much for increase in coverage as well as service differentiation due to their size and variety in their activities. Amas, apart from being a traditional forwarder, was a specialist in transporting plants, bulbs, furniture, removals, etc. Z&B also had certain specialities like undertaking project transportation contracts world-wide, solving difficult dismantling, packing, moving and mounting problems, etc. The French companies acquired were also both general forwarders and specialists in certain business fields, such as the transport of furniture, works of art, etc.

Some of the other small companies acquired were specialized in warehousing /distribution such as Allservice/WMS, DMP and LCI. Another group of companies were specialized in furniture transports such as ITM, Beyer and some of Amas companies. Further NAC, ACE and Rambaud and some of the companies in the Amas Group were specialists in airfreight. The larger companies in the Group like NTS, Amas and Z&B all provided airfreight, seafreight, rail, trucking as well as warehousing and logistical services which seemed to be either complementary to or competing against the services offered by the specialists and to each other.

They were large enough to specialize in certain areas and at the same time offer general services.

Table 7.3. IF Group (facts at the time of the takeover)

Company	Services[4]	Offices in HC[5]	Subsid./SO abroad[6]
Sweden			
NTS Group	Gen forw./Specialist (air/sea/truck/rail)	34	F, W-G, N,Dk,SF,I,E.
J.A.Larsson	Specialist (plants and bulbs)	1	
Sped.AB Jerre	Gen forw/specialist (Rail/air)	6+2	F, S- F
Allservice/WMS	Wareh/distrib.	1	
ACE	Gen forw.(air)	4	Dk,N,S-F
Forsblad & Son	Specialist	1	
West-Germany			
Schier&Otten	Gen forw/Specialist (sea/air)	3-5	
Z&B	Gen.forw/Specialist (air/sea/truck,project)	12 1 subs.	I, UK, A, Saudi, Africa Head Office(Switzerland)
Fenthol&S.	Gen.Forw (truck)	5	East-Germany
DMP	Wareh/distrib.	1	
Benelux			
Amas (NL)	Gen.forw/Specialist (air/sea/truck)	1+20 [7]	
Sasse&Co (B)	Gen.forw/specialist (air/sea/truck)	3	
U.K.			
Norfreight	Gen.forw/specialist (sea/truck)	4	Eire
Bondelivery	Wareh/ distr.	15	
LCI(UK)	Wareh/distrib.	13	

---

[4] Dominating activities of the company
[5] In home country
[6] Subs.= subsidiaries, SO= sales offices, Abroad i.e. outside homecountry
[7] Amas had a number of subsidiaries in Belgium

France			
Beyer	Gen forw/Specialist (truck,air,sea)	40 3 subs	W-G, B, Lux
Rambaud	Gen forw(air/sea/truck)	3	
SMTS	Gen forw(air/sea/truck)	7	Algeria, Maroc
All transports	Gen forw/distribution	1	
Denmark			
ITM[8]	Specialist (furniture)	1	

The list above covers the number of offices that each of the acquired companies had in their respective home countries including airfreight offices and in addition the number of subsidiaries in home country and abroad(listed separately. As can be appreciated, many of these companies covered large parts of their home countries while others were concentrated to a single place. Many of the companies had separate subsidiaries in the home country apart from a net of offices also. Almost half of the companies presented above had foreign subsidiaries and there were probably some representative offices abroad not included. In total these foreign subsidiaries covered 18 countries of which 14 were European at the time of the takeover.

This meant that in some countries IF was represented by many different companies. First, the country might be a home country for acquired companies. Second, there could have been a number of foreign subsidiaries to other IF companies situated in the same country. Third, other companies could cover the country via direct traffics from their home country. Finally, the company could be represented by an agent. Therefore in different areas in several countries IF was represented several times. Many of the companies acquired thus had parallel traffics West-Germany-Holland or Belgium-Holland or UK-West-Germany or France- Belgium, etc. It also extended to overseas traffics since most of the companies concerned had international traffics which included airfreight and seafreight. It led IF to have a number of different agents representing it in the same country.

The total number of agents in Europe for one of the transport companies might easily have been anywhere between 15-40. For instance, in 1989, NTS Sweden had 40 agents, and NTS Denmark had 31, including sister companies (see lists in appendix 5). Other examples are NTS France and Z&B which had agents in 13 countries and some 21 countries respectively(see lists in appendix 5). Most of these companies, as well as others like Sasse, Amas, Beyer and SMTS

---

[8] Acquired by Amas in 1990

had more than one agent for general forwarding in many countries. Then, of course, airfreight and niche specialities, etc. would have added some extra agents to the picture.

As a result of the acquisitions made during these first 3 years the number of agents and the number of offices increased immensely. When IF started in January 1988 it only had 22 offices in 7 foreign countries including the offices of the recently acquired Danish companies. A year or so later, the number of places where IF had its own offices outside Sweden via subsidiaries had increased to somewhere between 150-200 .

In the same way the number of agents had increased. Due to this, the number of companies that IF Group companies were working with in each country could be very high. For example, NTS Sweden, Denmark and Norway alone had more than 20 agents, excluding cooperation with some offices of sister companies, in West-Germany in 1989 (see list in Appendix 5).To a large extent these agents were competing with some of the IF companies in West-Germany. For instance if a Z&B office, not having any regular services to/from Scandinavia, had wished to establish a traffic on Scandinavia, it might have found it impossible to use NTS, NTS already being tied up to some other agents. This sort of situation was not helped by the fact that IF had declared that each subsidiary should be free to act as it wished concerning agents.

In a country as big as West-Germany, where the number of acquisitions was high, the number of offices belonging to subsidiaries increased from 4 to around 25 in the second year. Cities such as Hamburg, Bremen and Berlin each had at least 3 such offices, for example belonging to Z&B, Schier&Otten and NTS. The number of agents in Germany increased since most of the companies acquired, Beyer, SMTS, Sasse&Co, Forsblad & Son, Amas quite apart from the 20-30 agents for the NTS companies, had traffics to/from West-Germany.

When a new company joined the Group the fact that IF already had a number of subsidiaries and offices in the different countries raised the suspicions of many of the existing agents for the company acquired. Some of the agents having an alternative available immediately left their cooperation with the company in question. This happened for instance to Z&B which lost an agent in the US and one in the UK. Both agents were themselves part of other international groups, in this case ASG and Rhenus. This also demonstrates that it was not only European agents but agents in other parts of the world who could become involved, as was the case for a company like Z&B who had their own representation on other continents.

Further it became difficult to be an agent for an IF Group company in Holland, for example, due to Amas' 20 or so offices in the country covering almost all types of services possible. In spite of this, NTS in Sweden retained its existing agent in Holland for general forwarding and continued to cooperate with Copex for special transports of plants, bulbs, etc. Companies like Z&B and ACE (airfreight), etc had other agents.

NTS Sweden had almost the same representation in 1989 as it had when it joined the IF Group in the beginning of 1986 (see lists of NTS Sweden in Appendix 5). Some countries in the Near and Middle East had been added. In total, the changes were a small reduction in the total number of agents and very few new agents. However NTS changed their important agent in Finland to the old Bilspedition agent. Further a few of the former agents, Z&B in West-Germany and Copex in Holland,became part of the Group. In both cases there were other agents in the same country as well. NTS also changed for a while from Ziegler in Belgium to Satraco.

As far as airfreight was concerned, the acquired companies had their own agents in the countries in Europe. These parts of the companies had an international net of agents. Some of them were merged like NAC and Jerre airfreight and others started to cooperate like ACE and the aircargo operations of Amas and Sasse & Co. On the other hand, Z&B aircargo (ZAC) was sold during 1990 to another airfreight company in Germany, Senator. IF then acquired 45% of the shares in Senator.

Changes developed over time when it came to subsidiary-to-subsidiary cooperation due to the fact that some of the existing agents left the cooperation with the acquired companies when they joined the IF group. Other reasons for an increase in the cooperation within the Group were the Group meetings and the will for the companies to increase their business activities together.

Organization and investments

The organization was in a constant state of change during the first two years of IF's existence since the Group was growing at a very rapid pace.

Buying the new companies in Germany, Benelux, France U.K.and in Sweden meant, of course, a lot of organizational changes for the IF Group .The formation of a holding companies for handling the management problems of those companies acquired in those countrries was one such example. Many new tasks - board meetings, group meetings, strategic planning meetings, etc., for the many companies acquired - devolved upon the individual members of the IF management. Constructing a basic organization embracing all the new companies and linking in decision routes, etc., imposed a heavy strain on management capacity during the first two years. Investment in management systems was also quite high at many other organizational levels in the newly acquired companies, due to the need to adapt to the demands imposed by IF. Z&B had to change its organizational structure in 1990 into three different companies, for example, and convert to working in a different manner, in order to so conform. The airfreight part was separated from the project company and the general forwarding company was sold. The accounting systems had to changed and the personnel reorganized as a result.

Management education within the Group was another area in which IF invested. Apart from the huge investments made in acquiring companies during the first two years, the largest investment would seem to have been in communication and information systems for the Group. All the investments made were concentrated to European countries.

(During 1991, IF made strenuous efforts to consolidate existing activities, to search for synergies in order to broaden the cooperation between the group companies and to restructure where necessary. Most of the European companies were probably affected in one way or another, especially in countries with a heavy concentration of subsidiaries.)

Summary of period 1988-90
During the first years of IF's existence they acquired more than 20 international, transport and distribution companies. Several of them were former agents or partners to NTS and their subsidiaries.

Most of the acquired companies had their own subsidiaries and/or agents in other European countries. One company, Amas, had 21 international subsidiaries in Benelux region. As a result of the development IF group covered the countries in Northern and Middle part of Europe by a combination of home-based companies, foregn subsidiaries and agents. In some countries like Germany, Benelux, France and U.K. the numbers became very large. IF had holding companies in these countries.

During the first years the cooperation between the acquired companies did not seem to increase. There were changes going on within the acquired companies such as reorganization and new design of communication systems. Only in a few special cases, as in airfreight, did new cooperations between the acquisitions take place.

Finally, after a short time some of the newly acquired companies also got activated and started to search for new acquisitions in foreign countries.

7.1.3. Specific event 1 - Züst & Bachmeier A.G.(Z&B)

Before the event
Z&B, an old Swiss forwarding company, was established in Chiasso in 1911 by Mr Züst, who worked as a broker at the Swiss-Italian border. His business idea was to derive advantage from the large differences existing between customs tariffs for finished and semi-finished goods by adapting the goods to the most favourable situation. He was able to offer customers lower car prices, for example, merely by taking the wheels off a car before transporting it over the border and putting them back on once on the other side.

During the first world war trade between countries diminished and trade between Switzerland and Italy became too limited for Z&B to exist profitably so other services had to be developed. Mr Züst decided to start railway traffics via Chiasso to/ from Italy, Switzerland and Germany. In order to guarantee an equally good service at both ends a number of small offices in Düsseldorf, Leipzig, Chemnitz and Berlin were established in Germany. This was mainly achieved through buying small German transport and forwarding companies of good reputation and merging them into Z&B. During the period of the 1920's and the beginning of the 1930's it was relatively cheap to buy small companies in Germany with Swiss capital because of the war debts and the high inflation in the country. It was cheaper to buy than to start from scratch. Later in the 1930's, when the offices in Stuttgart and Hamburg were to be established the situation in Germany had changed and these offices were therefore directly established by Z&B.

Mr Züst established also a few affiliates in Italy between the two world wars. It was not possible to find any transport or forwarding companies to buy in Italy having the right know-how during this period so there had to be greenfield investments.

All Z&B offices, whether in Germany, Italy or Switzerland, were totally concentrated on international services mainly in a south-north direction in Europe and had no interest in domestic traffics.

During the 1930's Z&B initiated overseas traffics as an increasing number of customers were developing in overseas markets. An example was Krupp which produced the bulk of the rails for the American railways at that time requiring to be transported to the United States. The overseas goods were transported via several Italian, German or Dutch/Belgian harbours utilizing the offices of Z&B where available or agents, as in Rotterdam and Antwerp.

Z&B opened its first airfreight offices in the interwar period. Project transports had their beginnings in the transportation of materials and tools to the oil industry in the Middle East (mostly Iran).

At the end of the 1930's and before the second world war, Hitler decreed that foreign capital should be removed from Germany. The Z&B offices in Germany had to continue on their own and generate their own capital through profits. In 1940, the offices in Berlin and Leipzig were closed down. The others continued for as long as possible.

After the war, the offices in West- Germany came to life again as some of the employees returned from the war. Since Z&B was a Swiss company with Swiss capital it was easier to find suitable facilities, permission to continue as a transporting and forwarding company, etc.

This created an advantage for the firm during this period. The capital that Mr Züst had to withdraw from Germany before the war could now be invested in West-Germany.

During this period, new traffics were developed utilizing new means of transportation. Almost all long distance transports were by rail to begin with. Then Z&B in Germany gradually started to use also trucks as a means of transportation for some longer distances. For the Head Office in Chiasso rail remained the most important means of transportation. This change gradually created a difference in development and a gap in understanding between the German offices and the Head Office in Chiasso. Most offices in Germany had not had railway traffics for years by the end of the 1980's.

During the immediate postwar period most of the transports were for aid organizations and other aid programmes. The more traditional aid transports in combination with the Marshall Aid and the reconstruction of the German industry created a very high growth in international transports and especially so for overseas transports. Returning refugees helped with contacts. Z&B, which had some overseas traffics even before the war, continued its development in overseas markets. At the same time, some Z&B employees who had left the country during the war and settled overseas became Z&B contacts in some of its overseas markets like in the U.S. and in South America. Other countries like Japan and Egypt came to be markets of interest for Z&B in the immediate post-war years.

It was not until the 1970's though that Z&B started to look beyond the borders of Switzerland, Italy and Germany to establish offices of its own.

As the market grew in West-Germany, new offices were opened in several different places like Nuremberg(1950), Frankfurt(1951), Wuppertal(1952), Mannheim(1953) and Munich(1957). These offices all started on a small scale and were not small acquisitions like some offices were before the war. In Italy, on the other hand, Mr Züst acquired an old established company Ambrossetti in 1948/49. The firm Ambrossetti, founded the same year as Fiat, had a good reputation and very good relations to the Fiat Group as well as to the family Agnelli. The Z&B offices already established in Italy were merged with Ambrossetti and the company was renamed Züst & Ambrossetti. This way Z&A became a sister company to Z&B in West-Germany and Switzerland.

In 1959, Mr Züst decided to retire. He gave 5% of the total shares to the managers. The managers could then buy the shares in the respective companies. The outcome was that each company found itself with a large number of owners, who at the same time worked in the company. The companies in Italy and Germany were no longer sister companies. After a period, this finally led to the end of the cooperation between Z&B and Z&A and Z&B started a new office of its own in Milan.

After the transfer of ownership, the total company was divided in two, each part being much smaller than the original both in coverage and resources, which over a period had many important implications for the development of Z&B.

The overseas traffics continued to increase during the 1960's and 1970's as a result of the internationalization of German industry. As an international forwarder, Z&B's overseas transports came to be the predominant part of the business. Project transports developed further during this period as well logistical consulting and service systems.

In 1963, Z&B bought a packing company in Witten " Korrosion Schutz und Verpackung" which gave Z&B a vital complementary service. This company has played an important role for overseas and project business in Z&B over time.

Many German projects were going on during the 1960's and 1970's in the Near and the Middle East. During this period contracts were signed covering transports and international trade with all the East European States except for East Germany. This also led to increased transports to/from the Middle East and overseas countries. Negotiations had been going on for a long time out of the Nuremberg office. This situation gave Z&B the opportunity to organize transports and arrange many different types of business for these States. These contacts with the Eastern European States have been very positive for the growth of Z&B. The Z&B offices in Iran and Iraq were established partly as a result of this trade. Nuremberg developed over time to be the main center for project business in Z&B.

Striving to be very close to customers, Z&B tried to fulfil the demands of customers even though such demands might seem unachievable. The example of how the company built a separate railway siding (on its own initiative) in order to store a number of waggons during the war for the Chilean government, and then transporting them over to Chile directly after the war, is part of company history. This effort by Z&B was recognized with a decoration awarded by the Chilean Government. This deep-rooted company policy also meant that out of necessity it must be a full service company. Z&B therefore started early with airfreight as a complementary service. It even handled goods for customers with European transports to countries and places to which it had no traffics. In these cases, co-loading with some other transport company was the method generally used. This was more often the case in east-west directions since the company was based on south-north transports.

Basically all services before the second world war were in the south-north direction in order to serve the trade between Italy, Switzerland and Germany. As the development of overseas and airfreight intensified the east-west destinations increased, not only to/ from other continents but also within Europe.

Airfreight started in the beginning of the 1950's as a complementary service in the company mainly for overseas transports for goods like spare parts, etc., and a number of airfreight offices were opened during the 1950's.

During the 1970's and the beginning of the 1980's a number of offices were established in the overseas markets like Lebanon(1974), Iran(1976), Iraq(1982),Saudi Arabia (1977), the U.S. (1979), South Africa (1985) but also in the U.K.(1974) for overseas purposes. Two more offices were established in Europe, in Vienna and in Zurich. The office in Zurich, which specialized partly in East African traffics, was closed down in 1985 after 7 years' of existence. Z&B also set up a representative office in Beijing in the late 1980's.

Even though Z&B might have offices in a country it often had agents as well, as in the northern parts of Switzerland, in the U.K. and the U.S.. By setting up an office of its own in a country such as the U.K. where it still had agents for its transports between the U.K. and Germany, a loss of confidence was experienced between the existing agents and Z&B.

Over time, the different Z&B offices had developed traffics to different international destinations but since they had no domestic traffics they all focused on their own business to/from Germany. In this way the different offices had little business in common. As separate profit centers, the offices had also become independently self sufficient and, as a result, the company had no common strategy.

The individual offices knew very little about the activities of the other offices. On the other hand, the individual offices maintained a very close connection with their customers and commonly held on to their customers even if they moved away to some other part of Germany. This complicated the situation further.

However, when overseas activities increased for business areas, such as airfreight, the demands from agents overseas emphasised the importance to have a common agent for the whole of Germany. This would seem to have forced Z&B to create a common coordinator for all six Z&B airfreight offices in Germany.

In other service areas, the problem was partly solved by letting those offices specialized in a specific area act as main coordinator in that respect for the whole of Germany for certain destinations. However, there was still insufficient coordination between offices.

During the early 1970's, the Head Office in Chiasso appointed a managing director for Germany, Mr Scherer, to be located in Stuttgart,and two regional managers, one for the southern region of Germany and one for the northern region. The southern region included Munich, Nuremberg, Stuttgart, and Mannheim but the region was also responsible for managing the former offices in Saudi-Arabia (Jeddah), East Africa, and Iran (Teheran). In the northern region, the offices of Hamburg, Bremen, Düsseldorf, Wuppertal and Frankfurt were included as well as the management of the offices in the U.K.(London), South Africa (Johannesburg) and indirect via the London office,the former office Iraq (Bagdad). Vienna and New York were both independent companies under the name of Z&B, owned by the managing director in West-Germany.

The owners of the companies taken over from Mr Züst in the late 1950's were already getting elderly in the 1960's. When taking over the shares at the end of the 1950's, a special clause in the contract stated that the owners were supposed to be active in the company. Naturally this could no longer be the case in 1970´s and 1980´s once they had retired. The company, therefore, found itself very restricted in its possibilities to expand since part of the profits had to go towards dividends and because none of the owners were willing to put any more money into the company for investment in communication systems, etc. Another problem was the fact that the shares in the company were evenly spread so that decisions had to meet with general approval.

As the company grew and the need of capital increased these problems became a severe draw-back and Z&B's ambitions to be a full service forwarder could not fulfilled. The internationalization of the customers demanded that Z&B set up some international offices of its own in areas like South America, where the companies seemed to lack the necessary know-how and/or where they were unable to find satisfactory agents. Limited resources created problems for Z&B in finding the partners it wanted. Large competitors like Schenker, Kühne & Nagel and Danzas, invested heavily during the 1960's and 70's and increased their growth.

The practice of working close to the customer out of individual offices hindered overall marketing coordination which added to the limitations of the middle-sized company that Z&B undoubtedly was.

The Z&B agents in Europe were usually strong locally and largely privately owned and during the 1980's these agents faced the risk of being bought by other, larger companies.

In the last years before the acquisition the problems were enhanced. There were discussions of a management buy-out but there was a problem in raising the capital needed.

The effects of the financial constraints under which the company was labouring grew worse over time.It needed larger resources to be able to compete on certain projects but there was no possibility of growth through investments. The old policy of not owning any equipment, building or terminal became a disadvantage at this stage since the fixed assets to borrow against were limited.

In earlier years, when Mr Züst managed the company, many investments and many new services were started. After that period, when the owners grew in number and in age, only limited investments were made which made it difficult for the company to fully capitalize on the growth in trade between Germany and the rest of the world.

The Event

IF acquired 100% of Z&B early in 1989 as a continuation of its international expansion on the European Market in transport, forwarding and distribution.

At that time the Z&B company had existed for more than 77 years and many of the existing shareholders were over 80 years of age.

The acquisition included all offices in Germany as well as the Z&B packing company in Witten, the office in the U.K., an office in South Africa, a small representation in East Africa and the Head Office in Chiasso as well as 54% of the Vienna office. (The rest of the Vienna office as well as 100% of the New York office continued to belong to Mr Scherer personally.) The Milan office remained an independent company with the name of Z&B.

The total number of employees was around 400 and the Group had a turnover of around SEK 750 million.

At this time, the distribution of Z&B services was around 35-40% in seafreight, 35-40% in airfreight and 20-30% in international inland transportation in Europe.

The company could offer all different types of services internationally, anything from specialized export packing and heavy transport to airfreight and airmail.

The contact with Z&B were made via an independent consulting firm which made a search of the German market to find suitable companies for IF. NTS had, however, a twenty year old cooperation with Z&B in Nuremberg.

The construction of the company being Swiss but having the main part of its business spread over many different profit centers in Germany made it unusually difficult to obtain an accurate overview of the development of the company.

Since the greater majority of the managers of Z&B in Germany had no shareholding in the company and lacked the capital to mount a management buy-out, the development of the company remained in the hands of the old retired managers. The younger managers had a distinct interested in changing the situation so that the company would be able to invest in order to survive.

Shortly after the company was sold Mr Scherer, the managing director of the company for 15 years (1974-89) and a shareholder, decided to relinquish his position in Z&B and concentrate on Italy as well as the U.S. and the Vienna office in Austria.

Z&B was a very old company compared with the IF Group starting in 1988 and had a tradition of involvement in Germany and Switzerland extending over many years. Although Nuremberg had trucking traffic together with NTS, most of the largest offices had no regular traffics to/from Sweden which remained relatively unknown to Z&B. The focus for Z&B were the overseas traffics, sea or airfreight which also left it less well equipped to manage the Common Market development on its own.

After the event

Since these acquisitions were made in the beginning of 1989 the intervening time span had been short (at the time this was written in 1990). During the period, the changes for the Group as a whole were large, notwithstanding the fact that the individual companies continued to be free to act without any demands being placed on working with the other companies in the Group. The effects were reflected at many levels in the Group. Some took the form of different kinds of cooperations started within the Group. In other cases a cooperation was not wanted or was not possible. In certain areas problems were foreseen since the sister companies already had agents that represented them in a specific part of the German market.

Internally

As intended the IF Group started the takeover by going through a strategic planning process with Z&B. This made it possible to create common goals and objectives for the company. The planning process involved all the managers of the company and this was a radical change, as such, since the company had not had any common planning previously. A new managing director of Z&B Germany had to be appointed. A manager form the IF Group was appointed for a period of 6 months.

After the first year the company was reorganized into two separate companies, one for general forwarding and one for airfreight. It was also the intention that project forwarding should become a separate company in the following year. To begin with the managers of the Düsseldorf office for general forwarding, the Stuttgart manager for airfreight and the Nuremberg manager for project business became the new managing directors of these various companies. This was because of their special know-how in the different offices. Each of the companies was to have a separate board of directors consisting of some Swedish directors from the IF Group and from the general forwarding company and the manager of NTS Germany also. Together they would function more like a working team. The offices that had shown a loss for a period were to be reduced in size. One of these offices reduced its number of employees by 75 per cent.

The reorganization of the company was implemented during 1990 and partly during 1991. There was also a reconstruction of the reporting, budgeting, planning and informations systems during 1989. The creation of an EDP system for general forwarding had its beginnings.

All these activities have had deep effects on the company. The intention was to make the personnel more inter-changeable between the separate offices through better coordination and better distribution of knowhow according to the different activities of the various Z&B companies.

Airfreight would find this less of a problem since a certain level of coordination already existed between the different offices in Germany as a result of the demands from the overseas agents. However, different offices were coordinating different traffics. It was the original intention to coordinate airfreight with the Nordisk Air Cargo organization but, in the event, Z&B airfreight was formed into a separate company merging in 1990 with Senator Airfreight GmbH in Germany. In 1991, IF bought 45% of Senator Airfreight GmbH.

Externally
Z&B had to change its agents in the U.K., the USA and Holland. The two agents in the UK and USA were both associated with other Groups (the Rhenus Group and the ASG Group). The agent in Holland left because Amas beecame part of the IF Group. IF has found new agents in the UK and the USA. Even though Z&B had an office of its own in the U.K. the office was specialized in overseas traffics and did not have the resources or knowledge to handle land-transports to/from Germany. Many of the existing agents stayed however.(See list of countries covered at the time of the takeover)

Neither the customers or the competitors reacted very much on the event, no doubt due to the frequency with which similar events have been happening in Europe during the last decade. Many of the privately owned forwarding companies have been acquired by larger companies which, in turn, has resulted in a concentration within the industry in Europe.

Z&B expected a closer contact with the other companies in the Group and wanted to start several new types of business with the contribution of know-how from other specialists in the Group.

IF's purchase during 1990 of two companies in Germany with domestic traffics and terminals and almost as many employees together as Z&B in Germany will, of course, effect Z&B either directly or indirectly via customers and competitors.

The formation of a German holding company containing all the different German IF Group companies will have its effect on all the companies involved.

Summary of the Z&B event

Züst & Bachmeier(Z&B) was a privately owned Swiss forwarder, which had been developing through establishment and acquisitions of companies in Germany and Italy as well as through many agent cooperations before and after the second world war. As the founder of the company retired, the managers took over and the company was divided into Z&B, the Swiss-German part, and Z&A, the Italian part.

In the beginning of 1989 IF acquired Z&B. The Z&B office in Nürnberg had been an agent to NTS in Sweden for more than 20 years. The first year after the takeover the company was reorganized into two separate units i.e. general transports and airfreight. Another unit for international projects was to be constructed the year after. The takeover caused some of the agents left the cooperation with Z&B. In these cases Z&B found new agents. Cooperation with other companies in the group did not change during these first years, except in airfreight.

7.1.4. Specific event -The acquisition of Amas

Before the event

Amas is the holding company for a small group of companies in The Netherlands and Belgium. Amas Holding b.v.was founded in 1972 and its business area has mainly been trading and forwarding.

The privately owned Amas was sold in 1981 to the British Bowater Group, primarily active in paper production and trading. Bowater had created a separate freight services division which included companies like Rhenania (with large boats and vessels for canals and rivers, etc), Mondia (a large removal firm based in Strasbourg) and Amas. Together these companies formed a group of around 3,000 employees out of which Rhenania had the major share (around 2,000).

Companies within the Amas Group had been confined to The Netherlands and Belgium but, on the other hand, there were many different companies. At the border between The Netherlands and Belgium there were a number (11) of import brokerage offices under the names of van Huls and Belcomex belonging to the Amas group and together they had a high market share of customs clearance (around 30%). The other companies represented different types of transports such as Internationaal Expeditiebedrijf Copex b.v.(Copex) in Hillegom (roadtransports), Copex Air (airfreight), Copex IGS (sea-transports) and Schut Copex (industrial packaging and removals) Apart from these different Copex companies there were other companies within the same type of business or in closely related businesses. In total the Group had 21 companies before the take over by IF. Many of these companies had originated with or had been initiated by the existing companies while other companies were added through acquisition. Many activities between the companies became overlapping as they developed over time and competition increased within the Group. For example, three companies had IATA licences in airfreight, i.e Copex Air, Mondia Europe and Copex in Hillegom. There were many other areas of competition in road transport, ocean freight, special transports, etc. The Group profile, as such, was very low during these years, each company had its own profile.

Examples of complementary activities developing over time were a number of airfreight services closely related to Copex Air, like Skylink (airport handling services), Speed (a broker in airfreight space), Air Agencies Holland (airline representative), etc. These companies were initiated by Copex Air which, in turn, evolved out of Copex in Hillegom.

Closely related companies to Copex IGS (Rotterdam), having competing as well as complementary business, were Terwee Okker, Amsterdam (ocean forwarding), Neptune, Antwerp (bulk shipments), Cobimar, Antwerp (ship´s agent) and finally Schut-Copex and Hofsteange b.v. (project removals and furniture transports) and Meubeldistributie- en Service Centrum b.v. (furniture distributions).

 There were some trading companies over and above this which were separate from the others. The trading side of Amas, for paper as well as for packaging machinery and materials to supermarkets and industrial clients, had gradually reduced in importance within the Group and only two trading companies were left at the time of the take over .

The Copex Group, engaged in different areas like airfreight, seafreight and road-transports, formed an important part of the Amas group of companies.

The cornerstone of the Copex group of companies was <u>Copex in Hillegom</u> which started in 1921 as a cooperative for flower bulb exporters in Hillegom. The flower bulb exporters wanted to control the documentation as well as the transportation of the flower bulbs.

The exports of flower bulbs expanded to many different countries during the 1920's. The most important countries for export have been not only the European countries but over time also the U.S. and Japan. However, there were several other overseas destinations of lesser importance.

Copex in Hillegom expanded and established its first subsidiary in 1947 at Alsmeer. The exports from Holland at that time included not only flower bulbs but many other different products like tree cuttings, plants, flowers, etc.

Further subsidiaries, specializing in seafreight, were then set up in Rotterdam and Amsterdam in order to handle the expansion of overseas exports.

Copex in Hillegom has always been a company specializing in perishables or agricultural products, even if the Copex companies have slowly started taking on more general cargo and spare parts for the automotive industry.

For a specialist in perishables the time aspect of the transport and the handling of the goods were extremely vital. This made the choice of agents very important and most agents to Copex Hillegom were specialists in perishables and green products.

As Holland gradually changed from being an exporter to more of being an importer of plants and flowers and other agricultural products, the quality of agents became even more essential for Copex. Holland developed into being an important trading country in agricultural products for large parts of Europe.

Before the war, most transports by Copex in Hillegom were by rail or by sea but after the war there was a development into transports by air and truck.

Over time as the share of general cargo handled by Intern.Exp.Copex increased, some of the existing specialist agents proved to be inadequate. Therefore separate agents were sometimes appointed for general cargo parallel to the existing specialist agents.

In 1988, before the take over, Intern.Exp.Copex had agents in large parts of the world. In Europe, there was a combination of direct transports to other countries and representation by agents. Copex had their own direct services (round trips) for agricultural products within a radius of 500-600 km. This meant that they had direct door-door transports to parts of Germany, France, Belgium and the U.K.using termo and refrigerated vehicles. In more distant markets like Italy, Spain, Portugal, Austria, Sweden, Norway, and Finland they had to rely on agents. They had two agents in Sweden, J.A. Larsson in Malmö (later part of the IF group) and Anton Pettersson (Scansped Group) in Stockholm, both specialists in agricultural products (see appendix 5). In many countries they were represented by several agents, for instance a combination of direct transports and agents.

Copex started airfreight services in Hillegom as a complementary service directly after the war in 1945. In 1953 a special office was established at Alsmeer (the location of the flower market) to handle airfreight, which had gained very much in importance, and this became the beginning of Copex Air. Three years later the office in Alsmeer was closed due to intense competition and the airfreight department concentrated on general aircargo instead. The growth of aircargo continued but it was still considered as a complementary service and therefore the agents used were mainly sea and trucking forwarders. Airfreight to start with was almost exclusively export consignment handed over to the airlines and this continued until the beginning of the 1960's when Copex decided to appoint specialized aircargo companies as agents more systematically. During the 1950's and 1960's Copex, as well as its agents, was very dependent on the airlines for the handling of the goods, documentation, rates, etc., but for as long as imports continued to constitute only a limited part of the total business the customs clearance was handled by the Dutch airline K.L.M. on the instructions of Copex. Then imports started to grow and a few years later Copex opened a separate office at Schiphol airport largely for handling imports.

As the development continued Copex came to realize the need to have not only loosely connected agents on bilateral agreements but a network of cooperating specialized agents. This made Copex take the initiative to form IASA, International Air Shipping Association. IASA was founded by 12 European air cargo agents in 1971. The idea was that these agents should form a network representing each other instead of having only bilateral agreements. This network should be world wide, so agents from different parts of the world could become members. Many of the companies joining IASA had no appointed agents in Europe before. As a result of this, the growth of Copex accelerated

The formation of IASA gave rise not only to very high growth but also to new services and the formation of Speed. Speed is a small company specialized in buying space from airlines and selling it to forwarders. Speed started as a result of a cooperation between the French agent and Copex and for the specific purpose of operating regular charter transports to Nigeria in 1976. The company then developed into being neutral broker of aircraft space for forwarders and became well established on this market.

Other services developed as a result of the specialization of the total Copex company in agricultural products, which made it necessary in 1986 to have Amas represented at the flower market in Alsmeer once again. Accordingly Mondia Europe b.v. was created to specialize in handling the export and import of flowers. Copex Air and Mondia decided jointly about agents, sales abroad, etc. In 1988 Mondia had become one of the leading air cargo companies in the flower market.

The growth of Copex Air continued and in 1986 Copex had become one of the three largest airfreight forwarders in The Netherlands. The size of Copex made it necessary to find new facilities. Amas then decided to build its own facilities at the airport. This building was ready in 1988 and as the area exceeded the needs of Copex Air, another company Skylink, offering a complementary service, was created in 1988. This company also offered warehousing and handling services to airlines and to some off-line trucking companies, brokers and forwarders, on a neutral basis.

Amas had always preferred to start new companies when creating new business ideas. The basic reasons for this (according to top management) were to keep flexibility as well as retaining the good managers.

The event

The former owner Bowater, which had been buying several companies world-wide, ran into economic problems. Many of the companies were in bad condition. They wanted therefore to sell their freight service companies Rhenania, Mondia and Amas.

When the story as to how NTS broke away from Scansped became public knowledge some top level people in Amas contacted people in NTS whom they knew to ask about IF policies and whether there might be a possible interest. It was only after discussions between Amas and the management of IF, that Bowater became involved and the outcome was that the company was sold to IF at year-end 1988/89.

Mr Leibbrand, the president of the Amas Group, was one of the persons that wanted the Group to be sold to IF rather than to any of the other large companies, like Nedlloyd, Franz Maas, etc., which had policies of merging acquired companies. Amas saw a risk in this, both for themselves and for their agents. If taken over by a large multinational they expected it would lead to changes of agents for them as well as for the agents. IF on the other hand had the reputation of allowing acquisitions to keep their own name and culture. IF was also only interested in companies not owning the means of transportation. Accordingly Amas was sold to IF. Mondia and Rhenania were sold to other companies.

The Amas Group had started to work more as a group in the last years before the takeover and therefore Amas held out for a guarantee that they would be granted a special status and allowed to continue working as a group within the IF Group.
The company had 5-600 employees at the time of the takeover.

After the event

After the takeover Amas companies continued as before. The main difference arising out of the acquisition was a closer coordination within the Amas group. The common profile for the group became enhanced and the group was divided into a number of internally more closely cooperating divisions. New investments in computerized communication systems were made and a number of companies were acquired and added to the group.

Many of the existing agents were afraid to start with that Amas would be forced to switch to Group members as its agents in other European countries. Amas explained about its guarantee and most agents seemed to be satisfied. However, as a result of the takeover, Copex in Hillegom changed to the IF Group company in Denmark, NTS Denmark.

During the period that Amas has been owned by IF, several new companies have been added on the initiative of Amas. Amas has not founded new companies on its own but has acquired established companies like Sasse & Co, Satraco and ITM in Denmark. The one exception was Rocotrans, a neutral railway-trucking/container broker, which was a company founded by Amas and starting its business on January 1, 1989.

ITM in Kolding, Denmark, acquired during 1990, was a specialized company within furniture forwarding. This company had in turn to invest in a small Swedish service company in Varberg since they lost their Swedish agent Tibro Lastbilscentral as a result of the takeover by an IF company. (Tibro Lastbilcentral was cooperating very closely with ASG in Sweden.) Acquiring ITM was in line with Amas specialization in furniture forwarding and means that Amas has ambitions to internationalize itself within this field within the IF Group.

Another company acquired was Sasse & Co, a 150 years old Belgian international general forwarder of sea, air and roadtransports with offices in Zavantem, in Antwerp and in Brussels. The number of employees was around 150. Sasse & Co contributed to a better coverage of the Benelux market for Amas. In airfreight Copex Air has introduced Sasse to IASA Group and therefore Sasse has became an observer company within the IASA. Before the Sasse acquisition, the representation of Amas in Belgium was limited to specialized customs clearance offices at the Dutch border, to Cobimar, a small ship´s agent and to Neptune specializing in bulk shipments. These companies are now part of the Sasse organisation. As for road transports they were performed via direct traffics from Holland.
Another change has been that Amas has sold off one of the trading companies for exporting paper in order to concentrate to a greater extent on forwarding and transportation.

The airfreight division has developed into the services of being General Sales Agencies i.e. representing airlines without offices in Holland. For this purpose Air Agencies of Holland (AAH) was bought. However the AAH situated in Rotterdam had restricted its services to passengers while Amas wanted to expand into serving airlines for cargo as well. Therefore the airfreight division set up a branch office of AAH at Amsterdam airport .

Basically being a member of IASA meant that Copex Air could not cooperate with the other airfreight companies within the IF Group. However IASA agreed in 1990 to cooperate with ACE in Sweden, where they lacked a member at that time.

ITM in Denmark became a part of the Amas International furniture transport and distribution division and not of NTS Denmark. Though Amas did discuss a cooperation with NTS in Sweden. This did not happen because of the differences in culture and type of goods and customers.

Furthermore the acquisitions made by Amas other countries has increased the number of subsidiaries in many European countries. Through the acquired companies new agents will also be tied to the IF group via Amas even though some of these have already reacted and left their existing partner like Tibro Lastbilcentraler.

Neither the customers of Amas nor the competitors seem to have reacted, since most of the transport companies in Holland were part of one group or other. At the same time Amas remains as separate Group within the IF Group continuing on its own, as before.

Summary of the Amas event

Amas was a group of around 20 companies situated in Holland and Belgium. The base of the group, Copex in Hillegom, had been established in 1921 in Holland. Over time new international activities were developed by Copex both in Europe and overseas and new companies were spun off and acquired in Holland and Belgium. When IF acquired Amas in early 1989, Copex was an agent to NTS in Sweden.

After the event the Amas group has continued as a separate holding company for Benelux within the IF group. The main changes during the two first years were investments in new communication systems and an increased coordination of the activities within the Amas group. Further, Amas acquired two companies, one in Denmark specialized in furniture transports and another one, a general forwarder, in Belgium. Both have been incorporated into the Amas group.

7.2 General case analysis

7.2.1 Period 1988-90 - Acquisitions

Integration

IF, being part of the Ratos Group and the parent company for a planned group of companies in transports and distribution, started its activities by legally integrating NTS through a takeover from the Ratos Group.

The expansion of IF was totally dominated by acquisitions. During these first years IF has made many acquisitions, large and small, but all in distribution and transports. After two years, IF consisted of around 20 larger companies. IF was *joining nets* each time a new larger acquisition was made. Some of the smaller companies acquired, which basically only concerned a single transport system or a local complementary service, should be seen as the net *opening up*.

The joining nets all continued during the period as separate part-nets within the total IF net. Very few exceptions existed. However, one exception was airfreight. The airfreight companies were mostly either merged or cooperating very closely after a very short time period.

A large number of the joining nets were foreign based international companies with the same type of services as the first NTS net which meant that they were O/C (overlapping in services and complementary geographically).

Most of the companies acquired were, however, in one way or another marginally connected to existing earlier acquired companies at the system level. This was the case for Z&B, Amas, Jerre&Co, J.A. Larsson and Sasse &Co. The initial acquisition of NTS was made through existing contacts between the Ratos Group and NTS.

In the total net level there existed not only legal but also social and control integration of the separate nets. Control integration increased very quickly through introduction of a specified common planning system and decisions on recruiting and training of management in the dominating companies within the separate part-nets. The social integration increased through new board members from the Group, meetings within the total group, etc. Through such increased integration some of the agents´ nets were *drifting closer*.

In general during this period there was very little integration going on directly between the acquired part-nets. However, the creation of holding companies within countries with several subsidiaries increased legal, control and social integration between part-nets.

Several changes were instead taking place within the part-nets, both through reorganization and through new acquisitions to these part-nets. Reorganization was made of the NTS group of companies, of Amas, of Z&B, etc., within a relatively short period of time from the acquisition. A higher execution integration followed within the part-nets. As for the acquisition of companies, they were increasing their execution integration very strongly with the rest of the companies within the part-net.

NTS, as most of the other acquired nets, cooperated basically with agents but had a few subsidiaries in other countries. Since the integration was very low between the part-nets the cooperation between the agents at system level continued almost unchanged during these first years. In spite of the increased integration with the IF Group at net level and NTS and Copex did not enlarge their existing cooperation at net level. NTS kept their other existing agent in spite of the conflicts. This would seem to have been true also in other cases like for Z&B and other companies in Amas.The larger changes in the net of representatives were taking place through the internal part-net reorganization.

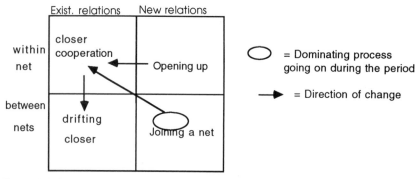

Figure 7.4. Internationalization - integration 1988-90

Even though IF was a very young group of companies in terms of internationalization, the companies acquired were not young. Several of the international companies acquired had existed since the beginning of the century and had been developing internationally over the years through a combination of cooperation with agents, small acquisitions and greenfield investments. The international development of Z&B showed a pattern of making use of different types of cooperations and aspects of integration over time. Not only Z&B but also Amas, Norfreight Ltd, Sasse & Co, Fenthol & Sandtmann, Schier & Otten, ACE, etc., had their international nets of representatives in Europe and had gone through a long period of internationalization.

Finally, as can be seen from all the acquisitions made, the legal and control aspects seem to be very important. To a large extent, the social and execution aspects will have to be developed in the next step.

Extension

Through the NTS takeover, IF became extended to all important countries in Europe directly from the start, either through agents or subsidiaries. Through NTS, IF also became extended to many overseas markets via shipping or airfreight.

Therefore the acquisitions of a series of international companies did not change *first degree* of extension but well the *secondary degree* of extension. This was especially the case for the first foreign acquisitions but since many of the acquisitions had traffics to/ from the same countries the secondary degree of extension was also soon at a maximum.

The speed of extension could not possibly have been much higher.

Penetration

During the first two years of IF's existence the turnover more than doubled for the Group through the acquisitions. The amount of resources and relationships increased at a very high speed.

Through the takeover of NTS IF gained access to established relations in most European countries as well as many countries overseas which did not change *size of the relations* very much. Then the acquisitions increased the *spread of the relations* both directly through being established in the foreign country and indirectly through having cooperation with agents in those European countries.

The result was that IF covered many countries via a combination of subsidiaries to Swedish companies, home-country companies and agents to a large number of foreign companies. For example, in Holland Amas had around 20 different companies NTS had three agents, Z&B had its own agent, Jerre Rail its own agent , NTS France its own agent etc. The situation in West-Germany, Belgium, the UK, etc., showed similar complexities because of the acquisitions.

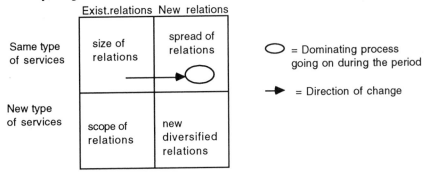

Figure 7.5. Internationalization -penetration 1988-90

Through this wide representation within many of the largest European countries the penetration seems to be very high in some countries.

As a result of these acquisitions of companies mostly working internationally the penetration seems to increase also in other countries outside Europe. Many of these international companies had agents or representative offices or even subsidiaries in some of the most important areas outside Europe like North America, Far East, Middle East, etc.

Conclusions and effects on representatives

Through the takeover of NTS, IF achieved a high degree of internationalization from the start. The internationalization process was totally dominated by joining nets through legal integration. However the acquisitions in general continued as separate part-nets being O/C and integration did not increase directly between them but via group management.

Through these acquisitions involving some other nets were drifting closer. Penetration increased enormously over the period through the fact that countries were covered not only by many subsidiaries but also by agents and former subsidiaries to the larger operating companies.

Effects on representatives grew more complicated with each international acquisition since the degree to which the net included negatively connected systems increased over time.

Since many of the joining nets continued as separate part-nets within the total net the changes were small in the beginning with the exception of a few cases seeing their present cooperation without future as being part of O/O (overlapping both in services and geographically) nets. Due to this, some agents decided to leave almost directly after the IF takeover. For Z&B one agent in US (an ASG subsidiary) and one in the UK (subsidiary to Rhenus Group) left very quickly. Z&B had to find some other agent since they were not prepared to take over themselves even though they had a company in UK. Others were worried because they were competing with other IF companies in their international traffics.

The fact that the companies were only legally integrated in the total net and only loosely integrated between part-nets made fewer agents leave than would otherwise have been the case. On the other hand, IF companies that wanted to add complementary services very often could not do so since the sister companies were already tied up with existing agents .

Not only were different agents negatively connected but also so were the different subsidiaries within countries working within separate sub-nets within IF group.

Also, the fact that so many companies have been acquired during such a short time has made many of the IF companies unaware of activities going on in the Group - as the picture became clearer the effects increased. As the acquired groups started to reorganize and restructure within their part-nets larger effects on the representatives became more obvious.

Effects 1988-89 on suppliers, owners and competitors

The effects on the suppliers were limited since IF had declared its intention not to own the means of transportation. However, some of the companies acquired during 1989 have not only been forwarders but to an even larger extent trucking companies, having terminals like Fenthol &Sandtmann. Also DMP has terminals and warehouses in Germany as well as contracted distribution. This change means that integration has increased with the trucking companies in the countries involved.

Z&B has also been highly integrated for a long time, both legally and executionally, with a small specialized packing company in Witten in Germany which had a specific importance for the project business.

As for the specialized railway companies, Jerre Rail and NTS Rail both have a close cooperation to the railway as well as different companies having waggons for rent like VTG. This has been changing over the years as the companies started to charter full train sets which meant taking over activities that the railway company normally performs. This will change the asymmetry between the railway and the rail transport agencies in the Group.

The increased complexity of the total IF net caused a higher amount of internal conflicts within the net not only in Europe but also overseas.

An important effect of all these acquisitions taken together is the increased turbulence on the transport and forwarding industry within Europe as well as the rise in prices for acquisitions within the industry. The need of coverage within Europe in order to adapt to the deregulation of the Common Market obviously made many other companies in the industry more aware of the time pressure. In both cases the competitors were affected.

Interaction between the dimensions of internationalization

For IF, integration through joining of nets was totally dominating both for extension and penetration I-->E-->P. After the first acquisition most extension basically only changed in secondary degree I-->E2-->P and after that only penetration increased as a result of joining new nets I-->P.

8. Conclusions of general case analysis and comparison of the cases

Period 1 1945-54	Period 2 1955-69	Period 3 1970-79	Period 4 1980-90
AS G -Start through rail expansion -Single systems integration - New coop.-->closer coop. -No legal integration - Extension to 11-12 European countries of first degree -Increase in volumes and increase in spread relations -A net is gradually created	**ASG** -Trucking takes over Single system integration new and cessation of rail cooperations -Net is opening up -Penetration through new diversified and scope of relations -Continued first degree extension to Europe and start oversea **Bilspedition** -Starting through trucking expansion -System as well as net integration. -New coop->closer coop -Open.up and joining nets -Certain legal integration -Extension of first degree to around 14 European countries. Secondary degree of extension through subsid. in Dk and N -Penetration through size of relations changing towards an increase in spread of relations	**ASG** -Specialization and diversification of services. Changes at systems and net levels positive and negative -Creation of separate part-nets -Extension first degree continued Europe and oversea. Secondary degree starting -Penetration via spread, scope of and new diversified rel. **Bilspedition** -Specialization and diversification of services -Creation of part-nets -System integration New coop->closercoop -> enlargement -Net integration Joining net and open up -Increased legal integr. especially Sweden -Extension first degree European countries and oversea and secondary degree - Investment abroad increases and decreases -Penetration via scope of and new diversified relations	**ASG** -Part-nets develop differentiated. Opening up and closer coop. through greenfield inv and small acquisitions -Moving towards closing up in airfreight part-net -Changes in secondary degree of extension -Penetration increase and decrease via spread, size of and scope of relations **Bilspedition** -Joining nets through acquisitions of large O/O nets -Leaving nets and closer cooperation within net through merging of the overlapping nets. -Extension secondary degree changes -Increases and decreases in scope of and spread of relations and increase in size of relations due concentration **IF** -Start by "joining nets" through acquisitions of around 20 larger internat. transp. comp -Extension into European region and oversea - Penetration through a change from size of into a spread of relations via nets acquired

Start of the internationalization in the three cases

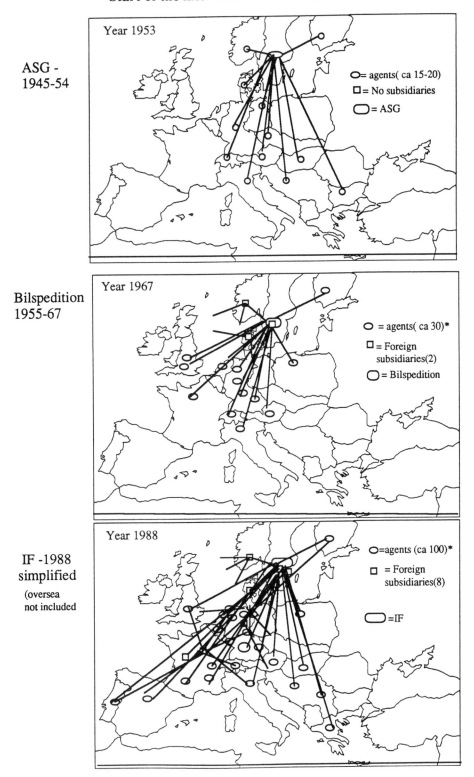

ASG -
1945-54

Bilspedition
1955-67

IF -1988
simplified

(oversea
not included

* =including the agents of the foreign subsidiaries

Internationalization at the end of 1980s in the three cases Europe -landtransport

ASG

Simplified

Year 1989

O = Agents (est. 75-100) incl. agents to subsid

□ = Foreign subs.(5)

⬭ = ASG

Bilspedi-tion
(after the merger)

Simplified

Year 1989

O = Agents(30-50) incl agents of subs

□ = Foreign subsidiaries (18)

⬭ = Bilspedition

IF
Simplified

Year 1989/90

O = Agents incl agents of subs(200-250)

□ = Foreign subsid.(35-40)

⬭ = IF

Comparison between case patterns

<u>Comparison of the start of internationalization</u>
(See the first map)

ASG started internationalizing during the 1940's, some 10-15 years earlier than Bilspedition and about 45 years before IF was created, and carried on during and after the war. When discussing the earliest stages of the internationalization process in the respective companies, the first decade after the war for ASG is compared with the period 1955-67 for Bilspedition and with IF's first year of existence.

ASG's internationalization process was predominantly a process of *integrating* single system relations based on informal bilateral agreements with local agents, through which a net was created. In the case of Bilspedition, a combination of single systems integration and net integration was used, involving legal integration to a certain extent. Finally, in IF's case, net integration was based on the legal aspect almost totally. IF's first acquisition was the net of NTS. This was a C/C net while the other smaller Swedish companies added during the first year were basically C/O and O/O.

Looking at the initial stage, only the first degree of *extension* took place in ASG while in Bilspedition not only first degree but also, to a limited extent, the secondary degree of extension took place, due to the internationalization of its Scandinavian subsidiaries. In the IF case, the acquisition of NTS and the other smaller Swedish international companies added both the first and secondary degrees of extension almost from the outset to most European and many overseas countries through their subsidiaries.

The level of *penetration* also differed very much between the three focal companies. After the first year, IF had many more relations and resources in most European countries, either directly or indirectly engaged, than ASG and Bilspedition ever had at their respective beginnings. ASG had 12-15 agents, Bilspedition had 2 foreign subsidiaries and an estimated 30 agents as compared to IF's 8 foreign subsidiaries and about 100 agents including those of the subsidiaries. Further, as ASG was first in the field, its penetration was very limited since only one type of service was involved initially and the only local agents used were relatively small. Bilspedition would seem to have achieved a somewhat greater degree of penetration by acquiring ATA and later Trailer Express but these companies were still small at that stage and their resources limited. In IF's case almost all types of services were covered right from the start and the subsidiaries were internationalized to a larger extent.

Patterns of internationalization over time

ASG pattern

Basically ASG's development over time was a process of gradual internal growth achieved through *integration* of single systems leading to opening up and closer cooperation at the net level. During the 1970's, after almost 20 years of continued growth, ASG created C/O part-nets through reorganizing its existing activities. Legal integration was very limited until the 1980's when ASG made a few greenfield investments and a couple of acquisitions which were merged into existing part-nets.

Extension of first degree was the dominant feature during the first periods while during the 1970's and 1980's second degree developed as the important feature. *Penetration* became more important for the total net than extension during the 1970's. Although integration was important at the single system level for the first three periods, interest for integration at net level was increasing over the periods and took first place in importance during the 1980's. Several changes in integration were made during the 1980's at the expense of penetration.

Bilspedition pattern

The internationalization of Bilspedition has been based on a combination of single system and net *integration* through joining of nets but with the proportion of net changes increasing over time. Therefore its growth has stemmed partly from internal development and partly from acquired external development. During the 1970's C/O part-nets were created out of the different acquisitions.

The nets of those companies acquired were primarily other Swedish international transport companies. These companies were mainly O/C in the 1960's, C/C combined with C/O in the 1970's and finally O/O during the 1980's. However, during the 1980's the number of instances of joining O/C nets with foreign acquisitions increased slightly.

Bilspedition would seem to have given priority to *extension* during the 1960's while during the 1970's a combination of extension and penetration was important through C/C and C/O nets adding new services. Initially in the 1980's *penetration* remained as a very important dimension since the O/O nets acquired were not merged. However, from the mid-1980's onwards integration at net level would seem to have been given highest priority, partly at the cost of a period of decreased scope and spread of relations in the dimension of penetration.

IF pattern

IF achieved growth solely through acquisitions and legal *integration*. The nets joined during the first year were Swedish following which a large number of foreign companies with O/C nets were joined. At this stage, there was a change towards the creation of separate C/O part-nets within the nets joined. The foreign companies were not merged but continued as separate part-nets. Since most acquired nets were international, they were increasingly becoming O/O as the number of joined nets grew. Merging into specific part-nets was only done in exceptional instances as when smaller companies, such as airfreight, were involved.

IF would seem to have given high priority to extension and penetration for the established total net and to have given integration lower priority. In this IF differed from both Bilspedition and ASG as we can see from figure 8.1.

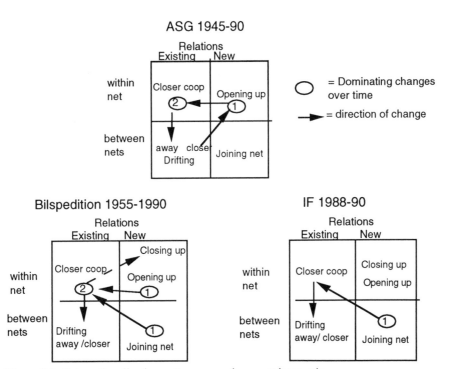

Figure 8.1. Internationalization patterns over time -net integration

Finally there are large differences between the three cases, both in the total size of the nets domestically and internationally and in the number of subsidiaries and foreign agents (see the second map). In total, Bilspedition was double the size of ASG and triple the size of IF.

Effects - owners, suppliers, representatives and competitors

Owners

--The original owners of ASG and Bilspedition were international transport companies, a fact which played an important role, in terms of opportunities and restrictions, in determining how ASG and Bilspedition developed. SJ and Svea shipping line, ASG's original owners, were not only positively connected to the international development but by recommending ASG to their international contacts they also took an active part. On the other hand Svea did not want ASG to develop sea-transports and Fallénius & Leffler put restrictions on GBS developing into forwarding.

--Before Bilspedition internationalized, the owner-structure had been changed to 2/3 the trucking companies´associations in Sweden and 1/3 customer industries.

--The advantages and disadvantages of having owners positively connected in the transport systems were that the reported profitability of ASG and Bilspedition was not the prime mover. Instead they seem to have had a more direct influence, both positive and negative, on the fields for expansion. On the negative side, SJ delayed ASG developing trucking services for several years through their ability to influence the issue of international trucking permits. On the positive side, the trucking companies positively connected to GBS transport systems made a an intensive drive among trucking companies in 1964 to provide GBS with the necessary capital for expansion.

--When Bilspedition and ASG became registered on the stock exchange the dominant positions of the trucking companies in Bilspedition and of the Swedish Railway in ASG were reduced. As a result, the demands on profitability increased and restrictions on fields for expansion were reduced.

--In the IF case, the explicit intention of the Ratos Group in creating IF was to develop into the field of transport and distribution, Ratos having other international investment activities. Since they were not positively connected to IF's transport systems, the requirements for return on investments focused on profitability.

--Finally through the acquisition of the Scansped Group in 1985/86 Bilspedition acquired Fallénius&Leffler, their original owners.

Suppliers

Since one of ASG´s most important suppliers was SJ, who were also the owners, the international development in railway traffics had positive effects on SJ and so their reactions were positive.

Further, for as long as ASG and Bilspedition were small internationally, the suppliers to a large extent set the rules, being the owners of the means of transportation. The roles changed when ASG and Bilspedition increased in size because then they became more important to the suppliers. This was enhanced by the fact that the railways, the shipping lines and the airlines, after a period of growth, ran into capacity problems which they had difficulty in handling. These seem to have come in waves if taken over a period, capacity becoming a problem for the railways in Europe in the early 1950's and for shipping lines and airlines during the late 1960's and early 1970's. For the shipping and airlines the lack of capacity turned into over-capacity during the latter parts of the 1970's as they had invested in new ships and aeroplanes. The fierce competition which resulted, however, continued to give the control to those forwarders having large volumes of goods.

- The containerization and use of unit loads as from the late 1960's further enhanced the importance of ASG and Bilspedition at the cost of the shipping and airlines specifically. As a result, the two companies gave priority to just a few suppliers which then cooperated more closely with ASG and Bilspedition. ASG and Bilspedition increased their control of the total transport system. During the 1970's the forwarder's legal responsibility changed so that they had to bear full responsibility towards the customer and this contributed to their change.

-During 1970's, the trucking companies were also suffering from a large over-capacity and both Bilspedition and ASG had to assume more responsibility towards the trucking companies in order to rationalize within the transport systems .

-During the 1980's, Bilspedition even acquired some of the suppliers, such as the shipping lines Transatlantic, Cool Carriers, etc., as well as part of the domestic airline Linjeflyg. The incidence of trucking companies being directly acquired also increased over time.

- In the case of IF, the suppliers comprised a large number of companies from different areas and there is not much evidence to show that any reactions took place from the suppliers' side since the companies taken over continued as separate entities.

Representatives
- The representatives have been affected differently depending on how the focal companies and the agents have developed over time. The direction of that development both in services and geographically has been of importance for positive and negative connectedness towards the focal companies and between representatives again over time. Conflicts between different agents as well as between agent and focal company seem to arise from a change in priorities between type of services and specific traffics.

-As many agents have internationalized over a period of time their interest and resources diverged into other areas. ASG had some problems during the 1970's as agents seemed to be less interested in their traffics-in-common due not only to their but also to ASG's development in other areas.

-Profitability and control of the transport systems as between the focal companies and the representatives seems to have been another problem leading to conflicts. A local sales office belonging to the focal company would basically mean a lower degree of control for the agent since the customers are contacted directly by the focal company thereby exacerbating the conflicts of interests with the agents. It is worth noting that ASG and Bilspedition closed down all of their European sales offices after just a couple of years.

-Having a local subsidiary with the same name as the focal company even though it operates in quite another field of services or geographical area than the representation, means a restriction placed on the agent's expansion and a risk of future negative connectedness. However, the possibilities to expand into new fields services are facilitated.

-When international nets are created and integration increased within them then the continued development of O/C and C/O nets can easily change into O/O nets over time through internationalization and diversification. This was the case between ASG and Schenker and between Bilspedition and ASG and their agents. As a matter of fact, most of their largest competitors with O/O nets have been or still are agents in some place or other in the world. This goes for Schenker, Panalpina, Kühne&Nagel, Nedlloyd, Emery, Danzas, etc.
In the IF case, the fact that a company was acquired by IF led to the fact that some agents belonging to O/O nets left the cooperations with the acquired companies. Both ASG and Bilspedition nets had been or were cooperating with some of the acquired companies such as Z&B, Sasse & Co, Satraco, etc.

Competitors - (ASG-Bilspedition -IF and other competitors)
-Over time ASG and Bilspedition seem to have kept a close watch over the development of each other closely.
-- When SJ became engaged in ASG by acquiring 50% the shares in 1941 Fallénius & Leffler sold 50% of the shares in Bilspedition to the Swedish trucking companies association the year after. Bilspedition had decided to be the private alternative to ASG.
-- When the Rego shipping lines acquired 25% of ASG in 1967, Bilspedition then joined the newly established constellation of important shipping forwarders, which was a strong competitor to ASG and an important contributor of freight to Rego shipping lines.
-- As the Bilspedition Truckers Association (BTF) became part-owner of Bilspedition in 1965 the corresponding organization in ASG acquired 5% of ASG from the 100% of the Swedish Railway the same year.
-- During 1970's the specialization and diversification of ASG and Bilspedition was very similar. However, ASG was still somewhat larger than Bilspedition internationally .
-- As ASG started a number of subsidiary companies in 1980 and 1981 for air and seafreight after leaving WACO, Bilspedition acquired Wilson & Co, one of the largest sea and airfreight forwarders in Sweden, in 1982/83. Later when Bilspedition became registered on the stock exchange they acquired Scansped, one of the largest international transport and forwarding groups in Sweden at the time, and at the same time Fallénius & Leffler, their original owner.

-NTS, leaving the Scansped group at the time of the takeover, then became the base for the creation of IF group. The establishment of IF created a strong Swedish alternative to ASG and Bilspedition. On two occasions during the wave of acquisitions in the 1980's Bilspedition acquired some part of ASG's important representatives in the Nordic countries, thereby leaving ASG with no alternative but to change representatives at short notice and with great difficulties.

-When ASG and Bilspedition started their international activities, their former customers, the Swedish forwarders, became their competitors. In the case of ASG, they even went to the lengths of forming a constellation to try to force ASG out of international activities by bringing their influence to bear on the Swedish Railways.

-As ASG, Bilspedition and IF grew into larger international nets, many of these competitors were acquired by them and some of their former agents, like Schenker, Kühne &Nagel, Nedlloyd,became their new competitors, growing into large international nets.

9. Event analysis - Dynamics and context

Up to now, we have analyzed internationalization concentrating on dominating changes for the focal companies over time. Even though the general case analysis shows that there exists an interaction between the development of the focal companies and the context, the' multiplexity' of the focal companies makes it difficult to follow in greater detail how the interaction takes place. However, the event analysis will make it possible to depict the underlying sequences of changes that were taking place between the focal company and a specific part of the context by following, instead of the focal company, the development of each event over time.

Further, in the changes of the relations studied in the event, the focal company is just one of several transport companies in focus. Therefore, the specific events will not only contribute to a deeper understanding of but also facilitate a generalization of the sequences of changes going on during the internationalization process.

The changes in the events will be analyzed with reference to the integration dimension since this dimension best reflects the changes in interaction with other transport organizations. It is also this dimension which initiates the process of internationalization, which leads to changes in extension and penetration.

The event analysis will be concluded in two steps which, taken together, suggest a more general pattern of changes in systems and nets when transport companies internationalize.
The first of these steps abstracts integration changes in the direct relations to the companies in focus into typical sequences. These typical sequences experienced through the events at system and net level will then be compared with similar changes in the general analysis.

The second step the conclusion involves the effects of these typical sequences on the structure of the net and network.These effects concern the indirect relations and include typical changes taking place due to actions and reactions to the event. Here we shall see that the patterns of sequences of changes and effects might give rise to an international domino game in the total network.

We end the event analysis by discussing how these more general patterns of integration changes, developed in the two concluding steps, will influence extension and penetration and based on this, a typical pattern for internationalization will be discussed, taking context into account.

Finally, there is a summary of the important empirical results from the the general as well as the event analysis in section 9.5..

9.1. Event analysis

The specific events are very different in terms of size, point in time for the event and time span. The first event goes back to 1946, when ASG signed an agreement with one of its first agents and the last events studied are from 1989. The majority of events, however, take place during the end of the 1980's when the variety seems at its largest.

While the ASG events are of different types, such as establishing a an agent relation, acquiring a company, making greenfield investments and leaving/joining an international net, the Bilspedition events are concentrated to one major merger between three large international company groups. Since the total merger, described in the Scansped Europe event, involves such a large part of the international changes of the Bilspedition Group, it is already discussed in the general case analysis. Therefore the events concerning the merger, analyzed here, are only parts of the total event and concern the mergers in Sweden, Belgium and the changes in West-Germany. The IF events study two companies acquired by IF during 1989. The companies which are middle-sized international companies have a long international history. Finally, there will be a certain interaction between ASG, Bilspedition and IF companies in the events.

Specific events time span   (/ = Event)

	1940	50	60	70	80	90
ASG-Switzerland	/--					
ASG Belgium				----------------------/------------------------		
ASG West-Germany			/--------------------/--------------------------			
WACO				/-------/------------------		
Scansped- Sweden					------/-----	
Scansped-Belgium					----- /----	
Scansped- West-Germany					-----/---	
IF -Züst & Bachmeier			-- ------------------------------------/---			
IF-Amas					------------/---	

Figure 9.1. The events

When discussing each event and within the context, the discussion will be divided into three phases - before the event, the event and after the event. Before the event involves the relations of importance that existed before the event while after the event concerns the relations changed as a result of the event. The changes will be described, if possible, in terms of short and long run changes. The event will describe the important actions taken by the organizations involved.

9.1.1. ASG events

ASG-Switzerland- start of cooperation with an agent

Before the event: ASG was a large domestic transport company, whose transport systems were connected to those of SJ (Swedish Railway) and Svea Shipping Line. Natural was an established international transport company which via its earlier contacts with Svea was seeking a new agent in Sweden.

The event: The event was the development of a *new (system)cooperation* with Natural after half a year of negotiations. The alternative for Natural in Sweden was Wilson. Wilson cooperated at that time with Danzas in Switzerland but wanted to change to Natural.(See figure 9.2).

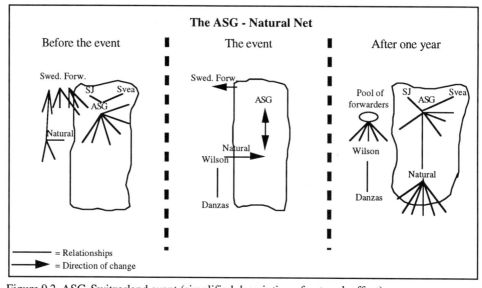

Figure 9.2. ASG-Switzerland event (simplified description of network effect)

After the event: ASG and Natural *cooperated closer* in order to increase efficiency and meet the new situation. Natural and ASG had one of the largest traffics between Sweden and Switzerland. New direct traffics were then added as well as road transports and new functions some years later. This lead to *enlargement* of the cooperation. Railway transports gradually decreased in importance until other types of traffics (combi-traffics or trucking traffics) had totally dominated. During these almost 50 years both Natural and ASG have continued their internationalization to and from other countries, with other agents and into other fields of services. During the 1980's airfreight was also added into the relationship but then s ASG acquired part of a Swiss airfreight forwarder the cooperation for airfreight ceased. Therefore first a an *increase* and then a *decrease in the field of cooperation* took place. In this aspect ASG airfreight was negatively connected to Natural airfreight. During 1980's the cooperation came to include not only ASG Sweden but also ASG Norway as well as Finland and ASG started to cooperate with a sister company of Natural's in Portugal. During 1970's and early 1980's ASG and Natural were *drifting closer* on net level while there were tendencies of *drifting away* during the end of the 1980's.

Effects: Effects at net level were that a group of Swedish forwarders, in their services formerly complementary to ASG, formed a new anti-constellation. The part-ownership of ASG by the Swedish Railway (SJ) and Svea Shipping Line seems to have had an important bearing on the reactions of the other international transport and forwarding companies. They were cooperating with Svea as well as SJ in their international traffics. A result of this was that the other nets tried to convince SJ that ASG should refrain from internationalizing and remain domestic. The fact that ASG and Natural succeeded in the creation of a new concept, the door-to-door sales concept, affected the other transport companies in their marketing as well.

System level changes: New cooperation --> closer cooperation --> enlargement-->closer cooperation--> enlargement --> decrease in field of cooperation --> closer cooperation--> enlargement--> decrease in field of cooperation

Net level-changes: Drifting closer--> ....and later.....-->drifting away

ASG Belgium - a greenfield investment

Before the event: ASG started a *new (system) cooperation* early 1950's with an agent, Ama, and had continued for more than twenty years. Ama had grown over a period and developed many new traffics to Sweden together with ASG leading to *closer cooperation* and *enlargement*. Then in the mid-1970's Ama was sold to the owner of West-Friesland, a competitor to ASG-Ama traffic. The takeover created problems in the ASG-Ama cooperation. The development of the cooperation ceased, leading to *a decrease in field of cooperation* and *looser cooperation*.. A few years before the event, ASG had set up a European Representative Office in Brussels which came to be important as a contact for planning the event.

The event: ASG Belgium was established with the help of key personnel from Ama. Two other transport companies joined as minority owners, E. Depaire (partly owned by Belgian Railways) and Gyssens & Co, through which ASG obtained contacts and physical facilities. This was necessary for a quick switch. Temporary sales personnel were sent down from Sweden for the purpose of retaining the customers. The result for ASG in Sweden was a *switch of representative* in Belgium. The former agent Ama, which became a competitor, successfully sued ASG for damages.

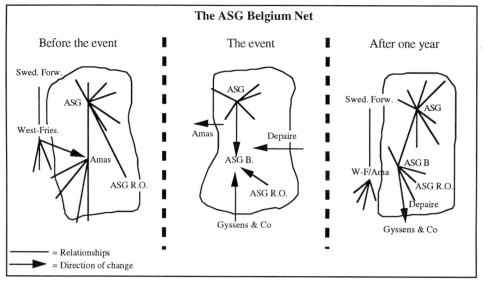

Figure 9.3. ASG Belgium (simplified description of network effects)

<u>After the event</u>: ASG continued to send resources of all types to ASG Belgium for a rather long period in order to increase efficiency of the traffics and the office, which led to a *closer cooperation*. The minority owners left within a few years and the European Representative Office was closed down. Within a short time ASG Belgium also started traffics to Norway and Denmark. In the Norwegian traffic ASG Belgium cooperated with the ASG Sweden agent. Nevertheless, the office in Belgium has stayed a rather small company with basically Scandinavian traffics. Some other international traffics have been added and from discontinued from time to time.

<u>Effects</u>: The effects at the net level were limited. At the system level some new companies became positively connected to ASG Belgium through establishment of new traffics. On the other hand, some important representatives of the parent company in Sweden, such as the agent in Denmark and the subsidiary in Hamburg, became negatively connected to ASG Belgium in their international traffics.

<u>System level changes</u>: New (system) cooperation--> closer cooperation--> enlargement--> decrease in field of coop.-->looser cooperation-->Switch of representative-->closer cooperation--> enlargement

ASG in West-Germany (Hamburg and Stuttgart)

Establishment of ASG Hamburg

<u>Before the event</u> : ASG had started several international railway traffics to/from West-Germany. The agent in Hamburg area was Wendschlag & Pohl. Then, as trucking traffics were developing, ASG started a *new (system)*

cooperation with another agent who was not only a regular agent but also a support office for the total international traffics. The trucking traffics started through co-loading with the traffics from Holland and grew into traffics of their own.

The event: Within a couple of years, ASG took over by letting the owner and manager of the existing trucking agent start ASG Hamburg, which caused a *switch of representative*. The old trucking agent company ceased to exist some years later.

After the event: . ASG Hamburg´s, Scandinavian traffics grew during the 1960's, both in number of traffics, in size as well as in added new functions like warehousing, special transports, etc., which led to a *closer cooperation* and *enlargement*. During the 1970's, they started new traffics to other European countries and in some of them they had the same agents as ASG Sweden. This was a form of *opening up* on net level.

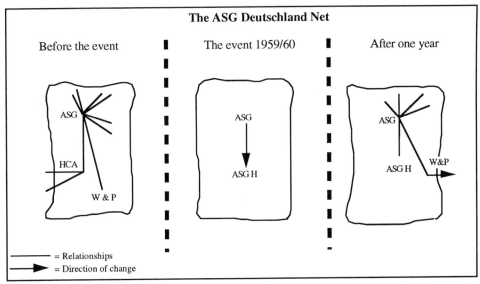

Figure 9.4.1. Part event 1- in ASG Deutschland event (simplified description of network effects)

Effects: ASG and the railway agent in Hamburg ceased their cooperation shortly after. Other agents in adjacent areas also perceived a certain negative connectedness to ASG Hamburg due to the risk of ASG collecting/distributing directly via Hamburg and later due to competition in international traffics. Another cause for conflicts were the German sales offices which could take over the customer contacts from the agents. During this period, Atege Stuttgart was one of the more important of the around 20 West-German agents. This was the situation before the Stuttgart event.

System level changes Hamburg: Switch of representative---> closer cooperation--> enlargement

Net level changes (as ASG Hamburg internationalizes): Opening up--> closer cooperation

Acquisition of Atege Stuttgart

The event: In 1976 ASG acquired the existing agent in Stuttgart. This legal integration implied a *closer cooperation* between ASG and Atege on system level. On net level Atege's agents came to be included in the net of ASG. ASG Hamburg was changed to ASG (Deutschland) GmbH which became the formal owner of Atege Stuttgart. However both continued as separate companies and ASG (Deutschland) was seen as a holding company.

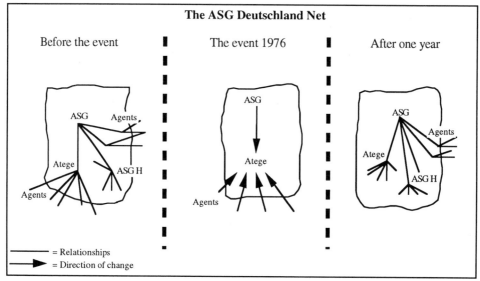

Figure 9.4.2. Part event 2 - in ASG Deutschland event (simplified descritption of network effects)

After the event : Through this acquisition ASG increased their resources in and coverage of West-Germany. Over time the two German companies have slowly started to cooperate. As ASG acquired the resources of another comany in Bielefeld in 1988, the number of offices of ASG (Deutschland) had increased to nine.

Effects: As ASG continued to grew in West-Germany, the ASG agents in the country became worried. Many of them were also negatively connected to Atege in other international traffics. Further when ASG acquired ERT in 1979 the negative connectedness increased within the ASG net, since the ERT and their agents and ASG and their representatiors were competitors in West-Germany.

System level changes Stuttgart : Closer cooperation
Net level changes (Stuttgart acquisition) --->Drifting closer (to a number of agents in other countries).

<u>Waco (World Air Cargo Organization) -ASG/ISA</u>

The specific event studied concerns when ASG was leaving the airfreight net of WACO based on exclusive cooperation between large airfreight agents world-wide.

WACO and ASG

<u>Before the event</u>: ASG net had grown in the number of different services as well as the number of countries covered in Europe as well as overseas. A separate net (part-net) for airfreight within ASG was created through *opening up*, letting many of the gradually increasing number of WACO agents complement the existing agents in airfreight. As ASG started to *cooperate* more *closely* with these WACO agents, through creating a new common communication system, etc. and adding more exclusive WACO agents. The net was changing towards *closing up*. As a result of this ASG was also *drifting away* from some of its existing partners like Schenker, Emery, etc. since the cooperation decreased with their subsidiaries in other parts of the world. Finally U.S agent Emery departed from their cooperation with ASG. A new Waco agent, IFI, was identified and ASG switched to that agent. After a while IFI offered ASG the opportunity of acquiring 50% of the company. This changed the situation in Waco since ASG not only represented the Nordic countries in the Group but such an important country as the U.S as well.

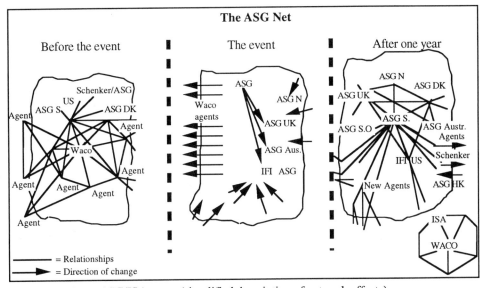

Figure 9.5. Waco -ASG/ISA event (simplified description of network effects)

<u>The event</u>: ASG had to leave the WACO group, involving a large number of agents world-wide which at that stage had a close cooperation. Around 20 agents had to be *switched* as ASG was *leaving* the WACO *net*. The net was *opened up*. New representatives had to be found to ASG Sweden's existing traffics and also for the airfreight subsidiaries in Denmark, Norway and the U.S. ASG set up a company in the U.K. taking over part of the

personnel from the former agent. A similar thing happened in Australia where ASG made a greenfield investment but added two acquired small companies.

After the event : The ASG airfreight subsidiaries cooperated to a large extent with each other which *increased the degree of cooperation* within the airfreight *net* and the net was moving towards *closing up*. In some cases, where the established sister companies lacked the know-how or were tied up with some other agent or were not themselves established, they had agents of their own. As Schenker-ASG in HongKong split up, ASG set up its own office there. ASG also established a representative office in Singapore moving the salesman from Schenker Bangkok to Singapore. Later ASG acquired 100% of its U.S. joint venture and part of a company in Taiwan, which was reached formerly via Schenker in HongKong, and acquired a seafreight company in the U.S.

Effects: The whole Waco organization had to change agents in Sweden, Denmark, Norway and in the US as a result of ASG leaving the organization and new competitors to WACO were set up by ASG in Australia and the U.K. All the former WACO agents became negatively connected to ASG and its subsidiaries. As the new subsidiaries internationalized this situation was enhanced. On the other hand a row of new agents, became positively connected. Some of the existing landtransport agents enlarged their cooperation with ASG into airfreight.
Having its own offices affected ASG's relations to the seafreight agents situated in the same country. In some cases the seafreight agents became airfreight agents as well.
As the negative connectedness to Schenker increased and it became a necessity to split up Schenker-ASG, the Schenker and ASG nets became negatively connected world-wide (O/O).

Net level changes: Opening up--> closer cooperation--->closing up-->drifting away -->looser cooperation-->Leaving the WACO net--> Opening up--> closer cooperation-->closing up

System level: Switch-->closer cooperation-->looser cooperation-->switch -->closer cooperation

WACO and ISA event

Before the event: ISA, the airfreight company owned by Wilson &Co, had had problems with their international net of representatives. They had their own office in Denmark and had had joint ventures in Brazil and Singapore which had not worked out. ISA was offered to join the WACO group after ASG either as an associate or full member.

The event and after the event : ISA decided to *join* the WACO *net* as a full member. The Waco group changed to ISA, as their Scandinavian agent. Joining the WACO net meant switching around 25 agents. On the other hand, the quality and size of agents increased for ISA through the WACO net. This cooperation lead to a *closer cooperation* in many aspects and then moving over to *closing up* of the net.

Effects: All the former agents became competitors. Competition on the Swedish market increased with ISA selling the WACO concept.

Net level changes: Joining a net --> closer cooperation--> closing up
System level changes: switch--> closer cooperation--> enlargement

ASG events

The ASG events are all very typical for ASG over time. ASG started cooperating with agents as in the Natural case, later they made some acquisitions or greenfield investments which were all basically tied to existing agents. Finally during the 1980's net changes were dominating.

9.1.2. Bilspedition events

The events which are studied in the Bilspedition case are part of the same basic process of change i.e.the merger with Scansped, Wilson and ATA international groups. The total Scansped Europe merger has already been discussed and as a part of the general case analysis due to its importance for Bilspedition changes in general. The events presented here concern changes in specific countries, which are part of the total merger.

Scansped Sweden merger

Before the event: Bilspedition had through acquisitions *joined the nets* of the large Swedish international transports groups Wilson and Scansped, both overlapping in their activities to ATA as well as to each other. The three different groups continued as separate part-nets within the total Bilspedition net to compete internally. The groups suffered economic problems.

The event: As the three groups were merged, they had to *leave* 56 agents in their existing *nets*. The priority was set for the use of existing international subsidiaries as representatives. Subsidiaries existed in 11 countries in Europe and in most countries there were several of them which were also merged. Leaving existing agents and switching to subsidiaries increased the level of integration leading to *closer cooperation*. The parts of the net that remained were*closing up*. The total number of relations had decreased because of the event.

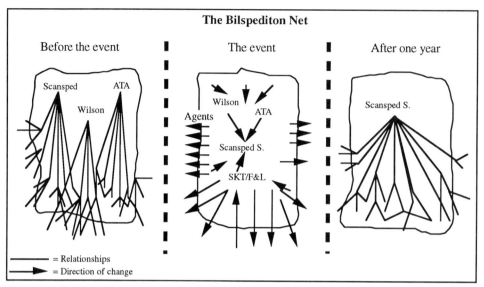

Figure 9.6. Scansped Sweden merger (simplified description of network effects)

<u>After the event</u> : There was a reorganization within the Group and it took at least a year before that was settled. The total volumes decreased since many customers stayed with the former agents. This was the outcome in spite of market growth in terms of volumes. The existing representatives had to take care of the volumes of at least three companies in the area which caused capacity probelms but also increased the frequency of the traffics.

<u>Effects</u>: The very large number of former agents to Scansped and Wilson leaving the net became negatively connected to the new merged Scansped in Europe. In very few cases, only, did the remaining agents of the former groups chose to leave the new larger Scansped, as in Finland where Scansped had to find a new agent. Moreover the agents staying on were often negatively connected to the traffics of the Scansped subsidiaries.

At the network level, the merger of the three Swedish parts of Wilson, ATA and the existing Group of SKT/F&L/TK (three already merged companies) had a very large effect on the Swedish part of the network. The agents leaving had to find another alternative practically over night. As mentioned earlier, the result was the establishment of around 10 new transport companies since there were not many agents left in Sweden who were not already tied up to someone else. Many of the new companies, which included former Scansped personnel, became the Swedish representative to the former Scansped agents. Some of the former agents acquired part of Swedish transport companies, like Danzas which acquired 50% of Rationell Transport. In other cases the existing international Swedish transport companies got many possibilities to change or complement their existing net of agents. The effects on the network were not as large abroad since the agents were spread out over so many areas in Europe.

In some cases it seemed possible for some large and locally very strong companies to continue cooperation and to accept a higher degree of negative connectedness between the nets.

Other already negatively connected transport systems like that of ASG and Natural reacted because of the increase in competition both in Sweden and in Switzerland.

In many cases the Group was forced to make further investments in terminals and new agents as well as in buying new companies. The new net of representatives was not really settled at the end of 1989. Yet further changes were taking place, especially since Bilspedition bought another large international transport group in Finland named Speditor.

<u>Net level changes</u>: Leaving (part of the) net-->closer cooperation (remaining part)-->closing up

<u>System level changes</u>: Switch--> closer cooperation-->enlargement

Scansped Belgium merger

<u>Before the event</u>: In Belgium the Bilspedition Group had three separate international transport companies that were competing. They were representatives of the different groups i.e. Castra of Skt/F&L/TK, Scanroute J/V of Wilson and ATA of ATA group. Castra was a subsidiary of van Casteren in Holland owned by the Bilspedition group and ATA was a former West-Friesland company in Belgium acquired by Bilspedition in 1986. The competition on the Nordic countries was especially fierce . The merger of Scansped Sweden necessitated the merger of the companies abroad.

<u>The event</u>: The three companies were supposed to merge but the other part owner of Scanroute J/V C.Geerts acquired the other 50% of the company so the merger eventually involved only ATA and Castra. Castra, formerly a subsidiary to van Casteren, was now separated from Holland. When merging they had to leave a number of their existing agents and stayed on cooperating with the subsidiaries as well as some of the agents. The changes were not so large since they were slightly different in their profiles. There merger led to an increase in *closeness of cooperation* between the two former companies. Since the new merged subsidiary was larger than any of the former subsidiaries, the representatives remaining form earlier had to adapt much the larger volumes. This resulted in closer cooperation with them.

258

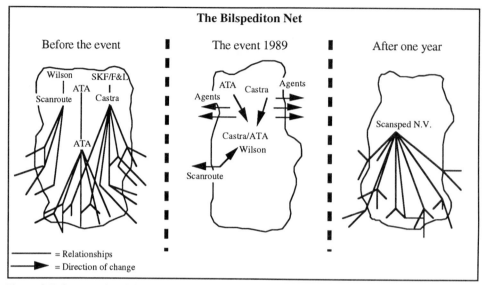

Figure 9.7. Scansped-Belgium merger (simplified description of network effects)

<u>After the event</u>: The agents staying on met a larger company with more problems. The fact that some agents left, forced the company to find new alternatives. However, since Scansped had subsidiaries of its own in many countries and finding an agent became increasingly difficult, it would try to use the subsidiaries as representatives. This caused a change towards *closing up*.

<u>Effects</u>: Many agents left or had to leave as the new merged Scansped in many cases chose to cooperate with its sister companies instead of the existing agents to the former companies.

In some areas where Scansped continued cooperation with the agent even though a sister company existed, as in the UK, a negative connectedness between the sister company and the agent was created. In other cases, the existing agents became indirectly negatively connected because they were part of other groups, like a Nedlloyd subsidiary in France being agent to Scansped Belgium. The fact that the subsidiary in Belgium took the name of the Scansped (as the other subsidiaries also did) increased the connectedness effects in that they demonstrated their Group loyalty.

Effects on the network as a result of the event in Belgium only seem to be significant for the Belgian companies having traffics to/from Scandinavia.

<u>Net level changes</u>: Leaving the net--> closer cooperation --> closing up

<u>System level changes</u>: Switch -->closer cooperation--> enlargement

Scansped Germany

Before the event: In West-Germany there was only one German subsidiary and a small office in Travemünde. ATA in Hamburg, established in 1980, had earlier joined the net of former West-Friesland, an international transport company which Bilspedition acquired from United Transport Corp. in 1976. Basically ATA in Sweden cooperated wih ATA GmbH while Wilson and Skt&F&L/TK together had around 31 different agents in West-Germany.

The event: ATA GmbH changed its name to Scansped Germany and became a representative of the new Scansped Sweden together with 10 out of the former 31 agents. Therefore the cooperation ceased with several agents of Wilson and SKT/F&L/TK in the Scandinavian traffics. Instead the *cooperation* became *closer* with the sister companies. The size of the Scansped Germany increased and the volumes more than doubled overnight.

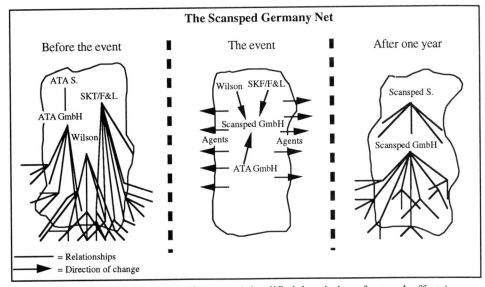

Figure 9.8. Scansped event in West-Germany (simplified description of network effects)

After the event: The size and number of offices in West-Germany was not enough for the sister companies so a new relatively large international transport company was acquired leading to anohter *joining of nets* and later in 1990 another transport company was acquired. The reason for the first of these acquisitions was that Scansped Holland lost their agent Panalpina in the Stuttgart area. Since Scansped in Stuttgart did not posess the right know-how and as it was impossible to find a suitable agent that was not negatively connected, Scansped had to invest in acquired a company in the area, Tekatrans, an international company with strong traffics to/from Holland and Belgium.

Effects: As for Scansped Germany five of their existing agents in other European countries left the cooperation as a result of the change and became negatively connected to the Scansped Group. Four of these agents found another agnet and one was acquired by a large international Group. Therefore new representatives had to be chosen for Scansped Germany. It is interesting to note that the Scansped Germany changed to agents and not sister companies in each of the countries, in spite of the fact that there was a Scansped sister in the country. Both the fact that these agents looked for new agents and that Scansped changed had an impact on the structure of the network. Traffics by sister companies to/from Germany were often negatively connected to the traffics of Scansped Germany and its agents.

 As a result of the merger many former agents in Germany had to find new agents in Sweden and some of Scansped Germany agents in West-Germany.

System level changes: Switch --> closer cooperation

Net level-changes: Closer cooperation--> ...moving towards closing up

The Bilspedition merger events are all connected to the development of Scansped Europe and merging the three groups of companies Wilson, SKT/F&L/TK and ATA. The three different events, analyzed here, show similarities in that a number of agents had to leave or left and that Scansped concentrated on much fewer representatives in Europe including a larger number of subsidiaries. In all three case there were new investments involved in the different countries for Scansped but also for the departing agents and their new partners. The total effects of the events, merging in nine countries at the same time, affected many other international transport companies in the network in one way or another. Including effects on subsidiaries, around 100 agents in Europe were involved and when they all started to look for new agents many changes must have taken place, that have not been recorded in this study. Since most of these new partners to the former agents were probably also tied up to some other agent.

Net level changes : Leaving (part of) net--> closer cooperation (remaining part)--> closing up

9.1.3. IF events

The IF events each concern the acquisition of an international transport company . IF was established less than a year before these events were taking place.

Züst & Bachmeier acquisition

Before the event: Z&B was an old international transport company with head office in Switzerland but with its main activities in Germany. The company had grown through a series of smaller acquisitions and greenfield investments in Italy and Germany. Then from these countries they internationalized. The total Group was split into two companies i.e. the Swiss-German(Z&B) and the Italian part(Z&A). However after that split Z&B continued to expand internationally by *opening up* their net establishing many *new (system) cooperations*. As the company needed more capital for their expansion, they were looking for new owners.At the same time IF , recently established as a Group, was searching for potential acquisitions in Europe. Z&B in Nuremberg had been an agent of an IF group company, NTS in Sweden, for 20 years.

The event: Z&B was joining nets with IF. The IF acquisition included a small packing company in Witten, offices in the UK, in Africa and part of the Vienna office.

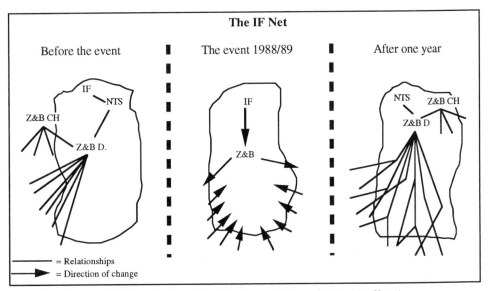

Figure 9.9. IF - the Z&B acquisition (simplified description of network effects)

After the event: A holding company was created in West-Germany which came to include all the German companies of the IF group. NTS also had a company and had also recently acquired a small seafreight company, Schier& Otten. These companies continued as separate entities. The net of Z&B and NTS and Schier & Otten in Germany were to a large extent complementary but had some overlapping activities.

In practice Z&B did not change very much as a company during the first year. The company continued as before and except for a very small number of new cooperations within the Group. After two years, the company in Germany was reorganized and divided into three separate companies being part-nets with their own international representation. One of these companies, Z&B airfreight *joined* another net, Senator, and together they created a joint venture in Germany for airfreight.

Effects : The main difference was that the agents of Z&B came to be included in the IF net. As a reaction to the acquisition three of their former agents left the cooperation, as their nets were drifting closer to the IF net and therefore got negatively connected, and three new agents took their place. Two of the agents leaving were

IFI, ASG´subsidiary in the US, and a British subsidiary to the Rhenus Group. The third was the agent in Holland, an effect of Z&B now belonging to the same Group as Amas. Some of the agents to Z&B also became negatively connected to other traffics and activities within the Group.

Net level changes: Joining nets

System level: Switch

The Amas event

Before the event: Before the acquisition the Amas group was part of a freight services division of a large international paper production and trading company. Amas around 20 companies were concentrated in Holland and Belgium. Copex in Hillegom was one of the most important companies in the Group from which many of the other companies have spun off such as Copex Air, Copex IGS, etc. It had expanded in Europe and Overseas over the years through establishment of many new (system) cooperations. Since IF wanted to get a better coverage of Europe and the owner of Amas had economical problems, both were interested in future cooperation.

The event: IF acquired Amas including all the small companies in Holland and Belgium. Therefore Amas and IF were *joining nets* and many agents were added into the net

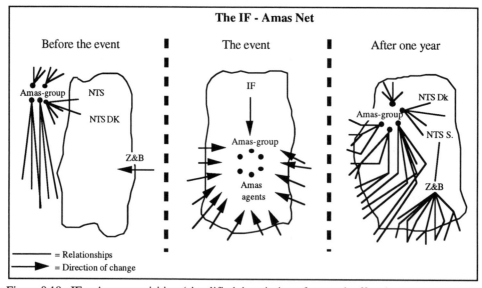

Figure 9.10. IF - Amas acquisition (simplified description of network effects)

After the event: The changes of arising out of the acquisition mostly came after more than one year when Amas started to restructure the companies and their activities leading to a *closer cooperation* within the Amas group. They also acquired new companies like an international transport company Sasse& Co in Belgium and ITM in Denmark. Then there were mergers of part of Amas' existing activities and Sasse's activities. Increased cooperation between Amas group and other IF group companies were very limited. However one example of closer cooperation followed in 1990 as a result of IF acquiring ACE, a Swedish international airfreight forwarder. An Amas airfreight company of Amas recommended ACE as well as Sasse as new members to an international airfreight agent organization IASA. And so the *closer cooperation* developed in the area of airfreight.

Effects: The effects were not very large to begin with since most agents continued cooperating with Amas in the same way. Rather the problem was that there was some overlapping between Amas and other parts of the IF net as well as within Amas part-net. As Amas started restructuring and acquiring other companies the effects increased since some of the agents' nets were *drifting closer* as the agent entered and cooperation increased and other nets were *drifting away* as the agent left the IF net. This will have effects basically on the transport companies established in the Dutch and the Belgian transport network.

Net level changes: Joining nets--> closer cooperation-->drifting closer
System level changes: Switch

The IF events mainly seem to have had effects on the network and the net and less at system level since the acquired companies continued as before but through their joining of a net their agents and subsidiaries are included. Any system effects were the result of these net changes. As time passed new net effects showed through the addition of new acquisitions to the Group. A net effect that occurred in both events when the IF group was drifting closer to some nets of the Amas´ and Z&B´s agents and drifting away from those leaving.

9.2.Patterns of changes

The analysis of the events above seems to confirm that there is an interaction between changes and effects which will lead to further changes in the degree of internationalization in both the short and the long run for the companies involved in the event. The focal companies are subject to sequences of changes over time which seem to be repeated. These changes seem to apply not only to the three different focal nets under study but also to other transport companies.The intention in this section is to examine the direct relations in the event analysis in pursuit of typical sequences of changes.

The different events described and analysed cover the basic types of integration and form sequences of changes. Since these events are commonly seen in the general case analysis, the sequences of changes shown in the events are assumed to be similar. Therefore, these events would reflect the way the focal companies internationalized.

We can notice that the three early events were dominated by changes at system level while in the events of 1980´s net level changes dominated. This is in line with what we found in the general case analysis in chapter 8.

Further, it can be understood that net level changes cause effects at the single system level which was the case with Waco, Scansped, Z&B and Amas. On the other hand some single system integrations involve net aspects like the acquisition of Atege Stuttgart. Others did not involve any net aspects at the time of the event, as in the case of ASG Hamburg but did so later on.

The changes will be analyzed first at the system level and then at the net level and will be divided into a typical growth sequence and typical change sequence. However, being typical implies that these sequences of changes are the most common but they do not always have to take place in this way. Further, the typical sequences of changes do not say anything about the time length of each change. As the growth sequences seem to be more frequent and more detailed in the descriptions it seems easier to interprete in terms of typical changes while the change sequences are more imprecise.

9.2.1.System level sequences

The growth sequence at system level, which seems to take place in all the events of new relationships whether they are based on a switch of representatives or a (new) system cooperation, leads to increasing integration of the relationship as well as the transport system. The change sequence is seen in many of the events before the switch of relationships takes place. It leads to a decrease in integration.

Growth sequence- at system level
The first four of the ASG events (ASG-Natural, ASG Hamburg, ASG Belgium, Atege Stuttgart) all started with new relationships. The development included either a new (system) cooperation or a switch to a new relationship. Then there was a change to closer cooperation and further to an increase in the field of cooperation (enlargement). The ASG-Natural cooperation and the ASG cooperations with the first agents in Belgium and Hamburg are

typical examples of 1a sequence while the event changes of ASG Hamburg and ASG Belgium are typical of 1b sequence.

<u>Sequence 1 - growth sequence at system level</u>

a) New (system) cooperation--> closer cooperation--> enlargement
b) Switch (new relationship)--> closer cooperation -->enlargement
c) Closer cooperation--> enlargement

Switch of representatives as in 1b also took place in large numbers during the Scansped and Waco events leading to closer cooperation with the new agent. Some of the agents that ASG changed to in the WACO event were already existing agents in land-transportation which made them move directly into enlargement.

All new cooperations of the focal companies seem to develop according to either of the aternatives (1a-c) in sequence 1. In some cases, by stopping at closer cooperation and not going into enlargement they might not complete the sequence.

The 1c alternative would be normal in a situation when a closer and/or enlarged cooperation already exists and it increases further through an acquisition of an agent like when ASG acquired Nordex in Norway, shares in the Danish agent, etc. Another situation which makes 1c important when many of the traffics are moving towards a higher degree of integration over time due to technical development or increase in customer demands.

Change sequence-at system level
Another typical sequence complementing sequence 1 over time is sequence 2. This sequence is seen in the ASG Belgium event, the Waco event and many other similar events over time for ASG, Bilspedition and IF. Sequence 2 can be seen as a movement backwards of sequence 1 leading to decreasing integration. However, the whole sequence is not shown in the events. In most events it is only registered at the stage of looser cooperation. Therefore decrease in field of cooperation might actually take place almost at the same time or in some cases show a movement back and forth before leading to switch or cessation of (system) cooperation.
Further, in the general case analysis it never dominates a whole period since new growth sequences have taken over rather quickly. With very few exceptions the change sequence is directly followed by the growth sequence after leaving the existing systems and/or the relationships. Rather than changing the total system the normal situation seems to be, that the companies are switching to another representative, as in the WACO and Scansped events. Therefore the basic sequence leads here to a switch to another representative while 2b is cessation of (system) cooperation. Alternative 2b was frequently used as the cooperation with

the railway agents ceased and trucking agents and systems increased which happened in the ASG Hamburg event .

Sequence 2- change sequence at system level

a) Decrease in field of cooperation<-->looser cooperation-->switch (leave relationship)
b) decrease in field of cooperation<-->looser cooperation-->cessation of (system) cooperation
c) decrease in field of cooperation<--->looser cooperation

Sequence 2c on the other hand shows the case of a decrease in the degree of integration without leading to a switch or a cessation of (system) cooperation. This happened in the ASG case during the 1970's when they reactivated some of the existing agents of the European land transportation Some of these relations continued into a new more intensified level after a period of dissatisfaction with the cooperation.

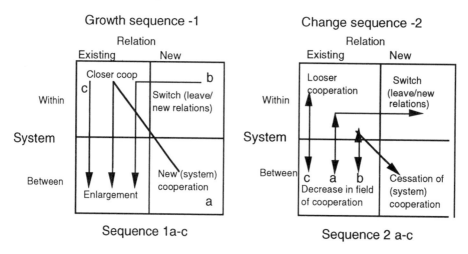

Figure 9. 11. Growth and change sequences at system level

These two sequences 1 and 2 seem to be a basic pattern for development at system level since it is repeated in most of the events taken place. The very fact that these sequences are repeated leads to the creation of a net and is the base for net effects. The design of the net will be decided by how these sequences are combined and repeated. Normally, as new services are added a combination of new representatives and existing representatives will take on the new services. Further, over time switches of representatives take place, as well as closer cooperation and enlargement into the new service with the existing representation. This continues over time as a company adds new types of services (figure 9.12.).

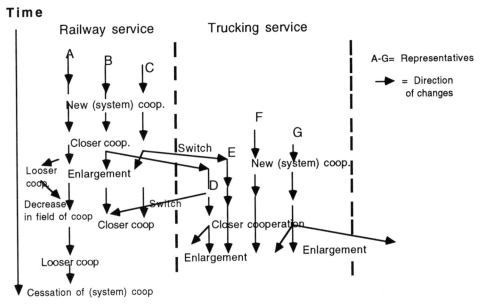

Figure 9.12. Creation of a focal company´s net by growth and change sequences at system level (a simplified description)

As is shown above is the possibility of repeating these sequences over time lead to an increasing number of representatives and probably also an increasing awareness of an interdependence between them leading first to the creation of a net and then to opening it up.

The changes at net level will be discussed next.

9.2.2.Net sequences

The net changes are more controversial than those at system level since they often involve sequential as well as parallel changes occurring in the net. As discussed earlier the sequences shown are typical sequences, which means that only the most common types of sequences of changes are presented.

Growth and expansion sequence at net level

There are two ways that lead to growth and expansion of a net and these are based on what happened in the IF and ASG events and the ISA event in the WACO case. The basic sequences of changes taking place in the general case analysis at net level (ch.8) for the three cases include the same sequences, only that there are parallel changes taking place as well and some are not fulfilled as in the IF case.

The first case 3a is when a net is opening up adding new single relations from outside the focal net. Over time this leads to a gradual expansion in the number of representatives which changes into closer cooperation. This increased closeness might either lead to drifting closer to some companies which then might be included through another opening up or it might lead to a closing up of the existing net. This sequence took place twice in the Waco event. The first time when being an associate member in WACO and the next time when leaving and creating a new net. ASG opened its existing international net in order to add new representatives which led to closer cooperation and closing up (3a). In the general cases analysis showing the total net of ASG, this sequence normally ended by drifting closer (3b) rather than closing up. In spite of the fact that opening up is often accompanied by dissolution of some of the existing relationships a sequence starting by opening up would seem to be a typical way to grow over time adding new services and representatives (see figure 9.12).

Over time these changes mean gradually adding a number of new representatives whether agents, small local acquisitions or greenfield investments. During part of the 1960's and '70's ASG as well as Bilspedition used this way to develop, adding many single new transport systems.

The second way to expand begins by joining nets. This is shown in 3c. ISA joining WACO net and IF acquisitions where they joined nets with Amas and Z&B. Joining of nets mostly leads to closer cooperation between several companies within the focal net and finally, as in the case of ISA and WACO, Scansped event, the existing net were closing up. The joining of nets has not arrived at the closing up stage yet in the IF case.

Sequence 3- growth sequence at net level
 a) opening up--> closer coop -->drifting closer
 b) opening up-->closer coop.--> closing up
 c) joining net --> closer coop.--> closing up

In the Scansped event expansion was taking place before the merger when there were several instances of joining of nets and the closer cooperation only took place within the part-nets. As the merger started the net was contracting rather than expanding which takes us over to the change sequence at net level.

Change sequence - at net level
Sequence 4 is a sequence of changes used in many cases by the focal companies in order to switch from one situation to another. The sequence involves a negative development in terms of integration for certain organizations and for certain systems. This happened to ASG in the Waco event as well as in the Scansped events.

In other cases when the net is not so highly exclusive and integrated as in the WACO case 4a seems to be more the norm. The cooperations between ASG and Schenker as well as between ASG and Emery show these changes over time. Very often the sequence starts from a closing up of a net. The same sequence can be applied to the Scansped event where so many companies ceased cooperation. Most of these agents must have gone through a similar process seeing the Bilspedition net closing up through the earlier mergers and then the cooperation becoming less motivated and looser and then the break coming with the result of leaving the net. In other cases the parent company left but the subsidiaries still cooperated however with changed priorities. Since the order of the stages of drifting away and looser cooperation is not always clear, these two stages are shown with arrows in both directions. Sometimes the stages take place almost at the same time or there is a movement back and forth before the looser cooperation finally leads to leaving the net.

<u>Sequence 4 - change sequences at net level</u>

a)   drifiting away <-->looser cooperation-->opening up (dissolving/ widening)

b)   drifiting away<-->looser cooperation --> leaving the net.

The sequences shown above are mostly over time combined into patterns of development for the different companies. For instance sequence 4 is mostly combined with sequence 3 depending on the situation for the specific company.

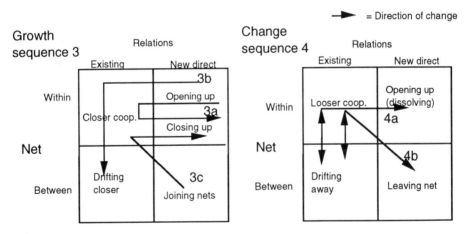

Figure 9.13. Net integration sequences

The Scansped event is an example which combines the two net sequences, starting with sequence 3 as they joined the net then sequence 4b and then changing over to sequence 3 again. In the case of merger the sequences are both parallel and sequential processes.

In conclusion there are typical sequences both at system and at net level which seem to be combined into patterns of changes. These patterns form a combination of sequence growth-change-growth at system level and growth-change-growth at net level. However during the first period of internationalization only growth sequences are present.

Furthermore these patterns lead to structural effects on indirectly related organizations and on the total performance. The typical effects of these sequences will be discussed in the next section.

9.3. Sequences of effects - contextual changes

In this section, the patterns developed as a first conclusion of the event analysis will be applied to a wider perspective involving not only the direct relations but also the indirect relations to companies in focus in the net and network.

Through studying the structural effects involving the indirect relations we will find that the same patterns apply to indirect relations influencing or being influenced by the event. Finally performance effects are briefly discussed at network level.

In this section, the companies discussed include only the representatives and therefore owners and suppliers are not involved in this concluding analysis.

We start by looking at the effects on the companies either getting indirectly related through the change or being directly influenced from the change. It relates to a kind of first and second level of indirect relations seen from the established direct relations. This takes place within or very close to the focal nets. Then we study indirect relations further away from the focal event which lead to special network effects like the domino effects. This is illustrated both by the WACO and Scansped events but also from a combination of the events seen in the general case analysis.

Systems and nets

Following the typical patterns of growth and change at system and net level, the companies becoming or being indirectly related seem to follow the same sequences leading to the same patterns as the direct relations, such as the former agent of ASG Belgium at system level and the former agents to ASG and ISA in the WACO event and former Scansped agents at net level. First they get positively connected, and then changing into negative connectedness and finally becoming positively connected to a new system or net.

These conclusions also seem to apply to the effects arrived at in the events. If ASG is switching representative so does the representative, since they both must find a new representative taking care of the goods at the other end. Typical changes at net level as in the WACO event are that both the ASG companies and the companies staying in WACO had to find new representatives.

Therefore all of them moved into sequence 3 but with other partners. Further, the changes will probably be almost simultaneous in time.

In some events, such as the Scansped event, there will be many companies searching among existing transport companies for new partners suitable as representatives. Since there was a lack of suitable alternatives, new representatives were created through establishment of 10 new transport companies in Sweden, some of which being greenfield investments based on personnel from the merging Scansped companies.

The companies becoming, as well as being, indirectly related will show the same pattern, combining the growth and change sequences both at system level and net level.

These sequences demonstrate that there are some typical effects at system and net level in terms of the same sequences for these indirectly related transport companies.

Network level and domino effects

Over time more companies will be interconnected since companies follow these growth sequences of integration and since nets of companies are created within the total network through this process.The general analysis of the focal cases shows the same. Basically this would also lead to a higher integration of the total network. Due to this inter-connectedness the influences of events will be stronger and spread faster. Therefore also indirect relations relatively far away from the companies in focus for an event will be affected also and "domino effects" start to show.

In the Waco and Scansped events, both taking place during the 1980's, the effects involved a large number of the indirect relations. In the WACO event, after ASG bought part of the American WACO agent both ASG and WACO passed through the change sequences leaving their existing agents. Then they both went into a new growth sequences with new agents. The new agent of WACO, which was ISA, had in turn just passed through a change sequence leaving 25 of their former agents in order to join WACO. Further, many of ISA´s former agents would probably be try to find new representatives with whom they develop new growth sequences. In this way the effects continue and domino effects arise. The patterns of growth - change-growth sequences at system (1-2-1) and at net level (3-4-3) are repeated for both ASG, other WACO agents and ISA and their former agents.

The number of events that followed the Scansped merger were numerous. The same thing applies for all the IF acquisitions, counting all the representatives leaving and joining. However, no event has really followed what happened over several nets. The Waco event description followed two nets, ASG and ISA, but that was all.

However, in the Scansped event and general case analysis there would seem to be one incident that came back several times which showed how these domino effects continue across several different international nets. This incident was the Nedlloyd group´s acquisition of a large international transport company Uniontransport in West-Germany which had effects on the Scansped acquisition of Tekatrans in Stuttgart.

There was a whole chain of events related to the Scansped acquisition of Tekatrans. In that particular case both ASG, Bilspedition and many other companies were involved (see figure 9.14.). To begin with, Nedlloyd, a large Dutch international transport Group, was cooperating with several agents in Germany. In 1988 they acquired Uniontransport in Germany, a large German company with good coverage of the country. Nedlloyd therefore ceased their cooperation with their German representative Panalpina (another large international Group) in Stuttgart. As a result, Panalpina, which in turn was agent to Scansped Holland in the Stuttgart area, started its own activities in Holland and in doing so ceased its cooperation with Scansped Holland.

Scansped Holland had to find another suitable representative in the Stuttgart area. Scansped's own subsidiary in Stuttgart lacked the necessary resources, however, and none of the existing Scansped agents in Germany were willing to solve the problem. Scansped's international expansion caused large parts of the nets of the international agents and Scansped to be increasingly overlapping. Scansped solved the situation by acquiring Tekatrans, an international transport company with strong traffics to/from Holland and Belgium. In turn, Tekatrans had to break with its agents both in Holland and in Belgium and their salesman moved into the office of Scansped in Belgium. From there the chain probably continues on.

The Nedlloyd acquisition of Uniontransport also had effects on ASG since ASG was cooperating with another company acquired by Nedlloyd, van Gend & Loos (vGL). vGL was an old agent of ASG's from the 1950's and cooperated also with ASG Hamburg. Due to the same acquisition of Uniontransport, ASG Hamburg lost its Dutch agent vGL but found a new agent called Bayer which was part of the Belgian Ziegler Group.

Patterns of growth sequences at system and net level interrupted by change sequences which continue into new growth sequences (1-2-1 or 3-4-3) lead to *domino effects* in the total network showing the same typical sequences as those of the direct relations.

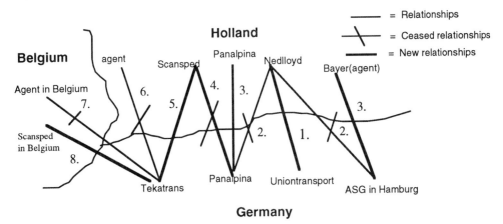

Figure 9.14 Domino effects in international network

Speed is vital for the companies affected by these domino effects. The time it takes to find a new representative and the time that is available for the change seem to be critical. The need for speed increase with the number of representatives simultaneously looking for alternatives. Since there is so little time and the problems of finding a suitable representative not already part of an international overlapping net are large, more costly alternatives are often chosen in order to get out of a precarious situation. Both Scansped and Panalpina, having their own companies in the specific area, had to acquire a company or add the necessary resources to their existing subsidiary in the area to solve the situation they found themselves in. Therefore, as the speed of changing from growth to change sequence are becoming more crucial when a large number of representatives are involved, finding new representatives can be more costly .

Furthermore, it seems that the expectations of the sequences of changes fuse the speed of events so that either some sequences are not followed through or are speeded up.

When many companies are going through change patterns, the effects on performance of the domino effect will therefore be quite marked, not only for the acquisitions and green field investments but also for the high costs of establishing new relations to representatives, suppliers and customers.

Finally, in looking at the chain of the domino effects as regards the Nedlloyd Group, the Scansped Group and the Panalpina Group, all three increased their degree of internationalization in the sense that they increased the degree of integration within their nets and at the same time increased their degree of overlapping between the nets. The domino effects fused both Nedlloyd, Scansped and Panalpina into a movement towards closing up.

9.4. Patterns and internationalization

In the model of analysis we developed we assumed that the process is intitiated through coordination to foreign resources and activities. From this has followed that integration started the process of internationalization. Further, as has been shown from the general case analysis, changes in extension and penetration then follow from integration. Thus the patterns of integration will have important implications for the extension and penetration of the companies over time. However, even though integration intiates the process of internationalization, changes in penetration might lead to continuation of the process through influencing integration to increase.

In the pattern of changes at system level (1-2-1) the first growth sequence (1) seems to be of basic importance for increase of *extension* at system level and at net level. Extending through the first growth sequence at system level seems to have been the normal situation in Europe for ASG and to a large extent for Bilspedition until the early 1970's. Since extension will only increase for the focal company or the focal net if there is no earlier extension between a specific pair of countries then the second growth sequence in the above pattern, involving switching to another representative will not further increase extension.

As regards to the typical net level pattern, when both first and secondary degree of extension are involved, the question is rather whether the new systems and nets in the second growth sequence are C/C or O/C. If they are, then there might be increased degree of extension otherwise only integration and penetration will be involved.

The very existence of these patterns shows that the companies are very reluctant to decrease extension and specifically so the first degree of extension. Even though they change, their intent rather seems to be to secure the extension involved. There are very few examples in the cases of decrease in the first degree of extension. As for the secondary degree of extension, the importance of securing this degree, increase with the number of subsidiaries in the net.

Unlike extension, *penetration* will continue to change as a result of a growth sequence. However, there is a difference between the first and second growth sequence since the first sequence sets the stage in terms of the degree of penetration, while the second resets the penetration, with the level of the first in mind. Moreover, since the changes in the sequences are speeded up and especially so the change sequences (2 and 4), it seems to be more relevant to compare the end product of the two growth sequences than to follow each stage in the sequences for direct changes over time. Further, the intention of the companies, when switching at system level or leaving and joining nets at net level, seems to be to secure a certain level of penetration through the new alternative and then continue in the second growth sequence.

In the cases of ASG Belgium and WACO the interpretation is that the degree of penetration for the focal companies would be the engaged resources before the event compared to those after the event, The strength of the former agent in Belgium and former agents of the WACO net compared to the new greenfield investment and the new net, will then decide how penetration has changed.

Under certain circumstances, as in the case of WACO, when comparing before and after the change sequences (2 and 4) penetration even decreased. Similarly, as Scansped merged its three international groups this also caused decrease in penetration since the number of agents decreased in the country and the reorganized subsidiaries often could not cover the country in the same way. As the internal competition between the overlapping part-nets within Bilspedition had created such large inefficiencies in the total net, the cost of a decrease in penetration seemed perhaps necessary to bear. However, as penetration would normally follow on to integration it would catch up again, over time. In these two cases it was not possible to secure the degree of penetration directly after the event. However, one could expect that, after the second growth sequence was fulfilled, penetration might have returned to a similar level as before the event.

The domino effects in the total network imply that penetration change in one country will lead to changes in penetration in other countries and that the companies sometimes have to change at such short notice that an alternative securing existing extension and penetration is not available. Therefore they have to settle for alternatives that lead to decreases in the short run and /or pay a high cost in the form of investments.

9.5. Conclusions of empirical results

9.5.1. General case analysis - conclusions

1. The patterns of the three different cases differed
- ASG, the earliest of the three to start internationalizing, had gradual development of system integration over time. Net changes increased during the 1980's.
- Bilspedition - starting in the mid 1950's had a combination of gradual systems integration and net changes. From the 1980's it was mainly net changes that took place.
- For IF starting in 1988, net changes dominated entirely.

2. Internationalization was initiated by increased integration leading to increased extension leading to penetration. Over time, extension became less of an issue. Penetration became more

important. Increased penetration also increased possibilities for increased integration. Finally in the 1980's integration within and between nets dominated in importance over extension and penetration. Integration seems to have caused further integration without any related changes in to extension and penetration.

3. As a net was created and developed in services over time the negative connectedness increased between representatives. Development of part-nets (parts of higher interdependence within the total nets of ASG, IF and Bilspedition) in the 1970's decreased the conflict between the representatives.

4. The separate part-nets increased the number of parallel processes going on within the net. In the 1980's the some of part-nets were changing towards closing up for ASG and Bilspedition.

5. The owners, being positively connected transport companies were taking an active part in the internationalization of ASG and Bilspedition. Moreover, being owners and suppliers in combination made them place restrictions on suitable areas of development rather than on declared profitability.

6. The establishment of sales offices or subsidiaries via either greenfield investments or acquisitions differed in importance over time. The sales offices and greenfiled investments were more important during the 1960's and 70's. During the 1980's acquisitions predominated.

7. As the representatives grew domestically and internationally the negative connectedness increased between local representatives and international representatives. Conflicts between representatives and between focal companies and representatives appeared because of negative connectedness between their traffics.

8. The role of the focal transport companies towards many of their suppliers increased in importance over time. Suppliers' capacity problems seem to have had a large impact on this. Further Bilspedition acquired several important large suppliers and its former owners as well in the 1980's.

9. As the focal companies and the agents diversified and developed internationally their nets became increasingly overlapping. This caused many cooperations to cease over time.

10. Competitors such as ASG and Bilspedition have acted and reacted continuously on the changes taking place in the other over time and especially so to changes in ownership.

9.5.2. Event conclusions

11. There are some typical growth and change sequences of integration forming the base of international change, which were repeated over time.

12. These sequences exist at system and net level and seem to form patterns consisting of combinations of growth -change- growth sequences. These sequences at system level lead to the creation and then development of a net.

13. As companies become increasingly connected through these sequences, new changes may develop into domino effects on the total network.

14. International interconnectedness causes interaction between changes in different countries which leads to further changes in the internationalization of the involved companies.

15. Changes in indirect relations in network might have large effects on the focal company through domino effects.

16. As interconnectedness increased, agents not being part of international overlapping nets become increasingly difficult to find and acquisitions become more common. Moreover the existence of a subsidiary often increases conflicts with internationalized agents and therefore forces further investments.

17. Expectation of the changes in the sequences combined with the domino effects speed up the change sequences.

18. Joining of nets increased in importance as a way to internationalize as the number of international nets and interconnectedness spread within the total network. Creating a net through gradual single system integration disappeared since the agents were already tied up internationally.

19. Different types of joining of nets lead to different effects on the extension and penetration. Adding an O/C net would increase extension while adding a C/O net of complementary services would increase penetration. Finally as the internationalization continues the nets become increasingly O/O over time. The O/O nets if not merged would add much to penetration while merged nets add integration and partly decrease in penetration.

20. The pattern of integration sequences very seldom implies a decrease in first degree of extension while both integration and penetration might decrease. As for changes in secondary degree of extension these have been subject to decreases in change sequences.

Part IV   Theoretical results

10. Theoretical discussions

Up to now the study of the case companies has consisted of empirical observations on behaviour within the theoretical framework of the model of anlysis. The aim of this chapter is to apply the existing research to the empirical results and discuss how it supports and explains the findings of the general and event analyses. Indirectly, the extent to which the findings are coherent with existing network-, distribution- and internationalization research would also be a test of the usefulness of the model. Further it seems important to point out to what extent there might be limitations in existing research as to its ability to explain the same findings.

The chapter will start by discussing the basic empirical results on patterns of internationalization found in the study and then examine more in detail each of three dimensions of integration, extension and penetration. In each of the dimensions the explanations for changes taking place between the different aspects of the concept will be discussed as well as research that is specifically tied to that dimension of internationalization.

10.1. The basic patterns of internationalization - support, explanations and limitations of existing research

There are four basic findings of the study concerning patterns of internationalization which will be discussed from the perspectives of internationalization, network and distribution research.

First, there was a gradual expansion of companies dominating for earlier periods while changes in leaps and radical net changes were dominating during 1980´s.

Second, the dimensions of internationalization were interacting and the process was initiated by integration of relationships at network level leading to integration of systems or nets. Integration then caused extension and penetration. During the first period extension seemed to be more important than penetration. Over time as extension of first degree became less of an issue penetration increased in importance. Further during the 1980's integration at net level became dominating in importance.

Third, there were sequences of changes of integration which were typical in the international development. These could be seen as growth and change sequences and they seemed to be combined into patterns of growth-change-growth sequences of integration. These were depicted not only for the focal companies but also for other transport companies in the network.

Finally, as companies were becoming more interconnected and more strongly tied to different nets _domino effects_ will developed in the international network involving a large number of companies.

As we shall see, theories and models from the three research areas support and explain part of the results in different ways. We start by looking at the traditional Uppsala School research from the 1970's and continue to the research on MNE and internalisation of intangible assets. Second, we discuss the network approach and add the developments from the Uppsala model by Johanson& Mattsson (1988) and Forsgren (1991).The network part will also include a discussion concerning closure of a community (Astley,1985). Finally we are discussing some of the underlying reasons for the patterns from distribution research involving economies of scale and scope (Dixon & Wilkinson, 1986).

Internationlization theories

Uppsala School internationalization model
The Uppsala School internationalization model (Johanson & Wiederheim-Paul, 1974; Johanson & Vahlne, 1975), based on a sequential experiential learning process, supports the early gradual development in the patterns of internationalization and specifically the growth sequence at system level. The assumption of increased degree of commitment over time would also support and explain the change from extension to penetration dimension. As companies learn and do more in a specific country the resources and the relations will increase. Further, the continuation of the process when increased commitments lead to increased knowledge of the company would give an understanding of how penetration might lead to increased integration over time, if we assume that the knowledge created is included in its relationships.

The model also implies an increase in the directly controlled resources over time which is in line with the development of an increasing number of subsidiaries in foreign countries for the focal companies. However, as we can see from the cases the same gradual development and increasing commitment seemed to be equally important in their application to the cooperation with the agents over time. The limitation of the model seems to be its lack of ability to explain the new patterns of internationalization during 1980's, which is less gradual and more radical than in earlier years.

Internalisation of intangible assets
Another important explanation for the patterns of sequences might be found in the discussions on transactional market imperfections which imply that internalisation is necessary in order to protect the intangible assets of the firm (Buckley & Casson,1976; Caves,1976; Magee,1976). Magee (1976) takes this reasoning a little bit further through discussion of appropriability of

knowledge and information for individual companies, which can be seen as investments being subject to depreciations in value over time.

Applying the theory of internalisation of intangible assets to a net of company relations and its different aspects of integration rather than to a single company and only legal integration, it would be a plausible explanation for the increasing number of net changes and to the domino effects. A net would then be assumed to be protecting the common intangible assets of the net from being dispersed through company relations to other nets. The probability of leakage and possibilities to prevent leakage would be a base for a decision to leave or to join a net or to break a single relation due to its connectedness to other nets.

Moreover, in the network perspective companies develop knowhow in their relationships over time, which can be assumed to spread between relationships in the net. The knowhow developed this way about marketing, transport system design, communication systems, etc would be intangible net assets which will be protected by the organizations benefiting from this asset. This would explain not only the leaving of relationships or part of nets but also why nets are moving towards closing up.

In some cases, the reason for starting a relation or joining a net might be that of assumed spillover from one relation to another. This seemed to be an important reason in many relationships where one company is more advanced in some aspects than the other one.

In the 1960's and 70's, using the terms of Dunning(1989), the increasing investments in terminals, technical facilities, etc. of the focal companies and their agents seem to have given rise to ownership advantages due to structural imperfections based on size, technology, etc. while during the 1980's the advantages can be seen as being based more on transactional imperfections. Therefore the importance of intangible assets has increased. One such evolving ownership advantage has been the global network and the coordination advantages that come out of that.

The internalisation theory thus seems to be relevant for explanation of changes both of nets and of relationships.

<u>Network approach</u>

Network and internationalization

Johanson & Mattsson (1984) have argued that the Uppsala model does not seem to take the internationalization of context into account. They claim that the internationalization of the network or the "market" plays a vital role for the way a company internationalizes and therefore the Uppsala model seems to be more valid for companies establishing internationally in the early stages of "market" internationalization. The model would explain why net changes came to dominate over time as well as the difference between the gradual development of ASG and net changes of IF. In the case of companies starting or continuing their internationalization process in an international context the authors state that other factors would have to be taken into consideration such as suitable agents already being tied to competitors, a higher need for coordination etc. These factors increase the interest for joint ventures or acquisitions. This situation seems to fit both IF being a 'late starter' and the situation of ASG and Bilspedition being 'internationals among others'.

Further, Johanson & Mattsson comment upon the fact, that "integration not only in a vertical sense but also in a lateral, decentralized sense " seems to be very important for such companies. In line with this reasoning they argue that extension and penetration are more important during the earlier gradual development while integration increases over time. Similar reasoning can be found in Bartlett (1986) and Martinez & Jarillo (1987) concerning the increasing importance of coordination and integration in MNEs.

This approach taking both the internationalization of the company and of its context into account seems to be far better when it comes to explaining the changes in the patterns over time than if only the internationalization of the company is focused.

A limitation of the model is that it shows different alternative situations for companies as the context internationalizes but not how companies over time might move between them.

Secondary degree of internationalization

Secondary degree of internationalization is applied to the phenomenon of internationalization of subsidiaries (Forsgren,1991; Forsgren & Holm,1991). As the subsidiaries of an MNE internationalizes the company grows into a multi-center firm in terms of decision location. Acquisitions will contribute to this development. A similar development is shown in this study, only that these subsidiaries also seem to follow a gradual or radical development pattern depending on the degree of internationalization of the context. The early subsidiaries developed gradually internationally through cooperation with agents while for those companies starting later the acquisition of a company already having established relations internationally was more likely. Internationalization of subsidiaries facilitates the understanding of the increasing interconnectedness of the network and the increasing complexities over time leading to repeated integration patterns of growth and change sequences.

However in this study secondary degree of internationalization is not only applicable to subsidiaries of the focal companies but also to agents and suppliers. The complications for the focal companies to handle internationalization of subsidiaries in a situation where most other companies are also internationalizing seem sometimes to be so large that radical solutions have to be chosen. A typical radical solution would be to buy another international company. However, this will change the negative and/or positive connectedness between relationships and give rise to new restrictions and opportunities which might lead to domino effects as a result of increasing degree of overlapping of nets. The domino effects are initiated by pre-empted reactions to expected changes of the involved companies. Therefore the secondary degree of internationalization will precipitate the net level changes.

Community ecology

Similar sequences of changes as in this study are assumed to exist within the community or human ecology as typical changes when a community is changing over time. Even domino effects are mentioned as a possibility when a community is disturbed (Astley,1985).

Astley argues that closing up towards a higher degree of integration and exclusiveness within a net will increase the risk of a radical change. Change towards closure of a community unfolds through succession which means simultaneous changes in structure within and between populations. These changes involve development along two axes, the competitive and the symbiotic. He further says "if complex communities experience disturbance beyond a certain threshold level, they may disintegrate because of a domino effect"(Ibid p. 237). It seems as if it is important to know to what extent the community has reached a closure. Once closure is reached the change will be more extensive. Astley also comments upon what will happen after such a change which in turn gives support to the combination of growth and change sequences at net level. "A severe disturbance upsets the equilibrium and destroys the community and recovery of an equilibrium condition eventually occurs through ecological succession"(Ibid p.237). The last sentence would indicate that moving into new growth sequences would be a normal development before as well as after a community had been fully or partly destroyed.

These comments will also take us to the effects of these different sequences combined, which form patterns not only for the focal nets but also for other nets in the network. Astley mentioned that a domino effect was present when the community was seriously disturbed. A similar effect was shown in the dynamics of the transport companies except that it did not only stay within one net of basically complementary organizations but continued between different nets of organizations. This would indicate that many nets of the transport companies are interdependent on each other which causes the domino effect to occur between these nets. In this case the effects of the closure of community apply to the total network of transport nets rather than to a single net.

Distribution theories

Economies of scope and scale

Chandler (1990) pointed out the concepts of economies of scale and of scope in combination with transaction cost efficiency as very important driving forces for internationalization. Even though this was based on coordination within a legal unity it seems to be relevant for coordination within a net of cooperating transport companies as well.

Further Dixon & Wilkinson (1986) argue that the underlying factors that affect effectiveness and efficiency in a distribution system are economies of scale and of scope. They show how these economies influence both technical and administrative sub-systems in a distribution system leading to positive and negative sequences of changes as one of subsystems or both reach an optimum.

For transport companies economies of scale can be applied to 1) a growth within an existing transport system 2) more transport systems of the same type within existing relationship, 3) more transport systems of the same type but linked to other relations. The last two alternatives will also involve elements of economies of scope in that the services are different and especially so in alternative 3 if it is a transport system to another country.

Economies of scale will lead to increased efficiency as volumes grow. As volumes increase there would be economies of scale for transport companies in the utilization of resources in the technical subsystem of the transport system. As for the administrative sub-system, when volumes increase more can be communicated and coordinated at the same time and the routines for communication could become more efficient. Second, it would also be possible to invest in larger and more advanced communication systems which is important for transport companies and increasingly so during the last decades.

Economies of scope on the other hand are based on joint utilization of resources for more than one type of system. Economies of scope can be 1) new types of systems within the same relation 2) new types of systems in other relations. The opportunities of joint utilization differ between the cases depending on the type of resources that can be used jointly.

There seem to be especially important gains in economy of scope in the marketing resources since the customers might need different types of service, customers might be situated in distant geographical places and might coordinate their purchases of transports. This is accentuated as the customers internationalize and the manufacturing industry decreases the number of suppliers.

Since economies of scope and scale seem to be different depending on the total volumes and number of services of a company, the structure and number of relations of the single company will be of importance. Therefore economies of scope and scale could differ between the organizations. These dissimilarities in potential gains of economies of scale and scope between single companies probably would increase the dynamics of a net and push for increased interaction between integration, extension and penetration as well as gradual development.

Over time the focal organizations seem to have been aware of the necessity of utilizing economies of scale and scope. Therefore they have reorganized into more specialized departments or divisionalized or separate companies, thereby getting a quicker access to the economic gains. This has also been suggested by Chandler as a common way to cope with the problems of costs for coordination and administration internally within large groups. However it is perhaps not only a solution to internal problems but also to contextual problem in the sense that what the firm is coordinating is not only its own resources but also the resources of other companies. The creation of these separate "part-nets" might be even more important for the increasing effectiveness in the coordination of the indirectly controlled resources.

On the whole, economies of scale and of scope facilitate the understanding of both a gradual development, interaction between integration and penetration and typical patterns of growth and change sequences at system and net level. However at net level scope seems to have a greater importance than scale.

Summarizing, each of the existing theories seem to support and explain different parts of the findings but none of them follow the development of a company and its sequences of changes over time from one stage to another taking context into account. Moreover the implications of domino effects for the internationalization of companies do not seem to have been studied.

10.2. Integration changes - Support, explanations and limitations of existing research

Integration has been shown in this study to be a process of basic importance for internationalization.

There are several important findings of integration which will be discussed more in detail.

- The content of the growth and change sequences at system level and at net level
- The variation of relative importance of the different aspects of integration have varied over time. Legal integration has increased very much during the 1980's leading to higher integration of the nets and part-nets created.
- The effects of increasing integration on positive and negative connectedness between direct and and indirect relations.
- The speed of the change sequences increase.

We shall start by discussing the different supports for the content of the sequences by presenting the life cycle of the relationship and trust in and conflicts of relationships. Then after having shortly commented upon the effects of economies of scale and scope and their contribution to the explanations of the content of the sequences we finally turn to discuss predominately net level sequences through raising the subject of acquisitions and mergers. The changes of positive and negative connectedness and the changes in different aspects of integration will be intervowen in the discussions.

Life cycle of relations

The studies on the evolution of a relation made by Dwyer, Schurr & Oh (1987) and Liljegren (1988) show a very similar behaviour to that of the growth and change sequences at system level. According to Dwyer, Schurr & Oh the relation starts with an awareness and an exploration phase realization of the problem, finding out possible alternatives and trying a cooperation Liljegren calls this the build up phase. In the first phase a new cooperation is built up. The next phase concerns expansion/ development and commitment which are actually a mixture of closer cooperation and enlargement. In the growth sequence at system level, closer cooperation includes increased integration in the existing relations and in the system while enlargement means an increase in the existing field of cooperation. It seems to be important whether the cooperation involves just closer cooperation within existing services or adding more services. Adding more services of the same or different type is important from the network perspective, since it changes the connectedness to other companies.

The studies of the evolution of a relation over time by Dwyer et al (1987), Liljegren (1988) and Gadde & Mattsson (1987) all include one or two phases of disintegration. Dwyer et al had one phase called dissolution. In the case study of Liljegren (1988) the relation studied did not dissolve but entered a phase of uncertainty which reactivated the existing relation. In spite of this Liljegren claims that there are two phases for dissolution, that of breaking a relation and that of withdrawal. Gadde & Mattsson (1987) observed in their study a gradual disengagement before exit. In very few cases there were direct switches to another supplier and to dissolution of the relation. The exit pattern could also be more complicated, being alternately strengthened and weakened. This combination of growth and change sequence at system level would give a empirical pattern of change similar to that found in this study.

Many other authors have touched upon the life-cycle of relations. Among them are Van de Ven & Walker (1984), who in their study of the development of relationships over time argued that the creation and expansion of the relation also contains the seeds of its disintegration. They claim that increasing formalization and monitoring in a relation cause conflict and dissension among the organizations struggling to maintain their autonomy, that the increasing transactions within the relation over time lead to a shift and that the domain of the organizations will shift from being complementary to becoming overlapping. These changes lead to an increase in conflicts and competition which in turn will lead towards a dissolution of the relation. This would actually support not only the changes taking place in this study at system level but also changes going on at net level leading to more overlapping nets.

Trust and conflicts

Trust and conflicts are very important factors explaining stability and change of relationships over time.

As has been shown in the cases many relationships existed over a long period. The average time for ASG agent relations was 20-40 years. The same observations have been found in many other studies of the network approach.

Trust in different studies can be seen both as a motive and as an effect of a long term relationship (Young, 1992). The combination of these views on trust would help to explain the establishment as well as the continuation of relations. Heide&Miner (1990) comment that the very expectation of a continued relationship leads to a significant positive effect on cooperative behaviour including trust.

In most cases the discussion of trust is limited to single relationships and will therefore have implications at single system level rather than at net level.

However, according to Granovetter (1985), being embedded in a social network leads to a certain advantage in terms of trust. The organizations gain better and richer information through using the experience and knowledge being stored in the direct or indirect relationships. As a result of this, trust would play an important role at net level and also as a source of information and could, as such, help to explain the changes at net level as well.

The degree to which trust and stability are present in a relation is often dependent on complementarity and competition in that relationship. According to Mallen (1964) if conflicting objectives outweighs the cooperating the effectiveness will be reduced. When that takes place, a change sequence will be followed through.

However, the intensity of the conflict as well as the possibility that it will turn into a real conflict and not just a potential one is dependent on the age of the relationship, trust and communication (Anderson & Weitz, 1987). This indicates that a change into a continuation of the cooperation would be a natural development for long term relations of high trust and communication level rather than dissolution.

Håkansson (1987) widens the reasoning, saying that a relation has five significant and well documented characteristics which are duration of the relationship, adaptions made, technological content, range of contact and social content. These characteristics as well as the stake in the relationship will play a role when discussing the probability of dissolution of a relationship. This indicates that whether the conflicts lead to dissolution depend on a combination of all these characteristics.

The nature of relationships, showing duration, stability and trust, would indicate that a gradual change in the growth sequence at system level and that the "opening up" alternative at net level would be more natural for cooperations than "joining of nets" involving larger acquisitions. However this does not explain the cases of dissolution of some long term relationships or the radical changes taking place more often during the 1980's.

In order to find explanations to these phenomena the concepts of positive and negative connectedness between nets might be of some help. In this study, changes in other direct or indirect relations in the network seem to be of importance for the balance between trust and conflicts within an existing relationship. If the changes increase the negative connectedness between two nets, this would escalate the conflicts within the existing relationship bridging the nets. The probability of this increases with secondary degree of internationalization.

According to Cook (1982) exchange networks are dynamic, as a result of actors´ attempt to restructure power in networks. The number of desirable alternatives for coordination and the number of possible ones are in constant change due to power-balancing between the actors. This changes the interconnectedness in the network over time. Change in the power balance within and between the nets would perhaps help to explain a change in balance between trust and conflict in long term relationships leading to a final dissolution of the bridging relationship. Therefore at net level the degree to which nets are overlapping or complementary seems to be important for understanding the changes going on and why changes in trust and conflicts take place.

Economies of scale and scope and the content of the sequences
Over time, the companies coordinating the transport systems will develop in know-how of what, with whom and how to coordinate and communicate. As for the technical sub-systems, over time the development implies a creation of specialized equipment, utilizing the capacity of the means of transportation more efficiently and specialization of the roles between the companies more clearly. This process will necessitate a "closer cooperation" in a relation. Further, adding new transport systems relying on economies of scale or of scope based on existing competence would then lead to an "enlargement" of the relation.

At net level using economies of scale or scope would be adding systems into new relationships and thus gradually create a net or "opening up". As for "joining nets" it can be explained by making use of economies of scope or of scale depending on the type of nets which are joined.

O/O and O/C nets would be explained by scale economies while C/O and C/C nets would be explained by scope economies.

Network changes, acquisitions and mergers
Until the 1980's the cooperations seem to have been based on informal or rather loose formal agreements concerning exclusiveness for a certain local area which enhanced the importance of the social aspect of integration. The development was gradual. During the 1980's the legal investments through acquisitions were totally dominating which led to more radical changes and joining of nets.

If legal integration is an important way to increase efficiency through reducing costs and increasing environmental control (Williamson,1985; Andersson & Weitz,1987) then why were there so few acquisitions during the 1960's and 1970's when large investments and specialization took place? One of the reasons for this might be found in the utilization of economies of scope which actually involves a tendency for decreased specificity in the resources at the systems level.

Dixon & Wilkinson (1990) argue slightly differently. They maintain rather that there would be an interval within which an intermediary would be the choice and then, as volume and number of transactions increased further, an investment would take place. This would indicate that many of the relations in the 1960´s and 70´s were still too small in size.

Even though Williamson (1985) argues for acquisition of critical resources which include a very high asset specificity for a relation he does not comment upon the issue of integrating the resources or not. On the other hand Chandler (1990) found that integration between the acquired companies was necessary in order to increase efficiency. Otherwise the gains of economies of scale and scope were not realized.

Astley & Fombrun (1986) had found horizontal, vertical and diagonal interdependencies when studying development of large cooperations. This was also reflected in waves of mergers and acquisitions taking place over time. During the 1980's when the vast majority of acquisitions were made of the three focal transport companies these were not of single companies but rather of nets and even though one of the above mentioned interdependence types dominated the others were mostly present as well. This is also in line with the reasoning by Cook et al (1989), who argue that very seldomly are there only positive or negatively connected nets but that the normal situation would be a mixed net which would play an important role for the changes over time.

However, looking at the acquisitions in this study in terms of Astley & Fombrun (1986) there have been a total domination of horizontal acquisitions if acquisitions of agent´s nets are included as horizontal. While Bilspedition showed a tendency to acquire overlapping (O/O) nets from competitors, ASG and IF acquired partly complementary nets (C/O or O/C) through acquisition of agents. At the end of 1980´s Bilspedition added some acquisitions of vertical nets through acquiring some shipping lines.

The diagonal type of acquisitions has been rather infrequent and took place mostly during the 1970´s in a period of diversification and specialization.

On the other hand it is important to note that the acquisitions of the nets during the 1980´s often involved small parts being vertically or diagonally dependent to those of the acquiring firms. Even though the vertical or diagonal parts might be small in some of the individual acquisitions, when there are numerous acquisitions they will finally accumulate to a larger share of the total activities. As they have grown to a more important role, they have to be dealt with. After a period of time, effects on the diagonal or vertical parts perhaps would call for action in terms creating separate part-nets within the existing net or having the parts disposed of Therefore an expansion in one horizontal direction would probably bear the seed for future expansion either in a diagonal or vertical direction. This happened in several of the cases, as with IF´s development of airfreight services during the first years.

Moreover, the increased efficiency differs, depending on whether the acquisition was C/C, C/O,O/C or O/O. Letting fully owned companies continue to compete internally, which Bilspedition did, obviously did not lead to any increased efficiency but rather the reverse. In spite of their common ownership and the management´s expressed will, the O/O part-nets did not cooperate. This contradicts what Williamson (1985) says about hierarchies and internal control but supports what Chisholm (1989) found in his study on internal rivalry in hierarchies.

Quite often, according to the empirical findings in this study the cause to a merger or a contraction in a net might not derive from the focal companies but is a result of the agents leaving, realizing the overlapping activities between nets. The focal company might have to solve the situation by increasing cooperation between the existing representatives and accelerate the process towards "closing up".

Mattsson (1987) saw both expansion and contraction as important change processes in the network. Changes in networks could have many dimensions, becoming more or less hierarchical, more or less tightly structured, more or less homogeneous more or less exclusive. Both expansion and contraction would involve these but the degrees would be different. A net contracting such as concentrating the international activities to fewer units would lead to a higher structuredness, more hierarchization and more exclusiveness than a net expanding through opening up or joining of nets. Basically a contracting net would change towards "closing up".

Explanations of speed and timing and increasing integration
Over time, the process of going in and out of the growth and change sequences will give the focal companies a certain experience of the costs of changing agents in different situations, which will probably also affect the way in which they act, i.e how far they will go in adjusting, the speed and timing of the change, etc. The very fact that they expect certain problems to occur when there is a "switch", for instance regarding the relationship between the focal company and the customers of the leaving agent, seems to lead to an increase in the speed with the objective to take the agent by surprise. This happened both in the Belgium event and in the large Scansped merger.

Movement in one or other direction might also be influenced by the expectations of future behaviour. Granovetter (1985) states that experience and information are richer and cheaper in networks. This knowledge can be vital for expectation on future behaviour and for decisions on changing positions. Taking Bilspedition as an example sooner or later it merged most of its overlapping companies or part-nets . This would give reason to believe that it would do the same when acquiring a new company in spite of any assurances it might give to the contrary. This would also increase the speed of changes.

Johanson & Mattsson (1992) use this argument when they discuss how a change in "network theories" for the organizations being part of the network, influences strategic actions. Those "network theories" would probably be based on the expected behaviour of companies in growth and change sequences in the network and on how the sequences are combined into patterns. A possibility to change the network theories would be to change the actors perceptions´ of in what phase, in what type and with whom the sequences take place. This would be complemented with the knowledge and information from the network of how the specific companies move in the patterns.

The speed of the sequences also seems to increase over time. Therefore the timing of the new cooperation is important when discussing the speed.

The increasing pace of internationalization seems to be true also whether the internationalization includes acquisitions or cooperations or switching. Once the focal companies as well as the agents and subsidiaries develop several types of services the opportunities for "enlargement" increase. In most cases this decreased the time for growth sequences at system level. In some cases when there is a need for switching, speeding up the dissolution might cause some practical problems when there is a very high interdependence between the focal company and the agent. How fast would it be possible to change even though there is an available alternative? The difficulties will probably increase with the size of the cooperation and therefore a start with a decrease in the field of cooperation would seem likely.

There will probably be many changes leading to spirals of increasing integration. First, there are internal reasons which originate from interaction between the integration aspects, interaction between the dimensions of penetration and integration and increasing effectiveness through economies of scope and scale. Second, there might be changes in the basic conditions like regulations, technology, infrastructure, which push for a continuation of increasing degree of integration over time or the development of new types of transport systems, new more efficient equipment, new communication systems, etc. Another important reason might be the changes in customer demands as a result of increased international competition for customers giving rise to demands for higher levels of reliability and speed in the existing transport systems.

The existing research on life cycle of relationships and trust and conflicts support and explain the changes mainly taking place at system level. Explanations to net level changes seem to be few and limited when it comes to explaining net level changes and its interactions with those at system level. Further the explanations to the increased speed of the sequences over time and the spiral of changes would need to be developed theoretically. The expectation of changes and the "network theories" could probably add to the understanding.

10.3. Extension changes - Support, explanations and limitations of existing research

The main results concerning extension which will be discussed here are:

- To begin with, extension was gradual as the single systems were integrated involving new countries while later, extension of net changes went either in leaps and bounds or was almost non- existent.

-Extension basically concerned that of first degree during the early years. The secondary degree of extension increased over the years as the number of subsidiaries increased.

- Internationalized organizations being directly or indirectly related to the focal company's total net (including the domestic parts) played an important role as regards the choice and the number of countries.

- The Nordic countries and northern or central Western European countries were among the first for ASG and Bilspedition while IF extended itself to the whole of Europe and to many overseas countries simultaneously.

The theoretical discussion will start by bringing up the concept of psychic distance used by the Uppsala School and combine this with indirect and weak relationships of the network approach. Then we continue to discuss the importance of regions and homebases. Finally we end up by discussing speed and timing.

Psychic distance and indirect relations

The Uppsala school combined extension with penetration through presenting the model of increasing commitment and knowledge. Their explanation for choice of country was based on a general knowledge of a specific country called the psychic distance. Psychic as well as cultural distance was supposed to be low to countries nearby compared to more distant countries, which also was supported in empirical studies (Hörnell, Vahlne, & Wiedersheim-Paul, 1973; Johanson & Vahlne, 1977). The findings by Nordström (1991) indicate that psychic distance would play a role but a more limited one and that there is an acceleration of the establishment sequence for the companies entering more recently. Further he comments that there seems to be a levelling out of the psychic distances between countries over time. This seems to be very similar to some of the empirical findings for the first degree of extension in this study. However, besides the psychic distance there are other vital factors, which also seem to increase in importance as the transport companies become more international and secondary degree of extension increases.

In the case studies the existence of direct and indirect international relations to the focal company in other countries would seem to have played a very important role. The concept of psychic distance is based on general factors of internationalization. However, the links in these case studies seem to be specific rather than general in character, and the indirect relations specifically seem to play an important role.

In the network approach, Granovetter (1973) argues that weak ties might be used as bridges to other parts of the network. When trying to develop into new areas it would be natural to look at these relations. Especially since there is knowledge about other organizations available through the network that reduces uncertainty, thereby taking away one of the reasons for the existence of psychic distance. This could be interpreted as supporting the importance of direct and indirect international relations in a focal company's total net in the choice of new countries. It seems reasonable though to expect psychic distance to play a more important role in the cases where direct or indirect relations are too distant or not available.

It is when customers, suppliers and agents become internationalized that the possibility of finding a direct or indirect international relations with other countries increases and the importance of psychic distance therefore decreases. This is also in line with the assumptions that the 'late starter' is less likely to develop according to the establishment sequence based on psychic distance.

"The extension patterns will be partly explained by the international character of indirect relations and the existence of entry opportunities" (Johanson & Mattsson, 1988 p 20)

Regions, extended homebase and secondary degree of extension.

Another factor to note is that the focal companies, as they become increasingly connected, are becoming more interested in regions than single countries. The Nordic countries e.g. are declared to be a homebase for ASG and Bilspedition. Europe is often seen as a single market as to which certain critical points are supposed to be covered. The changes in the European regulation and standards contribute to this. This would mean that extension for the 'late starter' will have another meaning and will be more dependent on the international network structure both of other transport companies and that of manufacturing companies. The sense of a base would include a secondary degree of extension between the countries being part of the base.

Finally, an important factor when discussing extension for transport companies specializing in transports by truck, by rail, by air, or by sea is that there are certain limitations on their economic and physical coverage. Over time certain of these limitations have been overcome by technological development but, for instance, when ASG started. ASG extension was dependent on the economic reach of the railway while Bilspedition, starting later with trucking and trailer traffics, was able to extend to areas more suitable for trucking.

Timing and speed

The speed of extension for a company starting to internationalize is dependent on when they start. These variances seem to support the differences between "early starters" and "late starters".

As for companies continuing to internationalize, the speed with which new nets are added and the degree to which these nets are C/C, O/C or C/O lead to changes in extension. All three might lead to secondary degree of extension while only C/C and O/C would increase first degree of extension.

Summarizing, it seems that there is support both for gradual change and for the increasing speed of extension. However the changes due to net sequences have not been developed in existing research in terms of extension. Explanations are either limited to gradual changes of extension concentrating on establishment sequence or not formerly applied to extension in the internationalization process..

10.4. Penetration changes - Support, explanations and limitations of existing research

Only more important changes in penetration will be discussed. These are:

-On the whole, the three focal companies studied have increased their degree of penetration over the total period studied due to increased investments.

-The acquisitions of companies gave rise to further investments.

-Penetration in one country became over time increasingly dependent on penetration in another and changes in one country had their effect on other countries.

-The early gradual change was made together with agents. Over time greenfield investments and acquisitions increased. During the late 1980's acquisitions totally predominated.

-The importance of the aspects of penetration differs over time. In the early years of internationalization penetration increased gradually through size and spread of relations. This was in the 1960's and 70's followed by increased variety of services either contributing to new diversified relations or scope of relations of penetration Then during the 1980's integration at net level predominated over penetration and there were increases as well as decreases, both in size and scope as well as spread of relations.

-Penetration in the sense of increasing growth in size of relation often resulted in further increases in integration level and therefore initiated new changes in internationalization.

The changes in penetration are mainly explained by the research on network advantages and the establishment chain.

Network advantages
The network advantages of a global organization are treated by a number of authors (Chandler,1990; Johanson & Vahlne,1990; Kogut, 1983; Magee,1976; Vernon & Wells, 1976). They have been discussing the advantages in terms of information and knowledge, lower transactional costs, economies of scope and scale and possibilities to utilize locational advantages.

These types of advantages would facilitate the understanding as to why focal companies have continued to increase their degree of penetration of countries and why penetration was allowed to decrease during later periods at the expense of integration.

In this study, however, certain network advantages like economies of scale and scope and part of the technical and informational externalities were relatively quickly reached for the focal companies through creation of a net of agents. Basically the most important advantages during the early years seems to have been economies of scale and scope in marketing and production in the home countries for the focal company, as well as agents which made it possible to cover extended areas with a number of basic services.

As penetration increased over time new network advantages developed and increased in importance, such as using the same communications system, setting a specific quality standard for the net, creation of a common image, etc., all of which necessitated a certain investment in each country. Interpreted in the terms of Johanson & Vahlne (1990) these changes woud lead to changes in the "advantage package" and to lower transactional cost activating the "advantage cycle".

The necessity of common investments for the net in order to gain these network advantages would contribute to an understanding of the concentration of agents that took place at the end of the 1970's and during the 1980's as well as the increasing number of subsidiaries. There was a need to give priority to certain types of investments which seemed more important than some of those existing. In order to be able to get the net to make these investments there seems to be a concentration to fewer agents and more subsidiaries, which has decreased the spread of and partly the scope of relations. This concentration of the net has also lead to an increasing homogeneity and perhaps hierarchization. Further as a result of the common investments, new information and knowledge advantages and new levels for economies of scale and scope seem to have been established.

As for the locational network advantage, presenting a possibility to arbitrage between international restrictions, the Common Market is deregulating and homogenizing its rules and this could offer an explanation for the priorities given to the European countries.

Choice of representation or establishment chain
As we discussed earlier, on the whole, the establishment chain, implying increasing commitments over time, was supported by the empirical results in this study, but it must be said also that the increasing of commitments was not only driven internally but also externally through actions taken by other firms.

Even though establishment in foreign countries has changed in the direction of more subsidiaries and less agents over time there have been combinations of representations which are of interest in relation to changes in penetration over a period. From the mid-1950's to the early 1980's a number of sales offices existed in Europe which in combination with the existing agents represented the focal company in the specific area. During the 1960's and the first years of the 1980's greenfield investments in foreign countries seem to have been more common than acquisitions. During the 1980's acquisitions dominated but, looking at the total penetration, they were often combined with the existing agents and former greenfield investments or former acquisitions. The new acquisitions mostly caused conflicts with the existing setting in the country, which resulted in further changes of penetration.

The establishment of sales offices only brought about a temporary increase in penetration. This contradicts the establishment chain hypothesis. The first sales offices created during the 1960's and 70's increased marketing and coordination of the focal company services in the country concerned. The number of direct relations to customers also increased for the focal company and this, in turn, gave rise to conflicts with the agents. After a period the contribution of the sales offices seemed to decrease and the sales offices were closed. However, the direct relations established by the sales office very often continued to exist with the focal company but directly from the home country at head office or divisional level.

Even though the number of subsidiaries increased over time there seem to be differences in the choice between greenfield investment and acquisitions. Forsgren (1985) argues that location, industrial structure and degree of internationalization would be crucial for the choice between these alternatives. Further he found that a greenfield investment would make it easier to keep existing relations to customers, suppliers etc, while acquisitions would make it less possible to do so. In many cases the companies started with a greenfield investment and then continued into an acquisition.

In the case of transport companies, however, in most instances a greenfield investment was taking over representation from an earlier agent leading to a competition between the new company and the former agent. Therefore many of especially the foreign customers and suppliers kept their relation to the local agent rather than to the focal company. On the other hand since many of the acquisitions were of agents these rather increased the possibility of retaining existing customers and suppliers.

Further, as the transport companies and the focal nets get more internationally interconnected, the choice between greenfield investment and an acquisition will rather depend not only on the location, the industrial structure and the degree of internationalization of the focal company but also the degree of overlapping between the acquired and focal nets. The choice between greenfield investments or acquisitions in a foreign country became quite another one in cases where they would have to fulfil an international role. However, in an international role, both an acquisition and a greenfield investment might create large connectedness problems but in different ways. For greenfield investments the problems are to find new relations in other countries not already tied up and for international acquisitions the problem lies in adapting the acquisition's existing foreign representatives in other countries to the new international net.

During the 1980's, as the companies had the capital available, they obviously chose mostly to acquire international companies. In this way they acquired a number of international O/C, C/O or O/O nets leading to many positively and negatively connected relations and transport systems. The degree of overlapping within existing nets gradually increased over time.

In this study, the greenfield investments often involved taking over some of the personnel from the former agent, which increased the possibilities of retaining existing relations to customers and suppliers. This is less possible in the case of acquiring a company, which is not the former agent. Moreover, when companies merge and many agents lack new representatives, the personnel might well take the initiative to start a new company together with agents, as in the Bilspedition case.

Timing and speed

First, in line with the reasoning in Johanson & Mattsson (1988), timing and speed differs depending on the firm being a "late starter" or an "early starter". Second, as companies are internationalized, however, the speed of penetration seems to be subject to the degree of overlapping and complementarity of the joining nets and existing part-nets rather than gradual growth. Basically acquisitions of any net will lead to increased penetration. The only exception is merging O/O nets. Over time, as acquisitions have increased, penetration has also increased but, as the number of O/O nets increases, mergers as well as the speed of penetration will be reduced and even decreased.

Third, the changes taking place in other countries will also have to be taken into account due to the necessity to balance resources between countries.

Fourth, as was discussed by Dunning (1989) specific location advantages are supposed to be combined with internalisation and ownership advantages. This is of very particular importance for transportation companies since the rules and regulations for transports as well as for transport companies have been many and rigid. Through the creation of the internal market within EC the size of relations in the dimension of penetration seem to play a more important role. Indirect relations from the focal companies' point of view or more direct relations within the net seem to be increasing in value.

In summary the establishment chain of the Uppsala School seems to support the overall changes of increasing commitment over time. However, this model does not comment upon what aspects of penetration that are changing and not on the decreases in some aspects of penetration taking place during 1980´s. The explanations to the changes of 1980´s are based on the degree of overlapping and complementarity between nets and the use of network advantages. The network advantages are difficult to get without making certain investments for the net in specific countries. Further, such investments also seem to be important prerequisite for continued integration This leads us to understand the importance of the interaction between integration and penetration.

11. A dynamic network model for internationalization

This model is based on a combination of empirical patterns of internationalization and basic driving forces to these patterns taken from the theoretical discussions.

The development according to the traditional gradual pattern of internationalizing has over time set the stage for a new different pattern of internationalizing through net changes. This has an impact both for continuation and start of internationalization. The new pattern increases the complexities and investments.

How the gradual pattern over time will lead to the new pattern used in the 1980's will be expressed in three different sequentially dependent phases. The behaviour is described in terms of integration, extension and penetration i.e. the three dimensions of internationalization.

The dominant patterns of changes in integration are based on the sequences presented in the event anlysis, both for systems and net level. Extension is shown as a result of integration which is also the case for penetration. Increases in penetration will further have an impact on integration which causes a continuation in internationalization once started. For all three dimensions speed and timing will be taken into consideration as an aspect of starting or continuing operations during the three phases.

The model will concentrate on the dominating changes over the period and not on all the parallel processes going on.
Finally, the driving forces to the internationalization process and their importance over time will be presented.

Phase 1 - gradual increase at system level (traditional pattern)

Period 1945-65

Integration: The changes are made through growth sequences at system level which are repeated over and over again. First the sequence concerns new cooperations in new countries and then it continues into several new cooperations within single countries. A gradual internationalization takes place.

Extension: The number of countries increases very much during this period. The majority of countries are geographically close.

Penetration: The growth in volumes is high and therefore the size of the relations grows. The spread of relations increases as the result of extension but also directly due to integration. The growth in volumes especially caused further increase in integration.

During this period the companies, whether they are starting to internationalize or continuing internationalizing, will be expected to follow the same growth sequence of integration only that they will have reached different stages in that sequence.

Phase 2 - Increased specialization and diversification of services (predominantly traditional pattern)

Period 1966-79

Integration: Single systems integration is combined with net changes. Through the patterns of internationalization at single system level (1-2-1) a net has been created. Opening up at net level increases internationalization. Now and then joining of nets interrupts and causes a sudden leap in the gradual changes. Drifting closer and away to/from certain representatives´ nets seem to increase as many new nets have been created.

Extension: The number of countries increases further and this time to countries not covered earlier in Europe. Then there is a continuation to the overseas countries as new services are developed. First degree of extension is still most common but secondary degree of extension increases during the period.

Penetration: There is an increase both in scope of relations and in new diversified relations through adding new types of services. Specialization will sometimes result in a decrease in size of relations taking goods from existing services. However, after a period both diversification and specialization will lead to an increase in size of relations through growth. Further the increasing internationalization of the subsidiaries will also add to an increase in size of relations. During this period there will probably be a difference between the development of a company starting to internationalize and a company continuing internationalization in the sense that the former will have more joining of nets in the process.

Phase 3 - net changes (new pattern)

Period 1980-90

Integration: Growth and change sequences at net level are totally dominating and within these sequences joining and leaving of nets will be the most common depending on the situation. The growth and change sequences at system level are results of changes at net level. Positive and negative connectedness and the increasing degree of overlapping between nets in the total network will lead to domino effects and a movement towards closing up for the nets.

Extension: The patterns of sequences will maintain the first degree of extension. The change will take place in secondary degree of extension. Moreover, extension is concentrated on large economically important regions like Western Europe or the Nordic countries or the Far East, etc rather than on individual countries.

Penetration: Penetration might decrease in favour of integration for an internationalized company since concentration to fewer agents and to subsidiaries will take place. A certain continued diversification in services like time-guaranteed transports, logistical services, etc., will also be behind an increase in scope of relations.

Starting up during this period will generally be achieved through joining of nets, first a C/C net and then others. Continuation can be made both through opening up or joining of nets but there will be an increasing amount of the latter.

Driving forces for the process
There are a number of driving forces which appear as important in the theoretical discussions. These are divided into driving forces being either predominantly internally or predominantly contextually driven. Some of these are subject to analysis in this study while others not. The internal driving forces are generated through the relations at system level and/or at net level. The contextual driving forces are generated from organizations being part not only of focal relationships and nets but to a larger extent of other relationships and nets being part of the same total network. Finally there are some important contextual driving forces added to this model which have not been subject to analysis in this thesis. The most important of these are customers´ internationalization and technical development.

Since this study includes changes taking place for the companies both internally and in the context we have chosen to combine the most important internal and contextual driving forces. The basic criteria for the choice of driving forces from the study have been that they are 1) repeated as important explanations in many different discussions 2) underlying many of the explanations, 3) initiating other driving forces to change and 4) seem to exist over all periods. All of these driving forces are accepted to continue to the extent that they might create a higher effectiveness for a focal transport company.

Some of the contextual driving forces are added even though they are not directly studied in this thesis. However, the reasons for their presence among the driving forces are that their importance has been mentioned several times in the study and that they are vital prerequisites for the internationalization processes of transport companies.

These driving forces interact in the development of this process of internationalization.

The most important driving forces are:

Internal -	Trust in relations Economies of scale and of scope Intangible assets (creation, development, access to, protection of)
Contextual -	Number of direct and indirect relations Positive and negative connectedness Expansion and internationalization of agents, suppliers, etc.
(Not directly studied in this thesis)	Customer internationalization and customer demands Technical development (means of transportation, equipment, etc) Rules and regulations International trade and economic situation Infrastructure

Even though they are all important driving forces they differ in importance during the phases.

Internal driving forces

Trust in relations and the stability it creates, is an extremely important prerequisite for the growth of single relations. Since internationalization of transport companies to a large extent is based on establishment and development of a large number of relationships trust is a vital force. This was especially the case during the first two phases of internationalization when single system integration was still vital for the development. Later when large nets are present each single case is of lower importance but the type and number of organizations by which they are trusted still affects the trustworthiness of the focal company in the network.

Economies of scale and of scope are both very important over the whole period but from different aspects. During the first period gains, of economies of scale dominate through growth in existing systems and adding more of transport systems of the same type. During phase 2, which involves specialization and diversification of services, economies of scope are present between different types of services and relations. In these cases economies of scope are gained through utilizing the same facilities, market knowledge and marketing resources, communication systems for different services, etc. During this period specialization resulted in economies of scope sometimes being reached at the cost of economies of scale. In phase 3 both economies of scale and scope are of importance since the demands of the customer on higher frequency in the transport systems have increased the importance of scale and the offering of alternative services is vital.

Intangible assets

The creation, development and protection of and obtaining access to intangible assets are important driving forces over time. During the 1950´s and 60´s the existing intangible assets of the focal company are developed and new assets are created in the more vital relationships. As the focal companies become related to an increasing number of organizations the intangible assets will be developed and spread over many relationships and their transport systems. In this way intangible assets create a higher interdependence between the companies in the net.

Over time, furthermore, the intangible assets, being strategic for the net, will be of importance to protect, especially from organizations being part of negatively connected nets. On the other hand, obtaining access to new strategic intangible assets might be important for future development and therefore new relations have to be added to the existing net. As valuable intangible assets are developed and become more specialized over time through different investments in know-how and relations, the companies in the nets are more aware of the risk of leakage and spillover which can take place. Therefore companies in a net will react more to changes in relations that will have an impact on negative or positive connectedness between nets. Through developing and protecting these intangible assets we create network advantages.are created

Contextual driving forces

The number of direct and indirect relations is an important contextual driving force. When starting to internationalize the number of relationships with international activities will increase the opportunities for the focal company to become internationalized. Later the number of direct relations will increase in trust, due to economies of scope and of scale and the development of intangible assets will increase the degree of internationalization over time. On the whole, the number of direct and indirect relations will play a very important role for the development into new areas and services. However, the ties to other companies are not only important for the possibilities to expand but they also create restrictions for developing into specific areas and services. Finally, as the total number of direct and indirect relations grows, the possibility to protect the intangible assets decreases which in turn might lead to closing up of the net.

Positive and negative connectedness and direction of changes of these are important for the development during all phases.
In the beginning, the very fact that the focal company in its relationships is positively connected to internationally related companies, either being directly part of the same transport systems or with other types of connections, seems to increase the probability that they internationalize over time. When changes occur in the conditions of effectiveness for the transport system the focal transport company might take the opportunity to internationalize or might be driven to do so. It

might even lead to a situation where these other companies are pushing them towards internationalizing.

In phase 2, the connectedness will lead to new conflicts and cooperations, due to the diversification and internationalization of subsidiaries, agents, suppliers and other partners. Therefore the situation will have to be rearranged in order to avoid conflicts leading to decreased effectiveness, the risk of the agent breaking the relation and to protect against leakage of intangible assets. As for the new cooperations, there might be a possibility to gain access to valuable intangible assets and reach economies of scope and scale by adding new resources.

In phase 3, when most transport companies are internationalized and/ or are part of international nets then the negative and positive connectedness between nets will be increasingly important for internationalization. These changes will be discussed in terms of the other nets which are overlapping or complementary in type of service and area covered (C/C, O/C, C/O or O/O). For companies starting to internationalize during phase 3 this is made through a C/C or O/C net while the changes and the effects of the nets being O/O,C/O,O/C or C/C will be of extreme importance for a company continuing the process. Further, the direction of net development in terms of connectedness is important. The companies might be drifting away or drifting closer and the expectations on future continued development in the same direction would cause companies to take certain proactive actions. Such expectations of changes positive and/or negative connectedness might lead to domino effects in the total network.

Expansion and internationalization of subsidiaries, agents, suppliers and competitors. The same type of changes and driving forces as described above are assumed to be applicable to the agents, suppliers, competitors etc. Especially the expansion of subsidiaries and agents into other areas geographically as well as into other services will either result in changes in the degree of overlapping or degree of complementarity between the organizations which will then forward internationalization in new directions. The fact that the agents, suppliers, etc., internationalize leads to an increase in the interdependence of the total network as well as helps to create possibilities for closer cooperations with certain trusted organizations while others will be left outside. This will lead to the development of nets.

Customer internationalization and customer demands are an important driving force for the internationalization of the transport companies. Changes in demands on more international transport and higher control of international systems have caused transport companies to internationalize and integrate their systems. The internationalization of single customers will be especially important in the beginning of the internationalization process while as transport companies grow internationally the demands of the customers will be of higher importance. The demands on new and more effective transport systems will stimulate the transport companies to move into new areas and services over time. Further, some of the services developed are based on taking over parts of the activities formerly performed by customers like warehousing, packaging, distribution, etc. As customers develop into MNE with international or global distribution networks this will have an impact on the continued internationalization of transport companies both in terms of what regions are of importance to cover and the service offers needed to be considered an important supplier.

Technical development creates opportunities and limitations for the transport companies. New types of systems have another reach, as in the geographical reach of the airplane in comparison to land-transports, etc. In other cases the development and diffusion of container technology changed the possibilities for the freight forwarders to control their goods and to further integrate in their systems. Therefore the technical developments create new opportunities as well as change the possibilities for differentiation within the systems and nets. Technical development leads to development of new services as well as gains in economies of scale and of scope, which will have effects on the existing services and changes of roles between transport companies.

Rules and regulations are important driving forces. If they are changed there are always some companies that can take advantage of the changes. After the war, trucking traffics were strictly regulated to shorter distances but when this was changed it started a wave of development of trucking transports. The expected harmonizations and deregulations have caused and will cause large changes in the opportunities and threats for the transport companies during the early 1990's.

Infrastructure, international trade and economic situation will also have an impact on the opportunities for transport companies and to the extent that they develop positively over time. More trade, better infrastructure and industrial growth would increase the possibilities for many transport companies to start or continue internationalization.

Conclusion

The patterns of changes and the driving forces seem to lead towards closing up after a long period of increased interconnectedness. If it continues this development would lead to a clustering of the network into separate nets and also increase the total level of integration in the network for transport business. The intention to develop and protect these clusters might lead to the domino effects. These domino effects break up existing clusters and lead to the formation of new clusters. However on the whole the clustering seems to increase. A simplified illustration of a the growth sequence and change sequence at net level is shown in figure 12.1.

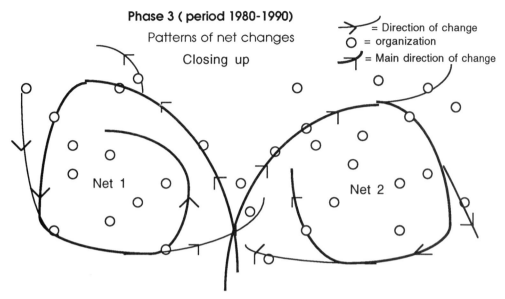

Figure 12.1. Patterns of changes at net level. Illustration of two nets closing up

The question is to what extent will this closing up continue? What factors might put an end to this tendency? Based on this, what conclusions concerning changes of the total network are possible to draw for the transport companies in the future? This will be discussed under continued research.

What are the available strategies for the future in such a situation? This will be discussed under Managerial Implications.

12. Managerial implications

The main interest in this chapter on managerial implications of the results, will be in formulating strategies based on the dynamic network model of internationalization. Furthermore interest will be focused on the new patterns of internationalizing. The strategies thus formulated should be regarded merely as ideas as to how it would be possible to adapt the reasoning in this thesis to management issues. Being mainly ideas to implications also signifiy that they are still formulated in the conceptual framework of this study and will therefore not be described in the everyday management language.

The model presented in chapter 12 will serve as a base both for an understanding of what changes are going on in the network and formulating strategies for a specific company and net. Further the basic concepts used are clarified in the model of analysis (chapter 4)

The strategies will differ depending on stages in the sequences of changes for transport companies showing typical ways of growing and changing found in the study (chapter 9). We will discuss the strategies for each stage of the sequence separately in terms of its driving forces and its specific problems and strategies. This will serve as a base for a more general strategy formulation. The type and strength of driving forces are especially important both for choosing suitable organizations for cooperation and for continuation of the stage. The final generalization of strategies will summarize the sequences of changes in the form of general comments and three basic factors. These are content, speed and timing.

12.1. Expansion and growth (the growth sequence at net level)

Joining of net (s)
This is a very open stage where the number of direct and indirect relations to other organizations is high and the level of integration in the net relatively low. An example of joining nets is when a focal international company is acquiring another international transport company. The interaction with companies outside the existing net will be very high. Positive and negative connectedness will be shifting. Former competitors may turn into partners and vice versa. The effects on suppliers, competitors, partners etc. will not have had time to settle though.
During this stage the potential gains due to economies of scale and of scope from the change have not been realized and the new strategic intangible assets of the net not developed. The spillover and leakage of existing strategic intangible assets are probably high since trust in many relationships is not yet established and the borders of the net are not yet clear.
Important strategies for the specific company in this stage would be to search for knowledge and information about the total network through the existing relationships as well as to search

for valuable intangible assets such as critical knowhow, design of transport systems etc. that could be developed and spread in net at a later stage in the sequence. It seems important to establish trustworthy relations to the representatives showing these future capabilities.

A way to identify a suitable net to join would be through using the contact net of the existing direct and indirect relations to owners, suppliers, representatives etc as well as the knowledge and information of those contacts.

Closer cooperation

The stage of closer cooperation is focusing more on existing relations than the former one and is also less exposed to changes and effects outside the net. The strategic intangible assets should be developed in existing relations and adapted to or changing the existing systems. An example could be creating a new communication system that is to be used by a large number of companies cooperating in the net. The gains from economies of scale and of scope in existing relationships will be exploited and standardization and formalization will be present to a larger extent. This stage will be very important for the establishment of trust in the relationships but at the same time internal conflicts will become more obvious. This will affect the degree of positive and negative connectedness between representatives in the net. One of the effects of this stage might be that the focal company will drift closer to other nets through the closer cooperation with some of the existing agents. This will be a possible indicator of future relations to develop .
Exploitation of all possible economies of scale and of scope and the development of strategic intangible assets within the existing relationships, would be typical strategies in this stage.

Closing up

A net closing up will become increasingly interconnected. A typical example would be when a focal transport company, their subsidiaries and very close agents to a larger extent cooperate with each other excluding others. It is probable that a common image for the net is created. During this stage there is intensive homogenization within the net in terms of systems design but heterogeneity in terms of the roles of companies and their representation for different areas. This implies that economies of scale and scope are continuously exploited and the profitability increasing. The possibility for a company to change its position is limited in the network since the network effect of such a change would be considerable.

The strategic intangible assets are well protected, due to greater distance to other nets. The disturbances from organizations outside the net will have to be strong in order to impose changes since the companies are so interconnected. During this stage there will be a spread of the intangible assets and a continued homogenization and hierarchization will take place. The existing positive and negative connectedness within the net will be very clear. Companies not willing to adapt and to invest in common resources, will have to leave.

Very high stability and trust could be a problem, in that it might lead to a stagnation and decrease in the value of the intangible assets. It should therefore be necessary to increase the search for new strategic intangible assets and to continue development within the existing relationships. In spite of the high stability and the relatively low impact of much of the changes in the context, companies should be very much aware of what changes are going on since a disruption to their stability would be costly.

If the closing up will achieve successful results other actors of other nets will probably imitate the way of internationalizing. This will in turn be a reason for continuing the process of closing up.

12.2. Reducing cooperation (The change sequence at net level)

The change sequence on net level is usually less clear in its form than that of the growth sequence. However it is very important when it comes to forming strategies, since it concerns divesting in the set of existing cooperations and preparations of a new base for growth.

Drifting away

Drifting away from another net is based on decreased priorities put to cooperation with certain agents which also are tied to one another or to other nets.

This stage is important merely for its first indication of changes in priorities going on. It does not change relationships more than marginally but it points at the direction of changes in terms of overlapping or complementarity of nets. Being aware of these changes would seem to be very important for a company. Risk of leakage or spillover of important intangible assets might be the reason behind these changes. It has an impact on the distance to indirect relations. Drifting away seems to be an indicator of cooperation between companies when cooperation is either already loosened and/or becoming looser in the future.

Looser cooperation

The stage of looser cooperation might develop due to depreciation of valuable intangible assets, decreasing economies of scale and of scope or to disappearance of certain network advantages. Further it might be a result of decrease in trust, change in priorities and an increase in competition between companies.

However depending on the length and strength of the cooperation such companies may be interested in finding a new common solution. Sometimes there will be a change and a looser cooperation will not continue into leaving net.

Crucial factors here are if cooperating companies desire to continue their relationships or not, the cost of breaking a relation and the number of alternative cooperations available. If this stage shall continue into that of leaving the net, it has to be planned. If there is a a reason and will to continue the relationships it will be likely to continue into a stage of closer cooperation instead of dissolution.

A strategy for this stage might be to look for the underlying changes causing this situation and see if it is possible to regain lost economies of scale, of scope and of intangible assets or if new alternatives have to be found.

Leaving the net

This stage will differ very much in time depending on the amount and type of resources and relations involved in the restructuring. Leaving a number of cooperations almost simultaneously will normally be costly. Furthermore, the compatibility between probable new resources and of the existing resources will be of importance. The learning cost for a new alternative and the possibilities to exploit the existing skills and know-how will be important.

Where will the existing net or part net go ? Will a substitution be found easily for the focal company or will it be necessary to wait and invest in order to find new representatives? In some cases there may even be special costs associated with breaking contracts when leaving the net. The divestment costs for leaving a net will vary, depending on the situation.

There is a high instability in this phase, not only for the companies involved but also for other indirectly involved companies. The effects on the context will be large and domino effects might be present. Therefore the necessary investments might increase drastically compared to what is expected. The costs involved of a drawn out process might be very high. Thus a quick outcome can be vital.

12.3. General strategies and dimensions adapting to specific company situation

An important general strategy would be *to follow the growth sequence through* in order to get the necessary gains. If disruptions are likely it would seem important to go through the change sequence as fast as possible. In order to avoid too many disruptions, the creation of part-nets, smaller net within the total focal net, will make it more likely to be able to follow the growth sequence towards closing up. However the general strategy will have to be modified depending on the situation of the company in question. Further there are the three basic factors of content, speed and timing according to which strategies are changed or modified to fit the situation of a specific company.

Content

The content of a stage can be changed in order to make the stage include or exclude more/less of or different resources and relationships in different areas.

This will be important in the cases when companies seem to think that the stage offers more or less than intended or expected. For example in the case of joining nets, more and different resources are added with the purpose of increasing the gains in economies of scope and scale within the existing relations. This would lead to an increase in content. In other cases the reverse situation might be present.

Speed

Speed can be slowed down by the actor and therefore delaying the next stage or it can be accelerated. Both cases seem to be of high importance in relation to changes of the context. Slowing down/delaying can be used when there exists a wish to delay the next phase. Delaying can be made through twisting rules in contracts, or finding any excuses not to enter the next stage. One important reason might be that a company can foresee that they have to leave the net but finding new alternatives is difficult. Another reason might be that the company does not want to become more dependent on a specific net.

Speeding up on the other hand, aims to get all the possible gains from the on-going stage but during a shorter period. This seems to be extremely important when it comes to the costly stages like joining nets, leaving net or looser cooperation. Speeding up into stage of closer cooperation and closing up is necessary in order to get a better profitability.

Timing

Being part of a changing context makes timing extremely important. Following what is happening to other companies and other nets is vital in order to make use of the opportunities and risks that will stem from these. As the context constantly changes, the timing of when to join or leave a net or when to proceed into the next stage in the sequence seems to have a large impact not only on the possibility to act but also on the effects of the action. Therefore the timing for a specific company of moves in and out of the stages in the sequences, will influence the possibility to use the changes going on in the total network instead of being subject to the effects of them.

12.4. Conclusions

An important conclusion for the specific company as well as for the net is to continue the growth sequence from the stage of "joining nets" into that of "closing up". The changes taking place on the way are likely to have a positive impact on profitability and create a stronger postition of the company and net in the total network. For a single company the main factors used for changing their position would be the content, the speed and the timing of the stages in the sequence.

Further, the choice of cooperation for each company will be determined by the type and strength of driving forces involved.

The change sequence which basically concerns a potential divestment should by necessity be as short as possible either by a return into closer cooperation with the same partner or by dissolving the cooperation with the adaption to the new partner in mind.

The strategies formulated here assume that the companies are aware of their situation in a net as well as of their relations to other nets.

13. Continued Research

The findings of this thesis pose a number of questions that would be of interest for continued research. Some questions of importance concern the problem of generalization based on case studies while others concern development of existing theoretical research. We have chosen to focus on questions related to the network model of internationalization, the industry dynamics involving domino effects, on forces that serve to stop the further internationalization processes and finally on the interaction between the transport companies and some of their customers in the process of internationalization. We start by discussing the model of internationalization involving the changes of patterns of sequences and driving forces.

The dynamic network model of internationalization

First, to what extent can the model be generalized and applied to other types of companies? In the model of internationalization the companies concerned change their pattern of internationalization over time. The sequences that they are part of differ depending on the context. The notion of companies being part of nets and changing through these rather than as separate companies would be of interest to study for other type of service companies like banks, insurance companies, advertising agencies etc. Is the same phenomenon present for them as for the transport companies?

Further, it would be of interest to know whether the suggested network model on internationalization can be applied to manufacturing companies. Many researchers applying the industrial organization approach have formulated a need for further research which takes the higher interdependence within the context into account. At the same time network researchers have formulated an interest to continue into creating a dynamic model of internationalization. Distribution researchers look upon distribution systems as networks in order to be able to combine sets of distribution systems and to discuss the interaction within and between these.

Second, a question of importance concerns how the model is related to that of the choice of, development of and the interaction of the driving forces. Are there any other driving forces which seem to be of equal importance as the ones mentioned here?

Third, there seems to be many interesting questions for further studies as regards each of the specific driving forces. Some of these will be further elaborated here.

Trust, which is a very important concept in the network approach, is a relationship phenomemon. An interesting question is to what extent other relationships in a network have an impact upon trust in a specific single relationship. It seems in this study that the knowledge and information that are available in networks (Granovetter 1985) will play both a positive and negative role for trust between the companies in the network.

Another question is the protection of intangible assets and the boundaries of a net. What is of importance as regards the intangible assets when it comes to setting border of a net? If the intangible assets are important for the choice of actors taking part in closing up they would probably also have an impact on the design of the net as well as its borders.

Further as was discussed in the dynamic model of internationalization the scale of economies and scope of economies seem to play different roles over time. Are these changes typical for other service companies as well as for manufacturing companies?

Another matter is the influence on internationalization of direct and indirect relationships. There has been a number of network studies concerning the importance of having a high number of indirect relaions for development into new areas. This seems to be a fruitful way of looking upon internationalization for companies especially as they start to internationalize.

Finally, the behaviour in the past seems to set restrictions on how the company can internationalize. For example the degree to which companies develop overlapping nets with their agents through subsidiary internationalization will have effects on the possibilities of future growth of their existing relationships and their abilities to select new representatives in other areas. Therefore the past behaviour of establishing subsidiaries limits their possibilities to develop in the future. This past dependence would be of interest for further studies.

Industrial dynamics and domino effects
The domino effects is a phenomenon worth studying to a much deeper level. The high interdependence between companies that is the cause of these effects lead to a new type of industry dynamics. Similar types of effects might be experienced in several other industries like banking, insurances and advertising. In this thesis we have only followed some cases and from the perspective of internationalization. An interesting question would be to find out the costs of domino effect-related network changes and how the negative effects could be reduced. Finally studies of domino effects should involve their influence on the total network.

Another interesting field to study would be to continue on the idea of "network theories" developed by Johanson & Mattsson (1992) and discuss to what extent the domino effect induce and is a result of changes in "network theories" of the actors in a network.

What are the forces that will stop the movement towards closing up and further internationalization?
What are the forces that will lead to a decrease in terms of internationalization and how will that influence the situation of a specific company? We have seen in this study that sometimes companies decide to decrease in one dimension of internationalization for a shorter period in order to get future gains. However in some cases there might be decisions to decrease the

degree of internationalization for a longer period. Some of the interesting questions related to this concern the basic reasons for such a development and if the driving forces are the same.

Interaction between transport companies and their customers in the process of internationalization

We know that international transport systems are interdependent with manufacturers' international distribution systems. It would be of interest to find out when and to what extent the changes going on in the transport systems are caused by underlying changes in the international distribution systems and how the manufacturing industry takes transport alternatives into consideration when internationalizing? Such studies on the interaction between transport and manufacturing companies would indicate what importance the effectiveness of the transport systems and the design of net of the transport companies will have for manufacturers´development. and also indicate how internationalization of a transport company influences that company´s capacity for customer orientation and its cooperative strength

References

Achrol, R. & L. Stern, 1988. "Environmental Determinants of Decision-Making Uncertainty in Marketing Channels".Journal of Marketing Research , Vol. XXV (Febr.), pp. 35-50.

Aharoni, Y., 1966. The Foreign Investment Decision Process. Boston, Mass., Harvard University.

Alderson,W., 1954. "Factors Governing the Development of Marketing Channels". In Clewett, R.M.(ed), Marketing Channels for Manufacturing Products. Homewood, III; R.D. Irwin.

Alderson, W., 1965. Dynamic Marketing Behavior. Homewood, Ill; Richard D. Irwin.

Aldrich, H. & D.A. Whetten, 1981. "Organization Sets, Action Sets and Networks: Making the Most of Simplicity". In Nyström, P.C. & W.H. Starbuck (eds), Handbook of Organization Design, Vol. 1. New York; Oxford University Press.

Anderson, E.& H.Gatignon, 1988. "The Multinational Corporation´s Degree of Control over Foreign Subsidiaries: An Empirical Test of a Transaction Cost Explanation". Journal of Law, Economics and Organization IV:2.

Anderson, E. & B. Weitz, 1986. "Make or Buy Decision: Vertical Integration and Marketing Productivity." Sloan Management Review, (Spring).

Astley, W.G., 1985. "The Two Ecologies: Population and Community Perspectives on Organization Evolution". Administrative Science Quarterly, 30, pp. 224-241.

Astley, W.G. & C.J. Fombrun, 1983. "Technological Innovation and Industrial Structure". Advances in Strategic management, Vol,. 1, pp. 205-209.

Axelsson, B., 1992. "The Future". In Axelsson B.& G. Easton (eds)Industrial Networks- A New View of Reality. London; Routledge.

Bagozzi, R.P., 1975. "Marketing as Exchange". Journal of Marketing, 39 (Oct), pp. 32-39.

Bailey, E.E.& A.F. Friedlaender, 1982. "Market Structure and Multiproduct Industries". Journal of Economic Literature,Vol. XX (Sept), pp. 1024- 1048.

Ballou, R.H., 1987. Basic Business Logistics. Englewood Cliffs. N.J.; Prentice Hall.

Bartlett, C.A., 1986. "Building and Managing the Transnational". In Porter, M.(ed), Competition in Global Industries. Cambridge, Ma; Harvard Business School Press.

Betancourt, R. & D.A. Gautschi, 1986. "The evolution of Retailing A suggested Economic Interpretation". International Journal of Marketing 3, pp. 217-232.

Bilkey,W.J. & G.Tesar, 1977. "The Export Behaviour of Smaller - Sized Wisconsin Manufacturing Firms", Journal of International Business (Spring/Summer), pp. 93-98.

Bilkey, W.J., 1978. "An Attempted Integration of the Literature on Export Behaviour of Firms". Journal of International Business, No. 9, pp. 33-46.

Breyer, R.F., 1950. "Some Observations on "Structural" Formations and the Growth of Marketing Channels". In R. Cox et.al.(eds), Theory in Marketing. Chicago; R.D. Irwin.

Browne, M.J., 1991. Prospective Freight Mega-Carriers: The Role of Information Technology in their Global Ambitions. 24th Hawaii International Conference of System Sciences Jan., 1991.

Buckley, P.J. & M.C. Casson, 1976. The Future of the Multinational Enterprise. London; The Macmillan Press.

Bucklin, Jr. J.C., 1960."The Economic Structure of Channles of Distribution". In M.Bell (ed), Marketing: A Maturing Discipline. Chicago; American Marketing Association, pp. 379-385.

Burt, R.S., 1980. " Models of Network Structure". Annual Review of Sociology 6, pp. 79-141.

Calvet, A.L., 1981." A Synthesis of Foreign Direct Investment Theories and Theories of the International Firm". Journal of International Business Studies, Vol. 12, No..1, pp. 43-59.

Carlson,B., 1990. Den amerikanska avreglreringsvågen. Stockholm; SNS Förlag.

Casson, M., 1987. "General Theories of the Multinational Enterprise: A Critical Examination". In The Firm and the Market. Cambridge Ma; MIT Press.

Casson, M.1990. Enterprise and Competitiveness- A Systems View of International Business, Oxford; Clarendon House.

Caves, R.E., 1971. "International Corporations: The Industrial Economics of Foreign Investment". Economica ,Vol. 38, pp. 1-27.

Caves, R.E., 1982. The Multinational Enterprise and Economic Analysis. Cambridge; Cambridge University Press.

Chandler, A.D., 1962. Strategy and Structure . Cambridge, Mass; MIT Press.

Chandler, A.D., 1977. The Visible Hand- The Managerial Revolution in American Business. Cambridge, Mass; Harvard Press.

Chandler, A.D., 1990. Scale and Scope - The Dynamics of Industrial Capitalism. Cambridge, Mass; The Belknap Press of Harvard University Press.

Chisholm, D., 1989. Coordination without Hierarchy: Informal Structures in Mukltiorganizational Systems. Berkeley CA; University CA Press.

Coase, R.H., 1937. "The Nature of the Firm". Economica 4 (Nov).

Cook, K.S., 1982. "Network Structures from an Exchange Perspective".In Marsden, P.V.& N. Lin (eds), Social Structure and Network Analysis. Beverly Hills; Sage Publications.

Cook, K.S., & Emerson R.M., 1978. "Power, Equity and Commitment in Exchange Networks". American Sociological Review 43, pp. 721-739.

Cook, K.S , R.M. Emerson, M.R. Gillmore & T. Yamagishi, 1989. " The Distribution of Power in Exchange Networks: Theory and Experimental Results." American Journal of Sociology, Vol. 1989, No. 2, pp. 275-305.

Coughlan, A.T., 1985. "Competition and Cooperation in Marketing Channel Choice: Theory and Application" .Marketing Science, 4:2 (Spring) pp. 110-129.

Cox, R., 1965. Distribution in a High-Level Economy. Englewood Cliffs N.J.; Prentice Hall.

Cummings, TH.G., 1984. "Trans-organizational Development". Research in organizational behaviour, Vol..6, pp. 367-422.

Comén, L-G, 1988. The Airfreight in Sweden and World Wide - Forecasts and Trends. Stockholm; TFB. (Swedish Transport Research Board) Report 1988:7.

Dixon, D.F. & I.F.Wilkinson, 1986."Toward a Theory of Channel Structure". In Research in Marketing,Vol. 8, pp. 29-70.

Dunning, J.H., 1977. " Trade, Location of the Economic Activity and the MNE- A Search for an Eclectic Approach". In Ohlin, B., P-O Hesselborn & P.M. Wijkman (eds) The International Allocation of Economic Activity. London; Macmillan.

Dunning, J.H., 1988. "The Eclectic Paradigm of International Production - A Restatement and some Possible Extensions". Journal of International Business Studies XIX, (1) pp. 1-31.

Dwyer, F.R., P.H.Schurr & S.Oh, 1987. "Developing Buyer-Seller Relationships". In Journal of Marketing Vol. 51, pp. 11-27.

Dwyer, F.R. & A. Welsch, 1985. "Envronmental Relationships of the Internal Political Economy of Marketing Channels". Journal of Marketing Research 12 (Nov.) pp. 397-414.

Easton, G. 1992. "Why Networks?" In Axelsson, B & G. Easton (eds), " Industrial Networks - A New View of Reality". London; Routledge.

Easton, G.& P.Smith, 1984. " The Formation of Internorganizational Relationships in a Major Gasfield Development". Research Seminar on Industrial Marketing, Stockholm School of Economics, Sweden.

Englund, M., 1990. Inter-organisatoriska Informationssystem.- En utvärdering av potentialen i fem svenska fall av datoriserad kommunikation med kunder. Stockholm; IMIT at the Stockholm School of Economics.

Eisenhardt, K.M, 1989. " Building Theories from Case Study Research". In The Academy of Management Review, Vol. 14, pp. 532-550.

Emerson, R.M., 1962. "Power Dependence Relations". American Sociological Review 27, pp. 31-40.

Emerson, R.M., 1972. "Exchange Theory, Part II: Exchange Relations in Networks". In J. Berger, M. Zedditch & B. Andersson (eds), Sociological Theories in Progress.

Emery, F.E. & E.L. Trist, 1966. "The Causal Texture of Organizational Environments", Human Relations, 18, pp. 21-32.

Etgar, M., 1977. Channel Environment and Channel Leadership. Journal of Marketing Research. 14 (Febr.), pp. 69-76.

Fombrun, C. J., 1982. "Strategies for Network Research in Organizations ". Academy of Management Review, Vol. 7: 2, pp. 280- 291.

Fombrun, C.J., 1986. "Structural Dynamics within and between Organizations" <u>Administrative Science Quarterly</u> 31, pp. 403-421.

Forsgren, M., 1985. "The Foreign Acquisition Strategy - Internalisation or Coping with Strategic Inter-dependencies in Networks?". University of Uppsala. <u>2nd Open International I.M.P. Seminar on International Marketing,</u> Sept-4-6.

Forsgren, M.& J. Johanson, 1990. "Managing International Networks". In <u>Swedish Council for Management and Work Life Issues.</u> Report No. 11.

Forsgren, M., 1990. "Managing the International Multi-Centre Firm". <u>EMJ,</u> Vol .8 No 2.

Forsgren, M. & U.Holm, 1990. "Internationalization of Divisional Management in Swedish International Firms". In <u>Swedish Council for Management and Work Life Issues</u>. Uppsala; Uppsala University.

Forsgren, M. & N.Kinch, 1970. <u>Företagets anpassning till förändringar i omgivande system. En studie i massa och pappersindustrin.</u> ACTA Universitatis Upsaliensis; Studia Oeconomica Negotiorum.

Frazier, G.L., R.E. Spekman & C.R. O´Neal, 1988. "Just-In-Time Relationships in Industrial Markets". <u>Journal of Marketing</u> (Oct.), Vol. 52, pp. 52-67.

Gadde, L.O. & L-G Mattsson, 1987. "Stability and Change in Network Relationships". In <u>International Journal of Research in Marketing,</u> 4, pp. 29-41.

Goshal, S. & N. Nohria, 1987. "<u>Multinational Corporations as Differentiated Networks</u>", Cambridge Mass; MIT.

Granovetter, M., 1973. "The Strength of Weak Ties: A Network Theory Revisited". <u>American Journal of Sociology,</u> Vol .78:3, pp. 3-30.

Granovetter, M., 1985. "Economic Action and Social Structure: The Problem of Embeddedness". In <u>American Journal of Sociology</u> (November).

Gundersen, H., 1975. <u>NSB- med Linjegods i lasten</u>. Oslo; Pax Förlag A/S.

Hammarkvist, K-O., H. Håkansson & L.-G. Mattsson, 1982. <u>Marknadsföring för Konkurrenskraft.</u> Malmö; IVA, MTC och Liber Förlag.

Hedlund, G. & Å. Kverneland, 1984. "Are Establishment and Growth Patterns for Foreign Markets Changing?" Stockhom School of Economics; Institute of International Business.

Heide, J. & A. Miner, 1990. The Shadow of the Future: The Effect of the Anticipated Interaction and Frequency of Delivery on Buyer-Seller Cooperation. Working Paper.

Henders, B., 1992. Positions in Industrial Networks - Marketing Newsprint in the U.K. Uppsala Universitet (Dissertation)

Hertz, S., 1992. "Towards more integrated Industrial Systems". In Axelsson, B. & G. Easton (eds), Industrial Networks - A new View of reality. London; Routledge.

Hirsch, S., 1976. "An International Trade and Investment Theory of the Firm" Oxford Economic Paper, Vol. 28, pp. 258- 270.

Hymer, S.H., 1960. The International Operations of National Firms: A Study of Direct Foreign investment. Cambridge, Mass.; MIT Press.

Håkansson, H. &C. Östberg, 1975. Industrial Marketing and Purchasing of Industrial Goods: An Interaction Approach. Chichester; J.Wiley.

Håkansson, H., 1982. International Marketing and Purchasing of Industrial Goods: An Interaction Approach. Chichester; J Wiley.

Håkansson, H., 1987. Industrial Technological Development: A Network Approach. London; Croom Helm.

Håkansson, H. & A. Lundgren, 1992. "Industrial Networks and Technological Innovation". In Möller, K.E. & D.T. Wilson (eds), Business Marketing : An Interaction and Network Aproach. Boston; PWS Kent (forthcoming).

Hörnell, E., J-E. Vahlne & F. Wiedersheim-Paul, 1973. Export och utlandsetableringar. Uppsala; Almqvist & Wiksell.

Johanson, J. & L-G.Mattsson, 1984. "Internationalization in Industrial Systems -A Network Approach". Paper presented at Prince Bertil Symposium, Nov 7-9 at the Stockholm School of Economics, Stockholm.

Johanson, J. & L-G Mattsson, 1992. "Network Positions and Strategic Actions - An Analytical framework".In Axelsson, B.& G.Easton (eds), Industrial Networks- A New View of Reality. London; Routledge.

Johanson, J. & L-G. Mattsson, 1987. "Interorganizational Relations in Industrial Systems -A Network Approach compared to Transaction Cost Approach". Interorganizational Studies of Management and Organization, Vol. XVIII, No. 1 pp. 34-48.

Johanson, J., L-G.Mattsson, P.Sandén & J-E. Vahlne, 1978." The Role of Knowledge in the Internationalization of Business". In Social Sciences Faculty Book in Honor of the 500th Anniversary of the University of Uppsala, pp. 27-45.

Johanson, J. & I. Nonaka, 1983. "Japanese Export marketing: Structures, Strategies and Counter Strategies". In International Marketing Review, No. 1, pp. 12-25.

Johanson, J. & J-E. Vahlne, 1977. "The Internationalization Process of the Firm- A Model of Knowledge Development and Increasing Foreign Market Commitments". Journal of International Business, 8 (Spring/ Summer), pp. 23-32.

Johanson, J. & J.-E. Vahlne, 1990. " The Mechanism of Internationalization". In International Marketing Review, Vol.7, No. 4, pp. 11-23.

Johanson, J. & F. Wiedersheim-Paul, 1974. "The Internationalization of the Firm - Four Swedish Case Studies". Journal of Management Studies, 3 (October), pp. 302-322.

Kang, Rae Cho, 1985. Multinational Banks - Identities and Determinants. UMI Research Press.

Kindleberger, C.P., 1969. American Business Abroad: Six Lectures on Direct Investment". Yale University Press.

Klein, S., G. Frazier, V. Roth, 1990. "A Transaction Cost Analysis Model of Channel Integration in International markets". Journal of Marketing and Research (May).

Kogut, B., 1983. "Foreign Direct Investment as a Sequential Process". In Kindleberger, C.P. & D. Andretsch (eds), Multinational Corporations in the 1980s. Cambridge, Mass.; MIT Press.

Knickerbocker, F.T., 1973. Oligopolistic Reaction and Multinational Enterprise. Boston. Harvard University.

Knoke, D.& J.H. Kuklinski, 1983. Network Analysis. Beverly Hills; Sage University Press.

Laage-Hellman, J., 1989. Technological Development in Industrial Networks. Uppsala University; Department of Business Studies; Uppsala (Dissertation).

Laage-Hellman, J. & P. Smith, 1992. "Small Group Analysis in Industrial Networks". In Axelsson, B. & G. Easton (eds), Industrial Networks- A new View of Reality" London; Routledge.

Liljegren, G., 1988. Interdependens och dynamik i långsiktiga kundrelationer- Industriell försäljning i nätverksperspektiv. Stockholm; EFI/ MTC.

Lincoln, J.R., 1982. "Intra (and Inter-) Organizational Networks". Research in Sociology of Organizations Vol. 1, pp. 1-38.

Lindholm, S., 1979. Vetenskap, verklighet och paradigm. Stockholm; Almqvist & Wiksell Förlag AB.

Lindqvist, M. "Infant Multinationals - The Internationalization of Young Technology - Based Swedish Firms. Institute of International Business; Stockholm School of Economics (Dissertation).

Ljungström, B., 1986. Strategier för planering av transportsystem. Stockholm. TFK Rapport 1987:7.

Lovelock, C.H., 1984. Services Marketing. Englewood Cliffs N.J.; Prentice Hall.

Lundgren, A., 1991. Technological Innovation and Industrial Evolution - The Emergence of Industrial Networks. Stockholm; EFI (Dissertation).

McInnes, W., 1964. "A Conceptual Approach to Marketing". In R. Cox et. al.(eds), Theory in Marketing. Homewood Ill.; R.D. Irwin.

Magee, S.P, 1977. "Information and Multinational Corporation: An Appropriability Theory of Direct Foreign Investment". In Bhagwati, J.(ed), The New International Economic Order The North-South Debate. Cambridge, Mass.; MIT Press.

Mallen, B., 1964. "Conflict and Cooperation in Marketing Channels". In G. Smith; Reflections on Progress in Marketing. Chicago; American Marketing Association.

Marret,C., 1971. "On the Specification of Interorganizational Dimensions". Sociology and Social Review, pp. 83-89.

Marsden, P.V., 1981. "Brokerage Behaviour in Restricted Exchange Networks". In Marsden, P.V. & N. Lin (eds), Social structure and Network analyses. Sage Publications.

Martinez, J.I. & J.C. Jarillo, 1989. "The Evolution of Research on Coordination Mechanisms in Multinational Corporations". Journal of International Business Studies, (Fall).

Mattsson, L-G., 1969. "Integration and Efficiency in Marketing Systems". EFI, Stockholm; Nordstedt & Söner (Dissertation).

Mattsson, L-G., 1984, "An Application of a Network Approach to Marketing: Defending and Changing Market Positions". In N. Dholakia & J. Arndt (eds), Alternative Paradigms for Widening Marketing Theory. Greenwich CT; JAI Press.

Mattsson, L-G., 1986. "Indirect Relations in Industrial Networks. A Conceptual Analysis of their Strategic Significance". 3rd International I.M.P. Research Seminar at Lyon, Sept 3-5.

Mattsson, L.-G., 1987a. "Conceptual Building Blocks of Network Theory". Working paper.

Mattsson, L-G., 1987b. " Managing of Strategic Change in a 'Markets as Networks' Perspective". In A. Pettigrew (ed), Management of Strategic Change. London;Basil & Blackwell.

Mattsson, L-G., 1988. "Interaction Strategies - A Network Approach". American Marketing Association (Summer), Marketing Educators' Conference, San Francisco, Aug. 7-10.

Mattsson, L.G., 1992. "Marketing Perspectives and International Business". Conference on Perspectives on International Business: 'Theory, Research and Institutional Arrangements', University of South Carolina, May 21-23.

Miller, J.W., 1982. The Philosophy of History - with Reflections and Aphorisms.London; W.W. Norton & Company.

Mitchell, J.C., 1969. Social Networks in Urban Situations. Manchester;Manchester University Press.

Nordström, K.A., 1991. The Internationalization Process of the Firm - Searching for New Patterns and Explanations. Stockholm School of Economics, Stockholm; Institute of International Business and K.A. Nordström (Dissertation).

Normann, R., 1985. Service Management - Ledning och strategi i tjänsteproduktion. Stockholm; Liber Förlag.

Palamountain, Jr. J.C., 1955. Distribution: Its Economic Conflicts. Reprinted from The Politics of Distribution. The President and Fellows of Harvard College.

Pavitt, K. 1971. "The Multinational Enterprise and the Transfer of Technology". In Dunning J.H (ed), The Multinational Enterprise. London; Allen & Unwin.

Pettigrew, A.M., 1985. "Contextualist Research : A Natural Way to Link Practice with Theory". In Lawler et. al. (eds), Doing Research that is useful in Theory and Practice. San Francisco; Jossey Boss.

Pfeffer, J. & G.R. Salancik, 1978, The External Control of Organizations - A Resource - Dependence Perspective. New York, N.Y; Harper & Row, Publishers.

Porter, M.E., 1990. The Competitive Advantage of Nations. London and Basingstoke; Macmillan Press.

Ramberg, J., 1983. Spedition och fraktavtal. Stockholm; P.A. Nordstedt & Söners Förlag.

Rask, L-O., 1984. Det strukturella armodet - organisationsteori för åkeriföretag. Lund; Studentlitteratur.

Regnell, H., 1982. Att beskriva och förklara. Lund; H. Regnell and Bokförlaget Doxa AB.

Reve, T., 1986. "Organization for Distribution". In Research in Marketing Vol .8, pp. 1-26.

Revzan, D.A., 1961. "Marketing Organization Through the Channel". In Wholesaling in Marketing Organization. Chichester; John Wiley & Sons.

Shepherd, W.G., 1984. "Contestability vs Competition". The Americal Economic Review, (Sept), Vol. 74, No. 4.

Silverman, F. & J. Jones, 1976. Organizational Work- The Language of Grading the Grading of Language. London; Collier Macmillan.

Stern L.W., 1969. Distribution Channels: Behavioral Dimensions. Boston; Houghton Mifflin.

Stern, L.W. & A. El-Ansary, 1988 (3rd ed), Marketing Channels. Englewood Cliffs, N.J.; Prentice Halls International Inc.

Stern L.W. & T. Reve, 1980. "Distribution Channels as Political Economies - A Framework for Comparative Analysis". Journal of Marketing, Vol. 44 (Summer).

Stopford, J.M. & L.T. Wells, 1972. Managing the Multinational Enterprise. New York; Basic Books.

Stock, J.R. & D.& M. Lambert, 1987. Strategic Logistics Management. Homewood Ill.; R.D. Irwin.

Sölvell, Ö., 1987. "The Entry Barriers and Foreign Penetration- Emerging Patterns of International Competition in two Electrical Engineering Industries". Institute of International Business. Stockholm School of Economics (Dissertation).

Tarkowsky, J. & B. Ihrestähl, 1988. Transport administration. Lund; Studentlitteratur.

Toyne, B., 1989. "International Exchange - A Foundation for Theory Building in International Business". Journal of International Business Studies XX (1), (Spring) pp. 1-17.

Törnebohm, H, 1977. Kontextuellt tänkande. Rapport no 89. Avd. för Vetenskapsteori, Göteborgs Universitet ; Göteborg.

Van de Ven, A. & G. Walker, 1984. "Dynamics of Interorganizational Coordination". Administrative Science Quarterly, (Dec.), p p. 598-621.

Van de Ven , A., 1976. "On the Formation and Maintenance of Relations among Organizations". Academy of Management Review, 1 (4), pp. 24-36.

Vernon, R., 1966. "International Investment and International Trade in the Product Life Cycle". Quarterly Journal of Economics, Vol. 80 (May) pp. 190-207.

Vernon, R., 1979. "Product Cycle Hypothesis in a New International environment". Oxford Bulletin of Economics and Statistics,41, pp. 255 - 267.

Vernon, R. & L.T. Wells, Jr, 1976. Economic Environment of International Business. Englewood Cliffs, N.J.;Prentice-Hall.

Weick, K.E., 1979. The Social Psychology of Organizing (2nd ed), Newbery Award Records Inc., New York; Random House.

White, H.P.& M.L.Senoir, 1983. Transport Geography. Essex England. Longman Group Ltd.

Wilkinson, I.F., 1990."Toward a Structural Change and Evolution in Marketing Channels". In Journal of Macromarketing (Fall).

Williamson, O.E., 1971. "The Vertical Integration on Production: Market Failure Consideration". American Economic Review 61, May.

Williamson, O.E., 1985. The Economics of Institutions of Capitalism. New York; The Free Press.

Young, L., 1992. The Role of Trust in Interorganisational Relationships in Marketing Channels. University of New South Wales (Dissertation)

Zeithaml, V.A., A. Parasuraman & L.L. Berry, 1985. "Problems and Strategies in Services Marketing". Journal of Marketing (Spring) ,pp. 33-46.

Appendix 1

<u>ASG case</u>

Primary sources of information

Interviews: B. Jönsson (President, formerly responsible for European Division)

B. R. Hansen (Vice Pres. - responsible Overseas Division)

R. Teltscher (Dir. European Division)

B. Stödberg (Man.Dir. of the subsidiary Road Ferry /former Traffic mgr.

of Continental Division, board member of ASG Belgium)

A. Brunninckx (Man.Dir. of ASG Belgium)

L. Enquist (Traffics Mgr. of special European markets)

J. Andresen (Man.Dir. of ASG Deutschland)

R. Müller (Man. Dir. of Atege Stuttgart)

R. Hertz (former Manager of Overseas Division)

W. Rueger (responsible for Sweden traffics by Natural AG)

H. Bell (Director of Natural AG)

R. Wilton (former Man.Dir. of ISA)

H. Larsson (former Man. Dir. of ISA, Vice Pres. of Bilspedition)

Other persons contributing with information material

E.   Westling (form. Man. Dir. of ASG Belgium, former Mgr. of European Repr. Office)

A.   Lundström (Finance Mgr. member of the board of many international subsidiaries)

M.   von Baumgarten (ASG advertising, information)

M   Hellström (Administration)

Secondary sources of information

Annual Reports 1967-90

Sales Material, pamphlets etc

Earlier reports on specific topics (concerning agent representation, WACO, company planning etc)

Lists of representatives: Europe 1976, 1979, 1988 and 1990

Overseas 1974, 1976, 1983, 1988, 1989,

Protocols from meetings

ASG Internal magazines

Articles, interviews in papers, etc

Bilspedition case

Primary sources

Interviews: M. Lundberg (President, Bilspedition Group)

E. Sterner (Man.Dir. European Division Scansped)

B. Madsen (President Scansped Group)

L. de Leeuw(Man. Dir. Scansped Belgium)

I. van Beurden (Administration, Scansped Holland)

L. Törnqvist (Man. Dir.Scansped Sweden)

J.P. Blumröder (Finance Dir. Scansped Germany)

H. Kuhlmann (Man. Dir.Gebr. Hellman, Osnabrück)

Other sources contributing with information

S   Osvald (Dir.Group Corp. Communications)

D.   Fagring (Dir. of information Scansped Group)

R.   Rux (Scansped Group)

A-C   Kutzner (Administration Scansped Sweden)

Secondary sources of material

Annual Reports 1960-91

ACC Group - ett kvartssekel

Special information 1983, 1985, 1990/91 invitation to buy new shares

Pamphlets and sales material (Scansped Group, Scansped Belgium, Scansped Holland, Bilspedition and Gebr. Hellman)

Scansped Magazine

Lists of international representatives: Bilspedition 1967, ATA 1988, Wilson 1988, SkandiaTransport/ F&L 1988, Scansped 1989

Articles in magazines and papers: Affärsvärlden, Dagens Industri, etc.

Inter Forward

Primary sources

Interviews::   H. Bergström (President Inter Forward)

A. Sörås (Senior Vice President Inter Forward)

G. Stolpe (Senior Vice President Inter Forward)

E. Scherer (Former Man. Dir. Züst & Bachmeier)

N. Fischer (Dir. Züst & Bachmeier, Stuttgart)

G. Wild (Dir. Züst & Bachmeier, Nürnberg)

A Herzog (Fin. Dir. Züst & Bachmeier)

H. Johannecken (Man. Dir. Züst & Bachmeier)

L.W.H. Leibbrand (Man.Dir. Amas Holding)

H. Wildeman (Man. Dir. Intern. Exped.Copex)

A.M. Hageman (Man.Dir.Copex Air)

Other sources contributing with information

K. Åström (Fin. Dir. Inter Forward)

L. Larsson (former Man.Dir. NAC, special responsibility Züst& Bachmeier reorganization)

R. Teltscher (Dir. NTS Gen. Cargo)

G. Glimstedt (Controller Inter Forward)

Speeches and discussions at the Inter Forward Group Conference June 1989 in Stockholm

Secondary sources

Annual Reports 1988-1991 Inter Forward, NTS 1989, Ratos 1988

Inter Forward Group Conference material

Sales Material and Pamphlets (Amas, Z&B, Copex Air, IASA, NTS Denmark)

Lists of international representation 1985, 1989

Articles in magazines and papers

Interview Guide

Letter to President

Internationalization of the transport companies from a network perspective   - S. Hertz
(Economic Research Institute at the Stockholm School of Economics)

Febr. 1989

Interview guide

General

The interviews are semi-structured and therefore I only present the different areas that I
would like to talk about. It is up to the person interviewed to decide how they want to
comment on the area in question.
Hopefully I can perform these discussions with persons from different levels in the
organisation (for ex.1-2 persons at group level, 2-4 persons at divisional level and 3-6
persons concerning a specific event more in detail). If the company agrees I would also
like to meet some long-standing customers and find out how they have reacted to
changes made by the transport company over a period.
Each interview will take at least two hours.

Group level

My main interest here is to find out historically how the Group has grown internationally
over a period and how the network of companies with which the Group is cooperating or
competing has changed over a period. It would also be of interest to be given a
description of the important events for the Group over a period when internationalizing.

Question areas:

1.   Facts about the Group

Type of services (basic, complementary)
Type of resources(means of transportation,terminals,know-how, personnel, etc)
Type of organization (functional,divisional, etc.)

Changes over a period concerning services,resources and transport systems in amount
and size and in strategic importance for the Group.

Material like annual reports ,organization charts and other descriptions of the Group and
its development over a period are important as a complement.

2.   Business policies for internationalization of the Group concerning

services offered
resources (owned,controlled in other ways)
representation abroad
management
financing
info/communication system
etc.

Change over a period and reasons for change.

External or internal reports and statements concerning policies are examples of material that could support the discussions.

3.   The Group and the network

3.1   Task environment

Customers
Partners/agents
Suppliers
Competitors
Others (like different authorities,banks etc)

Relationship characteristics (cooperative ventures,conflicts, dependencies,contacts etc.)
Number of years that other companies have existed in the specific categories. Strength in
the relationship to the Group.
Changes in respect of the companies within these categories in the exchange in
responsibility, in payment/compensation, information/communication and in the flow of
goods, etc

3.2   Other parts of the network of interest

Other types of transport companies (not direct competitors)
Other types of industry
Other types of suppliers within the field (not mentioned above)
Other partners/agents
Others

Existing connections between these other parts of the network and the companies in the
task environment (over a period of time).
Change over a period in how these companies have been connected in groups or smaller
nets of companies.
Positive or negative relations between the different constellations of companies.

Material that could be of help would be details of change in market shares over a period,
brochures, possible other reports of historical value concerning cooperations , contracted
agreements, conflicts, etc.

4.   Specific events of importance for the Group

Criteria for importance of the events. Possible reasons for the change.
Materials of interest here can be historical reports, statements, etc.

 Level II - a specific unit of the Group (like a division)

The interest is focused on how the unit has changed internationally over a period.

1.   Facts about the unit

Type of services/traffic systems
Volumes
Sales
Profitability
Investments (in different types of resources)
organization
etc

Development over a period of these variables.

Materials of type annual reports,brochures, etc would facilitate.

2.   The unit in the Group over a period

Reasons for being a separate unit
Cooperation and conflicts with other units in the Group
Borderlines between the units

3.   Business policies of the unit

Type of resources
Type of representation abroad
Type of management
Type of info./communication system, etc

Changes over a period

4.   The international representation

Location of the different type of traffic systems/services
Location of fully or partly owned or controlled in other ways representation
Location of partners
Location of suppliers involved
Other companies of importance

Characteristics of the relationships
Changes over a period in location of,type of,importance of, etc
Reasons for change over a period
Conflicts with the unit over a period
Criteria for choice-change over a period
Cooperations and conflicts between the different partners,suppliers, etc

Lists of representation abroad from different periods of time would be valuable.

5.   Customers

Long term relations /short term relations
Type of
  Development
  Geographical spread
Importance to the unit

Changes over a period.

Internal or external articles or reviews, etc., that present different customers and their
relationship to the unit would be of interest.

6.   International net

Characteristics of the systems
Flow of goods
Technical development
Marketing
Personnel
Responsibility
Compensation/payment
etc

Changes in efficiency over time

Materials that could be of help are internal or external articles that discusses the changes in and objectives of efficiency.

7.   Activities

Who controls what in the different systems generally?
Who is doing what?
Who has the customer contacts?

Changes over a period

8.   Initiatives to change in services /traffic systems

Starting new
Divestment

Reasons ?

9.   Cooperative ventures/conflicts

Between different groups of companies that the partners or suppliers are connected to?
Effects on the unit?

10.   Specific events of importance

New partners
New suppliers of importance
New technology
New services, etc
with high importance on the unit

Causes, adaptions, etc

Level III A specific event concerning a specific country

What is important to know in this case is what happened before, during and after the event.
It is probable that the persons who have the detailed knowledge about the event have only parts of what has happened. Therefore the interviews have to be adapted to the specific person and his/her knowledge.
The different questions that I would like to cover in these interviews are presented below in a summarized version.

Question areas

1. Reasons for the event

2. The importance of the country to the Group or the unit in question

3. Initiative to the event

4. Before the event

4.1 Facts

Type of traffic systems/services
Type of activities performed
Resources involved for the different activities
Organization
etc

Different internal and external reports and statements are important as a complement

4.2 Relations of importance for the traffic systems/services in the specific country

Partners (in the country or in other countries)
Suppliers   -"-
Customers   -"-
Other parts of the Group
Other actors

Characteristics of the relations
Long term relationship
Conflicts in the relationship

5. During

Different stages of the event
Actions taken
Resources involved

Timing, size and effects short term

6.   After the event

6.   1 Facts

See 4.1

6.2   Effects on relations see 4.2.

        Change in cooperative ventures, conflicts, dependencies, etc

7.   Effects on business policies for the unit and the Group

Example on event level

(Slightly adapted to the situation, the same interviews were made in Swedish and German.)

I   The international development of the Amas group before the t akeover of Inter Forward

1.   The start of the Group/ company

When was the company established? Why?
What was the basic business idea?

2.   How has the company or the Group developed internationally since then?

2.1.   What type of countries have come to be involved?
        In what order?

2.2.   What type of businesses have been developed?

2.3.   What means of transportation has been involved ?
        How has this changed over a period?

2.4.   What type of agents did the company have? Have there been any changes in the policies towards agents?

2.5.   When was the first subsidiary or representative office started ? Where? Why?
        How has this changed over time?

2.6.   What did the network of agents and subsidiaries look like before IF took over?

3.   How have the relations to the suppliers of transport services changed over a period?

4.   Resources and investments

4.1.   What are the basic areas for investments?
4.2.   Where have you invested internationally? In what?

5.   Industry and Customers

What type of industry and companies were your customers at the start ? How has this changed over time?
Who are the most important customers today?

6.   What were your basic strengths and weaknesses before the takeover?

II The takeover

1.   What was the basic reasons for selling the Group/company?

2.   Why Inter Forward? Did you have any contacts with IF companies before the takeover?

3.   Did you consider any alternatives?

4.   How did it come about? (in practice)

III After the takeover

1.   What were the effects from the takeover ? (Direct and indirect effects)

1.1.   Externally?
        The agents?
        The customers?
        The competitors?
        The suppliers like trucking companies, etc?
        Other?

1.2.   Internally?

Organization?
Marketing?
Services? traffics?
Administration?
Financially?
Communication systems?
Reactions from employees?
etc

1.3.   Were the effects as expected?

--

How do you think that EEC changes will affect your Group/ company?

Direct via changes in regulations, rules, etc

Indirect via agents, customers, competition, etc

Have any of the companies cooperated in some country with any of the Bilspedition companies, for example Scansped Group or ASG companies?

Appendix 2: Glossory and lists of transport companies

Glossory of transport terminology

Loads/ goods

Break-bulk =	Traditional method of freight handling. heterogeneous cargo packed into cases cartons, drums etc of an infinite sizes and shapes. Each package handled separately when loaded. This is basically performed in terminals and more or less mechanized.
Consolidation goods =	Normally 100- 1000kg
Full load=	The total capacity of the carrier is filled.
Unitload=	when package loads is partially consolidated into larger units of uniform dimensions and which can be easily transferred at low cost from one transport morde to another.
FCL=	Full Container Load
LCL=	Less than container load
Parcel load=	1-100kg
Part load=	1-5 tons
Bulk=	Consisting homogeneous cargo shipments of single commodities such as pertroleum, vegetable oils, grains,ores etc.,

Type of transports

Traffic =	Transport system utilizing any mean of transport
Long-distance transport=	More than 200 km
Local transport =	Pick up/ Collecting and Delivery (sometimes distribution is used)
Direct traffic=	A direct transport system from one area to another. From there on local transports will take place
Direct goods/ transport =	Goods without terminal handling
Customized traffics=	A transport system especially designed for a specific customer.
International traffic=	Consists of both local and long distance transports
Full load traffic=	A traffic that goes direct from a shipper to a receiver.

Unit load traffic=	A traffic based on unit loads of containers, trailers, flats etc. Such a traffic can easily use and switch between different means of transportation
Consolidation/ groupage traffic or LCL traffic =	A transport system based on is break-bulk goods. If it is a trucking or LCL traffic it might also include part loads.
Combi-traffics =	A combination between different means of transportation like air-sea, road-rail, air-road, etc. In most cases it is based on unit loads.
Project transports=	The transport company taking on these type of transports normally include both consluting, planning, transport and customs clearance for large specific industrial projects like turn-key investments etc.. The transports are taking place during a time limited period and might involve several different countries.

Organizations

FIATA =	Federation internationale des Association Transitaires Assimilés The international forwarders Association
IATA =	International Air Transport Association- a voluntary organization for scheduled airlines.
NSF=	Nordic Forwarders Association
Shipper=	Consignor=Sender of the goods
Receiver=	Consignee= Receiver of the goods
Forwarder=	A forwarder does no normally own the means of transport. They have traditionally been an organizer and avdisor to the shipper or receiver of transport as well as the performer of the transport documentation.
Border Broker=	A forwarder located at the border specialized in handling customs clearance and brokerage.
Customs Broker=	A forwarder specialized on import documentation
NVOCC=	Non-Vessel -Operator-Common-Carrier

Documentation

Terms of delivery=   Regulate the responsibilities of and costs to be carried by seller and buyer. Mostly used is the internationally accepted Incoterms.Examples Ex Works, Free Carrier, Free-on -Board, Ex ship, Delivered at Frontier, Delivered Duty paid etc

Terms of payment=   Cash on Documents(COD), Letter of Creditt(L/C), Cash on Delivery (C/D) etc.

NSFAB=   Common Conditions for forwarder´s responsibilities in the Nordic Countries.

Bill of lading=   Freight document

Airway bill=   Freight document for airtransport

Facilties, equipment

Container =   Standard sizes 20´(6,06m) and 40´(12,12m)

Trailer =   Standard size 12,5 m -on wheels.

Flat=   A standard sizes length: 6,06m, 6,6m and 7,15m. Legs can be attached.

Terminal =   A station for sorting and reloading of basically break-bulk goods and for changing from local to long-distance transports. Shorter warehousing is often included. Possibilities for shippers and receivers to collect or leave their goods. The goods can be repacked

Pallets=   A wooden, aluminium or plastic base made for goods which is adapted to and facitlitates handling by fork lifts.The EUR pallet (1200mm x 800mm)

Operational structures of transport systems

Network system =   Direct traffics between different local terminals. In Europe this is the dominating operational structure until the end of 1980´s.

Central terminal=   There are several local terminals but only one central terminal. All traffics go via the central terminal and all long distance traffics go to/from the central terminal. Some of the large parcel companies are using this type of operational system.

Hub-Spoke system/

Sattelite system=   A heirarchical system where the londistance transports go between head terminals. Is similar to a very concentrated network system. Common in U.S.for domestic transports.

Others

Cabotage=   The right for a foreign transport operator to take on domestic t ransports in their traffics.

Sources

Abrahamson & F. Sandahl, 1992. *Internationella Transporter och Spedition* Malmö; Almqvist & Wiksell

Jensen, A., 1987. *Kombinerade Transporter i Sverige- system, ekonomi och strategier.* TFB Report 1987:9

Ljungström, B., 1986. *Strategier for planering av transport system.* TFK: Report 1986:7 (Huvudrapport och bilagor)

Ramberg, J., 1983. *Spedition och Fraktavtal.* Stockholm; P.A. Nordstedts &Söner.

Tarkowsky, J.& B. Ihreståhl, 1988.*Transport Administration* . Lund; Studentlitteratur

White, H.P. &M.L. Senior,1983.*Transport Geography.* London; Longman

Cont Appendix 2

The largest transport companies in Europe - passenger and freight (ranked by sales) in 1988

Company		HQ (Country)	Type of activities	Sales ($)[1]	Employees	Profit[2]
1.	DB	D	Rail	15,2	268.176	(-1.789)
2.	SNCF	F	Rail	7,8	223.202	(- 163)
3.	BA Plc	GB	Air	7,6	43.617	478
4.	Lufthansa	D	Air	6,6	49.056	133
5.	P&O Co	GB	Sea/road etc.	6	55.600	565
6.	Air France	F	Air	5,8	42.663	290
7.	BR	GB	Rail	4,6	154.748	201
8.	Danzas AG	CH	All types	4,6	13.400	72
9.	SAS	S	Air	4,4	35.600	604
	(Schencker)	W-G	All types	4	11.500	450)
10.	SB	CH	Rail	3,2	37.210	28
11.	SJ	S	Rail	3,1	41.700	(1)
12.	Bilspedition	S	All types	3	9.500	83
13.	Swissair	CH	Air	3	17.910	51
14.	Iberia	E	Air	3	27.305	0
15.	Alitalia	I	Air	2,9	18.453	59
16.	Kühne & Nagel[3] CH		All types	2,9	8.868	23
17.	KLM	NL	Air	2,8	22.257	157
18.	NFC Plc	GB	All types	2,7	31.800	161
19.	Chargeurs SA	F	All types	2,6	22.126	191
20.	Nedlloyd	NL	Sea/road etc.	2,5	21.500	73
22.	van Gend & Loos NL		All types	2,4	7.900	n.a.
24.	Panalpina AG	CH	All types	2,2	6.800	2
25.	Lep Group Plc	GB	All types	1,9	8.300	33
26.	Hapag Lloyd	D	Sea/air etc.	1,8	7.700	63
35.	Swedcarrier	S	All types	1,4	10.500	58
44.	Kühne & Nagel	D	All types	1,1	3.700	16
46.	TDG Plc	GB	All types	1,0	13.100	74
	(ASG	S	All types	1,0	4.500	25)
50.	SCAC	F	All types	1,0	9.400	1

Source:: U.N International Classification Standard by ISIC: Industrial codes 71, Transport and Storage

---

1	Billion dollars
2	Million dollars
3	International

List of the largest transport companies in Europe (ranked by sales) in 1977

Companies		HQ	Activites	Sales(DM)[4]
1.	DB	D	Rail	16, 9
2.	SNCF	F	Rail	11,6
3.	BR	GB	Rail	6,5
4.	FS	I	Rail	5,7
5.	BA	GB	Air	5,2
6.	Lufthansa	D	Air	4,6
7.	Air France	F	Air	4,5
8.	Danzas AG	CH	All Types	4,0
9.	P&O	GB	Sea/Road	3,8
10.	SJ	S	Rail	3,7
11.	Schenker	D	All Types	3,6
12.	NS	NL	Rail	3,2
13.	Kühne & Nagel[5]	CH	All Types	3,0
14.	Swissair	CH	Air	2,7
15.	SB	CH	Rail	2,6
16.	KLM	NL	Air	2,6
17.	SAS	S	Air	2,5
18.	Chargeurs	F	All Types	2,4
19.	SNCB	B	Rail	2,4
20.	Hapag-Lloyd	D	Sea	2,2
21.	Nedlloyd	NL	Sea/ road etc	2,2
22.	ÖB	A	Rail	2,1
23.	Panalpina	CH	All Types	2,1
24.	Altialia	I	Air	2,0
25.	RATP	F	Rail/bus	1,9
32.	Scansped	S	All Types	
44.	ASG	S	All Types	
50.	Bilspedition	S	All Types	

[4] Bill. German Mark (Exchange rate)
[5] International AG

APPENDIX 3

Enclosure 1

Countries	**Subsidiaries (minority and majority) in Europe**

Denmark
ASG Dk -59(air)   100%_____
TK Nord-89/91(land)   10%_65%
West-Germany
ASG Hamburg-60(land)[6] 100%_____
Atege Stuttgart-76(land/air)   100%_____
ASG Bielefeld-87(land)   100%____
ASG Deutschland-76/ -91(hold.comp)   100%_____70%
Horst Wiedeman GmbH-89   _100%
Atege Germany -91   30%
Finland
Finnexpress-68(land)   25%_____20%_____/
 decrease of shares-75
ASG Finland-88(air/sea)   100%___
-90-(land included)
Norway
NG-Globe-71-74   70%___
Air Contact -77   100%_
Flygods-79(air)   65%_____100%_____
 increase in shares- 85 named ASG(Norge)A/S
Nordex-85 (land)   60%_100%___
 increase in shares -86 and named ASG(Transp. & Sped) A/S
ASG two Norwegian comp. merged
Belgium
ASG Belgium-77(land)   76%_____100%_____
 increase of shares -83
U.K.
ASG U.K.-80 (air)   100%_____
Switzerland
Nova traffic-84 (air/ sea)   _____
Holland
ASG Intern B.V.-89(holding)
100%
Sweden based
Road Ferry(land)   50%_____100%_____
Confracta-72/73(land)   37,5%_____50%/
increase in shares -88
sold -89 to Faxxion(J/V)   40%_
ERT -79(land)   100%_____
                    1959/60--------------------70--------------------80------ --------------90
                                                                                                        Year

6In 1976 ASG Hamburg formally changed its name to ASG (Deutschland)
GmbH and Atege Stuttgart became a part

ASG - Net of representation of Europe (agents, Group companies etc)
1967 landtransportation(excl air)

Number of

Austria	2
Belgium	1
Bulgaria	1
Denmark	1
East Germany	1
Finland	1
France	8
Great Britain	2 (1 sales office)
Greece	1
Hungary	1
Ireland	
Italy	1
Yugoslavia	1
Luxembourg	
Netherlands	1
Norway	1
Poland	1
Portugal	
Rumania	1
Sovjet Union	
Switzerland	1
Spain	1
Czechoslovakia	1
West-Germany	20-25(1 subsidiairy)
Sweden	
Total	48-53

ASG - Net of representation of Europe (agents, Group companies etc)
1976 and 1989 landtransportation(excl air)

Number of	1976	1989
Austria	2	2
Belgium	2 (1 sales office)	1 (Group)
Bulgaria	1	1
Denmark	1	1
East Germany	1	1
Finland	1 (J/V)	1 (J/V)
France	8	1
Great Britain	1	1
Greece	1	1
Hungary	1	1
Ireland	1	1
Italy	1	1
Yugoslavia	1	1
Luxembourg		
Netherlands	1	1
Norway	1	1
Poland	1	1

	1989	1976
Portugal	1	1
Rumania	1	1
Soviet Union	1	3
Switzerland	1	1
Spain	1	1
Czechoslovakia	1	1
West-Germany	18(2 Group)	3(1 Group)
Sweden		
Total	**49** (2 Group,1J/V,1 S.O)	**28** (2 Group,1 J/V)

ASG - Net of representation of Europe (agents, Group companies etc)
airfreight   1989 and 1976 (within brackets same as landtransp.)

	Number of 1989	1976
Austria	1(same)	1_(same)
Belgium	1	1
Bulgaria	1 (same)	
Denmark	1(Group)	1(Group)
East Germany	1_(same)	
Finland	1(Group)	1J/V (same)
France	1	1
Great Britain	1(Group)	1
Greece	1	
Hungary	1 (same)	
Ireland		1
Italy	1 (same)	2_(1 same)
Yugoslavia	1	
Luxembourg		
Netherlands	1	1
Norway	1(Group)	1
Poland	1(same)	
Portugal	1_(same)_	1
Rumania		
Sovjet Union		
Switzerland	1(Group)	1
Spain	1	1
Czechoslovakia	1_(same)	
West-Germany	1_(same)	1
Sweden		
Total	20 (5 Group)	15 (1 Group, 1 J/V)
No of the agents	9	2

the same as landtransports

ASG West-Germany -1989[7] (ASG Hamburg,Atege Stuttgart, ASG Bielefeld)

Net of representation of Europe (agents, Group companies etc)
(excl air)

Number of

Austria _____1_____
Belgium_____1(not the Group company)_____
Bulgaria_____ _____
Denmark_____ 2(1 same as parent)_____
East Germany_____ _____
Finland_____2_____
France_____ 5(Stuttgart, Bielefeld)_____
Great Britain_____ _____
Greece_____
Hungary_____
Ireland_____
Italy_____ 1(same as parent)_____
Yugoslavia_____ _____
Luxembourg_____
Netherlands_____ 1(changed from parent agent to a new)[8]___
Norway_____ 2 (1 Group company)_____
Poland_____1_____
Portugal_____
Rumania_____
Sovjet Union_____
Switzerland_____2_(1 the same as parent)_____
Spain_____
Czechoslovakia_____
West-Germany_____
Sweden_____ 1 (Parent company)_____
Total   19

Natural - Switzerland

Net of representation of Europe (agents, Group companies etc)
(excl air/sea) 1989

Number of

Austria _____ 1_____
Belgium_____ 1(subsidiary)_____
Bulgaria_____ _____
Denmark_____ 2_____
East Germany_____ _____
Finland_____ 1_____
France_____direct distribution_____

---

[7]In the beginning of 1976 before the acquisition of Atege ASG Hamburg was the only subsidiary in West-Germany and their only had three international traffics Denmark, Holland and Sweden. As the new terminal was opened in Hamburg the international traffics were increasing in number.

[8] The former ASG agent van Gend &Loos was acquired by Nedlloyd Group. AS Nedlloyd acquired Uniontransport in West-Germany the cooperation with ASG had to cease. ASG started to cooperate with a subsidiary to the Belgian agent instead.

Great Britain_____	1 (sister company)_____
Greece_____	1_____
Hungary_____	
Ireland_____	1_____
Italy_____	direct distribution_____
Yugoslavia_____	
Luxembourg_____	1_____
Netherlands_____	3_____
Norway_____	1 (ASG)_____
Poland_____	
Portugal_____	1 (sister company- same agent as ASG)_____
Rumania_____	
Sovjet Union_____	
Spain_____	3 (1 sister company)_____
Czechoslovakia_____	
Turkey_____	2_____
West-Germany_____	1_____
Sweden	_1 (ASG)___
Total	21 + Italy and France (direct distribution)

Net of representation outside Europe

1989, 1981 and 1976 airfreight and seafreight

Countries	**1989**	**1981**	**1976**
North America			
USA_____ __	6(2 Group) [9]___	4 (1 J/VGroup, 1 S.O)_3_____	
Canada_____	1_____	2__	_____3 (1 S.O.)_
Far East			
Hong Kong_____	1(Group)_____	2 (1 Group)____ _	1(J/V Group)__
Singapore_____	2 (1 Group)[10]___	3(1 S.O.) _____	2_____
Japan_____	3 (1 Group)_____	2 (1 Group)_____	1_____
Taiwan_____			1_____
China_____	2 (1S.O)_____		
Thailand_____	1_____	1_____	1(J/V Group)___
India_____	1_____	2_____	1_____
Australia			
Australia_____	2 (Group)_____	1(Group)_____	1_____
New Zealand_____	1_____ _____	1_____	1_____
Africa			
Tanzania_____	1[11]_____	1(Group)_____	
Kenya_____	1[12] (J/V Group)_	1 (Group)_____	

---

[9] Within brackets means out of which 2 are ASG Group companies

[10] A company was acquired during 1989 by ASG

[11] ASG company sold to personnel and continue as agent

[12] ASG Kenya was changed from fully to partly owned

South Africa	1		1
Nigeria	1	1	1
Uganda	1		

South America

Brazil	1	1	
Argentine	1	1	
Colombia		1	1
Venezuela	1	1	

Middle East

Iraq	1	1	
Iran	1	1[13]	
Jordan	1		
Kuwait	1		
Saudi Arabia	1	1	1
Total	**33**	**26**	**19**

---

[13] To Iran there were also a trucking traffics

Appendix 4

Bilspedition- organization 1960´s

Before 1967

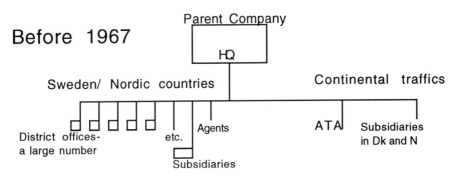

Parent Company

HQ

Sweden/ Nordic countries

Continental traffics

District offices-
a large number

etc.

Agents

Subsidiaries

ATA

Subsidiaries
in Dk and N

1967
Eight districts and centralization of invoicing, bookkeeping as well as selling
and traffics to the larger central offices of the district.

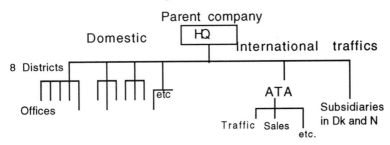

Parent company

HQ

Domestic

International traffics

8 Districts

Offices

etc

ATA

Traffic Sales

etc.

Subsidiaries
in Dk and N

1970

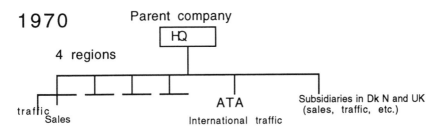

Parent company

HQ

4 regions

traffic
Sales

ATA

International traffic

Subsidiaries in Dk N and UK
(sales, traffic, etc.)

Continued centralization to the regional offices for sales, bookkeeping, etc.
Sales for domestic as well as international traffics became centralized to the regional
offices in Sweden. ATA basically became only an operational company without sales.

Bilspediton -organization 1970´s and 80´s

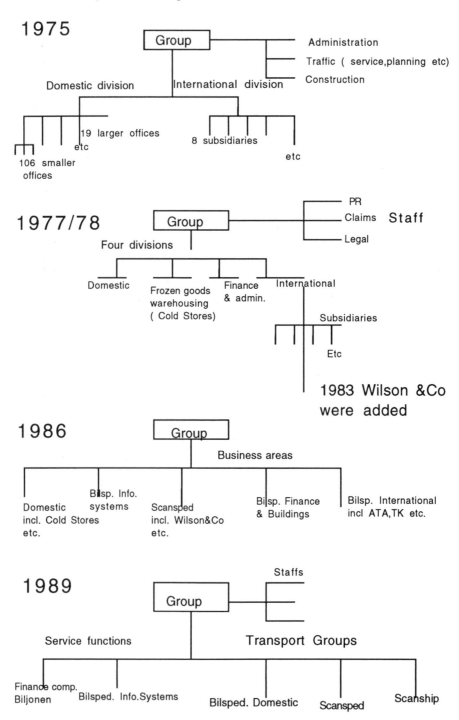

Cont. Appendix 4 - Enclosure 2

In 1967/68 GBS (Bilspedition) had the following representation in Europe

Country	Representation
Austria	Scandinavia-Austria Express Autotransport GmbH Wien
Benelux	Rederij van Swieten N.V., Amsterdam (ceased 1969)
Denmark	Nordisk Bilspedition A/S (subsidiary)
France	Mory. S.A. , Paris
Finland	Kaukokiito Oy
Hungary	Hungarocamion (start 1968)
Italy	Transmare S.I.T.R., Milano
Luxembourg	Lentz, Luxembourg (start 1968)
Norway	Skandinavisk Bilspedition A/S (subsidiary)
Poland	Pekaes, Warsaw
Switzerland	Autotransit A.G. Internationale Spedition , Basel

West-Germany
   Hamburg   Otto Longuet, Intern. Sped (ceased 1969)
   Ashaffenburg Joh. Birkhart, Intern.Sped.
   Stuttgart   Franz Lebert & Co Intern. Sped.
   Hannover   Karl Nelke Sped.
               Bilspedition Sales office (start 1968)

U.K.   Continental Ferry Trailers Ltd (ceased -69)
              Atlas ExpressLtd
              Eurofreight, London
              Trailer Express Ltd (1968 - a subsidiary)

International subsidiaries of Bilspedition

Time -year   60_____70_____80_____90

Denmark
1.Nord. Bilsped/ATA -57   (50%)---- 61(100%) --/
2. SGS -70(50%),-83(100%)   50%------------------------------------- 100%
3. Flygspedition 71/72(59%)   -50%-- -100%---
1974 (100%)
4. Eurotrans -79-83(100%)   100%--/
5.Danish Express Co -83-86   100%---/
6 Scandinavian Aircargo-85-86(100%)   100% -/
6. Scanflight A/S-87   100%---
7. Adams Transport -87(100%)   100%-----
8. Scansped Denmark-88(100%)   100%-

Norway
1.Skand Bilsped/ATA-57(50%)   50%---100%--------------------------------60%--------/
1961(100%), -84(60%)
2. SGS -70(50%),-83(100%)   50%-------------------------------100%----------
3. Linjegods -84(20%)   20%
4. Skandiatransport-85(100%)   100%----/
5. Scandinavian Rail Cargo-85(100%)   100%----
6 Scanship-86(100%)   100%
7. Skand. ADR Transport-86(57%) -88(100%)   100%-------
8.Scansped-88/89(100%)   100%-

Finland
1.Autotransit OY-87-88(49%)   49%---/
2.Scansped Oy-88(95%)   95%
3.Speditor Group-90 (100%)   100%
4.Transocean OY-88(100%)   100%-

Belgium
1.Autotransit NV (73)87-88(100%)   100%--
/
2.West-Friesland NV-86-87(100%)   100% -/
3.Scanroute NV-87-88(50%)   50%--/
4.Castra NV -85-89(100%)   100%--/
5.SA Carion freres-85-89(100%)   100%--/
6.Scansped/carion Freres-90(100%)   100%--/

Holland
1.Trailer Exp/ATA-72-88(100%)   100% ------------------------------/
2.West-Friesland-85/86   100%-
3.van Casteren-85-88(100%)   100%--
/
4.Multiport BV/Continex -82/83   100%-/
5.Transit Internationale -82-88(100%)   100%--/
6.Scansped Holland BV-89-(100%)   100%-
7. Autotransit Representation Office Europe
8. Cool Carriers -87(100%)   100%
9.Incotrans BV-87(50%),-88(100%)   50%100%

France
1.Nord Express SA-85-88(100%)   100%------/
2.Carion Freres SA-85-88(100%)   100%------/
3.Scansped/Nordexpress-89(100%)
100%
4.Scansped/Carion freres-89(100%)
100%

Italy
1.Autotransit Srl-77(40%),82(100%)   ----------------------------------/
sold-89
2.IncotransSrl -88(100%)   100%

Poland
Scanpol-90(50%)
50%

Switzerland
1.Autotransit AG -79-88(40%)   40% ----------------------------------/
2.Incotrans AG-87(100%)   100%--
3. Scansped AG-89(100%)   100%-

UK
1.Trailer Express Ltd-68-75(100%)   100%------/
2.Autotransit Ltd -80-89(100%)
3.Wilson &CO -85- 89   100%---/
4.Skandiatransport Ltd-85-89(100%)   100%-/
5.Transocean Shipp.Ag-88(100%)   100%-
6.Cool Carriers-88(100%)   100%
7.Global Equipment Management-88(100%)
100%

West-Germany
1.Bilspedition Represen.Office-68-71
2.Autotransit GmbH -80-88(100%)   100%--------------/
3.Wilson GmbH -83-88(100%)   100%-----/
4.ADR Transport GmbH -86(57%),88(100%)   100%--
5.Incotrans GmbH-88(100%)   100%-
6.Teka Trans GmbH-89(100%)   100%-
7.Nellen&Quack GmbH-90(100%)
100%

Sweden based (international companies)
1.ATA -62(10%),-64(50%),-65(100%)   50%-!00%--/
2.Trailer Express -68/69(100%)   100%-/
3.SGS-71(partowned),-83(100%)   100%-----------------------------------
4.Scandinavian Ferry Trailers-69(100%)   100%----------------------------------/
5.Flygspedition -71(50%),-72/73(100%)   100%---------------------------------
-
6.Alpen&Parelius-76(100%)   100%-/
7.Coldsped -71(50%),79(100%)   50%----100%----------------------

8. Coldstore 75-79(100%)   100%----------------------
9.Wilson&Co -83-(100%)   100%------------
10.InterScandinavian Airfreight -83-86(100%)   100%---/
11.Wilson Shipping-83(100%)   100%-----------

-

12.Nyman&Schulz-83(100%)   100%----------
13. SkandiaFallenuis-85-88(100%)   100%----/
14 Transportkompaniet-85-86(100%)   100%--/
15. ADR Transport AB-86(57%),-88(100%)   57%--
100%
16.Anton Pettersson Sped.-85(100%)   100%-----
17. AB Aug Andersson-85(100%)   100%------
18.Kungsholms Express-85(100%)   100%------
19.Scanflight-88(100%)   100%------
20.Scansped AB-85(100%)   100%-----

-

21.Scansped Equipment AB-85(100%)   100%-----

-

22.ABSkandiatransport-85(100%)   100%------
23 G.Smiths Ab-85(100%)   100%------
24.ACL AB -87(100%)   100%--
25.RederiABTransatlantic-87(100%)   100%--
26.Cool Carriers AB-87(100%)   100%--
27.RederiAB Transocean-87(100%)   100%--
28.Simon Edström AB-87(100%)   100%--
29.Transocean Shipping Agency AB-87(100%)   100%--
30.Lindblom &Co-90(100%)   100%

Outside Europe Bilspedition had only 25% in Wilson &Co Inc., until 1985.   In
1989 they were situated in HongKong, Canada, Mexico, Japan and Australia.
Except for one company in HongKong and one in the US these companies
belonged to the Scanship Group.
Subsidiaries to non transport organizations are not included.

**Net of representation of Europe of the Swedish companies of ATA[14],
Wilson and SKT/F&L[15] - before merger 1988**
(excl air)

(number of)	ATA	Wilson	SKT/F&L
Austria	1	2	4
Belgium	1(Group)	1(J/V)	1(Group)
Bulgaria		1	
Denmark	1 (Group)	1(Group)	3(3 Group)
East Germany		1	1
Finland	1(Group)	5	2
France	2(1 Group)	2	6(1 Group)
Great Britain	1(Group)	4 (1 Group)	2(1 Group)
Greece		1	(1via)
Hungary		1	1

[14] ATA was at that time the dominating part of Bilspedition International
[15] SKT/F&L as well as Wilson were both part of Scansped even though they
competed   internally

Ireland		1	
Italy	1(Group)	2	3
Yugoslavia		1	8
Luxembourg			1
Netherlands	2(2 Group)	4	1(Group)
Norway	2(1Group,1J/V)	1(Group)	1(Group)
Poland		1	
Portugal	1	1	4
Rumania		1	
Sovjet Union			
Switzerland	1(Group)	1	2(1 Group)
Spain	1	2	1
Czechoslovakia		1	
Turkey			1
West-Germany	2 (2 Group)	16 (1 Group)	16
Sweden			
Total	**17 (13 Group)**	**51(5 Group)**	**58 (9 Group)**
Summary	126 (out of which 25 Group companies, 2 J/V and 99 agents)		

Net of representation in Europe of Scansped Sweden, after the merger 1989 (land-transports)

(number of)

Austria	4
Belgium	1(Group)
Bulgaria	
Denmark	3 (3 Group)
East Germany	1
Finland	1(Group)
France	7(2 Group)
Great Britain	2(1 Group)
Greece	
Hungary	1
Ireland	1
Italy	3
Yugoslavia	4
Luxembourg	
Netherlands	1(1 Group)
Norway	7 (1Group, 1J/V)
Poland	1
Portugal	2
Rumania	
Sovjet Union	1
Switzerland	3(1 Group)
Spain	1
Czechoslovakia	1
West-Germany	12 (2 Group)
Sweden	
Total	**57 (14 Group and 43 agents)**

Net of representation in Europe of Scansped Belgium, before and after merger in the end of 1988 (land-transports)
(number of)

	early 1988		early 1990
	ATA	Castra	Scansped
Austria		x[16]	x
Belgium			
Bulgaria			
Denmark	1(Group)	1(Group)	1(Group)
East Germany			
Finland	2	1(Group)	1(Group)
France	1	3	3(1 Group)
Great Britain	1	1	1
Greece		x	1
Hungary			
Ireland			
Italy	1	1	1
Yugoslavia			
Luxembourg			1
Netherlands		1(Group)	1(Group)
Norway	1	1(Group)	1(Group)
Poland			
Portugal		1	1
Rumania			
Sovjet Union			
Switzerland		1(Group)	1(Group)
Spain			
Czechoslovakia			
West-Germany		3	2(1 Group)
Sweden	1(Group)	1(Group)	1(Group)
Total	**8(2 Group)**	**15(6 Group)**	**17(8 Group)**

Net of representation of Europe of Scansped Holland before and after the merger in the end of 1988 (land-transports)
(number of)

	early 1988		early 1990
	ATA	van Casteren	Scansped
Austria		1	1
Belgium			1(Group)
Bulgaria			
Denmark	1(Group)	1(Group)	1(Group)
East Germany			
Finland	1(Group)	1(Group)	1(Group)
France		5 (1Group)	5 (1 Group)
Great Britain		1	2
Greece	1		1
Hungary			
Ireland	1		1
Italy		1	1
Yugoslavia			
Luxembourg			direct

---

16 Via Mother company in Netherlands

Netherlands			
Norway	1(Group)	1(Group)	1(Group)
Poland			1(Group J/V)
Portugal			
Rumania			
Sovjet Union			
Switzerland	1(Group)	1(Group)	1(Group)
Spain			
Czechoslovakia			
West-Germany		9	4 (1 Group)?
Sweden	1 (Group)	1(Group)	1 (Group)
Total	7(5 Group)	22(6 Group)	22(9 Group)

Net of representation of Europe of Scansped West-Germany before and after merger in the end of 1988 (land-transports)
(number of)

	early 1988 ATA/ Bilsp.Intern`l	1989 Scansped
Austria	2	3
Belgium	1	2(1 Group)
Bulgaria		
Denmark	1(Group)	1(Group)
East Germany		
Finland	1(Group)	1(Group)
France	1	1
Great Britain	1	1
Greece		1
Hungary		
Ireland		
Italy	1	1
Yugoslavia		
Luxembourg		
Netherlands	2	3(1 Group)
Norway	1 (Group)	1(Group)
Poland		
Portugal		
Rumania		
Sovjet Union		
Switzerland	1	1(Group)
Spain	1	
Czechoslovakia		
West-Germany		
Sweden	1(Group)	1(Group)
Total	14(4 Group)	17 (7 Group)

Appendix 5 Inter Forward

Net of representation of Europe[17] NTS Sweden
(number of)

	1989	1985
Austria	1	1
Belgium	1 IF Group	1
Bulgaria	1	1
Denmark	1(IF Group)	1
East Germany		
Finland	1	1
France	3 (IF Group)	5(1 NTS Group)
Great Britain	1	1
Greece	1	1
Hungary	1	1
Ireland		
Italy	1	1
Yugoslavia		2
Luxembourg	1	1
Netherlands	3(1 IF Group)	3
Norway	1(IF Group)	1(NTSGroup)
Poland	1	1
Portugal	1	2
Rumania	1	1
Sovjet Union		
Switzerland	1	2
Spain	1	1
Czechoslovakia	1	1
West-Germany	16(2 IF Group)	13(1 NTS Group)
Sweden		
Total 1989	**40 (7 IF Group)**	**42 (3 NTS Group)**

Net of representation of Europe -1989

(number of)	NTS DK	Jerre Rail(S)	NTSRail(S)
Austria	1	1	x[18]
Belgium	2(1 IF)	1	
Bulgaria	1		x
Denmark			
East Germany			x
Finland	1	2(1 IF Group)	
France	2(1 IF Group)	1(IF Group)	2 (IF Group)
Great Britain	1		
Greece	1		
Hungary	1		x
Ireland			x
Italy	2	3-5	x (1 IF SO)

---

[17] Not including airfreight and rail agents
[18] Number of agents unknown

	NTS DK		
Yugoslavia			
Luxembourg	1		
Netherlands	1(IF group)	1	
Norway	1 (IF Group)		
Poland	1		
Portugal	1		
Rumania	1		x
Sovjet Union	1		x
Switzerland	1		x
Spain	1	1	x(1 IFSO)
Czechoslovakia			
West-Germany	8(1 IF Group)		x
Sweden	1		
Total NTS DK	**30(5 IF)**	**10-12(2 Group)**	**12 countries(3 Group)**

Net of representation of Europe - 1989 (spring)

	Z&B	NTS F	Intern. Exp.Copex (Amas)
Austria	1(IF Group)	x	x
Belgium	x	x	direct
Bulgaria	x P[19]		
Denmark		x (IF group)	x(IF Group)
East Germany		x	
Finland	x	x	x
France	x		x+direct
Great Britain	x(1 IF Group)	x	x+direct
Greece	x		
Hungary	x P		
Ireland	x		
Italy	x(1 IF Group)	x	x
Yugoslavia			
Luxembourg			direct
Netherlands	x	x	
Norway		x (IF Group)	x
Poland	x P		
Portugal		x	x
Rumania	x P		
Sovjet Union	x P		
Switzerland	x (1 IF Group)	x	
Spain	x	x	x
Czechoslovakia			
Turkey	x		
West-Germany		x (1 IF Group)	x+direct
Sweden	x (IF Group)	x (IF Group)	x(IFGroup)
Total Z&B	**18 countries (at least 5 IF Group)**		
NTS France	**14 countries**	**(at least 4 IF)**	
Copex	**13 countries**	**(at least 2 IF)**	

---

[19] P = agents for project transports

IF Group Foreign subsidiaries in 1990

Austria
 1. Z&B(100%)(T) 2y
  2. Impazel(Trading Co)[20]
    Amas

Belgium
1.Satraco(100%)[21]
2.Belcomex de Wolf (Amas)
3. Neptun (Amas)
4. Belcomex n.v.
5. van Huls(Amas)
6.Sasse Co(Amas)
7. Subsidiary to Beyer, France

Denmark
1. NTS Denmark(100%) 0y
Tid. Erritzoe, Hansen
 2. ITM (Amas)

Finland
1. Railcarriers(66%)
1.J.Jerre OY

France
1 NTS France
2.Woodtrans
3. Nortrans S.A.
4.Beyer
5.Rambaud
6.SMTS
7.All Transports

Great Britain
1. Norfreight(100%) -88
2. Z&B(100%) -88
3. London Carrier International -90
4. Bondelivery

Italy
1. NTS Rail(repres)

Luxembourg
1.J.Jerre International S.A.
2.Subsidiary to Beyer, France

Netherlands
Amas (1988)
Gen &spec forw. division
1.Copex Hillegom B.v.

---

[20] Winded up 1990
[21] Sold 1990

2.Schut-Copex
3.Copex IGS B.v.
4.Terwee Okker
5.Hofsteenge b.v.
6.Meubeldistrib.&Serv.b.v.
7.Mondia Europe
Airfreight Division
8.Copex Air b.v.
9.Speed b.v.
10.Skylink Handl.Serv.b.v.
11.Air agencies Holl.b.v.
12.Mondia Europe b.v.
13.Copex Hillegom b.v.
Customs clearance division
14.Belcomex b.v.
15 van Huls

Norway
1.NTS Norway A/S

Spain
1.NTS rail (repres.)

Switzerland
1. Z&B (100%)-88

West-Germany
1. Z&B 100% -88
2. Z&B Verpackunsges.-88
3. Schier&Otten100% -88
4. NTS Germany100%-85
5. Fenthol&Sandtman 100% -89
6. DMP 100%
7.Subsidiaries (2) to Beyer France

Appendix 6

Epilogue of the cases for year 1991 and 1992

Since 1990 ASG, Bilspedition and Inter Forward have endured a period of decreasing results, due to economic downturn in important markets and overpriced acquisitions.. They have met these changes by restructuring their Groups in different ways. However, here I will only shortly comment upon some of the changes in their international activites.

ASG, which has had a conservative approach regarding acquisitions outside their core business, has focused much of their interest to the Nordic countries. In 1992 they made an agreement with Danzas, a large multinational transport group. Danzas will represent ASG world wide in areas where ASG does not have their own offices. ASG became the new agent of Danzas in Scandinavia and the Baltic States. The idea were continued international expansion with limited economic risk.

For Bilspedition the problems have mainly derived from activities outside their traditional forwarding and transport activities such as real estate, airline and shipping operations. These engagements have caused Bilspedition severe losses and therefore most of them have been sold during the last two years or are for sale. However, the Scansped Group, which have continued their growth and concentration of the international net and its profitability has improved.

The economic development has forced Inter Forward to cease their expansion by acquisitions. If has entered a period of consolidation and increasing coordination between the acquired companies. They have started merging and restructuring the groups of companies existing within their most important markets. The company has received more capital from its owners for the task.

Sources: Annual reports and some news paper articles.

EFI - reports since 1987

Published in the language indicated by the title

Andersson, T., Ternström, B., Private Foreign Investments and Welfare Effects: A comparative study of five countries in southeast Asia. Research report

Andersson, T., Ternström, B., External Capital and Social Welfare in South-East Asia. Research report

Benndorf, H., Marknadsföringsplanering och samordning mellan företag i industriella system. EFI/MTC

Bergman, L., Mäler, K-G., Ståhl, I., Överlåtelsebara utsläppsrätter. En studie av kolväteutsläpp i Göteborg. Research report

Björkegren, D., Mot en kognitiv organisationsteori. Research report

Claesson, K., Effektiviteten på Stockholms Fondbörs

Davidsson, P. Growth Willingness in Small Firms. Entrepreneurship - and after? Research report

Engshagen, I., Finansiella nyckeltal för koncern versus koncernbolag. En studie om finansiella måltal. Research report

Fredriksson, O., Holmlöv, PG., Julander, C-R., Distribution av varor och tjänster i informationssamhället.

Hagstedt, P., Sponsring - mer än marknadsföring. EFI/MTC

Järnhäll, B., On the Formulation and Estimation of Models of Open Economies. Research report

Kylén, B., Digitalkartans ekonomi. Samhällsekonomiska modeller för strategiska val. Delrapport 2 i "Nordisk Kvantif"

Lundgren, S., Elpriser: Principer och praktik. Research report

Schwarz, B., Hederstierna, A., Socialbidragens utveckling - orsaker eller samvariationer? Research report

Swartz, E., Begreppet federativ organisation belyst i ett organisationsteoretiskt, juridiskt och empiriskt perpektiv. Research report.

Westlund, A.H. Öhlén, S., Business Cycle Forecasting in Sweden; A problem analysis. Research report

1988

Andréasson, I-M., Costs of Controls on Farmers' Use of Nitrogen. A study applied to Gotland.

Björkegren, D., Från sluten till öppen kunskapsproduktion. Delrapport 3 i forskningsprojektet Lärande och tänkande i organisationer. Research report

Björkegren, D., Från tavistock till Human-relation. Delrapport 4 i forskningsprojektet Lärande och tänkande i organisationer. Research report

Björklund, L., Internationell projektförsäljning. En studie av ad hoc-samverkan mellan företag vid internationella projekt. Research report

Bojö, J., Mäler, K-G., Unemo, L., Economic Analysis of Environmental Consequences of Development Projects. Research report

Brynell, K., Davidsson, P., Det nya småföretagandet? - en empirisk jämförelse mellan små high-tech företag och konventionella småföretag. Research report

Dahlgren, G., Witt, P., Ledning av fusionsförlopp. En analys av bildandet av Ericsson Information Systems AB.

Forsell, A., Från traditionell till modern sparbank. Idé organisation och verksamhet i omvandling. Research report

Hirdman, V., The Stability and the Interest Sensitivity of Swedish Short Term Capital Flows. Research report

Hultén, S., Vad bestämmer de svenska exportmarknadsandelarnas utveckling?

Häckner, J., Biobränslenas konkurrenskraft i ett framtida perspektiv. Research report

Jennergren, P., Näslund, B., If the Supreme Court had Known Option Theory: A Reconsideration of the Gimo Case. Research report

Jennergren, P., Näslund, B., The Gimo Corporation Revisited: An Exercise in Finance Theory. Research report

Jennergren, P., Näslund, B., Valuation of Debt and Equity Through One- and Two-State Contingent Claims Models - with an Application to a Swedish Court Case. Research report

Jonung, L., Laidler, D., Are Perceptions of Inflation Rational? Some Evidence for Sweden. Research report.

Lagerstam, C., Business Intelligence. Teori samt empirisk studie av elektronik- och bioteknikbranschen i Japan. Research report

Liljegren, G., Interdependens och dynamik i långsiktiga kundrelationer. Industriell försäljning i nätverksperspektiv.

Näslund, B., Några synpunkter på börsfallet i oktober 1987. Research report

Olsson, C., The Cost-Effectiveness of Different Strategies Aimed at Reducing the Amount of Sulphur Deposition in Europe. Research report

Philips, Å., Eldsjälar. En studie av aktörsskap i arbetsorganisatoriskt utvecklingsarbete.

Sellstedt, B., Produktionsstrategier. En diskussion med utgångspunkt från litteraturen. Research report.

Skogsvik, K., Prognos av finansiell kris med redovisningsmått. En jämförelse mellan traditionell och inflationsjusterad redovisning.

Wahlund, R., Skatteomläggningen 1983 - 1985. En studie av några konsekvenser. Research report

Wahlund, R., Varför och hur olika svenska hushåll sparar. Research report

Vredin, A., Macroeconomic Policies and the Balance of Payments.

Åkerman, J., Economic Valuation of Risk Reduction: The Case of In-Door Radon. Research report.

1989

Andersson, T., Foreign Direct Investment in Competing Host Countries. A Study of Taxation and Nationalization.

Björkegren, D., Skönhetens uppfinnnare. Research report

Björkegren, D., Hur organisationer lär. Studentlitteratur.

Blomström, M., Transnational Corporations and Manufactoring Exports from Developing Countries. Research report.

Carlsson, A., Estimates of the Costs of Emission control in the Swedish Energy Sector. Research report

Blomström, M., Foreign Investment and Spillovers. London; Routledge

Bordo, M.D., Jonung, L., The Long-Run Behavior of Velocity: The Institutional Approach Revisted. Research report

Davidsson, P., Continued Entrepreneurship and Small Firm Growth.

DeJuan, A., Fiscal Attitudes and Behavior. A study of 16 - 35 years old Swedish citizens. Research report

Edlund, P-O., Preliminary Estimation of Transfer Function Weights. A Two-Step Regression Approach.

Fridman, B., Östman, L., eds. Accounting Development - some perspectives. In honour of Sven-Erik Johansson.

Gadde, L-E., Håkansson, H., Öberg, M., Stability and Change in Automobile Distribution. Research report

Glader, M., Datorer i småföretag. Teldok

Jakobsson, B., Konsten att reagera. Intressen, institutioner och näringspolitik. Carlssons Bokförlag

Jonung, L., The Economics of Private Money. Private Bank Notes in Sweden 1831 - 1902. Research report

Jonung, L., Batchelor, R.A., Confidence about Inflation Forecasts: Tests of Variance Rationality. Research report.

Kylén, B., Hur företagschefer beslutar innan de blir överraskade. Ett försök till förklaring av svarsmönster i svagsignalsitutationer.

Lagerstam, C., Jämförelse av skydd med samlad valuta/aktieoption och skydd med separata aktie- och valutaoptioner samt härledning av optionspriser. Research report

Lagerstam, C., On the Pricing and Valuation of Forwards and Options on Futures and their Relationsship. Research report.

Larsson, B., Koncernföretaget. Ägarorganisationer eller organisation för ägare?

Lindberg, C., Holmlöv, PG., Wärneryd K-E., Telefaxen och användarna. Teldok

Löwstedt, J., Föreställningar, ny teknik och förändring. Tre organisationsprocesser ur ett kognitivt aktörsperspektiv. Doxa Förlag

Löwstedt, J., (red) Organisation och teknikförändring. Studentlitteratur.

Tollgerdt-Andersson, I., Ledarskapsteorier, företagsklimat och bedömningsmetoder.

Schuster, W., Ägandeformens betydelse för ett företag - en studie av ICA-rörelsen.

Schwartz, B., Företaget som medborgare. Samhällskontakter och reklam som legitimeringsinstrument. Research report

Spets, G., Vägen till nej. Anade och oanade konsekvenser av en OS-satsning. Research report.

Stymne, B., Information Technology and Competence Formation in the Swedish Service Sector. IMIT/EFI

1990

Björkegren, D., Litteraturproduktion - en fallstudie. Delrapport 2 i forskningsprojektet Det skapande företaget: Management of Narrativation. Research Report.

Bojö, J., Economic Analysis of Agricultural Development Projects. A Case Study from Lesotho. Research Report.

Brunsson, N., Forsell, A., Winberg, H., Reform som tradition. Administrativa reformer i Statens Järnvägar.

Drottz-Sjöberg, B-M., Interests in Humanities, Social Science and Natural Science. A Study of High School Students.

Eklöf, J.A., Macro Ecoonomic PLanning with Quantitative Techniques - and Effects of Varying Data Quality. Research Report.

Flink, T., Hultén, S., Det svenska snabbtågsprojektet - de första 20 åren. Research Report.

Hesselman, A., Ett lokalt ekonomisystem. En fallstudie inom byggbranschen. Research Report.

Jennergren, L.P., Näslund, B., Models for the Valuation of International Convertible Bonds. Research Report.

Jonung, L., Introduction and Summary to The Stockholm School of Economics Revisited. Research Report.

Lagerstam, C., Hedging of Contracts, Anticipated Positions, and Tender Offers.

Lindkvist, H., Kapitalemigration

Normark, P., Strategiska förändringar i kooperationer fallet Lantmännen. Research Report.

Patrickson, A., Essays in the Latin American Fertilizer Industry.

Sjöstrand, S-E., Den dubbla rationaliteten. Research Report.

Steiner, L., Ledningsfunktionen i tillväxtföretag. Ledningsteamens sammansättning och funktion i tillverkande företag inom informationsteknologiindustrin.

Warne, A., Vector Autoregressions and Common Trends in Macro and Financial Economics

Wärneryd, K., Economic Conventions. Essays in Institutional Evolution.

1991

Bergholm, M., Hemdistribution med hjälp av datorkommunikation. Research Report.

Bojö, J., The Economics of Land Degradation. Theory and Applications to Lesotho.

Brytting, T., Organizing in the Small Growing Firm - A grounded theory approach

Edlund, P-O., Soegaard, H., Business Cycle Forecasting: Tracking Time - Varying Transfer Functions. Research Report.

Ericson, M., Iggesundsaffären - Rationaliteter i en strategisk förvärvsprocess

Horn av Rantzien, M., Endogenous Fertility and Old-Age Security. Research Report.

Jennergren, L.P., Näslund, B., Options with Stochastic Lives. Research Report.

Jonung, L., Gunnarsson, E., Economics the Swedish Way 1889-1989. Research Report.

Jungenfelt, K., An Analysis of Pay as Yo Go Pension Systems as Dynastic Clubs. Research Report.

Lundgren, A., Technological Innovation and Industrial Evolution - The Emergence of Industrial Networks.

Nilsson, A. G., Anskaffning av standardsystem för att utveckla verksamheter. Utveckling och prövning av SIV-metoden.

Nilsson, J., Ekonomisk styrning i ett multinationellt företag. Research Report.

Normark, P., Swartz, E., Bolagisering av ekonomiska föreningar. Research Report.

Rutström, E., The Political Economy of Protectionism in Indonesia A Computable General Equilibrium Analysis.

Sjöstrand, S-E., Institution as Infrastructures of Human Interaction. Research Report.

Söderqvist, T., Measuring the Value of Reduced Health Risks: The Hedonic Price Technique Applied on the Case of Radon Radiation. Research Report.

Wahlund, R., Skatter och ekonomiska beteenden. En studie i ekonomisk psykologi om främst skattefusk och sparande utifrån 1982 års skatteomläggning.

Wahlund, R., Studenternas betalningsvilja för studier vid Handelshögskolan i Stockholm. Research Report.

Westelius, A., Westelius, A-S., Decentraliserade informationssystem. Två fallstudier inom ekonomistyrning. Research Report.

Westlund, K., Affärsetik. En studie av etiska bedömningar. Research Report.

Wirsäll, N-E., Julander, C-R., Den lättrörliga detaljhandeln.

1992

Charpentier, C., Ekonomisk styrning av statliga affärsverk.

Edlund, P-O., Karlsson, S., Forecasting the Swedish Unempolyment Rate: VAR vs. Transfer Function Modelling.

Eklöf, J., Varying Data Quality and Effects in Economic Analysis and Planning.

Eliasson, M., Julander, C-R., Productivity in Swedish Grocery Retailing. - changes over time and a causal model.

Ewing, P., Ekonomisk styrning av enheter med inbördes verksamhetssamband.

Fredriksson, O., Datorkommunikation i Distributionssystem.

Erfarenheter och effekter vid införandet av två multilaterala interorganisatoriska informationssystem - exemplet BASCET Infolink AB.

Fredriksson, T., Policies Towards Small and Medium Enterprises in Japan and Sweden. Research Report.

Gerdtham, U., Jönsson, B., Sjukvårdskostnader i de nordiska länderna. Research Report.

Hedvall, M., Produktkvalitet som konkurrensmedel i producentvaruproducerande industri. Research Report.

Holmberg, C., Effects of Feature Advertising and Other Promotions Research Report.

Jansson, D., Spelet kring investeringskalkyler. Norstedts

Jennergren, L.P., Näslund, B., Valuation of Executive Stock Options. Research Report.

Ljung, A., Intressentstrategier - En long-itudinell studie av utvecklingen i två svenska företag.

Kokko, A., Foreign Direct Investment, Host Country Characteristics and Spillovers.

Mårtensson, P., Mähring, M., Information Support From Staff to Executives. - An Explorative Study. Research Report

Paalzow, A., Public Debt Management. Research Report.

Persson, P-G., Basket Analysis. A New Way of Studying Short Term Effects of Promotions in Grocery Retailing.

Sjöstrand, S-E., On Institutions and Institutional Change. Research Report.

Södergren, B., Decentralisering. Förändring i företag och arbetsliv.

Rabiee, M., A Review of Demand for Telecommunication: An Analytical Approach. Research Report.

Thodenius, B., Användningen av ledningsinformationssystem i Sverige: Lägesbild 1991. Research Report.

Tollgerdt-Andersson, I., Sjöberg, L., Intresse och kreativitet inom tjänsteproducerande företag. Research Report.

Wahl, A., Kvinnliga civilekonomers och civilingenjörers karriärutveckling.

1993

Ekvall, N., Studies in Complex Financial Instruments and their Valuation.

Söderlund, M., Omvärldsmodeller hos beslutsfattare i industriföretag - en studie av svenska leverantörer till fordonsindustrin.

Whitelegg, J., Hultén, S., Flink, T., High Speed Trains. Fast tracks to the future.